MULL: THE ISLAND AND ITS PEOPLE

The 'Rosy' Map, of 'Mull island', on which the area of the Ross of Mull was quaintly named Rosy, was published in John Smith's *General View of the Agriculture of the County of Argyll* in 1798. The orientation of sea lochs, the shape of coasts and bays, the relative proportions of islands like Ulva and Gometra, and the squat character of the whole island make it an amusing map today, but useful in its presentation of place names which were significant in the eighteenth century, and for the prominence given to areas such as Tontire and Lermulach.

MULL

The Island and its People

JO CURRIE

Birlinn

First published in Great Britain in 2000 by
Birlinn Ltd, West Newington House,
10 Newington Road, Edinburgh EH9 IQS

www.birlinn.co.uk

ISBN 1 84158 177 1

The publisher gratefully acknowledges
financial assistance from The Russell Trust

British Library Cataloguing-in-Publication Data
A catalogue record for this book is available
from the British Library

Typeset in Monotype Bell by Carnegie Publishing, Lancaster
Printed and bound by Creative Print and Design, Ebbw Vale, Wales

Contents

List of illustrations   vii

List of maps   ix

Abbreviations   x

Acknowledgements   xiv

Preface   xvi

Part I   The Historical Background

1 A backward glance   3

2 *Ne obliviscaris*: the Campbells and the Macleans   11

3 Dukes and exiles   22

4 'Lose not heart, beloved people'   39

Part II   The People

5 John Lochbuy and his sons, Gillean and Archy   55

6 Murdoch Maclaine, linen merchant   75

7 The Lord of Ulva's Isle   89

8 Dr Johnson, Mr Boswell and other tourists   104

9 Archy Lochbuy's honeymoon   119

10 Three men called Allan Maclean   137

11 Murdoch Maclaine's inheritance   151

12 'Marianna in the moated grange': the Torloisk family   170

13 A servant of two masters: James Maxwell of Aros   188

14 'His people are distractedly fond of him': Staffa's story   199

15 Hail to the Chief: young Murdoch of Lochbuy   211

16 A Writer to the Signet: Donald Maclean WS   230

17 'The duke does not care a fig': the Macquarie brothers' bid   245

18 *Tha tighinn fodham eiridh*: it comes upon me to arise   265

19 Of hubris in the affairs of men   278

20 The organ grinder comes: Sandy Campbell's quest   293

21 The fly on the wall: Lauchlan Maclaine's diary   305

22 The tent in the gravel pit   324

23 *Doctair ruadh nam blàth shùilean*: the tale of the red-haired
    doctor   336

24 'No Jews, negroes, gipsies, foreigners, or people born in
    England'   346

25 'I cried for madder music and for stronger wine'   361

26 The potatoes fail; Mr Somers investigates; Mr Clark has a
    remedy   370

27 'I dreamt I dwelt in marble halls': the new men   381

28 *An t-sòbhrach Mhuileach*: the Mull primrose   397

    Bibliography   407

    Landownership maps   415

    Genealogical tables:

        1 Maclaines of Lochbuy   419
        2 Later Maclaines of Lochbuy and Macleans of Drimnin   420
        3 Macleans of Duart and Brolass   421
        4 Macleans of Torloisk and Pennycross   422–3
        5 Maclaines of Scallastle   424
        6 Gregorsons of Ardtornish   425
        7 Campbells of Argyll   426
        8 Family of Lauchlan Maclaine   427
        9 Macleans of Drimnin and Kinloch   428
       10 Clarks of Ulva   429
       11 MacQuarries of Ulva and Ormaig   430–1
       12 Macquarie brothers   432
       13 Maxwells and Macleods   433
       14 Macdonalds of Boisdale, Staffa and Inchkenneth   434

        Indexes

        1 Place names   435
        2 Personal names   444

List of Illustrations

Appearing in Text Pages

Letter from the Commissioners of the General Assembly   9

Ode to the Second Duke of Argyll   25

Shoemaker's bill – shoes supplied to Miss Mally Maclaine   57

Broadside summary of the case of Maclean *v.* Maclaine, 1759   59

List of men from the Lochbuy estate   125

The first page of a rental of the estate of Lochbuy   133

Three Writers to the Signet   165

Tha tighinn fodham eiridh   264

Captain Lauchlan Maclaine's assessment for the support of the poor   275

Cholera poster in Gaelic   313

Presumed silhouette of Lauchlan Maclaine   317

Appearing in the Monochrome Plate Section

Aros Castle, scene of the meeting of chieftains, 1609

John, second Duke of Argyll

Duncan Forbes of Culloden

Lieutenant-Colonel Jack Campbell, later fifth Duke of Argyll

The Rev. Dr John Walker

Highland soldiers of the 1750s

Lachlan MacQuarrie of that ilk

The Sapient Septemviri: the senate of King's College, Aberdeen

Early nineteenth-century engraving of Staffa

Sir Allan Maclean, 'the Knight'

Jane Campbell, wife of Murdoch Maclaine of Lochbuy

Murdoch Maclaine of Lochbuy

The twins, Archibald and Murdoch Maclaine

Old Torloisk House, *c.* 1785

Faujas de Saint-Fond

Prospect of Staffa, 1798

A Mull cottage, 1798

The Marquis of Northampton

George William Campbell, sixth Duke of Argyll

Archibald Macarthur, piper to Ranald Macdonald of Staffa

Sir Henry Steuart of Allanton

Thomas Campbell, poet

Carsaig House

Alexander Campbell, the 'organ grinder'

John Campbell of Ardmore, 'Factor Mór'

Old Ardtornish House in the mid-nineteenth century

Oban during the regatta, 1835

Angus Gregorson, nephew of Young Murdoch of Lochbuy

Francis William Clark of Ulva

Quinish House, late nineteenth century

Gillean Maclaine, grandson of Gillean of Scallastle

The Rev. Angus Maclaine, minister of Ardnamurchan

Donald Maclaine of Lochbuy

The three daughters of Donald Maclaine of Lochbuy

Catherine Maclaine of Lochbuy

Dugald MacPhail, author of *An t-eilean Muileach*

A nineteenth-century Mull cottage

Appearing in the Colour Plate Section

Old Moy Castle

James Boswell

Murdoch Maclaine, later 19th of Lochbuy, *c.* 1758

Gillean Maclaine of Scallastle, *c.* 1770

Lochbuy House

Marianne Maclean, later Mrs Maclean Clephane

General William Douglas Maclean Clephane

Three places of worship in Torosay, 1787

Craignure Church

Margaret Douglas Maclean Clephane

Lord Compton

Ranald Macdonald of Staffa

Lachlan Macquarie, Governor of New South Wales

Elizabeth Henrietta Campbell, wife of Lachlan Macquarie

Portrait of Lachlan Macquarie Junior of Jarvisfield

View from Ulva to Benmore, 1813

The Breast, Tobermory, 1813

Aros Bridge, 1813

Achnacroish House

Old Gruline House

Colonel Alexander Campbell of Possil and Achnacroish

Harriet Maclachlan, wife of Colonel Alexander Campbell

Miss Susan Campbell daughter of Colonel Alexander Campbell

List of Maps

The 'Rosy' Map	*frontispiece*
Place-names past and present	xii
Map of the Destitute Areas of the Hebrides	383
Mull Proprietors, 1700	415
Mull Proprietors, 1800	416
Mull Proprietors, 1825	417

Abbreviations

Archive Sources

ABDA	Argyll & Bute District Archives, Lochgilphead
EUL	Edinburgh University Library
GRO	Gloucestershire Record Office
HMSO	Her/His Majesty's Stationery Office
ICP	Inveraray Castle Papers
NAS	National Archives of Scotland, formerly SRO
NLS	National Library of Scotland
OPR	Old Parish Registers in General Register Office for Scotland, Edinburgh
RCAHMS	Royal Commission on the Ancient and Historical Monuments of Scotland
SGS	Scottish Genealogy Society
SHS	Scottish History Society
SRS	Scottish Record Society
TP	Torloisk Papers
UAHC	University of Aberdeen Historic Collections

People

ACP	Colonel Alexander Campbell of Possil, Achnacroish
AM	Brigadier-General Allan Maclean of Torloisk
AMB	Sir Allan Maclean, 'the Knight'
AMD	Dr Allan Maclean, the 'red-haired doctor'
AMLB	Archibald Maclaine of Lochbuy
CM	Colonel Charles Macquarie of Glenforsa, of Achnacroish, of Ulva
DM	Donald Maclaine, merchant and seedsman in Edinburgh
DMLB	Donald Maclaine of Lochbuy
DMWS	Donald Maclean, Writer to the Signet
FWC	Francis William Clark of Ulva
GM	Gillean Maclaine

JB	James Boswell
JC	Jane Campbell of Airds
JG	John Gregorson, Sheriff
JMG	John Maclaine, Tacksman of Gruline
JMLB	John Maclaine, 17th of Lochbuy
LM	Lachlan Macquarie, Governor of New South Wales
LMD	Lauchlan Maclaine, the diarist
LMQ	Lachlan MacQuarrie of Ulva
LMT	Lachlan Maclean of Torloisk
MM	Murdoch Maclaine 19th of Lochbuy
MM2	Murdoch Maclaine 20th of Lochbuy
MM3	Murdoch Maclaine (1814–1850)
MMT	Marianne Maclean of Torloisk (Mrs Maclean Clephane)
RM	Ranald Macdonald of Staffa
SJ	Samuel Johnson

Places

D/A	Duart or Argyll estates
LB	Lochbuy
PG	Pennyghael
PX	Pennycross

Mull placenames past and present

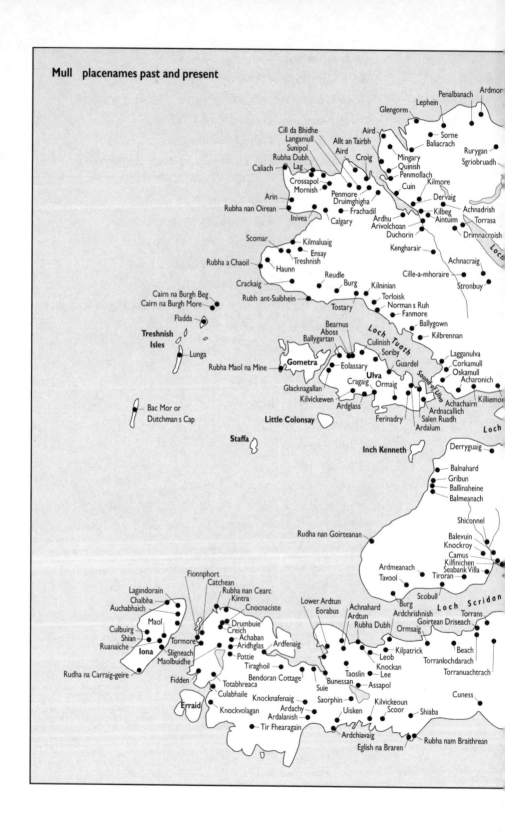

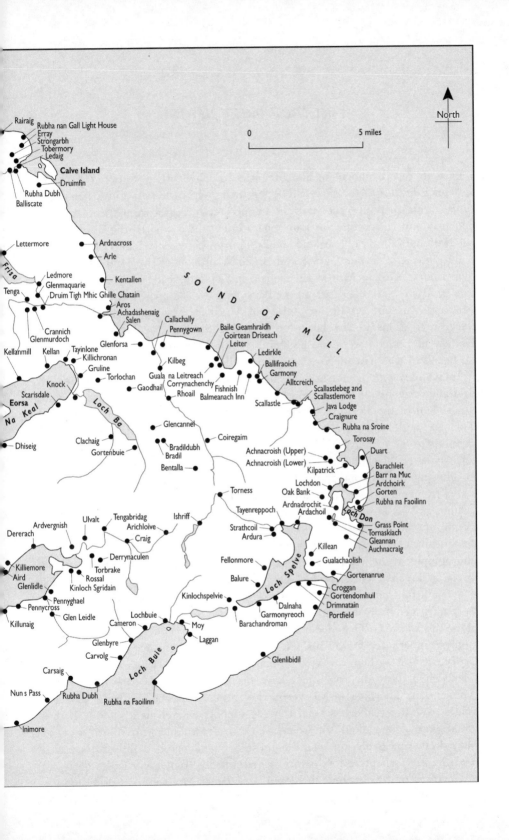

North

0   5 miles

Rairaig
Rubha nan Gall Light House
Erray
Strongarbh
Tobermory
Ledaig
Calve Island
Druimfin
Rubha Dubh
Balliscate

Lettermore
Ardnacross
Arle

Ledmore
Glenmaquarie
Kentallen

Frisa

Tenga
Druim Tigh Mhic Ghille Chatain
Aros
Achadashenaig
Salen
Callachally
Pennygown
Baile Geamhraidh
Goirtean Driseach
Leiter

S O U N D

O F

M U L L

Crannich
Glenmurdoch
Glenforsa
Tayinlone
Ledirkle
Ballifraoich
Garmony
Kellanmill
Kellan
Killichronan
Kilbeg
Gruline
Guala na Leitreach
Alltcreich
Torlochan
Corrynachenchy
Gaodhail
Fishnish
Scallastlebeg and
Scallastlemore
Knock
Rhoail
Balmeanach Inn
Scallastle
Java Lodge
Craignure
Scarisdale
Eorsa
Na Keal
Loch Ba
Glencannel
Coiregaim
Rubha na Sroine
Torosay
Dhiseig
Clachaig
Gortenbuie
Bradildubh
Bradil
Achnacroish (Upper)
Achnacroish (Lower)
Duart
Bentalla
Kilpatrick
Barachleit
Barr na Muc
Torness
Lochdon
Oak Bank
Ardnadrochit
Ardachoil
Ardchoirk
Gorten
Rubha na Faoilinn
Ulvalt
Tengabridag
Arichloive
Ishriff
Tayenreppoch
Loch Don
Ardvergnish
Craig
Strathcoil
Ardura
Grass Point
Tornaskiach
Gleannan
Auchnacraig
Dererach
Derrynaculen
Killean
Fellonmore
Gualachaolish
Killiemore
Aird
Torbrake
Rossal
Balure
Gortenanrue
Glenlidle
Kinloch Sgridain
Loch Spelve
Croggan
Gortendomhuil
Pennyghael
Kinlochspelvie
Dalnaha
Drimnatain
Pennycross
Glen Leidle
Garmonyreoch
Portfield
Killunaig
Lochbuie
Cameron
Moy
Barachandroman
Glenbyre
Laggan
Carvolg
Loch Buie
Carsaig
Glenlibidil
Nun s Pass
Rubha Dubh
Rubha na Faoilinn
Inimore

Acknowledgements

I have to record enormous indebtedness to the Scottish National Archives staff in Edinburgh (formerly SRO) for their help over two and a half years of research there, to the staff of Gloucestershire Record Office for their courtesy and cushioning on four separate lengthy visits, to the librarians of the National Library of Scotland and Edinburgh University Library (my former colleagues), to Alastair Garvie and Bruce Whittaker of the Mull Museum in Tobermory. Also to Murdo Macdonald in Lochgilphead, to Susanna Kerr in the Scottish National Portrait Gallery, and to Thomas Smythe of Perth Military Museum, whose 'unveiling' of Murdoch Maclaine was the first of many revelations in the hunt for portraits. Staff of the National Portrait Gallery in London were most helpful, as was the archivist at Castle Ashby on behalf of the present Northampton family.

Individuals with private archives have been both encouraging and interested, first and foremost of these being Captain Alwyne Farquharson of Invercauld, descendant of the Torloisk Macleans, who, very early on, allowed me to tour Torloisk, and later gave me access to his papers at Invercauld. Particular gratitude goes to David Sillar, descendant through the Gregorsons of Ardtornish of the Maclaines of Lochbuy, whose warm enthusiasm and generosity in allowing me to copy the only existing photographs of bygone Lochbuys was a tremendous help in picturing social life on the Sound of Mull. Charles ('Chubby') Ives in modern Ardtornish gave me permission to copy his photograph of the demolished Old Ardtornish House. The late Jock Luard, descendant of the McVeans, kindly gave me the use of his collection of photographs at the Mull Museum. David Clapp gave me a copy of his portrait of the ambivalent Gillean Maclaine, who now looks smugly from his frame in a delightful Connecticut farmhouse. Jane Jenner-Fust and her fellow trustees were most generous in giving permission to use their extraordinary collection in the care of the GRO, and were wisely philosophical about Gillean's misdeeds, amply compensated for by his son Lauchlan's endearing diaries.

My friend Meg Duncan came on many Mull holidays, when we walked and talked about how the past must have been, and she read early drafts with acumen. Iain Thornber in Morvern, who had corresponded with me on many points over the years, has been a great support as well as a mentor with a fund of knowledge about 'the Country'. Olive Brown and Jean Whittaker read early drafts and made important suggestions, and Jean and Billy Munro also read the early chapters for historical inaccuracies (remaining faults being all my own). Attie MacKechnie in Fionnphort, James McKeand in Scour, and my late cousin, Cathie Crawford in Eorabus shared insights (and jokes) with me. Meg Douglass introduced me to several abandoned settlements in Mull, and arranged for me to meet the Thomsons at Aros Mains, and thus to view James Maxwell's house. The Harmers at Gruline were almost the catalysts of the scheme to write a book, which was not planned when I talked to them. James Corbett at Lochbuie took me on a personal tour of the house Murdoch built, where young Murdoch gave his large dinner parties, and which Donald Lochbuy filled with vast pieces of furniture from Java. My own youthful associations with Ardfenaig were reinforced by the very real interest of Malcolm and Jane Davidson.

The generosity of owners of portraits and illustrations has been tremendous, notably Chris James's kindness with his water colour of Achnacroish. Colin Carter-Campbell gave copies of Possil portraits, Robin Campbell and Duncan Robertson were generous even in the face of some unkind views of their ancestors.

I am grateful to the Mitchell Library, Sydney, New South Wales for help with portraits of the Macquarie family, and for permission to reproduce them, including one which I have identified as Young Lachlan without their authority, but with the backing of Lauchlan the diarist's descriptions of this young man. His Grace the Duke of Argyll kindly gave permission to reproduce portraits of the family of Argyll who have been less than fairly represented in this book because the records at Inveraray were unavailable to the public at the time of writing, so that a new and independent assessment of the Campbell role in Mull's story has not been attempted. It is my sincere hope that a new and original interpretation of relationships between the dukes' factors and the dukes' tenants, particularly in the mid-nineteenth century, will be made possible in the not too distant future.

JC Edinburgh, 15 June 2000.

Preface

As this book goes to press in the year 2000, no full history of the island of Mull has yet been attempted, except for a two-volume work by J. P. Maclean published in Ohio in 1922; this was more an anthology than a history, embodying no research in original sources, but using the published findings of its time.

I make no apology for not writing a full history of Mull. For that, one would have to be an archaeologist, a medievalist, a Latin scholar, a Gaelic specialist and, not least, a professional historian. But I have always been struck by the fact that most writers on Mull say very little about the eighteenth and early nineteenth centuries. Indeed, for some of them, the material which is now available in record offices and private collections was simply unknown or inaccessible, having appeared only in the last eighty years. I have tailored my coat to my cloth by using this material, although it might seem that the survival of papers belonging to the lairds and their families would swing the social balance of the picture in favour of the lairds. Surprisingly, however, we are shown almost as much of the lives of the small tenants, crofters and cottars as those of the men with the so-called power, who so often had very few options, least of all the luxury of being able to emigrate and start a new life.

Having a Mull ancestry and a compulsive interest in the people and their social, as well as their blood relationships, my first purpose in offering a distillation of this wealth of letters, diaries, bills, official reports, petitions, rentals, wills, poems and songs, is to re-people the island, and to allow my readers to imagine it as it once was, while my second purpose is to demonstrate that its history is quite different from that of any other island of the Hebrides. My third hope is that I can provide hundreds, or even thousands of descendants of the Mull diaspora with a clear picture of how their forebears lived in the eighteenth and nineteenth centuries: one which is not based on analogy with other islands and Highland areas.

The first question that visitors to Mull ask, after disembarking from the Oban to Craignure ferry, and setting out on the road to Fionnphort or Tobermory, is generally about the ruins of habitations which they see dotted about the landscape. These broken-down houses arouse feelings of indignation or compassion in the beholder, and particularly in the descendants of Mull people who were known to have left in the nineteenth century. There is an idea, engendered by popular clearances literature and reinforced by sad songs, that each cottage was once the home of a family cruelly evicted by rapacious landlords or brutal factors. The sternly beautiful scenery of glen and shore is darkened by the outlines of these humble abodes. The tourist will turn and stare at the pile of stones, wondering that any human life could be supported on such barren ground, and conflicting ideas might come into his mind about eviction. Was it a dreadful or a good thing, in the long run? What miseries must it have caused at the time, and what longings for this superlatively beautiful and haunting land? Why had the people allowed themselves to become helpless victims of such ruthless men? Why had they no recourse to the law? 'Did they not have a Domesday Book like ours?' asks the English traveller.

But the timescale of Mull is not what it seems. The few ruins visible from the road are more likely to be of houses inhabited as recently as the late nineteenth and early twentieth centuries than dwellings carrying a history of eviction. The traveller must look farther afield for earlier townships and for explanations. He must expunge the word 'clearances' from his vocabulary for the time being, and consider other possibilities. Mull's past is different from the past of Sutherland or Skye, at once more diverse and more dramatic. Population loss was not sustained in one fell swoop, but in waves which came and went over a century. And if the truth be told, there were very few houses of stones and boulders in eighteenth century Mull. People lived in huts of turf and heather, in which they required less peat to keep warm than in the 'improved' days of stone. And, in startling juxtaposition to these conditions of life, there operated in Mull, before Adam Smith had put pen to paper, an economic system which we now call the Free Market Economy.

A strict social order prevailed, with elements which we may still recognise: 'He putteth down one and setteth up another.' Some hut-dwellers were destined to go up, some to go down in the social order, some of their own volition, others pushed by the cruel economic conditions of the times. Poverty, relative or absolute, was everyone's enemy. We have heard about indigent cottars and penniless lairds, and how the combination of the two, looked at in the most detached manner possible, brought about a confrontation which resulted in the clearances. Some might say there was no confrontation, and that a ruthless band of lairds simply removed helpless people from their ancestral homes. But we must be aware that removals, sequestrations, evictions, warnings and clearances were all in operation in Mull, varying with circumstances, under conditions which varied from one estate to another, and which were different in each decade, so that all these emotive terms must be treated with caution.

The huge exodus of indigenous population was only identified as a systematic clearance by analogy with other areas towards the end of the nineteenth century, when official enquiries were held into the causes of the people's landless state. Little reference was made to the eighteenth century's role in the process, produced by economic factors such as non-circulation of cash, as well as human shortcomings. The model of the Sutherland and Skye clearances has been used in an assumption that landowners, estate factors, the Victorian fashion for sporting estates and pure greed acted in a similar way upon the fortunes of a hapless people all over the Highlands and Islands.

It is to be hoped that this book, relating in a chronological way the changes Mull people suffered from 1600 to 1870, will show that men and women of all castes and persuasions were victims of each other, and of intolerable economic forces beyond their control. Few judgements are made on the wide social front. The reader should assess events and attach blame, if that is desirable, from the incomplete but telling records which have come down to us.

Today's traveller finds a landscape spectacular in its bleakness, the habitat of rare birds and animals and of residents who would once have been called 'strangers'. Only a remnant of native people remains, the Gaelic language is rarely heard, and there is little in the way of a yardstick to enable us to imagine the past. To bring back that extraordinary past is the purpose of this book.

For those who come to the book with a deep knowledge of Mull history, I have to explain certain policies that have had to be adopted for consistency. Genealogists may find discrepancies in the numbering of clan chiefs and lairds. I have had to use numbers only because there were so many people with the same Christian names, but where Macleans are concerned, I have decided to remain with the system used by Maclean Sinclair in his 1899 publication *The Clan Gillean*.

In the spelling of surnames I have used in the text the variety of versions used by the bearers at different times, but in the index the scope has been reduced to avoid cross-references. In deference to custom, women are mainly called by their maiden names, which, until the end of the nineteenth century, they never lost. Place names are spelt variously throughout the text, but they can be found standardised in the index. Although the recent family of Maclaines of Lochbuie have used this spelling, the territorial designation 'Lochbuy' was so dominant in the eighteenth and nineteenth centuries that I have preferred this when applying it as a personal name, in the manner of the time. The persistent use of territorial designations combined with Christian names, such as 'John Killean' (for John Maclean, once a tacksman in Killean, or the son of one), long after a man had ceased to have any connection with the place name, is such standard practice in Mull life and custom that I have used it also, but hope that the index will clear up the problems.

If Iona seems to appear only fitfully in this history, it is because E. Mairi MacArthur, in her *Iona, The Living Memory of a Crofting Community, 1750–1914*, has already written an excellent book covering the same period, and other writers and artists have done it more justice than I could.

Lastly, the genealogical tables must be regarded in many cases as the nearest approximations to accurate family trees that any one person can produce in less than ten years. It is inevitable that my more specialised readers, and members of the families concerned, will find deficiencies. If I had sought incontrovertible conclusions, the book would never have been finished.

PART I

The Historical Background

1

A backward glance

The history of Mull and its people derives almost entirely from the nature of the land, and from the significance it had for the people. Poor and unproductive as the land was, by some standards of comparison, it was still desirable to those who had no other home, as well as to men who coveted territorial power. The climate of Mull, with its sudden changes, the rock-festooned coast, the boggy and mountainous interior and the infertility of much of the soil deterred all but the hardiest of conquerors. The fatal disposition of warring families to destroy each other for the sake of possessing this barren land continued long after lawless killing was brought under control. In the eighteenth and nineteenth centuries, enmity between clans, and within clans, found a new means of expressing itself. Instead of putting each other to the sword, the clansmen entered the courts of law, and proceeded to annihilate each other by means of bankruptcy, sequestration, eviction and ruin. In these two centuries, since nearly everyone in Mull was related, internecine struggles were enacted in the name of land possession and the collection of land-related debt. It is necessary, therefore, to survey briefly the background to the exodus of the indigenous people which ensued.

Although Scotland was not included in the Norman Conquest of 1066, Normans began to infiltrate Scotland around 1080, and by 1150 were holding the most important offices in the Lowlands.[1] By the twelfth century the south of Scotland was run within a feudal framework, with the system becoming less pronounced as one crossed the Highland line, and when one crossed the seas to the islands, Celtic tradition and habit obtained. These two modes of life were not incompatible, and in fact had many similarities. The Norman feudal system recognised the king as chief authority, and the king granted land by charter both to members of the new Norman aristocracy and to the Scottish chiefs of old, and the remoter Scottish chiefs had, if anything, increased power confirmed by law. The clan organisation of Celtic society remained much the same, while law, dispensed from southern centres of power, was imperceptibly changing, or imposing itself on a previously lawless people.

Mull was under the rule of the MacDougalls of Lorn until the wars of independence, when clan Donald gained the upper hand, and as Lords of the Isles the Macdonalds held power until 1493, thirty years after their fourth hereditary head, John, had made a pact with Edward IV of England, whereby he was to become the liege of Edward, and in return, was to be given half of Scotland north of the Forth, if, and when, Scotland was conquered by England. This pact (not discovered until 1475) was subscribed at Ardtornish Castle, in

Morvern, on the mainland, directly opposite Garmony in Mull. The second significant act of John, Lord of the Isles, was to quarrel with his own illegitimate son. Father and son fought in Mull, at Bloody Bay, near Tobermory, around 1480. Bloody Bay is a name that can well be forgotten, or committed to oblivion; Ardtornish, on the mainland side of the Sound of Mull, and visible from the Mull ferry today, is a name which will return in this story.

Charters had been granted by the four generations of the Lords of the Isles of lands in the Mull group and after the 'age of turbulence' [2] which followed the forfeiture of the Lords, many of the charters were renewed in the name of the king into the mid-sixteenth century.

In 1540, the Scottish King James V made a voyage round the coasts and isles of his kingdom, and after summoning some of the island chiefs to meet him on board his ship, had them placed in captivity – a display of power which was followed up by the annexation of the lands of the Lordship of the Isles to the crown. In the year of his death, however, he granted a charter of former Lordship lands to Hector Maclean of Duart and his son Hector. These lands, which extended from Duart Castle itself to Torloisk on the north-west coast, when joined with former grants, made the Macleans of Duart the largest landholders in Mull, so that when James' daughter Mary, Queen of Scots, succeeded to the throne in December 1542 as a six-day-old baby, more than half of Mull was 'possessed' by the Macleans of Duart, and the rest by the Macleans of Lochbuy, the MacQuarries of Ulva, the Macleans of Coll, the MacKinnons of Mishnish and the abbey of Iona. Seven years later, the island was described by Dean Munro, Dean of the Isles, as 'ane grate roughe iyle' – 'rough' because it was full of mountains and bogs, mostly uncultivated, and with an interior which only an intrepid *Muileach* would care to traverse.

The abbey of Iona held its lands of Ross and Icolmkill (an English approximation of the Gaelic name for Iona, and the name used habitually until the Latinised name, Iona, was taken up again in the nineteenth century) from the crown, but after the Scottish Reformation in 1560, the monks left Iona, and the abbey and the nunnery became ruinous. Shortly after the Reformation, a feu charter of Iona and the Ross of Mull was granted by Bishop Carswell to Hector Maclean of Duart, and this was re-granted in 1588 by James VI to Hector's grandson, Hector Maclean of Duart.[3] But by 1648, the rents of the bishopric were under the control of the Marquis of Argyll, for reasons which will be made clear in the following chapter on the struggles between the Campbells of Argyll and the Macleans of Duart.

At the end of the sixteenth century, the island of Mull was shared by the Macleans of Duart, Lochbuy and Coll, with members of their extended families such as the Torloisk and Brolass Macleans, as well as MacKinnons and MacQuarries. In 1598, James VI introduced an act requiring all who claimed to own land in the Highlands and Islands to produce their title deeds before the Privy Council of Scotland. Crown charters were the necessary deeds, but Highland chiefs were slow to ensure that they had such documents in their possession. There was still a tradition around that conspicuous trappings such as castles, gentlemen's retinues, horses, cattle, galleys, weapons and wine casks were a more positive proof of power than written charters. They were without doubt more colourful, but the story of the following century, the seventeenth, was to show that the pen was to be incontestably mightier than the sword.

In 1608, James VI of Scotland, who was now more importantly James I of England, appointed a commission to summon the various chiefs of the Western Isles to a meeting at Aros, in Mull, at which they were to be acquainted with the intentions of government in regard to the organisation of their domains. Of the eleven chiefs who presented themselves, Mull was represented by six. Unlike chiefs further afield, the Mull lairds could have little excuse for not going to a meeting in Aros, but nevertheless their number was significant for the later diversity of ownership in Mull, in contrast to the more straightforward suzerainty of other islands.

The proceedings of the meeting at Aros Castle were recorded for the Privy Council by the convenor, Andrew Knox, Bishop of the Isles.[4] They consisted mainly of an intimation of government's plans before these plans were more formally presented. The chiefs learned that their castles should be at the disposal of the king, that they should pay rents directly to the crown and feu duties to the feudal superior (southern Scottish practices which had been in place since the reign of King David were only now catching up with the Hebrides), that they should abide by the laws of the rest of the kingdom, and that their children should be required to attend schools in the Lowlands, so that they might be integrated, in language and in customs, with other Scottish heirs of estates. But these directives were not as shocking to the chiefs as the order from on high that their birlinns, or larger boats, their galleys and all vessels of war were to be destroyed. Fortunately Bishop Knox was aware of the social and commercial necessity of birlinns for chiefs who had no other means of travelling to and from their islands. Knox interceded on their behalf for a modification of this clause. How could the chiefs pay the aforesaid rents to the king if they had no vessels to transport their cattle to market, or to effect other such peacable transactions? The abandonment of this draconian scheme was one of the few examples in the history of the islands of an amelioration which took the insular position of the chiefs into account.

The next stage of the scheme for the harmonisation of insular and mainland habits of life was enacted at Icolmkill, or Iona, in the following year. The chiefs attended in a slightly different grouping, and the intentions of government were modified in a manner which suggests the intervention of someone more concerned for the social and moral conditions of island life than for the long-term political advantages of government. Bishop Knox, who had first-hand knowledge of the isles, may have injected moral imperatives into the contract with the chiefs. Go-betweens who stand between a remote and ignorant power and a people living in an unkind environment can often make such practical compromises.

In the eighteenth century, in a similar way, Archibald Campbell of Stonefield was to intercede for the hard-pressed tenants of Mull when faced with the demands of a high-handed absentee duke.[5] When the new vision of life was codified in the Statutes of Icolmkill, it resembled the Ten Commandments rather than a political manifesto, and included the following guidelines:

1. The chiefs were to rebuild and support kirks, and ministers were to be planted in the islands.

2. Inns were to be established to protect inhabitants from having to supply food to strangers.

3. The number of gentlemen in chiefs' houses was to be reduced.

4. Sorning [the billeting of strangers on inhabitants] was to be abolished.

5. The importation of wine was to be prohibited to certain islanders of insufficient standing, to prevent drunkenness, but whisky might be distilled for home use.

6. Every gentleman of a certain standing (defined by the number of his cattle) must send his oldest son or daughter to the Lowlands, to be educated in English.

7. No one must carry firearms, even for shooting game.

8. Chiefs must not receive in their houses vagabonds, bards, beggars or jugglers, all being flatterers.

9. Chiefs must be answerable for their followers' behaviour, and report annually to the Privy Council.[6]

It has been said that the Statutes of Iona changed nothing in island life, that they were not implemented, and even that they were totally disregarded.[7] As the commissioners considered remedies, the scene shifted, and the islands which were giving government most trouble changed before their eyes. It is true that the conditions to be rectified were possibly common to all the islands, but the commissioners seem to have abandoned their political improvements, and as a stopgap, concentrated on domestic and moral problems which were to be found in all the islands. Thus we have a much more valuable picture drawn from the negative aspects of island life, and can fairly safely argue that in Mull, as in other places, there were, in the early seventeenth century, sorners, bards, vagabonds, jugglers, drunken commoners, beggars, strangers demanding hospitality, illegal carriers of firearms, ministers who were not backed up in their efforts by their chiefs, and chiefs who did nothing to punish the sins perpetrated around them. The picture is clear, and one that we must retain in our mind's eye when we look at the eighteenth and nineteenth centuries.

Even if the Statutes of Iona were afterwards disregarded, the Privy Council did hold the chiefs in check for a decade, but following the death of James VI in 1625, the priorities of English and Scottish government changed. An important event for the story of Mull was the establishment of the Register of Sasines in 1617 as a legal register of heritable property. Mull lairds were slow to realise its importance. In the seventeenth century they had not yet come to their inveterate habit of resorting to law in every eventuality. The first lairds to register were Murdoch Maclean of Lochbuy in 1643 and Hector Maclean of Torloisk in 1658. Others were not made aware of the register until well into the eighteenth century, when doubtless owing to their litigious tendencies, and most probably because they were raising loans against the collateral of their estates, their men of business in Edinburgh reminded them that a sasine was required.

The Macleans of Duart are conspicuous in the Register of Sasines by their absence. When Sir Lachlan Maclean of Duart was created a baronet in 1631 by Charles I, he had no sasine, although he did claim the right to a crown charter, granted in 1495, for his lands in Mull, which was a confirmation of an earlier charter from Donald, Lord of the Isles. Despite the new baronetcy, the Macleans of Duart were, as early as 1631, accumulating debts which were taken on by the astute Earls of Argyll, with Duart lands as security. In 1637, the Earl of Argyll quietly 'expeded' a charter to the lands of Aros and Brolass which Sir Lachlan Maclean of Duart had 'resigned' in 1634. Throughout the seventeenth century, therefore, the Duart Macleans lived above their income, with the help of the Campbells, who bided their time. What the Duart Macleans were doing to exceed their income in this way is largely unknown, but may be guessed at. They had been allowed by the Statutes of Icolmkill, or Iona, to keep eight gentlemen in their retinue, but who could enforce such a ration? Certainly the Privy Council was not sending inspectors to Duart, especially since Duart was garrisoned by the king's men, and, in theory, behaving itself. Sir Lachlan Maclean had given tacks on his estate to Maclean kinsmen, who paid rents to the Earl of Argyll direct. Sir Lachlan was receiving only small rents from his own lands, but life and private wars had to go on, and his expenses were as before.

Sir Lachlan was, as it happened, a partisan in the civil wars of his time. The civil wars were the Scottish end of the English struggle between Cavaliers and Roundheads, and played themselves out at the Battles of Inverlochy and Kilsyth in 1645. In the latter, the royalist Sir Lachlan was able to muster 750 Macleans and 350 MacQuarries, and won a short-lived victory.[8] But this small rout of the Covenanting forces brought only revenge from Argyll and General Leslie, who invaded Mull in 1647, putting an end to the island's resources of men and supplies. So grievous was the suffering of the poor in Argyllshire, that the General Assembly of the Church of Scotland issued a letter asking for contributions to enable the innocent victims to survive. Shortly afterwards, Sir Lachlan Maclean of Duart died, and the King himself was beheaded in

London. But the worst was still to come. At the Battle of Inverkeithing in July 1651, the new chief of the Macleans, Sir Hector, was killed with at least 700 Maclean clansmen and 200 other names, crippling the island of Mull for two generations.

And so the second half of the seventeenth century crept in upon an island with its fighting men – including many MacQuarries – killed, its lands and women and cattle ravaged, its crops unsown, and with two senior clansmen, Donald Maclean of Brolass and Murdoch Maclean of Lochbuy, in charge of the very young, very new Maclean chief.

A description of the island survives from 1680, when it is to be hoped some regeneration of population had repaired the ravages of Inverkeithing thirty years before. Without reference to the political and financial feud of the Macleans and the Campbells (which will be dealt with in the next chapter) the writer of the 1680 description presents an estate agent's view of Mull, or a document fit for tourists, had any existed or dared to go there.

The island had many woods, of birch, hazel, rowan and holly; it had many foxes, harts and hinds, salmon, herrings, cod, wildfowl; the men were tall, fair-complexioned, valiant and of a naturally martial disposition, and wore plaids and 'trowes'; the women wore white blankets belted about them, and bracelets of 'pretious stones' around their necks; Duart Castle still had a 'spatious hall'; the best harbour was at Lochbuy, and the best roads for ships to ride at anchor in were near Duart and Bunessan and at various points in the Sound of Mull; cattle were bred in abundance though pasturage was poor; medicinal plants grew in the mountains and medicinal springs were at Ben Buie and in the Ross of Mull; seven churches could be counted, but no burying grounds, for heaps of stones were built up where men had been killed; horses were small, but of good mettle; mussels, clams, oysters and other shellfish were plentiful on the north-west coast, and Inchkenneth was so fertile that cows and sheep required no bull to produce their young. Aros Castle was, in 1680, uninhabited.[9]

It should not be surprising that most of the warfare and plunder in Mull was caused by disputes over land, between families that had long been enemies, particularly where that land should be governed by indistinct laws, or laws in transition, or laws which could be ignored by the power of the sword. The Highlands and Islands of Scotland were slow to be influenced by the Normans and the feudalisation which transformed southern Scotland as early as the twelfth century, yet aristocratic models in the two areas were not dissimilar. Great men in the islands had their fortified castles as had great men in the Lowlands. Their lands were held indirectly of the king, yet the king himself was rarely apparent in the few dealings (except for his 1540 kidnapping of the chiefs) they had had with him before 1600. Gaelic-speaking lords had a system of inheritance not unlike the southern one, for they were not unaware of the benefits of feudal laws. But Scottish government turned its attention at intervals to the problem of the threat from such unorthodox bonds as the Treaty of Ardtornish, and the unfettered activities of Highland chiefs. The crown had interfered with the Lordship of the Isles, and had moved to curb the power of

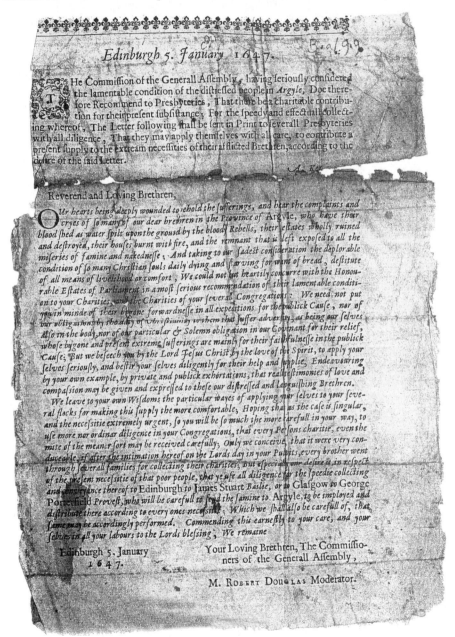

Letter from the Commissioners of the General Assembly of the Church of Scotland, sent to presbyteries in 1647, recommending a collection in aid of the distressed people of Argyll. (*Edinburgh University Library*)

chiefs in the Statutes of Iona. But in the seventeenth century, struggles between Campbells and Macleans had been allowed, on the whole, to evolve and to abate with only occasional interference from the Scottish Privy Council on legal points, interpreted according to the law of the times, and that law had in itself evolved from the increasing importance of charters and sasines. Decisions about the validity of claims to land were increasingly made in favour of the Campbells, whose peculiar talent was to keep their territorial gains within an impeccable legal framework. Thus the Argyll Campbells, for example, insisted upon the Lowland concept of feu duty, due to the superior who stood between the king and the possessors of land, and when this feu duty, unrecognised by holders of land under the Lords of the Isles, remained unpaid, a huge retrospective debt was built up, which the superiors could produce before the Privy Council in evidence of the clan's recalcitrance. The family of Argyll therefore became creditors claiming enormous cumulative payments, not only from their old enemies, the Macleans, but also from other clans whose feudal superiors they had become during the gradual, but legal and almost imperceptible fusion of feudal legislation and old Highland custom. If rents had not been paid to the superiors to eradicate debts, feu duties and rents were combined, with compound interest, into an ever-increasing sum, which, as we shall see in the following chapters, was to cause the downfall of the clan MacQuarrie and its dependants, as well as the Macleans of Duart.

That the clan Campbell should have had the perspicacity to operate on a financial and legal front against its enemies, who remained entrenched in their Celtic habits of chieftainship, and their misconceived and outdated ideas of heroism in battle, may seem simplistic, in view of the variations of personality in heads of families, but the accounts of these families which follow give ample proof of inherited traits of cunning, irresponsibility, guile and foolishness, which were to have their effect on the fate of the lairds and their tenants, and which were to influence the whole history of Mull for two centuries.

Notes

1. Ritchie, quoted in Walker, D. M., *The Scottish Legal System*, p. 78.
2. Munro and Munro, *Acts of the Lords of the Isles, 1336–1493*.
3. *Argyll 4*: Iona, p. 149.
4. Seneachie, *Historical and Genealogical Account of the Clan Maclean*.
5. *Infra*, p. 35.
6. For a variety of presentation of the clauses of the Statutes *see* Campbell, *Canna, The Story of a Hebridean Island*; Grant, *The Macleods, The History of a Clan, 1200–1956*; Goodare, 'The Statutes of Iona in context' in *SHR* 77, 1: 203.
7. Goodare, op. cit.
8. Sinclair, *The Maclean Bards*.
9. NLS. Sibbald Papers. Adv. MS. 33.3.20. ff. 11–13 and 34.

2

Ne obliviscaris: *the Campbells and the Macleans*

'Let it not be forgotten' might be the English translation of the Latin motto of the Campbells of Argyll, and it certainly could not be forgotten by the unfortunate clans who suffered from Campbell ambition and cunning in the seventeenth century. Students of Scottish history are familiar with the humorous jibes at Campbell tactics which recur in every academic account of the civil wars in Scotland. The heroes who dared to oppose the Earls of Argyll, such as the Marquis of Montrose and Alasdair MacColla, are treated with particular affection because of the general consensus, not only among contemporaries, but among historians, that the Campbells of Argyll were a particularly unlovable breed, who passed on from generation to generation not only the name of Archibald, but a personality with the same components of self-righteousness, deviousness and acquisitiveness. The Campbells themselves changed allegiance, and yet remained the same. They were frequently on the wrong side. On the national stage they suffered the death penalty and forfeiture twice in the course of the seventeenth century, but in their more local ambitions to control the Highlands they acted in a Campbell way, which meant that with unceasing application they hunted their prey, and their prey mainly consisted of two or three clans who would not give in. Of these clans, the most resistant were the Macleans.

In the 1640s, when confrontation between the west Highland clans and clan Campbell was at its peak, Montrose, who was an outsider, and Alasdair MacColla, an insider, had joined forces in the Royalist cause, and had in 1645 advanced through Argyll, hitherto regarded as impregnable, destroying houses, killing cattle and burning what they could. On 2 February 1645, they carried off the extraordinary feat of routing Campbell forces at Inverlochy, near present-day Fort William, in a mighty slaughter. The Mull Macleans did not play a large part, although Sir Lachlan Maclean of Duart and Maclean of Torloisk were participants, and the Gaelic poets who celebrated the victory reproached the 'Mull heroes' who did not turn up at Inverlochy with virulent sarcasm. To the bard Ian Lom Macdonald, the battle was not one of a series of encounters between Royalists and Covenanters, and not related to the sassenach quarrel between Cavaliers and Roundheads, but a head-on encounter between Campbells and their enemies. But even for onlooking Mull Macleans, the slaughter at Inverlochy was sweet, and they wished they had been part of it – wished that it might happen again. By 15 August 1645, Donald Maclean of Brolass, brother to Duart, had added more than 1,000 men to Montrose's army, led by Sir Lachlan Maclean of Duart, to join Montrose and MacColla at Kilsyth, where again the battle was won. It was a dramatic event, and one which would be described by bards and participants for years to come. To be a player in an epic poem by a Gaelic bard, and to be able to relate feats of bravery to grandchildren, was an important achievement. Gaelic accounts did not mention the larger issues such as the sanctity of kingship, or the political balance of power in Scotland and England. Pride in victory was about the vanquishing of the soft 'dulse-eating rabble',[1] and the humiliation of Campbells and their allies.[2]

Highlanders seldom viewed warfare as an ongoing commitment. When they were needed, and when a detested enemy was the target, they ventured from their glens or islands, fought with fierce determination, and withdrew, especially if harvest time was approaching and their families needed them at home. Thus it was that in mid-September 1645, Montrose was without his Mull heroes when he was surprised by General David Leslie at Philiphaugh. The men lost by Montrose were mainly Irish.

In 1647, Argyll and Leslie engaged together to stamp out opposition in Argyll. After cruel punishments in Kintyre and Islay, Leslie landed in Mull and confronted Sir Lachlan at Duart. Sir Lachlan was forced to surrender not only his castle, but the faithful Irishmen who had protected Duart, and who were duly put to death. The atrocities committed by both sides in Argyll in this year, with innocent people murdered, villages burned, and even Inveraray destroyed, moved the Commissioners of the General Assembly of the Church of Scotland to send the letter reproduced on page 9, expressing their heartfelt sorrow in beholding the sufferings and hearing the complaints and cries of their dear brethren in the province of Argyll.

Among Sir Lachlan's retinue at Duart in 1647, was the Rev. Farquhar Fraser, minister of Tiree, who had marched with the Maclean chief and Montrose, as chaplain to Sir Lachlan's men. He had been minister in Tiree for fifteen years, and was serving his own fighting men as well as his chief, so that his absence in the campaigns was not entirely dereliction of duty. Nevertheless, he was debarred from his charge for aiding the Royalists, and only after the Restoration and the death of Sir Lachlan was he compensated for his diligence among his people. His son, John Fraser, probably born at Duart in 1647, the year of complaints and cries, was later to be his successor in Tiree as well as in the chaplaincy, being preacher to Sir Allan Maclean of Duart between 1667 and 1677.[3] Another minister in the presbytery of Mull, Martin McGilvra of Pennyghael, was deposed from his incumbency at Iona for complying with the rebels, but reinstated at Kilninian before the deposers' backs were turned. Such excellent ministers could not be dispensed with, and in 1660 Mr McGilvra was able to turn his mind to the important task of translating the Old Testament Book of Nehemiah into Gaelic, which told of the repairing of the walls of Jerusalem.

The deposition of Mull ministers and the surrender of Duart to General David Leslie, were not, however, to be the most dire consequences for Mull of the Maclean allegiance to the Royalist cause, but only the goads which drove men to attempt the turning of the tide. Between the Cromwellian assumption of power in England in 1649 and the setting up of a commission to manage Scottish affairs in 1652, fell the shadow of Inverkeithing. This battle, fought on 20 July 1651, a year after the hanging of Montrose, receives little attention from historians,[4] which is why Mull requires a history of its own. The small Fife burgh of Inverkeithing was farther from home than the Macleans usually ventured in battle, but harvests were late in Mull, Morvern and Tiree, and there was time to fight with the new Duart chief, Sir Hector, before returning. The protagonists were very different from the bold fighters of Inverlochy and Kilsyth. This time the enemies were sassenachs,[5] led by General John Lambert, Cromwell's 32-year-old 'understudy', who had learned his art at Marston Moor, Preston and Pontefract. This time the conflict was between Scots and English, and the Macleans' nearest allies were the Buchanans. Surrounded by the English, the rash 25-year-old Sir Hector, whom even his most partial clan historian was unable to praise,[6] was defended by a Maclean kinsman, who leapt between Hector and his assailant. The kinsman was cut down. Another clansman threw himself before the chief, calling out *'Fear eile airson Eachainn'* ('Another for Hector'), until eight Macleans had, with the same cry, sacrificed themselves. Towards the end of the battle, Sir Hector himself was killed by a musket ball, and 700 Macleans, 100 MacQuarries and other Mull heroes lay dead.

It was said that thirty-five men returned to Mull.[7] The sons of Treshnish, Coll, Torloisk, Ardchrishnish and of the MacQuarries of Ulva, as well as commoners in great numbers, were wiped out; there were not enough men left to plough and plant in Mull, Morvern and Tiree for a generation,[8] and the loss explains much of the apparent passivity with which Mull faced its fate at the hands of the Campbells of Argyll in the next half century.

But where lurked Argyll? It is tempting to give the name to a composite figure representing all the earls of the seventeenth century, but there is one particularly salient Argyll: the squint-eyed Gillespie Gruamach (Archibald the Grim), eighth Earl and Marquis, who had, at this juncture, gone to earth. Son of the seventh earl who had been trusted and favoured by James VI, and who had added the peninsula of Kintyre to his domains, Gillespie Gruamach did not really resemble his father in the superficial or acquired aspects of his character; the father had, for instance, become a Roman Catholic, and from his earliest days Gruamach was a Presbyterian. But the verse of a Scottish poet

> Now Earl of Guile and Lord Forlorn thou goes,
> Quitting thy Prince to serve his foreign foes.

made fun of the Argyll title, and that of the heir, Lord Lorne, and indicates the family propensity to join forces with unexpected and often disastrous allies, in this case Philip of Spain. Gruamach was born in 1607, and was only eleven years old when his father was pronounced a traitor for his alliance with the Spanish king. Yet Gruamach, remaining in Scotland, was made a Scottish privy councillor even before his father's death in 1638. Although such a staunch Presbyterian, he did not sign the National Covenant. His principles remained fudged and vague, as well they might in a shifting age. But when some clans rose against the Covenant, Gruamach raised 4,000 of his own Campbells to oppose them. He had committed himself at last. By so doing, he made himself an enemy of Montrose, and of the Highland clans who hated him, but it was inevitable that they should be on opposing sides. Gruamach's financial activities as administrator of the Argyll estates and his predatory moves against the property of the Macleans, the Macdonalds and the Camerons, ensured, even if age-old hostility had not, the opposition of these families.[9]

After Inverkeithing, the Duart heir, Sir Allan, younger brother to the impetuous Hector, was but a child. Accounts of his age vary, but he was assigned guardians for about ten years. He must have been fostered, as was the custom of the day, in a friendly family. He married Julia Macleod of Dunvegan in Skye, and the son and heir, Sir John, was born in 1670. During Sir Allan's minority, the threats of Gruamach – beginning with reminders that he had bought the Duart debts – multiplied. Maclean of Brolass, tutor or guardian to Sir Allan, insisted that he had paid off about a tenth of the dues, but there is some doubt about this, both from lack of receipts on the Maclean side, and lack of confirmation by the Campbells. Meanwhile a new and inimical presence appeared at Duart. The Cromwellian vision of a Commonwealth of England, Scotland and Ireland included a garrison at Duart, and the Cromwellian officer Cobbett, testing the waters, found the country people so decimated, so demoralised and frightened, that they ran away from his troops. In their fright the people may have indulged in imprecations, for eight days after the landing, the Commonwealth forces lost some ships in the Sound of Mull, in that kind of violent storm which can be worse in July than in December.[10] Lillburne, the Cromwellian agitator, wrote from Dalkeith in 1654 that he had had a meeting with 'Marquesse Argyll' (Gruamach), who 'spoke very cordially, and I hope intends so' (even Lillburne was nonplussed by Gruamach's ambiguous manner, not helped by the squint). 'Hee is fearfull of his owne country and estate being ruined by the Enemy.' Indeed, Gruamach had never recovered from the surprise of his Argyll estates being overrun by Alasdair MacColla and Montrose in January 1645. His family motto, *Ne obliviscaris*, now applied to himself as well as his foes. In March, Lillburne instructed Captain Emerson, governor of the garrison of Duart, to reduce the people of Mull to obedience to the Lord Protector and to find out their inclination and temper. But the poor remnant of the slaughter of Inverkeithing posed no threat.

Gruamach, though 'fearfull of his owne country', had studied how to pass the time with profit. In 1659 he obtained a court adjudication from Edinburgh to say that both the superiority and the property of Maclean of Duart's lands were vested in himself.[11] But he had not chosen his moment well enough to have much joy from the decision. Oliver Cromwell had died in September 1658, Richard Cromwell had not lasted, and Charles II was restored to the throne in 1660. Gruamach was attainted, forfeited and beheaded on 27 May 1661; and for some reason – not compatible with dispassionate reporting – many Scottish historians have been unable to resist recording that his severed head was stuck on the very pikestaff recently decorated with the much prettier head of Montrose.

We have no evidence that there was rapture in Mull when news of Gruamach's death reached the people, but we do know that the Gaelic bard Ian Lom was overjoyed.[12] But Gruamach had a son, who, in that not unfamiliar manner of fathers and sons, was diametrically opposed to his father in politics, having espoused the Royalist cause in 1653, although in religion he did not differ from Gruamach. Young Archibald may have caused Gruamach's fear, and his disinclination to venture out, but the Macleans must have thought that the Argylls were simply hedging their bets on survival, and that father and son were in league. Sir Allan Maclean and his family had reason to suspect something of this kind, for, as a result of the court adjudication the Argyll family received Duart rents direct, and attainted and beheaded as Gruamach might be, the rents had not reverted to their rightful owners. The tutors and guardians of Duart had not seized the moment of Gruamach's execution to assert the Maclean claim, for the law was slow, and it was not even clear that Duart belonged to the crown. The marquis might be no more, but the great clutch of lawyers who worked tirelessly on his behalf, did not become idle overnight. The Argyll estates might be in limbo, but rentals continued to be made up, lands to be 'sett' and titles to be confirmed. In the year following the execution, the Mull lands were allocated by Hector Maclean of Torloisk and John Maclean of Ardgour. In 1663, only two years after the beheading, the whole of the Argyll estate was restored to young Archibald, Lord Lorne, his title revived as ninth Earl of Argyll. When seen as an act of indulgence on the part of Charles II to the 33-year-old professed Royalist, it could not surprise anyone. From the perspective of Sir Allan, now come of age, and also a Royalist by descent, it was preposterous and cruel.

Sir Allan Maclean's position was precarious. He was informed by his guardians that his debts to the Campbells of Argyll were in the process of being eradicated, but that no receipt had been given for the monies paid back. There was some doubt even among friendly clans about any money having been paid back. Sir Ewen Cameron of Lochiel refused to believe in the Maclean payments, saying in his memoirs

The unaccountable negligence of Maclean and his managers gave the Earl of Argyle a handle for seizing their opulent fortune by infefting himself upon the previous adjudication [with] legal diligence and fire and sword. It was unlucky for the Macleans that the Chief was a child and his tutor unfit ... for instead of settling matters by a composition, or attempting to redress them by law, he vainly squandered his pupill's money, and ruined the poor people by keeping them in arms against the Earl of Argyle's threatened invasion.[13]

Lochiel's view gives a quite different complexion to the story, which is usually given by Maclean apologists. The question was to be re-examined in the late eighteenth century, when in the process Allan Maclean of Drimnin *v.* John Duke of Argyll, the origin of the Campbell claim was investigated.[14] Whatever the truth about the repayments might be (and it is not an exaggeration to say that the whole history of Mull depended upon the turn events then took), the young Sir Allan Maclean of 1665 was a singularly tragic figure. He had no rents coming in, and therefore no money. The new Earl of Argyll was gathering his forces (he too was not without his debts), and was requesting a remittance of £121,000 Scots.[15] An appeal to Charles II in 1672 was put into the hands of Lauderdale, the Secretary of State for Scotland, who happened to be Argyll's ally, and only used his position to advance Argyll's cause. The Macleans were babes in arms when it came to state politics, especially in the corrupt forms of Lauderdale and the ninth earl. In 1674, Sir Allan died at the age of thirty-three, in the provoking way people had in those times, and no reason, regret or surprise at such an early death was expressed later by his few, incurious biographers.

The child of Duart who came into his empty inheritance now was Sir John (or Sir Iain) Maclean, aged four. He was fostered in the family of the Earl of Seaforth, and we do not know if he was sent to the lowlands for his schooling. Of what relevance were those far-off statutes of Iona now, with their guidelines for civilising island society? The most consistent enemy of the clan Maclean was the reigning Earl of Argyll, and it was the guardians of each succeeding Duart Maclean (usually Brolasses and Torloisks) who had the problem of negotiating with that enemy. When negotiation or resistance failed, the Argylls resorted to the Scottish Privy Council, and in 1674 that body granted a commission of fire and sword against the Macleans, giving the Campbells, backed by government troops, *carte blanche* to invade Mull. The poor people of Mull could only retreat into their own mountains with their cattle, and from the ensuing cruelties their long hatred of the Campbells was intensified. Within two weeks in September the Macleans capitulated. But Argyll's attempts to rewrite the terms of the charters went too far. The Macleans decided upon armed resistance. The child, Sir John, was taken to Cairnburgh, an island fortress in the Treshnish islands. There followed a series of plunderings and raids more typical of the fifteenth than the seventeenth century, and as these went on, so the Earl of Argyll continued to have his agents count the debts of Duart, until they reached the satisfactorily round figure of

£200,000. More than half of the tenantry of Mull were now registered as 'outlaws' due to the quite legal letters of ejection obtained by the earl against them.[16] From 1675 until 1679, alternate indemnities and threats were offered to the Macleans until they finally gave in. The end of the active struggles of the Macleans of Duart can therefore be dated to 1679, when the threat of the Dunbartonshire militia to be used against them served to quench the bravado which had sustained them since the fatal battle of Inverkeithing.

No sooner had the Macleans given up the struggle than a small setback in the ninth earl's career appeared, which might have set them free. Earl Archibald refused to sign the oath of the Test Act. It seems inconsistent with the character of such a great opportunist that he should stand by principle, but the Test Act and Oath of 1681 required all office bearers under the crown to adhere to Protestantism, as defined by the Confession of Faith of 1560, and this definition stuck in the earl's throat. The Confession had been superseded by the Westminster Confession of the 1640s, but it was the earlier statement of doctrine which was invoked. Then the earl did sign, but his signature was prefaced, and invalidated, by a number of qualifications which the reigning powers did not appreciate, and he was arrested for treason. Condemned to death, he escaped in an episode worthy of Toad of Toad Hall. He did not appear to have the kind of captors who might have pursued him with the rigour he would himself have applied to his enemies, but was at large for some time, in Holland. Here he was said to be involved in plots to assassinate Charles II and the future James II. When Charles died in 1685, Argyll was keen to raise support in Scotland for the rebellion against the Catholic King James. But his followers proved recalcitrant, and not as numerous as he had hoped. He was arrested near Renfrew, with his sentence still legally binding. The execution took place in 1685, on the same spot as that of his father, Gillespie Gruamach. He was fifty-six. He had, in a sense, managed to manipulate even death, so that it did not visit him until all the energies of his prime had been well invested in that cumulative Campbell wellbeing which was more important than mere life. The kindest thing that was said of him was written 300 years later, when he was described as a 'great planter'.[17]

A six-year-old boy was somewhere on the sidelines in 1685. His biographer, Robert Campbell, relates a curious incident on the very day of his grandfather's execution, when the child fell out of a window three storeys high, but the biographer did not say where, or how.[18] It was not regarded as an indication of the boy's deep distress, but as a good omen for the future of the Campbells, that he survived.[19] The child's father, the tenth earl, another Archibald, went through the same procedure as his own father, having the estates forfeited, and 'suffering my unjust sentence in banishment these thrie years and ane halfe'.[20] He was uncertain of the outcome until James VII was ousted, and William and Mary were called to the throne, by which time he had made sure of being on the right side, accompanying William of Orange from Holland on his triumphant arrival in England; his title and his lands were, of course, restored to him. To the Highland clans, many of whom had been financially indebted to the Argylls before the forfeiture, this development must have seemed disastrous and quite unbelievable. A rebellion broke out in Scotland, ostensibly against William and Mary, but possibly as much against the reinstatement of Argyll. Under 'Bonnie Dundee', the rebels fought at Killiecrankie, but with Dundee's death, all hope of a Jacobite ascendancy faded, and the next humiliation to the Highlanders was that the tenth earl himself undertook to extract from them an oath of loyalty to the new sovereigns.

Sir John Maclean's guardians had tried to take advantage of the ninth earl's strange inflexibility over the wording of the Test Act and his subsequent execution. They applied to the Privy Council for the restoration of Duart, and were successful in their appeal. But the Privy Council's order to the Argyll faction to restore the estates came when the estates were neither the Argylls' to return, nor the Macleans' to assume. The castle of Duart itself was occupied by Campbell of Inverawe, one of the commanders in the string of garrisons stretching from Inverlochy (Fort William) to the islands. The governor of Inverlochy was an Englishman, Colonel John Hill, who had kept his post through every twitch and change of government since Oliver Cromwell, and who prided himself on his neutrality. His role was precisely to take no part in clan feuds, these being the principal cause of disorder in the Highlands. Whether Campbell of Inverawe's refusal to surrender the stronghold was his own most natural Campbell inclination, or his happy interpretation of Colonel Hill's philosophy of governorship we shall never know. But it was a typical example of how Campbells always seemed to benefit (speaking of the dynasty, and not of the headless individuals) from changes in kings and governments, while Macleans lost out. There is many a slip 'twixt cup and lip, and in the years following the Privy Council's reprieve, Charles II died, James II and VII came to the throne, the so-called 'Glorious Revolution' put William and Mary in James' place, and Lachlan Maclean of Brolass, the principal guardian of the young chief of Duart, decided to begin to die. But on many occasions the Macleans seemed to live up to the image of the two ostriches which appear as supporters on their coat of arms: their heads were buried in the sand. (Sir John was literally buried on the tiny island of Cairnburgh for more than a year!) They were in the wrong place at the wrong time; Sir John had fought, naturally, at Killiecrankie. They were either too young to be wise (Sir John), or too old to act with speed (Maclean of Brolass). Complaints from the Argyll Campbells after the execution of the ninth earl about depredations, and the recurring phrase, referring to their cattle, 'carried away to Mull', suggests the Macleans took advantage of the Argyll interregnum by making gleeful cattle raids on the mainland rather than by consulting lawyers in Edinburgh.[21] Their moment had passed them by.

Colonel Hill, who corresponded with the laird of Culloden,[22] wrote from

Fort William on 24 November 1690 to report that the tenth earl 'My Lord Argyle' entered Mull with about 1,900 foot and sixty dragoons in order to extract from the inhabitants an oath of allegiance to the king and queen. The people had submitted, given up their arms, taken the oath of allegiance, but the weather had been so bad that the earl and his company had been unable to approach Duart from the sea. They needed heavier boats in which to carry their battering pieces and 'other engines of war'. Maclean himself, the governor added, was in 'Carnburrow, a Rock in the Sea that is inaccessible'. The earl had undertaken this task, Colonel Hill was careful to point out, at his own expense. Indeed the whole company was employed at the earl's own expense. 'He managed Generously & selfdenyingly, minding none of his own Concerns ... and treated the people with great Civility after their Submission.'

It seems clear from Colonel Hill's letter [23] that the earl did not prise Sir John out of Cairnburgh.[24] But in his report to the lords of the Privy Council in Scotland, this 'lord of Guile' was vague, self-righteous and very interested in having his expenses repaid.

> Att this tyme one came about who told us he understood Sir John Maclean was inclyned to submitt, but especially some of his followers wold, particularly the Tutor of Torloisk, and that he wanted an opportunity; upon which I sent over two Gentlemen to descourse ... Together they gave some full submissions ... I found it was his aversion to submitt to the present government ... mainly with the intent to have blown up the house of Dowart, and agreed to the most of what I demanded as to my own private interest, but wold not submitt to those terms ... Indeed I promised if they continued firm to King William I wold give the utmost of my interest in their behalf ... When I had received all their oaths, I went toward Dowart with a design to have besieged it, and lay in the open fields 10 days waiting for guns ... bot ye wynd proved so contrary and the weather so stormy that in all this tyme there could be no going over ... I doe propose no further advantage to myself by those garrisons but the publick service, for had I minded my own private concern, my rents, all that was owing me had been sent me over to Lorne without going to Mull ... I hope by this account your Lordships would be pleased ... to recommend [me] to his Majesties favour and that the whole expense I have been at may [be] considered.[25]

The Mull bard, Iain MacAilean, or John Maclean, wrote a song about the submissions, *Beir fios leat bhuam do Chearnaburg*, which explains the *Muileach*'s position with regard to oaths of allegiance taken in extenuating circumstances:

> Take a message with you from me to Cairnburgh
> To the lord of the excellent brave heroes,
> Although I made a change of master,
> My honour is none the worse of it.

> The oaths we took over there,
> When Argyll and his men were encamped
> By God's grace did our souls no harm
> For they were taken against our will.[26]

It is not known if the tenth earl made another expedition to Mull. Once again, it was seen by Mull people, and by modern historians as a Campbell conquest rather than a government exercise.[27] The earl makes his 2,000 strong force sound benign, but they were mostly Campbells, and they would hardly have been human if they had not avenged some of the 'depradations' of 1685–86. Coming in October 1690, the expedition served as an introduction to 'King William's Years' – the name given to the last decade of the seventeenth century.

Notes

1. Dulse, from the Irish word for seaweed, was Ian Lom's derogatory term for green vegetables, and in particular kale, which Highlanders despised, as fit only for soft Lowlanders, and which, in the food crises of the nineteenth century, they were reluctant to grow.
2. Stevenson, David, *Highland Warrior: Alasdair MacColla and the Civil Wars*, p. 159.
3. *Fasti Ecclesiae Scoticanae*, IV, 119–20. See also introduction to *Deuteroskopia, or a Brief Discourse Concerning the Second Sight*, by Rev. John Fraser.
4. In Gordon Donaldson's *The Edinburgh History of Scotland*, vol. 3. Inverkeithing is mentioned in a subordinate adverbial clause, while the clan histories of the Macleans devote no fewer than ten pages to the detail.
5. Sassenach: in Gaelic, an English person.
6. A. Maclean Sinclair, *The Clan Gillean*, pp. 195–6. 'His conduct in continuing the unequal fight so long, when he might have retreated or surrendered, was utterly unreasonable ... useless to the king and injurious to his clan ... We deplore his recklessness and folly.'
7. Ibid., p. 194
8. Macinnes, Allan I., *Clanship, Commerce and the House of Stuart, 1603–1788*, pp. 30–1, 109.
9. Argyll family relationships from Grant, Neil, *The Campbells of Argyll.*
10. Firth, G. H., *Scotland and the Protectorate.*
11. Campbell, J. L. and Thomson, Derick, *Edward Lhuyd in the Scottish Highlands, 1699–1700.*
12. Stevenson, p. 278.
13. *Memoirs of Sir Ewen Cameron of Locheill, Chief of the Clan Cameron*, pp. 195–6.
14. MacPhail, J. R. N. (ed.), *Highland Papers*, I, pp. 242–337.
15. Conversion from pounds Scots was later made by dividing by twelve.
16. MacPhail, 'Caption, the earl of Argyll against John Maclean and others, 1675. Some hundreds of names with places of residence, were denounced rebels: for not flitting and removing themselves, their wives, bairns, families, servants, sub-tenants, cottars, goods, gear and others furth and frae the lands ... pertaining to the said complainer.'
17. Lindsay, Ian G. and Cosh, Mary, *Inveraray and the Dukes of Argyll*, p. 23.

18. Sir Walter Scott, in his *Tales of a Grandfather*, identifies the window at Lethington, near Haddington.

19. Campbell, Robert, *The Life of the Most Illustrious Prince, John, Duke of Argyll and Greenwich*, 1745.

20. Declaration of the Earl of Argyll, 1685, Culloden Papers, published 1815.

21. *Account of the Depredations Committed on the Clan Campbell and their Followers during the Years 1685 and 1686, from a Manuscript* ...

22. Duncan Forbes of Culloden, father of the Duncan Forbes, Lord President, who was to interfere disastrously with Mull affairs forty years later.

23. *Culloden Papers*, no. XIX.

24. 'Cairn na Burgh More, rock of the big fort. Landing on both "Carnburgs" is difficult, and strong tidal streams don't help. It is easy to see how defensible they were. The larger Carnburg has its fortifications on the flat grassy top with a massive wall infilling a natural rock buttress on the perimeter. A further wall and stone gateway protects the castle and chapel.' Haswell-Smith, Hamish, *The Scottish Islands*. The island was, however, taken by Leslie in his 'visit' to Mull in 1647, and although supposed to be garrisoned by Maclean of Torloisk thereafter, its occupation by Sir John was kindly overlooked.

25. NLS. Argyll Papers. MS 3138. Report of the Earl of Argyle's Commission to Mull.

26. Sinclair, A. Maclean (ed.), *The Maclean Bards*, vol. 1, p. 91.

27. Dr John Bannerman in *The Beatons* calls it a devastating invasion of Mull by the Campbells.

3

Dukes and exiles

King William's years (1689–1702) were long remembered in Mull for a series of bad harvests and appalling weather, which brought famine and death in their wake. If there was any hope of deliverance from evil lurking in the breasts of the people of the islands, it came from rumours, which were constantly going the rounds, of help from France on behalf of the deposed King James VII, stories which were to persist through all the years preceding the Jacobite rising of 1715. Duncan Forbes of Culloden, in a memoir about the preservation of peace in the Highlands, saw quite clearly that King William would never gain the affection of Highlanders while such reports were encouraged by preachers,[1] and ministers had a hard time. With the departure of Sir John Maclean from Mull in 1692, and news of the treachery of the Campbells in the massacre of Glencoe in the same year, the atmosphere was tense. John Beaton, minister of Kilninian from 1679, having suffered in the tenth earl's 'expedition', was deposed in 1701, ostensibly for immoral conduct, but more probably for political reasons.[2] His successor in Kilninian, the scholar and poet John Maclean of the Treshnish family, was regarded with suspicion at a later date, when Duncan Forbes, son of the percipient memorialist, took a dislike to him.[3]

Martin Martin, describing the Hebrides in 1695, mentioned that the natives of Mull took large doses of aqua vitae, or whisky, as a corrective, when the season was very moist. As Martin was observing with approval the small black cattle and horses of Mull, an act was passed in the Scottish parliament which almost certainly went unnoticed on the island, but which was to have results more than a century later. This was the Act for the Division of Commonties, 1695, which allowed areas of land then held in common by neighbouring proprietors, to be annexed to estates, by agreement between owners.[4] A year later, in 1696, it was enacted that a schoolmaster should be appointed to every parish in Scotland, that a commodious house be provided for him, and his salary paid by heritors and tenants. 'Never was a law more studiously disregarded', said the social historian Henry Graham,[5] except, we might add, in Mull, where the laws enacted first by the General Assembly of the Church of Scotland, and then by parliament, several times over, for the establishment of a minister in every parish, with a manse, a glebe and pasturage for a cow were utterly ignored.

It had been observed by Forbes of Culloden in his memoir, mentioned above, that Jacobites called themselves Episcopal, 'but really are indifferent of that & all matters of that nature, and are addicted to nothing but King James.'

Martin Martin had remarked of Mull that everyone was a Protestant 'except two or three who are Roman Catholics', thus making clear the difference between the Argyll islands, Colonsay, Jura, Tiree, Coll and Mull, and the Inverness-shire parish of the Small Isles, containing Eigg, Rum and Canna, which were Catholic. The inhabitants of Mull, whose habit was to embrace everything opposed to the Argyll interest, must have had to do some double thinking in their religious affiliations, just as they had taken the oath of allegiance tongue in cheek. The Argylls did not become assiduous presenters and patrons of Protestant ministers until the second half of the eighteenth century, but they had influence in the General Assembly and the Privy Council which kept their islands Protestant. The ministers of the period 1690–1750 were loved and respected for their Gaelic culture and for their faithfulness to the Maclean way of life. Farquhar Fraser, minister of Tiree from 1633 until about 1680, had been Sir Lachlan Maclean's regimental chaplain. His son, John Fraser, born at Duart, won twenty-four families in Coll to Protestantism, not because of any Campbell hold on him, but through his own learning, charm and understanding of the minds of his congregation. Of such a breed were the early ministers in this story, and of such a breed did they continue, through the eighteenth and early nineteenth centuries. If the ministers had enemies within their parishes, they were not of the Campbell name, but Macleans, MacQuarries and Maclaines, these three, and the greatest of these was to be Lochbuy.

The tenth Earl of Argyll was much taken up with the things of the state after his expedition to Mull in 1690. In 1701 he was rewarded for his services to the monarchy with a dukedom, and died in 1703. His heir, John (at last the succession of Archibalds was, if temporarily, broken) was the child who had fallen out of a window on the day of his grandfather's execution, with his psychological development apparently unimpaired. Duke John was not a bright child, or at least he did not show a particular interest in book learning. His gifts lay in military matters, of which he had experience from the age of sixteen. He and his brother Archibald were prime movers in the preparations for the parliamentary union of Scotland and England. Duke John's military service in the wars of the Spanish succession, from 1701 to 1714, made him a hero second only to Marlborough in the eyes of the English, and when he was made commander of the government forces at the outbreak of the Scottish Jacobite rising of 1715, his popularity was enormous. He was one of the finest-looking young men of the age, with 'an expressive countenance, a commanding air, and the most easy engaging gracefulness of manner'.[6] This charming hero had had an entirely English education, unlike his younger brother and successor, Archibald, Earl of Ilay, who studied law at Glasgow University and Utrecht. When very young, he had married an Englishwoman of fortune, Mary Browne, but was separated from her both by intense dislike and by his long military service in Europe. His charm and good looks did not entirely conceal a quixotic temper, rashness, ambition and a haughty impatience of being contradicted. These characteristics gave him a rather elusive personality, and his favour, when granted, seemed all the more valuable to its recipients. At the time of the 1715 rising, when given command of government forces in Scotland, he knew more about European warfare than the military situation north of the border. His new responsibility was to stamp out a 'rebellion' against George I in the country of his hereditary estates. He was now about thirty-seven years old, and we have to remember that this duke was now the principal landowner in Mull, where, on his territories, many Macleans had been dispossessed in favour of Campbell tacksmen, but where also the other lands, amounting to just less than half the island, were owned by other Maclean families – Lochbuy, Torloisk, and Coll, and the MacQuarries and MacKinnons, 'vassals' of Argyll because of his feudal superiority.

Few of the planted Campbell tacksmen were resident in Mull, and the island was therefore the cradle of a rearguard action when it was found that George I, and not the Stuart heir, had been asked to be king. James Campbell of Stonefield, sheriff-depute of Argyll, was responsible for the administration of justice in the shire, and was to play a part in the aftermath of the uprising; but in the early months of 1715 he could not take responsibility for keeping the Mull heroes from the fray.

The standard was raised at Braemar on 6 September 1715 by the Earl of Mar. From the beginning, Argyll, for the government, had been entrusted with only 1,500 men, while Mar was reported to have a force of 10,000. Argyll's letters to Lord Townshend are full of understandable anxiety about the failure of government to comprehend the threat posed by the rebels.[7] But it is not the duke's reasonable complaints which are of interest, so much as his strangely defensive tone, his fear of doing something 'blameable', and the apprehensive whimpering of his style of writing, discordant with his status as a hero. His qualities of command were not here apparent. His touchiness about receiving 'reproofs' did not help the increase of his men, and it was fortunate that the Battle of Sheriffmuir, 'a confused running fight'[8] fought on 13 November 1715, was regarded by both sides as a victory; the Macleans saw it as a Maclean–Campbell confrontation, with their chief, Sir John Maclean returning from exile to take part, while the duke interpreted it as a scattering of the rebels, a temporary respite until he obtained reinforcements of Dutch soldiers.

Eventually reinforcements came, but not before Argyll's relations with the king's counsellors had been undermined, mainly by the very prolixity of the duke's letters. But to those who did not know of the correspondence behind the scenes, the duke's return to London in 1716 after the final defeat of the rising at Preston, was the triumphant arrival of a hero.

Throughout the eighteenth century, Mull Macleans were judged and admired for their part in the Battle of Sheriffmuir: regarded by all of them as a victory, and regarded by posterity as the unfortunate result of the overweening pride of John, Earl of Mar. As late as 1773 Johnson and Boswell

[I]

To His G R A C E the

DUKE of *ARGYLE*,

UPON HIS

Arrival at C O U R T, after the Defeat of the Northern REBELLION, *March* 6.

ETERNAL *Phœbus*! whofe propitious Ray,
Darting uncommon Luftre, crowns the Day
In which great ARGYLE from the *North* arrives,
And with his Prefence, Peace and Pleafure gives;
As thy bright Beams with conftant Glory fhine
Immortaliz'd above with Youth divine,
So may the Brightnefs of his Acts below,
While Time fhall laft, with equal Splendor flow.
And, fince thy Light which all the Globe furveys
Thro' its whole Round no greater Hero fees,
With genial Warmth inform *Britannia*'s Plains,
Moiften her blooming Vales with fpringly Rains,
That thy own Lawrel may in Plenty grow
To yield frefh Honours for the Warriour's Brow.

A 2   The

Ode to the Second Duke of Argyll, giving some idea of the importance of the 'great duke' at the height of his influence. (*Edinburgh University Library*) were to meet, in Mull, men who had been at Sheriffmuir as striplings. The Pretender, James, had arrived five weeks too late, in the typical Stuart manner; the defeat at Preston had resulted in the execution, forfeiture or shipping to America of the surviving Scottish participants.

Sir John Maclean died at Gordon Castle in 1716, aged about forty-five. A description of him in the memoirs of Sir Ewen Cameron of Lochiel gives some idea of the seductive charm of the Macleans of Duart at this time. He was

> of a person and disposition more turned for the court and the camp than for the business of a private life. There was a natural vivacity and politeness in his manner, which he afterwards much improved by a courtly education. In person well-made and graceful, he took care to set it off by all the ornaments and luxury of dress. He was of a sweet temper, and good-natured, his wit lively and sparkling, his humour pleasant and facetious. He loved books and acquired the languages with great facility ... he had elegance of expression, an inexhaustible fancy which on all occasions furnished him with such a copious variety of matter as rendered his conversation always new and entertaining. But with all these shining qualities, the natural indolence of his temper and an immoderate love of pleasure made him unsuited to the circumstances of his family. No person talked of affairs private or public with a better grace, or more to the purpose, but he could not prevail with himself to be at the least trouble in the execution. He seemed to know everything, and from the smallest hint so penetrated into the circumstances of other people's business that he often did great services by his excellent advice ... Sir John had the good fortune to be taken notice of at court by Queen Mary. She was naturally a good Princess, and had all the sweetness of the Royal Family of the Stewarts in her blood. She had a warm side to all her father's friends; but knowing *how much the Scots in general, but especially the Highlanders, were detested by the King, her husband,* she had too much reserve and modesty in her temper to interpose on their behalf. But she commanded when William was abroad. He [Sir John Maclean] told her that *most of his family's misfortunes were due to their loyalty to the Royal Family.* She promised to write to her husband. Prince William received Sir John with great kindness in Flanders.

The Maclean bards also succumbed to the spell of Sir John, and sang his praises. His son, Sir Hector, born in exile at Calais on 6 November 1703, succeeded to the forlorn hopes of the family. Meanwhile, a great disarming was taking place in Mull, Coll, Tiree and Morvern, which indicates to posterity the extent of Jacobite support (but not Episcopalian, as Forbes of Culloden had so rightly pointed out), in Mull.

In April 1716, James Campbell of Stonefield, the Duke of Argyll's sheriff-depute in Argyll, was at Duart supervising the disarming of all inhabitants, whether or not they were rebels.[9] His list is remarkable for the fact that it contains relatively few Macleans and many Camerons, MacLachlans and Stewarts, all mainland names apparently resident in Mull. Maclean tacksmen, tenants and subtenants in the former lands of Duart, we have to assume, had already been expelled from the island. Many of the men in the list were old and sick, and many reported having given swords and guns to others. Patronymics disguise the identity of many others from modern readers, although they are the forms of name then used. On the whole, the document implies that the main participants in the Battle of Sheriffmuir were taking their time about returning home, either from choice or from enforced absence. In Inivea, the poet John Maclean was lying low, making no statement to Stonefield, and no doubt reserving his opinions for an epic poem on Sheriffmuir. At Moy, seat of the Macleans of Lochbuy, Hector of Lochbuy was reported to be 'old and infirm'. He had disponed his estate in 1705 to his son Murdoch, and his other three sons had received in liferent the lands of Pennygown, Garmony and Knockroy. He had taken no part in the uprising, or the Battle of Sheriffmuir, and may have entered into a pact with the captain of the garrison at Duart, for before Sheriffmuir he and his son received a letter from Captain John Hardie.

> Well done, good and faithfull servants. For my own part I shall allways be proud to acknowledge that the preservation of Dowart is intirely owing to the good Management and Conduct of Lochbuy ... may you carry to your grave the character of a Britton who in its remotest parts scorned to flinch from his religion and principles, nor whose Judgement could be byased by ye giddy rabble whose unjust designs must first render them desperate and then miserable.
>
> Dowart Castle, October ye 1st 1715.[10]

So ran one of the first epistles in the surviving correspondence of the Lochbuy Macleans. It was not only the stranger in Duart, Captain Hardie, who wrote in English (for he could do none other). Although the books of the Old Testament, the Confession of Faith and the Shorter Catechism had been translated into Gaelic, Gaelic had not become the language of correspondence. It remained the language of the Bible and of the bards, both of which forms were more likely to be declaimed than written. Maighstir Seathan, 'Master John' Maclean, minister of Kilninian, son of Treshnish, was complaining in 1705, in his stirring poem, *Rainn*, of the demise of the language, after its glorious past:

> When the descendants of Gaedheal Glas and of Mílidh,
>   no faint-hearted race, came from Spain
> There was much talk in every land about the harshness of
>   their blades;
> About poetry too, and learning, which was not in short
>   supply.
> When that seed grew great, here and across the sea,

Gaelic obtained respect and was valued everywhere:
A widely-spoken, vigorous, sweet and melodious tongue,
A strong polished, beautiful and accurate language.
For a thousand years and more it held first place in the
  court of kings, before the speech of southrons raised
  its head.
It was in Gaelic that every poet and bard wrote when
  exercising his pen, every physician, eulogist and druid,
  craftsman and story-teller too – every noble art –
whom Gathelus brought over with him from Egypt.
Through it did the great divines, the honour and glory of the
  clergy, proclaim effectively the words of God.
It was Gaelic that Patrick spoke in Inse Fàil of the kings,
As did that gentle prophet, the holy Colum, in Iona.
The learning of the refined French, whose fashion every land
  has followed, derived its roots from Iona of the exiles;
It was the teacher of the people of every land and language:
Norsemen and Saxons sent kinsfolk and their children there.

Now, alas and alack, it has gone from us completely:
Few are those who love it. What a somersault the world
  has taken!
It has fallen from the Tower, together with its authors
And the princes who inherited it, who took an interest in
  defending it.
It has been sold in the court for a new speech dating from
  only yesterday,
And scornfully abandoned: people were ashamed of their
  own language.

Maighstir Seathan went on to praise the Welsh scholar, Edward Lhuyd, who had recently visited him on a philological expedition, for awakening interest in the Gaelic language, and saw in this a new beginning:

Now far-off lands will hear the fame of their deeds
And say to one another: 'Once upon a time there were Gaels'.[11]

The 18-year-old Sir Hector Maclean of Duart had been fostered in the family of the Macleans of Coll, and now it was time to send him to university. No curfew had been placed upon him, and it is likely that with his cousins of Coll he had crossed the sea from Coll to Quinish, their estate in north-west Mull. Like them, he spoke Gaelic. When he went to the college in Edinburgh he studied philosophy, mathematics and civil law, and may have met the father of James Boswell in his law classes. In 1721 he moved to Paris for 'the learning of the refined French'. His father's old enemy, the Duke of Argyll, was busy in

London, advising Walpole on Scottish politics. In 1729, Archibald Campbell of Stonefield succeeded his dying half-brother, James, as justice depute of Argyll.

The scene has now been set for what is said to have been the most significant change ever to happen, peacefully, in Mull life. But here we have to keep the personality of the second Duke of Argyll firmly in mind.

In the 1730s, the principal heritors in terms of acres were the Duke of Argyll and Maclean of Lochbuy, with Maclean of Coll, Maclean of Torloisk, MacQuarrie of Ulva and his kinsman MacQuarrie of Ormaig, and MacKinnon of Mishnish holding relatively small estates. All the heritors were resident except the duke, but his power exceeded by far that of all the other lairds put together, and therefore it is to him, his personality, his influence, his policies, and even to his duchess that we must return to see why events in Mull took the turn they did in the 1730s, 1740s and 1750s. Before returning to the world of the duke, in London and at Adderbury in Oxfordshire, it is necessary to have a look at the more primitive world of Mull in the first quarter of the eighteenth century.

The population of the island of Mull, with Iona and Ulva, was in 1725 probably about 4,000,[12] distributed through two large estates and four or five smaller estates, or, if an ecclesiastical delineation be preferred, through three parishes, the parochial divisions being more geographically laid out than the estate divisions. The parish of Ross, which was the long peninsula stretching south-west towards and including Iona, was largely composed of the old church lands of the monastery of Iona, or Icolmkill, added to the lands of Duart after the Reformation, and therefore claimed by the Argylls as part of the Duart estates. The parish of Kilninian contained lands owned by the Macleans of Torloisk, the Macleans of Coll at Quinish, the MacKinnons at Mishnish, and the MacQuarries in Ulva, and the Duke of Argyll in Treshnish, Mornish, the shores of Loch na Keill, Aros, and a broad strip of land from Kilmore to Tenga and Achadashenaig. The parish of Torosay, or Pennygown, stretched from the environs of present-day Salen to Lochbuy, and beyond, encompassing upland communities as well as the populated areas of Kilpatrick, Duart and Killean. The parish of Torosay was the most fractured in terms of estate ownership, since the Duart or Argyll estates penetrated the Lochbuy estates like long fingers, taking up the most fertile lands as if by some natural selection made in remote times.

In 1725 there were no roads. General Wade's roads through the Highlands, begun in 1726, did not extend to Mull. Tracks worn by human feet (and certainly bare feet) and by cattle connected settlements. Houses were made of turf, except for the few fortified residences such as the castle of Moy at Lochbuy, which were made of stone, and the house of Erray, near Tobermory, built for the laird of MacKinnon about 1725. The gentry, usually relations of the Maclean chiefs and chieftains, also inhabited turf houses, whose only claim to superiority lay in their length, number of compartments and furnishings. Camouflage was unintended, but these turf huts were not particularly visible to travellers, as their roofs tended to sprout grass and fresh heather, which provided grazing for goats and other animals. Turf roofs were supported by timber roof trees, and as timber was a scarce commodity, the roof trees were taken whenever a small tenant was required to move to a new location. The interior of these huts was smoke-filled from the peat which was used both for cooking and for heating, and which could only escape through the doors and the ribs of the roof. One of the most characteristic features of the landscape was the strong scent of peat smoke, which charged the air and which, along with the smell of seaweed, made the atmosphere of the Scottish islands distinctive and memorable.

The inhabitants of these huts – in 1725 mostly kinsmen of the indigenous families – lived on oatmeal, milk and some fish. Potatoes were not introduced until about 1752. Emaciated hens and small eggs provided some variety; mutton and beef were occasionally resorted to. Vegetables were not regarded as food, and wild fruit, such as bilberries and hazel nuts, may have been eaten in passing, but were not cultivated. After the disarming of 1716, there was an excuse that no game could be shot for want of firearms, and foxes, which could not be shot for the same reason, were predators which reduced the numbers of fowls.

Milk brought byproducts such as butter and cheese, but in the first quarter of the eighteenth century cheese was part of the rent paid to tacksmen. Rentals of the period show that a small amount of the rent was paid in cash, but cows, hens, sheep, butter and cheese still formed an important part of the tacksman's revenue. The tacksman kept the edibles, and passed the cash to the superior, or, in the case of the larger animals, like cows and sheep, the tacksman converted the beasts into cash. In the early eighteenth century the tacksman had an important role, as a kind of banker or entrepreneur. There were no local markets: to go to mainland markets was unthinkable, and storms and high seas could prevent sea journeys for weeks on end. So although rents were payable on fixed term-dates such as Martinmas and Whitsunday, small tenants could supply their tacksmen with rents in kind all through the year, which would be credited to them in stages, and there remained only cash to find to top up the rent in the final reckoning. This cash, so very hard to find anywhere in Scotland, since the economic machinations of the union with England had reduced circulating coinage to about £1 per head of the population in 1707, was rarer than ever in the remote areas of Scotland, and in Mull almost non-existent. It was only by giving their cattle into the hands of the drovers in the late summer that tenants could hope for a return in cash, and that not until at least the spring of the following year.

The drover trade in Mull was therefore of the highest importance in the economy of the island. The origin of the trade went back farther than records can show,[13] and was seriously interrupted by the warfare and depredations of the seventeenth century, but by the first quarter of the eighteenth century it had picked up again, and after the union of the Scottish and English parliaments in 1707 it had become essential to the economy of the Highlands, as cattle were the only exportable commodity. Drovers usually began by being cattle breeders at more than subsistence level, and in Mull the trade tended to be handed down in families like the Stewarts of Achadashenaig and the MacPhails in Glenforsa. They had to be an intrepid bunch of men, and honest in their dealings. To them was entrusted not only valuable cattle on their outward journey, but the cash they were paid at the markets of Crieff and Falkirk on their return. In years of troubles and rebellions they carried on with their journeys, and returned with cash in their pockets. Between the drovers and the tacksmen, the economy of Mull was sustained. The loss of either would threaten the survival of all Mull people.

These cattle, it should be added, were the most miserable specimens one could imagine. No care was lavished upon them. They were left out, in unenclosed ground, summer and winter. In the late spring, when food was scarce among the people, the cattle were often bled until they were quite weak, so that their blood, mixed with oatmeal, could provide a black pudding for their owners. In severe winters the cattle died; when there was a cattle sickness, they died. 'May you have increase in cattle' was a common Gaelic saying, but there was little in the way of animal husbandry to back it up. It was hoped that cattle which were dying and scraggy at the end of April would revive sufficiently in the following four months, when they could range freely in the unenclosed pastures, to face the long trek to the Lowland markets with the drovers. They were sold on to be fattened up by new owners in the south.

Tobermory did not exist, except as a well on the hill above the present town from which the place derives its name, and with a change-house or pub down on the sea front. Its potential as a harbour for ships passing down the Sound of Mull had been recognised long before, but as a trading post it did not attract investment. In 1730, Lachlan Maclean of the Coll family was asked by Alexander Murray of Stanhope, the mineral prospector, to draw up a feasibility study for such a port, dealing in meal, tobacco, sugar, herring, kelp, whisky, cheese, wool and linen, and 'highland blankets'. The sum of £700 was required as an investment, but the plan came to nothing, although it was well drawn up.[14] Murray of Stanhope was more interested in mineral speculation than in trade. If the mainland opposite Tobermory had been less wild, with a productive hinterland, Tobermory might have been a flourishing port in the 1730s.

There was little talk of 'improvements' in agriculture as early as 1725. The road engineer, Edmund Burt, who was stationed at Inverness in the 1720s in connection with Wade's road-making,[15] made some caustic criticisms of Highland methods of agriculture, but the fashion for 'improvement' did not take over until the second half of the century. Nevertheless, the careless indifference to the welfare of animals on the part of Mull tenants, which rebounded on themselves, cannot be excused. Murmurs from tacksmen and visitors testify to a quite culpable slothfulness. Since human children were not carefully spoonfed or protected from danger by enclosures, it is not surprising that cattle were left to sink or swim. Husbandry was an unknown skill.

Such was the situation when John, second Duke of Argyll, began to complain, or whimper, as he had done to his masters in the 1715 campaign, about the income from his insular estates. In the 1720s, he perceived that his islands of Mull, Tiree, and part of Coll, were not bringing in their due revenues.

The duke's domestic life had a bearing on his attitudes. In 1714, on his return from Europe, and while still married to Mary Browne, he had become infatuated by a lady-in-waiting to Queen Anne, Jane Warburton, who was a woman of no education and little natural ability. As he regarded all women as shallow, she shone above the rest by entertaining a partiality to him. When he returned from his humiliating Scottish campaign of 1715–16, she became his chief comfort at court, and when his estranged duchess died in 1717, he married Jane. Through all the ups and downs of his political career, his domestic life now sustained him. They had no son, but four daughters, foolishly spoiled by the vacuous indifference of Jane and the indulgence of the duke. If he ever dwelt upon his Scottish inheritance, it was in a spirit of disappointment and resentment. He was unhappy with his Mull tacksmen, whom he suspected of intercepting rents. Although they were nearly all Campbells, he took exception to their methods of dealing with tenants. In his emotional way, he had decided, without very much investigation, that they did not exert themselves on his behalf. By the mid-1730s they were being referred to as the 'late tacksmen'. That they should be expelled appears to have been the recommendation of a report by Archibald Campbell of Stonefield, now chamberlain of the estates, to the Duke of Argyll.[16] But what Stonefield had advised with caution, the duke had wholeheartedly embraced as a plan of action. He had no first-hand knowledge of Mull, and there is no evidence that he ever visited the island, even on a tour of inspection. He only knew that he was not receiving the rents which were his due. By this time he had at least two expensive households to maintain in London and at Adderbury in Oxfordshire, and his four unruly daughters, known as the 'bawling Campbells', were in the mid 1730s approaching an age when their lives would be full of parties and suitors. Revenue was his first object, although such rents as came out of Mull would not have been enough to provide gowns for his daughters. He was unable to understand why his Mull, Morvern and Tiree rents were never paid in full, and the excuses made by Stonefield about the drop in cattle prices, bad weather ruining harvests, and the abject poverty of small tenants carried no weight with him. Many corroborating stories were told to him, probably by Duncan Forbes, over the convivial cup at Inveraray and Adderbury. Duncan Forbes, then Lord Advocate in Scotland, and MP for Inverness-shire, was himself proprietor of a Highland estate, and frequently a guest of the duke in London, Adderbury and Inveraray from 1728.[17] The duke, a seasoned whiner, may have complained incessantly about his unsatisfactory lands of Mull, Morvern and Tiree, for Forbes, who already cherished the theory that middle-men were responsible for all the shortfalls in rent, offered himself, some time in the middle 1730s, as an investigator of the situation. His appointment as Lord President in 1737 almost jeopardised the proposed expedition to Mull and Tiree, but by that time it was a promise of long standing which must be honoured.

The basis of Forbes's relationship with John, the 'great' Duke of Argyll, was the favourable impression he had made during the rebellion of 1715, with his efficient organisation of affairs in Scotland, and his staunch support of the duke's tactics at a time when he was without intimate friends in his campaign to suppress the uprising.[18] The duke had offered Forbes the stewardship of the Argyll estates in 1716, so that a correspondence developed between the two men in which Forbes became 'dear Duncan'.[19] He was on more intimate terms with Duke John than with his brother, Lord Ilay, who should have had more in common with Forbes, being a lawyer and a man of intellect. Duke John was not a perceptive man, and perhaps Forbes enjoyed his role of advisor to a grandee who, in spite of his reputation and great influence, had a curious lack of confidence in himself, and a need for approval.[20]

Forbes planned to make his expedition a summer adventure. His son and only child John, then about twenty-seven years old, motherless since infancy, and who had not so far shown any great talent for anything, was to go with him. The duke's lawyer in Edinburgh, Ronald Dunbar MacMillan, and several lairds from mainland Argyll were to accompany the party as advisors and interpreters (for Forbes had no Gaelic), but chief among these was to be Stonefield himself, the careful, sensible, pragmatic chamberlain, whose commission as sheriff in 1729 had been signed by the duke, Dunbar and Forbes.[21] Before leaving, Forbes, who had a reputation as a very heavy drinker, and whose family's other claim to fame was to be the founding of the Ferintosh distillery, ordered several gallons of whisky and fourteen dozen bottles of wine.[22] They were to be away for over a month.

The party landed at Aros, and camped under canvas, just as the tenth earl's expedition had done forty-seven years earlier. Although Stonefield was known to the tenants, it was Forbes who, in a letter to the duke dated 24 September 1737,[23] called 'the tenants of that island' (meaning the Argyll estates only, of course) together, and told them of the ducal intention to free them from the tyranny of tacksmen and the duties of paying herezelds and of giving services. Herezelds were a form of death duty exacted from tenants in the form of a sheep or cow when the nominal tenant died, and not confined to the Argyll estates. Evidence from other estates in Mull[24] suggests that this payment was a not unfair exchange for the laird's obligation to supply meal and whisky for tenants' funerals, a very old tradition which had survived the legal abolition of herezelds. Services demanded of tenants included help for the laird or tacksman in the bringing in of the harvest, cutting of peat and other seasonal activities. Forbes went on to say that leases would be offered to the humbler tenants, and not just to the tacksmen as hitherto. These leases would be for periods of nineteen years, so that improvements could be made, but the leases would be offered to the highest bidders, and the tenants must be sure that their bids would be the result of frank and well-considered offers of sums which the bidders could well afford. Forbes was convinced that the 'late tacksmen' had squeezed smaller, poorer tenants to the limit, and so he did not expect any augmentation of rents from that class of people.

But he was surprised to find that his revolutionary proposals were not greeted with enthusiasm by his audience. They seemed to undervalue such favourable terms, and instead, the larger tenants offered less than they had previously paid the tacksmen. Forbes at once suspected a collusion or conspiracy, led, he was quite sure, by the minister of Kilninian, Mr John Maclean (Maighstir Seathan of the passionate poem on the Gaelic language) and those of the Maclean tacksmen who remained. Forbes conceived that there was a design to keep rents at their present level and to resist increases.

Like the duke, Forbes did not accept that many bad seasons had impoverished the people, or that low cattle prices deprived them of ready money. He had already made up his mind, in his confabulations with the duke, that these were the excuses of a devious set of people, supported by the gullible Stonefield. Stonefield, who must have been standing by his side during the Lord President's address, and who had the embarrassing task of translating it, could not oppose the plans of a Lord President who was not only an intimate of the duke but also steward of the estates.

With extraordinary vindictiveness, Forbes made an example of Maighstir Seathan. After a long debate in English (so that there could be no misunderstanding) with the minister, who had 'an advantageous farm' (as well he might have, since he had no manse or glebe) Forbes asked for a higher bid, and received one from one of his own party, a Campbell from mainland Argyll. Stonefield, whose warnings to the duke about clan hatred entering the arena of free market bidding had fallen on deaf ears, must have wished that the ground would swallow him up. A minister of John Maclean's standing, who represented all that was noble and good in the old Gaelic tradition, whose family had been in Treshnish for hundreds of years, had been knocked down like an aunt sally. 'You may believe,' Forbes wrote smugly to the duke, 'the minister, seeing himself by his own cunning beat out of an advantageous possession he had for many years enjoyed, was raving mad, and his fate caused some speculation in Mull before my return from Tirry.'

'Tirry' (Tiree) depressed Forbes with its poverty, which was again blamed on the 'harpies', the late tacksmen. The Thirisdeach people 'played the Mull game on me all to a man; their offers were all under the present rent.' Forbes returned to Mull, and received some improved offers from people intimidated by the thought of losing their homes and way of life. Some farms were left unset, because they did not achieve their full value, and these Stonefield would no doubt have to sort out. Forbes did not forget the chatty details which would amuse the duke, but left 'the odditys of your insular dominions' for entertainment at a later date. He did not omit from his letter a touching story of his son's illness when they were on Mull: young John had been seized with a sneaking fever, which Forbes had treated himself, and in Tiree had had rheumatic pains from sleeping in a tent. 'I had no medicine but rhubarb and gum pills. However I doctored him so well as to bring him home in the barge, and as I passed he was perfectly recovered.'

The duke's reply was full of gratitude for his friend's endeavours. He was sure that the problem had been solved, and did not spend any time on the details. He asked no further questions about Mull, but wanted to be given more impressions of Tiree. In the following year he rewarded Duncan Forbes for all the trouble he had gone to by arranging a commission for John Forbes, Younger of Culloden, in the Blues.

Archibald Campbell of Stonefield, who lived to the age of eighty-one,[25] must have been made of stern stuff. Not only had John, second Duke of Argyll, listened to none of his advice about the state of the weather, the markets for cattle, the attitudes of the tenants, the propensities of the Mull people to bid anything just to stay in their own places, the animosities which would lead to absurdly oversized offers, but Argyll had listened to an outsider (Inverness was quite a different matter from Argyll) who understood nothing of Mull, and had taken his advice. Stonefield now had to reap the whirlwind.

For seven years before the '45 uprising took up all his attention, he dealt with the implementation, and then the collapse, of the new system of free bidding for farms. One by one, those who had hardly been able to pay the old rents to the tacksmen, who had smiled that polite Highland smile when promising the impossible, fell by the wayside. In the late 1740s, rents actually had to be reduced if the whole of the Argyll estate in Mull was not to become waste ground. The only part of Forbes' plan that remained was the abolition of services [26] and a general increase in written leases.

Duncan Forbes had not quite comprehended the situation of Maighstir Seathan either, for although, as he told the duke, the minister could understand him very well, Duncan did not understand the minister. The person who was thrown out of Treshnish was the minister's half-brother, another John, tacksman of Treshnish. Known as the laird of Treshnish, he was descended from Iain Ruadh, hereditary constable of the fortress of Cairnburgh, and from a multitude of heroes of every conceivable battle from Inverlochy to Killiecrankie. No one's eviction could have been more calculated to extend hatred between Maclean and Campbell followers. The bard of the Macleans was quick to compose *Imrich Fear Threisinnis*, the Laird of Treshnish's Flitting, which, in many a ceilidh, was to set off a murmur of sympathetic droning voices as soon as the first words were heard, '*Fàilte do bhur n-imrich Luain, Eadar fhearaibh, chuain, is chlann ...*'

Here's to your flitting on Monday, with your men, your animals and your children. O may you be healthy, and may your cattle increase. Take that good place over there, and some day we will get our own back. It's not a proud flitting, but the loss of our ancestors' lands from spite, not by the sword.[27]

'That good place over there' was a piece of land on Icolmkill, or Iona. John of Treshnish went there with his wife Mary Maclean, and their children, Hugh, Ann, Florence, Neil, Una, Margaret and Mary, and the next instalment of their drama was not long in coming.

What significance did the campaigns of the second duke, and his personality, have for the history of Mull? He owned the largest part of the island, and his manner of governing his estate must have had some bearing on the fate of his tenants. Did his character and outlook affect in any way the life of neighbouring landlords and tenants? His fellow-landowners were the Macleans, MacKinnons and MacQuarries, and the questions we would like to ask would be concerned with the relationships of neighbouring heritors. Did the others regard the duke as a fellow landlord? He was the only absentee landlord; they all resided on their lands. Did they witness the arrival of the Lord President? Did they meet him? Had they heard of him? Did they discuss among themselves his manoeuvres? Did they speculate about the end results of his raising of the Argyll rents? What kind of leases did they give their tenants? Did they exact services? Were their tacksmen also 'harpies'? Did they know and respect Archibald Campbell of Stonefield, chamberlain of Argyll's lands, and their own sheriff-depute? Men and women must have married across the divide of the estates. How did they decide where to live? Was one estate better to be on than another? Could they change allegiance?

The answers are difficult to construct. It is certain that on the Lochbuy and Torloisk estates, if competitive bidding did not operate before 1737, it existed after 1750. As for tacksmen, they seemed to be even more necessary on estates where the proprietor was resident, for the very good reason that they could do the unpleasant tasks such as collecting the rents, policing the estate, and directing cash flow into the pockets of the laird. The introduction of leases in Torloisk and Lochbuy can be dated to the 1750s, but were generally restricted to the more important tenants and rarely given to joint tenants. On the other estates, much depended on the personality and efficiency of the laird himself, on the extravagance of the heir, and the length and stability of the reign of these petty princes. The people's marriages, across estate boundaries, seldom benefited them.

The second Duke of Argyll paid little attention to the changes in his insular domains. Instead, he was preoccupied with domestic troubles, and in particular with the behaviour of his daughter Caroline and his wife, for like many another man in his sixties, living in an entirely female household, he was much deceived by his womenfolk when it was his own inclination to put honour foremost.[28] For the last years of his life he suffered from a nervous and paralytic disorder, and was excluded from office in the new administration which followed Walpole's resignation. He died in 1743, and had had no sons. The Argyll estate passed to the 61-year-old Archibald Earl of Ilay, his younger brother, and also without a legitimate son. No two brothers could have been more different. Each despised the other, and Archibald's reply to Lord President Duncan Forbes's letter of condolence on the death of his brother is a masterpiece of restraint. The subtle third duke did not have a high opinion of Forbes,[29] and wrote as follows:

My Lord
I have the favour of your Letter of the 17th. The account you give me of the care that has been taken of the papers of the Family is one of the many instances in which I shall find myself obliged to return thanks to your Lordship for the kind concern you always had for my Brother, & extended also to those who should succeed to him. It is very unfortunate for me, and more for our Country, that the last has taken place so soon, & I shall always think myself as much indebted for the obligations of friendship which he owed, as for my own. The Dutchess of Argyll & I have agreed to beg the favour of your Lordship & the Justice Clerk to settle & determine all Questions that may arise about my Brothers Succession between the Dutchess, my Nieces, & myself; no man knows so well his intention as your self, & whatever that was, I shall think right; this must excuse my joyning with the Dutchess to ask that favour; as for the keys, I am unwilling that any body should receive them from you but my self. I must be in Scotland early in the summer, & in the mean time I believe either Lord Milton or Lord Striechen will be at the trouble to fetch any papers that may happen to be necessary, if that should happen. My Cosen Jack is just now come to me from Flanders, he and his two Sons, whom I must look upon as my Children, are very well. I have nothing farther to trouble your Lordship with, but to assure you that I am with the greatest Regard & Truth
My Lord, Your Lordships Most Obedient Humble Servant, Argyll.
London Nov. 29th 1743.

The 'Dutchess' was the flighty widow of the deceased duke, and 'Cosen Jack' was his heir, the fourth duke. Archibald himself had no 'Dutchess', and his great love, now about to enter his life if it had not already, was his project to build a new castle at Inveraray. Duke Archibald was a bookish man, interested in science, philosophy, mechanics, astronomy and architecture. These aspects of his character have been written about,[30] and it must be added that he was respected by the philosopher David Hume,[31] but his relationship with the Argyll estates, or with the Jacobite uprising of 1745, has rarely been mentioned. But as Archibald third duke is not to be classified as an 'exile', or an absentee landlord, his role as a more compassionate heritor than his brother, the second duke, will be noticed in the following chapter.

Notes

1. *Memoir of a Plan for Preserving Peace in the Highlands, written a short time after the Revolution*, Culloden Papers.
2. Campbell and Thomson, p. 23.
3. *Infra.*
4. Wightman, Andy, *Who Owns Scotland*, p. 9.
5. Graham, Henry Grey, *The Social Life of Scotland in the 18th Century*, vol. 2, p. 154.
6. Home, James A. (ed.), *Lady Louisa Stuart: selections from her Manuscripts.*
7. Tayler, Henrietta, 'John, duke of Argyll and Greenwich', *SHR*, 26, 1, 1947.
8. Pryde, George S., *Scotland from 1603 to the Present Day*, p. 59.
9. Maclean-Bristol, Nicholas (ed.), *Inhabitants of the Inner Isles, Morvern and Ardnamurchan*, 1716.
10. NAS. GD174/1217/1.
11. O Baoill, Colm (ed.), *Bardachd Chloinn Ghill-Eathain. Eachann Bacach and other Maclean poets*, pp. 101–3.
12. Webster's census of 1755 estimates the total of the three parishes of Mull at 5,287.
13. Haldane, A. R. B., *The Drove Roads of Scotland.*
14. NLS. Adv. MS 29.1.1. Lachlan Maclean to Alexander Murray, 29 January 1729/30.
15. Burt, Edmund, *Letters from the North of Scotland.* Although the editor of the 1998 edition dates his letters from the late 1720s, Burt's knowledge of local people suggests an even earlier residence in the area.
16. Argyll [George Douglas Campbell, eighth duke], *Scotland As it Was and As it Is*, pp. 246–53.
17. Menary, George, *The Life and Letters of Duncan Forbes of Culloden.*
18. See Menary, op. cit., and Campbell, Robert, *The Life of the Most Illustrious Prince, John, Duke of Argyll and Greenwich.*
19. Culloden Papers.
20. Tayler, op. cit.
21. NAS. GD14/9 Campbell of Stonefield Papers.
22. Cregeen, E. R., *The Tacksmen and their Successors …*
23. *Crofters Report*, Appendix A. 4. 1884.
24. Frequent references in the Lochbuy Papers, NAS. GD174.
25. NLS. MS 3737. Calendar of the Stonefield Papers. Appendix.
26. In the first *Statistical Account* of Mull parishes in the 1790s, the ministers stress that services are not exacted by the Duke of Argyll, but are still required by other heritors.
27. Free adaptation of the translation by Anja Gunderloch of the poem by John Maclean, 1738.
28. Home, James A. *Lady Louisa Stuart.*
29. Menary, p. 56.
30. Lindsay, Ian G. and Cosh, Mary, *Inveraray and the Dukes of Argyll.*
31. Hume presented his *Essays Moral and Political*, 'not to the duke of Argyll, but to Archibald Campbell, who is undoubtedly a Man of Sense & Learning.' Letter to Charles Erskine, 1748. Greig, J. Y. T., *The Letters of David Hume*, vol. 1, p. 113.

4

'Lose not heart, beloved people'

In 1740, when Duke John was suffering from the earlier symptoms of his paralytic illness, a memorial was addressed to him by Campbell of Kirnan, proprietor of an estate at Kilmichael-Glassary in Argyll, which Duncan Forbes of Culloden, as steward of the Argyll estates (and official interceptor of letters and memoranda) may never have passed on, for it was a document which no man could have received with equanimity. It was entitled *The present state of the shire of Argyll.*[1]

It spoke of oppression and grievances which had no hope of redress, and indicated that the author was not the only Campbell in the shire to be disgruntled. Since some of the tacksmen who had lost their holdings in Mull had gone back to base, it is easy to believe that there was strong resentment against the house of Argyll. Kirnan began by accusing the duke's forebears of building up their estates at the expense of their kinsmen and vassals, who had suffered from the forfeiture of the earls, but quickly moved on to more recent betrayals such as the misapplication of public funds, the illegal appropriation of bishopric lands, the wrongful distribution of land tax so that Inveraray escaped paying, and the numberless backhanders the collector of taxes awarded to himself. On behalf of the small fishermen of the shire, Kirnan deplored the illegal herring boat tax, imposed even when the catch was inadequate to pay it, 'for as these poor wretches must pay whether they have success in the ffishing or not, they rather chuse to Starve at home.' Kirnan's rhetorical question was how did it come about that the shire was so passive and the duke so absolute? The answer was, of course, that with heritable jurisdictions [2] the duke named the panel, picked the jury, and was himself the judge. If a trial was all one had to face, some might dare to oppose the duke, but being imprisoned in a loathsome dungeon in Inveraray for several months before obtaining a trial was more than anyone would face. There had been instances, added Kirnan, when a supposed criminal had begged the sheriff for God's sake either to be tried or hanged. Proper measures should be taken for the shire to air its grievances at the next session of parliament. The benefit of a grand jury and of habeas corpus [3] should be extended to Argyll. This might have the result of making the duke's subjects zealous in their attachment to the royal family and the government. It was the fear engendered by heritable jurisdictions which made the Scots mob pretend to adulate their haughty head (the Duke of Argyll), but if the privileges of habeus corpus were extended, the cause would be taken away, slavish dependence would cease, His Grace would be obliged to lay aside the monarch whom he now affected to mimic, and return to the more natural and private state of a subject.

Campbell of Kirnan had nothing to lose in thus addressing the 'great duke', for he had been bankrupt twelve years before, according to James Campbell of Stonefield, who reckoned his debts at £2,000 and the value of his estate to be 1,200 merks a year.[4] But he was only one of the losers in the Argyll confederation. A process of law against the tacksmen of Tiree was going ahead before the Lords of Session in 1728, which indicates that the duke was in conflict with his Campbell tacksmen for about ten years before Duncan Forbes visited the islands.

It was well for the second duke that he died when he did, two years before the Jacobite rising of 1745. Archibald the third duke was at once more down to earth, more intellectual, and more Scottish. At the outbreak of the rebellion he was happily planning his new Gothic castle at Inveraray, deeply involved with architects and gardeners, and looking forward to a new life of studious retirement.[5] But on 4 August 1745, Prince Charles Edward Stuart arrived in Moidart, and although government intelligence had predicted a rising of the clans, the crunch had suddenly come, rumours had turned into reality, and Duke Archibald's very life was threatened by a Jacobite plan to kidnap him.[6] Not having had very much reaction from his political allies in London to his warnings about an imminent rising, the duke felt that his presence in the metropolis was necessary to keep the politicians on the *qui vive* about developments in Scotland. But in spite of his constant advice, and the occupation of Edinburgh by the Jacobites, the government took a month to muster forces to confront the rebels.

From Mull, only about sixty individuals had joined the Jacobites from Maclean and other estates. A handful of men, including Maclean of Brolass, had offered to add a 'Maclean Militia' to the Argyll Militia, hastily convened to aid the government effort under the command of General John Campbell, grandson of the tenth earl and first duke of Argyll, and cousin of Duke Archibald. General Campbell was also heir to the dukedom, and his son, Lieutenant Colonel Jack Campbell, a young man of cherubic countenance and graceful manners (who was later to become the fifth duke) was at his father's disposal to serve as the general might think fit.[7] With such a small amount of active participation in the uprising, it is more useful to consider the effects of the long campaign on the island, rather than to follow the day-to-day events of the '45, or, since the following year was to be more significant and decisive, the '46.

The drawbacks in security of the government-commanded citadel of Fort William are well known. The fort could be approached from the Great Glen as well as from Loch Linnhe, and an approach from both ends, by land and sea, would pose a fatal threat. On 16 February HMS *Terror* arrived in the Sound of Mull, and her captain, Captain Duff, wrote from 'Topar Murry' that he had destroyed every boat on the coast of Morvern, lest they be used by the rebels, for unlike Mull, Morvern was a nest of Jacobites. The Sound of Mull was now patrolled by the *Greyhound, Furnace* and *Baltimore*, so that not even the most rabid of secret sympathisers from Mull would have dared to move a boat, even to fish. Scallastle Bay, north-west of Craignure, and commanding views up and down the Sound, was a centre of naval activity. When the governor of Fort William was persuaded of imminent attack, a message to Scallastle ensured the support of a ship which would run the risk of sailing up Loch Linnhe and running through the bottleneck at Corran Ferry, where rebels shot at ships at close range. Castle Stalker, that dramatic tower house in Airds Bay, overlooking the Strath of Appin, was a link in the chain of government posts, where Flora Macdonald was to pause briefly on being taken from Tobermory Bay (not having placed a foot on Mull soil) to a more secure spot. Although most people who are aware of the reprisals perpetrated by the Duke of Cumberland upon the families of the rebels tend to think that lands and houses were burned in the aftermath of Culloden, it was from Scallastle, in March 1746, that the operation known as the burning of Morvern was directed, almost as a diversion from the navy's normal duties.

The burning of Morvern, the territory nearest to Mull, and with a population closely related by ties of blood to the island, was not entirely random and mindless. Rumours had reached government command that a fresh wave of recruitment was in train there, and that rebel agents were scouring the land picking up waverers. Captain Duff of the aptly named HMS *Terror*, calling at Mingary on 9 March, received a letter from General Campbell, head of the Argyll Militia and heir to the dukedom, passing on an instruction from the Duke of Cumberland, now commander-in-chief of the government forces, that Morvern should be punished by having its lands razed and wasted. The *Terror* anchored off Ardtornish, opposite Scallastle, on the night of 10 March, carrying a detachment of Scots Fusiliers as well as its own men, and at four in the morning of 11 March, moved back up the coast to unleash them with orders to burn every house possessed by rebels. They began with Drimnin, where both Charles, the elder, and his son Allan were 'out', and where a 'ferm toun' or rural township full of small tenants was burned. By evening they had passed down through Fiunary to Loch Aline and Ardtornish, sparing the MacDougalls, who were known to be loyalist. The sinister *Terror* shadowed the men as they moved, hugging the coastline, and clearly visible by the Mull cottars of Fishnish, Garmony and Scallastlebeg, who, not knowing the rationale behind it all, must have feared that they were to be the next victims when they saw the ship return to Scallastle.

Archibald Campbell of Stonefield, who had seen his role changing since the third duke's accession, to a more trusted one of confidant, purveyor of advice and military intelligence, and co-ordinator of non-martial activities in the shire of Argyll, was occupied throughout the Young Pretender's visit to Scotland with business more urgent than the collection of rents. But not one single penny had been collected in rent from Mull and Morvern since the raising of the prince's standard, and the Campbell gentlemen who were able to factor the estates were involved in the Militia. Forbes of Culloden, no longer on the Argyll centre stage, had dashed to Culloden to protect his heritage. Sheriff Stonefield was the third duke's most faithful reporter of home affairs, for the duke had (some said pusillanimously) remained in London. He had received information about Cumberland's order for the burning of Morvern in February 1746, and had written to the duke expressing his very real anxiety for the welfare of the region and its people.

> The Inevitable Consequence of the Execution of this Order is that the Tender Innocent Babes must suffer with the guilty, and that it will most probably introduce a horrible Scene of Murder, blood and Rapin, not only in the Rebels Country, but likeways into all those Countrys that unluckily happen to be in their neighbourhood.[8]

The duke's reply indicated that he disliked the order as much as Stonefield, and when, in April, he began to hear imputations that he and Stonefield had been privy to the burnings, the ambivalence of his position was brought home to him.

> It's a pity the Rebells should impute to you and me the burning which I am sorry for, and never would have advised.

General Campbell, the future fourth duke, was not bothered by such qualms. As a professional soldier he saw the need for reprisals. In his February letter to Stonefield announcing Cumberland's plans, he had expressed himself of the opinion that everything should be burnt and destroyed, and 'in the Isles the ships ought to land some of their men and doe the like'. General Campbell perhaps had to over-compensate for the lingering distrust which the English, and Cumberland in particular, felt for the family of Argyll, by being harsh even in the treatment meted out to his own future tenants. But second thoughts must have revived his sense of justice, for he sent a memo to the ships in late March asking that they take care to inform themselves of the political colour of all intended victims so that the innocent would not suffer with the guilty.[9]

The people of Mull thus escaped indiscriminate retribution after the decisive battle of Culloden, and the sixty rebellious participants, now difficult to identify in spite of assiduous list-making, were killed, imprisoned, or could not have a case made out against them. Charles Maclean of Drimnin in Morvern, whose house had been consumed in the burning, lay dead on Culloden Moor, but his son Allan (whose descendants were to include a future Lady Lochbuy, and Charles Maclean, briefly proprietor of part of Brolass) being young and misled in his Jacobite leanings, was allowed to go free. Allan, who went on to study law in Edinburgh with Colquhoun Grant, another fervent Jacobite, was to be one of the exponents of the Jacobite dream, one of those who frequently toasted the prince and reminisced about the good old days of the uprising.

One Mull man, who has featured in our story already, was John Maclean, the laird of Treshnish, who had been cast out of his farm by Duncan Forbes in 1738, and had gone to the island of Iona. Having seen his family farm taken over by Campbells in the supposedly beneficial tenurial reorganisation, he had every reason to hate the Campbells, and in the old Mull manner, embrace every cause opposed to them; in this case the Jacobite uprising. He was arrested and imprisoned after Culloden for having piloted a rebel ship carrying foreign supporters of the prince. He protested that he had been going about his own business in Iona when a ship had anchored in the Sound, taken him on board, and ordered him to sail her to Barra; that against his will he had complied, leaving his family and peaceable friends, and had found himself embroiled. This dubious defence was offered to the authorities, and was followed in 1747 by a petition on his behalf from the ministers, heritors, feuars and tacksmen of Mull, a band of men whose integrity and solidity could not be doubted. If mid-eighteenth century Mull, Coll and Tiree had their humble equivalent of the Almanach de Gotha, this petition was either that, or a list of John's true friends, remarkable for their cohesion in times of strife.

The petition was presented as a certificate, drafted by the Rev. John Maclean of Kilninian (Maighstir Seathan), attesting the good character of John Maclean, who had been, against his will, taken on board a Spanish ship to Barra, but, returning to Iona, had mustered some of his own tenants for the Argyll Militia, who had presented themselves at Inveraray along with Allan Maclean of Brolass. His acquiescence on being taken on board the ship was due to the guile of his captors, and not to any voluntary act on his part. The signatories to the certificate were:

Allan Maclean of Brolass
Hector Maclean of Killunaig
Donald Maclean, Tacksman of Killunaig
Alexander McGilvra of Pennyghael
John Maclean of Killean
Hector Maclean, Minister of Coll
Hector Maclean of Coll
Hugh Maclean of Grishipol
Allan Maclean of Totranald (Coll)
Hector Maclean Younger of Totranald
Lauchlan Maclean of Toradon
Hector Maclean, Tacksman of Knock
Mackinnon of that Ilk in the Parish of Kilninian at Erray
Duncan Campbell, Innkeeper at Aros
Lachlan MacQuarrie of Ulva
Lachlan MacQuarrie of Ormaig
Hector MacQuarrie Younger of Ormaig
John MacQuarrie of Balligartan
Allan MacQuarrie of Culinish

Donald Maclean of Torloisk
Donald Maclean, Tacksman of Calgary
Alexander MacTavish, Minister (of Tiree and Coll)
Donald Campbell, Tacksman of Knock in the Parish of Pennigown
Archibald Campbell, Tacksman of Killiechronan, brother to Stonefield
Lachlan Maclean of Gruline
John Maclean, brother to Gruline [10]

Notable by their absence are the Macleans, or Maclaines, of Lochbuy.

In the summer of 1746, Mull was full of what might be called secret agents. The hunt was on for Prince Charles Edward Stuart, still at large, with a price on his head. Rumour had it that he was hiding in a Mull cave. One hundred men had been left in Mull to attend to his capture, but at last, in August, General Campbell withdrew these scouts as fresh sightings were reported of the prince. By 21 September 1746 it was clear that Prince Charles had effected his escape, and the bays of Mull abruptly ceased to function as naval bases. The people would now return to their normal lives.

One Mull man, Charles Maclean in Achnacraig, near Dervaig, was so affected by shaking hands with Prince Charles Edward, that he never gave his right hand to anyone to shake again. Since he lived to return to Mull, and to refuse his right hand for a lifetime, it is to be assumed that he was not punished for his partiality to the prince. His descendants in Kilbeg and Cuin cherished his act of heroism, as the descendants of the witnesses of the crucifixion might have passed down their forebears' hallowed experience. [11]

Early in June 1745, a dignified gentleman in his early forties, of below middle height, wearing clothes of a continental cut and walking with a slight limp, arrived in Edinburgh and took a room in the house of Moggie Blair, lodgings keeper in the Canongate. He was accompanied by a manservant who spoke English with a Highland accent. The gentleman seemed to sport a variety of names: one was Mr James Neilson, and another, in which letters were addressed to him, was 'Mr Cleland'. He seldom left the house, except on one evening when he went to dine at Newhaven, and stayed in the Canongate for five days, receiving visitors, and sending his servant on errands. On the sixth day he was arrested, and after a spell in Edinburgh Castle, he was sent with a courier to London, where, at Whitehall, on 13 July 1745, he and his servant were interrogated by no less a person than the Marquis of Tweeddale, Secretary of State for Scotland, and his assistant Andrew Mitchell, onetime college friend and correspondent of David Hume. The man was Hector Maclean – 'commonly known as Sir Hector Maclean' – chief of that name, who had spent many years in France, at Paris and Boulogne. His servant was Lachlan Maclean, born in the Isle of Mull and educated by his uncle, Allan Maclean. Sir Hector's answers to his questioner were non-committal, and quite vague, bordering, we might say (if he had not been so charming) on the derisory. He was not sure where he was born, but had been told it was 'abroad'. He had been bred a Protestant; he had three sisters in Scotland. His reason for leaving Paris was to do with a friend's elopement with an English lady. He had gone to Rotterdam to arrange a passage to Scotland, and was told there that a Mr Blaw was also hoping to return to Scotland. Sir Hector had written to Mr Blaw asking him to hold the ship, and had asked him to reply to him as Mr Neilson. Mr Blaw had replied to Mr Neilson, but said that he himself could not, after all, sail in that ship. Sir Hector and Lachlan sailed from Rotterdam to Newcastle and from there had gone direct to Edinburgh, where he had received visits from a friend, a Scotsman whom he declined to name. He had also seen Mr Blaw in that very house in the Canongate in which he lodged, Mr Blaw happening to lodge in the same place. The Marquis of Tweeddale listened courteously to this strange, confused, but polite account of the dignified gentleman's sojourn in Edinburgh, and decided to have his fellow-countryman placed in confinement in London. There Sir Hector Maclean remained for two years, and it is not known whether his faithful servant Lachlan ministered to him in his imprisonment. According to Seneachie, historian of the Macleans, Sir Hector had been betrayed by Blair, the landlady's 'gowk of a husband', who had hoped for a reward, and instead received his wife Moggie's reproaches as long as he lived for her loss of 'a kind and liberal lodger'.[12]

An island in conflict, even in passive conflict, takes time to settle down. The people of Mull, as a result of the navy's patrol of the Sound of Mull and its occupation of the bays of Tobermory and Scallastle, and also because of the search for the prince, were assailed by strangers. If they did not know anything of the personality of Prince Charles Edward Stuart it was interpreted for them by Alasdair Mac Mhaighstir Alasdair, the Jacobite poet of Ardnamurchan, who composed a song consisting of dialogues between Charles and the Gaels, so that Charles was perceived to speak in Gaelic to his followers.

> Misneach mhaith, a mhuinntir ghaolach
> 'S gabhaidh Dia dhinn daonnan càs,
> Cuiribh dòchas daingean, faoilteach,
> Anns an aon Tì a nì dhuinn stàth;
> 'S buannaichibh gu rìoghail, adhrach,
> Traisgeach, ùrnaigheach, caointeach, blàth;
> 'S bithibh dìleas do chàch a chéile,
> 'S dùinear suas ur creuchda bàis.[13]

The imagery of Alasdair combined faith with ongoing hope for the restoration of the true line of kings, in a form that the people knew and loved. But it was only the bards who dared now to express such sentiments. The ministers of Torosay, Kilninian and Ross were much too cautious to rock the boat. Maighstir Seathan was an old man, whose parishioners petitioned for his son

Alexander to come and be his assistant. The proscription of tartan in 1746 kept the male population subdued, for they were suddenly not allowed to wear the only clothes they possessed. Women could continue to wear plaid. After 1747, heritable jurisdictions were abolished, and the Duke of Argyll, with such large jurisdiction, was paid £21,000 in compensation. Also in 1747 the Argyll tenantry were so poor that they could not afford to pay Forbes of Culloden's higher rents, and they had to be lowered. Forbes himself died in this year. In about 1748, Captain Allan Maclean of Brolass, a firm supporter of Argyll, wrote to the duke asking humbly to have a lease of Brolass, his own family territory, for his mother and himself. 'It is well known', he wrote, 'that the lands of Brolass are by far the worst ... and the least capable of improvement of any lands of Mull, yet such is the memorialist's attachment to these lands that he is very desirous to become Your Grace's Tacksman ...'[14] It was so well known that there was a Gaelic proverb about the poverty of the soil. '*Diù Mhuile, Bròlas, 's diù Bhròlais, Cille-phàraig*': The worst spot in Mull is Brolass, and the worst spot in Brolass is Kilpatrick.[15]

Allan Maclean of Brolass (not to be confused with Major, later Brigadier-General, Allan Maclean of Torloisk) was granted a nineteen year lease of his own lands, which had been added to the duke's possessions as part of Duart. Shortly afterwards, Captain Allan married Una Maclean, daughter of the laird of Coll, and she corresponded with the duke in a most charming and deferential manner during her husband's absence in America, recounting all the small details of the tack.[16]

The years following the '45 also saw the demise of the MacKinnon lairds in Mull. They had been 'out' (that is, active supporters of the uprising) and may have been largely responsible for the untraceable number of sixty Jacobites attributed to Mull. An old family, they had been prominent for hundreds of years, retaining the area north of present-day Tobermory called Mishnish, and living themselves in Erray, in a house which still stands today. Apart from their participation in both Jacobite risings, male MacKinnons were in trouble with the presbytery of Mull over various sexual peccadilloes. In 1751, John MacKinnon of that Ilk was summoned to attend a presbytery meeting as an adulterer, and unlike most sinners so compeared, he actually turned up to discuss his shortcomings with the 'black crows' at Aros. He was asked to remove Susanna Maclean, his housekeeper, from his house, and after insisting that he needed her until April, he at last compromised by sending her to sleep at Portmore, a farm on his own estate.[17] The presbytery forced its point by summoning Susanna, reproving her sharply, having her personal belongings confiscated, fining her, and sending her out of 'the Country'.[18] In 1757, the sasine of Mishnish went to Norman Macleod of Macleod, but in 1774, John's son Charles was involved in the sale of the estate to the Campbells of Knock, who were somewhat confusingly referred to as 'of Mishnish' and 'of Knock' for another three-quarters of a century. And so the lively MacKinnon presence was removed from the circles of Mull landowners.

It was in about 1750 that the Macleans of Lochbuy began to standardise the spelling of their surname as 'Maclaine'. The immediate family of the current laird tended to write 'Maclaine', but cousins used 'McLean'. As for their territorial designation, the laird and his wife were 'Lochbuy' and 'Lady Lochbuy'. The spelling 'Lochbuie' did not begin to creep in until the mid-nineteenth century, possibly as a corrective, because of increased social intercourse with the unlettered sassenach who might pronounce the name 'Lock By'.

Since receiving John Hardie's congratulatory message about being 'good and faithfull servants' before the uprising of 1715, which, by its patronising tone might have raised doubts about the wisdom of their allegiance, Hector of Lochbuy and his four sons, Murdoch, John, Allan and Lachlan had controlled the estate, slicing it up between them like the Roman empire. But as the eldest, Murdoch the thirteenth, had four daughters and no sons, the title went to Hector's second son, John. It was a custom among Highland lairds to share the role of chieftain with the heir, so that, for example, John was 'John of Lochbuy' and his son Lachlan was 'Younger of Lochbuy'. A letter from Lachlan to his father, when he was away at school in Dumbarton in 1729 and probably about twelve years old, shows that he was already suffering from the family ailment of shortage of cash:

> I want nothing since I came heir [here] but a continuall flux that my purse has alwise, which I expect you will mend very soon. Desire my mother to send me out a coatt of good black ffelt and a night sark [shirt] or two, and if you can spare a bible ... and be sure to send some clase [clothes] to Sandy, for he is almost naked ... with my blessing to yourself, mother and my sister ... Lach: McLaine.[19]

A letter in October 1729 asks that his father be kind 'to my foster father and mamie', showing that Lachlan was, before going to school, fostered, as was the custom in the families of the gentry, by a relation or member of the clan. 'Sandy' seems to have been a servant, and it is not known that his nakedness was covered up before Lachlan appealed for a replacement. 'Send Archibald at the next occasion, for he is an faithfull servant.' Nakedness was the usual state of Highlanders of the poorer classes, as Edmund Burt tells us in his letters from the north of Scotland:

> The common habit of the ordinary Highlanders is far from being acceptable to the eye; with them a small part of the plaid ... is set in folds and girt round the waist to make of it a short petticoat that reaches halfway down the thigh, and the rest is brought over the shoulders, and then fastened before, below the neck, often with a fork, and sometimes with a bodkin, or sharpened piece of stick ... In this way of wearing the plaid, they have sometimes nothing else to cover them, and are often barefoot; but some I have seen shod with a kind of pumps, made out of a raw cowhide, with the hair turned outward, which being ill-made, the wearer's foot looked some-

thing like those of a rough-footed hen or pigeon: these … are not only offensive to the sight, but intolerable to the smell of those who are near them. The stocking rises no higher than the thick of the calf, and from the middle of the thigh to the middle of the leg is a naked space, which being exposed to all weathers, becomes tanned and freckled, and the joint being mostly infected with the country distemper, the whole thing is very dis-agreeable to the eye. This dress is called the 'quelt' [kilt]; and for the most part they wear the petticoat so very short that in a windy day, going up a hill, or stooping, the indecency of it is plainly discovered.[20]

It is well seen that Lachlan, in his black felt coat, would be embarrassed, like any schoolboy, to be seen in company with such an apparition in a Scottish Lowland town like Dumbarton. The gentry could afford to do as the Romans did when abroad, and until the kilt was proscribed following the '45 (and indeed after), their custom was to make an elaborate change of dress the moment they arrived back in 'the Country'.

In the mid-1730s the lairds of Lochbuy, elder and younger, were being severely criticised by a cousin for their unthriftiness, mainly their spending on horses and boats, and their tendency to sign bonds here there and everywhere, promising payment which they could ill afford, and which would put them in debt. Lachlan the younger had, about this time, married Katharine MacDougall, and his excessive spending was doubtless a result of setting up a separate establishment, although in the Mull of the 1730s domestic arrange-ments following the marriage of a small laird must have been touching in their modesty. But Lachlan's marital life was short, for he died in 1743, leaving an only son known to but a few as 'Hector the Infant', who survived his father by a year. Consternation reigned at Lochbuy, or at Pennygown, where most of the family lived. The next heir was Allan of Garmony's son John, and at precisely the time of the '45 uprising, John was seeking legal advice in Edinburgh about his inheritance, only to be informed in 1747 that as Hector the Infant's grandfather John was still alive – and who could not be heir male to his own grandson – the next heir would have to wait for the death of John, his uncle.[21]

This waiting chieftain of Lochbuy, John of Garmony, would, in 1747, be about forty-seven years old. Later he was to achieve a certain fame in Samuel Johnson's *Journey to the Western Islands of Scotland* as a 'true Highland laird, rough and haughty and tenacious of his dignity'. His succession was officially completed in 1751,[22] and like almost every other transfer of heritable estate in the history of Mull, proved to be hollow. Because of the level of debt, the estate was immediately placed in the hands of trustees. The new laird had to submit his estate to management, and take out a new loan to enable him to pay the most pressing creditors. In 1751, as will be seen in the following chapter, the trustees elected John's natural son, the Edinburgh trained 'writer' or lawyer Gillean Maclaine, as agent to collect rents from the lands.

Before he suspected that the line of Lochbuy would ever go through himself (for Lachlan the Younger and Hector the Infant were alive and well), John of Garmony had in 1742 married Isabel Maclean of Brolass, sister to Allan Maclean. She was later to be described by James Boswell as behaving 'like the landlady of an alehouse'. It is uncertain whether he had been married before, for the clan historian, A. Maclean Sinclair, did not always mention first marriages, or perhaps did not know about them.[23] But it seems that John of Lochbuy already had, at the time of his marriage, no fewer than three children. On his succession in 1751, Isabel had recently borne him a son, Archibald, and in 1752, in spite of the constraints on his finances, John completed a small laird's house next to the crumbling castle of Moy. Here he was to live out the rest of his days as a petty tyrant, and his wife probably needed all the talents of the landlady of an alehouse to keep him in check.

While John Maclaine of Lochbuy waited for lawyers to confirm his inheritance, the exiled Sir Hector Maclean of Duart, who had been released from confinement in London in 1747 with other 'French' prisoners, moved from France to Rome, where the Stuarts held court. He suffered a stroke in the summer of 1750, from which he partially recovered, only to be struck down again a few months later. By his death, unmarried, the title of Baronet of Morvern and Duart passed to his great-great-grandfather's great-great-grandson by a second marriage – Allan Maclean of Brolass. The Brolass Macleans had served their chiefs well, and most of the heads of Brolass in this complicated succession had been tutors or guardians or representatives of the chief in exile. Now, for the first time in nearly sixty years, a Duart Maclean actually resident in Mull was at the head of the Macleans.[24]

There was no danger of the old antipathies being revived between Campbell and Maclean. Sir Allan was a conciliatory kind of man. Good-natured and gentle, he had been on good terms with the Duke of Argyll. In 1750 he had married Una, daughter of Hector Maclean the eleventh of Coll, a 'judicious pretty gentleman' who managed his estates of Coll, and Quinish in Mull, in a prudent manner. Coll and Sir Allan had offered their services to Duke Archibald in the '45, so that, had they been princes, Sir Allan's marriage would have been seen as a great diplomatic alliance. As it was, Sir Allan had not an inch of land, but, as has been noted above, was a mere tacksman on his own ancestral and boggy acres.

'The Knight', as his Mull friends now called him with a mixture of indulgence, jest and scorn, played down his new status, and behaved with exemplary modesty which John Lochbuy and Lachlan MacQuarrie of Ulva would have done well to copy. He was a career soldier, first in Lord Drumlanrig's regiment, and then, by the influence of the Duke of Argyll, in Montgomerie's Highlanders. The Seven Years' War between the French and the British, from 1756 to 1763, was said to have taken 350 men from Mull, of whom only fifty returned.[25] The 300 who had not returned included those killed in America,[26] and also those who had taken up offers of grants of land. Sir Allan is said to have applied for 200,000 acres, but this has to be regarded as speculative, as many grants were declared forfeit in 1783, on the arrival of the loyalists.[27]

Sir Allan and his wife had three daughters, Maria, Sibella and Anna, and one son, Lauchlan, 'a promising child' who died in infancy about 1755. Una herself died in 1760. Gillean Maclaine, son of Lochbuy, writing to Murdoch Maclaine, merchant in Edinburgh on 16 June, mentioned the event in the light of what it meant to all. 'Lady Brolos Younger is dead & buried of a few days ago, so that Family is now, I may say, Extinct ...'[28]

In 1756, Maighstir Seathan, poet, scholar, minister of the gospel, died in the fifty-fourth year of his ministry and about the seventy-seventh of his age. He had gone to join his wife, Isibeal Nic Gill-Eoin, whom he had obtained from God on trust for forty-eight years. On losing her he had been desolate, but it availed him nothing to quarrel with the Lord of Hosts. Now he was to have a joyful meeting with her in the abode of happiness and good fortune.[29]

Notes

1. NLS. Culloden Papers. MS 2691.
2. Heritable jurisdictions were abolished in 1748, the Duke of Argyll as ever gaining from the act by receiving compensation of £21,000. Walker, D. M., *The Scottish Legal System*, p. 123.
3. The Scottish equivalent of habeas corpus, an Act 'anent Wrangous Imprisonment', had been enacted in 1701, by the Scottish parliament. Donaldson and Morpeth, *A Dictionary of Scottish History.*
4. NAS. Stonefield Papers. GD14/10/1.
5. Lindsay and Cosh, *Inveraray and the Dukes of Argyll.*
6. Lindsay and Cosh, op. cit., p. 48.
7. Fergusson, Sir James, *Argyll in the '45.*
8. NAS. GD14/68. Memoriall for the Duke of Argyll [from Stonefield] 1746.
9. Fergusson, p. 126.
10. NAS. Saltoun Papers MS 17677.
11. Maclean Sinclair.
12. Seneachie, *An Historical and Genealogical Account of the Clan Maclean* ...
13. Campbell, John Lorne (ed.) *Highland Songs of the '45.* 'A certain song': Lose not heart, beloved people/And God will always take our part/Put your firm trust in Him, gladly/He alone can give us help/And continue loyal, loving/Fasting, praying, mourning, kind/And be faithful to each other/Thus your death wounds shall be healed.
14. NLS. MS17677/56.
15. MacCormick, John, *The Island of Mull*, p. 142.
16. NLS. MS 17675/95.
17. NAS. Mull Presbytery Minutes, CH2/273/1.
18. 'The Country' generally meant the estate someone belonged to, but depending on

the perspective, could mean the whole of Mull, and where the presbytery was concerned, the presbyterial area of Mull, Morvern, Ardnamurchan, Coll and Tiree.

19. NAS. GD174/1226/1. Lach: McLaine [sic] to the Laird of Lochbuy, Mull, 1729.
20. Burt, Edmund, *Letters from the North of Scotland*, p. 232.
21. NAS. GD174/91/1–2. Memoriall for John Maclean [sic] of Garmony, 1729.
22. GRO. D. 3330. Uncatalogued MSS.
23. Maclean Sinclair was to omit any reference to Murdoch Maclaine of Lochbuy's first marriage, which lasted over twenty years, but his main source, 'a Seneachie', hinted that he had been refused information on the early Lochbuy genealogy by Murdoch the twentieth.
24. See table, Macleans of Duart and Brolass.
25. McKay, Margaret M., *The Rev. Dr John Walker's Report on the Hebrides of 1764 and 1771*, p. 30.
26. Brander, Michael, *The Scottish Highlanders and their Regiments*, p. 203.
27. Gibbon, J. Murray, *Scots in Canada*, p. 60.
28. NAS. GD174/1244/4. GM to MM, Garmony, 16 June 1760.
29. O Baoill, Colm (ed.), *Eachann Bacach and other Maclean Poets*. From the English translation of the poet's lament for his wife, Isabel Maclean.

PART II

The People

5

John Lochbuy and his sons, Gillean and Archy

We have left John of Lochbuy in his new, modest house at Moy, coming to terms with the disappointing realisation that the rents from the estate would not be his to do as he liked with, and that he was in the humiliating position of having to live on the pocket-money allowed him by his trustees. His predecessor, Lachlan, in spite of having sold off lands in Jura, had been prodigal in the extreme, and John the Grandfather, always referred to as a kind old gentleman, was a typical Highland laird of the times, hospitable and even careful with his money, compared with others of his name. There is no evidence that his purely domestic existence was within the old tower house of Moy.[1] In fact he probably corresponded very well to the chieftain described by Burt who emerged from his 'castle' to greet a guest bearing his Arcadian offering of a bowl of cream, and then accompanied the visitor back to a turf hut without any partition, where the family lived at one end and the cattle at the other.[2]

After the deaths of their son, Lachlan the Prodigal, and their grandson, Hector the Infant, John the Grandfather and his elderly, colourful wife, Isabel MacDougall, resumed the role which had previously been theirs, as heads of Lochbuy. Their son Lachlan had had one other legitimate child: a girl, Mary or Mally Maclaine. Mally was about four years old when her father died, and her mother Katharine had almost immediately remarried. The new stepfather was Allan Maclean of Kilmory, who did not feature largely in little Mally's life, since she was to undergo the standard upbringing of a girl of her class and time. She was fostered in the family of John Fletcher until she became a child of tolerable habits. And after the usual period of six or seven years away from home, Mally was not returned to Katharine her mother, but to her now-widowed grandmother, Isabel MacDougall, in Pennygown. Like other Mull children, she went to school. Like others, she was launched early into the difficulties of life. She had only just settled down with her grandmother when John of Lochbuy, casting around for augmentations of his pocket-money, decided to kidnap her and to take her 'Makalive' cattle for himself.

If John had been another kind of man, he would have approached Isabel MacDougall in a civilised manner, and suggested that he take Mally under his wing. The grandmother liked her drink, and was so frail that one glass would affect her immediately, but she was also a sensible rational woman, who could read and write, and who might have come to some arrangement about her granddaughter's cattle.[3] But John was a rough diamond, given to rash, unmeditated behaviour; his nephew, Donald Maclean of Coll, aptly described him as a Don Quixote.[4]

'Makalive' or Machtella cattle were the cows which were given with the fostered child to the fostering parents. The fostering parents kept an account of the increase of the herd, and at the end of the fosterage, or on the daughter's marriage, the herd became the bride's portion.[5] Like any other custom of antiquity, it worked well when the participants were accustomed to it, but any breach of the unwritten rules was dealt with swiftly by a posse of brutal clansmen swooping down upon cattle raiders. John Lochbuy, whose means were straitened by Mally's father's extravagance, surely thought that he might have room for a few unofficial reprisals. Capturing both the cattle and the now almost nubile Mally, he led them to Lochbuy, where, he claimed, he took the girl into his family to be treated like one of his own children. This treatment was not necessarily sweet or gentle, but included the same pinches on the arm, beatings, and resulting black and blue marks as were meted out to his own daughters by his wife Isabel, 'Lady' Lochbuy. Mally continued for a time to go to the local school, but was often barefoot, like the local children. Then she was sent to school in Inveraray, and finally this daughter of the chieftains of Lochbuy scraped up a little learning in some cheap seminaries in Edinburgh, where, at the tender age of eighteen, she met the recently widowed Allan Maclean of Drimnin, dashing Jacobite hero of the '45, friend of Colquhoun Grant, Writer to the Signet, and father of a handful of children not much younger than Mally herself.[6]

Allan Maclean of Drimnin had not been attainted after the '45, presumably because of his youth, and perhaps through the kindness of the Duke of Argyll, his superior in the lands of Morvern, where, it will be remembered, Allan's seat at Drimnin had been burned in the raids of the *Terror* in 1746 against the duke's wishes.

Allan's first wife, Ann Maclean of Brolass, had given him two sons and at least two daughters. The sons, Charles and Allan, were to play their ignominious part in the story of 'the Country', that area of consanguinity which embraced both Mull and Morvern, but at this stage they were young, and probably being fostered far from the scenes of their father's amorous adventures. Allan Maclean eloped with the 19-year-old Mally in 1759, insofar as a marriage with a fatherless girl could be called an elopement. He was unaware (as was she) of the clauses in her father's provision for her which stipulated that her marriage must be consented to by her parent or guardians, and that without this consent her portion could not be paid. With remarkable haste, the husband instigated a process against John, and the estate of Lochbuy, for the payment of the sum which should have been expended on her education, aliment and support during her minority.

John of Lochbuy, with the pugnacious litigiousness which characterised the first twenty years of his reign as laird, rose to the bait. Regardless of the expense of the enquiries into his treatment of his young kinswoman, and in spite of the fact that he had several other law pleas overlapping with this one, he entered the fray, convinced of his own rectitude. Since part of the married couple's claim was for the 'Makalive cattle' he had driven off, the Edinburgh lawyers, who claimed that the judge would not understand barbarous Highland customs, demanded explanations and examples of the old Celtic custom of fostering before they could proceed. Evidence had to be collected from witnesses of Lochbuy's ill-treatment of his ward, and there was no shortage of willing tenants to swear that she had been abducted 'crying and greetin'' from her grandmother's house, at the age of twelve. She had come to school,

Shoemaker's bill – shoes supplied to Miss Mally Maclaine of Lochbuy in 1750–52, produced in court evidence that she had not been without shoes as a young girl in the laird's care. (*NAS. GD1/1003/3/5*)

said the schoolmaster, Lachlan Maclean, always neat, but without shoes or
stockings, which condition was inappropriate to her rank.[7] Bills from shoe-
makers were produced by Lady Lochbuy to show just how many pairs of
shoes Mally had had while at school in Inveraray.[8] The lawyers for Drimnin
then turned their attention upon Lochbuy's claim of having been *in loco parentis*,
and witnesses were found who were happy to remember that his style of
addressing his ward was hardly that of a fond parent: 'Turn out, you little
bitch!' was quoted as typical.[9] The case had descended into the sordid and the
trivial. It was fortunate that in the 1760s the press had not established a
sensationalism in its reporting which would make these incidents known to
the nation, but the legal community in Edinburgh took note. Honourable
lawyers pitied the reputation of an old family. John Murray, acting for Lochbuy
in the late 1760s, was to warn the laird too late that 'it is not bairn's play to
deal with Drimnin.' [10] Mally Maclaine, or Maclean, as she was to be from her
marriage, was awarded costs in her case against Lochbuy, but the main profit
must have been for the lawyers. Lochbuy, who had several processes running
in the courts at the same time, was inevitably the loser. Colquhoun Grant,
friend and legal agent of Drimnin, was reputed to be very rich from the
takings. We shall return to Mally's marriage in Chapter 16: the arrival of her
oldest son, Donald Maclean, born in 1770, introduced a very important player
into the drama of Mull in the nineteenth century. Meanwhile, two other
performances in the Court of Session were to influence events.

On 13 October 1758, John of Lochbuy incarcerated two kinsmen, Allan
Maclean of Kilmory and Hector Maclean of Killean, in the empty castle of
Moy. As hereditary chief of the barony of Moy, he might have had the right
to do so ten years earlier, but Heritable Jurisdictions, or the right of a
landowner to dispense justice within his own estate, had been abolished by
parliament in 1748, as one of the measures taken to curb the power of Highland
chiefs after the Jacobite uprising. If John did not know that the Act had been
passed, his prisoners did. Indeed, Hector Maclean of Killean was not even a
tenant of Lochbuy, but the son of John Maclean, tacksman of Killean, who
was in the employ of the Duke of Argyll.[11] It has been suggested that the
two men provoked Lochbuy into this rash move, in revenge for the many
wrongs he had done them, knowing that it could land him in the deepest
trouble. A criminal process was instigated in 1759, Killean and Kilmory against
Lochbuy, which, of course, Lochbuy chose to defend. The papers in the
case [12] show that Allan and Hector were not the first to be imprisoned in this
fashion since the abolition of the Act, but they were the only ones who were
opportunistic enough to use the episode against its perpetrator. John Mac-
Millan, 'a reputed rogue' in Tormagulen, Hector Campbell in Rossal, and
Charles MacKinnon in Kilfinichen, among others, had suffered this rough
justice. To justify his actions, Lochbuy called scores of witnesses to speak for
his own 'goodness', for he had supplied 'Coall & Candle, Sheets & Blankets

EORGE, by the Grace of God, King of Great Britain, France, and Ireland, Defender of the Faith ; To Our Lovits
Macers of Our Court of Justiciary, Meffengers at Arms, our Sheriffs in that Part,
conjunctly and feverally, fpecially conftitute, Greeting. Forafmuchas, it is humbly meant and complained to Us, by Our Lovits, Hector M'Lean, Son of John M'Lean of Killean, and Murdoch M'Lean, Son of the decea'd Allan M'Lean of Killmory, with Concourfe
our right trufty Robert Dundas of Arnifton, Efq; Our Advocate, for Our Intereft ; and alfo, by the faid Robert Dundas, for himfelf, and
ur Intereft, upon John M'Lain of Killean, and Sheriffdom of Argyll, John M'Phie, and Donald M'Lean, Servants
the faid John M'Lain of Lochbuy, Donald M'Lean, Son to   M'Lean Piper to the faid John M'Lain ; Duncan M'Lean Schoolmafter
Teacher of the faid John M'Lain his Children ; Murich M'Pherfon, Innkeeper in Moy in the faid Ifland of Mull, and Charles and Lauchlan M'-
adens, and Charles M'Lean Tenants or Refidenters upon the Lands of Kinlochfpelve, in the faid Ifland of Mull, and belonging to the faid John
Lain : THAT WHERE, by the Laws of this, and of all other well governed Realms, the violently invading and feizing the Perfons of any of Our
eges ; the forcible carrying them in Captivity, and the committing and detaining their Perfons, within any private or lockfaft Houfe, Caftle,
other Place, by way of Imprifonment, without any Order or Warrant of Law, are Crimes of a high Nature, dangerous to the Liberty of
e Subject, to the Peace and good Order of Our Government, and therefore feverely punifhable; ESPECIALLY when fuch Crimes are committed
Perfons of bad Fame and Character, who are habite and repute common Oppreffors, or the Minifters and Inftruments of fuch Oppreffors : AND
ien a Number of fuch Perfons are affembled together, and furnifhed with Arms, by a Perfon of Rank and Eftate in the Country, pretending Autho-
y over the Perfons fo affembled, to which he is not intitled by Law ; and MORE ESPECIALLY, when fuch Crimes are committed in an Ifland, or
er remote Place of the Highlands of Scotland, where the Bearing of Arms is prohibited by Law, and where the diftant Situation of fuch Ifland from
r Courts of Juftice, may render the Commiffion of fuch Crimes more dangerous to the Liberty and Security of the Subjects: YET TRUE IT IS
ND OF VERITY, That the aforefaid John M'Lain of Lochbuy, and the other Perfons above named, all and each of them, or one or other of them,
ve prefumed to commit, and are guilty, Actors, Art and Part, of all and each of the Crimes above mentioned, aggravated as aforefaid : IN SO FAR
, upon the thirteenth Day of October One thoufand feven hundred and fifty eight, or upon one or other of the Days of that Month, or of
Mouth of September preceeding, or of November following, the Complainer Hector M'Lean, and the decea'd Allan M'Lean of Killmory,
ther of Murdoch M'Lean the other Complainer, having repaired to the Houfe of the faid John M'Lain of Lochbuy, in the faid Ifland of Mull.
Sheriffdom of Argyle, in order to prevail upon him to reftore a Horfe, belonging to him the faid Hector, which the faid John M'Lain had
lawfully detained from him, for above the Space of twelve Months : And the Complainer, Hector M'Lean, having accoringly applied to the
John M'Lain for Reftitution of the faid Horfe, received from him many opprobrious Names, fuch as, Villain and Rafcal ; and the faid John
Lean did threaten, that if the faid Hector made any more Noife, he would lodge him *over by*, pointing to an old ruinous Caftle, called the Ca-
of *Moy*, belonging to him the faid John M'Lain, and near to his Dwelling-Houfe ; and the Complainer Hector M'Lean having expreffed
ne Contempt of the above Threatening, knowing that the faid John M'Lain had no legal Power or Authority to commit any Perfon as a Prifon-
to his Caftle, the faid John M'Lain did thereupon order his Servants to feize the faid Hector M'Lean, and carry him to the faid Caftle ; and
faid decea'd Allan M'Lean of Killmory having interpofed, to prevent the faid Hector, his Nephew, from being carried a Prifoner to the a-
e Caftle, the faid John M'Lain did thereupon repeat his Orders to his Servants, and commanded them to lay hold of the faid Hector M'Lean,
of the faid Allan M'Lean his Uncle, and to carry both of them Prifoners to the faid Caftle, and, if they offered to make any Refiftance, to
them Neck and Heel: And, in confequence of thefe Orders, the faid John M'Phie, and Donald M'Lean, Servants of the faid John M'Lain
Lochbuy, Donald M'Lean the Piper's Son, Duncan M'Lean, and Murich M'Pherfon, all above complained of, all and each, or one or other
them, did violently feize upon the faid Hector M'Lean Complainer, and the faid Allan M'Lean of Killmory, in order to have conducted
in Prifoners to the faid Caftle of Moy; but Mrs. M'Lain, Wife of the faid John M'Lain of Lochbuy, having refufed to deliver to him the
y of the faid Caftle, he the faid John M'Lain did thereupon order the faid John M'Phie, and the other Perfons laft above named, to carry the
Hector and Allan M'Leans Prifoners to Dowart Caftle, in the faid Ifland of Mull, where a Garrifon of our Troops is kept, and immediately
went into his Houfe and brought forth two Guns and a Sword, and delivered the fame to fome of the Perfons laft above named,
ordered them to proceed with their Prifoners to the faid Caftle of Dowart; and the faid Perfons complained upon, or one or o-
r of them, having, in obedience to thefe unlawful Orders, carried the Prifoners about three hundred Yards from the Houfe of the faid
in M'Lain towards Dowart Caftle ; the faid Hector M'Lean Complainer, and Allan M'Lean of Killmory, then Prifoners, fat down
n the Ground, and refufed to go any further, until they fhould fee a proper Warrant for carrying them to Dowart ; and, foon
r the faid John M'Lain of Lochbuy, on Horfe-back, came up with the Party, and afked the Reafon of their ftopping : To which
faid Hector M'Lean and Allan M'Lean Prifoners, or one of them, made Anfwer, That they would not go further, until they faw a legal
rant for carrying them to Dowart ; upon which the faid John M'Lain, after abufing his Prifoners with bad Names, and attempting to knock down
the one and then the other of them, with the Butt-end of his Whip, ordered the Perfons above named, in whofe Cuftody they were, to take
of their Prifoners, till he fhould bring a Party of the Military from Dowart ; and having left them for about an Hour, he again returned with
ral other Perfons, particularly the above named Charles and Lauchlan M'Phadens, and Charles M'Lean : and thefe three Perfons having joined
Party which guarded the Prifoners, did, with them, forcibly carry the faid Hector and Allan M'Leans Prifoners towards the faid Caftle of Moy.
t the faid John M'Lain of Lochbuy having, in the mean Time gone to his own Houfe, and brought from thence the Key of the faid Caftle, did
wards rejoin his Party near to the faid Caftle ; and immediately required the faid Hector and Allan M'Leans to enter Prifoners into the faid
tle, moft audacioufly ufing Our Royal Name, to authorize his illegal Requifition ; and the faid Hector and Allan M'Leans having refufed to
r, until he fhould produce a legal Warrant for their Commitment, he thereupon repeated his former Orders to the Party, and commanded
m to carry their Prifoners by Force into the Caftle ; and the faid John M'Lain of Lochbuy did himfelf lay hold of the faid Allan M'Lean, in or-
to thruft him into the Caftle ; whereupon a Struggle enfued, in which the faid Allan was brought to the Ground ; but the faid John M'Lain
ing again repeated his Orders, and opened the Door of the Caftle, the other Perfons above complained of, or one or other of them, did there-
n feize the faid Hector and Allan M'Leans, and forcibly thruft them into the Caftle ; whereupon the faid John M'Lain locked the Door, and carried
the Key in his Pocket: And the faid Hector and Allan M'Leans were confined and detained Prifoners in the faid ruinous Caftle, expofed to the Incle-
ncy of the Weather, and ill provided of Neceffaries, from Friday, when they were committed, till the Sunday following ; and during their Con-
ement, John M'Lean of Killean Father of the Complainer, Hector M'Lean, and Mrs. M'Lean Wife of the faid Allan M'Lean of Killmory,
ne to the Houfe of the faid John M'Lain of Lochbuy, and begged of him to liberate the Prifoners, or at leaft to allow them to go in and fpeak
h them; both which he refufed. And having kept them in this illegal Confinement during the above Space, he was at laft prevailed upon to fet them
iberty, by the Entreaties of Mr. Niel M'Leod Minifter at Rofs, and Mr. Alexander M'Lean Surgeon, both in Mull, upon their granting an Obligation,
ail-bond, that the faid Prifoners fhould prefent themfelves at the Caftle of Moy, Dowart, or Inveraray, any Day the faid John M'Lain fhould ap-
t, betwixt and the firft Day of December then next. AND by thefe violent and illegal Proceedings, the faid Hector M'Lean Complainer was
ived of his Liberty, and highly injured in his Perfon ; and the faid Allan M'Lean of Killmory, Father of the other Complainer Murdoch
Lean, being an old difeafed Man, fuffered greatly in his Health, and died within a few Weeks after he was difcharged from the above illega
finement. AND the faid John M'Lain of Lochbuy, John M'Phie, Donald M'Lean, Donald M'Lean the Piper's Son, Duncan M'Lean,
rich M'Pherfon, Charles and Lauchlan M'Phadens, and Charles M'Lean, are all and each of them guilty Actors Art and Part of the Oppreffion,
lence, and Crimes above libelled. AND FURTHER, the faid John M'Lain of Lochbuy is habite and repute, and notouly known in the Country,
e an Oppreffor of the People living upon his Eftate and in the Neighbourhood, and to have committed many Acts of Violence, and wrongous
rifonment fimilar to that above libelled, and to be a Harbourer and Protector of Thieves upon his Eftate ; and the laill other Perfons above
plained of are habite and repute to be Thieves, or Perfons of bad Character, and to have been employed upon former Occafions in executing the
cut and illegal Orders of the faid John M'Lain of Lochbuy their Mafter : AT LEAST, Time and Place forefaid, Hector M'Lean Complainer,
the decea'd Allan M'Lean of Killmory were violently and illegally feized, and carried Prifoners to the aforefaid Caftle of Moy, and therein com-
ed and detained Prifoners, during the Space, and in the Circumftances above defcribed ; and the faid John M'Lain of Lochbuy, John M'Phie,
ald M'Lean, and Donald M'Lean the Piper's Son, Duncan M'Lean, Murich M'Pherfon, Charles and Lauchlan M'Phadens, and Charles M'Lean,
nd each, or one or other of them, are guilty Actors Art and Part, in committing the faid violent and illegal Acts. ALL WHICH, or Part thereof,
hat the Perfons above complained upon, were guilty Art and Part thereof, being found proven by the Verdict of an Affize, before Our Lords
ice-General, Juftice-Clerk, and Commiffioners of Jufticiary, the faid John M'Lain of Lochbuy and the other Perfons above complained of, fhould
unifhed in their Perfons and Goods, to the Terror of others to commit the like in Time coming ; and ought and fhould be decerned and ordained,
junctly and feverally, to make Payment to the faid Hector and Murdoch M'Leans, Complainers, of the Sum of L. 500 Sterling, in Name of
tthment and Damages ; and alfo of the Sum of L. 300 Sterling as the Expence of this Profecution.

OUR WILL IS HEREFORE, *&c.*

Broadside summary of the case of Maclean *v.* Maclaine, 1759.
(*Edinburgh University Library*)

and plenty of good Straw' to the prisoners, despite being called 'a Senseless Bugar' by the men. There was now a new charge: that exposure to wind and weather during the two-day imprisonment had caused the death, a few months later, of Kilmory.[13]

Attentive readers will recognise Allan Maclean of Kilmory (a 'quarrelsome, ill-natured coxcomb' in Lochbuy's words), as the second husband of Katharine MacDougall, mother of young Mally Maclaine, and might rightly conclude that this quarrel ran very deep, as quarrels did in 'the Country'. Lochbuy took the opportunity, in the course of the trial, to air every past skirmish between these rival families, including the thrashing of John the Grandfather and his son Lachlan, by Hugh, Allan and Lachlan Kilmory in the mill of Cameron many years before. For every recital of evils done, Lochbuy produced witnesses from his tenantry, who all had a free trip to Edinburgh to give evidence.

He also chose to use the court to publicise the iniquities of the family of Killean, whose latest felon, Hector, now accused him, Lochbuy, of wrongful imprisonment. Hector Maclean was in the habit of trying Lochbuy's patience. In July 1757, he had come to the house at Moy and asked Lady Lochbuy where her own daughter Bell and her step-daughter lay, but without waiting had forced open their door, tried to lie with them, and on their refusing, had called Peggy a whore. The next day he had spread around the island the story of how he had found Peggy in bed with a man. 'Tho' my daughter Tibby lay alongst with her', Lady Lochbuy said indignantly, 'this story he had the assurance to tell me in my own house, where my brother Brolass and several other gentlemen were at the time. I told Hector never more to come to my house ... but he came more than once ... my husband never countenanced him. I know he was much provoked by him and Kilmory before he confined them.'[14]

All this was called up in defence of the imprisonment of Kilmory and Killean. If making Hector Maclean of Killean's behaviour public served to clear Lochbuy's system of enmity and hatred, perhaps the finding against him was a small price to pay. He was ordered to make payment of £500 to the complainers, and £300 as the expense of the prosecution.[15] Elsewhere, in the real world, in this 'year of miracles' 1759, Quebec fell to James Wolfe and Fort Ticonderoga and Montreal were captured by Jeffrey Amherst. Both victories involved men from Mull.

In all the correspondence which survives from Gillean Maclaine himself, his admirers, his detractors, his cousins, his wife and children and grandchildren, there is no clue as to his mother's identity, or his early upbringing. A natural son of John of Lochbuy, he was, by certain accounts, born in 1724, but his own testimony puts his date of birth as 1733.[16] Again, from his own account, he claimed that his father had expended little on his education, but had left him in Edinburgh to shift for himself at the early age of fourteen, when he found an occupation in the office of a clerk of session [17] and earned his bread for five or six years writing at the rate of a penny a page. By his own industry, he acquired enough knowledge of the law to be admitted a notary public, and with this qualification, was invited by his father in 1751 to return to Mull to look after the affairs of the estate of Lochbuy at an annual salary of £18, and the added inducement of the tack of the farms of Garmony and Ledirkle.[18] Gillean later claimed that he was extremely reluctant to do this, having other views for his future, but he had agreed to commence as factor to Lochbuy at Whitsunday 1751.

Gillean's experience both in Edinburgh and in Mull made him qualified for the task, for he was almost certainly raised in Mull, at Garmony, where his grandfather Allan Maclaine of Garmony had had the liferent. His grandmother, Julia Maclean of Torloisk, probably had charge of him there, as is suggested by his attachment to her at the time of her death.

Gillean was in Garmony at the time of his marriage in 1771. In 1751, his father John took up residence in the nearly completed Moy House, near the Castle of Moy. Throughout the 1750s, Gillean spent his time between Mull and Edinburgh, travelling regularly on behalf of his father, whose processes in the Edinburgh courts multiplied in that decade.

Having intimate knowledge of his father's business concerns, and being asked by the laird to make all his legal affairs watertight, Gillean proceeded to draw up documents concerning the administration and inheritance of the estate. His father, John, who was a simple country laird with much respect for, if little understanding of, the law, trusted him to such an extent that he did not read the papers he was asked to sign. Gillean's explanations were long and convoluted, and full of legal terms which the father found tiresome. Likewise, Gillean, an acute young man who had to make his way in the world, found his father's incomprehension exasperating, but was not slow to realise that John's inability to concentrate on the detail of the law was something he might exploit. Between his farming activities, his factoring, and his visits to Edinburgh, he set about revising and recording Lochbuy's wishes for the estate, and defining his own role as his father's trusted administrator.[19]

One of Gillean's records concerned the rent of his own farms of Ledirkle and Garmony, and the addition of the land of Scallastle to the group. Scallastlemore and Scallastlebeg, just north of present-day Craignure, had been leased to a Kilmore tacksman called Alexander Campbell, who had built a brewery, and begun to distil spirits. He had cut no peats, but used the woods around Scallastle for fuel. Next, Alexander Campbell had built himself an 'ordinary dwelling house', using the best local oak, but the house had 'tummilled to the ground' within two years. He and his servants had cut down forty 'Plumm Trees' and other fruit trees within the garden. In 1756, Alexander Campbell's brewery had not saved him from becoming bankrupt. He had turned to smuggling, plying his trade between Scallastle, the Isle of Man and Ireland. But it was a dangerous way of life, and he was drowned off the coast of Ireland before the end of 1756.[20]

Susanna Campbell continued with the tack of Scallastle, and, as was the usual fate of widows, she had to sell implements, cattle and other possessions in order to survive, with her four young children. The Scallastle woods were bought by an English company at Bonawe, but Susanna found Gillean ready to evict her because she had not enclosed the woods to keep out her cattle. Mistress Susanna had influential friends and relations,[21] but none could prevail against Gillean's determination to move her from Scallastle. Since her husband's arrival in Mull, 500 trees had been cut down, he said simply, and put the matter into Mr Orme's hands, in Edinburgh. Gillean also asked Mr Orme to proceed against Campbell of Airds for debt, and Hector Maclean of Torloisk for cutting down trees in Gruline. Susanna's friends were disabled from acting on her behalf by being selected for these processes themselves.[22] When Susanna was duly evicted, the Campbells' tack had some years to run, but Gillean, in his capacity as manager of the estate, was able to buy up the remainder of the lease of Scallastle, adding it to Garmony and Ledirkle to make a very satisfactory estate within an estate, complete with excellent kelp shores: Gillean was probably the first person in Mull to see the commercial potential of these. He made out three consecutive nineteen-year leases for himself, something unheard of on the estate of Lochbuy, which secured the farms for Gillean up to the age of eighty-five. Furthermore, the farm of Scallastle was to be sett at a smaller rental than it had paid in 1742, when it was sett in a public roup. This was because, Gillean said later, his father liked people to build now in stone and lime, 'a thing very unusual in this part of the country', and the Scallastle house was to be two storeys high. The expense of all this would be offset by a moderate rent, Gillean argued. The reason for assigning himself three nineteen-year leases, and not simply a lifetime's occupancy, was given, in one of the many court cases resulting from this allocation, as one of tradition. The Duke of Argyll was in the habit of granting nineteen years. And so indeed he was, as we have learned from the innovations of Duncan Forbes of Culloden in 1737, but not often, as far as we know, in multiples of nineteen. At least the business of Gillean's acquisition tells us that the method of free market bidding had operated in Lochbuy in 1742, only five years after Forbes had introduced it on the Argyll estates.

The audacious scheme not only flaunted all tradition by its magnitude, but it completely ignored what Gillean must have known – that Scallastle was to be part of Lady Lochbuy's jointure should she be widowed, and was set apart for that purpose.[23]

But Gillean's tidying up of the affairs of the estate of Lochbuy did not rest there. He had also produced documents for his father's signature which affected the destination of the estate after his father's death, and to these we must return after considering the early life of John's son and heir, Archibald.

Archibald Maclaine of Lochbuy was born about 1749, after his sister Isabella, and possibly other infant siblings who had not survived. The beloved son of the family, he had been sent to the High School at Dalkeith, near Edinburgh, which was then enjoying the reputation of being one of the best schools in Scotland. He was placed under the supervision of his cousin, Murdoch Maclaine, merchant in Edinburgh, and it was to Murdoch's house, and to his even more attractive shop, with its sweetmeats, that Archy went on high days and holidays. 'Archy, the very plague of my heart, – for to keep him from the Raisin Cask and Figg drawer it would require more servants than I am able to maintain', Murdoch wrote in January 1765.[24] But only two months later, this childish Archy was indentured to a Writer to the Signet, Alexander Orme,[25] for a term of five years, to learn the business of a law firm and to keep the secrets of his master. In the autumn of 1765 he matriculated in the arts classes at the University of Edinburgh at the age of sixteen, which was then above the average age for a 'bejan' or first-year student.[26] His first year was filled with Latin and Greek, and the cost of a Greek dictionary was duly put through the ledger of his cousin Murdoch. In his third year he studied moral philosophy with Professor Adam Ferguson, who had just published *Essays on Civil Society*. If John of Lochbuy was himself poorly educated, or unable to understand a legal document or philosophical argument, he was ensuring that his son and heir would be well equipped for the life of the intellect, and Archy was reported by all to be making good progress. He completed three years of the arts course. At that time it was positively unfashionable to proceed to graduation, and the custom of prospective ministers and lawyers was to stop at the end of the third year of the four-year Master of Arts curriculum. Neither the church nor the legal establishment required graduation. A modicum of theology or law might be imbibed with the arts subjects, but specialisation was mainly confined to the period after the arts examinations.

In the summers between his indenture and the end of his college course, Archy returned to Mull. In 1765, his father had raised an action of Reduction in the Court of Session at Edinburgh against Gillean. This had been a long time in coming to a head, and when the action was finally brought, it is hard to believe that Archy did not know about it, working as he did in one of the law offices employed by his father, and privy to the rolls of the Court of Session which announced forthcoming processes. A Reduction was an action to make null and void legal writings which would prove injurious to the pursuer, and in this case Gillean was the defender; hoist, one might say, on his own petard. For Gillean had made a fatal mistake.

On 8 January 1759, a letter to John of Lochbuy from his son disturbed the father, and made him request to see all the revised legal documents. It ran:

Dear ffather,
As you have of this date signed a nomination and testament wherein I am named Tutor & Curator for my Brother Baldie [Archy] and also a Factory and Commission during his Minority, also a Bond, payable to me, for £500

sterling at first term of Martinmas or Whitsunday after your decease, also
a Tack ... of the Lands of Scallastle, Garmony and Ledirkle, I hereby declare
it lawfull for you at any time in your life to revoke the above deeds except
the Tack, and to augment, alter or diminish the same by a Writ upon
Stampt Paper under my hand, to be Intimate [intimated] to me ... and I
further declare that in case you shall think proper any time during your
lifetime to live by yourself and family at Garmony or Ledirkle, then in that
case it shall be leisome [morally permissible] and lawfull for you to assume
the possession thereof, upon paying Meliorations [improvements on rented
property] and putting me in possession of Pennygown and Leiter. But in
case you don't alter these deeds or assume said possession, I declare the
said Writs to be good and valid. I am, &c.[27]

John's mind was full of his grievances against Kilmory and Killean, but
something in this communication alerted him to an excess of interference on
the part of his natural son. Having spoken to some Mull friends, he asked
Gillean if he might have another look at the documents he had signed, and
to his very great surprise, and further suspicion, Gillean refused, saying that
because the papers concerned him, he could not let them out of his sight, and
indeed it was unlawful to do so. Lochbuy consulted his man of business on
this point, and was warned that Gillean might have overstepped the mark.

Gillean had chosen to 'remind' the laird of Lochbuy of decisions he was
supposed to have made between 1751 and 1758, which had been formalised
by the son. The older man had cast envious eyes on Gillean's farm at Garmony,
which in the 1750s had been improved, with what funds he knew not, out of
all recognition, and was now more attractive than Moy itself. He had suggested
to his son that he might like to live there, and Gillean had decided to treat
this request with indulgence if his father was seen to understand the covenant
between them. The letter was intended to make the situation clear, and it
misfired. Those who are familiar with the kind of dialogue which frequently
occurs between an old, dull-witted, but stubborn parent and an incisive son
may recognise this situation, but John was not a man in his dotage. He was,
however, a man who both trusted and feared the law. He was now in the
midst of the case with Kilmory and Killean, but at all times he had prosecutions
going on against tenants for unpaid rents, unfulfilled leases, or damages to
property. Now, as he pondered Gillean's words, the iron entered into his soul
again, and he resolved to take legal advice in Edinburgh.

Gillean was not without enemies in the legal fraternity. As an action for
Reduction began to build up, there were many who relished the idea of stabbing
him in the back. The preparations began in March 1764, when Gillean was
asked to deliver up the deeds which he kept in his own house, for cancellation.
He delayed his response for one term, and finally delivered up the documents,
all of which were graced with the handsome, flourishing, unmistakeable
seventeenth-century signature of his father. By 1765 the Condescendence had

been completed, a statement of facts for John which would have to be proved in court if not admitted by Gillean.[28] But many Mull people had anticipated the accusations long before the father had noticed anything. Daniel Maclean, a writer and 'man of business' in Glasgow, had written to his cousin, Hector Maclean of Torloisk, writer in Edinburgh, and laird of the Mull estate of Torloisk, as early as 1759

> I know there is a Macer gone to Mull to summon poor unluckie Lochbuy; the abominable bastard Gillean has ruined him. I wish that vagabond could be banished. I am told he has lately been guilty of forgery and detected. You are the only one of the clan in a public capacity, and why won't you endeavour to redress the wrongs of a poor child [Archy Maclaine of Lochbuy] who, if it is not prevented, must suffer for the folly of his father and the Knavery of a supposed, bastard brother.[29]

Then there were people like Susanna Campbell, widow of the former tacksman of Scallastle, and her son, Neil Campbell (now entering the legal profession himself), who had fallen prey to Gillean. The lawyer Hector of Torloisk was the one man who might have exposed 'the abominable bastard', but he was ill in 1765. 'I hear my good friend Hector is dying', Gillean had the gall to write to Murdoch Maclaine. 'May God forgive him his sins.' Gillean had gone to considerable lengths to ensure that Hector did not know too much about Lochbuy affairs. He believed Hector 'held him at ill will'.[30] Hector died in the summer of 1765, in Glasgow, in the house of his cousin and associate, Daniel Maclean; he was about forty-seven years old.

The lawyers for John of Lochbuy now presented the facts. From the early 1750s, they said, Gillean had organised a settlement of the entire estate, first to Archy, and then, failing heirs of Archy, to Gillean himself and his heirs. But in 1759, he had drawn up a disposition of a personal bond for £500 to himself, a commission to take over the total rents of the estate, and to grant tacks, a nomination of himself as Baron Baillie of Moy, a tack of Scallastle, Garmony and Ledirkle with kelp, relieved of cess duty. And, as Gillean anticipated the possibility of a Reduction, he ensured that John signed another deed binding his other heirs to accept the changes, and not to attempt to interfere with the new arrangements.

A hundred little arts were practised by Gillean, said the lawyers, to retrieve the letter which gave a summary of the business, the letter which had alarmed the father. Finally, Gillean was satisfied that his father had carelessly lost the letter, and proceeded to draw up further safeguards, awarding himself costs of 5s. a day, ferry money, and other perquisites. But (like some villain in a melodrama) Gillean had become so pleased with himself that he had boasted of his position of strength all over Mull, and some of his father's friends had been alarmed, suggesting to Lochbuy that he should check his legal papers. It was at this juncture that Gillean had refused to give up the deeds.

No mention had been made by Gillean of John's girls, Peggy, his natural daughter, or Isabella and Catherine, his lawful daughters, except to proclaim that they must give power to their half-brother to intromit with the funds and direction of the succession. Yet the estate had been burdened with gifts and payments to Gillean beyond anything it could ever hope to pay.

As the case against Gillean was being prepared, and the ease with which he had altered the family papers was revealed, questions arose in the minds of the lawyers about his father's gullibility, and then it was suggested to them that John was not just gullible, but 'facile'. This was the eighteenth-century way of saying that he was mentally unsound, or suffering from diminished responsibility. The condition was as difficult to prove then as it has been in modern times, for the spectre of insanity lurked within the definition. Nevertheless, John's lawyers attempted to bring his 'facility' into the case, but it would not do, as James Boswell was to observe in his journal.[31] The case ended in a partial Reduction of the deeds, affecting the inheritance, but leaving Gillean favourably endowed, with his Scallastle, Garmony and Ledirkle lands, his bailliedom, his salary and his kelp shores. This settlement would make Lochbuy a house divided, and was to cause property problems lasting until the sale of Scallastle in 1872. Gillean remained in control of certain aspects of the estate, but turned his legal mind upon the more challenging difficulties of the Ulva sale. Here his notoriety and ruthlessness qualified him in the minds of impatient creditors to accelerate the settlement which the MacQuarries had been blocking for nearly a quarter of a century.

John of Lochbuy and his natural son managed to live in relative peace until their settlement was reached. It was the tenants who suffered, when, for instance, John rode down to the kelp shores of Loch Spelve in 1766 and tore the kelping tools out of their hands, thrashing them with his whip, and shouting imprecations at Gillean, who was happily not present, or he would have had his head broken.[32] The father was not inclined to be silent about the causes of his anger. 'Gillean would cut your throat', he warned Murdoch Maclaine in 1765, as the debate proceeded in the Court of Session. The only person he would not take into his confidence about the whole affair was his own son and heir, Archy, who was not to be told of the pitiful financial condition of the estate he was to inherit. Archy, it will be remembered, was a university student and an apprentice writer in the chambers of Alexander Orme, WS. When he came home to Mull, he was not allowed to stay with Gillean at Garmony on his way to Communion at Salen lest he be influenced by his half-brother's powers of reasoning, or given the other point of view, or even told just how great a debt hung over the estate. It was the opinion of John Murray, assistant to Alexander Orme, that the heir should be told of the true situation and, of course, Archy knew: he could hardly not know what was going on. John Murray wrote to Lochbuy:

Dear Lochbuy,

Your son is now become a man. He is in that time of life when it is full time you should make him entire master of all your transactions and you ought to have his opinion on every action of your future life. I know you study his welfare more than your own. – Then consult with himself about the means of bringing about that welfare. He will now prevent you from writing to such people as will take hold of to prevent your interest, and he will give you such humble, tho' at the same time sincere advice as you ought to weigh well before you do anything contrary to it. Two will see more than one. I beg you will keep copies of every letter you write to people about business. When Archy comes here I shall introduce him to Mr Lockhart, and shall make him known in all your affairs. Pray why have I not heard from you ere now? [33]

In March 1768, Murray was urging genteeler company for Archy, and less pocket-money 'as there are some young folks in Town who ramble too much, and with whom he has been too intimate', but the laird responded by showing less confidence in Murray, for he liked to do things his way. There was not a house in Edinburgh that Murray entered where he did not feel uncomfortable when Lochbuy was mentioned. Murray had to advance money to begin parts of the legal process, but Lochbuy did not pay. 'I will be knocked up entirely as your Cousin Mr Murdoch can inform you', Murray wrote plaintively.

Gillean was being replaced as factor of the Lochbuy estate by another John Maclaine, a cousin of the family, who had hitherto had the tack of Bradil, on the shoulder of Glen Forsa. From now on he was to live at Gruline, and to be called, simply, 'Gruline'. He was either a widower of long standing or a bachelor, for he had no wife; his sister Miss Ketty kept house for him. Their parents had been Allan Maclaine, tacksman of Suie in the Ross of Mull, and Marion Campbell. Through his mother and another sister, he was related to the Campbells of Knock, an Argyll possession close to the farm of Gruline. He seems to have been the antithesis of Gillean – a soft-hearted man, and one who helped his tenants in times of trouble. Among the *dramatis personae* of eighteenth-century Mull, he was to play a sad, small part.

After the death of Hector Maclean of Torloisk, in 1765, Gillean took over much of the legal business of that lawyer and laird. He acted, in so far as anyone could act, in the stultified affairs of Lachlan MacQuarrie of Ulva. His involvement with the MacQuarries of Ulva and Ormaig introduced him to his second cousin, the 21-year-old Maria MacQuarrie, in 1768.

In Edinburgh, Archibald Maclaine of Lochbuy finished his three years as an arts student, and seems to have decided not to make a permanent career of the law. It is not clear that he finished his indenture with Orme, due to be completed in 1770, but he certainly preferred the company of the 'ramblers' who had worried John Murray, to that of his fellow writers. In May 1769 he was one of a party who drank grog with the governor of Duart Castle, in Mull, and falling into a dispute with Governor Lane, Archy challenged him and drew his sword. Gillean was also of the party, as were Sir Allan Maclean and Lachlan MacQuarrie of Ulva. In a letter to Murdoch Maclaine in Edinburgh, Gillean described the incident:

> [Sir Allan Maclean, MacQuarrie and Archy] came last week to Dowart ... and drank whisky grog with Governor Lane.[34] The latter and Archy quarelled, and so sharp they would be, as they were going to engage in the Governor's own room. McQuary came upon them, and to prevent a quarrel McQuary broke the two small swords, one being the officer's and the other the sergeant's. Then Archibald went for the Knight's sword, which McQuary likewise broke. So you see he is a friend to sword merchants. Then the whole party at Dowart turn out, the Corporall giving some abusive language to Archy which the Knight resented by giving the Corporall a Box on the Ear, but you won't hinder Mr Corporall to return the Compliment, but, being low of Stature only reached the Knight's Arm. Mr Corporall was drubbed by the Knight's whip, and put to the Black Hole till he ordered him to be relased ... But I fear this Brother of mine [Archy], and your Cousin, will not mend matters. In short all the young Generation of our friends are worse than the old. At least they don't promise well. You need not take any notice of this behaviour of Archibald at present, tho' indeed I doubt not as already publick enough. The Knight has no honour by it ...[35]

But another undated letter, much crumpled, tells a further tale of Archy's temper:

> All I could do to defend myself ... the Knight keep'd his House and looked on. The Knight's own behaviour I thought so little of that I bade them farewell within a mile of my own house [at Garmony]. The Knight returned to Callachilly and Archibald followed me to my own house to fight me, and had nigh strangled me with the silk napkin at my neck, which he would have effectually done ... In short, his behaviour was so like a Madman that it would take me too much paper to describe it. He has laid himself open for a criminall prosecution of the Worst Consequence if I chuse it, which will depend upon his Father's Immediate Conduct. His Father has been here since, and is Sensible of his son's Madness.
>
> Sir Allan wrote me, exclaiming against Archibald's conduct ... so you see what a figure we make here. For myself I bore all without a Reproaching Syllable, and ordered my servant to conduct him out of Town.[36] I proposed to Lochbuy a Submission of all Disputes ... and drop any further Processes, and I presume even Ross or Lockhart will not advise an Appeal. So you see there's great encouragement to settle in this Country ...[37]

So Gillean found his trump card, and tells posterity, in his own words, why his father did not pursue the entire programme of Reduction. It is quite possible that this arch-deceiver exaggerated Archy's 'madness' and took care to inform Murdoch Maclaine in Edinburgh. If he frightened his father with the prospect of a 'criminall prosecution' of Archy, no evidence of this has reached us. But John of Lochbuy could not allow himself to be pronounced facile in the Court of Session, and his heir shown to be mad also. After 1769 Gillean was a changed man, with a new future. It was immediately after the attempted strangling that he became attracted to Maria MacQuarrie of Ulva.

John Maclaine of Lochbuy was now an old man, in his seventieth year. The Argyll families noted a perceptible cessation of hostilities between John and Gillean. Archy was brought into the fold as Archibald Younger of Lochbuy. John Murray, now in India, wrote, 'the re-establishment of his family appears to me no very difficult matter provided method and uniformity in conduct are observed'. The heir spent more time in Mull. There were anxious moments for the fond father when Archy almost lost his life in an accident off Ulva in 1774, in which Donald Maclean Younger of Coll and eight others were drowned.[38] At about the same time, John at last passed on the estate of Lochbuy to his son, who appointed trustees, and the trust deponees were granted sasine of the lands. Having divested himself of the duties of being a landowner, Archy prepared to do what his feet had been itching to do for some years – to go to America. There were times when he thought that the army might offer him the best means of getting there, and he was asked how many men from the estate might go with him. He produced a list of eighty-eight potential recruits. But the immediate commission offered was not good enough, and he thought he might go as a private person. He had not chosen the right moment. The American colonies had revolted in 1775, and the British had evacuated Boston in March 1776. On 14 May the 42nd Regiment sailed out of Greenock for America.

On 3 June, John of Lochbuy and his natural son, Gillean, travelled together to see Archy off in the *Nelly of Greenock*. It was to be the last time they would see him.

Seven years earlier, when Gillean played his trump card, the attractions of Maria (or Marie, Mairi or Mally) MacQuarrie had impressed themselves upon his much jaded palate. He met her in Edinburgh, where she had been staying in the house of Murdoch Maclaine, and in Ulva, where he was trying to persuade Lachlan MacQuarrie, her father, to bring the matter of the sale of Ulva to a head. As the marriage of Gillean, the household of Murdoch, and the island of Ulva will be dealt with in later chapters, it is expedient to follow Archy to America, and to watch John of Lochbuy's decline after parting with his favourite son.

Archy wrote to John from Londonderry on 14 June, and John wrote back on 23 July to announce that Lady Lochbuy was very ill, and to say that he hoped Archy would look back at his past follies with 'abhorrence and contempt'.[39] These communications were not of great interest to the young man who arrived in New York in August 1776 a few weeks after the American Declaration of Independence had been issued from Philadelphia.

Long Island was buzzing with activity. General Howe had recently arrived with 9,000 men from Halifax, Nova Scotia, reinforced by a large number of German mercenaries. His brother, Admiral Howe, now naval Commander-in-Chief in North America, brought ten ships and twenty frigates, and together they planned to take New York, and the Hudson River route to Canada. Here also, Archy met his kinsman, Lieutenant-Colonel Allan Maclean of Torloisk, and Major Small, commanders of the 1st and 2nd Battalions of Royal Highland Emigrants. Maclean, who did not approve of Archy's independent way of doing things, nevertheless told him that there was a commission awaiting him, but that he must go immediately to Halifax to join the forces there. It would seem that Archy did this, as he must have had to undergo some military training, but the records are silent on this point, and the next we hear of him is in the following year, 1777, when he has joined the ponderous march of General Burgoyne's troops, increased by native Indians and German mercenaries, as they advanced towards Lake Champlain. The Indians had to be repeatedly warned against scalping the enemy, but when encamped, their trophies were hung up to dry like so many pieces of clothing on a washing line.[40] In a misjudged raid upon an American store of ammunition at Bennington, a detachment of about 800 men from Burgoyne's army was infiltrated by men calling themselves Loyalists, who betrayed them to the American militia. The engagement which followed was described by a German officer, Lieutenant Glich [41] as 'defying all power of language'. Men fell by direct blows from bayonets, rifle butts, sabres and pikes, and some who were not mortally wounded escaped into the woods. Among those left, to be taken prisoner and marched to Boston, was Archibald Maclaine of Lochbuy.

The first surviving account of this unfortunate event from Archy's own pen is in a letter to Murdoch Maclaine, in which he did not mention the actual fighting at Bennington, but described the aftermath.

> I had the misfortune to be taken prisoner near Bennington on the 16 August. When taken prisoner, I was deprived of all my baggage, and stripped of my coat, watch, even shoe buckles, thrice knocked down ... beat and bruised till I spit blood, obliged to walk thirty miles barefoot after a march of 140 miles before being sent aboard a guardship turned into a dungeon, obliged to lye on board without a rag of cloathes to cover me ...[42]

On 16 December 1778, Archy wrote to Allan MacDougall, now his man of business in Edinburgh, telling him that he was back in New York, on parole, and waiting to be exchanged, and that he was to return to Canada in the spring to join General Maclean's regiment.[43] This is confirmed in a later account of Archy's, which informs us that he was sent to New York and exchanged in 1778.[44] His letter to his lawyer was inspired by a need for money, but as his father was now totally without funds, there was no need to write to him. Poor John Lochbuy received only second-hand intelligence of his son's circumstances, and in December 1777 heard from the newspapers of Burgoyne's setback, without knowing that Archy was remotely connected with the Bennington disaster.[45] MacDougall was considerate enough to pass on any news he received, but one source was no more authoritative than another in old Lochbuy's eyes, so that when he received a letter from Alexander Maclean of Coll in January 1778, apparently commiserating on the death of his son, John was distraught. After the first shock, he took up his pen to write to John, tacksman of Gruline.

> Moy, 12 Jany. 1778
> Dear Poor John,
> This is to inform you of the sad New Year gift I have received this afternoon. A letter from Sandie Coll[46] from Eberdeen of date the 28th December, informing me of my lovely son's death, which is sad news for me and all his family & clan, but worse for me than the whole. However, God's will be done. I must submit. Upon receipt of this you'll come here and bring John Killean's[47] gelding with you. Upon receipt of this you'll write to Torloisk[48] to see what New [news] he got. Write Gillean also, and send him here if he is come from Ulva. Whither or not, write him of this sad Newes. I remain, poor John,
> > My hand can scarcely keep my pen.
> > Your very much Distressed friend to serve you.
> > John Maclaine of Lochbuy.[49]

As the letter from Sandie Coll has not survived, it is not clear that it gave some mistaken account of Archy's death. Letters from others, in America, London and Edinburgh, conveyed more hopeful information. MacDougall assured the father in February that his son was about to go to Canada, and what was even more positive evidence of his being in life – he had drawn on the estate for £180. But from the moment of his 'sad New Year gift' John Lochbuy went downhill. In March, John Gruline was writing to Archy that his father was failing fast. Dr Andrew Maclaine was attending him night and day. On 4 April 1778, old *Beul na Cabhraigh* died.[50] At his bedside were Gillean, Dr Maclaine and his old friend 'Sanders' Maclaine, Callachilly. In his will there was nothing to leave but a personal bequest of £60 to the little grandson whose presence will be explained in another chapter.

Perhaps his greatest claim to fame was his brief appearance in Dr Samuel Johnson's *Journey* and James Boswell's *Journal*. 'Rousseau,' Johnson had once remarked to Boswell, 'was a very bad man'. Boswell had asked if he was as bad as Voltaire. 'Why, Sir,' Johnson had replied, 'it is difficult to settle the proportion of iniquity between them.' These two bad men, Voltaire and Rousseau, died in the same year as John Lochbuy, who might be rated a harmless dull man in comparison.

In the Seven Years' War, as has been said, 350 men went from Mull, and only fifty returned. It is not thought, although it is not known particularly, that more than fifty to eighty Mull men were killed in action. But many remained in North America, where Colonel Allan Maclean of Torloisk appealed to their Loyalist sentiments in 1775, when raising his Royal Highland Volunteers. Men from 'the Country' were the backbone of the reinforcements which Allan Maclean produced at the eleventh hour in the siege of Quebec, saving Canada as a future British possession.

It may be asked why Highlanders should be loyal to the British government after settling in America. The answer would appear to be that they had seen savage reprisals meted out to those who had taken part in the 1745 uprising in Scotland, and knew the power of government to punish them. There was no reason to suppose that King George III would not be the victor in the American wars, although with hindsight the impossibility of policing even the New England part of the colonies is obvious. But Highlanders in both the northern and southern colonies were determined to stay on the right side this time, and were to suffer gravely for this pragmatic decision.

Commissions were made easier to obtain, and in times of crisis were dependent upon the recruitment of a quota of men. Archy Lochbuy, in later attempts to get a company under his command, had to pledge himself to provide forty-five men. Officers could poach men from other people's estates, or from towns where there was no traditional connection between the recruiter and the recruited. But from the end of the American war, after 1783, men became scarce and unwilling. By the end of the eighteenth century, many men enlisted only to get a passage to Canada for themselves and their families.

At the time of John Lochbuy's death, hardly anything was happening in Mull except 'levying', according to John Maclaine, tacksman of Gruline. Levy money stood at £12–£20 per man.[51] This was the high point of Mull's military service, not to be exceeded even in the Napoleonic wars, in which the officer class was well represented, but the ranks were thin. The old order had changed.

Notes

1. In spite of an assertion in *Argyll 3*, that the tower was lived in until *c.* 1752, that is, until John the seventeenth built his house, family correspondence between 1730 and 1751 seems to be from Pennygown.
2. Burt, p. 193.
3. NAS. GD1/1003/3/12. Evidence of Lachlan Maclean, schoolmaster, Leiter.
4. Boswell, *Journal*, p. 390. Boswell dismissed 'Young Col's' description as 'extravagant'.
5. See Mackinnon, *Descriptive Catalogue of Gaelic MSS*, for Makalive cattle. Pottle, p. 260.
6. All information about the marriage of Allan Maclean of Drimnin and Mary Maclaine of Lochbuy, including their legal dispute with Lochbuy, is in NAS, GD1/1003.
7. NAS. GD1/1003/3. Ibid.
8. NAS. GD1/1003/3/5. Bills to Miss Mally Maclean from John Galbraith, cordiner at Inveraray, 1750–52.

9. NAS. GD1/1003/3/12. John's words were reported by two separate witnesses to the abduction.
10. NAS. GD174/1273. Murray to JMLB, 7 November 1767.
11. Killean, where a derelict medieval church stood, was a no-man's-land, associated with Iona Abbey in the fourteenth century, being on the pilgrim route as one of a string of churches including Lismore, leading to Iona. Considered after the Reformation as church land, the Duke of Argyll was unable to lay claim to it, but claimed the rents of Gualachaoilish as part of the debts of the Duart estate. Macphail, *Highland Papers.*
12. NAS. GD174/124. State of the criminall process ... 1759.
13. Criminal process, 1759, Killean and Kilmory *v.* Lochbuy. NAS. GD174/124/1–11.
14. NAS. GD174/13. Evidence of Isabel, Lady Lochbuy.
15. EUL. Session cases.
16. NAS. GD1/1003/15/8. Copy representation of Gillean Maclaine, 1766, in which he states that he came to Edinburgh aged thirteen or fourteen, in 1747.
17. Clerks to the Court of Session were qualified lawyers. Their scribes painstakingly copied out documents to be presented in evidence in Court of Session processes.
18. NAS. GD1/1003/15/8.
19. NAS. GD1/1003/15/8–10.
20. NAS. GD1/1003/8.
21. Her brother Donald Campbell was tacksman of Barr; Donald Campbell of Airds and John Stewart of Achadashenaig were friends.
22. NAS. GD1/1003/7/3. Memorandum for Mr Alexander Orme.
23. NAS. GD1/1003/15/8. Culloden had opened the Argyll estate rents to competitive bidding in 1737 (see Chapter 3). The roup of Lochbuy in 1742 is cited in the process Maclaine *v.* Maclaine, 1766.
24. NAS. GD174/1252/6. Letter, MM to John Maclaine, 8 January 1765.
25. WSS were a body of law writers privileged to prepare papers under the signet, for the higher courts. Alexander Orme was admitted as a Writer to the Signet in 1755, and became Principal Clerk of Session in 1777. Gillean, although working in the office of a WS, had not been indentured, and therefore became an ordinary 'writer'. The cost of Archy's indenture was £41 13s. 4d. in 1765. NAS. GD174/145.
26. Edinburgh University Archives, EUL. Matriculation albums and Morgan Transcripts, 1764, 1765, 1766.
27. NAS. GD1/1003/15/2. GM to JMLB, Moy, 8 January 1759.
28. NAS. GD1/1003/15/3. Condescendence for John MacLaine of Lochbuy, Esq., 1765.
29. Torloisk Papers. B391 Daniel Maclean to Hector Maclean, 27 July 1759.
30. NAS. GD1/1003/15/8. Memorial for John Maclaine of Lochbuy.
31. Boswell, *Journal of a Tour* ... Thursday, 21 October 1773. 'Lochbuy some years ago tried to prove himself a weak man, liable to imposition, or, as we term it in Scotland, a *facile* man, in order to set aside a lease which he had granted, but failed in the attempt.'
32. NAS. GD174/1244/21.
33. NAS. GD174/1273/3. John Murray to JMLB, Edinburgh, 9 December 1767.
34. Duart Castle still had a military governor as part of the government's security arrangements after 1745.
35. NAS. GD174/1244/30–31. GM to MM 17 May 1769.
36. 'Town' was the township of Garmony, a group of cottages on the farm.
37. This letter is so fragile and eaten away that it is illegible in many places. NAS. GD174/1244/31. GM to MM, n.d.
38. Fleeman quotes, p. 196, a paragraph from the *Weekly Magazine,* xxvi (6 October 1774)

p. 62, describing the sole survivor as 'Mr Maclean of Lochbuy'. This should have read 'Mr Maclean Younger of Lochbuy'.

39. NAS. GD174/1306. This letter was forwarded to America.

40. Hibbert, p. 172.

41. Lieutenant Glich's account quoted by Hibbert, p. 177.

42. NAS. GD174/2110. AMLB to MM, Boston, 18 October 1777.

43. NAS. GD174/1315. AMLB to Allan MacDougall, 16 December 1777.

44. NAS. GD174/2131/3. Memorial, AMLB to Lord Amherst, 30 September 1779.

45. NAS. GD174/1261/6. JMLB to MM per John Maclean of Killean, at Montreal, December 1777.

46. Alexander Maclean the fifteenth of Coll, 1754–1835, laird of Quinish in Mull as well as of Coll, who lived partly in Aberdeen.

47. John Maclean of Killean, then living in Brolass.

48. Lachlan Maclean of Torloisk (1720–1799) was in the habit of receiving newspapers.

49. NAS. GD174/1314. JMLB to John tacksman of Gruline, Moy, 12 January 1778.

50. *Beul na cabhraigh* – mealy mouth – so nicknamed in a letter from John Murray to MM, 18 November 1775.

51. NAS. GD174/1316/1 JMG to AMLB, Gruline, 23 March 1778.

6

Murdoch Maclaine, linen merchant

Murdoch Maclaine, son of Lachlan Maclaine of Knockroy (near Tiroran), was a nephew of John the Grandfather who had outlived his own grandson, Hector the Infant. Murdoch was therefore a cousin of John Maclaine of Lochbuy, but as John was thirty years older than Murdoch, they were men of different generations. When John inherited in 1751, Murdoch was twenty-one, and already a merchant in Edinburgh. Just as little is known of his birth, childhood and early education as of Gillean's. Murdoch must have known his cousin, Lachlan the Prodigal, the one with the 'constant flux' in his purse; he seems to have spent his boyhood years in Mull, but we do not know where (although we might reasonably assume Knockroy). His father and mother probably died before 1750, and his older brother Allan may have died in America during the Seven Years' War. The only other siblings we know anything about were Peggy, and an unnamed sister.[1]

Murdoch's education was not academic. For most of his life he wrote a poor hand, showing no sign of knowing Latin, in which Highland gentlemen were often fluent. Edmund Burt's observation about Highlanders not paying very much attention to spelling when they wrote English applied to Murdoch. 'If they read English authors, I wonder their memory does not retain the figures or forms of common words, especially monosyllables, but it may, for aught I know, be affectation,' Burt wrote.[2] It is certain that Murdoch's mother tongue was Gaelic, but not a scrap of Gaelic was written by him.

At the age of about fourteen, Murdoch began an apprenticeship with an eminent linen manufacturer in Edinburgh.[3] He was taught the arts of weaving damask, diaper and plain linen, the heckling and dressing of flax, and the spinning of yarn. He must have witnessed the entry into Edinburgh of Prince Charles Edward Stuart, the Young Pretender, in 1745.

In 1746 the British Linen Company was instituted, and the industry seemed to be on a fair course for success, but in 1754 linen received a blow by the expiration of its bounties, and, recovering in 1756, was hit again by the American wars, which cut off its chief outlet. By his own account, Murdoch, observing 'a great stagnation in trade', applied for a lieutenancy in the 114th Regiment in 1761. Some sources say that he was in America towards the close of the Seven Years' War, when he served under Allan Maclean of Torloisk, but others[4] indicate that the 114th saw no overseas service. At the end of the war, he had diversified his trade, becoming a general merchant, but still trading in cloth.

In about 1757, he married Anne Learmonth, daughter of Charles Learmonth, late merchant in Edinburgh, who was a trader in her own right, a woman of substance with business ability and property. The marriage was childless, but Murdoch and Anne took into their house in Writers Court, in the Old Town of Edinburgh, the children of relations from 'the Country' of Mull, Morvern and Tiree. Among these were Murdoch's nephew Donald Maclaine, whose parentage remains uncertain, and who learned Murdoch's trade of shopkeeping, then Lachlan, and later, Charles Macquarie, his sister Peggy's children from Oskamull. As has been mentioned, Archy Lochbuy was also a protégé when on holiday from school in Dalkeith. Donald, Lachlan and Charles were Gaelic speakers with no knowledge of English when they first arrived. All three were to play an important part in the history of Mull, and Lachlan in the history of Australia.

The merchant from Mull was patronised by the lairds and tacksmen of Mull and Lorn and Morvern. Murdoch's ledger from 1759 to 1768 reads like a list of all the notables of 'the Country', in which every bonnet laird has his page, showing which little luxuries were essential to his life. Mrs Maclean of Torloisk required cloves, ginger and breakfast tea, writing paper, oranges and gilly glasses, while Miss Susanna Campbell of Airds had need of hair powder, acorns, raisins, almonds and Scots fir seeds. John MacQuarrie, Younger of Ulva had his pistols cleaned in 1764, rum, sugar, lemons and whisky on account, and a play ticket. Mr Gillean Maclaine had sent for Florence-oil, sugar, vinegar, mustard and barley, pepper, cinnamon, nutmeg, honey and lemons. Mr Duncan Maclean, Lochbuy's servant, was repeatedly billed for 'a big Blew Coat from years ago not paid'. But the strangest charge was to Sir Allan Maclean, Knight, of Brolass, for the cost of a nurse for an infant who died within months, and whose shroud and burial costs were also entered in the books more than five years after the death of his wife. Hector Maclean of Torloisk, the Edinburgh lawyer and dandy, received a new scabbard for his sword, and John Stewart of Achadashenaig a mattress costing 7s. 6d. Thus had Murdoch truly diversified from the linen industry.

But being a reliable agent in Edinburgh for the Argyll gentry also brought tedious tasks and reproaches. Gillean Maclaine, seeming friendly in his letters to Murdoch, was not above betraying that friendship. In a memorandum to his legal agent in 1766, Gillean, referring to himself in the third person as 'the Defender', observed:

That at present the Action [for Reduction] is carried on altogether by Murdoch Maclean [sic], Merchant in Edinburgh, a relation of Lochbuy's, who would willingly supplant the defender in the Esteem of his father, and who has himself an eye upon those farms the defender possesses, for which he has made application to Lochbuy. It is that Gentleman who has taken upon him to plead the facility of Lochbuy in the present process, and the representative humbly craves your Lordships that this fact likewise may be enquired into, whether any authority has been given by Lochbuy himself for founding on that Plea.[5]

Two or three years later, Gillean stayed with Murdoch and Anne, and on his return to Mull wrote to Murdoch requesting 'a negligee of a tolerable good silk, not expensive, but neat, a Hatt and Cardinall[6] of the present mode, either silk or Sattin' for the girl he was trying to win, Mally MacQuarrie of Ulva. And when they were both around forty years of age, these two cousins were corresponding about Gillean's choice of Mally as a future wife, a subject not usually associated with the epistles of eighteenth-century men. In the future, other friends were to write to Murdoch about their love affairs, giving the impression that he was a man who liked to discuss the attractions of women.

A portrait of Murdoch Maclaine survives, in the uniform of the Black Watch, or 42nd Regiment. He is aged about thirty-two, fair complexioned, with brown eyes and a very long, narrow nose, which was to be passed down to future offspring. It was at this age that he was to become one of the most widely known of Mull personalities, operating on a variety of social levels – the servile merchant to some, the brilliant entrepreneur to others, the patron of the under-privileged, the recruiter of Mull men for the army, the negotiator of bills of exchange, the purveyor of news, the correspondent of all, the carrier of letters, inspector of educational establishments for Mull parents, and even marriage broker and matchmaker, if that was not the distinct preserve of Anne, his wife.

His fatherless nephew, Donald Maclaine, had been taken in by Murdoch and Anne, had assisted in the shop, and made an inventory of its contents in 1769.[7] The shop was always addressed 'Att the back of the Fountain' or 'behind the Fountain Well', but the house was at the Exchange, or in Writers Court, called 'the Thermopylae of Writers Court' for its role in the '45, when the tavern known as Clarihughs had been the haunt of an elderly Jacobite general. This association provoked many jokes at Murdoch's expense, for although now a lieutenant of the King's Royal Highland Volunteers, he had not as such seen any action. A letter in 1765 congratulated Murdoch on his 'late victory after driving the enemy out after their first assault at Clarihughs, and your house entered by storm.'[8] But the Fountain was close to the law courts, and the shop was in the very centre of the Old Town with its tall, tightly packed tenements.

Donald Maclaine was being groomed to take over the business as Murdoch became more involved in military matters. It is difficult to know if the direction the business was taking was influenced by market forces or by Donald's inclination, but it veered now towards seeds and plants of a surprisingly exotic kind. The inventory of 1769 shows a stock of sugar peas, Rouncevale peas, broccoli seeds, silver onions, cresses, Dutch parsnips, spinach, asparagus, 'collyflowers', cypress and larch, shallotts, garlic, leek, cucumbers, melon and cinnamon bark, to name but a few delights. There was also an ironmongery collection of shears, scythes, spades, weeding irons, picks and shovels, and all that the thirsty gardener required in glasses and decanters. Among the shop's chests of drawers and counters and scales, there were twelve gallons of rum, presumably because this was in a barrel, and part of the furnishings.

In 1769, Miss Marie (or Mally) MacQuarrie, from Ulva, then twenty-two years old, was a guest, perhaps a paying one, in Murdoch and Anne's house, and as her charges for shoes, shoe repairs and pattens in the shop's ledger demonstrate, very busy trotting around Edinburgh. If she was receiving an education, it was not in writing or orthography, as her subsequent letters clearly show, but more likely in women's skills such as sewing and playing upon the spinet. In this year, Gillean Maclaine was still embroiled in the case for his Reduction, which had been in preparation since 1764; and was what people called, even then, a dripping roast for the lawyers. If Murdoch had been responsible for asking if John of Lochbuy might not be called facile, or simply daft, as he was called in Edinburgh, it had been a suggestion which took the lawyers into labyrinthine ways, as they probed at the evidence. Archy, in his law office by day, and mixing at night with his rambling friends, had still not been informed of the true state of his father's finances. But the son had little concern for the legal problems of the estate. He continued to ramble with the ramblers, and ignored Murray's attempts to introduce him to a 'genteeler set'.

John Murray was a young Writer known for his decency and uprightness, and interested in the welfare of the family of Lochbuy. He deplored his client's total inability to supply documentation for the legal cases which he leapt into in rash moments. Murray's letters to Lochbuy remained unanswered, and the facts the case depended upon were never forthcoming, drawing out the action interminably. It was now Gillean who turned the tables by requesting a compromise and attempting a reconciliation with his father, as it appeared to observers who did not know about the trump card. Gillean – who had in 1766 accused Murdoch of supplanting him in his father's esteem – was now concerting with Murdoch to restore his own reputation.

Whether the house in the 'Thermopylae of Writers Court' was large enough to accommodate Gillean as well as Miss Mally MacQuarrie cannot now be ascertained. The Maclaine household was a meeting place for people of 'the Country', and Murdoch was a sociable man. In 1769 there were stirrings in the bachelor heart or loins of Gillean, which were not perhaps entirely for Mally; on his trips back to Mull (for after all, he was still a farmer, responsible for running a farm at Garmony and organising all the kelp he could lay his hands on) he wrote to Murdoch, man to man, of other amorous adventures in which he was 'more luckie than prudent. A Maidenhead was the thing.' In the same letter [9] he wrote of being at Ulva trying to persuade the MacQuarries of Ormaig to sign away their part of Ulva, for their procrastination was delaying a sale which was already being prepared to pay Lachlan MacQuarrie's debts as well as their own. Gillean blamed Maclean of Coll and Lachlan

Maclean of Torloisk for pushing all the MacQuarries into selling. 'I find Coll and Torloisk must have their money'. Gillean too, like almost everyone else in Mull, was owed money by the MacQuarries, so that the sale, when it came, was to be everyone's salvation. Murdoch's Edinburgh ledger was also full of charges carried forward for goods supplied to the Ormaigs and Lachlan MacQuarrie of Ulva.

But a tentative interest in Mally, shown by Gillean in Edinburgh, now seemed to grow in direct proportion to Gillean's involvement in the affairs of her father, and in inverse proportion to his entanglement with his own father, which paled into insignificance beside the massive complications of the Ulva title, and the lackadaisical indifference and lazy good humour of the chief of the MacQuarries. Correspondence between Gillean and Murdoch and Anne (for he liked 'good Mrs Maclaine' and her matchmaking) quickened, so that the pirouetting of the Mull gentry in these two years before they closed in on their genial prey is amply described for posterity. But more interesting still was the fact that Murdoch Maclaine, merchant in Writers Court, Edinburgh, or back of the Fountain Well, or at the Castle on his military duties, should be at the centre of communications, and those members of Argyll families who had taken up residence elsewhere, who followed trade or waited for a war, or studied medicine or theology or law, wrote to Murdoch to discover what was happening in 'the Country' and in the law courts where Gillean's Reduction was pending. In July, Hugh Maclean of Kingairloch wrote from Greenock.

This is the day agreeable to what the Publick pappers say that our unluckie Cousine Ormaig's Lands are to be sold. A hard case that such should happen ... I am heartily sorry for the unluckie fate of these People, who, all of them, were so Stench to the interest of our Clan. I have a letter from Edinburgh some days ago telling me that Gillean has been in Edinburgh a considerable time past reconoituiring the ffield before his ffather Lochbuy was there. I dare say a Lochbuy is with you before now. I suppose there will be a good many of our Mull ffriends at Edinburgh just now.[10]

The gossip-loving Kingairloch and other friends might have rejoiced in the description of Gillean drawn up two years before, by Counsel for Lochbuy:

There is scarce a man of character of the name of Maclean who did not look upon the Ruin of Lochbuie as certain and infallible unless some happy incident occurred to remove Gillean from his Ear and break that unhappy Ascendant by which the other was effectually blinded ... [Gillean] is universally known to be active, designing, uncommonly acute, industrious, crafty and persevering in his own Interest. These natural abilities, brought to perfection by his education as a Writer, in which capacity he is by no means delicate in method if the end can be attained ... All these schemes and proposals, in themselves so important, were kept a dead secret from the whole friends of the Family without exception, and particularly from the late Hector Maclean.[11] Gillean not only acted as Lochbuy's factor, Writer and confidant, but intermeddled and swayed him in every Domestick Transaction.[12]

But for Gillean all this was in the past. Mally MacQuarrie was unlikely to understand the ways of courts, and he began to see that her confidence in him must be cultivated. Murdoch's wife Anne, an avowed matchmaker, was his greatest ally. Back in Ulva (where Gillean spent most of his time, between Ormaig and Ardnacaillach, dealing with the two proprietors) he wrote:

> I have been at Ulva ... and nothing final done ... only Mr MacDougall has got the unanimous consent of old young and middle-aged Ormaigs to sell that little Property by Publick sale. I owned when the old man signed I was sensibly touched for him. Had our Aunt [13] been alive it struck in my head they were a second edition of our old father & mother Adam & Eve when they were drove out of Paradise.[14]

Mally was upset by the lecherous advances of her uncle, Archibald Maclean, a merchant in Laggan Ulva, and Gillean became her champion. Her distress and vulnerability increased his regard for her.

> He is such a scandalous talker that no person heeds what he says, and for that reason I am vexed that his niece takes it so much to heart ... Upon the whole I'm truly vexed to see that goode Girle so much Crush'd in her spirits, for she is the only person of the Family most sensible of its misfortunes. I remember you spoke to me seriously at parting to make it up with her, and I have been since thinking of it, & I have reason to believe she may make a good companion, as she does not want good natural parts, and I likewise think she wishes me well ...[15]

The setbacks Gillean encountered in his wooing of Miss Mally MacQuarrie are not revealed. The time between his perception of her as a good companion and their marriage was at least eighteen months, an unusually lengthy courtship. It seems unlikely that Mally viewed the fact that he made a local girl pregnant in the interim with misgiving. The old parish registers of Mull record a handful of baptisms every year of infants conceived, in the phraseology of the time, 'in fornication', and the baptism is quite regularly followed by the marriage of the father to another woman. But in Gillean's case, the young woman who bore his child in June 1771 gave birth in Edinburgh, although she was a Mull girl. Most of these fathers admitted paternity, and the child was given their name, so that everyone knew of the relationship. It was customary for a 'gentleman' to bring up his natural child after it was weaned, and natural sons were often brought into the new family circle and educated with their half brothers and sisters. Gillean himself had been educated by his father before John's marriage to Isabel Maclean of Brolass.

The natural son born in Edinburgh on 9 June 1771 to Janet MacPhail was christened Lauchlan Maclaine, and he will feature in later chapters. On 1 July 1771, Gillean and Mally were married in the parish of Kilninian in Mull, the word 'publickly' added in the entry in the register suggesting that it was a celebration open to all, at the home of her father in Ulva. But it was not a ceremony which had been intimated beyond the parish, for Murdoch Maclaine in Edinburgh did not know of it when he wrote about the same time to ask how Gillean's matrimonial plans were progressing. Gillean replied:

> Dear Coussine,
> Your last I received wherein you seem to think I keep'd up my Matrimoniall Offers as yet, but that's all over, for I am once fairly yoked ... my wife wants Custard dishes and half a Dozen Tarte panns ... and if opportunity casts up for sending home the Drawers and little Articles of Mally's ...[16]

The yoked pair remained in Garmony, where Murdoch and Anne stayed in August of that year. The next letter to Murdoch was written from Scallastle on 27 July 1772.

> Dear Cousine
> I received your last of the 2nd currt. about Money Matters which you had a Title to expect Ere now and you know I always paid when able. But this year I am difficulted to procure as much as will keep my family in Meal, for not an ounce is to be got without ready Cash. As you come to the Country soon, all I can say is that if in my power then you shall have some cash, if I can depend upon others promises ...[17]

Gillean's family meant his household – himself, his wife, their in-servants and their out-servants, as well as any relations who might be staying. Their firstborn son, Allan, was to make his appearance on 6 August 1772. Gillean's shortage of money was not confined to himself. First of all, the winter of 1771–72 was called the Black Winter, with a continued frost detaining the snow upon the ground for eight weeks in Mull. 'Against a calamity never known', Dr Johnson wrote, 'no provision had been made, and the people could only pine in helpless misery.' [18] Cattle died because they had no byres, and no winter provender.[19] Without cattle the drovers were empty-handed, and no cash came to Mull.

But 1772 also had a Black Monday, when the Ayr Bank (Douglas, Heron and Company) collapsed, causing panic all over Scotland, and a shortage of cash everywhere. In its three years of existence as a private bank, the Ayr Bank had actually eased the flow of money by cashing bills the two older banks were reluctant to touch. The combination of a ferocious winter and a run on the banks contributed to Gillean's desperation, Murdoch's slump in trade, and many drover bankruptcies. Hugh Maclean of Kingairloch was writing to Murdoch in May of 1772 that he was truly sorry for the sad description John Gruline gives of his country – the same all over Scotland, dearth of victual and great loss of cattle. Many of the Tenantry will be ruined. When my friend Torloisk came here upon his way for Edinburgh, I happened to be at Glasgow and missed seeing him. He has bought 500 bolls of meal to be shipped for the Sound of Mull.[20]

A year later, Kingairloch himself was unable to repay Murdoch, and John Gruline had not paid Kingairloch, so that there was an ever-increasing circle of relations owing each other money. Kingairloch wrote to Gruline:

> For a long time I have been greatly assisted in money given to me by my Cousine [Murdoch] I at present do owe to my Worthy Cousine more than double my account against you, and God knows it were a pity, nay, a very heinous Crime in anyone, particularly his Own Friends, to keep him unpaid, as I know him soe well that that man woud not have a single shilling when he woud not share with a friend. Sincere Affections to your Sister, and you, and honest Sanders Callachilly.[21] and his Family, my friend Donald Penny-gown [22] and his Family, with all others of the estate of Lochbuy.[23]

As in hard times in every age, there was a toy which was all the rage, and which took people's minds off their financial worries. In 1772 everybody, including Murdoch, wanted a parrot, and Greenock was a mart for parrots. In 1773, the Macleans in Erray, near Tobermory, were the proud owners of a parrot brought from Glasgow seven years earlier. It could speak very well in Glasgow, but in Mull it had rusted, and declined to say a word.[24]

1773 and 1774 were depressing years, and ones in which some Highland emigrants left the north-west mainland counties of Scotland for Nova Scotia. Murdoch Maclaine, who had spent the month of July 1773 in Mull, was back in Writers Court in mid-August, where he might have perceived James Boswell conducting Dr Samuel Johnson from Boswell's house in nearby James' Court to view the Parliament House at the beginning of their tour of Scotland. Adam Smith was writing *The Wealth of Nations*, and making a case of the failure of the Ayr bank, which had hit Scotland so hard. In North America, the Boston Tea Party of December 1773 heralded the formation of new militia companies in 1774 which provided for the defence of the colony of Massachusetts. As a result, the British army and navy increased their strength, and by June, the Scottish regiments were preparing to sail. Murdoch Maclaine, onetime linen merchant, having been a lieutenant in the 114th Regiment since 1761, was commissioned on 14 June 1775, as captain in the 2nd Battalion of the Royal Highland Emigrants, under the command of his kinsman, Colonel Allan Maclean of Torloisk.

Apart from joining the royal army with his regiment in the late summer of 1775, at Boston, Murdoch's first six months of service in America are unclear. If he was one of the Royal Highland Emigrants' reinforcements

introduced into Quebec by Allan Maclean when the city was under siege from
Americans under Montgomery and Arnold, on the bitterly cold night of 31
December 1775, he did not boast of it.[25] But immediately after this, plans
were afoot to send him on a mission to England. Major John Small, commander
of the 1st Battalion, wrote on 30 January:

> An officer of your experience, and in whose prudence and discretion and
> discernment I have the most ample confidence ... your application and
> intelligence respecting every part of the duty you are going to execute
> renders very minute orders or even advice from me almost superfluous.[26]

The duty he spoke of was Captain Murdoch's despatch from Boston on 1
February to settle all business concerning the Royal Highland Emigrants, and
to procure arms and clothing which he was to conduct to America himself.
The project involved seeing officials in the War Office in London ('men in
power'), as well as ordering from Scotland a suitable uniform for the regiment,
which was as yet unestablished, and therefore had not received the normal
endowments. Murdoch was to be rewarded with commissions for some of his
younger friends from 'the Country'. He reached London in the remarkably
short time of three weeks, for his expenses for 21 February–15 May in London
are given as seven guineas per week. He travelled then to Glasgow, where a
Maclean merchant was to make up and supply the uniforms. Returning to
London, he submitted charges for 'visiting the Great people on Regimentall
Business, and Drink Money to Porters and Servants about the Offices and
Great Men's Houses in order to procure easier access and reddier service':
£12 6s. 6d.[27]

Murdoch embarked at Glasgow in the autumn – in the company of his
nephew, the 15-year-old Lachlan Macquarie, and other young hopefuls – on
the *Newcastle Jean*, in convoy, bearing a precious cargo of guns, ammunition,
camp equipment, tents, uniforms, and even cash. In his correspondence with
John Small there had been some discussion of his authority in such a vessel,
and a contingency plan had been drawn up lest the ship be attacked as it
neared the coast of America. Accordingly, when the protecting convoy was
lost, and they entered disputed waters, Murdoch had to assert his leadership
by making out a plan of action. He had to be obeyed by sailors as well as
recruits, and his orders were to be law. The compact was agreed to by crew
and subordinates. On 24 October 1776 an American privateer challenged the
ship, and was fought off. A British government cargo worth £20,000 had
been saved, and young Lachlan Macquarie, stationed in the ship's magazine,
shared in the rapturous welcome as they sailed into Halifax, Nova Scotia.

From now until the war ended with the Treaty of Paris, six years later,
Captain Murdoch Maclaine was sent, with his company, to most of the scenes
associated with the northern and southern campaigns of the American revolutionary war – Massachusetts, Rhode Island, Philadelphia, New York and
Charleston. In 1779 he was back in England on military duties. His path

seldom crossed that of Archy Maclaine of Lochbuy, last seen on 1 February 1778, moving from an exchange of prisoners in New York to Halifax, and arriving there just after Murdoch's departure. Archy was given permission to go to Britain in late 1778, when the news of his father's death finally reached him. Young men with estates to settle were looked upon kindly by the army – so also were older officers whose wives died.

Donald Maclaine had kept Murdoch informed about Anne's health, but from as far back as 1775 she had been under the care of Dr Alexander Hamilton, the professor of midwifery and women's diseases at Edinburgh. Murdoch was able to travel to Edinburgh in December, when his wife's condition became grave, and he was with her when she died at the beginning of February 1780. As Donald had taken over the business, and Murdoch had made his career in the army, there was nothing to do but hold a roup of the household furniture and goods which had been Anne's. Murdoch had already returned to London *en route* for North America, when the sale was held in Edinburgh. Eight feather beds and two fourposters with chintz curtains, five mahogany tables, seven looking-glasses and four chests of drawers, with china, silver, blankets and linen fetched £183 8s. 9d. It had been a substantial house, and was now reduced to a good sum of money, which belonged by right to the husband.[28] He was almost fifty years old; his days as an Edinburgh merchant were well and truly over. The world was a changed place anyway, and the new world was where he was going.

Clinton, now Commander-in-Chief of the British forces in North America, and Lord Cornwallis, sailed from New York for the Carolinas on 26 December 1779 with 7,600 men.[29] It was a disastrous voyage with tempestuous seas and gale-force winds – an ominous beginning for the planned attack on Charleston. Murdoch appears to have spent most of 1780–81 travelling between Halifax and Charleston, describing one of his voyages as a 'very troublesome scamper of two months'. But the scampering was put to an end with the British surrender at Yorktown on 19 October 1781, although the battalions in the south had to wait for a long time while the dreary peace negotiations were dragging on in Paris, and it was not until 20 January 1783 that the Treaty of Versailles was concluded between Britain, France and Spain. Back in Windsor, Nova Scotia, in June, Murdoch bought a bay gelding to facilitate his travelling, for he was now supervising a more peaceful operation – the allocation of land around Colchester Bay to men of the 2nd Battalion of the 84th Regiment, as the Royal Highland Emigrants were now called. The British government, in its slow-moving manner, was not disposed to settle lands immediately upon the men whose recruitment had been conditional upon land grants at the end of the war. Allan Maclean, for reasons which will be seen in another chapter, had retired from the service immediately after the peace, and returned to London, and his promises of land (originally to be in New York, but that was no longer possible) to the men he had gathered to him on his pied piper journey up the Mohawk Valley in 1775, remained to be fulfilled. As the men in Nova Scotia waited to have their lots confirmed, they were undecided as to whether to clear ground which might not be theirs in the end.[30]

For the Highlanders among them it was a familiar situation, similar to those periods of uncertainty which they suffered at home as they waited for a tack to be confirmed by a landlord. Only an optimistic man, imbued with the idea that the hard work of clearing land was preferable to idleness, could take the risk of felling trees and planting corn. The Highlanders of the 84th, sick of war and privation, of which their battalion had had more than its share, preferred drinking their cares away to tilling someone else's land. By the spring of 1784, many had returned to Britain, including Murdoch himself, although he had applied for his 2,000 acres at Annapolis Royal. But from letters addressed to him from Nova Scotia, it was clear that he planned to return. A young woman called Polly, in the small town of Windsor, was among those who waited for him.

Murdoch's personality was convivial, and there is also a suggestion that he was a bon vivant, if purchases of delicacies in New York and Charleston in the course of his travels were for himself and his fellow officers. His nephew, Donald, a canny man who was always afraid of being taken advantage of, disapproved of his uncle's sociability, and while wishing that Murdoch could be home, took the opportunity in a letter to give him a piece of his mind:

> When you are here you are eaten up with a parcell of double-hearted people who would eat, drink, and be merry with you and call you a fine fellow, but would be d—d before they would relieve you were you in need of assistance. Some of them have got a good deal off me in my short time in Traid, who with others would see me sunk, because I don't trust them with my whole effects and entertain them at my Table as you did for many years. Such as these, my dear Sir, I despise ...[31]

There was no doubt that Murdoch was seeking a wife. There was a hint of 'love business' in London in the letters of his friends, and mention of his 'courting' of a Miss Park. In June 1784 he was in Edinburgh, still officially with the 84th Regiment, but awaiting his discharge, and with it, his reduced circumstances. Friends were telling each other that he at least would be capable of living carefully and prudently on his half-pay. In July he had a letter from Gillean, who had heard from a newly returned 'common soger' that Archy Lochbuy had married a woman in New York. 'It may be so', said Gillean, 'but till there are more certain accounts, I shall make no mention of it at all.' Before Murdoch left for Mull, a more certain account appeared in the newspaper. Archibald Maclaine of Lochbuy had been married at New York on 4 April 1784, to an amiable young lady of seventeen, Miss Barbara Lowther, with a fortune of £5,000.

Murdoch stayed at Scallastle from late August until October. It is not difficult to imagine the impact his visit made. Even in North America, he had retained his authority as chief purveyor of news. He had travelled in lands settled by Highlanders, with regiments of Highlanders, and he had served Mull's as yet most famous son, Brigadier-General Allan Maclean of Torloisk. He had seen his sister's sons in America, and he knew all that had passed in the famous quarrel between Torloisk and Young Lochbuy (which will be related in another chapter). The tenants of the Lochbuy estate looked to him for news of the absentee laird. Was Archibald bringing his bride back, and was he going to direct the estate? John Tacksman of Gruline was kind, but his hands were tied. Trustees and lawyers managed Lochbuy. Were there any opportunities for people who wished to emigrate? Gillean and Mally, who now had seven children, spoke of leaving Mull and going to live in Perthshire as soon as the Ulva sale was achieved, and various little matters to do with Sir Allan Maclean's recent death were settled at law.

In October another friend in Nova Scotia wrote urging Murdoch to return to Canada, as people were now flocking in, grabbing land. If his journey as an emigrant was delayed by the love business, by doubts about Canada, by the desire for a long, lingering farewell to Mull, or by other plans for a new life, we are unlikely to learn the cause. Early in November news arrived of a startling event which, if any man or woman in Mull had true second sight, should have been announced three months before. For Murdoch and Gillean it was like some turn of events in a Greek tragedy, and would put an end to all thoughts of leaving.

During the years when Murdoch Maclaine was trading from Edinburgh and following his military career in North America, life in Mull was slowly altering. Duke Archibald died on 15 April 1761, to be succeeded by John Campbell of Mamore as 4th duke and heritor of the former Duart estates – the Ross of Mull, Mornish, Treshnish, Gometra, Aros and parts of Torosay including Duart itself. Mr Neil Macleod, the new minister of Ross, the 'cleanest-headed man in the Western Isles' [32] discovered an irregularity in the payment of the rents of the old church lands of Iona and the Ross, which should have gone towards manse and glebe for the minister, and were instead being absorbed by the duke. The presbytery of Mull was alerted, and a visitation made to Bunessan and Iona, so that the ministers could measure out the manse and glebe for themselves.

In 1763 the Rev. John Walker came to Mull and reported on its commercial potential and religious life. He saw the *Schola Illustris* recently set up at Aros, where Latin, Greek, mathematics and book-keeping were taught, and he was told that the population of the island was 5,325, but declining as a result of the Seven Years' War. Of this number, 'only' about 335 could understand a sermon in English, and the remainder were preached to in Gaelic. Out of 191,600 acres of land, 80,000 had to be judged irreclaimable for agricultural purposes, as they consisted of mountain tops, boulders and steep declivities.

The reclaimable part might amount to 70,000 acres, and the remaining 41,600 acres were partly cultivated. Already Dr Walker had been told that the island was depopulated, and that large numbers had emigrated to Ireland. This depopulation was clearly confirmed by extensive fields which had once been in tillage, now lying unopened. Dr Walker blamed lack of mature timber on the browsing of cattle, and waxed lyrical over the fine harbour of Tobermory. He gave the number of black cattle exported annually as 3,400 and horses 1,500. Of kelp, a product still in its infancy, 100 tons had been sent off in 1762. Oatmeal had to be imported because of the inhabitants' 'injudicious attachment to pasturage and the neglect of the plough'. The potato, which lent itself to being planted on reclaimable land, was unfortunately taking up some of the best land. Dr Walker saw that some of the 70,000 uncultivated acres might easily be used for potato ground. As early as 1763, sheep farming was attracting gentlemen farmers by its better return for pasture, but predatory eagles and foxes made sheep farming a 'vain attempt' until the fox could be exterminated.[33]

In March 1764, a printed notice in English was issued to the tenants of the estate of Lochbuy. It contained twelve precepts, most of which echoed Dr Walker's comments. Its most important advice was that they should sow turnips, carrots, parsnips, kail, cabbage and other green crops to feed their milk cows and other cattle in winter. They should keep their cows and horses fat and in good order, and employ their servants in the long winter evenings at spinning, weaving and knitting. They were never to cut turves for firing or for covering their houses.[34]

The need for such advice gives some idea of the agricultural methods employed by the people. The tenants, who were the middle classes and the stratum of society immediately below John Maclaine tacksman of Gruline or Gillean Maclaine tacksman of Scallastle, carried responsibility for the tenants and subtenants of their lands, but as they were the only inhabitants of the estate who had leases, they were the only ones who could be appealed to in this paternalistic manner, and in English.

Notes

1. MM's sister was married to a Hugh Maclean, who died in 1760, leaving several children.
2. Burt, *Letters from a Gentleman in the North of Scotland*, XXII.
3. NAS. GD174/2059. Application and Petition of MM to succeed James Spalding as Surveyor of Manufactures in Scotland, *c.* 1765.
4. Reid and Chappell, *18th Century Highlanders*, p. 21.
5. NAS. GD1/1003/15/8. Copy representation of Gillean Maclaine, Writer in Mull, 1766.
6. Cardinal: a red cloak with a hood, worn by fashionable women in the 1760s.
7. NAS. GD174/564. Edinburgh 5 October 1769. Inventory of all the goods belonging to Mr Murdoch Maclaine ...

8. NAS. GD174. Letter, Sir Allan Maclean to MM, 1765.

9. NAS. GD174/1244/30 GM to MM, 17 May 1769.

10. NAS. GD174/1264/25. Hugh Maclean of Kingairloch to MM, 24 July 1769.

11. Hector Maclean of Torloisk, Writer in Edinburgh, and laird of Torloisk until his death in 1765.

12. NAS. GD1/1003/15/10. Condescendence for John Maclaine of Lochbuy, ... 1767.

13. Donald Macquarie of Ormaig's wife, Margaret Maclaine of LB, daughter of Hector Maclaine, twelfth of LB.

14. NAS. GD174/1244/30. GM to MM, 1769.

15. Ibid.

16. NAS. GD174/1244/32. GM to MM, Garmony? July 1771.

17. NAS. GD174/1244/33. GM to MM, Scallastle 27 July 1772.

18. Fleeman, p. 114.

19. Walker, *Econ. Hist.* vol. 1, p. 381.

20. NAS. GD174/1283/2. Hugh Maclean of Kingairloch, from Greenock to MM, 8 May 1772.

21. Alexander Maclean, Callachilly, father of Dr Andrew and Dr Donald Maclaine.

22. Donald Maclean of Pennygown, who had married Ann Maclaine, natural daughter of Lachlan Maclaine of LB, and half-sister of Mally Maclaine and Hector the Infant.

23. NAS. GD174/1283/3. Hugh Maclean of Kingairloch to JMG, from Edinburgh, 1 July 1773.

24. Pottle, p. 303.

25. NAS. GD174/2249. A memo, MM to the Duke of York, 1795, has a chronicle of his American service.

26. NAS. GD174/2100/2. John Small to MM, 30 January 1776.

27. NAS. GD174/2103/6. MM to RHE in Pennsylvania, 1776.

28. NAS. GD174/587. Copy of the Roup Roll of Captain Murdoch Maclaine's furniture, 23 March 1780.

29. Seymour, p. 145.

30. NAS. GD174/2154. Lieutenant Hector Maclean to MM, 1783–84.

31. NAS. GD174/1329/22. DM to MM, Edinburgh, 3 August 1782.

32. Pottle, p. 339.

33. McKay, pp. 150–66. Walker.

34. GRO. Printed notice, 'Advice to Tenants', 1764, in Maclaine papers.

7

The Lord of Ulva's Isle

The island of Ulva, off the north-west coast of Mull, and the smaller island on its far side, Gometra, have had different owners for a large part of their history. A charter of 1496 assigned Gometra to Lachlan, natural son of Hector Maclean of Duart, along with the coastal areas of Treshnish, Calgary, Inivea, Caliach, Lag, Sunipol, Gilchrist and Penmore.[1] But Ulva, for which no early charter survives, was in the possession of the MacQuarries from the thirteenth century until 1777, when it was sold to Dugald Campbell of Achnaba. About two years later, Dugald sold it to a kinsman, Colonel Charles Campbell of Barbreck, who, in January 1780, appointed John McNeill, Writer in Inveraray, as manager of the estate. This arrangement lasted for only five years, and in 1785, Ulva again changed hands, this time bought by Colin Macdonald of Boisdale, a kinsman of the Jacobite heroine, Flora Macdonald. Colin was a twice-married man, whose heir (to Boisdale) by his first wife was already married to a daughter of Hugh Maclean of Coll. Colin's eldest son by his second wife, Isabella Campbell, was Ranald Macdonald, born in the year of the first sale of Ulva, 1777. Ranald Macdonald's coming-of-age nearly coincided with his father's death, and Ranald became the youthful proprietor of Ulva and Staffa, while his older half-brother inherited the family estate of Boisdale in South Uist. This takes us up to the year 1800 in Ulva's history, but we shall pause to examine the long long reign and chequered story of the MacQuarries before coming to the romantic and colourful era of 'Staffa', who requires a chapter to himself.

Nothing is known of the personalities of the father and grandfather or other antecedents of the most famous MacQuarrie chieftain, Lachlan of that Ilk, who was born in 1715 to John MacQuarrie Younger of Ulva and his wife Florence Maclean of Assapol. Since fostering was the fashion in the first half of the eighteenth century, it is likely that Lachlan was brought up in the family of a kinsman. Whatever his education was, it equipped him to write amusing letters in English and to act the part of a civilised, courteous chieftain. Flippancy and fecklessness were prominent characteristics also, as were a love of liquor and story-telling; pride in his own status made him no different from most of his fellow lairds.

His father, John MacQuarrie, had died in 1735, when Lachlan was not quite of age, and guardians were appointed to manage the estate. These included Lachlan's uncle, Allan MacQuarrie of Culinish, a merchant in Belfast, who happened to be sailing in the Sound of Mull when his brother John died, and made a dash homewards in order to be part of the action. Allan MacQuarrie claimed that in the interval between his brother's death and Lachlan's majority (officially the age of twenty-five), he, as a trustee, cleared the Ulva estate of all its debts, but that Lachlan, as soon as he was able, appointed new curators, cronies of his own, and ousted his uncle.[2] Lachlan then became intimate with Hector Maclean of Torloisk, a lawyer in Edinburgh, who, with his knowledge of legal niceties, advised MacQuarrie to strip his uncle of his rented lands in Ulva.[3] Furthermore, Hector of Torloisk and Lachlan of Ulva hatched a plot to marry Hector's sister Alice to the laird of Ulva.

Alice Maclean of Torloisk, daughter of the cultured and talented Donald Maclean, and sister to Hector, was a poet of some merit. At the age of about seventeen she was in love with 'Young Ballinaby', a scion of the Campbells of Islay, who was probably her cousin on her mother's side. Marriages with first cousins were quite normal for that time, in an age when socialising was done mostly within related families anyway. But whatever hopes Alice had for her future were shattered, so the story goes, when she received a letter from her lover saying that he was going to marry someone else.[4] This letter was later to be revealed as being from Lachlan MacQuarrie himself, who, after thus tricking her, had asked for her hand in marriage. The nature of the deception, and the conspiratorial relationship between MacQuarrie and Alice's brother Hector fit both the personality of the chief of Ulva and the circumstances of the match. Alice's poem, *A' Bhean Mhuladach*, although universal in its application, includes the lines

> Though I will not tell of it
> It is in Islay that my sweetheart is;
> Though I will not speak of it,
> I gave love to him while still a child.
> Young lord of Ballinaby,
> You are my love among all men ...
> Though it is the Mull man and his goods for me,
> It is the Islay man who is my sweetheart.[5]

The poem is still sung today, with alterations which are quite consistent with the oral tradition of Gaelic poetry, in a version which may include Alice's own words

> When we would meet under the branches
> Our bed was composed of rushes and our pillow bog cotton
> The calling of the deer would waken us in the morning ...[6]

Alice Maclean bore eight children to Lachlan MacQuarrie of Ulva after about 1740, and died, in her thirties, in about 1755. Any other poetry that she may have composed cannot have had the poignancy of 'The Sorrowful Wife', and has not come down to us as hers, yet she has a reputation which cannot derive from a single poem.[7]

Once more, we cannot be sure if Alice had much to do with the early upbringing of her children, for it is certain that fostering was the custom among the Macleans of Torloisk in her own generation,[8] but after the '45, by accident or design, the strange tradition began to be dropped. It would seem that Alice's children, who ranged in age from twelve down to two at the time of her death, were not very well educated. Her oldest daughter, Marie, known in her young days as 'Mally', could barely write when she was in her twenties, and Alice's sons were not known for their literacy.

With eight young children left motherless, Lachlan employed domestic servants from his clan following of MacQuarrie women, and certainly ignored the spiritual, intellectual and moral development of his brood. Within five years, he was co-habiting with one of the maids, Ann MacQuarrie, who bore him three more children, Murdoch, Emmy and Sibella, before the kirk decided to take action, and the presbytery of Mull insisted that he should marry the woman. But his neglect of his first family must have been very great, since it provoked comments in the correspondence of other Mull families. Alice's brother, Allan Maclean of Torloisk, wrote to Hector Maclean of Torloisk as early as 1763, saying 'MacQuarrie is not content to ruin himself, but must destroy his children and prevent them from ever doing any good in the world.'[9]

As early as 1753, Allan MacQuarrie of Culinish, Lachlan's uncle and one-time guardian, having been threatened with eviction from his home in Culinish, Ulva, and having been defeated in the Edinburgh Court of Session in his appeal by the legal arts of Lachlan's ally and brother-in-law, Hector Maclean of Torloisk, sought to avenge himself by writing a telltale letter to the Duke of Argyll, informing His Grace that Lachlan had not paid him any compensation for his lands. It is uncertain whether the duke intervened in the family squabble, but he may well have investigated the debt, and claimed it, for in November 1754, Hector and Lachlan in concert (and in revenge, said Allan) stripped Allan of his lands of Culinish and Lagganulva, and Allan was moved to place an advertisement in the press, alerting the public to the fact that Lachlan MacQuarrie was now attempting to dispose of his estate, but had no right to do so, as it was still burdened with unpaid debt.[10] The feu duty owed went back to the superiority of the Duart Macleans in 1690, and at 700 merks a year, now totalled 45,000 merks.

The year of this disclosure was probably the year of Alice's death, for according to Allan's advertisement, Lachlan was thinking of transporting himself and his family 'somewhere else' with the price he was to get for the estate. But the estate was not sold in the 1750s or the 1760s, and in 1773, when Dr Johnson and James Boswell stayed with Lachlan, they pretended to be 'distressed to hear that it was soon to be sold for payment of his debts'.

There is no evidence to show that such financial worries contributed to Alice's demise. She may have died, as young women did, in childbirth. Her oldest son, John, Younger of Ulva, was not to come into this title officially. Her other children, Donald, Marie, Lachlan, Allan, Flora, Elizabeth and Jean had pride of birth, but little more. This family was then increased by Lachlan's 'concubine', who bore him Murdoch, Emilia and Sibilla out of wedlock, and Archibald, Margaret, Ann, Hector and Lachlan within the state of matrimony forced upon them by the presbytery of Mull, as mentioned above.[11] Ann MacQuarrie, Lachlan's second wife, died in the year of her youngest child's birth, 1778, in circumstances at least as trying as those of her predecessor. Lachlan, never slow to take comfort in another woman's arms, was reported in 1782 as living with his last wife's sister in Ulva.[12]

Ever since 1755, when Lachlan MacQuarrie had glimpsed his future 'somewhere else' with the advent of the fortune he was to get with the sale of his estate, fate had decided to deal him another hand. He lived on the credit of the expected bonanza, and every cask of brandy he requested from his neighbours and relations, such as John Lochbuy, was noted down and added up, until his creditors, themselves in debt, became impatient. An added delay in the sale of Ulva was a result of the share Lachlan's cousin, Hector MacQuarrie of Ormaig, held in the estate. Hector's father, Donald of Ormaig, had received his title in 1704 when he was perhaps forty years old. In 1751 he was still living, and passed his property to his son. The Ormaigs were famous for their longevity, but their tenacity was not appreciated by the creditors of Ormaig and Ulva. As most debts were only satisfactorily settled on death, the death of a debtor was to be hoped for, but Donald of Ormaig lived till he was over 100 (he was said to remember seven reigns) and his son Hector until he was approaching ninety. Hector and his wife, Anne Maclean, daughter of Sir John Maclean of Duart, were required to sign documents consenting to the sale of their property. 'The publick papers say our Unluckie Cousine Ormaig's lands are to be sold ... '[13] was the rumour in 1769, but a legal obstacle postponed the sale. The 'Ormaig Reversion' was the talk of MacQuarrie's creditors for a decade. Even the eventual sale of Ormaig was indecisive, for the old man would not sign the document placing the funds in the hands of his lawyer, Gillean Maclaine. Gillean wrote to Murdoch Maclaine about the situation.

> That unhappy man, Ormaig, & his wife did not sign the Discharge & Renunciation. He thinks he should get it all at once to drink & make merry while it lasted. There are still creditors unpaid ... The first thing that will happen is that Boisdale [14] will turn him out ... He says it would hurt his wife's soul to sign ... but it will hurt her body if he does not.[15]

Boisdale, however, was not disposed to turn Ormaig out. Instead, he deplored the behaviour of the Mull families (all of whom were owed money) to such a pitiful old man. 'Gillean has behaved very rascally towards them', he wrote to Murdoch Maclaine, hoping that Murdoch might do something immediately. 'If you do not it will be charity in you to get somebody to knock out his brains and take him out of pain, he and his wife and grandchildren, rather than see them starve downrightly.' As an outsider, Boisdale was amazed at the malice he saw in Mull, and the utter stultification of affairs which resulted from too many people being concerned in every matter.[16] Boisdale did not think highly of Lachlan MacQuarrie's skills as a manager, being willing to allow the now dispossessed laird of Ulva to remain in his tack, but knowing he was incapable of organising the manufacture of kelp.[17] Boisdale's commercial interest in Ulva was centred upon kelp-making, and MacQuarrie's sybaritic presence was undesirable.

Altogether, in the years between Johnson and Boswell's 1773 visit to Ulva, and Boisdale's purchase of the island from Colonel Charles Campbell in 1785, MacQuarrie was not a popular man, if he had ever been so. His correspondence suggests that he was quick to evict tenants who did not pay him, in spite of his own extreme faults in this direction. In 1778, short of ready money, he enlisted in the army at the age of sixty-three. There had been a small difficulty in finding a regiment unconnected with one of his many creditors, but the 74th, recruiting in 1777 in Argyll and Glasgow, offered him a lieutenancy. He sailed from Cork in June and arrived in Halifax, Nova Scotia in August 1778.

MacQuarrie must have looked back with some nostalgia upon his island, but his family was not being cherished in his absence. His second wife, Ann, suffered the attentions of an unknown arsonist, who set fire to her kiln house, her corn, and even her dwelling house at Ardnacaillach on Ulva.[18] Such vandalism was so rare in Mull that heritors and ministers of the gospel, fearing that they had a revolution on their hands, and alarmed for their own safety, formed a consortium to protect themselves from a similar attack, each contributing a guinea for the detection of the perpetrator.[19] Before a culprit could be found, the second Mrs MacQuarrie had died. Gillean, the old chief's son-in-law, wrote to break the news to the bereaved husband, who replied with an account of his fifty-day voyage, his colonel, his acquaintances and his concern for his daughter Mally, who had given birth in June.

> I am hopeful that Providence has been so kind as to spare her to her young family, and that my afflictions will have no additions, as truly I can ill bear them ... the loss of my dearest I shall never forget, and how great it adds to my afflicion that I cannot be in the duty I ought in gratitude to be in to her offspring. But I trust in God, if I have days, that he will inable me soon to be of service to them ... so let not any of my dear ffamily dispare, & I hope I need not recommend them to your care. For had it not been for the dependence I had on you, I would not leave them for the world. I am of the oppinion to keep them together & let Mr Walker [20] be continued with them as long as possible, as I have great hopes of his being a good Teacher, and of good Morrales. I shall send home some from my poor pay whatever Balance I ow him ...[21]

This letter indicates that Mally's life was feared for, that MacQuarrie's wife had died in or after childbirth (Ann's seventh child was two years old, and a younger son Lauchlan is recorded), and goes on to relate that a kinswoman, Peggie McQuarie, died on the passage to America in childbed, leaving 'a fine Boy' for whom MacQuarrie found a nurse aboard – 'no cheap affair'. It tells us that the elderly lieutenant had nothing but his army pay in the year following the sale of his lands. It also suggests that fathers were not expected to be responsible for the upbringing of young children, whose 'morrales' were left to be inculcated by mothers and teachers.

The flank companies of the 74th Regiment, or Campbell's Highlanders, went off to serve in the southern colonies, and battalion companies were sent to what is now the state of Maine, where they were to carry out Lord George Germain's plan to erect a fort at the mouth of the River Penobscot under the direction of Brigadier-General Francis Maclean, commander of the British forces in Nova Scotia.[22] Frank Maclean, of the Ardgour Macleans, had brought the 74th Regiment over to Nova Scotia. His old comrade in arms, Allan Maclean of Torloisk, was now military governor of Montreal, and constantly on the move between Montreal, Quebec, the frontier posts of Isle aux Noix and Point au Ferre, and Halifax. Well might MacQuarrie report to his son-in-law, Gillean, that

> this climat is so Highland that it agrees well with me. I have met with a great many worthie ffriends and acquaintances too Numerous to be Mentioned [who] study to make every Misfortune & Trouble as agreeable & comfortable to me as they can. All the McLeans and McDonalds that have been here are really an Honour to this Country, as their Brave & Sobber Conduct on various occasions has entitled them to the Generall good wishes of their superior officers and the esteem of all their Acquaintance.[23]

MacQuarrie's war service was, however, almost entirely in Maine, where the country was but a tree-clad version of home, and even the blackflies must have reminded him of the midges of Ulva. He was at Penobscot when the Americans attacked the settlement, and General Maclean with his two Scottish regiments held out for two weeks against the besieging force, before being relieved by the arrival of a British squadron on 14 August 1779.[24] This was a sad day for the Americans, seeking revenge on the Loyalists at Penobscot who had sided with the British. For the 64-year-old MacQuarrie, this unusual example of a successful concerted military and naval action in a war of otherwise endless blunders was an experience which he would not forget.

Francis Maclean did not live to remember the scene of his triumph, returning as a sick man to Halifax at the end of 1779. When hostilities ceased after the surrender of the British at Yorktown, the 74th Regiment returned to Britain, and unlike the senior officers of his acquaintance, MacQuarrie was not kept waiting around in North America. It was in May 1782 that he was observed in Ulva, living with his second wife's sister.[25]

After North America, he began a beggarly existence, rejected in turn by all the Mull landlords, who did not wish to see their various schemes for their properties 'mangled' by him. He took a lease of Little Colonsay, an island of 217 acres to the south-west of Ulva, with spectacular views of Staffa, Coll, Tiree, Iona, Inch Kenneth and the coast of Mull, and a rich flora of primroses, celandine and wild violets. He lived in a single, humble house, which he called 'this Hermitage', with few visitors. When his boat was watertight, he ventured to Ulva on those Sundays when the minister visited the island, to 'hear sermon', as he called it. On one such Sunday, he attempted to persuade Peggy Maclaine of Oskamull [26] to visit him in his hermitage, but to his great disappointment she was in the grip of a superstitious belief which made such an expedition impossible. He complained of this to her brother.

> Dear Cusine,
> I have been yesterday in Ulva hearing sermon, where I saw our Oskamull friends. Poor Peggy complains of sore eyes ... I was wanting her much to come here for some time, but she point blank refused comeing – some idle person was telling her that her great grandmother died in this island. Maclean of Duart's daughter, who was married to Coll, surely breathed her last here with Daughter your Grandmother. Her corpse could not be brought to Ulva for eight days. These things so frightened our living friend that she will never Cross the Sound of Collonsay. Dear Cusine, Yours or No bodies, Lachlan MacQuarrie.[27]

Once, when he was living on Little Colonsay, the hitherto compassionate Boisdale lost patience with him, and warned him. Lachlan had hatched a plan of going to live near Glasgow, which came to nothing. His 'boys', he said, were lost in this place.[28] He frequently asked the laird of Lochbuy for a farm, but a deaf ear was turned to his pleas. Farms were such a precious commodity that it was easier to maintain him on the charity of his relations than to trust him with anything resembling responsibility. His letters, begging everything from some pecks of salt to potatoes, meal, whisky and cash, were full of rakish literary references which would have warmed the heart of anyone able to recognise them, if they had not been exasperated by his constant sponging. At Christmas 1794, sick of Little Colonsay, he wrote,

> You'll sure think me half mad when I assure you that I fraughted a Boat to carry me to Crinan or West Tarbert ... a Don Quixote undertaking ... But, my Dear Friend, when I consider the situation of my family and my being in the Evening of my Time ... I shall spend the few coins I have on a tryal, and if disappointed shall endeavour to live in oblivion somewhere else from my Country.[29]

MacQuarrie observed a certain diminution of respect in the lower orders when he lost rank and status. In May 1804, when he had been removed from Little Colonsay to Gribun, the land of Major Macdonald of Inchkenneth, he complained to Lochbuy that the tenants there were disrespectful.

> The Tenants here are the most infernall. They have neither conscience or honour. The people not only threaten my servant but my own Person. I can't bear any longer with such usage.

Lachlan's teenage sons remained with him; by all accounts they were great strapping boys and layabouts, who were frequently offered help by relations, if they would get a modicum of education in the Lowlands to fit them for the army. Murdoch, son of the second marriage, was helped by his kinsman Lachlan Macquarie to become a midshipman, but disappointed his benefactor.[30] The same benefactor reported of Hector MacQuarrie that 'this foolish young man' would be obliged to sell out of the army to pay his own debts, and in 1801 added that while Hector 'has not all the vices of some of his brothers, he has all the extravagance, folly and vanity of his unfortunate family – vain, ostentatious, extravagant to a ridiculous degree ...' Hector died in 1802. 'My lovely son', Lachlan called him, when it was too late. Of all the boys, only Donald, Alice's son, who lived in Liverpool, seemed to prosper.

Of the girls, Mally MacQuarrie, Alice's daughter and wife of Gillean Maclaine, inherited her father's longevity, but not his carelessness about children. Her personality will be discussed in later chapters. Suffice it to say here that when her husband and father fell out, in 1782, and Lachlan challenged his son-in-law to a duel, her distress was great. The cause of the quarrel was, predictably, the kelp rights of Ulva, which Gillean had quietly appropriated on the death of Ann MacQuarrie during her husband's absence abroad. Gillean considered that this reimbursed him for the expenses incurred by his care of the young MacQuarries. But Mally had the wisdom to hold out against MacQuarrie's coming to live in her household, which would have compromised her fierce ambition for her ten children. MacQuarrie lived to the great age of 103, and in his last years was given asylum by Charles Macquarie, a more distant relation, at Pennygown. Old and blind, he retained one daughter, Ann, to look after his needs and to write his poignant letters, still begging from his old friends and pursuing old debts. He had, of course, outlived everyone. His former domain, Ulva, was once again on the market, and his greatest claim to fame was, like John Lochbuy's, his brief portrayal in Dr Johnson's *Journey* and James Boswell's *Journal of a Tour*. From the point of view of the fate of Mull, and Mull people, his legacy was disastrous. He was the first of many lairds, except for the much earlier Macleans of Duart, to lose his estate through sheer fecklessness, debt and weakness of character. Of his sixteen children, not one could be accounted well-bred, or even responsible. As a chieftain he failed his people, as a husband he failed his wives, and as a father he failed his children. His ineffectual amiability is well caught in the only portrait which survives of him, wearing his army coat, probably the only coat he then possessed.

What can never be known about Lachlan MacQuarrie is whether any of his failures are attributable to the Argyll family for calling in their feu duties when these had become too great for any mortal to be expected to pay, or to the malevolence of his uncle and guardian, Allan of Culinish, in drawing attention to the debt. The Argylls were always perfectly aware of the state of play regarding debts, and were unlikely to need Culinish's prompting. As they had already seized the lands of Duart for debt, the questions which must now be asked are: was debt endemic to the Mull scene? Were the small tenants and cottars of Mull who did not pay their dues in full, or on time, to their landowners, equally culpable in the domino structure of society? Did they in turn have someone to blame for their sorrows and privations?

Ulva's greatest asset was kelp. Before 1750, tacks of land invariably included shores from which people could fish, or take a boat out. After 1750, kelp began to be a profitable manufacture, and seaweedy shores suddenly took on a greater value than shores covered with small shells, previously valued for adding to the fertility of arable land. If we remember the population findings of Dr Walker, and consider that in the 1750s the number of people in Mull was about 5,000, or 750 families, that half of those families did not have seaweedy shores, and that half again were occupied with peat-cutting at the same time as they were required for the kelp, and half again were pregnant women or small children, we are reduced at best to a hundred or two potential kelp workers. Kelp then required the people to work at it, and the presence of the seaweed, combined with an idle population nearby, was a recipe for success for landowners who could find efficient managers.

Kelp is a kind of seaweed which when cut, dried and then burned, becomes an alkaline powder used in the manufacture of soap and glass. So important was the economy of the industry that Adam Smith devoted part of his *Wealth of Nations* to a consideration of its relationship to the rent of land. The rent of the land, Smith argues, is not necessarily related to any input from the landlord, such as improvement, but is dependent upon what the farmer can afford. The landlord will even demand rent for what cannot ever be improved, such as the kelp shore, which does not, in its natural growth, respond to human industry. Just as the fisherman who profits from the sea also needs a patch of land to live upon, so a kelper needs land, and must pay rent, which the landlord may augment. The rent of the land is therefore a monopoly price, and not related to what the landlord may or may not have laid out upon the shores.

The younger generation of Mull landlords were the first to exploit the profits of kelp. Gillean Maclaine, in Scallastle, was greatly exercised in rewriting his subtenants' leases in order to separate kelp shores from the lands they belonged to, so that he could control manufacture. He was therefore one of the first employers of labourers, a new category of lower beings, on an island where subtenants had previously been subsistence farmers, growing their own food and keeping a cow for their own milk. Again, Adam Smith can be referred to for an explanation of the relationship between wage-earning and increase of population. It was no accident that at the end of the eighteenth century in Mull, the wages from kelp caused an increase in the birth rate precisely in those areas where most kelp was produced – notably in Ulva, Ardmeanach and the Ross. From the 1780s, the Duke of Argyll's instructions to his chamberlain became mainly concerned with his kelp rights. 'You must immediately intimate to all the tenants who possess without leases that in future they are to deliver to my order all the kelp which they make on their farms, not under a certain quantity each, on being allowed a certain sum for each ton.'[31] But this method of extracting profit, this form of 'wages', was not always effective, and by 1799 the duke also was separating the rent of land from the rent of kelp shores in Oskamull.[32]

If Mull had been the best of all possible worlds, and if straight wages had been paid to the kelp workers, and competition allowed, the population explosion might have been greater than it was. But on the Argyll estates, the duke had a monopoly, and in Adam Smith's view 'monopoly is a great enemy to good management'. On the Lochbuy estates, quarrels between Gillean Maclaine and his father, John Maclaine of Lochbuy, provoked a situation in which even the tacksmen did not know if they had kelp rights or not, and the kelp labourers themselves did not know where they stood. In 1786, Gillean's kelp cutters in Ardmeanach were stopped by John Maclaine, tacksman of Tiroran, who was in bitter dispute with Gillean.[33] Such were the passions generated by the only profitable industry Mull ever had.

If the Lochbuy family had not been so constantly short of cash, and if the kelp had been managed more effectively, wages might have been regulated and paid. But thousands of tiny receipts in the family papers testify to a confusion of rent adjustments, patching up of leases and every other imaginable device to avoid just such a simple solution. In 1801, the tenants of Ardmeanach sensibly refused to work for Gillean's irresponsible son, Allan of Scallastle, unless they could have security for making his kelp.[34]

Colin Macdonald of Boisdale and his son Ranald apparently managed the kelp of Ulva better than their neighbours. A visitor to Ulva in 1807 explained that rents were not regulated there in such a way as to allow a man a comfortable profit from kelping after paying his rent. The poor tenant was unable to better his lot by endeavour. On the contrary, the kelp shores were competed for on the open market, as it were, and the rents paid in cash. If Sir John Carr [35] is to be believed (and his information came from the proprietor himself), it is not surprising that Ulva's population increased, and that the people were healthier and happier than they had been in the reign of Lachlan MacQuarrie of that Ilk.

'The bad Marcates and the want of a Boat, and Money being so scarce, all those things has hindered me from proceeding to Coll. I wish you could send me £10.' MacQuarrie wrote this, one of his less plaintive letters, in October

1799, when he was eighty-four years old, and a mere youngster compared to the venerable (though unvenerated) old man he was yet to become. His 'proceeding to Coll' was a much wished-for visit to his friend, Alexander Maclean of Coll, who was also the laird of Quinish in Mull, and therefore included in our list of Mull heritors. 'Coll is a very good hearted judicious young man,' the lawyer Allan MacDougall opined in 1786, 'always ready to render every service in his power to any of his friends of whom he conceives a good opinion.'

Alexander of Coll had been born in 1754, not the heir apparent to the estate, but son to Hugh Maclean, half-brother to the thirteenth laird. Alexander's father had become the fourteenth Maclean of Coll, and his mother was Janet Macleod of Talisker in Skye. Hugh and Janet lived much of the time in Aberdeen, in a circle of academics, an unusual set of people for anyone in Mull to be associated with at that time. Janet's brother, Mr Roderick Macleod, was a professor in King's College, Aberdeen, whose exertions in procuring Highland students made him famous enough to be caricatured in Kay's *Portraits* wearing Highland dress and brandishing a Lochaber axe. Alexander of Coll and his older brother Donald ('Young Col', who was so tragically drowned in the year following Johnson and Boswell's visit to Ulva) both matriculated at King's and it is to be regretted that the indolent MacQuarrie of Ulva did not aspire to sending any of his boys to answer the recruiting calls of academe. Yet MacQuarrie longed continually for the company of Alexander of Coll, and whether it was for his conversation or for his cellars, or simply for Coll's tolerance of himself, we cannot discern. In 1803, the old man was writing to Lochbuy, unhappily declining an invitation to visit Moy: 'It adds much to my disappointment at not being with you at this time, as my friend Coll is with you, whom I long to see.' [36]

This friendship, the desire of the moth for the star, is all the more surprising in that Coll was indeed 'judicious'. Unlike all the other heritors, he settled his accounts on time [37] and paid strict attention to the education of his sons. In 1799, moving with the times, he began building the new village at Dervaig, on his Quinish estate in Mull, which was intended to be a hive of industry in the new century.

Another difference between Maclean and MacQuarrie lay in the cultural traditions which the Macleans respected and the MacQuarries ignored, or perhaps never had. Admittedly, a family that employed a bard was going to see a return on its investment, a return indeed which would last longer than any estate. For bards sang of the births and the marriages of their chieftains, and celebrated their comings and goings in peace and war. The Macleans patronised bards, and enjoyed an attractive reputation as a result, but no such flattering unction was laid to the souls of any of the MacQuarries of Ulva, while Alexander of Coll's every act was celebrated by a poet, applauding his purchase of an island, or his marriage, or his hospitality.[38] It could be argued simply that no one has thought of preserving the poetry of MacQuarrie bards

as Macleans preserved theirs; in the country of the blind the one-eyed man
is king, and Charles MacQuarrie, that well-known author of religious tracts
such as *Dan, air bruadar Nebuchadnesair*[39] must stand unchallenged as the
writer and poet of the MacQuarries.

But to return briefly to the questions posed above, about whether Lachlan
MacQuarrie of Ulva was responsible for his own downfall or was the hapless
victim of the Argyll claim to a debt that had been allowed to run unchecked
for a century: the evidence for both theories is slight. Cryptic references in
two letters to MacQuarrie from John of Lochbuy in the late 1760s – 'I am
very much grieved in my heart how much both of you gentlemen [MacQuarrie
and Ormaig] are in the mercy of that family. However, you ought to make
the best of it, and you have no time to lose'; and another: 'there were so many
adjudications going on against you and your family which was very grievous
to me to hear' – only finish in the usual request for casks of rum or brandy.[40]
The few MacQuarrie papers which survive from the muniments of other
families include no discharges from the Dukes of Argyll, and even the lists
of dispositions and inhibitions which survive the many sales of the island of
Ulva[41] do not contain any mention of such a large sum being paid off. It
remains to be conjectured that Lachlan MacQuarrie of Ulva was as careless
with his receipts as his cousin and contemporary, John Maclaine of Lochbuy,
and that Gillean, as legal 'doer' for both, must have had difficulty in extracting
his own legal fees. Both sets of tenants, in Ulva and Lochbuy, suffered from
negligent and indifferent landlords who expelled many commoners for non-
payment of rent, and constantly threatened many more. Later chapters will
consider this groundwork, and its role in the collective memory of Mull people.

In the lifetime of MacQuarrie of Ulva, 1715–1818, boats were the chief form
of transport within and beyond Mull, but because of the scarcity of wood
there were very few boatbuilders. MacQuarrie, knowing the strict rules against
taking timber, approached Lochbuy in 1799 with his customary courtesy. 'I
hope you will permit me to Cull some small Sticks in Torrlochan for the
repare of my Boat.' Others were not so nice, and much wood was stolen in
desperation. Most boats were small, and illustrations show the kind of craft
employed to convey visitors to Staffa, or across the tidal waters of the Sound
of Mull, to be alarmingly fragile. Women, inevitably dressed in flowing
garments, were afraid for themselves and for their children. But the kind of
anxiety which must have followed the movements of husbands, even if they
were only hugging the coasts, must have been a constant torment. Sudden
squalls claimed as many lives as capsizings at piers.

Reports of men drowned at sea recur in letters throughout the eighteenth
century. The only good that came of the fierce storms and treacherous rocks
was the occasional booty from a stranger's ship wrecked on the coast, and
the Mull people were not even allowed to profit from these. 'Plunder night
and day' was the result of a shipwreck off Shiaba in the Ross of Mull in 1792,

in a decade of remorseless weather. In 1790 the minister of Torosay, Mr Patrick Macarthur, was drowned with twelve others in the Sound of Mull. In 1795, Alexander Maclean of Coll was trapped under a small boat when attempting to land on Staffa in high seas, but was dragged ashore, luckier than his brother Donald, who had drowned in similar circumstances with eight others, off Ulva, twenty-one years earlier. Most of those were local journeys, and with no roads, the transportation of goods within Mull had to be by overloaded boats which often sank within sight of the shore, as in the 'most melancholy accident' of 1768 when Archibald Maclean and Neil McOsenag, 'two of the Prettyest Commoners that this Island could produce', put too many herring barrels into Gillean's wherry at Garmony, and went down with their cargo.

Nor were long-distance vessels any safer, for the principal destination of the Clyde could be reached only by the treacherous route round the Mull of Kintyre, which a ship might navigate successfully only to be blown across to the coast of Antrim, like Mally MacQuarrie and her children, *en route* for Edinburgh in 1787. Passage between islands was fraught with danger, so that ministers from Tiree or Coll were unable to attend presbytery meetings in Mull, and Mull ministers found the crossing to Morvern boisterous.

But the most unfortunate result of the scarcity of ship materials (more nails were expended on coffins than on boats) was the effect of boatlessness on the fishing industry, which well-meaning mainlanders held out as the ideal solution to the problem of idleness and sloth. Because there was no native wood, there were no home-built boats, and fishing boats had to be ordered from the 'Low Country'. The economics of fishing alone, ably explained by Thomas Pennant in his *Tour in Scotland and Voyage to the Hebrides, 1772*, put the industry beyond the resources of Mull's subsistence farmers. The vagaries of the weather and the festoons of rocks around the shores made the regular pursuit of fish impracticable. But in the end it was to be the extraordinary fickleness of the herring itself which would put an end to hopes of rich rewards. The herring family which happened to frequent Hebridean waters was inconsiderate enough to have its season between May and September, and therefore conflicted with peat-cutting, stacking and carting, kelp-making and harvest. The provocative habit the herring had of swimming just below the surface of the sea in shoals required drift nets, and drift nets required heavy boats ... and so the cycle went on. A man might stand looking into a loch like Loch Scridain one day and see a goodly multitude of fish, and the next day they would have vanished, perhaps for ever.

As Campbell of Kirnan had once pointed out, a poor man had to pay herring tax whether he caught any herring or not. Later in the eighteenth century it was the salt laws which discouraged fishing. Not the duties on salt, but the convolutions of the laws themselves, which petty officers of excise interpreted each in his own way.[42] As a result there simply wasn't any salt in Mull in the late eighteenth century, and MacQuarrie's cry from the heart 'I wish Mrs

McLean could send some pecks of salt to me, as I have not what will season an egg' was a comment not confined to the little world of Little Colonsay.

Notes

1. Munro, Jean and Munro, R. W. (eds), *Acts of the Lords of the Isles, 1336–1493*, p. 226.
2. NLS. MS 17678 f. 27. Memorial, Allan MacQuarrie of Culinish to His Grace the Duke of Argyll, 1753.
3. Ibid. Allan MacQuarrie's version of what happened.
4. The story is told by R. W. Munro in *Clan MacQuarrie, a History*, but also related by Alice herself in her poem, *A' Bhean Mhuladach*, 'The Sorrowful Wife'.
5. Translation by Anja Gunderloch.
6. Translation of the song, as sung by Flora MacNeill, by Morag MacLeod.
7. Maclean Sinclair, *The Maclean Bards*, vol. 1, p. 257.
8. After Alice's brother, Lachlan Maclean of Torloisk, succeeded to the estate in 1765, his siblings (excluding Alice, who had died) sued him for their portions, the calculation of which was affected by the custom of foster parents giving 'Macallive cows' to the children's parents. GRO. Uncatalogued MS. 1770.
9. Torloisk Papers B228.
10. NLS. MS 17678 f. 45.
11. Kilninian and Kilmore OPR and Mull Presbytery Minutes, 7 May 1766.
12. NAS. GD174/1329/21. Letter, Donald Maclean to MM, 1 June 1782.
13. NAS. GD174/1264/26. Letter, Kingairloch to MM, 24 July 1769.
14. Colin Macdonald of Boisdale was the third purchaser of Ulva after the sale by the MacQuarries.
15. NAS. GD174/1371/11. Letter, GM to MM, 8 April 1788.
16. NAS. GD174/1425/2. Letter, Boisdale to MM, 6 September 1788.
17. NAS. GD174/1425/3. Letter, Boisdale to MM, 30 December 1788.
18. GRO. D3330. Box 17–18. Contributions for prosecuting the burner of the kiln at Ardnacallich, 1780.
19. Ibid.
20. Mr Walker, the tutor engaged at Ulva on LMQ's departure.
21. GRO. D3330. Box 18. LMQ to GM, Halifax, August 1778.
22. Hibbert, pp. 254–5.
23. GRO. D3330. Box 18. LMQ to GM, August 1778.
24. Hibbert, p. 255.
25. See note 12.
26. Peggy Maclaine was her maiden name. She was the mother of LM, future governor of NSW, and was then about seventy-two.
27. NAS. GD174/1427/50. Letter, LMQ to MM, 25 October 1801. Peggy and MM's mother was Flora MacQuarrie, daughter of the second wife of Lachlan MacQuarrie the fourteenth of Ulva, Catherine Maclean, who was the daughter of John Garbh the seventh of Coll, and Florence Maclean of Duart.
28. NAS. GD174/1427/8. Letter, LMQ to MM, 4 February 1792.
29. NAS. GD174/1427/22. Letter, LMQ to MM, 26 December 1794.
30. NAS. GD174/1373/7. Letter, LM to MM, 20 April 1790.
31. Cregeen, Eric R. (ed.), *Argyll Estate Instructions*, p. 186.
32. NAS. GD174/1478. Letter, James Maxwell to MM, 6 June 1800.
33. NAS. GD174/1371/7. Letter, GM to MM, 28 May 1786.

34. NAS. GD174/1538. Letter, Allan Maclaine to MM, 12 May 1801.

35. Carr, Sir John, *Caledonian Sketches*, pp. 492–3.

36. NAS. GD174/1427/69. Letter, LMQ to MM, 26 October 1803.

37. e.g. NAS. GD174/1628/388. Letter DMWS to MM2, 4 October 1824.

38. Maclean Sinclair, *Maclean Bards*.

39. 'Daniel, Nebuchadnezzar's Dream.'

40. GRO. Uncatalogued MSS in string bundle. Letters JMLB to LMQ, October 1766 and October 1768

41. NAS. GD174/31–4.

42. Carr, *Caledonian Sketches*, p. 489.

8

Dr Johnson, Mr Boswell
and other tourists

It is not often that readers of history or biography are asked to produce qualifications for proceeding to the next chapter, but here it must be stated that the reader who is not familiar with Dr Samuel Johnson's *Journey to the Western Islands of Scotland* and James Boswell's *Journal of a Tour to the Hebrides with Samuel Johnson, LL.D.*, is at a distinct disadvantage. These two works, now conveniently published together, are the archetypes of travel writing, and have never been out of print since they first appeared in 1775 and 1785 respectively. Although only a fraction of each deals with their travels in Mull, the shortcomings in their perceptions of the island must call into question for ever any insights that tourism in general might be thought to bestow on the casual traveller.

But tourists, by the very superficiality of their nodding glances here and there, and by the superciliousness which they often bring to a backward civilisation, have, both then and now, a valuable contribution to make to history. Without Johnson and Boswell we might not know that Tobermory was, in 1773, a fine harbour full of the bustle of sailing ships, with a tolerable inn by the shore. We might not appreciate that it took seven hours to ride on small Mull ponies from Tobermory to Ulva ferry, or that October brought to eighteenth-century Mull storms which would make rivers impassable, as there were no bridges. If we find the two friends unbearably unobservant when it comes to the ordinary people of the island, we must remember that Dr Johnson at least was short-sighted, and that the huts of the poor were barely visible, blending into the landscape and obscured by rain and mist. This infuriating pair of sightseers were intent on viewing antiquities, and the miles they had to go before they saw the ecclesiastical remains of Icolmkill, or Iona, were suffered in silence, or endured by discussing frivolous subjects which might have been saved for some coffee house in London. Maddening they might be, but some precious vignettes of Mull life drop from their pens.

After leaving the tolerable inn at Tobermory, they were invited to call on the relatives of their guide, Donald Maclean, 'Young Col'. The son of Hugh Maclean, laird of the island of Coll, and of Quinish in Mull, Col was, like his contemporary Archy Lochbuy, the heir to the estate of his father, but also conjoint laird. He was an intrepid talker, whether he knew anything of a subject or not, and indefatigable in his efforts to make Dr Johnson comfortable.

He was related to every heritor in Mull, and in 1773 the tradition of hospitality had not departed from the Hebrides. He was to introduce the visitors to four of his relations, and open doors to allow them to peer inside five Mull houses, which they were to describe for the delectation of generations of armchair travellers.

It was fortunate that their guide chose as the first port of call the old house at Erray, just outside present-day Tobermory, and then leased by Dr Hector Maclean, a man of Mull descent who had practised medicine in the army and in Glasgow. Dr Hector's wife, Catherine, was young Col's aunt, a brisk little old woman in a bedgown with a brown wig. This description of Boswell's was not published in his *Journal*, but in the version which was later to be discovered, to the great glee of all his adoring readers, among his more private manuscripts.[1] Dr Hector's daughter, Miss Maclean, 'a little plump elderly young lady in some dress which I do not recollect farther than that she had a smart beaver hat with a white feather', was a godsend to Boswell, who feared that Johnson would leave for the mainland without waiting to see Iona. But Miss Maclean proved to be an effervescent and learned elderly young lady, who could sing, play on the spinet, speak French, translate Gaelic, draw and sew. Dr Johnson pronounced her 'the most accomplished lady that I have found in the Highlands'. As the lexicographer was unwilling to believe that Gaelic could be translated literally, one of his greatest prejudices was allayed by Miss Maclean's straightforward intelligence and liveliness.

The house at Erray was described by Boswell, who was more inclined to notice material things, and less given to theorising than Johnson, as 'a strange confused house, built by MacKinnon the proprietor about sixty years ago', with a large unfinished cold kitchen leading to a narrow timber stair, which in turn led to a passage and a large bedroom with a coach roof. This is the most detailed architectural description there is of an eighteenth-century domestic structure in Mull. To be told also that it had bad portraits on the walls, prints of various eminent physicians, is an embarrassment of riches, for this kind of comment would be felt by a native to be both unnecessary and impolite. More savoury still is the point Boswell makes in his private journal that in the room where he slept with a rusty parrot,[2] he was shocked at the dirtiness of his sheets.

The next day, when rain prevented the tourists from continuing with their journey (and also postponed the doctor's return from a visit to a patient), Miss Maclean, in Boswell's words

> produced some Erse poems by John Maclean, who was a famous bard in Mull, and had died only a few years ago. He could neither read nor write.[3] She read and translated two of them: one a kind of elegy on Sir John Maclean's being obliged to fly his country in 1715; another a dialogue between two Roman Catholic young ladies, sisters, whether it was better to be a nun or to marry. I could not perceive much poetical imagery in the

translation. Yet all of our company who understood Erse seemed charmed with the original. There may perhaps be some choice of expression and some excellence of arrangement that cannot be shown in translation.[4]

The prurient Boswell saw no voluptuous charms in Miss Maclean (otherwise he would not have hesitated to record them in his private diary), and consequently failed to notice, under the smart beaver hat, the real woman. Exactly five years earlier, the presbytery of Mull had summoned Duncan Mackenzie twice, and Miss Maclean once, for immorality. In deference to her family and connections, the nature of the sin was not divulged, even in the minutes of presbytery, but it must be assumed she had not been called to account for giving Duncan several tunes on the spinet. Her rendition of the dialogue between the sisters was clearly given with feeling. It is known that her father disapproved of a match with Duncan Mackenzie, who was a commoner. Dr Maclean died in March 1784, and after a decent interval Miss Maclean married her lover on 6 June 1786.[5] Her affection for Duncan had endured for twenty years, and as Mrs Mackenzie, she was to charm visitors with songs and imitations long after the deaths of Boswell and Johnson.

After the rain had slightly subsided, the two travellers proceeded on the route by Sorne and Baliachcrach to Kilmore.[6] It was on this part of the journey that Johnson pronounced Mull to be a 'most dolorous country', and lost his oak stick. Young Col, their guide, was having his own problems with the itinerary, for one of the places he had it in mind to visit, was removed from the hospitality list because its head of household was on his deathbed. The party therefore had to continue in the direction of Ulva Ferry and rely on the goodwill of Lachlan MacQuarrie of Ulva. They were lucky to be able to attract notice in the dark, and to get to Ardnacaillich (as the site of Ulva House was generally called). 'To Ulva we came in the dark, and left it before noon the next day', Johnson wrote. As we know, MacQuarrie was fond of visitors, and liked to entertain them single handed. Neither Johnson nor Boswell mentioned MacQuarrie's wife, although they had been interested enough to describe other wives on their travels. Clearly their host had hidden his wife away, or she was in one of the many stages of child-rearing which kept her in the background.[7] Nor was there any comment, even in Boswell's private diary, about the children who were likely to be in bed after dark. But MacQuarrie fed his guests just the kind of information they wanted – first that after 900 years in the family, the island of Ulva was going to be sold to pay his debts (at which Boswell, who, as an Edinburgh lawyer must have known about it, feigned surprise), and second, that *mercheta mulierum*, the right of the lord of Ulva to have the first night of his vassals' wives, still existed in a watered-down form. But of more interest to those of us who are attempting to reconstruct Mull life in the 1770s is the fact that the windows in the 'spare' bedroom were broken and let in the rain – which, at that time of year, blew boisterously.

Next morning, Sunday 17 October, they were informed by MacQuarrie that there was nothing worthy of observation in Ulva. This extraordinary statement has to be tempered to what we know of the host, and what is known of the guests. The former was lazy, and not well-to-do; the latter were of the opinion that only ecclesiastical remains, historic monuments and antiquities were worthy of observation. Young Col was anxious to deliver them to the more urbane Sir Allan Maclean, at Inchkenneth, for they were island-hopping on the fringes of Mull on the way to Iona. Here Sir Allan's fine tall figure was complemented by the graceful presence of two of his three daughters, Maria and Sibella. Unlike MacQuarrie, Sir Allan was a tidy man, whose habitation on Inch Kenneth consisted of several single-storey huts, and whose army life had given him a taste for order in the wilderness. Here Dr Johnson admitted to 'some mournful emotion' as they contemplated the ruins of religious structures. The implication that feelings of sanctity no longer affected the natives of Mull in regard to this once holy isle is belied by the number of marriages which were celebrated here in the course of the eighteenth century.[8] The neglect of ecclesiastical buildings was a result of the departure of the church hierarchy, and of the monks who had once been responsible for tending chapels and tombs. Now, in 1773, the Church of Scotland was facing opposition on the part of impoverished heritors in the three parishes of Mull to any kind of contribution to church life, so that the preservation of historic church buildings was a Utopian concept utterly beyond any hope of achievement.

But Inch Kenneth, with its natural beauty, its oystercatchers, curlews and razorbills, its rich harvest of oysters and shell-covered shores, charmed our tourists so much that Dr Johnson wished he might stay longer − 'but life will not be all passed in delight'. Much of the delight was occasioned by finding here a parcel of recent issues of the *Caledonian Mercury* and the quietness required for reading all the news which had been wanting as they roved in the Hebrides. The island had remained private since the monks left its shores; as part of the lands of Brolass, claimed by the Dukes of Argyll but under tack to Sir Allan Maclean at the time of Johnson and Boswell's visit, it had always been the principal residence of the family of the Macleans of Brolass, and here again, Boswell had to be diplomatic in his references to its ownership, for he himself was involved in the preparations for the court case in which Sir Allan was to try to regain his ancestral acres.[9]

We now begin to appreciate that the two travellers were not quite what they seemed. Johnson was an English tourist who had wanted to see the Hebrides ever since his father had put into his hands a copy of Martin Martin's *Description of the Western Islands* when he was very young.[10] All through Johnson's account of his journey, he refers to and quotes Martin Martin, published in 1695, as the ultimate authority on the Hebrides. If Johnson saw a bird, and remembered that Martin had connected it with a certain island, its existence was confirmed. It was Martin who was responsible for implanting in Johnson the unaccountable prejudice that there were no 'Erse' or Gaelic manuscripts to be found in the islands,[11] and that therefore MacPherson's recent bestseller, *Fragments of Ancient Poetry Collected in the Highlands of Scotland and Translated from the Gaelic or Erse Language*, must be a fake. Martin had simply mentioned that he had seen no manuscripts, but as the great lexicographer was unable to believe that literature could be transmitted orally, the absence of manuscripts made the existence of a tradition of Ossianic verse untenable. With the doggedness of a prosecuting lawyer, Johnson questioned every minister he met about Gaelic originals, and every answer he received in favour of the oral transmission of the adventures of Fingal made him more convinced of his own reasonableness. 'He wished me to be deceived for the honour of his country', Johnson concluded, patronisingly, of a minister in Skye.

Johnson's very learning was therefore a handicap to him in the exercise of educating himself about the Hebrides, for if he had not read Martin Martin and MacPherson, he might have listened more attentively to what he was told, without the unnerving propensity to argue which he displayed at every turn. Boswell, who had had the idea of writing a biography of Johnson right in the middle of the tour, had turned himself nimbly into the role of listener, and to our great loss, recorded fewer of his impressions of the islands, and more and more of Dr Johnson's unchecked and outrageous opinions. Fortunately, the journal he kept, and those parts which he did not use for his life of Dr Johnson, survived, giving some further glimpses of Mull in 1773.

Of Sir Allan Maclean, 'the Knight' (who has already been seen through Gillean's eyes, boxing the ears of the little corporal at Duart Castle), Boswell records 'a strange unaccountable sort of hesitation whether he was to go with us or not' (to Iona). The poor Knight was not in fact the man of military precision who emerges from the two eighteenth-century published accounts. The positive character he is given there was not one subscribed to by his Mull friends, who could not say the word 'Knight' without prefacing it with 'poor'. But in his situation of having to play the host for several days, and accompany the awful Dr Johnson and sycophantic Mr Boswell from Inchkenneth to Iona, and from Iona to Moy, where John Maclaine of Lochbuy's poor mansion was marked out to be the next stop, he can be forgiven for being hesitant, and looking for a moment like a trapped animal. He was probably weighing up the claims on his time and the tradition to which he had to pay lip service, of the Highlander's hospitality. Visitors are inclined to think that a Mull man has nothing to do with his time but entertain them, that a Mull man's days are long and empty without the invigorating talk of a man from the outside world. But poor Sir Allan was a man who had been through the Seven Years' War, had lived in London and Edinburgh, and had in fact seen more of the world than Dr Johnson. In Mull, in the 1770s, many humble men who might appear to grow out of their huts, as if they had never seen any other spot, had seen service all over the world, and if asked, could happily compare the housing conditions of the cities of Lisbon and New York with those of home.

Boswell had been enchanted once or twice on his Hebridean journey with the song sung by boatmen, *Tha tighinn fodham eiridh,* which he called 'Hatyin foam eri'. On 5 October he reported that he had learned by heart all the Gaelic words of the first verse. Off the coast of Mull, Sir Allan's rowers sang Gaelic songs 'or rather howls', Boswell said, alluding to the pentatonic scale of notes which Sir Allan told them resembled the songs of North American Indians. They were rowed into Bunessan Loch, after seeing Staffa at no very great distance, with the surge high on its rocky coast. The inn at Bunessan, which has remained on the same site for 250 years, was kept by Lachlan Ban Maclean, former servant to Sir Allan. Lachlan Ban was twenty-two in 1773; already married to Mary Maclean of Torran, he was to have sons who would serve in the Napoleonic wars, but now he was under some strain, being asked for whisky for Sir Allan's boatmen, and being unable to supply it because he had just catered for a funeral. Lachlan Ban must have kept a good inn, for Sir Allan decided to take him along to Iona for the expertness with which he could prepare a bright fire, get good clean straw beds and make a tolerable supper. Accordingly, Lachlan came, and was sent ahead into the village of Iona to announce the arrival of the visitors. Sir Allan was greeted with affection, as chief of the clan Maclean, and after warming themselves in the house of 'Provost' Macdonald, Sir Allan, Johnson and Boswell lay down on beds of straw in a snug barn, with their servants at their feet. Sir Allan talked next day of 'recovering' Iona, referring now more openly to the process in which he was shortly to face the Duke of Argyll's representatives. For the ownership of the lands of Duart was shortly to be contested in the Court of Session, and Sir Allan, as successor to Sir Hector Maclean, of Duart, who had died in Rome nearly a quarter of a century before, was expecting to be successful.

Boswell found himself a little in revolt against the tourist mentality, seeing Dr Johnson examining inscriptions in the nuns' chapel, and considering that Dr Pococke, Dr Walker, Mr Banks and Mr Pennant had all done the same thing. Perhaps the same revolt had allowed him to pass by Staffa so complacently the day before, content with seeing the surf on its shores from afar. Joseph Banks had described Staffa well enough, and it was soon to be overrun with tourists. Disappointed with Iona, Boswell compared notes with Dr Johnson, who was not disappointed, because his expectations had not been high, based as they were on the writings of William Sacheverell, who had visited in 1697.

To the reader of Boswell's real journal, it is a relief to have pulled away from Iona, upon which Boswell had expended so much anxiety, and to the student of people a great delight to be approaching, by way of Loch Scridain, with Johnson and Boswell and Sir Allan, the house of Mr Neil Macleod, minister of the parish of Ross.[12] Mr Macleod, warned by the small servant-boy, Donald MacDougall, of the impending visitation, came out to greet his guests from the house known as Ardchrishnish. The ministers of Mull at this time had no manses, and Mr Macleod had the farm of Ardchrishnish as tacksman to the Duke of Argyll, and not by virtue of being in holy orders.

Mr Macleod had a black wig, a smart air, and his hat was covered with wax-cloth. In stark contrast to the lack of mention of Mrs MacQuarrie of Ulva, Mrs Macleod was pronounced by Boswell to be a very well-behaved woman, the daughter of a previous minister of the parish, who knew how to live in the minister's house. The three guests were given an excellent supper, and then a good clean bed each in the very same room. Mr Macleod, who expressed himself much obliged to Dr Johnson, had probably used his *Dictionary*. No mention was made of Mr and Mrs Macleod's children, who must have ranged in age from twelve to one. The travellers were mounted, and progressed the next day to Dr Maclean of Pennycross, one of the stoutest and most hearty men Boswell had ever seen, more like a farmer than a doctor, and here they had dinner on Thursday 21 October. From Pennycross they continued to Rossal, and here they crossed what Lachlan MacQuarrie of Ulva liked to call 'the Mull Alps'. It was a hard ride, and they must have been relieved to get on to the shore track from Glenbyre to Loch Buy. As it was so well into October, it must have been growing dark as they arrived at that small house of Moy, familiar to the reader of this book, where John Lochbuy had had his encounters with Killean, Kilmory and others, and was just about to meet the famous Dr Johnson.

But Lochbuy, not being familiar with the achievements of members of the literati, asked the sage if he was a Johnston of Glen Croe. Sir Allan was the brother of Lady Lochbuy, the very same lady who had pinched Mally Maclaine's arms till they were black and blue. Boswell thought the lady much older than her brother, Sir Allan, but she could not have been more than sixty-eight, and we can see from the Knight's assertion that she was an antediluvian, that Sir Allan was rather proud of his own youthful appearance. Young Col had told Boswell that he would have given a great deal to see Lochbuy and Samuel Johnson together, but Boswell observed:

> The truth was that Lochbuy proved to be only a bluff, hearty, rosy old gentleman of a strong voice and no great depth of understanding. He was not taller than the common size. He was a great deal like Craigengillan,[13] but had a longer face. His wife, Sir Allan's sister, but much older than him, was a strange being to be a lady at the head of a family which I was told has £1000 a year. She had on a mean bedgown, and behaved like the landlady of an alehouse ...[14]

Here, knowing the exact capability of Lochbuy's purse, we can afford to laugh at the informer who told Boswell he had £1,000 a year. We can also smile at the gullibility of journalists who think that a man with a fine estate must have the income to run it. And we know that only a few years earlier, Lady Lochbuy was buying so many shoes from Inveraray for her young ward, Miss Mally Maclaine, that she could not indulge in a new bedgown for herself. As at Erray, Boswell observed the daughter of the house:

> Their daughter was as wild as any filly in Mull. At least she had as little notion of good breeding. Mr Johnson tried to talk with her. But it would not do. The poor thing knew nothing. Though about seventeen, she had never read a play. Mr Johnson said my comparing her to a filly was not just, for she had not the friskiness of a wild animal.

This was Catherine Maclaine of Lochbuy, who, five years later, did not wait until her father was cold in his grave before marrying the penniless Hugh McGilvra of Pennyghael, an older man, who had not been John's favourite neighbour. This act of defiance of the dead was perhaps the only filly-like act Catherine ever performed, and she lived to regret it. Her struggle to gain a marriage portion from the Lochbuy estate was to take up most of her life, and she certainly was no more capable of reading a play in her mature years than she was at seventeen.

Boswell went on to mention a little legal matter which he had not missed in Edinburgh, and which demonstrates his awareness of affairs concerning 'the Country'.

> Lochbuy tried not long ago to prove himself a fool, or what we call a facile man, in order to set aside a lease which he had granted to Gillean Maclaine, his natural son, but it did not do, though I suppose there were foolish things enough proved. Mr Johnson told me that in England they will not allow a man to stultify himself, as they term it. Lochbuy some years ago was fined 500 merks, or paid that sum by way of damages, to some gentlemen whom he imprisoned in the dungeon of his old castle. Sir Allan said he still imagines that he has an heritable jurisdiction. I must do Lochbuy the justice to mention that he was very hospitable. Our supper was indeed but a poor one. I think a sort of stewed mutton was the principal dish. I was afterwards told that he has no spit, and but one pot in which everything is stewed. It is probable enough.

Indeed it was only too probable, and if Boswell had only known, the cause might be traced to Lachlan the Prodigal, or to Gillean, or to the drinking of too much of the admirable port which Boswell goes on to praise.

> He had an admirable port. Sir Allan and he and I drank each a bottle of it. Then we drank a bowl of punch. I was seized with an avidity for drinking, and Lochbuy and I became mighty social. Another bowl was made. Mr Johnson had gone to bed as the first was finished, and had admonished me, 'Don't drink any more *poonch*'.[15]

The stay at Lochbuy was concluded the next morning, with Lady Lochbuy offering Johnson cold sheep's head for breakfast, and Sir Allan being angry at her vulgarity. After breakfast, Sir Allan, Maclaine of Lochbuy and the two guests walked to the old castle of Moy and viewed the pit which had been the scene of the famous imprisonment. Lochbuy and Sir Allan accompanied the guests to the ferry at Achnacraig, and spoke of the young laird being absent at a black cattle fair. As the travellers sailed out, they saw the old castle of Duart to their left in the distance, a historic monument which they had not managed to visit. An hour or two later, they were at Oban, a small village 'if a very few houses could be so called', and two days later were dining with the fifth Duke of Argyll at Inveraray.

Dr Samuel Johnson's book, *A Journey to the Western Isles*, was published in January 1775, at the price of 5s., in a print run of 4,000 copies.[16] On the island of Lismore, to the east of Mull, the minister, Mr Donald McNicol, thirty-nine years old, a Gaelic poet and scholar, read the account, and could barely contain his fury. He wrote at once to Dr Walker, who had made the report on the Hebrides in 1764, complaining of the bare-faced impudence of this man who insisted that there was no written Gaelic more than 100 years old. Mr McNicol himself owned a manuscript genealogy of the Argylls of much greater antiquity, and there were Bibles, psalm books and song books galore to convince any other man that Gaelic was a written language.[17] Dr Walker encouraged his brother clergyman to publish his objections, but by the time McNicol's *Remarks on Dr Samuel Johnson's Journey to the Hebrides; in which are contained Observations on the Antiquities, Language, Genius and Manners of the Highlanders of Scotland* appeared in print in 1779, some thousands of readers had imbibed the sententious work of Dr Johnson and were infected by his anti-Gaelic views. Controversy had erupted in the 1770s over James MacPherson's three published works of 'translation' from the Gaelic, *Fragments*, *Fingal* and *Temora*, Johnson being MacPherson's most implacable critic and detractor. But MacPherson, who had created a hero in Fingal, son of the king of Morvern, and defender of the oppressed and the poor, had enjoyed a huge success, being translated into Italian, German and French just at the time when the concept of freedom was influencing the politics and subsequent revolutions of America and France. Apart from the verse epics of Walter Scott in the early 1800s, no poetic writings with a Scottish setting ever had such a universal popularity as MacPherson's prose renderings of the epics composed by Ossian. They prompted a new wave of tourism, and when the name of Staffa's great cave was misconstrued as 'Fingal's Cave', the passion for Ossianic verse was merged with the passion for geology begun by Joseph Banks. The readers of Johnson's *Journey* were caught up in this seductive mix of attractions, and as Mull, Staffa and Iona could be 'done' in a few days the tourist industry boomed. No one cared about poor Mr McNicol's defence of the Gaelic language, or his sincere desire to put the record straight.

As the 1770s rolled on into the 1780s, many of the Mull gentry would have been found in Halifax, Nova Scotia rather than Mull, and those who were at home in Mull were growing old. Yet so strong was the tradition of hospitality that anyone who could get a letter of introduction to a laird like Lachlan Maclean of Torloisk might rely on being entertained by him with the utmost generosity, and being introduced to his real friends, the ladies and gentlemen of his summer retinue. In 1784, the French writer, Faujas de Saint Fond, accompanied by Mr Macdonald, an officer from Skye, whom he had met at Oban, arrived at Aros. Faujas was a devotee of the Ossianic cult, and his description of Duncan Campbell, the Duke of Argyll's tacksman at Aros, is amusing in its unconscious attempt to represent the old man in his plaid in the form of an illustration from the Ossianic literature. We shall return to Faujas' impressions when we consider the Macleans of Torloisk in Chapter 12.

The tourist route in Mull was very different in the 1780s from the well-trodden tracks of recent years. Tobermory was still a tiny hamlet, and had no important landowner to play host to the visitor, although in 1788 Lord Mountstuart noted that it was marked out for building.[18] The great glen, Glen More, was not the main line to Iona, which was approached from the sea, or by genuine pilgrims from Loch Spelve. Even Achnacraig ferry was less used than Aros Bay, but when boatmen refused to go to Aros, the traveller walked or rode from Achnacraig. Gillean's house at Scallastle was therefore a frequent stopping place. When he spoke of leaving Mull in 1787, he received a letter congratulating him on the prospect of moving.

> I am very glad you have resolved to leave Scallastle, for you and your wife were not only perfect slaves, but your House was a compleate Cake House to all Comers & Goers.[19]

Enterprising commoners probably did better out of the visitors than the host families of the lesser gentry. They provided, or were employed to lead the small ponies hired by travellers for themselves and their baggage. They were asked to be guides on tracks such as the road from Achadashenaig to Loch na Keill, and up the side of that loch to Ulva ferry and Torloisk. They were boatmen who waited at Oban and Appin, or at Keill in Morvern to take the Fingal-enraptured young men from 'woody Morven' to the 'distant isle'. Boatmen figure extensively in the journals and writings of visitors, some for their risk taking, some for their refusal to sail in what seemed fair weather. But most are immortalised for their high charges, usually calculated at length in Gaelic beforehand, or suddenly embellished with a surcharge after a display of death-defying oarsmanship. Some passengers who had bargained for landing at Aros would be dropped at Scallastle Bay without any refund but their lives.

Citoyen Chantreau, a French tourist immersed in Ossian, who chose Aros for his anchorage in 1789, related an adventure of his own, fearful in its implausibility, in which he was invited to a wedding on the mainland, at

Bonawe, after which the bride's family and the groom's family dropped off all the guests, one by one, on their various islands; a storm blew up, certainly with that tragic unpredictability which is familiar to Mull, in which the bridegroom, Monsieur Kinedy, was lost to the fury of the waves between Penmore and Tobermory. The bride, Miss Susan Campbell, threw herself into the sea on finding her husband's body, and Citoyen Chantreau moved on to see Iona.[20]

In the year of Dr Johnson's successful publication, the war of independence began in America. Several Mull men were already involved by the autumn of 1775, and in December many more wrote in response to an announcement that Fraser's Highlanders were being raised. As men were required for the ranks, the offer of some of the redundant population of the Highlands was welcomed. Walter Scott was to look back on this period and explain the increase in population by the fact that landowners were no longer able to employ their small tenants and cottars in war, and were unwilling to support them as a redundant population in peacetime.[21] Scott quoted an old Highland chief saying in indignation:

> When I was a young man, the point upon which every Highland gentleman rested his importance was the number of MEN whom his estate could support; the question next rested on the amount of his stock of BLACK CATTLE; it is now come to respect the number of SHEEP; and I suppose our posterity will enquire how many RATS or MICE an estate will produce.

The Macleans of Coll may have thought in this way about the devaluation of men, for when the Fraser Highlanders were being raised, Alexander Maclean, Younger of Coll (brother of 'Young Col') wrote to General Fraser on behalf of a younger brother.

> I would have done myself the pleasure of waiting of you, but being unacquainted I thought it more eligible to take this method of acquainting you with my request. I can with confidence assure you that if you have not already made choise of all your officers, you cannot name one that can with so much case & expedition raise whatever number of men the commission he gets shall require; for this reason, that my father has not yet by raising his rents or other harsh usages, forced his tenants to leave their country, as too many other proprietors have done, the fact is there are actually at present too many people upon his Estate, & more of the antient attatchment subsists between him & his tenants than most Highlanders can now boast of; this consequently gives him a command of men. These are the arguments upon which I ground my hopes, tho' to you as a Highlander others might be urged ...[22]

Coll is displaying a certain amount of relative humanity, in suggesting the honourable profession of war where his fellow proprietors use tactics such as rent-raising and 'harsh usages' to tip their tenants out of the nest. This is the first indication that landowners were conscious of 'harsh usages' or that raising of rent was a device to get rid of people. Since this young Coll had five younger brothers who went into the army, one might suppose that they all took a quota of men with them. Fraser's 71st Regiment was later to absorb many Mull men, including Lachlan Macquarie, the future governor of New South Wales.

It is not known how many men went, and army records offer such minimal means of identification that it is useless to attempt to surmise. Nor did the only other custodians of information, the ministers, know very much about population, and where it went. On the Argyll estates, the population rose by more than 25 per cent between 1779 and 1792, and presumably this was a general rate of increase. When the ministers were asked to compile the *Statistical Account of Scotland*, each writing his description of his own parish, many were infected by the same weakness as Dr Johnson, and thought that the careful listing of ecclesiastical remains was more important than the nature and number of the population.

For the three Mull parishes in 1790, two ministers only responded to the clarion call of the general editor, Sir John Sinclair; the minister of Torosay, Patrick MacArthur, had just been tragically drowned in the Sound. Archibald MacArthur of Kilninian and Kilmore, wrote his own piece, and a hesitant one for Torosay, or 'Pennygown' as it was still often called. Mr Dugald Campbell of the Ross, more formally known as Kilfinichen and Kilvicheoun, was a more inventive kind of writer. The information they were giving was designed for contemporary readers of the cultured classes, and not for posterity; they were not instructed to explain things so that their world could be reconstructed in 200 years' time.

Mr MacArthur's essay on Torosay began on a dignified etymological note, and managed to include the complaint nearest to the clerical heart: the absence of manses and glebes. He also mentioned a population increase of 721 since Dr Walker's day. Stone bridges came in for special mention because they were new. When it came to his own parish of Kilninian, he had to say it did not furnish much matter (meaning that, like Ulva, it had no ecclesiastical monuments). Too much barley was used for whisky, but this was being rectified; the climate was very rainy; people were long-lived; the roads were very bad, and boats were few. The population had increased by 691 in thirty-five years. Tobermory was a new village of 300 souls, which, having been founded by the British Society, and not yet deemed a failure, Mr MacArthur felt required some cherishing. His excellent analysis of the supplementary requirements of the new village is laid out in detail, but went unheeded for the usual reason of lack of funds for investment.

The trades and occupations of the rest of the parish of Kilninian are carefully enumerated, and are interesting. In about 1792, there were three artificers, three smiths, thirty-eight male and thirteen female weavers, one wright or joiner, six boat carpenters, two coopers, fourteen tailors, seven brogue makers, six cowans (drystone dyke builders) and five merchants. Five change houses or pubs served this community, and mills of various kinds. Maclean of Coll and Macdonald of Boisdale were the two proprietors singled out for praise, for their compassion, as we can already appreciate.

Mr MacArthur's assessment of the people's moral character is favourable, since all save three families are Protestants, and these three had overcome their popish bigotry. He goes out of his way to say that no emigration to America has taken place from his parish, in spite of the unhelpful terms of landholding, for few have leases of any kind, and many are required to remove so frequently that no improvements can be effected. Services are still exacted (one supposes on the estate of Torloisk and at Mishnish, and perhaps Quinish, since we know that they were stopped on the Argyll lands). Mr Archibald concludes with a crescendo of lyrical prose worthy of Rousseau himself, aimed at the heritors of Kilninian, who are the only ones who can be held responsible for a less than happy society. These heritors were, it should be repeated, Maclean of Coll, Campbell of Mishnish, Macdonald of Boisdale, Maclean of Torloisk, Campbell of Knock and the Duke of Argyll. Tobermory's 'heritor' was the Fisheries Society.

Mr Dugald Campbell's account of his parish is forty-one pages long, and a joy to read. Both in his essays upon scenery and his observations on people, he is an able writer, of whom the great poet Duncan Ban Macintyre wrote:

> Nis on a dh' eug Calum Cille
> 'S nach bu dù dha féin bhith maireann,
> Tha aoibhneas air dùthaich Mhuile
> Dùghall a bhith 'n àite Chaluim.

> Now since St Columba is deceased,
> nor could by nature be immortal,
> 'tis gladness to the land of Mull
> that Dugald is in place of Calum.[23]

Certainly Mr Dugald would please sailors, fishermen, farmers, economists and biologists and naturalists for the amount of information he gives on all of those subjects. He also reports an increase in population. His division into trades and professions is six brogue makers, two boat carpenters, one wheelwright, two smiths, three millers, six merchants, many weavers and tailors – but only one boat of any size. His curious way of emphasising the rather inbred nature of the composition of his parish was to pronounce that he had 'no Jews, negroes, gipsies, foreigners, or persons born in England' among his flock. He did have two surgeons and six houses for retailing spirits, but no lawyers. Mr Dugald's parish had its share of people who had emigrated to America, and people who had left for the 'Low Country' only to return to

Mull the following year. The proprietors of the parish, who are not named by the minister, were the duke, Charles Maclean of Kinlochaline (who married one of Sir Allan's daughters shortly after Johnson and Boswell's visit), Sir James Riddell (who was not resident), the laird of Lochbuy, Maclean of Pennycross and Hugh McGilvra of Pennyghael, all of whom, with the exception of the duke, exacted services. And nearly thirty years after Dr Walker's strong insistence on enclosure, Mr Dugald reports failure to enclose as the main obstacle to good farming. Finally, in a section on enlisting in the army, the extent of military service in the Ross of Mull is shown to be very different from the rest of the island. Between 150 and 200 men and boys seem to have gone during the minister's incumbency to join the fencible regiments, and particularly to follow Charles Maclean of Kinlochaline and Maclean of Lochbuy. For 'it is to be observed that it is only with humane proprietors, and under whom they live easily, that they are disposed to inlist.' It remains to be seen whether anyone could live easily under Kinlochaline.

Although the estate of Lochbuy was mainly situated in the parish of Torosay, some parts of it reached out into Mr Dugald Campbell's parish of Kilfinichen and Kilvicheoun. As we know that John Lochbuy is dead, and Archy Maclaine of Lochbuy was last heard of in New York, marrying Miss Barbara Lowther – an amiable young lady with a fortune of £5,000 – the identity of a humane Lochbuy, almost by this time a contradiction in terms, will be revealed in the next three chapters.

Notes

1. Published in 1936 and edited by Frederick A. Pottle and Charles H. Bennett.
2. See Chapter 6.
3. This was not Maighstir Seathan, but Iain Mac Ailein, who had lived at Inivea.
4. Pottle, p. 305.
5. Mull Presbytery Minutes. CH2/493/1. September 1768. The marriage is in Kilninian OPR.
6. Not as Fleeman suggests (pp. 307–8) the line of the present road.
7. A daughter, Margaret, born in 1772, died in February 1773, and another daughter, Anny, was baptised in October 1774, so the second Mrs MacQuarrie was between babies.
8. For example John of Garmony and Isabel Maclean of Brolass in July 1742; Lauchlan Maclean and Catharine Maclean in 1763; NAS. GD174/82 and GD174/68, contracts being signed at the ceremony.
9. For details of the case, *Allan Maclean of Drimnin, pursuer v. John Duke of Argyle, defender*, see Chapter 10.
10. Boswell's introduction to the *Journal*, p. 1.
11. Johnson, *Journey*, p. 107. 'Martin mentions Irish, but never any Earse manuscripts to be found in the islands in his time ... I believe they never existed in any other form than that which we have seen [MacPherson's].'
12. The parish was officially Kilfinichen and Kilvicheoun, but was popularly referred to as Ross.

13. Boswell's most admired judge, John McAdam of Craigengillan, whose biography he planned to write.

14. Pottle, p. 343.

15. Pottle, p. 344.

16. For the intricacies of first and second impressions, see R. W. Chapman's introduction to the EUP edition of 1970.

17. EUL. Laing MSS. McNicol, D. Letter to Dr Walker, 22 March 1775.

18. NLS. MS 9587. Mountstuart, *Journal of a Tour round the Western Isles*, 1788.

19. GRO. D3330. AM to GM, London 23 February 1787. See Chapter 13 for remarks on the English visitor's habit of accepting hospitality without paying. It seems SJ and JB took no gifts, and expected hospitality, although JB returned this kindness in Edinburgh.

20. Chantreau, P. N., *Voyage dans les trois royaumes ... fait en 1788 et 1789.*

21. Scott, *Tales of a Grandfather*, 3rd series, p. 464.

22. EUL. MS La. II. 506. Alexander Maclean, Younger of Coll to General Fraser, London, 16 December 1775.

23. *Songs of Duncan Ban Macintyre*, pp. 344–5. Duncan visited Mull and Iona in about 1787. 'He was wandering about with the wife of his youth, Mairi Bhan Og, still fair, though no longer young. He then wore ... a tartan kilt, and on his head a cap made of fox's skin. He was fair of face, with a pleasant countenance and a happy, attractive manner.' Ibid., p. xxxiii. Johnson and Boswell's host, Mr Neil Macleod, had died in 1780, and Duncan heard Mr Dugald Campbell preach at Iona 'in place of Calum' [Columba].

9

Archy Lochbuy's honeymoon

Archibald Maclaine Younger of Lochbuy – known as Archy, and sometimes as 'Baldy' as all Hebridean Archibalds are bound to be called in their less dignified moments – has been glimpsed in these chronicles in the different characters which might be the many facets of any young man. He had been a thief in Murdoch's raisin cask and fig drawer, a happy schoolboy at Dalkeith, a student of philosophy at the College of Edinburgh, an apprentice Writer to the Signet, a would-be strangler of his half-brother Gillean, a rambler in low company through the streets of Edinburgh, a 'lovely son' to John Lochbuy, and a 'dangerous planner' of 'wild designs' to those members of his clan who took an interest in his welfare.

Too proud and independent to be thirled to a regiment, he had gone to America more in quest of a fortune than with any view of a career, but caught up in the excitement of the early stages of the American war, had offered himself to General Burgoyne as a recruit, had been imprisoned, exchanged and released. Finding himself ineligible for a commission in the regiments stationed in Nova Scotia because he had not pulled the usual strings at home, he found his position as a private soldier untenable, and incompatible with his rank as a Highland gentleman. Given the chance to return to Great Britain to settle his affairs after the death of his father, he left Canada for London in the summer of 1778, narrowly missing the arrival of Lachlan MacQuarrie of Ulva, who was carrying two letters for him which never reached their destination.[1]

Hearing that the new Lochbuy was in England, a feverish correspondence began between the creditors in Edinburgh, Inveraray and Mull about Archy's plans. Did anybody know, had anyone heard? Was Archy returning to take charge of the estate? How could the rentals be sett or leases signed without his consent? What was to be the plan for payment of debts? But nobody had heard from the young laird, who was in fact nearing thirty, and should be a responsible man, matured by his experience of war and hardship. The only sure sign that he was in existence was the regular withdrawal of cash from London. Allan MacDougall, Archy's man of business in Edinburgh, suggested meetings in vain. Even Donald Maclaine, now a seedsman and merchant in Edinburgh, wrote to Archy to persuade him that he was needed in Mull, that his lady mother had not seen him since her husband's death, and knew not where to live or what to do, or what her settlement would be. John Gruline, puzzled that his letter to Canada had received no answer, wrote to London, and was rewarded by being drawn on for cash. To everyone's astonishment,

Archy made no move to come to Scotland, and in April 1779, he wrote to Gillean to say that he had advised his mother to live with her son-in-law, that he did not think the old castle of Moy should be repaired, and that John Gruline could have the farm there. He then wrote a page of advice about the schooling of Gillean's oldest son, seven-year-old Allan:

> I hope my little friend Allan is turning out a good scholar. I wish he was now out of that Country and at some good and cheap school in England, as the sooner he leaves that the better, and I had rather pay one half of his expenses at a good school in England than that he should remain one year longer in that part, for these four or five years to come is the period of his life that is most essential to him to learn anything ...

Archy seems to have undergone that mysterious transmogrification which is frequently attributed to Scottish lairds at this period, whereby they began to speak with an English accent, sent their children to English schools, and aped English manners. If it was also true that an Englishman was not a gentleman unless he was in debt, he had heartily embraced the state of the debtor, and would not return to Edinburgh where broadly spoken lawyers still had the quaint idea that a good man paid his creditors, and where gentlemen who owed some money here and there were treated like sinners. When Murdoch Maclaine arrived in London again on regimental business, Archy prevailed upon him to take up his case and buy a company for him. He also gave him power of attorney. Arranging the funds with the estate executry, and leaving Murdoch to sign the documents, Archy duly sailed out of Portsmouth in April 1779.

At home, in Mull, John Maclaine of Gruline was left with the running of the estate of Lochbuy. Gillean had little to do with the larger estate, but the lands of Scallastle, Ledirkle and Garmony had remained in his hands when his tack was confirmed both before and after John Lochbuy's death. The widowed Lady Lochbuy did try to live with her daughter Catherine and her son-in-law Hugh McGilvra of Pennyghael, and of course never received any of the farms in her original jointure, which Gillean had successfully wrested from her.

In September 1779, Archy, in spite of his payment, and his cousin's efforts on his behalf, was refused a company in the 42nd Regiment, but a month later was offered a small light infantry company by his kinsman, Allan Maclean of Torloisk, whose Royal Highland Emigrants had now been established and upgraded. This unfortunate connection with Allan Maclean was to be the beginning of his downfall.

Allan Maclean of Torloisk was a complex man, as will be seen in Chapter 10, but at this point his public faults had been few, even if his private ones were many, and concealed from the world's gaze. His principal shortcoming, if it could be called that, was in seeing himself as the great recruiter of Highland soldiers, and as a father figure to his Argyll relations. From being an early supporter of the Jacobite cause, he had gone into the Dutch service, and, distinguishing himself at Bergen-op-Zoom, had entered the British army, serving with distinction in the Seven Years' War in North America. Many Highland soldiers had remained in America at the end of that war, settling in the Mohawk Valley and in the Carolinas. To his credit, Maclean had maintained a fatherly interest in those old soldiers of his, and his knowledge of their settlements as well as their sentiments of loyalty had made him the ideal person to reassemble them in 1775 for fresh service in the government cause. He recruited from the old 42nd, the old 77th and the old 78th with astonishing success, perhaps with blandishments which they were unable to resist, such as promises of land, but official documents appear to show that he had the sanction of the War Office for such promises. He and his American recruits had appeared at the eleventh hour when Quebec was under siege in December 1775, and as a result Maclean and his men were remembered for a perfectly timed piece of strategy and for saving Canada.

A great many of the Mull men who took part both in the Seven Years' War and the revolutionary war belonged to Maclean's and John Small's Royal Highland Volunteers. Murdoch Maclaine, taken under Maclean's wing at once because of his early co-operation with Allan from Edinburgh, was given a company in the 2nd Battalion, but as we have seen, he was found to have valuable gifts as an emissary and diplomat, and sent on special missions. Murdoch and Allan knew the rules of army life: Murdoch was at his best when tact and resourcefulness were required; Allan was at his best in action. Between his moments of action, Allan plotted to make himself more popular and indispensable to all his friends and relations. He arranged the promotion of this one and that one, always taking care to promote his cronies just so far, and no further. The ultimate aim of this man was to keep his own good name, and to have it made famous in London and in Mull, as that of a great benefactor to the cause of the Highlander's military reputation.

The blood relationship between Murdoch and Allan, and between Allan and Archy was not close, but they could all be shown to be third or fourth cousins, Murdoch and Archy being the closest in the triangle. It was an element in their friendship which hardly needed to be spoken, and which every *Muileach* understood, and still understands – except perhaps Archy. Archy had been seduced by a sassenach constituent in relationships: the idea of the English gentleman. And in admitting into his being this new concept, he had thrown out any understanding he had ever had of what made a Highland gentleman. Unlike Murdoch and Alexander of Coll, his own contemporary, he was unable to be a Highland gentleman and an English type of gentleman at the same time.

As captain by purchase of his light infantry company, Archy served mostly by moving his men from one frontier post to another along the northern line from Niagara, Detroit, Deer Island and the top of Lake Champlain, to

Montreal. At Montreal, he came into close contact with Allan Maclean, now the military governor, and his wife Janet, who, having no family, accompanied her husband everywhere. Archy called Janet Maclean 'the Madame', and described her as a prostitute, always an unwise impression to commit to paper. Even to Murdoch, he wrote from Quebec:

> Madam Maclean now behaves ten times more foolishly, if possible, than ever you saw her. She has drawn up with a German officer who is never apart from her one hour from 8 in the morning till 12 at night. In short they are the common ridicule of all Canada, & the husband more so as being silly enough to allow it. She made the Brigadier turn me out of the Light Infantry Company, as I did not pay a degree of Adoration to her which she thinks she is entitled to from everybody.[2]

About the same time, Archy wrote to Gillean describing his fellow officers as:

> a number of trifling upstarts out of the Dirt, who have neither money, men, or, I may say, any friends who could be looked upon as men of Interest. Yet by their friends being assiduous now get promotion in many of the new levies ... They are without any knowledge of the Service, and had they had the common education to qualify them even to sit in Camp with Gentlemen ... However, this I entirely gave up ...[3]

But in 1781 an incident occurred which should have taken the wind out of Archy's sails. In Montreal, on 21 March, Allan Maclean desired, through his brigade major, that Archy call on his commanding officer when in Montreal, for he had been reported to be in town for two nights without seeing Allan. Impatient of such reprimands, Archy ignored the note, and four weeks later was before a disciplinary board. Here he was so cocksure that he informed the board that in 1777 his commanding officer had erased the name of one of his favourites, Neil Maclean, in order to give the same commission as lieutenant to Archy. The board, much embarrassed, had been obliged to take note of this, which although not a heinous offence, was against army practice. Brigadier Maclean was in turn obliged to put Archy under arrest for having made the assertion. When Archy was re-examined before Brigadier Maclean, his story was found to be plausible by the board, whereupon the Brigadier accused him of other more serious offences, such as receiving pay in two battalions at the same time. A court martial was ordered and Archy was kept under arrest, using his time to write to the Duke of Argyll, requesting that the character of Brigadier Maclean should be made known to the king. Archy's self-confidence knew no bounds. He also planned to carry on his own defence at the court martial. He had not, after all, been trained in logic and the law for nothing.

The court martial was held in Quebec on 9 August 1782, the crime being 'conduct unbecoming the character of a gentleman and an officer' as demonstrated by Archy's denial of having received two sets of pay, his assertion that Maclean had made an erasure, and his falsification of the date of his original commission. The hearing lasted three weeks, with long-drawn-out explanations of Archy's purpose in coming to America. Allan Maclean denied meeting Archy in New York in 1776. 'Nor had I the least idea that an only son, his father old and infirm, with an estate of £1,100 a year, would come to America to look for a subaltern's commission in a provincial corps.' At the end, the prisoner was pronounced not guilty of the charge, but guilty of an assertion not supported by the evidence. So Archy was suspended from duty for six months, and was to be publicly reprimanded before the regiment. It was a decision aimed in the short term at preserving military discipline, but had to be sent to the king for final judgement. This judgement was received from London in May 1783. His Majesty, upon a general view of the conduct of the prisoner as it appeared at the trial, thought fit to dismiss Captain Archibald Maclaine from his service, although the captain would receive pay up to the date of his demission.

From the beginning of the breach with Allan Maclean, Archy had informed Gillean of his predicament in a breezy manner which cut no ice with his half brother, but omitted to communicate with the sensible cousin who had worked so hard to obtain a commission for him, and who had written many letters to which he had received no answer. In the undated copy he kept of a letter written to Archy in 1781, Murdoch did not hide his exasperation.

My Dear Cousin,
Your favour of the 27 August 1780 is the last I received from you, and tho' I wrote you in that year from Britain, and on my return to this Place, many letters, I have no intelligence of these getting your length, and I am very sorry for it, as I was so very Plain & Full in such matters as we are both interested in, that if I was sure of your receiving them, trouble might be saved to both, but as I am in doubts, I beg leave to inclose a Coppy of my letter ... I in the most anxious manner do beg and intreat for a meeting with you as soon as the nature of our present situations will admit. The manner I would have you follow is to ask for leave of absence to go to Britain, and if convenient, by way of Halifax, where I will most probably remain untill I receive information from you of your intention. It would be tedious & improper here to explain all my meaning, as I again repeat to you that nothing but an immediate meeting with me will please or satisfy me. If you have not Interest to procure the leave necessary I daresay your resignation will be accepted of.

The misunderstanding between General Maclean and you, which gives me Great Concern, is too Extensive & Dark for me now to enter upon. I'm sorry to allow that from its first appearance it sticks against you ... Whatever difference there may be between the General & you, I'm persuaded he'll forward your meeting me, and as I am now at liberty to go when I think proper, I only wait for your Answer ... I now wish you to proceed from

Cannada to Britain at once, especially if you determine against going to settle on your Estate, for in that event I am of Opinion that you will approve of trying your luck in the East Indies, especially as John MacPherson and John Stewart of Hampstead desire the General to send you after them, and as nothing but some mistake of your own will prevent them providing Handsomely for you ... it is the only course open for you, providing you decline settling at home, for in the 84th 1st Battalion *you cannot nor ought to remain.*

Archy's rash plan of going to India was countenanced by Murdoch only as a means of extricating the younger man from the mess he was in, but the court martial intervened to make it impossible to provide Archy with such a respectable means of escape. Dismissed from the service, Archy made his way to New York, and some time during the winter of 1783–84 he became friendly with a young man called Thomas Lowther, by whom he was introduced to a scheme for the purchase of land in Virginia, to which he subscribed his name. He was financing himself by drawing on everyone at home, including John Gruline, and Sir Allan Maclean, his mother's brother. Every attempt to borrow money in Scotland was accompanied by a letter (for he had to instruct the victim to pay, and not to refuse credit) which was the only indication his relatives received of his sentence in the court martial and his present plans. 'I have made a purchase in Virginia of 10,000 acres for £150,' Archy wrote to Murdoch in 1784, 'but say nothing of this.' He did not add that the purchase had been conditional upon the promise of supplying 100 families as settlers. One of Archy's schemes was, no doubt, to order the long-suffering John Maclaine, tacksman of Gruline, to round up 100 families from the estate, and send them out to America.

Drawn into the Lowther family circle, Archy had impressed Thomas's 17-year-old sister, Barbara Lowther. With considerable insight into Archy's nature, with a fancy for him which was all her own, and in the intriguing handwriting of an obliging friend, she sent a letter which was calculated to excite the animal in the young laird of Lochbuy without arousing his distaste for under-educated upstarts. The epistle which he received was undated and unsigned:

To have seen you and to admire you are the same. I conceived the fatal Passion last night. I thought of you while awake, and dreamed of you while asleep, but still resolved to stifle my attachment. But no words can express my sensations this morning. I went to Church with a determined resolution [and asked] God for strength and power to conquer the Flame, and resist the Temptation of your Person and Charms. But your appearance dissipated my Resolve, and yielded me a Prey to Love. In short (pardon my weakness), if you are capable of the tender Passion, and have ever experienced the Power of Love, you will meet me at six o'clock in the Churchyard this Evening. Either the world deceive me, or I am worthy of admiration. My

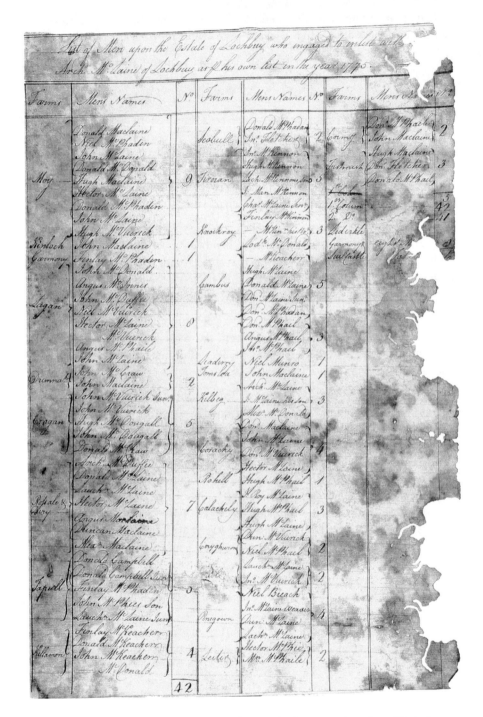

List of men from the Lochbuy estate who promised to go to America with Archy
Lochbuy in 1775. (*NAS. GD174/2096*)

Fortune and Rank are not inconsiderable. But come, my dear McLean, and judge for yourself. To live without you would be to cease to exist.[4]

This letter, so beautifully written, so faint and feminine upon the page, must indeed have stirred Archy, since he kept it, and presumably kept the appointment also. The next letter was signed with the initials BL.

The conflicting Passions which have rent my Bosom for these few days past are too much for frail nature to sustain … You may judge of my feelings when I saw you treated in the manner you was last Evening … [here much of the page is lost] … I wish much to see you. Meet me then tomorrow afternoon at Miss Pindar's, for I am determined you never shall be insulted again on my Account. Adieu, your BL.[5]

The next news of this passionate affair comes in a letter from Barbara's father, William Lowther, on 7 March 1784. He had been investigating the credentials of his daughter's suitor, and had been satisfied with a report of Archy from 'a Gentleman acquainted with you in Europe'.

… therefore my scruples are intirely removed, and if your Designs are really Honourable, which I have not the least Reason to Doubt, I am perfectly satisfied. Excuse the Anxiety of a Parent for the Happiness of his Children. But let me see no triffling & playing like Children when the family only are present. Every sentence may be spoke out.[6]

It was an odd reprimand to a man of thirty-four, that he should behave in company in such an immature manner, but Mr Lowther may have intended the rebuke to reach his daughter Barbara, who was clearly what James Boswell might have called a 'filly'. The letter did indicate that the parent was giving his consent, which should be noted, as within a short time, rumours were rife in 'the Country' that Archy had eloped with an heiress. But William Lowther seemed quite relieved to be quit of this troublesome nymphet.

The young couple were married at New York on 4 April 1784, the anniversary of old John Lochbuy's death. Archy was probably unaware of the significance of the date. Shortly afterwards, they moved on the first stage of their honeymoon to Jamaica. The bridegroom was later reported as having some property due to him there, but this was likely to be just one of his many 'wild designs', and nothing else was heard of it. The next plan was that he would go to the south of France, where he could 'live cheap'. At least this is backed up by evidence in the form of a letter written from Kingston, Jamaica, by the French consul, M. Pottineau Choffard to M. Caille, an official at Dunkirk, asking for a safe conduct through the French port for the young couple.

Monsieur,
Nous prenons la liberté de vous recommander Monsieur et Madame Maclaine que NS Choffard a eu le plaisir de connaître pendant le séjour qu'il a fait

dans cette ville. Leurs voyages doivent les conduire dans votre ville, et nous espérons de leur rendre leur séjour le plus agréable possible, sans pareille en toute autre occasion. Nous vous prions de disposer absolument de nous. Nous avons l'honneur d'être tout parfaitement, Monsieur, Votre humble et tout obéissant serviteur, Pottineau Choffard.[7]

The ship departed early in August from Jamaica on her way to London. She was called the *Hero*, and Archy had ordered provisions as his contribution to the captain's table. They included whole sheep taken on board to be slaughtered, as was the custom before refrigerated food containers were thought of, and considerable quantities of wine. Within twelve leagues of Cuba, Archy and Barbara were sitting at dinner with the captain, Daniel Sinclair, and another cabin passenger, also a Scot, named Daniel Munro. From the moment of embarkation, Lochbuy and Munro had conceived a mutual dislike, confined until now to verbal sarcasms, and fuelled by the prejudices engendered by vague notions they had of each other from imperfectly remembered past connections. It was all rather reminiscent of the night at Duart Castle when the effects of Governor Lane's grog had sent Archy off in search of his sword.[8] At the captain's table on board the *Hero*, Archy boasted that he had once made all the Glasgow magistrates drunk at a dinner party. Munro suggested he'd given them whisky punch. 'No,' said Lochbuy, 'better claret than ever was at your grandfather's table.' 'What do you say, Sir?' said Munro. Lochbuy repeated his words. Munro retorted: 'So says a fellow that was broke by a Court Martial.' Lochbuy threw a bottle at Munro's head; Barbara prevented Munro from throwing one back. Captain Maclaine of Lochbuy called for his sword, swearing that he would cut off Munro's ears, but the captain had wisely hidden it away. Munro returned to his cabin, and Lochbuy to his, but within minutes they were below decks, wrestling and thrusting, until Munro stuck his sword in Lochbuy, 'in and upon the left shoulder, near the left collar bone, a mortal wound of the breadth of half an inch and the depth of fourteen inches, of which he instantly died'.[9] As the newspapers put it three months later, Captain Maclaine was stabbed to the heart, while Ensign Munro was confined apart from the cabin passengers, one of whom (said the *Edinburgh Courant* dramatically) was the widow of the deceased. Then, to add to the drama and excitement of the case, on the vessel's arrival in Ireland, the murderer found means to make his escape.

Such a murder had to be tried by the Admiralty, but first the prisoner had to be caught, brought to London, and indicted. The *Hero* did not arrive in England until November, delayed by the hue and cry caused by the escape of Daniel Munro at Cork. Murdoch, as Archy's friend and relation was summoned from Edinburgh, but as he was in Mull, an express was sent there. If he had been waiting for a meeting with his cousin to determine the future of the estate before they went their separate ways for ever – Archy to Europe and Murdoch to his lands in Nova Scotia, there was now to be a much longer wait than he could ever have imagined. And for Murdoch it was not simply a matter of waiting for the trial and its outcome; he also had to put an end to the uncertainty about the succession of Lochbuy. As the only surviving son of Lachlan of Knockroy, he was himself heir of line. In London, in January 1785, Murdoch received a most surprising letter from Allan MacDougall, his lawyer in Edinburgh, who spoke of the extent of the Lochbuy debts, and then went on

> Speaking of this to Mr Gillean Maclaine, he informed me that he had in his possession an Entail executed by Lochbuy of his Estate, wherein, failing heirs male of Lochbuy's body, you and your heirs male were called to the Succession, whom failing Mr Gillean Maclaine himself, his children, and several other individuals. As I have not seen this Deed of Entail, I can give no Opinion about it, but unless very ample & proper powers are thereby given to the heirs of entail so as to enable them to pay off the Debts, it may create a Confusion. It might be very proper in Lochbuy to execute a Disposition of his estate to any series of heirs he thought proper that could not be gratuitously altered by those heirs, but the propriety of his executing a strict Deed of Entail, & how matters are now to be conducted so as to get your titles made up and matters put upon a proper plan of management is a thing of serious consideration & deliberation, & well merits the taking of advice of the ablest Counsel at the Bar for your government, but I will take upon me to do nothing in the affair without your instruction. I am always &c....[10]

Mr Allan MacDougall, who was fifteen years younger than Murdoch, and who had qualified with Colquhoun Grant in 1770, was too young to remember the case of Reduction against Gillean of twenty years before. What Murdoch thought of this development when he first heard of the entail is not known. Fifteen years later he was to express the opinion that Gillean had been the 'chief promoter of the entail, which was executed in the most private manner at his house, and left in his custody.'[11] The terms of the entail directed the succession to Murdoch (who would have succeeded had there been no entail), but failing his heirs, as Mr MacDougall had pointed out, it would go to Gillean and his heirs. As the entail was dated in May 1776, it should be remembered that at the time Gillean had prevailed upon Archy to make an entail (and on Archy's part the idea had been to have more cash available to him), Murdoch Maclaine was a married man, and Anne Learmonth was alive and well in Edinburgh. Murdoch and Anne were childless, but Gillean had a healthy four-year-old son called Allan Maclaine.

As the entail provided a means of paying off some of the debts of the estate legitimately through a clause which allowed marginal lands to be sold for the sole purpose of paying a predecessor's debts, with the permission of the other heirs of entail, it may have seemed to both Murdoch and his legal adviser as not a bad thing, although, as Mr MacDougall had rightly observed, likely to create confusion. But since the entail was produced, no doubts could be cast upon it, and matters had to proceed. Young Mrs Maclaine, who had had a honeymoon of four months and a widowhood of five, had to be interrogated about a possible pregnancy. For all that Murdoch knew, she might one day be acting the part of a Marie de Guise with an infant heir to Lochbuy.[12]

It is not known whether Archy's remains had been buried at sea, but Barbara arrived in London with her husband's effects. These included some letters, two regimental coats, one green coat, six waistcoats, six shirts, six pairs of silk stockings, a steel horseman sword, a pocket pistol, a pair of gold cufflinks, a shaving box and twelve guineas. The men who made the inventory of his possessions were Robert Wells, Barbara's father's friend and agent in London (alerted by Mr Lowther, who had learned of the tragedy long before the *Hero* reached England), and General Allan Maclean, who, since the peace, had retired to London. The general must have cast his eye over the letter about the passionate assignation in the churchyard, but he must have scrutinised more carefully incoming letters received by Archy at the time of the court martial. Murdoch's missive about the misunderstanding between Archy and his commanding officer was impeccably correct, which is more than can be said of Archy's own, in one of which he had told Murdoch that Allan Maclean had 'a little trick of keeping letters'.[13] But as all the letters in Archy's possession happened to side with Maclean, there was no need for the retired officer to slip any into his pocket, although he possibly had that in mind when he offered to help. Instead, Allan had reverted to his character of being the grave father to his afflicted clan. For the first few days he offered to take the widow under his wing, with his wife, the 'madame' who had also been traduced by the dead man. After that, Mr Robert Wells took his turn of looking after Barbara. He and his wife found the young woman very trying. She lied about money, did not keep appointments or answer letters, sailed out of rooms in high dudgeon, and behaved in an unbecoming, histrionic manner. There is a hint also that her appearance was bizarre, as Murdoch wrote to Allan MacDougall on 20 December 1784:

> Mr Wills, who approved much of the widow's going to Scotland with me, has just had a letter from hir father in New York, who after hearing of the Death of his son-in-law, writes to Mr Wills desiring he may take charge of the widow for *his*, hir father's behoof. Mr Wills now disapproves of hir going to Scotland ... Her connections and *appearance* would only contribute to additional reflections upon the conduct of my deceast friend, which I would now incline to smother ... She and all hir friends have declair'd hir non Pregnancy and therefore I hope you will proceed with the proper caution in such legal matters as is suitable in my situation ... As the widows of Lochbuy in general complained of the treatment of their husbands successors I would wish to avoid that error ...[14]

Daniel Munro came of a very respectable Scottish family, and his idea in escaping was not so much to thwart justice as to be given a fair trial under a legal system which he understood. He believed that a trial in Scotland would be fairer than one under the Admiralty's more rigid code. He remained at large for some time, but those who pressed for his trial suspected that he was being concealed in Glasgow. And so Murdoch began on a constant and repetitive trail back and forward between London and Glasgow, rather too much like his military jaunts between Halifax, Nova Scotia and New York. In London, he stayed with Allan Maclean and his wife, and Allan's unmarried sister, Miss Mary Maclean of Torloisk, who lived under the protection of her brother. In Edinburgh, his nephew Donald, in his limited way, was able to look after some of Murdoch's affairs. In Glasgow, Gillean's spies were skulking with their ears to the ground listening for clues about Munro.

'Munro's friends at Glasgow promise he will stand his tryall,' Gillean wrote. 'I wish he may.' As week followed week in the period before Munro was found, Barbara extended her circle of trouble-making. Robert Wells thought she was 'very sensible and clever', a phrase which does not have the same meaning as it would carry today, but implied that she was touchy and full of guile, knew her rights, and was what was to be called in a later age 'streetwise'. It was discovered that she had had no dowry, and the fortune of £5,000 which had been reported in the newspapers had not materialised. There had been no marriage contract. Such things, said Mr T. Lowther, were extremely rare in America. Mr William Lowther, whose business remains a mystery, had suffered crushing losses, and was unable to provide for his daughter. It fell to Murdoch to give her some kind of aliment and interim expenses, but she refused to sign receipts for the money, and went about telling people that he gave her nothing. She was quite irrational, a child in the body of a woman.

At last, on 21 June 1785, Daniel Munro was indicted 'for that he, not having the fear of God, but being moved and seduced by the instigation of the devil, on the sixth day of August in the twenty-fourth year of His Majesty's reign, with force and arms upon the high sea ... on board a Certain Ship called the *Hero*, did feloniously, wilfully and in Malice Aforethought ... make an assault with a certain drawn sword, and did Strike, Stab and Thrust the said Archibald Maclaine.'

Mr Maclaine was not open to the entreaties of his own wife. She kneeled and conjured him to be quiet, but on the contrary he declared he would not, and made use of every extraordinary declaration which was 'My dear, if you ever again open your lips on this subject to me, I will never again Cohabit with you'. Mr Maclaine was at this time in his own bed room ... making enquiry after his sword ... he took the ship's steward by the neck and said 'You rascal, where is my Sword?' Mr Maclaine came to the spot in a very violent passion. Mr Munro said the ship was not a proper place for such encounters, and promised a meeting on shore. Mr Maclaine bared his breast and dared Mr Munro to strike him ... when stabbed Mr Maclaine exclaimed with these words, 'Oh! oh! oh!' at which instant I perceived the sword broken in two; I instantly ran into the Ship's Cabin when I heard Mr Maclaine choaking with a rumbling in his throat, a torrent of blood issuing from his mouth, and expiring. The sword had entered the left armpit in a direction with his heart.[15]

Under English law there was no medium between wilful murder and acquittal, and the judge, Sir James Marriott, directed the jury to acquit the prisoner. The verdict of not guilty was returned, Daniel Munro walked free, and the relatives of Lochbuy were free also to walk away to their inheritance.

Barbara Maclaine was free too. No longer would she be shuttled between one family and another. Her last stay in London had been with the Rev. John Agnew, who, as if talking to a child, had warned her of 'improper hours, places and dangers about this city'. She had turned on him with the most ill-tempered abuse, saying that even Captain Murdoch Maclaine of Lochbuy had thought him an old dog: Mr Agnew wrote to Captain Maclaine to ask him to avow or disavow this remark.[16] A Mr Alexander Maclean of Kensington wrote to Murdoch too; the young widow had informed him that Captain Maclaine of Lochbuy had asked her to sign a receipt for £300, but had given her only £31. Surely, said this Mr Maclean, the Captain would not try to injure a young woman under his protection, the widow of his next-of-kin, by whose death he became possessor of a good estate. Yet a number of genteel people suspect him, which the writer hopes is not founded in truth.[17]

The legal proceedings were not over for Murdoch. Barbara was to raise an action in the Court of Session in Edinburgh against the estate of Lochbuy for her due portion. Refusing to settle the matter privately with Murdoch, because he had made her sign a receipt for £300, she was convinced that the courts would do more for her. She was still to visit her mother-in-law, old Lady Lochbuy, who lived with one of her daughters in Port Glasgow, and she might take it into her head to view the Mull estate which she had so narrowly missed possessing. In the meantime, in October, she went on a jaunt to Flanders, like any American in London, except that she went in the company of a man. When she did communicate with Murdoch, it was in the backward-sloping handwriting of a child. The young woman of the fatal passion was gone.

Among the papers belonging to Archy which were returned to England in 1784, was a letter in a primitive, but comprehensible form of French, from one Charlotte Lemaitre, and purporting also to be from a child with the name of Washington Maclaine. Archy had not departed from the Lochbuy tradition of sowing wild oats.

Mon chere et mable McLaine je vous ecrist cette lettre pour vous souter une bonne santez et jaispere mon chere petit que vous avez arivez heure-usement et que vous avez toute sorte de prosperiter dans votre voiage, votre cher fils ... [and there followed some pages of praise for her son].

Charlotte Lemaitre, 23 Septembre 1783. Washington McLaine, 25 Septembre 1783.[18]

Also among the papers was a receipt from William Lowther for £90 for a 'negro wench' called Dorcas.

In the nine years that had elapsed since Archy Lochbuy left Mull for America, the people of the island were not greatly affected by his absence. It is a testimony to his lack of influence on the tide of events that his name was not handed down in legends false or true. A new and good Duke of Argyll had inherited the Argyll estates in 1770, and was slowly making changes. Ulva was sold in a judicial sale in 1777. John Lochbuy died in April 1778, unregretted. The Rev. Neil Macleod, minister of the parish of Ross, had died in 1780. The act against the wearing of Highland dress was repealed. The roads appointed to be made in Mull were held up for lack of tools, although 152 men had been earmarked for their construction by statute labour. On 10 December 1783, Sir Allan Maclean died, so that the chief of the clan was now another exiled member of the family of Duart, with, some thought, a doubtful genealogy. The years 1782–84 were famine years, with snow lying on the ground for two months in 1783. The reduction of regiments in 1783 sent soldiers back to Mull, including Lachlan Macquarie, later of New South Wales. Lachlan Maclean, laird of Torloisk, completed in 1783 a brand new house on the site of the cottage of boulders and turf which his ancestors had enjoyed, and invited Faujas de Saint-Fond to stay there. The Stewarts of Achadashenaig, later to be called Glen Aros, were shining lights of industry and improvement in 1784, and MacQuarrie of Ulva had settled back into his customary habits of amiable fecklessness. An undocumented and almost surreptitious trickle of emigration had been taking place since before the American revolution through the back door of northern Ireland,[19] and the west coast Scottish ports of Greenock and Port Glasgow. There were large numbers of people from 'the Country' trading in Jamaica and Antigua. The names of the islands of the lesser Antilles group were as familiar to many as the names of the Hebrides.[20] As several had left Mull first to learn their trade in the lowlands, the move to the West Indies or America was not seen by them as permanent. Among this exodus there was a not inconsiderable number of surgeons with apprenticeships rather than university medical qualifications, among them being John McGuarie of Ormaig who left in 1774, Dr John Maclean in Brolass, his son Dr Allan Maclean who went to Quebec in 1779, Dr Donald Maclaine who served abroad before settling at Callachilly, Charles Maclean of Bunessan, an army surgeon, and Archibald Maclean, a surgeon in Jamaica who died in 1772.

These people were educated, but often came from penniless families. It would be difficult to describe them either as 'half-gentry' or 'middle class'. Their social position was defined by the fact that they spoke English as well as Gaelic, wrote English, and had often learned some book-keeping. They could not afford to buy an ensigncy in the army. They might take their wives

Rental of the Estate of Lochbuy Crop 1781

Penny Land	Possessions	Tennants Names	Wedders Cash	Particular Rents including conversion of Wedders £ s. d	Total Rents £ s. d
		Ardmeanach			
		1/8 Donald Campbell	1	4 5 "	
		1/8 Dun. Campbell	1	4 5 "	
		1/8 John Campbell Senior	1	4 5 "	
10.1	Tapul	1/8 John Campbell Junr.	1	4 5 "	
		1/8 Dun. Duffie	1	4 5 "	
		1/8 Angus McPhaden	1	4 5 "	
		1/8 Lauch. McLean Senior	1	4 5 "	
		1/8 Lauch & Ann McLeans	1	4 5 "	34 "
		1/8 Allan McKechran	1	4 " "	
		1/8 Chas. McKechran	1	4 " "	
10.2	Calumore	1/8 Samuel McKechran	1	4 " "	
		1/8 Allan McDonald	1	4 " "	
		1/8 John McSherrÌe	1	4 " "	
		1/8 Dun. McGilvra	1	4 " "	
		1/4 Dugd. McDougall	2	8 " "	32 " "
		1/4 David Obúrn	"	4 5 "	
		1/4 William Oburn	"	4 5 "	
10.4	Scobul	1/4 John McPhaden	"	4 5 "	
		1/4 Donald McPhaden	"	4 5 "	17 "
10.4	Tirouran	Chas and John McLains	8	" " "	30 " "
		1/8 Hugh McKechran	1	4 " "	
		1/8 John McKinnon Senr.	1	4 " "	
		1/8 John McKinnon Junr.	1	4 " "	
10.1	Camis & Shiconel	1/8 John McNeill	1	4 " "	
		1/8 Don. McPhaden	1	4 " "	
		1/8 Finlay McPhaden	1	4 " "	
		1/8 Lua. McDonald	1	4 " "	
		1/8 Chas and Hugh McLains	1	4 " "	
	Miln of Camis	Neill McLain		5 " "	37 " "
		1/4 John McKinnon	1	3 15	
		1/4 John McPhaden	1	3 15	
10.1	Knochroy	1/4 Lauch. McKechran	1	3 15	
		1/4 Neill McQuarie & Pr. McKinnon	1	3 15	15 " "
		Carried forward 36			£ 165 " "

John McLains

The first page of a rental of the estate of Lochbuy, compiled in 1781.
(*NAS. GD174/789/14*)

with them, and they might have half a dozen children abroad, yet still the ministers who composed the *Statistical Account* did not refer to them as 'emigrants'. When, in the 1790s, the ministers said, 'There has been no emigration from the parish in the last year', they meant that there had been no 'fever' of emigration which 'caught on' or 'set everyone afloat'. The word emigration seems to have been used with a specific and collective meaning, and did not apply to a few individuals working independently. It was applied to a large number of poor people who moved as a community and stayed as a community. These people, the commoners, lived within townships such as Tirergain, Knocknafenaig, Saorphein, Siaba, Ardchoirk, Fishnish, Scallastlebeg, Corrynachenachy, Tavool, Scobul, Soriby, Haunn, Inivea, Baliacrach, Sorne, Reraig, Tenga and Penmore, to name only a few. When the people moved, it was, as Boswell had observed in Armadale in Skye, like the dance which they called 'America'.

This brilliant metaphor of Boswell's[21] gives a different view of the Highlanders' collective decision to emigrate from the usual sad accounts, and the standard emotive paintings. In Mull there were two kinds, as has been said. The entrepreneurs were going in stages, but the commoners could have been counted if anyone had thought of doing it. The emigrant ships were leaving from Mull. Some are glimpsed in a throwaway remark in a letter, lying at anchor in small, isolated harbours. In retrospect it seems furtive, but no one in the 1780s possessed a social conscience. In 1785, a number of people from the township of Saorphein, near Loch Assapol, embarked on a ship bound for America. Nobody knew their plan, or their destination. But one passenger on that ship thought of giving the following information to John Maclaine, tacksman of Gruline:

New York, 5th Feb. 1786
Sir
I have taken the Liberty of Acquainting you of the unhappy news of our unlucky passage when I have loss all my family only myself alon stick on a spar or a piece of the mast where with it pleased God to save my Life; after which I have been sick; and confin'd for nine weeks in one place, about twenty miles from where our ship rack. She struck on the Beich by one o'clock in Morning, and stood so till six next evening when she broke all to pieces; same time I made the attempt by seting myself on the spar as above mentioned; and pleased God the wind Right to the shore. Run fatigued and stiffled with Cold, and Late in the Night so had remained on the shore all remaining part of the night exposed to wind and rain and worse of storm; bein badly wounded in time of the ship cracking almost ended my life. My father came to shore allys and children I saw none of them, by my bein unable to move. But I am informed by others that my Mother came ashore and is sick in the same place. A daughter of Neil McKinnon from Rossal escap'd all damages and hurt, and left there with a Gentleman who

promis'd to take care of her, in doing her the dutiful careing as his own Child, her Father, Mother, and all the rest of the Children was lost; by bein sick and hurt I was not Eable to go so as to see anybody, except my Father and Neil McKinnons youngest child; I was carried away in a Waggon to the above mention'd place where I remained nine weeks, but Recovering I got a passage free to New York; where I remain'd Ever since, and Expects to go to Arade in the spring ship's carpenter. Sir, I am your Humble Servt.

Hector McLaine

son to Hugh McLain from Kilbhickeoin, Ross.[22]

Emigration was undirected and risky in the 1780s, but it went on. Somewhere in America, two families may have cherished their incredible stories of a Maclaine and a Mackinnon ancestor surviving a dreadful shipwreck on an unknown coast. If there were other such shipwrecks, they have not been recorded.

Notes

1. GRO. Uncatalogued MSS. LMQ to GM, 31 August 1778. 'Your brother sail'd from this country 5 or 6 weeks ago. Yours & Gruline's letters I shall keep till I be bearer myself ...'
2. NAS. GD174/2147. AMLB to MM, Quebec, 16 August 1780.
3. NAS. GD174/1339/1. AMLB to GM, 84th Camp at La Prairie, 24 September 1780.
4. NAS. GD174/1357. Anon. to AMLB, n.d.
5. NAS. GD174/1358. BL to AMLB, n.d.
6. NAS. GD174/1363. William Lowther to AMLB, 17 March 1784.
7. NAS. GD174/1364. P. Choffard to M. Caille, Kingston, Jamaica, 18 June 1884. 'We take the liberty of recommending M. and Mme. Maclaine whom Secretary Choffard had the pleasure of knowing when they stayed in this town. Their travels will take them to your town and we hope their stay will be as agreeable as possible, without rival. Pray be at our disposal. We have the honour to be ... etc.'
8. See Chapter 5.
9. NAS. GD174/176/6. Admiralty Session, Old Bailey, London, 21 June 1785.
10. NAS. GD174/1330/7 and 13. Allan MacDougall WS to MM, 11 January 1785.
11. NAS. GD174/209/20. Papers in arbitration, MM and Allan Maclaine of Scallastle, 1800.
12. Marie de Guise-Lorraine was the formidable mother of the infant Mary Queen of Scots.
13. NAS. GD174/2147/1. AMLB to MM, Quebec 16 August 1780.
14. NAS. GD174/1369. Copy letter, MM to Allan MacDougall, London, 20 December 1784. It was typical of MM that he got names wrong, but his care about other details was exemplary.
15. NAS. GD174/176. Account of the death of Archibald Maclaine.
16. NAS. GD174/1376/6 . The Rev. John Agnew to MM, Salisbury Court, The Strand, 9 June 1785.
17. NAS. GD174/1376/7. Alexander Maclean to MM, 7 Young Street, Kensington, 31 August 1785.
18. NAS. GD74/1354. Charlotte Lemaitre to AMLB, Rivier de Soupe, 23–25 September

1783. My dear kind McLaine, I write this to wish you good health and hope, dear little one that you arrived safely and will prosper in your travels. Your dear son [and some pages of praise follow].

19. Hunter, *A Dance called America*, p. 31.
20. Numbers of tenants and relatives are mentioned by name in correspondence in the Lochbuy Papers as going to or returning from the Caribbean.
21. 'We performed with much activity a dance which I suppose the emigration from Skye has occasioned. They call it "America". A brisk reel is played. The first couple begin, and each sets to one, then each to another, then they set to the next couple, the second and third couples are setting; and so it goes on till all are set a-going, setting and wheeling round each other, while each is making a tour of all in the dance. It shows how emigration catches till all are set afloat.' James Hunter has used the concept for the title of his book on Highland emigration, *A Dance called America*.
22. NAS. GD174/1303. Hector McLaine to JMG, New York, 5 February 1786.

10

Three men called Allan Maclean

Three men called Allan Maclean were prominent in the eighteenth century. Two were Mull men, and the third belonged to Morvern, on the mainland coast of Argyll. All affected the course of Mull history, and all were outstanding personalities. Since they were apt to be confused even in their own lifetimes, they were referred to by a title, a military rank and a territorial designation respectively. All three have appeared in this narrative before, as minor players. The first, Sir Allan Maclean, was the urbane host of Samuel Johnson and James Boswell on Inchkenneth. The second, Colonel, later General, Allan Maclean of the Torloisk family was the hero of the siege of Quebec and the person responsible for the court martial of Archy Lochbuy. The third was the incorrigible Jacobite, Maclean of Drimnin, who eloped with Miss Mally Maclaine, the once barefooted daughter of Lachlan the Prodigal. They were in some degree related to each other, and were contemporaries. All are mentioned with admiration in the uncritical standard history of the clan Maclean.[1] It might be kinder to leave them with their honours thick upon them, but these honours obfuscate their true role in the Mull story, and may be better swept aside so that we may take a clearer look at the human beings.

Sir Allan Maclean

Born before 1720, Sir Allan Maclean was the only surviving legitimate son of Donald Maclean of Brolass, a loyal adherent of the Macleans of Duart. Like many of the Maclean women we are yet to meet, he tended to conceal his age, which makes it more likely that he was born well before 1720.[2] Yet another strange piece of evidence comes into play, for Allan matriculated at Glasgow University in the year 1737 as 'Allanus McLean a Broloss in Insula de Mull'[3] at a time when it would have been most unusual for an arts student to be more than seventeen years old. Whatever this said about his age, it is certain that he had an excellent liberal education, similar to the training in Latin, Greek, philosophy and logic given to Donald and Alexander Maclean of Coll at Aberdeen.

By his three sisters, Catherine, Isabel and Ann, Allan was closely related to the three lairds' families of Coll, Lochbuy and Drimnin, and by Una, the wife he married in 1750, he was doubly related to the Macleans of Coll.

Allan's father was designated a rebel for his pro-Jacobite activities, but was respected by his clan for his bravery and his wounds at Sheriffmuir in 1715.

Both father and son were celebrated by Maclean bards,[4] for their prowess in war and their noble bearing, although, since these attributes were conventions of Gaelic poetry rather than actual physical characteristics, they must be treated with a little caution.

The Brolass Macleans lived on their territory, although before the end of the eighteenth century there was no house of any quality in Brolass. Gribun and Inchkenneth being outlying parts of the parish of Ross, were also attached to the Brolass section of the Duart estate, which had been appropriated by the Campbells of Argyll in payment of the Duart debt. The farms which the family of Brolass actually lived in were Ormsaig (before Allan's father's death) and Inchkenneth,[5] but they lived there on a lease, like other tacksmen or tenants, although they had been granted the lands by the Duarts before the struggle for possession between Duart Macleans and Argyll Campbells got under way. In 1748, the lands of Brolass were sett, 'for silver rent and multure' as the charmed phrase had it, by the Duke of Argyll's chamberlain, Donald Campbell of Airds, in the following manner:

Ulvalt, Ardvairgnish, Dererach, Balnahaird, Killuman, Ballinaheine were all sett to small tenants in groups (for they were, in effect, joint townships); Killiemore, Ard (Camas) and Kilfinichen were sett to John Maclean of Killean (father of the notorious Hector who had been imprisoned at Lochbuy); Inchkenneth was sett to 'Lady Broloss', otherwise Isabel Maclean of Ardgour, the mother of Sir Allan, as her son was not yet married and was off at the wars; Balmeanach and Tenga, at Gribun were sett to Hugh Maclean; Kinlochscridain was possessed by John Maclean; Torranbeg and Torranuachtrach were sett to Hector Maclean, simply known as 'Hector Torran' but a significant patriarch in the Mull community; Killunaig was sett to a Donald Maclean; Beach and Carvolg (a pendicle) were possessed by Duncan McGilvra, brother to Pennyghael; and Ardchrishnish, where Johnson and Boswell visited Mr Macleod, was at this time sett to Macleod's predecessor and father-in-law, the Rev. Archibald Maclean. Kilpatrick 'the worse spot in Brolass' was yielding up its proverbially poor soil to the care of an outsider tenant, Archibald Macdonald in Tiree.[6] This was the entire community of Brolass, the happy family which Sir Allan would inherit as titular head and tacksman when he returned from his martial escapades. In the meantime, his representative, his mother, Lady Brolass lived on the island of Inchkenneth, well removed from possible taps on her door from complainers and people asking for rent reductions. It is fairly certain that the minister, Mr Maclean, acted the part of tacksman, and wrote letters to the chamberlain and the duke.

Such was the scene in Brolass of 1748, and it was really quite a healthy scene compared with some other parts of the duke's property ten years after the reforms of Duncan Forbes related in Chapter 3. Perhaps this relative order was a result of the fact that so many Macleans had remained, and the Campbells had not come in. For in the rest of the duke's lands, in Torosay and Kilninian parishes, and in the Ross, the report the duke received was a long sad story of farms which could not be sett at all, because the tacksmen were bankrupt, the tenants were bankrupt, and the subtenants could not pay the new rents.

In the Ross of Mull and Iona, good farms such as Ardalanish, Ardachy, Ardchiavaig, Saorphein and Bunessan were 'likely to be waste' because the tenants were too poor to pay. The whole of Aros district was reported to be 'in bad condition'. In Mornish, the tacksman of Penmore was bankrupt, and Cillchroisd, Oskamull, Treshnish, Inivea, Arin and Gometra were turning into waste ground.

So it was that this poor soil of Brolass now looked like the happiest part of Mull, with its community of Macleans, and its handsome tacksman, Allan Maclean, who became, by the death of his kinsman in Rome in 1750, Sir Allan, chief of the clan Maclean. In the early years of the eighteenth century, the Macleans of Brolass always fought on the other side from the Campbells, but a few years after Allan succeeded his father as representative of the family in 1725, he began a conciliatory relationship with the Campbells which has already been mentioned in Chapter 4. It is difficult to know whether this was a wise strategy, carefully thought out, or weakness on Allan's part. Weakness was certainly a constituent part of his character, referred to frequently in the correspondence of his many relations. He was also a man who in his domestic life was protected by women, for his mother lived with him, as well as his three sisters, and then when he married himself, he had three daughters, his only son, Lauchlan, dying young.

In 1757, he supplied 100 men from Mull for Montgomerie's Highlanders, for as chief of the clan Maclean he had influence, and was held in great affection. Like Allan Maclean of Torloisk, he was in the action at Ticonderoga in 1759. After the death of Una, his wife, in 1760, when he was granted home leave, he served for another three years before retiring from the army when his regiment was disbanded. Unlike the other Allan Maclean, he chose to return to Mull, for which he felt a great attachment, and settled on Inchkenneth, but not without several jaunts to Edinburgh, Glasgow and London. There is a faint hint in the correspondence of 'the Country' that Daniel Maclean, Sir Allan's second cousin, a merchant in Glasgow, was somehow holding the Knight to ransom, if a seasoned plotter like Allan Maclean, Torloisk could write to his somewhat depraved brother Hector:

> I shall say nothing of Daniel. His behaviour is such as I always expected. His manner of treating poor Sir Allan I cannot mention with any kind of temper, for tho' the Knight has failings, want of friendship is none of his faults.[7]

Daniel Maclean was one of those traders of the Maclean name whose mysterious business transactions were constantly taking him overseas. For a time, he was resident in Jamaica, as a customs collector at Montego Bay. He must have been aware, in the 1760s, that with the demise of Sir Allan's 'promising child', Lauchlan, the baronetcy of Morvern and Duart would revert to him

or to his heirs (as indeed it did). His treatment of Sir Allan may have had
something to do with the grant of land in America which was due to the
Knight at the end of his service in the Seven Years' War, which Sir Allan
applied for, but never took up.[8]

But Daniel Maclean was not the only person who took advantage of Sir
Allan, that 'good-natured thoughtless man'. The Knight might have a title,
but like most of the other gentlemen of Mull, he was penniless. As a mere
tacksman, he only collected rents and passed them on to the Duke of Argyll.
But he had his small luxuries to pay for, and his three daughters to educate,
and he was in a state of indebtedness which became more serious by the hour.
It was drawn to his attention that in view of the duke's doubtful right to the
Duart lands, he might now, as head of the old and dignified family of Duart,
claim the paternal estates through the Court of Session in Edinburgh. Did
not all the Gaelic bards proclaim that the Campbells of Argyll had taken the
lands by force, without paying for them? Everyone in 'the Country' knew that
the tenth earl had invaded Mull and forced the Macleans into submission.
And now that justice was dispensed by the impartial processes of law in
Edinburgh, and not by Campbell courts at Inveraray, it was a certainty that
the Macleans would see their rightful inheritance restored to them.

The Knight, although persuaded of the iniquities of all the transactions of
the Argyll family with his ancestors, was not as bold as his brother-in-law,
John Maclaine of Lochbuy, at rushing in where angels feared to tread. He
had always maintained a gentlemanly relationship with the house of Campbell,
and it was the more necessary to continue in this mode when his adversary
was the very model of ducal sophistication as personified by John Campbell,
fifth Duke of Argyll. The Knight's 'strange and unaccountable sort of hesitation' was put an end to by the sheer scale of his debt, and when he granted
a trust-bond for £20,000 Scots to his brother-in-law, the latter offered to act
for him in bringing an action against the Duke of Argyll. For legal and for
personal reasons, Sir Allan could not himself be the pursuer in the case, and
this champion he agreed to employ in the cause, this brother-in-law, this
namesake, was none other than Allan Maclean of Drimnin, whom we have
met before as the Jacobite lawyer and opportunist who eloped with Mally
Maclaine. When Mally was a barefooted girl, Drimnin had been married to
the Knight's sister, Ann of Brolass. The Knight, who had no son of his own,
was later to use his influence to recommend his nephew, Charles Maclean,
Younger of Drimnin, to General Fraser, who was raising a regiment for
America in 1775,[9] and Charles, two years afterwards, married Sir Allan's
daughter, Maria, who had read to Dr Johnson on Inchkenneth during the
visit of 1773. While this development was still in the future, these were the
kinds of bond of kinship which bound the two Allans, and it was only proper
that Drimnin should help the beleaguered Knight to fight his case against
Argyll.

The lawyers for Argyll and the lawyers for Drimnin were preparing their arguments before Johnson and Boswell visited Inchkenneth, and there is some dramatic irony to be revealed here, for Boswell the advocate was involved as Counsel for the pursuer, and was already conversant with the history of the acquisition of Duart before becoming Sir Allan's guest on the island. As a lawyer in a case which was *sub judice*, he was unlikely to discuss the matter with the Knight, who had distanced himself from the action, but his inside knowledge must have endowed his visit to Inchkenneth, as well as his visit to Inveraray a week or two later, with a certain amount of nervous tension, which he went some lengths to explain away. Boswell knew only too well that the outcome of the process would be like the terms of a great peace treaty. Even when a victory is won by the sword, the true victory lies in the terms of the ensuing settlement, which shows where real power lies. This would be the final pronouncement in a private war which had been waged for over 100 years, if not several hundred years, between Campbells and Macleans.

As has been mentioned in Chapter 1, clan Campbell had had the perspicacity to enter into combat backed up by the resources of law. It had retained, in cramped quarters in Inveraray and Edinburgh, muniments bearing witness to all its dealings, supervised by 'writers' who lived their lives in the service of the family. Every rental list was kept, every feu duty recorded. Charters, infeftments, resignations, processes of removing, decreets arbitral, petitions and reductions, letters of horning, letters of caption and ejection, of treason and of fire and sword, borne by lyons and heralds and macers, articles of capitulation – all from the year 1630 – were now produced and quoted, in their Biblical cadences, and with their irresistible logic. And when it was shown that the lands of Duart belonged irrefutably to the earls of Argyll and their heirs, upon the conditions laid out in the seventeenth century, it was pointed out that the Brolass Macleans had promised to act as peacemakers in a certain manner, binding all of the Macleans to be 'servants and followers to the earl and his family, received into his lordship's protection, and accepted kindly of by him'.[10] But the Macleans paid little heed to these overtures of kindness, as we have seen from the oath poem of the bard Iain Mac Ailean in Chapter 2.

From start to finish, the land of Brolass had been treated differently from the other Duart lands in Ross, Torosay, Aros and Mornish, both by a seventeenth century encumbrance and by virtue of the Brolass Macleans' role as go-betweens, and in 1749, Sir Allan Maclean had formally agreed to accept the confirmation of a former mortgage or wadset arrangement with the third duke. By this, the Knight could redeem at any time his very own lands, on payment of £20,000 Scots.

Readers will by this time, after experiencing the Reduction of Gillean Maclaine by his father, have grown used to the predilection of 'the Country' for humiliating the enemy within by Reduction. In 1771, the fearless Drimnin brought an action of Reduction against the fifth duke, to which the cool-headed

Jack Campbell responded by bringing the same against Drimnin and Sir Allan. Interlocutors and avizandums [11] followed, so that the process had now lasted six years, in the course of which Johnson had published his *Journey* (which the Knight must have had little stomach for reading) and the American revolution had taken place. For those who take delight in reading legal documents, the arguments for the defender were worthy of Cicero at his best, but for the purpose of this history, only the outcome can be of interest, and its purport for 'poor Sir Allan'.

Of the mutual actions for Reduction, it was the duke's which succeeded in the whole estate, but the Maclean one was successful in Brolass. The result was that although Drimnin and the Knight had set out to regain all of the lands of Duart, all that they received was Brolass, and the other Mull lands were confirmed as in the rightful possession of the Campbells. The duke was ordered to pay part of the mortgage capital, but this was reduced because of the costs of twelve years of litigation. Even before the judgement was made, the Maclaine grapevine was relaying the news. All the Knight's creditors, aware that Sir Allan would not have enough to pay his debts, began to plan for their share. Murdoch Maclaine, anticipating the problems to come, wrote to his nephew Donald from London on 28 July 1780:

> You must endeavour to recover Sir Allan's debt through that channel for himself ... his half pay is gone for three years to come. I'm not at liberty to tell you his misfortunes, but they are great, and you'll have them soon by other intelligence.[12]

In 1782, Donald wrote,

> Sir Allan is turn'd out of everything he had by his sons-in-law who has taken all to themselves and pays none of the creditors a penny ... Allan McLean of Drimnin Esquire manages poor Sir Allan like as the Paymaster does yourself. His claim against the Knight is only £5000 sterling, which he will draw soon from the D of Argyle, but devil a shilling for the poor unluckie Knight or his creditors, nor even for the unmarried daughter.[13]

On 1 February 1783, Donald wrote to Murdoch in America:

> All your friends and Relations are much about their Ordinary way. Nothing is done in any business of yours new to advise you. Sir Allan receives £6000 from Argyle to settle his plea anent Broloss & allowed to keep the lands of the old Rent during his life & after his decease the next heir pays I think nearly double rent at entry ... However, be all as it will, Drimnin *grips* at all this money ... Castle Duart may get a little feel, and of which Mr Charles must get £2000 sterling with his wife.[14] Duart Castle must get £5000 or £1000, and Drimnin & Colquhoun Grant [15] will keep the rest between them for their trouble in the long contested plea, and we pretty well believe that the poor Knight with his youngest daughter yet unmarried, with all the

Aros Castle, scene of the meeting of chieftains in 1609, but ruinous since the seventeenth century. Aros remained the principal administrative area for the Argyll estates, and the main port of embarkation for visitors until the nineteenth century. (William Daniell's *Voyage Round Great Britain*)

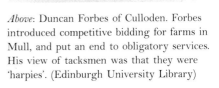

Hon.ble DUNCAN FORBES.

Above: Duncan Forbes of Culloden. Forbes introduced competitive bidding for farms in Mull, and put an end to obligatory services. His view of tacksmen was that they were 'harpies'. (Edinburgh University Library)

Left: John, second Duke of Argyll. (Campbell: *Life of The Most Illustrious Prince* ...)

Lieutenant-Colonel Jack Campbell, later fifth
Duke of Argyll. From an engraving by
Heath, c. 1745. (Scottish National Portrait
Gallery)

HIGHLAND SOLDIERS.

Highland soldiers of the 1750s, much as they
would have looked in the Seven Years' War.
(Grose's *Military Antiquities*)

The Rev. Dr John Walker, minister, botanist
and geologist, who made a report on the
Hebrides in 1764 for both the Commission for
Annexed Estates and the General Assembly
of the Church of Scotland. (Kay's *Edinburgh
Portraits*)

Lachlan MacQuarrie of that Ilk: 'His
ineffectual amiability is well-caught in this
portrait, wearing his army coat, probably the
only coat he possessed.'
(Major Nicholas Maclean-Bristol, Coll.)

The Sapient Septemviri, or the Seven Wise Men: the Senate of King's College, Aberdeen, the preferred circle of Hugh Maclean of Coll and his son Alexander. Roderick Macleod, Hugh's brother-in-law, is shown second from right, brandishing a Lochaber axe. He was the eighteenth-century equivalent of a university recruiting officer, his province being the Western Isles. (Kay's *Edinburgh Portraits*)

Early nineteenth-century engraving, showing a boat used for taking tourists to Staffa. This does not differ greatly from the ferry boat in service from Mull to Iona in the 1950s, except that the latter had an outboard motor. (Albyn's *Anthology*)

Left: Sir Allan Maclean, 'the Knight', charming host to Johnson and Boswell, and chief of the clan Maclean.

Murdoch Maclaine of Lochbuy and his wife, Jane Campbell of Airds, after their marriage in February 1786, from portraits by Raeburn, location unknown. (Copies reproduced by kind permission of Mr David Sillar, Berwickshire)

'Gillean has got two boys at one birth.' The twins, Archibald and Murdoch Maclaine, were born at Scallastle in 1777. Portrait by an unknown artist, *c.* 1783. (Wotton Auction Rooms, Wotton-under-Edge, Gloucestershire)

Old Torloisk House, built by Lachlan Maclean of Torloisk, *c.* 1785. A classical Mull house, it was unfortunately enlarged after the death of Marianne Maclean Clephane. From an original watercolour at Torloisk. (Royal Commission on the Ancient and Historical Monuments of Scotland)

Faujas de Saint-Fond, the French geologist and travel writer whose account of his stay at Torloisk in 1783 rivalled Boswell's journal in its wealth of detail. (Frontispiece to Faujas de Saint-Fond's *Voyage* ...)

Prospect of Staffa, drawn by Mr Watts in 1798 when he accompanied Dr Garnett to Mull. The proportions of this drawing were criticised, justifiably, by William Daniell, since the engraving looks more like a cake than an island. (Thomas Garnett's *Tour through the Highlands and Western Islands*)

A Mull cottage, drawn by Mr Watts about 1798. (*Observations on a Tour through the Highlands*)

The Marquis of Northampton after the death of his wife. Their second son William inherited Torloisk after the death of his grandmother, Marianne Maclean Clephane. From a portrait by Alexander Craig. (National Portrait Gallery, London)

George William, 6th Duke of Argyll (1768–1839), as Marquess of Lorne, from a drawing by Henry Edridge, 1801. (National Galleries of Scotland, and with kind permission of His Grace the Duke of Argyll)

Archibald Macarthur, piper to Ranald Macdonald of Staffa. Macarthur strutted about in front of Ulva House when there were visitors, and met the most important guests at Aros with a glorious *pibroch*. He piped before George IV on the king's visit to Edinburgh in 1822, and was given a cottage on Ulva for his retirement by Charles Macquarie. (Kay's *Edinburgh Portraits*)

Sir Henry Steuart of Allanton. A keen planter, he wrote a book called *The Planter's Guide*. As father-in-law of Ranald Macdonald, he came to the rescue of the bankrupt landowner in 1817, and eventually sold Ulva to Charles Macquarie. (Steuart's *Planter's Guide*)

The poet Thomas Campbell. His stay in Mull in 1795, when he was seventeen, as tutor to the children of Archibald Campbell at Sunipol produced no descriptions of the island, owing to his youthful obsession with his own feelings. (Bates' Maclise Portrait Gallery)

Carsaig House, where Donald Maclean WS spent the summer months. (Mull Museum, Tobermory)

Alexander Campbell, the 'organ grinder', who visited Mull in 1815 looking for original music and songs. (Kay's *Edinburgh Portraits*)

Administration of the Sacrament in the Gravel Pit, near Achnacroish, on 26 October 1845. Colonel Campbell of Possil had initially refused permission for a Free Church on his estate after the disruption, being against 'Reform' and disapproving of any opposition to the established church. At the time of this meeting, Colonel Campbell was paralysed by a stroke. The artist, J. Drummond, drew the worshippers from life, and among the congregation were Lamonts, MacPhails and other families from the Lochdon area. Many were to leave for Upper Canada in the 1850s. (Edinburgh University Library)

John Campbell of Ardmore, 'Factor Mór'. (Mr R. K. Campbell)

Old Ardtornish House in the mid-nineteenth century. This was the scene of many of Lauchlan Maclaine's Christmas and New Year parties, where he played the fiddle, and where his beloved Mrs Gregorson lived. (Mr C. M. Ives, Ardtornish, Morvern)

T. Allom.   M. J. Starling

OBAN, DURING THE REGATTA.

Above: Oban during the Regatta, at which, in 1838, a ticket for the Ball cost 7s. 6d. and beds one guinea a night. (William Beattie's *Scotland Illustrated*, vol. 2)

Below: Francis William Clark of Ulva. (Mr D. F. Robertson)

Angus Gregorson, nephew and factor of Young Murdoch of Lochbuy. He was remembered unfairly as a severe rent collector, but had a considerable sympathy for small farmers. (Gregorson photograph albums in the collection of Mr David Sillar)

Quinish House in the late nineteenth century, after it had passed out of the hands of the Macleans of Coll. (Mull Museum, Tobermory)

Gillean Maclaine, grandson of Gillean of Scallastle. He had a successful business in Java but was lost at sea returning to Britain with his family in 1840. From a portrait by an unknown artist. (The collection of Mr David Sillar)

The Rev. Angus Maclaine, minister of Ardnamurchan, benefactor. He and his brother made amends for the sins of their father and grandfather. From a portrait by an unknown artist. (The collection of Mr David Sillar)

Above left: Donald Maclaine of Lochbuy. Second son of 'young' Murdoch of Lochbuy, he went to Java to join Gillean Maclaine in his coffee exporting business, but returned to save the estate. (Mr David Sillar)

Above right: The three daughters of Donald Maclaine of Lochbuy – Emilie, Rosa and Christian, *c.* 1861. (Mr David Sillar)

Catherine Maclaine of Lochbuy, *c.* 1870. The only daughter of Murdoch and Jane to remain unmarried, she died in 1894 at the age of 100, but she was so accustomed to taking years off her age that both her death certificate and her memorial gave false information. (Mr David Sillar)

Dugald MacPhail, author of the Mull 'anthem', *An t-eilean Muileach*. Writing under the pen name Muileach, he was one of the most active of Mull exiles in the later nineteenth century, revered for his ability to arouse sentiments of home-sickness and loss in the diasporic community of the Scottish Lowlands. (*Modern Gaelic Bards*, published 1908)

A nineteenth-century Mull cottage in the Ross, showing the slanting chimney and roof style known as 'the cow with the crumpled horn'. (Ross of Mull Historical Centre, Bunessan)

Creditors, may starve for all they are to get of the above sum. I know you want above One Hundred, but knows not where your Clames lies ... I wish you had sold your Company some time ago. However it is needless for you to reflect less or more. Be happy, and come and live easie, quiet & peacably in your Own Country. Marrie a good woman and whether you get money with her or not, I think you are to procure yourself a worth companion in the deceant necessarys of life.[16]

It was left to Gillean Maclaine to make the most telling of literary allusions in reference to the Knight. Poor Sir Allan, he wrote to a friend in Dublin, was like King Lear, left alone in the world with his youngest daughter, Cordelia. And to his brother Archy, who, on hearing of his uncle's settlement, had tried to draw on him for £500, Gillean had to write, on 1 March 1784, 'Your uncle, Sir Allan dyed *suddenly* about nine weeks ago, and left his affairs in great confusion.'

By the death of Sir Allan Maclean, twenty-first chief of the clan Maclean and sixth baronet of Morvern, on 10 December 1783, the title, unsupported by any trappings such as castles, lands or possessions, went on its meandering way through the dead ancestors looking for a place to rest among the living descendants of John, son of Hector Og, son of Donald of Brolass, son of Hector Og of Duart, son of Lachlan Mor. It alighted upon a sixth cousin of the poor Knight, son of a Glasgow merchant who had died in the West Indies.

The Glasgow merchant, Daniel Maclean, has appeared as a shadowy figure in this story, and has to remain so. His name appeared on some rent rolls in the Ross of Mull, as an absentee tenant. It was he who had called Gillean Maclaine an 'abominable bastard'. It was he who had treated Sir Allan very badly, and perhaps ruined him. Yet, like many other Macleans of the eighteenth century, he continually pointed out the sins of others. Daniel's business debts were said to total £12,000 in the 1750s and '60s. He had married first a woman who was not of 'the Country', Mary Dickson, of no particular pedigree, the daughter of another Glasgow trader. This unprepossessing couple had two children who survived childhood, Hector and Janet. Janet married that other Allan Maclean, colonel, and later brigadier-general whom we are about to examine in pathological detail – Janet was the 'madame' so despised by Archy Lochbuy for her behaviour with German officers in Montreal. Hector Maclean was the son upon whom the title of Duart now devolved. In Mull he was obscure and unknown, so that as far as any *Muileach* was concerned, the title might as well have become extinct. 'Sir Hector' was, to them, and ever would be, the gentleman who died in Rome, who spoke the Gaelic fluently, who had lived among them in his youth, in Quinish and in Coll, and who had tried to take part in the '45. Sir Allan had also been a Gaelic speaker and had led Macleans in war. Sir Allan had lived in Mull for twenty years, had come among his people, had demanded services which they had been glad to give.

But who was this new Sir Hector? To the men who served in the 84th Regiment in Nova Scotia, he was known as a young ensign, who had arrived with Murdoch Maclaine and had been commissioned ensign by Allan Maclean in 1775 at the age of thirteen.[17] He was immediately attached to Major Small of the 84th, and remained with him until near the end of the revolutionary war, when he was sent home to Britain in a poor state of health. His return from America coincided with that of his brother-in-law, General Allan Maclean, and his sister Janet, the general's wife. The three settled in London, and from the time that Hector succeeded to the title in December 1783, he lived sometimes in the General's house, and sometimes in Yorkshire. When General Allan died in 1797, Sir Hector went on living in retirement until his own death in 1818. Although Allan Maclean and Janet visited Mull in 1790, it is not known that Sir Hector ever went to his ancestral home.

The passing of the title from Sir Allan was, to most of the Macleans in Mull, the end of an old tradition. Sir Hector was only 21 years old on his succession, but, except to the few who knew him as a mere boy in North America, he was a stranger. It can only be assumed that his life of retirement was the result of ill health and relative poverty or lack of ambition. His brother-in-law, General Allan Maclean, sometimes referred to him as one of the extended family who needed his support. But so little is known of Sir Hector's personality that the important question of whether, by hiding himself away, he was instrumental in bringing to an end the particular relationship between clan chief and people has to remain unanswered. Daniel Maclean, his father, had married as his second wife, Margaret Wall, so that Hector had a half brother, who was given the politically significant forenames of Fitzroy Jeffreys Grafton.[18] Born about 1770, Fitzroy, or 'poor Grafton' as General Allan called him, was apparently more outgoing than Sir Hector. He served in the West Indies from 1788, married a young widow in 1794, rose to the rank of lieutenant-general, and after a long absence from Britain, returned to London in 1815, just in time to find the sixth Duke of Argyll embarking on the sale of the old Maclean lands. Having two sons, he had some dynastic motive for being interested in the fate of the Mull estate, but what he did about it must be left to another chapter. In the meantime, his brother-in-law, General Allan Maclean of Torloisk, deserves some consideration as the second of the 'three men called Allan Maclean'.

Allan Maclean of Torloisk

He would have found it difficult to conceal his age, even if he had wanted to, being the third son of Donald of Torloisk, and having gone to school with John Gruline and other Mull notables. It was not in this area of life that his vanity lay. He was one of those men who liked to control and direct other men, and he might have made a much more effective laird of Torloisk than his older brother Hector Torloisk and his next eldest brother Lachlan, but

Allan fortunately had to find another field, and after a brief flirtation with the Jacobite cause, which he himself was successful in erasing from the annals, and from men's memories, he found his true calling in the British army, and most of all in the re-recruitment of his own discharged men in North America, as has been related in Chapter 9.

The ten Torloisks, children of the cultured and refined Donald of Torloisk, were born between 1715 and 1740 in the humble cottage which stood close to the present house, overlooking Loch Tuath and Ulva. The site had no trees when they were children, and in fact they probably saw little of it between infancy and the age of ten, for they were all fostered.[19] If early nurture was responsible for the great differences in their personalities, their foster parents' names are not revealed. By the time Hector succeeded his father, he was a lawyer in Edinburgh, and if Archy Lochbuy's opinion of him can be trusted, a rake. It was Hector who colluded with Lachlan MacQuarrie of Ulva to oust Culinish and to marry MacQuarrie to his sister Alice Torloisk. Lachlan, the second son, was totally different, a God-fearing young man who went to sea in the merchant trade between London and Jamaica, and whose greatest ambition was to own his own ship.[20] His journal of a voyage in the ship *Cecilia* in 1760 was a masterpiece of precise record-keeping.[21] But Lachlan's two brothers, Hector and Allan, mocked his simplicity and lack of guile, while Lachlan's marriage to a Fife heiress called Margaret Smith in 1763 prompted ribald remarks from the two bachelors, each of whom had a natural daughter. Hector Torloisk lived in Edinburgh, but did take an early interest in agri-cultural improvements in Mull, petitioning the Duke of Argyll in 1749 to be allowed to lease the duke's land at Penmore in order to join it with his contiguous lands and carry out extensive experiments in planting different kinds of clover, as well as flax-raising, 'and other improvements never yet practiced in that Country for which purpose I am resolv'd to send to Mull a skillful person in these branches of Agriculture, and to provide him with Ploughs & other labouring Utensills.' [22] Hector also set up a spinning school at Torloisk for the employment of his tenants' daughters in 1752, the year in which Murdoch Maclaine finished his apprenticeship in the Edinburgh linen trade, and became a merchant. Whether Murdoch and Hector collaborated, and were both stopped by the slump in trade in 1754, is not known.[23]

Hector had many irons in the fire, and in 1763 he and his brother Allan were conspiring to acquire land in St John's, later Prince Edward Island. Because of his military service, Allan was eligible for a grant of 6,000 acres, and 300 extra acres per head for every fifty settlers he could bring out from Mull with Hector's help.[24] But as no letters show the conclusion of such a deal, the outcome is unknown. In the 1760s, the population of estates in Mull had not begun the spiralling increase which would make men surplus to requirements, and Hector probably needed kelp workers just as Gillean did.

Allan and Hector had only two more years to hatch plots together, and the signs in their correspondence were that Hector was frequently ill. Never-

theless, Gillean was right to fear him, for Allan in London urged Hector to
pursue debtors and to keep the Mull residents of Edinburgh out of his plans.
'Keep Sir Allan out of your Councills ... do not trust Murdoch more ... do
not even let your own friends know the reason of their assembling till you
have them together, for they are so weak they are not to be trusted ... I shall
be in the state of Purgatory till I hear from you ...' And reporting the death
of John Maclean, one of the kin, in Jamaica, Allan told Hector

> I need not expatiate. You will Easily see all the Mischief that will be the
> consequence of this misfortune. If Daniel McLean goes off for Jamaica he
> will have a field day to cheat all his Creditors ... I am under a good deal
> of Concern & Anxiety.[25]

In this way, Allan referred to his own future father-in-law and the father of
two future chiefs of the clan Maclean. His own lifestyle in this inter-war period
was just as dubious as Daniel Maclean's. In December 1763 he was telling
Hector

> Three weeks will determine my fate with regard to my going abroad or
> remaining in Britain. I live with Doctor Lauch: We have a house in Lisle
> Street, Licesterfield. I wish we had one week of you. It would make me
> really happy.[26]

Doctor Lauch was the notorious Lauchlin Macleane, MD of Edinburgh University, who has been charged with being 'Junius', the polemical eighteenth-
century letter writer,[27] and if he was not Junius, he was certainly a schemer
of the deepest dye. Doctor Lauchlin was involved in the same land deals as
Hector and Allan Torloisk, and Allan's close association with him can only
confirm our suspicions about his integrity. A meeting of all three in Lisle
Street would have resembled a convention of devils, but the reunion was not
to be, for Hector Torloisk died in Glasgow in May 1765.

The Torloisk succession, and the story of how poor honest Lachlan Torloisk
was treated by his brother Allan Maclean following Hector Torloisk's death,
will be reserved for Chapter 12. Having set the scene with Allan's devilish
machinations and his unpleasant friend, it will not be difficult to see that
Archy Lochbuy's court martial, although richly deserved for his indiscretion
and hubris, was more in the nature of a confrontation between a remarkably
devious older man, well practised in the art of manipulation and self-deceit,
and a foolish, rash, childish younger man, than a mere court of justice, as it
might appear. In the wider world of 'the Country', Allan was ready to go to
any length to help a kinsman, but Archy had been right when he had said of
the 'Madame' that he had not given her the admiration she thought she was
entitled to. Neither had he given her husband his due admiration. It was
significant that the merchant Donald Maclaine in Edinburgh thought that
Archy was honest and good, Donald being a petty man, and a poor judge of

character. Archy had been right in spotting the erasure of a name on a commission, but to mention it at a board of investigation was bound to bring down on his head all the devious wiles of the brigadier, who immediately claimed that Archy had received double pay and had embezzled the funds of his company. But Archy was honest in his fashion, and those were not the kind of sins he committed. He had gambled excessively, and written the equivalent of cheques which he could not honour, but he was not an embezzler. He had thoughtlessly drawn on poor unfortunate men like Sir Allan and John Gruline, but he did not steal. When the king's advocate had dismissed Archy Lochbuy from the service, he had done so in the interests of army discipline, and to avoid an even more damaging court martial – that of the senior officer of one of the battalions of the 84th. Allan went home to London with remarkable speed, and began at once to justify himself by spreading rumours of Archy's embezzling and his abduction of Barbara Lowther, until suddenly he was freed from promulgating such untruths by the unexpected and glad news of Archy's murder.

In an extravagant and unhistorical account of these two men, it would have been made out that Allan sent a murderer to dispose of Archy, but enough is known of Archy's rash temper to endorse the stories of all on board the *Hero*. It can be seen why the brigadier-general turned up to 'help' write the inventory of the papers of the deceased Archibald Maclaine of Lochbuy.

Allan Maclean of Drimnin

The last of the three will not entirely redress the balance in favour of the name of Allan Maclean. His title of Drimnin, which is in Morvern, not Mull – though it looks across the Sound of Mull to Ardnacross – came from his seventeenth-century great-great-grandfather, Charles Maclean of Ardnacross, who bought the lands from the Duke of Argyll and passed them down through alternating Allans and Charleses until both the fourth Maclean of Drimnin and Lachlan his natural son died at Culloden, when the estate passed to this Allan, aged twenty-one. Young Drimnin was bred to the law, married Ann of Brolass, and was left a widower within ten years with a clutch of children. He then married Miss Mally Maclaine of Lochbuy in 1759.

Allan Maclean had been wounded at Culloden at the age of twenty-two, and although he had to lie low for a time, he was less conspicuous in Edinburgh as the eighth chieftain of the Macleans of Morvern than he would have been if he had resided at Drimnin, so that he made his home in town, surrounded by old cronies of the Jacobite persuasion such as Colquhoun Grant, in whose law office Drimnin learned his profession. When Mally's first son Donald Maclean became old enough to be indentured to a Writer to the Signet, it was Colquhoun Grant who was his master, while Allan MacDougall, Archy and Murdoch's lawyer, was Colquhoun's great friend. Mally's Donald married Colquhoun's daughter Lillias in 1793, and became a Writer to the Signet in

1796. Thus were all the old ties of 'the Country' perpetuated, and the interwoven circles of relationships were, in the not too distant future, to link up old and new branches of the family of Lochbuy.

But the first son of Allan Drimnin's first marriage was not to be as respected as Donald, the son of his second. Ann of Brolass's son Charles the Younger of Drimnin, persuaded either by his father Allan that Sir Allan's expectations from the case against the Duke of Argyll were very great, or smitten with the undoubted gifts and beauty of his cousin Maria, had married the Knight's daughter in 1777. The contract carried with it an assurance that Charles would inherit with his wife one-third of the restored estate of Duart. Even the baronetcy was talked of, but it would not do in the eyes of the Lord Lyon. Charles was to be most disappointed when the Argyll case was concluded, and only Brolass, the worst spot in Mull, was left to be divided between three daughters. Charles and Maria received their slice, and Charles bought out his wife's two sisters, so that when he was infeft in 1786, he was laird of the Knight's old tack – Inchkenneth, Balnahaird, Killumar, Ballinaheine, Tenga, Balmeanach, Kilfinichen, Killiemore, the Torrans, Ormsaig, Kilpatrick, Ulvalt, Ardchrishnish and the rest.

In order to buy out his sisters-in-law, Charles and his father had to borrow money, and a loan was arranged in 1785 with an Edinburgh portrait painter who had made a fortune painting nabobs in India, George Willison.[28] The artist, who included James Boswell among his subjects, was to have other links with Mull property deals which will emerge in Chapter 17. But Charles, although he was in the army, and had some pay to fall back on, was a spendthrift, and after the death of Allan of Drimnin in 1792, it was clear that he would be the last Maclean of Drimnin and Kinlochaline. In 1796, General Allan was writing to Murdoch Maclaine that he had heard 'Kenlochaline has just sold the south side of Brolass, from Kinlochscridain to Kilpatrick, to Pennycross [29] for £7,500'. Dr Archibald Maclean of Pennycross, who already owned Pennyghael, and who was certainly doing the logical thing in making sure that he would not be hemmed in by strangers, was, like most Mull landowners who really had no means, locking his own descendants into a relentless impecuniosity which was to stay their hands for almost a century.[30]

The Knight's daughter, Maria Maclean, who seems to have had no children, lived in Kilfinichen as her husband's finances proceeded on their downward spiral. Charles was stationed in Guernsey and Exeter, and returned to Mull at intervals. His attempts at recruiting his own tenants for the military failed, and when his appeals to cottars to give up one able-bodied lad from each family were met with refusal, he wrote to his neighbouring heritor:

> I have a parcell of rascalls on my property in this country who would not send their sons with me on this occasion, and whom, of course, I have turned adrift. Of course you will not give lands, or otherwise countenance such a worthless pack.[31]

The 'worthless pack' was just one sample group of small cottars evicted in the manner that Francis W. Clark was later to make famous on Ulva. Many lists of tenants warned to leave their possessions survive in Lochbuy documents, and in Ulva documents before Clark's time, but it is not clear that they were actually set adrift. Warning was often the penultimate step which forced cottars to pay their rents, and they were likely to beg or borrow the money before they were pushed out. But here their refusal to send a son to a regiment, combined with non-payment of rent, was reason enough to evict, and Charles Drimnin would get a better price for an estate unencumbered with scalags. No scheme of organised emigration aided their plight, but the kindness of relations was relied upon, and was forthcoming. Families broken up by eviction would descend upon cousins and grandparents within and across the boundaries of estates, so that life could continue in all its wretchedness.

In 1797, a roup took place at Kilfinichen of the household effects of Charles and Maria Maclean, the once hopeful children of two of our Allans. When a gentleman's family left Mull, or became bankrupt, a roup was the normal way to bring in cash. In an age when it was difficult to transport furniture through Mull, or even around Mull, by sea, a removal was unthinkable. In this particular roup, most of the possessions of the late Sir Allan Maclean and the late Allan Maclean of Drimnin must have been included by their heirs. These included a sideboard, dining table, eighteen dining chairs, twelve drawing room chairs, two breakfast tables and two tea tables, eight feather beds, a fine array of china, seventeen dozen bottles of claret and five dozen of port and sherry. The kitchen equipment was enough to run a large inn, with three dozen soup plates, blancmange dishes and cooking utensils. It was all a far cry from John Maclaine of Lochbuy's one pot.

No record remains of the buyers' names, as is the case with many later roups, such as those of Scallastle and Rossal, but the same limitations of transport which kept the goods in Mull would have operated to ensure that they did not leave the island. The chairs and tables of the Macleans probably circulated throughout the nineteenth century, going from roup to roup, from house to house, until they fell apart. The fate of Charles and Maria was much less certain.

Notes

1. Maclean Sinclair, *The Clan Gillean*.
2. Maclean Sinclair gives 1710 as Sir Allan's date of birth.
3. Addison, *Matriculation Albums of the University of Glasgow from 1728–1858*.
4. Allan in *Oran do dh-Ailein Mac-Gilleain, fear Bhrolais* and Donald in *Oran do Dhomhnall Mac-Gilleain, fear Bhrolais. Maclean Bards*, vol. I, pp. 215–20.
5. In a rental of 1679, Ormissaig was 'possest be Broloss' son and his goods', and

'Inshkaynich' was not paying a rent. MacPhail, J. R. N., 'Duart Papers' in *Highland Papers*, vol. I, pp. 314–15.

6. NLS. MS17677. A Rental of the Lands of Broloss, 1748.
7. Torloisk Papers. B337. AM to Hector Maclean of Torloisk, London, 23 February 1764.
8. Gibbon, J. Murray, *Scots in Canada*, p. 60.
9. EUL. Laing MSS. La. II 506. AMB to General Fraser, Mull, 18 November 1775.
10. Session Papers, 1775. Answers for Allan McLean of Drimnin, Pursuer, to the Petition of the Duke of Argyle, Defender.
11. Interlocutor: an interim decision only; avizandum: time taken in which to consider the case.
12. NAS. GD174/1338/1. MM to DM, London, 28 July 1780.
13. NAS. GD174/1329/24. DM to MM, Edinburgh, 2 September 1782. The unmarried daughter, Anne, who had been away at school when SJ and JB visited, remained unmarried.
14. 'Duart Castle' was John Maclean of Inverscadale, who married Sir Allan's second daughter, Sibella.
15. Colquhoun Grant, WS, lawyer in Edinburgh.
16. NAS. GD174/1329/26. Donald Maclaine to MM, Edinburgh, 1 February 1783.
17. Duncanson, *Rawdon and Douglas, Two Loyalist Townships in Nova Scotia*, pp. 394–5.
18. Presumably in honour of Augustus Henry Fitzroy, Duke of Grafton, whose meteoric rise to prominence c. 1756–62 led to his being Prime Minister from 1767 to 1770, when he was the butt of Junius's letters.
19. GRO. Uncatalogued MSS. Torloisk Disposition, 1770 in court case of Torloisk daughters *v.* Lachlan Maclean, their brother.
20. Torloisk Papers, B261 and correspondence.
21. Torloisk Papers, B261. *Journal of a Voyage Intended, by God's Permission, on Board the Ship Cecilia from Kingston in Jamaica for London, 1760.*
22. NLS. MS17677, f. 100. Saltoun Papers. The Memoriall & Proposalls of Hector McLean of Torloisk ...
23. NAS. GD174/2033–4. Abstract of the register book kept by the Spinning Mistress at Torloisk, 1752.
24. Torloisk Papers. B228. AM to Hector Maclean, 22 July 1763.
25. Torloisk Papers. B228. AM to Hector Maclean, February 1765.
26. Torloisk Papers. B228. AM to Hector Maclean, 3 December 1763.
27. Maclean, James N. M. *Reward is Secondary ...*
28. NAS. Argyll Sasines, 1781–1830, 216.
29. 'Pennycross' was Dr Alexander Maclean of Pennycross (1723–1800), father of Archibald, and grandfather of Sandy Pennycross.
30. Dr Alexander was married to Una, one of the MacGilvrays of Pennyghael, and a state of private indebtedness prevailed between the two families over various land exchanges for some time.
31. NAS. GD174/1440/3. Charles Maclean of Drimnin and Kinlochaline to MM, Brolass, 30 March 1793.

Murdoch Maclaine's inheritance

There is no record of Murdoch Maclaine's reaction to the first intimation of the murder of Archibald Maclaine of Lochbuy, but the sounds of rush and scurry are evident from the very absence of letters between men of 'the Country' written around 5 November 1784, when the news at last reached Britain with the arrival of the *Hero*, bearing the body of the victim, the murderer, and the child bride.[1]

Murdoch himself was so much on the move that his chief correspondents, Donald (now 'seedsman and grocer of Anchor Close'), Allan Maclean in London, Gillean, and the men left in Nova Scotia did not know where to find him at any given moment. His old address, when in London on military business, had been the Cecil Street or Exchange Coffee House, which, owned by a Maclean, served as a *poste restante* destination. Now he stayed with the brigadier-general, where also lurked the new young chief of the clan. But as Daniel Munro's absence was prolonged, and Murdoch kept having to return to Edinburgh to have the various problems of his succession to the Lochbuy estate resolved, there must have been many times when he wondered, with each new revelation of the state of the debt, whether it would not have been better to jump ship, and go to Nova Scotia to claim the land grant due to him as an officer of the 84th Regiment.

Lieutenant Adjutant Hector Maclean of the 2nd Battalion, 84th Regiment, had already settled on the Kennetcook river land, Hants County, Nova Scotia, and was expecting Murdoch to return.[2] There were also strong hints of an attachment between a young woman in Windsor, Nova Scotia, and Murdoch Maclaine – a young woman who asked blushingly about his return to Canada. But Murdoch, who had, before the news of Archy's death, committed himself to supervising a plan for overseeing the management of Lochbuy, must have known just how grave matters were, and yet did not consider that refusing the succession to Lochbuy was an option. It is difficult for us today to understand how a man aged fifty-five, without sons, could wish to shoulder such responsibility for an already ruined estate. It is impossible now to imagine any prestige attaching to the very obscure title of Lochbuy, tarnished as it was by the ineptitude of Lachlan the prodigal, John the irascible and Archibald the rash. But to fail to understand the importance of being head of a heritable estate is to underestimate the power of landed possessions in late eighteenth-century Scotland. By the provisions of Archy's entail, the succession was to go, failing the heirs of Murdoch's body, to the heirs of Gillean, and Gillean had heirs enough, in young Allan of Scallastle, thirteen years old, the twins

Archibald and Murdoch, aged eight, John seven, and a new infant, Hector, born as the Old Bailey was pronouncing that Daniel Munro was not guilty of Archy's murder. The entail also carried a clause intended to protect heritable estates for future heirs, which made it possible to sell off some parts of the estate for the sole purpose of paying off the debts. Lochbuy was a troubled estate, but it still seemed possible that it might be put on its feet again.

Murdoch's character was infinitely suited to the task awaiting him. The letters which passed between the Maclean kindred after he was served heir in 1785 were full of respect and confidence in his management. 'I am happy in the belief that your known Prudence, Frugality and Judicious Management will bring matters with the Creditors to be put on an easy footing,' wrote a John McLaine from Jamaica.[3] This seemed to be the view of all the people who had dealt with Murdoch as a merchant, an army officer and a go-between.

His first misfortune in his new role was that owing to his required presence at the murder trial in London, he was unable to be in Mull for the sett of his tacks at Whitsunday 1785. Tacks and leases ran from Whitsunday for a variable number of years, depending on the importance of the farm. John Maclaine of Gruline had been retained because of his knowledge of the estate, but his methods were inefficient, and his payments always in such arrears that he was continually at the centre of a clamour for money. He was in the habit of accepting rents in tiny instalments, and like the bulk of his subtenants and small joint tenants, was at the mercy of the drovers. Murdoch would have liked to select tenants for his key lands, especially since even the longer leases fell to be renewed in 1785. Luckily, one of the very few men he could trust to delegate the stewardship of the estate to, had arrived back in Greenock from Jamaica on 29 February 1784, and was facing a period of unemployment after the disbanding of his regiment. This was Murdoch's nephew, Lachlan Macquarie, now twenty-five years old, honest to a fault, and eager to oblige the uncle who had given him his first step in the army. 'Lachy' was to be an unofficial secretary and factor on the estate for nearly three years, travelling across Mull, carrying out commissions, going to Edinburgh, and even London, when required. It was Lachy who kept estate accounts, and a logbook of tacks and rents. He was to acquire a thorough knowledge of both the land and the people all over the island, so that, when the time came for him to have hopes of owning land himself, he was not simply a dreamer with a sentimental memory of the Mull of his childhood, but a realistic and experienced factor, who had marketed cattle and counted sheep stocks before being promoted captain in the 77th Regiment in 1788.[4]

Another problem which clouded Murdoch's future plans was that the paymaster of his regiment was claiming money from him, and from other officers of the 84th, which Allan Maclean of Torloisk now began to worry him about. As Murdoch had a clear conscience about his finances, he did not choose to pay much attention to Allan's agitation. But matters became serious when a judicial investigation was proposed, and the brigadier-general insisted that he come to London to testify, if he did not want to be ruined and his half pay stopped. For a man who was being besieged on every side with financial claims on both his personal finances and his estate, he was remarkable in that he was able to give thought to the urgent business of matrimony.

Murdoch's lawyer, Mr Allan MacDougall, Writer to the Signet, had produced a plan in February 1785 for managing Lochbuy, with sixteen pieces of advice which amounted to a ranking of priorities in dealing with debt, and included new borrowings which would pay off old creditors.[5] He reckoned without the acquisitive but slow cunning of the Mull relations; in the autumn of that year, Murdoch had chosen his future wife, and had approached her father, believing that it was feasible that he might be soon free of debt with that ability for good management which had always attached to his name. His choice of bride was from the circle of Argyll landowners he was now joining. To Jane Campbell, daughter of Sir John Campbell of Airds, he could now give the name of an old, and formerly much respected, family. Her father, descended from Donald Campbell of Airds, once chamberlain to the Dukes of Argyll, and her mother, a daughter of Archibald Campbell of Stonefield, were one of the first families in the county. They lived at Airds House, an early Georgian mansion house in Appin, built by Donald Campbell in 1738. The house, which still stands, is situated on Airds Bay, looking towards Lismore and the mountains of Mull, and was one of the main destinations on the mainland for people crossing from Mull in the eighteenth century. Sir John and Lady Campbell had a son and three daughters, all as yet unmarried. The oldest girl, Jane, was about twenty-four when Murdoch, aged fifty-five, began his courtship. It was likely that he had known the family well, as they had a house in Edinburgh, and had been customers in Murdoch's old ledger book. Jane may have met her future husband before his departure for North America in 1775, when, by all accounts, he had been a personable man, as shown in his portrait. If ten years had ravaged his appearance, he seems to have remained 'a gallant knight in the service of the ladies',[6] still capable of raising blushes and hopes. His letters to Jane, as they struggled to defeat the other calls on his time in order to meet at Airds in the New Year of 1786, are touchingly boyish, commending her for her rational and uniform conduct, when he expected her to be impatient of the delays he encountered in producing a satisfactory account of his financial situation for her father. 'My lovely fair', as he called her, had been informed by her father of the possible difficulties she might have as Lochbuy's wife, and had been warned by her mother that doing without certain luxuries was not easy. Jane was given ample freedom to change her mind, but remained resolute. She was a sensible, well-educated young woman. Her mother displayed a partiality for Murdoch which was understandable in a woman nearer his age than her daughter, but a revealing sentence in Jane's letter says little for her opinion of Gillean. 'My mother did not care to tell you that she did not at all like Mr Gillean Maclaine, that she would like much better your nephew, Lieutenant Macquarie, if you had mentioned him.' Lady Airds was never to know that her second daughter, Elizabeth, would many years later marry this preferred young man.

Murdoch Maclaine of Lochbuy and Jane Campbell were married on 14 February 1786 at Airds. About this time, and unknown to Murdoch, a boat arrived at Moy House, carrying Gillean and some Scallastle men. John Maclaine, tacksman of Gruline was living in Moy, as he had been for some years, with his sister Miss Ketty, but as he was on the mainland, Gillean asked Miss Ketty for the key to a closet, which she refused, saying she must ask her brother first. Then, said the teller of the tale

> He took a key from his pocket ... opened the closet, from which he took a writing desk, two trunks, and two swords. The trunks and desks she thinks were sealed at the time they carried them away. She says that Charles Roy Maclean was there, one of her brother's servants, who may inform you what other servants were about the house [7]

After the marriage of Murdoch and Jane, the couple remained at Airds. With John Gruline in residence at the old house of Moy, there was nowhere for them to live, so that the order of tasks was first to make the farmhouse of Gruline habitable, and move the sister and brother back there, then to make some small repairs and improvements on Moy, which was still as it was when Dr Johnson had stayed there. Then Murdoch and Jane would move into Moy and stay there while a new house was being built at Lochbuy. John Stevenson, one of the resourceful Stevenson brothers who had changed Oban from a hamlet with three houses to a thriving village and port, was engaged for both undertakings. Indeed, there was no other 'architect' or builder in 'the Country' able to take on such work. Stevenson had been involved in the building of several new houses in Argyll, and his method was to receive a rough sketch from the client, and to design a variation on his usual theme. Murdoch had allotted £200 to the house, but although Stevenson was a man of integrity, who did not take advantage of his monopoly of the market, this was deemed impossible, and there were delays in the agreement as Murdoch looked for funds. It was, Stevenson said, a very large house (by Mull standards, but not in comparison with Airds, where he was doing masonry work).[8] Six months later, Stevenson was offering to come and look at the stance, and at the quarries, for he used local stone, employing his own quarriers on or near the estate of the client, and moving the stone by boat. In the case of Lochbuy he proposed taking stone from Carsaig and slates from Easdale. The joinery work was to be done by Murdoch's sister Peggy's son-in-law, 'honest Farquhar Maclaine' from Oskamull. In May 1789, the joiners began the roofing, and in 1790 the floors of the dining room and drawing room, roughly similar in size, at about 23 by 16 feet. Stevenson was rushing from place to place, supervising work, complaining that 'Pennygail' did not pay him, and apologising for the torrential rain which fell on Lochbuy.

For John Stevenson, who was also a merchant and a kelp dealer, there were problems in being the only house builder in the area. He was also in demand as the only bridge builder, and was engaged to build the Clachan bridge as a preliminary to the laying out of the village of Tobermory. He needed cash flow, as all building businesses do, and MacGilvra of Pennyghael was notorious for his unwillingness to pay. It was fortunate that the Stevenson brothers were able to offer money for kelp as the only means of getting their own fees. In the year 1790–91, crops failed, potatoes rotted in the sodden ground and cattle prices fell. Like the Mull drovers, the Stevensons had come to be important to the economy of the island, but many of those in Mull who sold kelp undermined that importance by finding that Liverpool merchants paid a higher price.

After removing the writing desk and trunks from Moy in 1786, Gillean talked much of leaving Mull. What prevented him was his involvement in the Ormaig reversion, and his expectation of money from it. From resources which remained unexplained, he was able to maintain a house in Crosscauseway in Edinburgh, where his older children went to school, so that he and his wife, no longer called 'Mally' as every Mary in Mull was, but dignified by the name of Marie, lived apart for much of the year. They employed a tutor, who came to Mull in the summer, and returned to Edinburgh with Marie and the children in time for the beginning of the school and college term. This arrangement has had the happy effect of supplying us with letters passed between husband and wife, which show Marie as a poor writer and a timid woman, afraid of Gillean, and blindly attached to her young. Her father, Lachlan MacQuarrie, who always had a happy turn of phrase, referred to them as 'Marie Scallastle and her cubs'. She bore twelve children altogether, two dying in infancy, so that there were six born before 1779 and four between 1783 and 1788. In 1787, Gillean wrote to Murdoch to say

> My poor wife was yesterday brought to bed of a Fair Lady which was like to cost the Mother her life. However, she is now likely to recover. She protests against any more battles of that kind, and I am much of her opinion, and it's likely I shall stop process in that cause.[9]

But stopping process was something he was unable to do, in spite of the presence in his library of Daniel Defoe's anonymously published *Use and Abuse of the Marriage Bed*, with its recommendation of matrimonial chastity and condemnation of what Defoe called prostitution within marriage.[10] As this book also contained a passage on birth 'on the wrong side of the blankets' with animadversions such as 'No time, no merit of persons, no purchase of honours, or titles, can wipe out the remembrance of it', it must have made painful reading for Gillean in his reflective moments, and we are tempted to ask what construction he might have put upon its baleful message.[11]

The slightly smutty connotations which in the eighteenth century surrounded the conception of twins also gave Gillean a certain sexual notoriety. 'Gillean has got two boys at one birth', was how the news of the twins' birth was relayed in 1777, and the underlying innuendo was that he had 'entered double', an idea that was seized upon with glee by General Allan Maclean of Torloisk when Jane and Murdoch were thought to be expecting twins in 1791, and which prompted an anecdote about an old man who had thus caused his wife to bear twins.[12]

The two oldest of the little ones, Flora and Hector had stayed in Mull with a nurse when Marie wrote to Gillean in 1788, two weeks after the birth of Margaret Ann.

Edinburgh 13th September 1788

My Dearest,

Yours by Mr McLachlan I received ... I am now in good health & prity stout. In a fue dayes I shall be abel to take jurnie to Mull if you woud receive me. I am a little Dife [deaf] and when you scole me you need not expect a return ... Ould marie was her [here] and she brought me no jeas [cheese] she wantes Allan and Lauchlan to thathe [thatch] her house and see in her pototes before she goes home ther is fine wether her now ... I hope your hay harvest is over by this time Kelpe deliverit ... the young lady [the new baby] calls & I must answer.[13]

Gillean and Marie now had ten living children. Marie was forty-one, and still having children – what they called in the Highlands 'happy moments', except that they were now mostly unhappy, and made her ill. Jane Campbell, Mrs Maclaine of Lochbuy (she was not so apt to be called Lady Lochbuy with the old Lady Lochbuy still alive) had become pregnant in the spring following her marriage, but her husband, now dragged to London by Allan Maclean and the exigencies of the paymaster affair, was unable to stay in Mull, Airds or Edinburgh. Added to that was the uncomfortable fact that the brigadier-general was pressing him, on behalf of his sister Mary, to repay a loan she had made to Murdoch before the due date, because she could get a return of 10 per cent elsewhere. Every new day was bringing another creditor into the arena. Suddenly everyone in 'the Country' was suing for payment from the estate, including Archy's two sisters, Isabella and Catherine, who had had no portions, old Lady Lochbuy, whose annuity had not been paid, and faithful Gruline, whose payments on Archy's behalf, and to Archy, had not been refunded. In London, the paymaster of the 84th Regiment had caused the other senior officer, John Small to be arrested, and was spreading rumours of Murdoch's having tampered with the accounts. Allan Maclean wrote in June 1786, protesting that Murdoch did not have to oversee the repair of the tottering mansion of his predecessor, but must come to London to attend the enquiry. By August, the paymaster's impending charge was malpractice, and by September Murdoch's conduct was 'infamous' according to the brigadier-general. At last Murdoch consented to go to London and give evidence at the enquiry.

It is not known what the immediate findings of the court were, but it is

clear that Murdoch left London as soon as he could. His departure was followed
by a furious note from Allan Maclean:

London, 28th November 1786

Dear Sir

Your abrupt, clandestine & shabby departure yesterday by taking french
leave was to me not only a matter of surprise, but of real astonishment –
worst of all your offence to Miss Maclean. The only way you can redeem
yourself & recover her good opinion is to pay £100 immediately, and
discharge the whole bond at once. If you cannot get the £3000, remit her
£100 ...

and a week later another angry epistle:

You were in such a hurry to quit this place ... you must be over the hills
and far away. In fact I suppose you are in *Prick Haste,* and now that the
coast is clear, and the Cellar Empty, you want to be doing, but take my
advice and be not so rash. The more haste the less speed. Be cautious Young
Man. You will get a bellyfull of that business before you are many years
older. I am now to inform you that Colonel Small is immediately to commence
an action of defamation & libell against Major Macdonald. As you have full
as much reason as the Colonel to attack him in that way, and your proof
from the Court of Enquiry perfectly clear, I am desired to ask you if you
will join the Colonel in carrying on the action ... [14]

Such senseless litigation followed by the threat of more legal action goaded
Murdoch into sending an angry reply which has not survived. We only know
that when he returned to Airds he found that his young wife had had a
miscarriage.

There is no reason to suppose that there was any element of competition
between Murdoch and Gillean in the matter of procreation. Gillean had won
hands down, and the question was not uppermost in his mind. But when the
first Lochbuy child was born, in 1787, she was a girl, christened Jane after
both mother and grandmother, given to a wet nurse to be reared, as was the
custom among the lesser gentry, and sent to Airds where Lady Campbell
supervised her infant routine and wrote letters to Lochbuy reporting on her
progress. John Stevenson was only beginning on the house. Murdoch was
consumed with all the unpleasantness which was inevitable when those who
had been his friends, who had enrolled his help in their struggles for payment
from old Lochbuy, now turned into his own most inimical creditors. Turning
to the clauses of the entail which allowed him to sell land in order to pay the
debts of his predecessor, he met with approval from his lawyer, Allan
MacDougall, who considered that he had a perfect right to apply for permission
to sell a small portion of the estate. To their surprise, Gillean launched a
most virulent opposition, filing objections to what had already been spent on
the estate, and even to costs which had been paid from Murdoch's own purse.

As the next heir of entail, Gillean was empowered by the Entail Act to resist the sale, but it did occur to Murdoch that if he was acting *qua* heir, a marginal sale of land must benefit all heirs.[15]

Gillean had been suffering for some years from an unspecified ailment, the main manifestation of which was an acute pain in his side which prevented riding and walking. Marie bleated in every letter about looking after his health, and Gillean had told Murdoch as early as 1784 that his rheumatism was so severe he could not cross the threshold. He complained of pain frequently after Archy's death, and was restricted in his activities, except when they concerned the retrieval of writing desks and trunks of papers, or going to Edinburgh on urgent legal business. But in the letters written in her own hand, in her inimitable way, Marie expressed a pathetic but justified anxiety for the husband she had come to regard as the embodiment of all wisdom and authority. When she was too busy with her 'cubs', she employed her stepson Lauchlan, Gillean's natural son, who was being educated with her own children, as an amanuensis. Lauchlan, who was only one year older than Allan, Gillean and Marie's firstborn, actually enjoyed writing to his father, in his own way, at length and in detail. Allan rarely bothered. Allan was intended for the law, but Lauchlan was being educated in accountancy, book-keeping, and a shorthand system of the time, to fit him for a clerical post. From a single letter of Lauchlan's there is a strong impression of motivation in the house in Crosscauseway. Modern psychoanalysts might be tempted to say that Marie was compensating for the feckless father who had not cared enough to have her taught to spell, and Gillean for his accident of birth, which had placed him after both Archy and Murdoch, in spite of being much cleverer than either. It might also be added that Lauchlan wanted to please his father, who showed more partiality to him than Marie did.

Gillean's influence on Marie was powerful and authoritative. It is not difficult to see that he impressed her with his superiority to all the rest of the Lochbuys, and with his undeniable right to the honours he already possessed. The action for Reduction was probably presented to her as the reaction of a foolish old man. She had probably never had access to that 'universal knowledge' which described her husband as 'active, designing, uncommonly acute, industrious, crafty and persevering in his own interest'.[16]

The Scallastle family was so large, so autonomous, so self-contained, so sure of itself, so motivated and so inward-looking, that it did not question its view of the world. Yet it mixed with the best college society in Edinburgh, and on the day that Lauchlan wrote his most pleasing letter to his father in Mull, Professor William Robertson, Principal of the University, Enlightenment man, and author of *The History of America*, was taking tea with Marie. He asked with interest about the children's intellectual development, and advised Lauchlan to learn French.[17] And who else in Mull would ever have been interested in the collection of modern classic texts which Archy had brought home to Moy in 1770, and left there when he sailed to America? When John Lochbuy died, Gillean had removed them to Scallastle for the betterment of his family, and as his own rightful reward.[18]

His reward in the afterlife was coming fast upon him. Having inculcated the view that his family were the true heirs of entail to Lochbuy, and the inevitable heirs, since Murdoch had no son, Gillean succumbed to the great pains in his side, and died on 23 November 1788.

His oldest son succeeded to the long lease which had never been reduced or altered in the Reduction, which Allan knew nothing of. Allan did not apply himself to law, but contented himself with that dangerous thing, a little learning. Lauchlan was packed off to the West Indies to fend for himself as soon as Marie recovered sufficiently to speak. Her cries of poverty were not empty ones, for a widow's lot in Mull was a terrible one. Gillean had left no Will, a curious omission for one bred to the law, but perhaps a wise one, since such a document might draw attention to things better left alone. His repositories were sealed, and John Gruline guarded them in his ponderous and ineffectual manner, until he too died suddenly, leaving chaos behind him. If Murdoch thought for one moment that he had got rid of a thorn in his flesh (although their relations had continued cordial enough), he was mistaken. Allan Scallastle was to prove the greatest adversary of all to his plans for the estate.

Murdoch Maclaine, who had always paid his bills on time and dealt honourably with the world, now found himself in the dishonourable position of having no option but to act like Fabius Maximus, the well-known Roman delayer. Claims on the estate were impossible to satisfy, and many, such as the action for unpaid portions from the McGilvras of Pennyghael, were still affected by Gillean's revision of his father's intentions in providing for his daughters. A claim from Barbara, Archy's widow, was turned down by the courts in Edinburgh on the grounds that she had no marriage contract. She visited old Lady Lochbuy in Port Glasgow, and returned to America no richer than before. Old Lady Lochbuy tried living with her daughter Catherine (Boswell's filly) at Pennyghael, but complained of being 'plundered' by her son-in-law, Hugh. He had sold her cattle without consulting her, and acted as the ungenerous man he undoubtedly was. Lachlan MacQuarrie of Ulva begged for £10 here and there, and Murdoch gave him it, but this was not to suppose that Murdoch was dispensing largesse. It is more likely that he had a reserve of cash in MacQuarrie's name which could not have been safely given to the old man except in very small amounts. Allan Maclean of Torloisk, after some years of irking Murdoch with unpleasant threats over Miss Mary's money, was at last satisfied that a repayment was coming. 'You always mix evasions with your promises, and tell me without any remorse that you will pay all the expense of your house building before you pay any attention to the distressed situation of poor Mary.'

In 1790, Allan Maclean organised a jaunt to Mull for himself and his wife. They were, of course, to stay at Torloisk with Allan's brother, the laird, but as the relationship between the two brothers is to be considered in the following chapter, only the Lochbuy visit and its consequences will be related here. On Allan's last visit, in 1787, he had inspected Jane, the new young Mrs Maclaine. 'A prodigious favourite of mine on so short an acquaintance, and I am certain the longer I should know her the more I should esteem her, and I own you are *a lucky dog.*' Now he was bringing Janet, and wrote from Edinburgh:

Your cousin [Janet was remotely related to Murdoch] has often promised to be at your House if ever she went to Mull, and yet she is so terrified at being on horseback that I am at a loss how to accomplish it, for I do know if once she gets to Torloisk before going to Moy, she would not ride from Torloisk to Moy, not if the Duke of Argyll was to make her a present of his Mull estate. In truth, it is not airs that she gives herself, but she is miserable at the idea of being on horseback. She is indeed much afraid of water, but once in a good Boat, and the weather good, we might proceed from Oban to Loch Spelve, but I am Confident without your own presence I would be forced to land her on the first rock we could fetch at Achnacraig. By an accident we shall be obliged to remain here till next Monday the 31st May, but on the 5th June, please God, we shall be at Oban, but if you were idle, & had not a great deal to do, I should not be sorry to meet you there. I hope you have seen Robert Stewart.[19] If not, you and I must be at open war.[20]

From the evidence of the following letters, it seems that the visit, like most visits which are quickly forgotten, was a mixed success, with Janet sulking in her room at Lochbuy and refusing to come out, while Jane, who had just given birth to another daughter, exercised all her Airds diplomacy. Allan, as blunt as ever, called his wife a 'foolish wrong-headed woman' and her moods 'the whims of a foolish woman who has done her best to make herself and me ridiculous'. But the husband was no sooner gone, and on his way home, when his musings about what had passed in Mull enflamed his wrath:

Having spoke to you twice about the payment of Miss Mary Maclean, which you had positively engaged to pay last Whitsunday, in place of talking the matter over with Coolness and Moderation, you got into a most Violent Passion both times, & not only treated me Very Cavalierly, but called her a damn'd Bitch, etc., insomuch that in my Conscience I believe that had I had as Little Command of my temper as you, Pistoles would have ended the dispute. Permit me then, my good Friend, to tell you a truth, which is that you are the most altered man I ever saw. In short, you are grown so great & so mighty that you are not my old friend Murdoch Maclaine that I knew formerly. You are quite a different person, and that your own will and pleasure must be the rule with everyone you have to do with. As a Landlord & Companion you are an excellent fellow ... but I should ever wish to avoid having Money transactions with you. Let me however intreat that you will pay off Miss Mary Maclean at Martinmass next. If not I am certain she will be under the necessity of applying to the Court of Session. Should that be the case, you are not to blame that Villan Mr Campbell,[21] as his advice is not to be asked. My best respects to Mrs Maclaine. I hope this will find you, her, and the young ones [22] in perfect good health, and assure yourself that there is not, of your Name or Family, one man that more sincerely wishes the firm Establishment & Wellbeing of your Person & Family than myself, at the same time that I do most cordially dislike and reprobate the supercilious haughty new mode you have adopted, & by which you would compell Everyman to think and act as you would have them. In spite of which, believe me truly, My dear Murdoch, Your friend and humble Servant, Allan Maclean.[23]

This and other attempts ('for God's sake, Murdoch, keep the straight road. Do not march crooked ...') to restore Murdoch to his old self did not sit well on such an ambivalent man as Allan Maclean, but within a month or two he had forgotten Miss Mary Maclean in the excitement of new independent companies being raised, one of which was in the command of his young brother-in-law, Fitzroy Grafton Maclean. Fitzroy was already in the West Indies with his regiment, but thought that some Mull men might be raised on his behalf. Allan, whose great delight it was to raise men, was once more in his element, writing to Drimnin, Drimnin's son Kinlochaline, Alexander of Coll and his own brother Lachlan Torloisk. 'I wish you would write to your Nephew Donald at Edinburgh,' wrote Allan to Murdoch, 'to set every iron in the fire.' To Allan, all the Mull families had now become Fitzroy's, or Grafton's cousins, although as far as they knew, Grafton had not given them a thought in his life.

Murdoch was negotiating with the 'Villan', John Campbell, to make payment to his creditors as soon as he could sell the requisite part of the estate. The part to be sacrificed was Ardmeanach, on the north east of Loch Scridain, and for this, permission had to be obtained from the heirs of entail. Just as Gillean had opposed proposals to sell before his death, so now did his son Allan Scallastle (who in 1791 had left Edinburgh, and given up his plans for becoming a Writer), producing such a host of reasons that the lawyers were taken aback. Every setback in the selling of land was a delay in payment to the creditors, and created more bad feeling. It was a happy interlude in a depressing set of circumstances when, in 1791, Jane, who was thought at first to be expecting twins, gave birth to her fourth child, a son. He was not called after either Murdoch's father or Jane's but christened Murdoch. In the very next year a second son was born; the door was thus closed against the Scallastle family. It did not seem likely that Allan Scallastle, aided and abetted by his mother, would persevere with their ambition to possess the estate.

But with Allan home in Mull, the mother and son seemed not to notice that their chances were diminished, and if anything, they had stiffened in their resolve. They had refused to pay the rent of Scallastle, Ledirkle and Garmony from the time of Gillean's death, forcing Murdoch to a court action, which he undertook with good-natured reluctance, only to find that the law agents could get no replies from Allan. If Murdoch wrote to Marie – that once girlish Mally MacQuarrie who had long ago bought silks and pattens from his shop – she answered civilly but coldly that she had nothing to do with him, and had instructed her son to do no business with him. If Murdoch was Fabius Maximus, Marie was a stumbling-block.

Charles Macquarie, Lachy's younger brother, also returned from Edinburgh, where he had been under the watchful eye of his cousin Donald, having qualified himself as a notary public. He had turned out extremely well. Donald had written often about how clever he was. Now, like Lachy before him, he was learning about managing an estate, and lived at Moy. His mother Peggy lived at Oskamull, on the ducal territory, sharing a farm with her son-in-law, honest Farquhar. His brother Lachlan was in India, where Allan Maclean was quite sure he was going to expire in some manner or other. Allan went as far, in 1792, as to write to India House for a list of the killed and wounded, so that he could search for Lachlan's name with cheerful antici-pation.[24] For Murdoch, the advent of this second Macquarie brother was to be of great benefit, even if it was to last less than three years, and Charles was to take off in search of his true vocation. It is unlikely that Charles found his uncle 'a despotic Highland chieftain' as Allan did in the letter following.

> Present my best respects to Mrs Maclaine Lochbuy, for whom I have the highest esteem, and I must say that you have been luckier than you deserved to be in getting so amiable & good-natured a wife, who can with so much good humour bear with your oddities and whims, for let me tell you my good friend that you are greatly altered in temper & disposition since you are laird of Lochbuy ... not the Murdoch Maclaine I was acquainted with ... You are a despotic Highland Chieftain ... a pity you was not one of the disciples of the famous Mahomet, and if you had been, and was then trans-ported to the eleventh heaven ... surrounded with the Houris ... I am certain you would soon wish to be back again to the amiable good-natured woman at Moy. But all Allegory apart, it is a fact that all your old friends think you greatly altered ... not the jolly, good-natured, honest fellow you used to be ... Descend from your hills, and put yourself on a level with your old friends, that you & I may go on in our usual friendly way ... expeditiously & pleasantly, without complaint or murmuring.[25]

It was becoming a familiar refrain, but Allan did not consider his own behaviour to be partly responsible for the changes in his friend. In a way different from Gillean, he was always in the right. Charles, however, was to add another facet to the portrait of Lochbuy when he met Lord St Vincent five years later:

> He [Lord St Vincent] affects to be more *austere* than he really is. By the bye, he puts me in mind of what I have sometimes observed in you. When the side of his face next the person he is displeased at has a *frown* on it, the side farthest off *smiles*.[26]

Over the whole of Mull, the 1790s brought disaster and privation, not simply for the usual reasons of bad weather and low prices, but through the deaths of key figures who normally pulled the strings of Mull's fragile economy. John Maclaine of Gruline's death in 1792 caused his papers to be locked up until they could be examined by a competent judge of their import. His notes had been kept on tiny scraps, and his figures were illegible, so that his complicated transactions with the two stots of some miserable subtenant could barely be understood, except by the poor family who lost a year's income by his demise. His business was transferred to Lochbuy, and Charles Macquarie, a man of compassion and understanding, tried to unravel the credits and debits.

Three years later, another death caused even more havoc. Dr Andrew Maclaine, who lived at Pennygown, was a qualified surgeon who had become a cattle dealer because there was little profit in his medical practice. He had a lease of extensive lands in the Bentalla and Glenforsa parts of the Lochbuy estate, bred cattle, travelled up and down to the cattle markets at Doune and Falkirk, and had the reputation of being rich and clever. 'But for my old friend Dr Andrew, I suppose his attention is more taken up with money-making than friendship,' an expatriate Maclean wrote to Gillean in 1783.[27] Dr Andrew, like most Mull people, was related to everyone else. His brother Donald, also a doctor, lived in Sorne, and then in Pennygown, and was married to Mary McNicol, daughter of the minister of Lismore. Another brother, Hugh, was a vintner in Tobermory. Dr Andrew had married Janet McLachlan, sister of Eun McLachlan of Laudale in Morvern, whose father, Dugald was tacksman of Achnacraig in Mull. With such tentacles of relationships there were bound to be complex patterns of money lending, but the trouble was that when Dr Andrew went to the market in 1795, he took quantities of black cattle from every part of the island, and just about everyone was awaiting his return with anxiety, so that they could pay someone else. But Dr Andrew never did return, unless it was to be buried in Pennygown churchyard, for he collapsed at Glenorchy on his way home from the Michaelmas Falkirk Tryst. The £360 in cash found on his person had been used for immediate payments, and for the funeral, and then it had been discovered that this seemingly rich man was in an impending state of bankruptcy, and that everyone involved with him in business was going to be a loser.[28]

Dr Andrew's finances were largely in the hands of Allan MacDougall, that very same lawyer who acted for Lochbuy, who felt the shock waves of his cattle-dealing client's collapse just at a time when he was tottering on the edge of a financial disaster of his own, and the rumour of losses of £70,000 quickly sped around 'the Country', indicating that it was only a matter of time before Mr MacDougall failed. John Stevenson told Murdoch he should go to Edinburgh to find out what was happening, but before Murdoch could get off, the bankruptcy of MacDougall was confirmed, and a meeting of creditors arranged.

It might seem strange to us today that a lawyer should be broken in this manner, but in the late eighteenth century, lawyers arranged finance mainly for land and agricultural transactions which banks did not touch. As we have seen in the case of Miss Mary Maclean, many small amounts of money had to be found separately, and bonds negotiated in order to collect sums large enough for the needs of borrowers. A handful of lawyers such as MacDougall and Colquhoun Grant served an area like 'the Country' and could collapse like a house of cards. MacDougall and Dr Andrew were both men in their forties, with what might be called collateral employment. Allan MacDougall had been an agent for the government-sponsored Commission of Annexed Estates,[29] and was regarded by all as a most respectable and honest man.

It was in this climate that Murdoch was attempting to restore the fortunes of Lochbuy. In 1793, France had declared war on Britain, and among the seven fencible regiments formed in Scotland, the Argyllshire Fencibles commanded by the Marquis of Lorne, George William Campbell, recruited 100 men from the duke's estate in the Ross and elsewhere in Mull, and Murdoch joined the same regiment with about sixty. At the end of 1794, Murdoch was commissioned Lieutenant-Colonel of the Dunbartonshire Fencibles. Charles Macquarie was left in charge of the estate only until he too should join a regiment. Everyone's mind was on military preparations, and this state of affairs was to last for several years. In 1797, in reply to a letter from Murdoch, the Duke of Argyll wrote:

> From the alarm you express in your letter for the safety of Mull, I am induced to suppose that you have not heard that the report of the Enemy's having landed in Ireland has been some time since proved to be groundless.
>
> The intention of an Attempt to land in Ireland, tho for the present completely defeated, will call the attention of government to the Security of that Country by having a Naval Force on the North Coast of Ireland which will of course protect all the Western Islands and Coasts of Scotland. By this means I consider these parts to be in greater safety than ever they were in any former war. You seem also to forget that there is a Company of Volunteers in the Island and another at Oban. There are many objections to placing a thousand or five hundred arms at Duart Castle, without a large body of men constantly stationed there, and it might be an inducement to

Three Writers to the Signet, Allan MacDougall, Alexander Watson and
Colquhoun Grant (father-in-law of Donald Maclean WS). Allan MacDougall's
financial collapse affected Mull's economy. Colquhoun Grant was said to have made
money out of the litigious tendencies of the Mull gentry. (*Kay's Edinburgh Portraits*)

foreign Enemys or disaffected neighbours to come there on purpose to take possession of them.

     I am, etc.

       Your Humble Servant

         Argyll.[30]

The duke was always very conscious of disaffected Highlanders, and he instructed his chamberlain to refuse renewal of leases to the more recalcitrant ones. He may have thought it was the Campbell name which provoked refusals to serve, but Murdoch did not always have an easy time with his Maclean followers. He had received a petition in 1795 from tenants, cottars, crofters, followers and 'all other inhabitants' refusing to give their consent to their sons' enlistment, and pre-empting the laird's response by offering to give up their possessions and remove at Whitsunday.[31] The worm was beginning to turn.

But the real worm in Murdoch's life was Gillean's eldest son, Allan Maclaine of Scallastle. Throughout the 1790s, he had apparently employed all his waking hours in obstructing Murdoch's plans for selling off parts of the estate to pay its debts, and Allan, although by the birth of two males in the Lochbuy family he was farther than ever from inheriting, used his position as an heir of entail to veto all such proposals. When Murdoch finally decided to take the matter to the courts, Allan presented his lawyers with no fewer than thirty-eight objections, all of which required a response from Murdoch. The long series of notes which Murdoch made for his man of law shows that he had had to burn the midnight oil over the dark nights of winter 1799. Allan criticised every minute piece of expenditure on the estate, as if, Murdoch told his own lawyer, he was the rightful laird of an estate for which Murdoch was a mere factor or temporary custodian. Murdoch could not resist making remarks on the causes of this extraordinary attitude, and gave it as his opinion that Allan's mother, Marie MacQuarrie was behind it all. Referring back to the Reduction, which few now remembered as it had happened forty years before, Murdoch, calling himself 'the present Lochbuy', told Mr Campbell, his lawyer,

> At the earlie periote above mentioned, the Present Lochbuy & Hector Maclean of Torloisk were among the first friends to the faimily who had discovered Gillean's imposition on his Father, and were among those who laid to the means of reducing those deeds, and from that periote the present Lochbuy was alwise looked on with Jelous Eyes by Scalasdale and his widow, who, and not Allan, is the Promoter & Conductor of the present trouble given to him.[32]

At the end of his remarks, Murdoch, exhausted by the frivolous objections, added what he alone knew, since almost everyone else concerned was dead. It was that Archy had left Mull because he could no longer endure his friends there, or his family, or his brother Gillean who had resumed ingratiating himself with his facile father. Gillean, Murdoch wrote, abandoning any vow of silence he had ever taken on the subject, was a *'snaik in the grass'*, who embraced this opportunity of proposing the Tailzie [33] to Archy, and had chosen to leave Murdoch in his expected position in the line of succession to make the document more palatable. The Tailzie had been executed in 'a secret manner in Gillean's own house in Scalasdale, and kept a profound secret from every person in the Country, particularly the present Lochbuy, who was then abroad, and the witnesses did not know what they were signing.' [34] In America, Murdoch elaborated, for the benefit of his legal representative, the present Lochbuy had not been able to keep Archibald from expensive and disgraceful scrapes. He had lent him money, and had been given in return a lease of the old mansion house of Moy [35] and power of attorney for Archibald. It had been quite clear that Archibald had had no intention of returning to Mull.

So, in his exasperation, Murdoch Maclaine the nineteenth of Lochbuy gave his own account of the old events which had changed his life to the younger lawyer in charge of his case with Allan Maclaine of Scallastle. For Mr Campbell was too young to remember the Reduction, and too new to see the entail as another attempt on Gillean's part to change the destination of the estate. But Murdoch had not finished his observations. 'In this manner,' he continued, 'matters stood till after the death of Archibald Lochbuy, when, and not sooner, the Tailzie made its appearance and indeed surprised the present Lochbuy and all the friends not a little. The first resolution was to lay it aside by an action in court, as it was justly considered to amount to nothing else but to disconcert the operations of the present Lochbuy, and impede the payment of the honourable creditors. But this by varied advice, and the friendship expressed by Gillean and his faimily for the present Lochbuy, it was not executed.'

Murdoch had never harboured a grudge. He was even in the habit of inviting Allan Scallastle to a deer hunt at the end of a letter in which he had pleaded with the younger man to answer a letter or pay a bill. If his impatience with Allan was thinly disguised, he nevertheless seems to have resolved always to end on a note of kindness. With these examples of forbearance we must consider that he might have entertained a suspicion that the entail was fabricated entirely by Gillean. Murdoch must have known in his heart if the 'Tailzie' was true or false.

Over 200 years later we can only reserve judgement. Had not Daniel Maclean, as far back as 1759, written to Hector Maclean of Torloisk saying, 'I am told Gillean has lately been guilty of forgery, and detected'? [36] Had not Counsel for the Prosecution in Maclaine *v.* Maclaine pronounced Gillean to be 'universally known as active, designing, uncommonly acute, industrious, crafty, and persevering in his own interest, his natural abilities brought to perfection by his education as a Writer, in which capacity he is by no means delicate in method, if the end can be attained'?[37] Are not the boxes of papers of Gillean Maclaine which survive today swollen with copies of Entail Acts and of the Lochbuy Entail? And with copies of petitions written by Gillean in 1785 to the Lords of Council and Session requesting that Archy's Tailzie be recorded, and that it should take effect?[38] The Lords of Council and Session duly recorded the entail in the register, as requested, agreeable to the 'act 22nd parliament 1st, James VII, anno 1685 ... an Act concerning tailzies', where it was to remain uninspected until sixty years later, when little Murdie, wild with desire for cash, saw fit to ask to see it.

Notes

1. It is not known for certain that the body of the victim was returned for the trial.
2. NAS. GD174/2154. Letters of Hector Maclean to MM, 1783–85. See also Duncanson, op. cit.
3. This John Maclaine was the nephew of John Maclaine of Gruline, later confusingly to be known as 'Gruline' himself, when he returned to Mull in the 1790s. Maclean Sinclair mentions him in *Clan Gillean*, but does not seem to have known about the previous Gruline, his uncle.
4. LM's ledger of accounts in his regiment in Jamaica saw double service as a transaction book for the Lochbuy estate. GD174/2172.
5. NAS. GD174/841. Scheme for managing the estate of Lochbuy, 1785.
6. NAS. GD174/1396/1. Miss Mary Maclean of Torloisk to MM, London, 16 January 1786.
7. NAS. GD174/1479/11. John, younger tacksman of Gruline (the nephew) to MM, Gruline, 5 March 1800.
8. NAS. GD174/1410/2. John Stevenson to MM, Oban, 5 October 1787.
9. NAS. GD174/1371. GM to MM, 7 April 1787.
10. NAS. GD174/193. Inventory of Books found in a Press in a Parlour in the House of Mr Gillean MacLaine Writer in Mull, 8 May 1789.
11. *Use and Abuse ...*, Chapter V, the section on bastardy has an interesting bearing on the later opinions of Gillean's *legitimate* son, Allan Maclaine.
12. NAS. GD174/1387/64. AM to MM, Margate, 7 September 1791. The old man was Sir Stephen Fox.
13. GRO. Uncatalogued MSS. Marie Maclaine to GM, Edinburgh, 13 September 1788.
14. NAS. GD174/1387/11 and 12, AM to MM, London, 28 November and 4 December 1786.
15. NAS. GD174/209. Jottings of MM in the case Maclaine v. Maclaine, 1800.
16. NAS. GD1/1003/10. Evidence in the action for reduction of Gillean Maclaine, 1766.
17. GRO Uncatalogued MSS. Box 17. Letter, LMD to GM, Edinburgh, 9 June 1788.
18. NAS. GD174/209. Evidence in arbitration, Maclaine v. Maclaine, 1800.
19. Robert Stewart of Achadashenaig, then the sheriff of the Mull district, who was to arbitrate on a question concerning Pennycross.
20. NAS. GD174/1387/49. AM to MM, Edinburgh, 24 May 1790.
21. Mr Campbell. One of the trustees of the estate, in charge of the financial management.
22. Two more daughters, Margaret and Elizabeth, had been born to Jane and Murdoch in 1789 and 1790.
23. NAS. GD174/1387/53. AM to MM, Inveraray, 28 August 1790.

24. Allan appended to every comment on LM, 'if he lives'. NAS. GD174/1387/72. AM to MM, Ramsgate, 20 August 1792.
25. NAS. GD174/1387/70. AM to MM, London, 19 June 1792.
26. NAS. GD174/1484/69. CM to MM, Gibraltar, 21 November 1797.
27. GRO. Uncatalogued MSS. Lachlan Maclean to GM, Dantzig, 10 July 1783.
28. NAS. GD174/422. Financial affairs of Andrew McLean, surgeon.
29. Annexed estates had belonged to Jacobites who were 'out' in the '45, which, if not sold, were annexed to the Crown and administered by commissioners until 1784, when agents retained an interest in them.
30. NAS. GD174/2273/2. John, fifth Duke of Argyll to MM, Inveraray, 21 January 1797.
31. NAS. GD174/926. Declaration, 1795.
32. NAS. GD174/209/16. Remarks made on the objections offered by Allan Maclaine, tacksman of Scalasdale, November 1799.
33. Tailzie, the Scots word for entail.
34. The witnesses were supposed to be witnesses only to the fact that the signature was authentic, and were not privy to the contents.
35. 'As they were pleased to call it,' Murdoch said, with sarcasm.
36. Torloisk Papers. B391. D. Maclean to Hector Maclean, 27 July 1759.
37. NAS. GD1/1003/15/10. Reduction of Gillean Maclaine.
38. GRO. Maclaine Papers, Box 15 and other collections of legal papers.

12

'Marianna in the moated grange': the Torloisk family

Hector Maclean of Torloisk, the bachelor laird of the estate in north-west Mull, and Writer in Edinburgh, died in 1765, and his next brother, Lachlan, succeeded him. As Hector had not lived much in Mull, another brother, Archibald Maclean of Lagganulva, had looked after the lands, and Lachlan was at first happy that things should continue that way. He was a sea captain, sailing mostly from England to Jamaica, and to India and the Mediterranean. He loved his ship, and his maritime life: he had no desire to return to Mull.

Lachlan was the 'honest heart and good soul' who was despised in the correspondence of his two more sophisticated brothers, Allan and Hector, and Allan Maclean of Torloisk wrote to him shortly after Hector's death.

Tho' no man in the world loves you better than myself, yet I by no means rejoice at your being now Laird of Torloisk, since you got it by the death of the best and worthiest of Brothers. Indeed, my dear Brother, this blow fell with too much of severity to leave me capable of recollecting what I am about ... [Hector] came to the head of a small estate deeply involved in debt, with a large family of Sisters and Brothers to support. He paid all the debt, recovered the estate to a better condition than ever it was in before ... and lived genteely among the first company in Scotland. He has transmitted to you now a clear estate of £230 a year free of all debts ... I hope you will transmit it to your son in the same condition ... Your Brother has not left a sixpence to his only daughter,[1] but I know you have a humane heart, and will pity the distressed. All friends are unanimous you should go to Mull, live there, and manage your own estate. Archibald[2] has been too long in the Management, and as I see from your own letters that you are heartily tired of the sea ... it will be necessary to sell the Ship ... You'll need to be very frugall ... You must build a house at Torloisk, for your Beds and Bedsteads will go for a mere triffle. You had better sell your man James. He will by no means do in Mull ... I also beg you will not think of bringing your sister-in-law with you to Scotland at this time. In short, keep everything together ... Sell your Negro man ... Your Brother made no Testament. You are too good a Christian, and a too honest man to oppose some good offices he intended to some of his friends. I know you well. Sure I am that you have a good heart and that you will most chearfully agree to every honest and reasonable thing your Brother meant to do. My Brother Archibald and I have not agreed well since Hector's death ... I did all I could for you, and he found fault. But that gives me no concern. I have nothing at heart but your interest ...[3]

Allan, however, found after correspondence with Hugh Maclean, the lawyer in whose Glasgow house Hector had breathed his last, that the deceased laird had debts in Jamaica of £2,000, and that Hugh had already performed some of the 'intended good offices' by buying a commission in the army for a friend's son. Allan had himself remembered some uncompleted business in his own purchases of land on Hector's behalf, in 1764, and claimed repayment from the estate, and therefore from Lachlan's diminishing inheritance. On 1 July 1766, Allan wrote to Lachlan from London.

Your manner of writing me, my Dear Brother, would give me infinite concern, were I not very secure in my own innocence, and a good heart will feel distress when wrongfully accused, but a certain consciousness of not being guilty must relieve me, tho' accused, even by a Brother, and that of crimes of so black a nature that my soul abhors them.[4]

Lachlan had apparently mentioned the bad influence of Allan's London friends. Allan had blandly suggested that they find an arbiter, 'and,' he added, 'I can't think which of my friends you refer to.' On the outside of this letter Lachlan wrote, 'from Major Maclean, a very strange letter full of professions without sincerity.' On Allan's other letters of the period, Lachlan also scribbled his perplexed reaction, such as 'fatuous letter'.

But Lachlan had settled down at Torloisk, more impoverished than he could ever have expected to be when he gave up his ship and his lucrative trade. Like Murdoch Maclaine twenty years later, he was confronted with the claims of all his relations, and had the discomfort of seeing all five of his surviving sisters concerting together to sue him for the Makalive cattle which Hector had not paid for.[5] An extensive legal process was also to decide differences between Lachlan and Allan, and yet, even if relations between all these siblings were not of the warmest, they were not entirely broken off, for Allan, as we have seen from his visit to Mull with Janet, remained close enough to his brother to come and stay with him. An arbiter also had to be sought in 1771 to resolve the problems between Lachlan and his next brother, Archibald, merchant in Lagganulva, who had been collecting the estate rents for some eight years without remitting them to either Hector or Lachlan. Archibald was not suspected of peculation. As unofficial factor, and the only merchant in north-west Mull, he had simply mixed his transactions together, and kept insufficient account books. Lachlan, in the end, reduced Archibald's due debts, and then discharged the remaining sum. It was a good thing that Lachlan obliterated the debt legally, for Archibald's two natural children, John and Allice Maclean, were to be liabilities in years to come.[6]

Lachlan had been married in 1763 to Margaret Smith, the daughter of a Fife family, and one daughter, Marianne, was born in 1765. For reasons unknown, the Torloisks were unable to have more children, and Marianne became the heiress to the estate. Lachlan was a prudent laird, and Margaret, by all accounts, a refined woman of taste. After Lachlan's first shock over the debts of the estate, he managed his affairs carefully, and by 1782 was able to embark on the building of a new house to replace the cottage of dry stones and thatch in which he had been born. This new house was constructed in a simple, graceful style, its only decoration a small classical pediment in the centre of the south front, a delightfully pretty house which remained much the same until the mid-nineteenth century, when it began to be systematically disfigured by the dictates of Victorian taste, and the 'marble halls' mentality' which was to place several unsightly buildings on the Mull landscape. It was to this house that the French naturalist and traveller, Faujas de Saint Fond, came in 1784, as part of his journey through England and Scotland to the Hebrides. The French edition of his book was published in 1797 (delayed by the French revolution), and an English edition two years later. As Lachlan of Torloisk died in 1799, he may not have seen this lyrical account of his hospitality, but it is worth some study in the interests of this story. Lachlan also was host to visitors like William Thornton, Lord Mount-stuart and Dr Garnett.

Faujas arrived at Aros on 24 September 1784, where he was greeted by Duncan Campbell, the Duke of Argyll's chamberlain in Mull, an old man of seventy-seven, who impressed visitors with his voluminous tartan plaid and hoary beard. Mr Campbell served port wine, sea biscuit and myrtleberry jam to his visitors.[7] Faujas was particularly interested in food, and his observations on the fare produced from his hosts' cupboards show either that there had been a distinct improvement since Dr Johnson's visit, or that the French palate was being pandered to.

When Faujas began on the journey from Aros to Torloisk, he could not help commenting, as so many travellers did, on the length of Scottish or Highland miles, which were here 'nearly double the length of those in England'. It was Faujas also who remarked on his companion's (a Mr Macdonald) change into Highland dress as soon as he landed on Mull, and the outfit was described in detail, for Faujas loved costume as much as he loved food. Even the guides' garments were described down to the colours in their bonnets, but where Burt[8] had found Highlanders' bare legs and plaids unpleasant, Faujas thought the Mull guides wore their plaids with grace.

When the two travellers arrived at Torloisk with their guides, it was after dark, but Lachlan Maclean, his wife Margaret, his daughter Marianne and several other ladies and gentlemen were engaged in a little musical concert. Marianne played Italian music on a harpsichord. Civilities and delicate attentions flowed from the family, and Faujas learned that 'all the inhabitants of this island ... about six thousand souls, have only one family name, that of

Maclean'. This information came no doubt from Lachlan, and although slightly exaggerated, given that there were a few other surnames, was almost true in the case of this estate.[9] Dr Johnson had made the same observation about Mull in general. Lachlan also told Faujas that Macleans were distinguished from each other only by Christian names and the place they lived in. He was himself a perfect example in being known as 'Lachlan Torloisk'.

Although the account of Faujas' stay at Torloisk deserves to be read in full, readers may find it for themselves.[10] Here we are mainly interested in the house, its owners, and its servants, what was worn and what was eaten. The contrast between the comfort of Torloisk and the hut William Thornton and other visitors had stayed in on Staffa was great. One had feather beds and sumptuous fare, and the other had a smoky interior, pigs, cows and hens sharing the only room, armies of lice sharing the visitors' straw beds, and milk and potatoes for dinner.

Torloisk, on the other hand, was a 'commodious habitation in the modern style, without parade, but in which great neatness and quiet simplicity prevail'. The house was situated on a dry platform without trees or verdure, so that to make himself a small kitchen garden, Lachlan had had to dig away part of the rock and import soil to fill the space. As Lachlan showed his French guest round the policies, he grew emotional as he pointed out the hut in which he (and his siblings) had been born. 'That is the ancient habitation of my fathers, and I feel inexpressible regard for this modest site, which reminds me of their virtues and frugal life.' Faujas judged that this sentiment painted the character of Mr Maclean of Torloisk better than all he could say of him.

What Faujas did go on to describe, with the eye of a Frenchman for a pretty woman, was Lachlan's one ewe lamb, Marianne, 'pretty, with a graceful figure, interesting from her talents, her acquirements, and her modesty' playing upon the harp, and well-versed in the language, poetry and music of the Hebrideans.[11] She told Faujas that she could not conceive how the English writers, strangers to the Celtic tongue, should have so obstinately persisted in doubting the existence of the ancient poems of Ossian. Altered as the poems might be, through being handed down, there were still large parts of them intact. Miss Marianne, he hoped, would publish her researches on the poems and airs of the Caledonians. Faujas recognised in Marianne a bluestocking not unlike those of the French *salons*. What is remarkable is that this intellectual young woman should have been reared in Mull, a first cousin of Marie Maclaine of Scallastle.[12]

The Frenchman's interest in the domestic servants of Torloisk is even more revealing. The barefooted servant maids wore their long dark hair in snoods of green and red wool. They had tartan wool petticoats worn with fitted bodices, and their teeth were very fine. As for the food served by these attractive domestics, breakfast consisted of smoked beef, Mull cheese, English cheese, fresh eggs, salted herring, porridge, milk and cream, oatcakes, currant jelly, myrtle or blaeberry conserve, tea and coffee. Jamaica rum was also available. Dinner was at four in the afternoon, with Scotch broth, black pudding, broiled beef, roast mutton, potatoes, game birds, pickled cucumber, cream with madeira and creamy puddings. When many decanters appeared on the mahogany table after dinner, Faujas was pleased to note that the ladies did not withdraw, but remained to partake of the 'merry feast'. His only mild criticism was that from ten o'clock in the evening till midnight, an abundant supper almost identical to the dinner was presented.

Unlike Dr Johnson and James Boswell, Faujas was observant in little matters such as the cottages of the commoners, which, as there were no 'real' villages in the island, were scattered about on the coast or clustered in the interior. These were, he said, built of basalt boulders, with very thick walls less than five feet high, and doorways only three feet high. Most of the people did not have doors in their doorways. Clods of turf covered the stone huts. As late as 1784, the fireplace was still in the centre of the house, with peat smoke finding its exit through a hole in the roof rather to the side of the fire. Faujas had to admit that Eskimos and Laplanders were more artful in their constructions than any *Muileach*.

The common people went bareheaded and without shoes, fearing neither rain nor frost, although fathers of families might wear a bonnet, and their wives a coarse cloth cap. They grew a few oats and potatoes, which, with milk, formed their main diet, varied by home-smoked salmon and herring. The women were (unlike the selected maidservants at Torloisk), small, ugly and ill-made, with a few exceptions, but as the sun was almost always hidden by clouds, their faces were pale and overlaid with peat smoke. But men and women were notable for their fine healthy teeth.

Of small birds, Faujas says that he saw only the ortolan bunting, which the editor of the English translation took occasion to doubt, and it is likely that the geologist had mistaken the more probable greenfinch for the little bird which was a gourmet delicacy in France.

Faujas was not the only tourist entertained by Lachlan of Torloisk and his wife Margaret. Fourteen years later, Dr Thomas Garnett, accompanied by his illustrator, Mr Watts, was surprised to meet with elegant society there.[13] Shortly after this 1798 visit, Lachlan died, but Margaret continued to give hospitality to visitors such as Mrs Murray. We are privileged to read about Torloisk through these three writers, but many less articulate guests must have stayed under that attractive roof. Margaret was often mentioned warily by men of 'the Country' as being too much of a gentlewoman for Mull. 'I'm afraid Mull will not agree with such delicate fine women', Hugh Maclean of Kingairloch was telling Murdoch Maclaine in 1772. Margaret was the one with style, and Lachlan had a reputation for frugality. One of Lachlan's nephews is on record, writing in a disloyal vein from Edinburgh to another uncle, Brigadier-General Allan Maclean, when Lachlan was visiting his Fife relations.

Old Moy Castle, ancestral home of the
Maclaines of Lochbuy. (Author)

James Boswell, painted by George Willison,
father-in-law of Charles Macquarie.
(By kind permission of the Scottish National
Portrait Gallery)

Murdoch Maclaine, later 19th of Lochbuy,
c. 1758, wearing the uniform of the 114th
Foot. (By kind permission of the Black Watch
Museum and Archives, Perth)

Gillean Maclaine of Scallastle, c.1770, from an
original portrait by an unknown artist.
(By kind permission of Mr David Clapp,
Essex, Connecticut)

Lochbuy House, also known as 'Moy', built 1786–88. (Mr Iain Thornber, Morvern)

Marianne Maclean later Mrs Maclean Clephane, after a portrait by Raeburn. (By kind permission of Capt A.A.C. Farquharson of Invercauld)

General William Douglas Maclean Clephane, husband of Marianne, after a portrait by Raeburn. (By kind permission of Capt A.A.C. Farquharson of Invercauld)

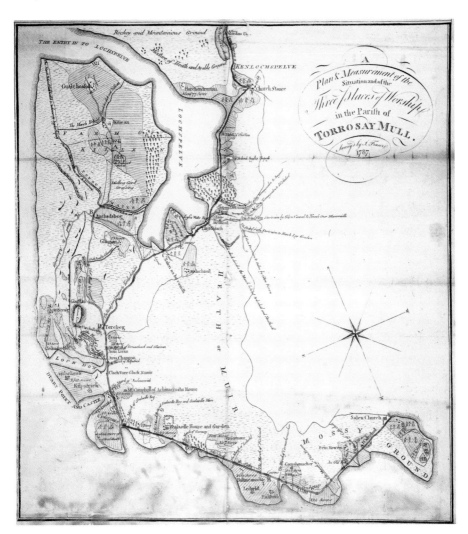

Three places of worship in Torosay, 1787. A survey of the parish of Torosay by a Mr Fraser,
presented upside down. The plan is of interest as it shows roads and foot tracks, and the
position of populous townships such as Fishnish, Ledirkle and Ardchoirk. The once-famous
garden of Scallastle is prominent in this last year before Gillean's death. (National Archives of
Scotland)

Interior of Craignure Church where in May 1836 Mr Clark preached his sermon on the eclipse of the sun. (Author)

Margaret Douglas Maclean Clephane at the time of her marriage to Lord Compton, after a portrait by Raeburn. (Castle Ashby)

Lord Compton at the time of his marriage, after a portrait by Raeburn. (Castle Ashby)

Ranald Macdonald of Staffa. (Mr Alastair de Watteville)

Lachlan Macquarie, later Governor of New South Wales, aged 44, from a portrait by John Opie. (By courtesy of the Mitchell Library, State Library of New South Wales)

Elizabeth Henrietta Campbell, wife of Lachlan Macquarie, from a watercolour by an unknown artist. (By courtesy of the Mitchell Library, State Library of New South Wales)

Portrait (believed by the author to be) of Lachlan Macquarie Junior of Jarvisfield. (By courtesy of the Mitchell Library, State Library of New South Wales)

View from Ulva to Ben More in 1813, Ulva House was constructed after Colin Macdonald's purchase of the island in 1785. Ranald ('Staffa') Macdonald entertained in style here and is probably one of the figures depicted in the foreground. From a collection of drawings by William Daniell. (William Daniell's Voyage Round Great Britain)

The Breast, Tobermory, in 1813, shortly before the development of the lower village. Daniell noted the 'neat women'. (William Daniell's Voyage Round Great Britain)

Aros Bridge, 1813. James Maxwell lived in this area, and most visitors arrived here or at Grass Point, in the tourist boom of 1775–1825. The Stewarts of Achadashenaig lived in a 'commodious habitation' (now Glenaros) to the right of this picture. (William Daniell's Voyage Round Great Britain)

Achnacroish House, principal residence on the Duart estate, in the time of Charles Macquarie. (Mr Chris James, Torosay Castle)

Old Gruline House, home at different times of John Gruline, Miss Ketty, John Gruline the Nephew, Charles and Marianne Macquarie, Lachlan Macquarie and his wife Elizabeth Henrietta, and Lachlan Junior. (Author's photograph, by kind permission of Mr and Mrs Harmer, Gruline)

Colonel Alexander Campbell of Possil and Achnacroish. A generous and good landowner, he refused a site for a Free Church in Torosay, which drove the congregation to 'the tent in the gravel pit'. (Mr Colin Carter-Campbell)

Harriet Maclachlan, wife of Colonel Alexander Campbell. She dispensed medicines and distributed food in Torosay parish during the famine years. (Mr Colin Carter-Campbell)

Miss Susan Campbell, daughter of Colonel Campbell, from a miniature. She was admired by the diarist Lauchlan Maclaine, who referred to her as 'my flame', and blushed in her company. (Mr Colin Carter-Campbell)

Torloisk & his family are at Auchternairny. Still, I have let them know that I am come here, and if they wish me to go there, they will certainly invite me. If they do not ... He himself is such a miserable man that I am sure he would even begrudge that meat and drink that would be expended at Auchternairny, as he expects his daughter will get it some time or other. His conduct is such that I'm really ashamed of him. He is nothing but *an old Woman.*[14]

Lachlan's way was to be careful. He was instrumental in hastening the settlement of the Ormaig reversion when in 1769 he found that the rents owed to him by the MacQuarries were unpaid, and the longstanding debts owed long ago to his brother Hector by both MacQuarrie families were being ignored. It was Lachlan Torloisk who raised an action in the Court of Session, pointing out that the two MacQuarries, Ulva and Ormaig, were colluding to avoid the sale of both estates by a pretence which cheated all of their creditors, by postponing the sale of Ulva by as long as possible.[15] Having lost faith in the integrity of all his neighbours, and all his own relations, it was small wonder that Lachlan turned to the society of cultured guests, and concentrated on the education of the daughter whom he had chosen to inherit his lands, in preference to male relations who were likely to betray his interest, and call him an old woman.

His behaviour was, as Hector and Allan had discovered, that of 'an honest heart'. Lachlan entered into every transaction which was honest and above board. He entered into a submission with the Duke of Argyll to determine the boundaries of their respective estates. He willingly took part in the affairs of the presbytery, which most of the other heritors avoided, lest they should be involved in the unwanted expense of the building of churches or the insolent petitions of the ministers for manses, for which proprietors were responsible. It was Lachlan who steered his daughter Marianne away from a marriage within the families of Argyll, and who was perhaps responsible for many of the animosities which she was to display in the forty years of her reign at Torloisk. Although the Torloisks were related to nearly every Mull family, the only one they were to regard with true affection was that of Maclean of Pennycross. The Boisdale Macdonalds were regarded with particular hatred. When Colin of Boisdale died, after Marianne had assumed the running of Torloisk, this new heritor, Mrs Clephane, wrote to her cousin, John Maclean of Lagganulva (natural son of Archibald) without ceremony or greeting.

Boisdale is dead. And that is saying much to you in a few words. God forbid however I should wish you joy of an event which however favourable for you, I believe neither you nor any good Christian can seriously rejoice at. I consulted two Edinburgh lawyers who were here to see Staffa and do business, about your stated account with Kenlochaline.[16] They say it must be sworn to before a Justice. I shall endeavour to send you for that purpose when Achnacroish [17] or Pennycross [18] comes here, which I expect will be next week ... when I shall hope to find you at home. This, if anything, will save MacQuarrie [19] from the Philistines. I mean B's death.[20]

Marianne, the pretty, graceful, musical bluestocking of Torloisk, had married William Douglas Clephane of Kirkness in September 1790. Their sons were to have been heirs to Torloisk and Kirkness, but like her mother, Marianne was destined to have no sons. General Clephane was appointed lieutenant governor of Grenada in August 1803, and it is not known if Marianne intended to join him there. She would not have had time to sail out, for her husband, 'a bad subject for a warm climate' survived for only two months, his funeral in Grenada being described as 'the most sumptuous ever seen on that island'.[21]

From the lovely young girl of Faujas' visit, and the belle of the Perth ball, Marianne had become, even in her husband's lifetime, an acerbic lady laird, who did not suffer fools, but, by her own account, was surrounded by fools. Her cousin, John Lagganulva (as he was called, although his house was now at Kilbrenan), came in for her sharpest criticism. He was clearly feckless, in the manner of so many Mull men, and 'such people' as his mother, Marion Maclean, who went about shouting abuse at Mrs Clephane, did not help.[22] John Lagganulva had married one of the MacQuarrie girls, one of Alice's daughters, so that Marianne was related both to the husband and to the wife at Kilbrenan. Mistress Flora was a decent young woman, who, like her sister Mally, could write and spell minimally. Marianne blamed the husband for neglecting their son Lachlan's education, and wrote to him fiercely:

Dear Sir,
Your son Lachlan will probably go for Ireland in two days, where I wish he may maintain himself in the situation he is placed in. The bad habit young people have in the Highlands of speaking nothing at home but Gaelic makes them find it hardly possible to change their tongue when they come here [Edinburgh], and Lachlan has suffered so much by that, and that you have not yourself tried to give him some notion of reading and spelling that I am apprehensive it may be a serious loss to him ... Dr McLean was in hopes it was strangeness to speaking that prevented him, which time would wear away. But since Langamull's son [23] is gone, his writing shows he does not understand English, a thing you have yourself to blame for.

The land you desire to have you shall have on one condition – that you confine yourself to your income of £40 ... you will have £27 to get in money. But if a single debt exceeding that sum appears against you, after this term, especially to MacPherson, Wilson, or the Aros shop, or to D. McNeil,[24] you must give up this bit of land and apply the rent to the discharge of this debt. Tell your wife that for a line from her in matters not concerning her, a summons will be sent to her, of which she may make thread papers if she chuses. With best wishes to you and her. I remain dear Sir, Your most obedient servant,

M. D. Maclean Clephane.[25]

These were the strong words of a widow of about forty years of age who was determined to rule her estate with a rod of iron. She was even more critical of her neighbour, sometime tenant and uncle by marriage, Lachlan MacQuarrie of that Ilk, who, like his brother-in-law's son, owed money to wine merchants while pleading that he could not pay the rent. Her reasons for continuing to dislike Ranald Macdonald of Staffa, Boisdale's son, were not simply founded in clan enmity, as Walter Scott liked to think,[26] but rooted in her father's differences with Boisdale in the case of the Ormaig reversion, and in perpetual squabbles over the lands of Lagganulva, which were divided between the owner of Ulva and the proprietor of Torloisk. Because of this bitter hostility, two families who were culturally compatible, and living as near each other as the swoop of a seagull, were for ever barred from meeting. One would have thought that at least the younger generations might have welcomed overtures of friendship, but instead, their rivalry was increased by some competition over the favour of Walter Scott.

On the death of General Clephane, Marianne's three daughters had been assigned a guardian who was to be one of the most influential men in Scotland, in a sphere quite foreign to the experience of other Mull families. This was Walter Scott, not yet famous, son of an Edinburgh Writer to the Signet, himself a 32-year-old lawyer. Marianne, educated by Lachlan to have a mind of her own, brought up her three daughters in a certain state of defiance of the Douglas side of the Clephane family, determined to secure for Margaret, her oldest girl and heiress, the inheritance she was due in Mull and in Fife, but unwilling to submit to her mother-in-law. According to Marianne, her daughters met with 'hostility, persecution and malevolence' at their grandmother's. 'I entered this family,' she told Walter Scott, 'with the strongest wish to be really one of it, because they were truly dear to him who connected me to them, and spent thirteen years in every endeavour to please and benefit them, in vain, and when that bond ceased, they have never lost one opportunity of annoyance.[27]

The Maclean Clephanes, as the girls were called, received an education befitting the daughters of a *femme savante*. They spent part of the year in London, Harrogate, Tunbridge or Edinburgh, returning to Mull in the summer to receive guests at Torloisk. Walter Scott had had enormous success with *Marmion*, and his new poem, *The Lady of the Lake* was showing signs of being equally popular. For the latter he had enrolled the help of the Torloisk young ladies, who had sent him *coronachs*, or Gaelic dirges. Anxious for background material for his projected poem *The Lord of the Isles*, he accepted an invitation from Ranald Macdonald to visit Ulva. It was a relief to him to find that the Maclean Clephanes were not to be in Mull. As he wrote to a friend:

> We deeply regretted the absence of our kind and accomplished friends the Clephanes, yet, *entre nous*, as we were upon a visit to a family of the Capulets, I do not know but we may pay our respects to them more pleasantly at

another time. There subsist some aching scars of the old wounds which were in former times inflicted upon each other by the rival tribes of Maclean and Macdonald, and my very good friends the Laird of Staffa and Mrs Maclean Clephane are both too keen Highlanders to be without the characteristic prejudices of their clans, which in their case divide two highly accomplished and most estimable families living almost within sight of each other and on an island where polished conversation cannot be supposed to abound.[28]

In August 1813, Scott sent up two young men on a tour of the Highlands which was to include some authentic island life. One of them was Spencer Joshua Alwyne Compton, twenty-three years old, and already an MP. He was the son of the ninth Earl and first Marquis of Northampton, but had rejected his father's high Tory politics for liberal causes. He was a Cambridge graduate, and had interests in literature, the fine arts and science. The intrepid bluestockings of Torloisk were slightly in awe of his reputation for speaking his mind, and for being crotchety and argumentative, but were surprised to find him quite philosophical about not being able to get to Staffa because of storms and high seas. Margaret told Scott:

> I was just going to have mentioned how well we all thought of Lord Compton, taking a certain dislike of contradiction in very small trifles that one was hardly aware of the possibility of being taken up. To be sure he has never been contradicted in all his life, so he is unused to it, but he seemed unprepared for the possibility of such a thing. Well ... we all set off together for Staffa. The wind came contrary, and the rain poured down in deluges. We were obliged to put back after we had gone half way, and as so many days of disappointment have passed since he came here, I expected at the least that he would have been very sulky and snappish, in place of which he did all in his power to make everybody happy and merry, and told good stories all the way back ... I do beg his pardon for thinking worse of him than he deserved ... We shall miss them much when they leave us.[29]

But Scott had done well when he sent Lord Compton and his friend Pemberton to Torloisk. It had been a lucky accident, for his first choice of host had been Ranald Macdonald in Ulva, a more congenial, light-hearted guide than the over-serious Misses Clephane. But 'Staffa' was not to be on Ulva that summer, and Scott had written to Marianne instead. Lord Compton passed the test which Marianne claimed was applied in Mull – that of stripping men of their rank and prestige, and judging them by their intrinsic worth. He appreciated Margaret's substantial gifts, her playing on the harpsichord, her literary taste, her lively mind and rather plump dark beauty. What Lord Compton, who was much involved with Wilberforce in the anti-slavery movement, thought of social conditions in Mull is unrecorded. His reforming zeal was to operate in a different sphere. In 1814, Scott himself paid his long-promised visit to Torloisk during the tour of inspection he made on board the lighthouse yacht, the *Pharos*. Although it was August, the mist was thick, and the crew of the *Pharos* were unable to find a landing place near Torloisk. Instead they took shelter at Gometra, and in the early evening Scott and a companion rowed across Loch Tuath in heavy rain. They arrived at Torloisk in darkness, and were greeted by the Maclean Clephanes, who insisted on inviting the rest of the party across for breakfast next morning. Scott commented on Mrs Clephane's improvements. The grounds had been dressed to smooth their ruggedness, and Mrs C. had formed 'extensive plantations' of trees. But, leaving all too soon, forced onwards by the timetable of the *Pharos*'s journey, they were thrust into an embarrassing situation, outlined by Scott in the present tense in his diary.

> When we come on board, we learn that Staffa-Macdonald is just come to his house at Ulva; this is a sort of unpleasant dilemma, for we cannot now go there without some neglect towards Mrs Maclean Clephane; and on the other hand, from his habits with all of us, he may be justly displeased with our quitting his very threshold without asking for him. However, upon the whole matter, and being already under weigh, we judged it best to work out of the loch, and continue our purpose of rounding the northern extremity of Mull.[30]

Mrs Clephane's life seemed to be much complicated either by feuds, or by a social rigidity which caused embarrassment to many of her guests. She might speak with approval of the Highland habit of judging men by their intrinsic worth rather than their rank, but many guests were to comment on the stifling, or cool atmosphere of her reception, or her way of dismissing them.[31] Such treatment was doubtless common in London, but was hardly suited to an island where visitors arrived wet, hungry and cold. On the other hand, her efforts on behalf of Lord Compton could hardly be curbed. When he left his watch at Torloisk, she directed a small army of men to search every inch of the plantations of trees, and when the watch remained unfound, intended to place advertisements in the Edinburgh, Glasgow, Greenock and Inverness papers, a service guaranteed to publish his presence in her house, but an oversized hunting ground for the lost watch.[32]

In the year following Lord Compton's visit, Margaret observed in a letter to Scott that there was 'no rhyme for Mull but dull',[33] and talked of spending the winter of 1814–15 in Edinburgh. How and where the romance developed is unknown, but by the spring of 1815, Scott, although embarking on his new career as a novelist, found time to act as a legal emissary in his capacity as Margaret's guardian, travelling to London and Castle Ashby to draw up the marriage contract, meeting Lord Northampton and his lawyers, and speaking peace to the difficult Douglas relations. 'I wish much to have the Entail of Torloisk, a copy of your mother's marriage contract, or the original, and rentals of your own little property and of Torloisk,' he wrote to Margaret. And to Marianne he reported, after many investigations and discussions, 'I have the pleasure to inform you that the *free income* of the Northampton estate is £18,000 per annum at least – no bad prospect for our young lady ... and it is an improving property.' [34]

To her mother, Margaret's marriage on 24 July 1815 was a most happy triumph. It did, however, have the effect of removing her in mind and spirit, as well as in body, from Torloisk. Margaret did not have an easy time at Castle Ashby, where she had to live with her mother-in-law, Lady Northampton, who was 'full of a hundred littlenesses'. The Northamptons were not in the least bit cultivated. 'I am fond of things they never heard of, and languages they don't understand', the bride wrote. She and Compton had to go off and read Milton together to escape the littleness and fidgets of the family.[35]

In 1820, defeated at the general election, Lord Compton, whose health was not good, decided to live in Italy with his wife and children for at least part of every year. His houses there became refuges for political agitators for freedom, and his wife, who wrote and spoke Italian, was a valuable asset. Three sons, Charles, William and Spencer Scott were born between 1816 and 1821. Marianne, with her remaining two daughters, Anna Jane and Wilmina, suffering from the economic problems of estate management in Mull and still staggering from the costs of the wedding in 1815, postponed the much-longed-for tour to Italy.

The years immediately following the marriage were some of the worst that Mull had ever known, and Mrs Clephane was not impervious to the needs of her tenants.

> This country is now suffering grievously from the want of money, as well as the total stop to all sales of any of their commodities. The people are in distress for food, having expended this provision in the long severe winter ... yet they make no complaint, but show a fortitude of endurance more interesting by far than complaint. I am glad we are here, for by employing them we have been able to help some of them, and if you should ever ramble this way you will see they have done some service.[36]

In Mull, the impoverished Mrs Maclean Clephane planted and improved the 'dry platform' they perched upon, made alterations in the kitchen quarters, but left the pretty house built thirty-five years before fundamentally unaltered. Anna Jane had written to Scott in 1816 about the changes that were about to transform the island. The Duke of Argyll's lands were for sale: 'I wonder at it, for we always thought they were entailed.' And when Scott helped Archy Park, brother of the explorer Mungo Park, to find a job as comptroller of customs at Tobermory, Anna Jane reported the situation there.

> Mama is rejoiced at the prospect of your stout yeoman, Archy Park, taking up his residence in this Country. I only hope our precious Tobermorrians

will not take umbrage at his honesty as to plague him, for I think within these two years they are worse than ever, and the Collector, his superior, is a perfect missionary to all the Country, even daring to laugh at the Sheriff (at which proceeding *you* ought to be the judge of the full enormity), and even to ridicule Mr Maxwell.[37]

Mrs Clephane 'rejoiced at the thought of seeing an honest man at Tobermory'. She rather wished that the job had gone to her own favoured candidate, Sandy Maclean of Pennycross, whose father had been 'totally ruined' by the hard times. Sandy was a kind of 'stickit lawyer' for which profession he had been meant. She was not above trying to lure Archy Park into her parlour, for now there was a rage among heritors for having Lowland men as shepherds and managers. But Archy was shocked at Mrs Clephane's 'stylish' farming, which must be an expense if she persisted in removing rocks, and covering their places with imported earth.[38] Archy noted that Colonel Campbell of Mishnish was letting out crofts near Tobermory of from two to eight acres each, at two guineas per acre. This was too high a price for a prudent Lowlander. By 1817, Mrs Clephane had given up hope of going to see Margaret. 'This country is in a ruined state. Nothing of our exports will sell, and the last harvest is now almost consumed. The poorer families begin to want bread, and have nothing to purchase it ... There is no question about paying rents, for to keep life is the sole object. I gave them twenty-five shillings last year, and possibly may require to do so again, for it is of no use to me to run up an arrear only to drive these poor mortals to despair.'

Determined to employ a Lowlander as factor and overseer, Mrs Clephane found Alexander Shiells, from the parish of Earlston in Berwickshire, and made extensive enquiries about his character. Recommended for sobriety, strict integrity, intelligence, good manners and a knowledge of accountancy, she offered him £60 a year and a house at Langamull to be her factor, to run her home farm, and collect her rents. He was to move in at Martinmas 1822, a year in which Mrs Clephane was much exercised with the legality of her ownership of Torloisk, suspecting, not without reason, that the Argyll Campbells had acquired charters which they had doctored. Like many of her fellow Mull heritors, she was indignant at the effrontery of ministers who thought they had a right to demand a manse and a glebe in their parish, and an action had been raised in 1819 in which she confronted her own minister, the Rev. Donald MacArthur, in an effort to deny him the use of a spot of land at Kilninian farm, where, she said, her family went sea bathing.[39] This year had also seen the greatest slump in the price of kelp since the end of the French wars. It was not an auspicious time for Mr Shiells to become Torloisk's factor.

Mr Shiells and Mrs Clephane were not a popular combination. In the 1820s, the farms attached to Torloisk were Kilbrenan, Ballygown, Fanmore, Kilninian, Tostary, East and West Burg, Reudle, Ensay, Druimgigha, Kengharair, Kilmory, Lagganulva and Langamull.[40] Most of the farms had anything from four to fourteen heads of household as tenants, so that the number of families on the estate was probably about sixty. During the 1820s, in an effort to combine smallholdings into larger farms, small tenants were removed from their possessions so that a more efficient farmer could move in, and one of the farmers so favoured was Andrew Shiells, the factor's son. By the early 1830s, resentment was beginning to surface, and Alexander Shiells received an anonymous letter, in English.

> This is a letter to thee, wretch that thou art, to take thy flight away from this place, or else thou and all thy effects shall be given a sacrifice to the burning fiery flames. Do not look for any mercy, for thou will obtain none, for we are as fond for thy life as a young lion for her prey when she is hungry. If you do not believe this, let thy blood and the innocent blood of thy family be upon thy head, for we are sworn by God, if time and opportunity be in our power, that you will not escape punishment.[41]

The style owed much to the method of teaching English in schools and Sunday schools by the medium of the English Bible. Mr David Thomson in Torloisk, another 'stranger', also received an indirect message for Mrs Clephane, known to many of the people by the familiar plain name of Mary Maclean Torloisk: not for them the ornamental 'Marianne'.

> This warning is sent to you in order that you may let Mary Maclean of Torloisk know if she will keep Alexr. Shiels in this place any longer than may, that we will burn hir property with fire. She was bad enough hirself. She had no need to bring belzebub prince of the devils to reign here, for since Mull was separated by the earthquake from the mainland, such a reech [wretch] as Shiels never came to it bud Robison who was at groulen [Gruline] ... He is a good slave driver. I think we should recommend him to John Maclean Jamaica for one ...[42]

Margaret, Lady Compton, latterly Lady Northampton, died in Rome in 1830, after giving birth to a daughter, to the surprise and grief of her husband and her mother, who had both been ailing much more than Margaret. Mrs Clephane and her remaining unmarried daughter, Anna Jane, spent time at Castle Ashby with the Compton children, and Anna Jane occasionally returned to Mull alone. Alexander Shiells therefore required to be an incisive letter writer, telling of rent arrears and bad behaviour. He reported on the Macleans of Kilbrenan, who had placed a legacy in the hands of Mrs Clephane rather than allow it to be touched by their alcoholic son, Lachlan. When Mrs Maclean Kilbrenan, once Flora MacQuarrie of Ulva, died in 1836, Mr Shiells described the goings on at the burial, alas only too typical of Mull funerals:

> Dear Madam,
>
> I wrote you ten days ago with a note of the accounts which I hope you have got ... Just after I sent them, Mrs Maclean of Kilbrenan died. She

died on 3rd February, and was buried at Kilninian on the 8th, at their
ground, alongside of Miss Jane.[43] They take up all the ground. There is
not one inch for Lachlan, and I have no doubt I might say I know that his
death is anxiously wished for. And I have no doubt that ... giving him his
own will of a cask or two of whisky, that might be accomplished in good
time. I am sorry to say that at the funeral there was sad drinking and
plenty fighting, which, from the drunken state many of them were in, I am
not much surprised. However, it is completely disgraceful. Your people seem
not to be the best in Mull in that respect. I might almost say I think them
the worst. John Maclean the schoolmaster's two sons, Alexander and John,
were the worst, but especially John. They both struck a strong lad [who]
never struck them in return. I had almost gone to the Procurator Fiscal
about them, but it being not quite so bad as the row the Mackinnons had,
I am certain he would not take the case in. There seems to have been one
general squabble all along the road, for the funeral was late, and it had got
dark.[44]

Mr Shiells was unfamiliar with a custom which was sanctified as a rite of
passage in the lives of all, and one which had little to do with the particular
character of the deceased. Mrs Maclean of Kilbrenan's attitude to drunkenness,
a state personified for her in her late husband [45] and in her son Lachlan, was
distinctly disapproving, but the option of a small private family funeral was
not open to her. It would have been bad form to exclude the entire population
of the Torloisk estate from the ceremony, which was not always presided over
by a minister, but began with drinking and dirges, moved on to the procession
of relatives, friends and acquaintances to the place of burial, and, if there was
an inn on the route, was extended by a stop of some hours' duration. Edmund
Burt had blamed the *coronach* for inciting 'mischievous encounters and bloody
broils' [46] for, as he said, 'all that have arms in their possession accoutre
themselves with them upon those occasions.' On this occasion, another mour-
ner reported on Mrs Maclean Kilbrenan's obsequies. Her corpse, he said, was
deposited at Kilninian alongside her late husband and her sister Jean, and
afterwards there were beef, fowls, bread, cheese and whisky for 200 people,
with an elegant and more private dinner at Kilbrenan for the family.[47]

Funerals were often the only opportunity for a starving family to eat well,
and in this year of 1836, hunger was as rife as it was to be in the following
more famous decade. But eating was often a way of being repaid for favours
to the dead which had gone unacknowledged. Where the dead had been
irreproachable in their generosity, or had lived away from home, the *fête
champêtre* became a battle ground for the resolution of old animosities. Young
men just happened to have brought their wooden clubs with them, concealed
in the sleeves of their coats. Every funeral offered the chance of settling old
scores, like Hector McNeill's burial in Torosay in 1824, when a Maclaine
from Ledirkle attacked John Currie, a Ballameanach tenant, in a savage manner,

and nearly murdered him, and Charles Maclaine in the same dastardly manner cut and bruised Mary Currie, his sister, for endeavouring to save her brother from their blows.[48] 'There is scarcely a person on the Poor Roll,' Dr MacArthur, the minister of Kilninian told the Poor Law Enquiry in 1843, 'who has not two or three pounds lying in the hands of some gentleman, which they never touch, but keep it to pay their funeral expenses.'[49] Mr Shiells' accounts for Miss Jean MacQuarrie's funeral show that 96 lbs of mutton were consumed at 4d. per pound, and four stones of oatmeal at 2s. 6d.[50] The only appeal for food or money which a landowner could not reject was the standard note asking for as many as ten gallons of whisky for a burial. In 1842, Lachlan MacFadyen apologised for increasing the number of gallons required from Murdoch Maclaine of Lochbuy, by explaining that it was the relations' last and only chance of drinking at the dead man's expense.[51] In 1824, when Lachlan Macquarie's body was brought back to Mull, Donald Maclean WS expressed a hope that there would be no 'excess' – 'so disgraceful on such occasions.' If there was excess, the diarists and letter writers were circumspectly silent.

A few days after Mrs Maclean's funeral, the other tenants were bidding for Kilbrenan by the usual method of offering what they thought was the highest rent, and the drunken Lachlan Kilbrenan was planning to leave Mull, free now from the restraining hand of his mother. But, Shiells said realistically, things looked extremely ill. 'I hear many of the small tenants are already near out of potatoes.' And he told Mrs Clephane, 'I hear most all the tenants in Ulva are under sequestration for rent due to the trustees.' As a parting word, Shiells informed his mistress that the small tenants were allowing their cattle to eat her grass. 'They eat into yours, and keep your cattle in starvation.'[52] It was not a letter to endear a lady to her tenants, or to postpone the day of judgement in the matter of her own inevitable sequestrations. What was more, Alexander Shiells had very much understated conditions in Mull.

A severe hard season, 1836 had found the people with no seed potatoes to plant. Snowstorms and hard frost in October had begun the winter, and not even the famous 1782, or 1807 or 1817 had been worse than this. The poor collected shellfish on the shore, always for them a last resort rather than a delicacy. This year was to be more decisive than the year of the potato blight, for even those who escaped sequestration saw that they had only a temporary respite. In February, a young heritor called Lachlan Macquarie Junior of Jarvisfield married a Miss Campbell from Islay, and Sheriff John Gregorson remarked, 'I hope he will become a resident proprietor, for absenteeism is the bane of the Country.' Mrs Maclean Clephane, although she would not have admitted culpability, was an absentee through no fault of her own. She tried to be at Torloisk, but her grandchildren were at Castle Ashby, and a grandmother's duty to her beloved eldest daughter's children came before her concern for her tenants. She was seventy-one years old. On the other side of

Loch Tuath from Torloisk, Ulva's new owner had driven a hard bargain with the island's trustees, and was about to do the same with his tenants. It seemed unlikely that Francis William Clark would be any more of a kindred spirit for Marianne than 'Staffa' had been in his day. She had few friends on the island, and it was left to Anna Jane to return to Mull in the five years that remained of her mother's life.

The Mull presbytery reported that unprecedented sickness and destitution, low attendance at school, and scarcity of food, fuel and clothing had characterised 1836, 'the merited chastening of the Almighty'. On Sunday 15 May at 3 p.m. a solar eclipse occurred, which the people did not fear to look upon with the naked eye. The minister of Torosay, Mr Clark, had that morning seized the occasion to preach a Gaelic sermon on a dramatic text, Luke 21: 25–26, to a very large congregation. 'And there shall be signs in the sun, and in the moon, and in the stars; and upon the earth distress of nations, with perplexity; the sea and the waves roaring; men's hearts failing them for fear, and for looking after those things which are coming on the earth; for the powers of heaven shall be shaken.' [53]

Notes

1. An illegitimate daughter. Her identity is unknown.
2. Archibald Maclean of Lagganulva, the fourth brother. He was unmarried, but had a son and a daughter.
3. Torloisk Papers. B337. AM to Lachlan Maclean of Torloisk, Edinburgh, 23 June 1765.
4. Torloisk Papers. B337. AM to Lachlan Maclean of Torloisk, London, 1 July 1766.
5. GRO. D3330. Uncatalogued MSS. Disposition of 1770, referring back to 1739, of the sisters of Lachlan Maclean of Torloisk. For a similar legal dispute over the cattle of fostered daughters see Chapter 5, and the case of Mally Maclaine.
6. GRO. D3330. Uncatalogued MSS. Discharge of Lachlan Maclean of Torloisk to Mr Archibald Maclean, his brother, 1771. The presence of this documentation of Torloisk affairs in the Scallastle family's papers is due to Gillean's involvement on behalf of the siblings.
7. The nearest French equivalent. It was more likely to be bilberry, or blackcurrant.
8. Burt's *Letters* ... see Chapter 4 for his description of the plaids and bare thighs of Highlanders.
9. In a rental of Torloisk of 1755, Macleans outnumbered all other names, but there was a plurality of McNeills, Macdonalds, Rankens and MacFarlanes. Torloisk Papers. B70.
10. Faujas de Saint Fond, B., *A Journey through England, and Scotland to the Hebrides in 1784.*
11. See Chapter 19 for a description of Marianne in 1787, by another admirer. 'Her divine mind beamed through her lovely eyes.'
12. Marianne's father Lachlan being a brother of Alice Maclean, Marie's mother.
13. Garnett, T., *Observations on a Tour Through the Highlands* ...
14. Torloisk Papers. B345. Lachlan McLean, Edinburgh to AM, 26 March 1786.
15. EUL. Session Papers. Petition of Lachlan McLean of Torloisk, 24 February 1775.

Ormaig owned one third of Ulva, and Lachlan Macquarrie two thirds. Torloisk had instigated a process in 1769 which was 'most obstinately opposed by Ormaig under various false and frivolous pretences.'

16. Charles Maclean, of Kinlochaline, son of Allan Maclean of Drimnin.
17. Alexander Campbell of Achnacroish, an Argyll tacksman.
18. Archibald Maclean of Pennycross.
19. Lachlan MacQuarrie, formerly of Ulva, who was at this time renting a farm from the Boisdales.
20. GRO. D3330. Box 26. Mrs Maclean Clephane to John Maclean, Lagganulva. n.d., n.p.
21. *Gentleman's Magazine*, 1803. ii. 1256.
22. GRO. D3330. Box 26. Mrs Maclean Clephane to John Maclean, Lagganulva, 11 January 1802.
23. One of the four sons of John Maclean of Langamull. John Maclean was drowned in 1810.
24. All merchants who sold alcohol. John was following in his father's footsteps.
25. GRO. D3330. Box 26. Mrs Maclean Clephane to John Maclean, Lagganulva. Edinburgh, 17 May 1804.
26. cf. p. 38, note 3, *infra*.
27. NLS. MS 3885. f. 220. Mrs Maclean Clephane to Walter Scott, Torloisk, 25 November 1814.
28. Grierson, H. J. C. (ed.), *Letters of Sir Walter Scott*, vol. i, 1808–1811.
29. NLS. MS 3884. f. 213. Margaret Maclean Clephane to Walter Scott, Torloisk, 1 August 1813.
30. Scott, Walter, *The Voyage of the* Pharos, entry for 29–30 August 1814.
31. See Chapter 21, in which LMD records many snubs from MMT in his diary.
32. NLS. MS 3884. f. 226. Mrs Maclean Clephane to Walter Scott, Torloisk, 15 August 1813.
33. NLS. MS 3885. f. 130. Margaret Maclean Clephane to Walter Scott, Torloisk, 12 July 1814.
34. Grierson, HJC (ed.), *Letters of Sir Walter Scott*, vol. iv, 1815–17. 'I could say nothing until I saw the marquis's rent roll and the burdens affecting it ...' The amount of Scott's work on the preparations was prodigious.
35. NLS. MS. 3886. f. 192. Lady Compton to Walter Scott, Castle Ashby, 1815.
36. NLS. MS. 3887. f. 108. Mrs Maclean Clephane to Walter Scott, Torloisk, 20 August 1816.
37. NLS. MS. 3888. Anna Jane Maclean Clephane to Walter Scott, Torloisk, 20 January 1817. Mr Maxwell was the Duke of Argyll's chamberlain in Mull – see following chapter. The superior, Campbell McCallum, was 'never sober'.
38. NLS. MS 3888. f. 10. The Pennycross Macleans, according to MMT were a 'falling family'. Archy Park's impressions of life in Tobermory on his arrival in the New Year of 1817 are in his letters to Scott, NLS. MS. 3888.
39. Torloisk Papers. B74. The litigation actually lasted from 1808 until 1822, and was typical of the resistance shown by most of the Mull heritors to the valid claims of ministers. Sea bathing, however, was an unusually frivolous defence.
40. Torloisk Papers. B66. Rental of the estate of Torloisk, 1827–28.
41. Torloisk Papers. B66. A. Shiells to Mrs Clephane, February 1833, enclosing copy of this letter.
42. Torloisk Papers. B66. Anon to David Thomson, n.d. Thomson and his wife, Janet

Stirling, had been at Torloisk from at least 1818, when a daughter, Janet, was baptised on 4 October (Kilninian OPR).

43. Miss Jean MacQuarrie, her sister, who had lived with the Kilbrenans, and died 21 November 1835.

44. Torloisk Papers. B456. Alexander Shiells to Mrs Clephane, Kengharair, 12 February 1836. The schoolmaster, John Maclean, married Margaret McCallum in 1802. Their sons Alexander and John were born at Ballygown in 1802 and 1808. They had six other children.

45. Her husband John was the man MMT had warned about debts with wine merchants.

46. Burt, *Letters from a Gentleman* ... XXIII, p. 244.

47. GRO. D3330. Box 25. LMD. Diary. Monday 8 February 1836.

48. GRO. D3330. Box 25. LMD. Diary. Monday 19 April 1824.

49. Poor Law Enquiry. Evidence, p. 122.

50. GRO. D3330. Uncatalogued Letters. A. Shiells to Rev. Angus Maclaine, July 1838.

51. NAS. GD174/1712/68. Angus Gregorson to MM2, Oban, 1 June 1842.

52. Torloisk Papers. B456. A. Shiells to Mrs Clephane, Kingharair, 12 February 1836.

53. GRO. D3330. Box 25. LMD. Diary. Sunday 15 May 1836. 'Gaelic service – excellent discourse Luke 21: v. 25 given to a pretty large congregation. This discourse was appropriate as a Solar Eclipse was to take place at the hour of 3 o'clock PM. This took place and was visible with grand effect to the naked eye.'

13

A servant of two masters:
James Maxwell of Aros

We have dwelt long on the earls and the early Dukes of Argyll, and commented on the collective personality attributed to them, even when they were individually very different kinds of men. For the Mull people who lived on their lands, they were remote figures, represented by chamberlains, factors and tacksmen, whose courts at Inveraray were to be avoided, and whose letters of fire and sword had threatened most of their ancestors. But after the '45, the third and fourth dukes began to appear more benign, and by the time young Jack Campbell became fifth duke in 1770, the ducal lands in Mull were the best administered of all the Mull estates. The other estates were Lochbuy, Mishnish, Torloisk, Ulva and Quinish. Of these, Lochbuy and Ulva were in a parlous state of debt, Mishnish was soon to be sold, Lachlan Maclean was attempting to put Torloisk back on its feet, and Quinish was awaiting the attentions of 'Young Col', Donald Maclean Younger of Coll, whose property it would be when he completed his apprenticeship in farming in England.

Jack Campbell, who, in his new dignified situation must now be called John, had been a soldier, fighting on the government side at Culloden, and subsequently attaining the rank of field marshal. In 1758 he had married Elizabeth Gunning, widow of the Duke of Hamilton, and when he came to the title there was a precious two-year-old heir, George William Campbell, who had followed one daughter and two dead baby sons. Another future duke (had he only suspected it) was the son born in 1777, John Douglas Campbell, mainly known as Lord John Campbell. Duke John was a great-grandson of the ninth earl, who had imperturbably asked if he might take a nap on the afternoon of his execution.

The fifth duke lived in London and at Inveraray, but if he seldom if ever visited Mull, he took a very great interest in it. Names of places and of people came second nature to him, and he personally appointed his tacksmen in the principal farms. His great aim was to have an industrious and virtuous tenantry, to treat them with fairness and to reward them for effort and loyalty. His Mull estates were those lands which had belonged to the Macleans of Duart, and followed historical divisions of a kind which appear rather erratic to us, because they were not joined up on the landward side; but when you look with the eye of a sailor at Duart land acquisitions, they begin to make sense: bring your boat into Tobermory, and you take the land from the shore up to Baliscate. Bring it to Duart, and you acquire Achnacroish (now Torosay

Castle), sail into the neck of Loch Spelve, and you have Killean. In the north-west, Ulva, Torloisk, Quinish and Mishnish are taken, so you settle for Penmore, Sunipol, Calgary, Killunaig, Killiechronan and Knock. The Ross of Mull is all for the taking, since it belongs to the church.

The fifth duke's lands were divided into farms, and the principal farms were Achadashenaig (now known as Glen Aros), Aros, Ardnacross, Baliscate, Sunipol, Frachadil, Treshnish, Killiechronan, Knock, Achnacroish, Kilpatrick, and Achnacraig. Brolass and the Ross of Mull were very different territories, and still retain the character of farm 'towns'. In 1771, when the duke was new, there was no house where he could have laid his ducal head on a pillow, so that any visit he might have made would have been a voyage by sea and a putting in at ports. He relied mainly on his chamberlain or tacksmen to carry out a series of meticulously numbered instructions. Before 1787, Donald Campbell of Airds and Duncan Campbell in Aros carried out instructions. In 1787, when Duncan reached the hoary old age referred to by Faujas de Saint Fond, he was given honourable retirement.

On the recommendation of James Ferrier, however, in 1787 the duke appointed a new representative, a young man called James Maxwell, to be his chamberlain in Mull. Maxwell came of a family in Kintyre with Renfrewshire origins, for a deliberate policy of plantation had been followed by the dukes in their Kintyre lands, whereby good hardworking Ayrshire and Renfrewshire farmers were brought in to demonstrate successful farming methods, and show the Gaelic-speaking natives how things should be done. Maxwell was just such a young man as the fifth duke loved to encourage: he had studied at Glasgow University, worked for the Commissioner of the Argyll estates, James Ferrier, in Edinburgh, and had then become a sheriff substitute at Campbeltown. With some knowledge of the Mull estate, he was an efficient, responsive and responsible man.

At first, there was nowhere for James Maxwell to live, there being no house fit for a chamberlain on the whole of the east coast of Mull within the ducal estate, for old Duncan Campbell was still living at Aros in his retirement. The east coast was the only possible centre of operations for a man who would have to make frequent trips to Inveraray, and Baliscate was the first choice, after some complicated rearranging of leases. Maxwell would live there until the small tenants of Ardnacross were moved to Ardtun in the Ross of Mull to make a place for him there.[1] But Baliscate had problems in 1789, not least because of the fact that its arable land was needed for the settlers in the new town of Tobermory. Then, just as plans were under way for the removal of the Ardnacross people, and the building of a house there, the old tacksman, Duncan Campbell, died at Aros, and his land became available for Maxwell. Ardnacross or Baliscate would have been more useful for the new chamberlain, who was deeply involved in the planning of the new village of Tobermory, but this burst of activity was, it was to be hoped, of limited duration. Aros, as a principal landing place for boats from the mainland, was then a more important centre than the new village, which, it has to be remembered, was set high on a hill, and not placed around the harbour. Some twenty years later, the engineer Robert Stevenson, who was Walter Scott's companion on his voyage in the *Pharos*, was to lament that the village founded in 1789 by the British Fisheries Society, had not been built on the island of Calve, where the fishermen would not be so 'retired into the depth of the bay'.[2] Maxwell may have felt the same, but plans were too far advanced when he came to office to be altered.

Maxwell was not settled in Aros until 1791, when, after a lengthy sacrifice of his domestic comforts, he was able to bring his wife, Janet McNeill (of Highland Kintyre stock) and their two young sons to a house of their own, designed by him and built within a few yards of the ruined castle of Aros. This house, now known as Aros Mains, and still closely resembling the Maxwell concept of 1790, lay below a typical township of the late eighteenth century, where, in the census of 1779, his predecessor had enumerated fifty-seven souls.[3] If anyone should imagine that life in Mull for a chamberlain in the 1790s was leisurely, James Maxwell's schedule was ample evidence that it was not. Apart from being the fifth duke's representative in the construction of Tobermory, he travelled to Iona to inspect the shocking state of the abbey (with a view to enclosure), the state of schools, and sites for a spinning school. He made the kelp industry efficient on the duke's shores. He arranged cutting and replanting of woods in both Mull and 'woody Morvern', and was drawn into the serious matter of establishing boundaries with all the other heritors of Mull. These marches were to have march dykes built on them to 'prevent disputes', but also to accord with an Act, passed almost 100 years earlier, which was to have dire consequences for the poor of Mull.

The Act for the Division of Commonties, 1696, was designed to establish that no land in Scotland belonged to 'nobody', or, in other words, that no land traditionally assigned for pasturage to be held in common among the common people, could remain in such vague ownership. We have seen so much of the antics of the Lochbuy and Ulva families in the eighteenth century, that it is clear they had other things to think about than the ascertaining of boundaries in the inland reaches of the island of Mull. A form of transhumance had always been practised, which was satisfactory to lairds and people alike. In summer, the herds and the maidens – subjects of a thousand Gaelic songs and poems – had led their cattle to the hills, living in sheilings and watching their herds with half an eye, returning to their townships in time for the harvest. The only heritors who attempted to follow the injunction of the Act were the Dukes of Argyll, and perhaps the Torloisk Macleans, when it suited them. The fifth duke, however, believed in anticipating trouble, and with increasing sales of Mull lands, new buyers had to have a clear title. Before James Maxwell was appointed, Ulva had been on the market, Charles Mackinnon of Mackinnon had sold Mishnish to John Campbell of Knock, and Lochbuy was preparing to sell what he could under the terms of his entail.

To James Maxwell fell the thankless task of seeing each of the neighbouring heritors, arranging for a representation of old men to remember how, in their fathers' time, 'the Country' had been divided, and taking down their opinions in writing.

Maxwell had no Gaelic, being a Lowlander. He attempted to understand a little, but wisely forbore claiming that he understood anything that might have a legal significance. As his reputation for integrity and fairness grew, he was increasingly asked to be an arbiter in disputes between heritors, but where the Gaelic language was used in evidence, he would frequently refuse. In one such case he wrote frankly to Lochbuy:

> Dear Sir,
>
> I would with all my heart undertake the execution of the Commission in the question betwixt Mr MacMillan and you, if I was so much master of the Gaelic language as to be able to examine witnesses in it, but this not being the case, I am obliged to decline, as there is no other Commissioner joined with me who could help me out when I might happen to be at a loss.[4]

He was not at a loss when, accompanied by an interpreter, he followed Donald MacEachern in Assapol to the spot where his father had habitually turned the cattle at Arinucadeur, as the boundary of Brolass was approached, or listened to Hugh MacFarlane in Ardchrishnish describing the march of Kilpatrick, Ross.[5] The duke's unrelenting endeavour to have boundaries entered properly into the records, and Maxwell's care in naming every (Gaelic) rock or burn in folk memory, combined to eradicate unpleasant ideas that the Campbells had simply walked in and taken over Maclean lands. The duke's unfailing courtesy in appealing to the memories of old men, and in continuing to allow his tenants hill pasturage in common, gave the house of Argyll, at least temporarily, a certain reputation for good management, and in this reputation Mr Maxwell played a very large part.

Tobermory was not the only new village being constructed in Mull which required Maxwell's supervision. The duke, who tried to promote industry and self-sufficiency among his people, was planning new villages at Bunessan, Creich and Kintra, where fishing was to be encouraged. He promoted flax growing, weaving, road-making, cattle-raising, kelp manufacture and everything designed to banish indolence.

Maxwell was himself a sincere Presbyterian, and took an interest in the church at Salen as well as the presbytery in general. The duke was always well disposed to the church, being patron, and choosing and presenting most of the ministers. Maxwell was known to sway the duke in favour of many plans which the other heritors would not agree to. At the end of the eighteenth century, Alexander Fraser, Dugald Campbell and Archibald MacArthur, ministers of Torosay, Kilfinichen and Kilninian respectively, had continued their predecessors' struggles to have granted to them what both ecclesiastical and secular law had decreed – a manse, a church and a glebe in every parish. Lochbuy was most implacably opposed to the church. Torloisk, who was, unlike Lochbuy, a God-fearing man, was reluctant to dip into his pocket. Coll had already contributed to Kilmore, his end of Kilninian parish. It was left always to the duke to make a conciliatory gesture to the ministers, whom, in his greatness, His Grace did not resent as the lesser landlords did, for their impudence and presumption. When Mr Fraser arrived in 1792, Maxwell wrote to him saying that the duke would be happy to concur with the other heritors in providing a manse and a glebe in Torosay, but this happy concurrence was to be invalidated by the refusal of Lochbuy even to reply to Maxwell's proposal. In 1800, at the height of the struggle between Lochbuy and the presbytery, Mr Ferrier in Edinburgh and Maxwell plotted together to force the reluctant Lochbuy to agree to one method of supplying a glebe. Killean, formerly church land under the control of the duke, was to be sold. Ferrier suggested that if the duke and Lochbuy bought this little snippet of land together, they might then cut out of it the land for manse and glebe, then resell it, and split the profit.

Maxwell passed the message to Lochbuy (better it should come from him than from the duke!) and the pleasing plan was accepted. The Killean land was sold for £1,540.[6] Gualachaolish was cut out of Killean, and Mr Fraser was installed in this not very convenient or 'centrical' farm until fresh struggles broke out in the nineteenth century, to be related in Chapter 22. 'I am glad to understand,' wrote Maxwell to Lochbuy, 'that the farm of Killean has been kept out of the hands of the Roman Catholicks.'[7]

Mr Maxwell's social life fell into two categories – the socialising thrust upon him in his capacity as the duke's resident representative in Mull, and the family and friends he chose to spend his time with. During his service as chamberlain, from 1787 until 1829, the tradition of island hospitality still prevailed. For at least the first half of that time, before the advent of the steamboat, Aros was, with Achnacraig (as Grass Point was then called), the main landing place for travellers going to see Staffa, the Disneyland of the eighteenth century.

Gillean Maclaine in Scallastle, whose house had been described in 1787 as 'a compleat cake-house for all comers and goers', did not live to see Mr Maxwell, to whom he might have been grateful for taking over some of his burden of hospitality. Among visitors who called on James Maxwell and his wife were Sir John Carr in 1807, who pronounced their house comfortable, and Walter Scott in 1810, both on their way to see Ranald Macdonald, or 'Staffa', at Ulva. These were only two of a very large number of travellers, and their descriptions of Ulva and its laird will be presented in the next chapter. In the meantime, a rather more practical view of the constant stream of visitors to Aros, by James Maxwell's grandson, must be quoted.

Alas! for the hospitable Highland mansion which happened to be situated at a convenient resting place for the tourist *en route* to some spot of interest! There was then prevalent among southern tourists a sort of romantic idea of the unlimited extent of Highland hospitality, and of the means at its command. It was no unusual occurrence for the traveller to land at any hour of the day or night which winds, tides, or boatmen might determine; to walk up to the house of the Highland gentleman; to get a dinner, supper and all, plentiful and comfortable; to retire to bed, without a thought where the family had packed themselves so that the travelling party might have accomodation; and finally to obtain next day, or, if it rained, days after, carts, horses, boats, men with baskets of provisions, crammed with roast fowls, cold lamb (salt never forgot), cold salmon, grouse, milk, brandy, sherry, and bottles of whisky. The potato digging, the hay cutting, or the reaping of crops might be put a stop to; what of that? they are *so* hospitable in the Highlands! And then these summer visitants bade farewell with shaking of hands, and waving of handkerchiefs, and with the usual stereo-typed hope expressed that, 'should they ever come to England and visit Land's End, how glad, etc …' But the reception was nevertheless all put down to a *habit* of the Country, a thing called Highland hospitality, something like speaking Gaelic, smoking tobacco, or wearing the kilt.[8]

There were four hospitable houses on Mull and Ulva where English visitors did not hesitate to call. The first was Mr Maxwell's, the second Mr Stewart's of Achadashenaig, the third Colonel Campbell Knock's, and lastly Ranald Macdonald's house on Ulva. The lady wives of these kind hosts (with the exception of Mr Macdonald's, who had not yet married him) excused their own weakness and forbearance by asking what else they could do. There were no inns that were not wretched holes, and all the travellers were well-to-do gentry, accustomed to better conditions. And they could not be expected to take the risk of sailing from Oban round the dangerous points of Caliach and Treshnish to reach Staffa and Iona. And if they arrived with a letter of introduction from His Grace the Duke of Argyll, what chamberlain, tacksman or fellow-heritor could refuse?

The fifth Duke of Argyll, whose relationship with his chamberlain was considerate, as was his treatment of his tenantry, was not guilty of imposing his friends on Maxwell. But after nineteen years of what might be called a prudent partnership, Duke John died in 1806, and his eldest son, the Marquis of Lorne, became George William, sixth Duke of Argyll. He had caused his father much anxiety – as is so often the lot of a careful father – by his extravagance. He was a bachelor, and one of the fast set surrounding the Prince Regent; what else needs to be said? Except that James Maxwell's grandson Norman Macleod happened to attend the funeral of a later duke, and left a description of the Argyll burial place at Kilmun:

Then came the magnificent coffin of the great duke John of Greenwich, the companion of Marlborough, and second in command in all Marlborough's great battles ... and his brother ... the long-headed, sagacious and able man who built Inveraray Castle, and then the good old duke and field marshall for whom Mr Maxwell long acted as chamberlain on his Mull and Morvern estates, a truly good and great man; and beside him the coffin of his duchess, the loveliest of all the ladies in the kingdom ... then came the leader of the gay, Duke George, the extravagant and foolish, and yet the favourite of all – a kind, easy, good-tempered, gentle, noble-looking man. I never met a man who took such hold of my mind; he gave me my first presentation; he presented me at court, and was kind, courteous and attentive to me at all times.[9]

It was George William, 'the extravagant and foolish', who gave all his friends letters of introduction to the house at Aros; kind as he was, he perhaps did not think of the strain on a poorer man's purse. It was George William who came himself, on impulse, in the year following his father's death, to visit Mull, 'diffusing uncommon joy all over the island' and going to see the people of Iona 'who had during a century, never been so honoured'.[10] The new duke took one look at the road from Achnacraig to Aros, and promised to construct a new road in these 'uncouth parts'.[11] In the event it slipped his mind, which was otherwise occupied. In London, he lived in the society of artistic and often highly talented people, such as Matthew 'Monk' Lewis, the playwright, but he himself, although not lacking in intelligence, was inclined to languor and boredom. His marriage to Caroline, Lady Paget, took place when he was over forty (although his lifestyle was that of a very much younger man) and when she had obtained a divorce from her husband; even in a licentious age, this 'unnatural' relationship shocked their friends. Duke George did not return to Mull, and spent money on extravagant changes at Inveraray. In fact, by 1810, the year of his marriage, his finances were in serious disarray. Shortly afterwards, in 1812, his lands in Clackmannanshire were sold to pay his debts, and the rest put under trustees.[12]

For Mr Ferrier, who looked after all the estates from Edinburgh, for Mr Maxwell in Mull, and for all the residual Campbell tacksmen, during the years between 1812 and 1816, when a special act of parliament permitted the first sales of Argyll estate lands, a terrible shadow hung over the future. Among the people, there were the usual warnings and evictions for non-payment of rent, but the destinations of the evicted were so mixed as to be almost untraceable. Some Highland soldiers returning from the so-called 'second American war of independence' of 1812–14, gave a glowing account of America which promoted emigration. Some small tenants moved in with relations. Some families were cleared, as in Mornish, prior to the sale of land to prospective buyers who did not wish to purchase a parcel of poor people with their property.[13] The drift of the dispossessed into Tobermory began. Respectable tenants on Argyll lands, unable to appeal to the duke, wrote instead to the trustees about their plight. One of these was Duncan Campbell, tacksman of Treshnish at Kilmaluag, who petitioned the accountant Charles Selkrig:

> Your memorialist & his predecessors have been for some generations tacks-men of Treshnish from his Grace the duke of Argyll, that they always paid their rents regularly. But from the great distress of the times your memorialist has fallen in arrears a whole year's rent at Whitsunday next. That this was brought on by the great and annual fall in the price of black cattle for the last four years ... that the management of the farm from the very boisterous shores is attended with a very great expence in boats and hands [14] that to his great distress he was obliged for the last three years to sell double the number of cattle usual to make good the rents. That lately, Mr Maxwell, his Grace's Factor, has been under the necessity in order to secure his Grace's interest, to sequestrate his stock. That the amount arrested by regular valuation to cover £184 due at Martinmass last and Whitsunday first, would have five years ago sold for near £600.
>
> Under these circumstances, your memorialist craves the indulgence to be allowed a deduction of rent, and that his cattle may not be sold till Whit-sunday, when it is to be expected they will bring a better price. If this is granted, he is promised by his friends that they will come forward with cash to stock the farm, and give security for the rents, but should it be refused, he has nothing to look for but starvation for himself, his wife, and six young children, and also lose the benefit of his great outlays on the farm.
>
> Duncan Campbell [15]

From this pathetic appeal, the situation of most of the middle class of Mull farmers can be imagined. From this date, coinciding with the Battle of Waterloo, in which not a few Mull men lost their lives, the nature of emigration changed. Those who could afford to lose their 'great outlays' on their farms simply had to go, but these were largely families like Duncan Campbell's. Lochbuy's tacksman in Tiroran, John Maclaine, after thinking of emigrating for about twenty years, took the plunge in about 1816. Mr Maxwell was in the painful position of having to press the tacksman class for rents because he could squeeze the smaller tenants no further. If times were hard for the people, Mr Maxwell's job had become extremely distressing to him. In fifteen years the old duke's optimistic little kingdom with its utopian plans for new industry set in planned villages, had changed to a country of half-starved people who had to sell the cattle which provided their sustenance.

James Maxwell, who, with Mr Robert Stewart of Achadashenaig (died 1813), was regarded as the most honest man on the island, and was always asked to resolve disputes, value property and stock, seal up the repositories of the recently dead, and pronounce on church affairs, was unable to have friends (other than his neighbours the Stewarts) on Mull. He was a new kind of man:

a middle-class, well-educated professional who did not belong to the gentry of 'the Country'. His own family, the Maxwells in Cattadale, Southend, Kintyre had left for America in the wave of Argyll emigrations around 1800.[16] But he and his wife, Jessie McNeill and their six children made friends in Morvern, on the other side of the Sound of Mull, with a remarkable family, the Macleods of Fiunary. The Macleod family, originally from Swordale in Skye, had struck down roots in Morvern when the Rev. Norman Macleod was presented by the fifth Duke of Argyll to the parish of Morvern in 1775. By the time the Maxwells came to Aros, the Macleods were living in the manse at Fiunary, with six children, and another six were to be born by 1801. The two families became very close, spending time in each other's houses, so that the Macleod boat, the *Roe*, was as often to be seen at Aros as on the Morvern shore below Fiunary. A little window in the gable wall of the Aros house allowed the Maxwells to send signals to the Macleods, whose manse was set on the hill opposite.

When Maxwell was 'off duty' he shed his serious demeanour, and came into his own as a fun-loving wit and raconteur. When George William brought his friend Tom Sheridan to visit Mull, the latter told so many stories and sang so many songs that Maxwell inherited this 'large literary property', recounting them for many years to his guests after dinner. Being fond of poetry, he most particularly enjoyed Walter Scott's stay in 1810. These were the happy days before the financial problems which accompanied the expected sale of the duke's land.

Two of James Maxwell's children, John Argyll Maxwell and Agnes Maxwell, married children of the minister of Morvern, and his son Robert married Catherine Stewart, eldest daughter of Robert Stewart of Achadashenaig. Agnes' marriage in 1811 to Norman Macleod Junior, who became minister of Campbeltown, Campsie and St Columba's Gaelic church in Glasgow, made her the wife of a very famous man, known all over the country as *Caraid nan Gaidheal*, the friend of the Gaels. As we shall see later in this story, his contribution to Gaelic literature was to have significance for the increasingly marginalised Gaelic-speaking community in Mull, and his ideas on education were to change school policies overnight. His periodical, *An Teachdaire Gaelach* ('The Gaelic Messenger') first appeared in the year of his father-in-law's death, 1829. Its preface was so inspiring that it came like a message from God himself to the embattled Gaels, and yet was so modern, so innovative and racy in its style, its themes and ideas, that Highlanders still at home as well as those who had been forced to leave, suddenly became subscribers to a magazine which gave them pride in their heritage as well as food for thought on the latest questions of the day. Allan Lamont, schoolmaster and postmaster at Clachandow (Lochdon), who was agent for the Mull subscribers, found his workload increased as the *Teachdaire* went out to cottages from Achnacraig to Ardmore. A new spirit was felt in the community, most sadly to perish only two years later, when Dr Macleod, who had stolen the time 'from my night's sleep', was unable to continue through lack of support and help in the production of the magazine, and from a certain opposition in 'sundry quarters'.[17]

By the time the *Teachdaire* had run its sparkling course, the duke, George William, retained only his Ross of Mull lands and Knock. Large pieces of Morvern and the southern and eastern reaches of Mull had gone very frequently to sons of the eighteenth century tacksmen like the Gregorsons in Ardtornish and the Stewarts in Achadashenaig. Other swathes had gone to the Macquarie brothers and to Maclean of Coll, who added Tenga and Druimfin to his Quinish possessions. Mornish had gone to Captain Allan MacAskill, not by any means an outsider, as will be seen later. The landowners were still mostly Gaelic speakers until the advent of Colonel Campbell of Possil (who might be called a 'lapsed' Gael) at Achnacroish, and Mr Auldjo at Pennyghael. The Macleans of Torloisk had a keen academic interest in Gaelic, translating verse for the benefit of their friend, Walter Scott. There was even a certain desire among heritors of the old families to keep 'the Country' Gaelic-speaking and free from 'Strangers'.[18] Better the devil you know than the devil you don't know because he does not speak Gaelic. The demise of the *Teachdaire* seemed to symbolise the end of an age. It was often the most benevolent landlords who unintentionally hastened the language change, and while the charitable goodness of Colonel Campbell of Possil gave to the poor with one hand, his very kindness dealt a blow to Gaelic culture with the other. On Sunday 29 July 1832 an ominous thing happened in the church at Craignure: Divine Service was attended by a small and select congregation, largely composed of house guests of the Possils, and not by the usual large number of commoners; it was the first time that an English service was performed without any Gaelic discourse in it. This was noted by one man with grave displeasure and foreboding. It was the beginning of the end.

Just as the fifth duke's noble efforts to promote industry in Mull had failed as a result of the profligacy, dashing though it might appear, of his son George William, so James Maxwell's life's work was to melt into nothing in the sales of Argyll land from 1816 to 1822. In the last resort he opposed the chopping up of the estate into very small pieces, which was what most potential buyers wanted. Money was shorter than it had ever been, but the disposal of the estate gave families like the Stewarts and the Ardtornish Gregorsons the chance to stay in their homes. Priority was given to sitting tenants, most of whom spent years trying to raise the purchase money in an age before mortgages, when a pile of loans had to be negotiated, partly by the buyer and partly by his lawyer. All the new heritors began their new lives encumbered with serious and increasing debts.

James Maxwell must go down in history as the most incorruptible of all the men with Mull associations, a title for which there were few contenders. 'I never knew any man that I considered more upright in his proceedings,' Donald Maclean WS wrote in 1822.[19] However, when the time came for Mr

Maxwell to give his services as an arbiter in the matter of the final settlement between Scallastle and Lochbuy, Sheriff John Gregorson and Murdoch Maclaine, whose interests were both at stake, unwisely decided to reward Maxwell's impartial but pleasing decision with the gift of two silver cups. Mr Maxwell's acceptance of the 'flattering testimony' contained a mild comment on these gentlemen's notions of saving money through resorting to arbitration instead of going to court.

> I truly regret that you have thought it necessary to make so costly an acknowledgement for the exercise of my good offices in settling the Scallastle question; because a principal motive in undertaking such references is to save my friends from expense, and in this case your generosity has defeated that intention.[20]

Notes

1. Cregeen (ed.), *Argyll Instructions*, p. 153.
2. *Voyage of the* Pharos, p. 100.
3. Cregeen (ed.), *Inhabitants of the Argyll Estate*, 1779.
4. NAS. GD174/1478/3. James Maxwell to MM, Aros, 16 December 1797.
5. Cregeen (ed.), *Argyll Instructions*, p. 139.
6. NAS. GD174/1329/90. DMWS to MM, Edinburgh, 24 May 1800.
7. NAS. GD174/1478/6. James Maxwell to MM, Aros, 6 June 1800.
8. Macleod, Norman, *Reminiscences of a Highland Parish*, pp. 241–2.
9. Macleod, John N., *Memorials of the Rev. Norman Macleod Senior, DD.*, pp. 211–12.
10. Carr, Sir John, *Caledonian Sketches*, pp. 471, 485. This suggests that no duke had come to Mull since the beginning of the eighteenth century, not even the fifth duke, whose very impressive familiarity with the island in his instructions was possibly learned from maps and an efficient supply of information.
11. Ibid.
12. Lindsay and Cosh, *Inveraray and the Dukes of Argyll*, pp. 307–12.
13. John Campbell's evidence to the Royal Commission (Highlands and Islands, 1892) spoke of eight families being removed from Caillach, eleven from Arin, four from Inivea *c.* 1814.
14. In taking cattle to graze on the Treshnish Isles. The farm of Treshnish was on Mull.
15. EUL. MS Gen. 886* Duncan Campbell to Charles Selkrig, n.d. From the baptisms of his children amounting to six, the date is construed as 1815. Duncan was born in 1766.
16. McKerral, Andrew, *Kintyre in the 17th Century*.
17. Macleod, John N. *Memorials of the Rev. Norman Macleod Senior, DD.*, p. 90.
18. NAS. GD174/1828. DMWS's letters show bias against incomers in his property deals.
19. NAS. GD174/1628/295. DMWS to MM2, 6 August 1822.
20. NAS. GD174/1671. James Maxwell to MM2, Aros, 8 March 1825. Maxwell's descendant, Dr George MacLeod, Lord MacLeod of Fiunary, was to resurrect the family's links with 'the Country' by his founding of the Iona Community in 1938.

'His people are distractedly fond of him': Staffa's story

The dislike evinced by Marianne Maclean Clephane for Colin Macdonald of Boisdale, proprietor of Ulva, seems to have been shared by most of the old families in Mull, and this was because, as an outsider, Boisdale had criticised the creditors of the MacQuarries of Ulva and Ormaig for their harsh treatment of the two aged representatives of these families, Lachlan MacQuarrie of Ulva and Hector MacQuarrie of Ormaig. But Boisdale's patience had not been tried over a period of several decades. From the 1750s, the two MacQuarries had simply stalled all their creditors, talking of an eventual sale of Ulva to pay their debts, but always finding reasons for not proceeding. The background was this:

The sale was known to be imminent when Dr Johnson and James Boswell visited, but the estate affairs were so complicated that the buyer, Dugald Campbell of Achnaba, had to await settlement of several court adjudications before entering into possession of the property, and so long did it take that he died before all the claims on MacQuarrie had been cleared.[1] The old chief owed arrears of rent and other debts to most of his fellow landowners, many of them relations. Some were disponed and assigned to further creditors of the creditors, and were complicated by MacQuarrie's holding of certain lands jointly with his kinsman, Hector MacQuarrie of Ormaig. Each of the creditors, themselves in debt, had to wait for a ranking of their creditors to be completed before proceeding with the next part of their application for payment from the sale of the island estate. After the death of the buyer, another Campbell, Colonel Charles Campbell of Barbreck, acquired rights in Ulva and Ormaig[2] and sold them on to Colin Macdonald of Boisdale, who had married Isabella Campbell as his second wife. Colin's heir by his first wife was Alexander Macdonald of Boisdale, who inherited the Boisdale estates, but his heir by his second marriage was Ranald Macdonald, born in 1777, to whom Colin made over, on his coming of age, the lands of Ulva and Staffa.[3] Colin died in 1800, having installed his wife and daughters at Ulva House, and Mrs Murray, the bold traveller and writer of guidebooks, stayed a month with them in 1800, describing a new house, larger than the one Johnson and Boswell had stayed in.

Ranald Macdonald was a slim, comely young man, trained for the law, but, because of his position as proprietor of the popular island of Staffa, rather more interested in his role as a Highland host than his legal career. In the first fifteen years of the nineteenth century, his mother and sisters looked after the mansion house which had been built in a style similar to Lochbuy, but in a magnificent setting, with views of Ben More and Loch na Keill. He acquired neighbouring islands and coastal lands as tacks expired – Little Colonsay in 1801, Inchkenneth with Gribun in 1803, Burg and Gometra in 1807. He found Ulva overpopulated with poor tenants, and arranged for some of them to go to America, although no documentation survives of the actual names or numbers. A few clues suggest that there was a legal dispute with an emigration agent over conditions on board the vessel which bore the poor people of Ulva across the Atlantic.[4] The correspondence of Mull people in the early 1800s is full of allusions to 'Staffa's' quickness to evict for reasons other than non-payment of rent, such as collusion with recruiting officers. But as absolute sole lord of his property, with tenants-at-will, he had every right so to do.

His little kingdom, full of charm like Prospero's Isle, was ideally placed to be a showpiece, and since everyone went to Ulva in order to proceed to Staffa, the geologists, economists, agriculturalists, mineralogists, writers, planters, poets and playwrights solicited invitations or introductions from the two Dukes of Argyll in turn, and arrived at the Inn or on the doorstep of Ulva House. The wars with Napoleon had put an end to the Grand Tour in Europe, but what could be better than a tour of the Hebrides with a sketching pad and a copy of *The Poems of Ossian* in one's saddle-bag?

Staffa (he was rarely called anything else) loved publicity. He was eager to show the reading public that Ulva had changed since Johnson and Boswell published their not very flattering impressions. He was probably also motivated by his intense dislike of the Macleans of Torloisk to inspire visiting authors to write volumes which would put Faujas de Saint Fond's description of that family (published in an English translation in 1799) in the shade. He gave much thought to his presentation of his estate, and treated James Macdonald, Sir John Carr, William Daniell, Walter Scott and Necker de Saussure to personal tours. Such guests were met by boats decked with flags and entertained by pipers. Singing boatmen rowed them to the Isle of Staffa with the laird himself as guide. Sir John Carr, who had recently published a bestselling work on Ireland, arrived in Mull in 1807. Steeped in the Ossian tradition, he saw with dismay that 'woody Morvern' had lost its trees. When he arrived at the inn on Ulva, the 'merry peasants' were dancing, but offered to stop if he was disturbed by the noise. The Macdonald family at Ulva House were both amiable and refined. Their piper strutted before the windows of the house; their table was plentiful and elegant. In the boat going to Staffa, the rowers sang Boswell's much-loved song, 'Hatyin foam foam foam! Hatyin foam foam foam! Hatyin foam foam eri' as Carr took it down phonetically. This was the song which impressed all the travellers, *Tha tighinn fodham eiridh.*[5] When Fingal's cave had been seen, and the party returned to Ulva, Sir John began his journalistic investigation, and the voice of Staffa can be heard in the ensuing pages of the book – Staffa's political views, his agricultural plans, his ideas on enclosure, fishing, baking, volunteering for the army.[6]

If we can accept Staffa's presentation of his island, it has to be said that it was a veritable paradise.

> The natives of Ulva ... have an opportunity of living in great comfort and happiness. Their food consists of fish, of which they have upwards of twenty different species within a few hundred yards of the shore; of mutton, lamb, and beef, of which they consume a good deal; of geese, ducks, hens, chickens etc. Indeed at certain seasons of the year they consume a considerable quantity of poultry; eggs and milk they have in great abundance all the year round.
>
> The worthy Laird of Ulva arranges all the lots of land upon his property in such a manner that the holder of the smallest lot has his two cows ... and up to six, ten or twelve cows. In consequence, many of them not only provide their families with butter and cheese, but have a surplus to dispose of. The bread generally made use of is from barley and oatmeal, of which they also make porridge, which forms their breakfast or supper, along with milk ... As every small tenant has a garden attached to his house, he in general plants a quantity of cabbages, and of late turnip, which, with potatoes, are the principal vegetables ... and in general every tenant has a row-boat for himself, with which they fish, make kelp, etc.

If your host tells you of the excellence of his island domain and the happiness of his people, it is churlish to question any aspect of his account, and Sir John Carr did not have the same need for further information that we have today. But the key question here is whether 'tenant' applied only to one layer of the Ulva population, or whether all the people were tenants. Elsewhere in Mull, tenants were a middle class of society, below whom were the poor cottars or 'scalags', who were at the mercy of tenants rather than landlords. It is not known that poor cottars paid any rent to the laird. Rentals of estates contain only the names of tenants. If a tenant was evicted for failure to pay his rent, he had to take his cottars with him, or at least expel them from the land he had leased. Poor cottars, until the first census of 1841, remain unnamed and unlisted. For Ulva, no list of tenants survives of an earlier date than 1824, and when this is compared with an estimate of the number of people on the island, it can be seen that tenants were only one stratum of the population.[7]

A further question which leads on from this extrapolation is about how a tenant acquired those cottars, scalags, or subtenants. Did he need them, or were they his own poor relations? The answer would appear to be that they were simply descendants of people who had been there all along, but, through sickness, old age, or misfortune, had not aspired to seek tenant status. Inevitably, they were related in some degree to the tenants, and blood relationship could never be denied or ignored. Some were useful in giving their labour in the kelp season, and kelp, at the time of Sir John's visit, was the most important part of the Ulva economy.

Ranald Macdonald also entertained the Genevan geologist Louis-Albert Necker de Saussure in 1807. Necker was attending Edinburgh University, and in the summer vacation undertook a tour to the Hebrides which was more scholarly in its motives than Carr's. His book, *Un voyage en Ecosse et aux Iles Hébrides*, was published at Geneva in 1821, and covered much larger issues, such as the damage done to the reputation of Highland literature by Dr Johnson, the question of the authenticity of Ossian (to which he devoted nearly 100 pages), and the origins and nature of the Gaelic language. He also explored the relationship between landowner and people, the necessity for emigration, and the characteristics of Celtic music. He deliberately avoided the kind of domestic detail which had intrigued Faujas de Saint Fond, feeling that it was an intrusion into the privacy of his host. There is no doubt that Staffa discussed these subjects with him, but unlike Carr, Necker had conceived a strong affinity with Highland life, and had already learned a great deal about the background. He went to see the island of Staffa twice, and therefore had ample opportunity to hear the bagpipes played in the boat, discerning a strong connection between the natural beauty of the rocky coast lashed by violent waves, and the sad, wild, bitter-sweet, plaintive melodies of the oarsmen. To him, there was in this music and song a oneness with the primitive poetic strains of Ossian. He was not naïve in this. He had gone into all the stages of the controversy over MacPherson's 'translations', and decided very wisely that if the author or translator had only used the word 'adapted' instead of 'translated', he would have had no trouble. Necker was impressed with the use of music in all tasks. There were spinning songs, waulking songs, milking and rowing songs. The account of Necker's stay in Mull is full of sounds – music, wind, waves, rain and the sound of reels danced on the white sands of Iona, in honour of the sixth duke, whose visit he witnessed.

Staffa accompanied his guest to Tobermory, which was, in 1807, a most promising small town, with clean, slated houses, a shop, a good inn and a fine harbour. But he did observe (or Staffa pointed out) that because the feuars had small plots of land, they neglected fishing, the very *raison d'être* of the place, and already the fishing village was seen to be a failure.

Necker was almost the only traveller who attempted to understand the nature of Gaelic, for Dr Johnson's high-handed condemnation of the language had struck him as irrational and unworthy. The Genevan heard the recitation of the death of Oscar from an old man whose memory did not fail him.[8] To Necker, it was quite natural that Gaelic was an oral medium. He found the characteristic constructions of the language fascinating. Initial mutations, periphrastic verbs, the formation of adjectival properties – all were meaningful in the larger social and historical context.[9]

Although Necker's enthusiasms were entirely his own, he must have been indebted to Ranald Macdonald for some information on subjects like emigration, in which 'Staffa' was deeply involved. The statement that it was 'getting out of control' [10] rings true of Mull, from all these hints and unsubstantiated remarks which we find everywhere, unimportant for the people who utter them, but a haunting refrain for those of us who want to know more. Ranald Macdonald, in a Gaelic poem by John Maclean, is said to have had a lawsuit with a man called James Robertson, who forced people to emigrate against their will. [11] Unfortunately, the conventions of Gaelic praise poetry do not admit of much historical fact, and the circumstances of the case are not fully divulged. But in the years between 1800 and 1807, emigration was beyond the control of the landlords, and perhaps Staffa had presented himself to Necker as a heritor who lived among his people. Necker blames the emigration fever on those landlords who, after switching to a cash economy, go and spend their rent money on the pleasures of the cities, instead of investing in their lands. It is difficult to judge whether at this time Staffa could be accused of luxurious living in Edinburgh; he certainly went back and forward, as Murdoch Maclaine of Lochbuy had done in his time, and as Mrs Clephane most certainly did. As for the sixth Duke of Argyll – after his ceremonial visit to Mull and Iona, he did not return. His habitat was the south of England, with a very occasional visit to Inveraray. If we are to judge Ranald Macdonald, perhaps his friend and fellow lawyer, Walter Scott, always a gentle and wise commentator, will help to clarify his role as a landowner.

Walter Scott – who was not to be Sir Walter Scott until 1820 – visited Ulva in 1810 (as mentioned in Chapter 12) during the absence of Staffa's neighbours, the Maclean Clephanes. His friendship with Ranald Macdonald was an offshoot of his professional closeness to Staffa's half-brother, Hector Macdonald. [12] Scott made little of Staffa's invitation in his letters to the Maclean Clephanes, knowing that they would be unhappy about their rival having all the honour of introducing him to the Hebrides, and explaining customs which they would have preferred to elucidate. But, as he wrote to Lady Abercorn: 'My friend Ranald Macdonald of Staffa promises me a good barge, six rowers, a piper, and his own company for pilot, which is a strong temptation.' On 19 July Scott was writing to Joanna Baillie [13] from Ulva House, where he and his wife and daughter were being entertained with great kindness.

We rode across the isle on highland ponies attended by a numerous retinue of gillies, and arrived at the head of the salt water loch called Loch-an-Gaoil [14] where Staffa's boats awaited us with colours flying and pipes playing. We proceeded in state to this lonely isle where our honoured landlord has a very comfortable residence, and were received by a discharge of swivels and musquetry from his people. Yesterday we visited Staffa and Iona ... The [boat] men, cheered by the pipes, and by their own interesting boat songs, which are uncommonly wild and beautiful, one man leading, and the others answering in chorus, kept pulling away without apparently the least sense of fatigue, and we reached Ulva at ten at night, tolerably wet and well disposed for bed ... Our friend Staffa is himself an excellent specimen of Highland chieftainship; he is a cadet of Clan Ranald, and lord of a cluster of isles on the western side of Mull, and a large estate, in extent at least, on that island. By dint of minute attention to this property, and particularly to the management of his kelp shores, he has at once trebled his income and doubled his population, while emigration is going on all around him. But he is very attentive to his people who are distractedly fond of him, and has them under such regulations as conduce both to his own benefit and their profit, and keeps a certain sort of rude state and hospitality in which they can take much pride. I am quite satisfied that nothing under the personal attention of the landlord himself will satisfy a highland tenantry, and that the substitution of factors, which is now becoming general, is one great cause of emigration. This mode of life has, however, its evils, and I can see them in this excellent and enthusiastic young man. The habit of solitary power is dangerous even to the best regulated minds, and this ardent and enthusiastic young man has not escaped the prejudices incident to his situation. He beards the duke of Argyll, the Lord Lieutenant, and hates with a perfect hatred the wicked Macleans on the other side of Mull who fought with his ancestors two hundred years ago.[15]

Staffa was not such a very young man. He was thirty-three years old in 1810, and therefore about the same age as Archibald Lochbuy (when he left the world's stage) and about five years younger than Duke George William when he was rapturously received in Mull and Iona in 1807; young, handsome, eligible chieftains seemed to command great affection in the people. In the very same letter to Joanna Baillie, Scott had reported meeting Mackinnon of Mackinnon at Aros

a young gentleman born and bred in England, but nevertheless a Highland chief. It seems his father had acquired wealth, and this young man who now visits the Highlands for the first time, is anxious to buy back some of the family property which was sold long since. Some twenty Mackinnons who happened to live within hearing of our arrival, came posting to see their young chief, who behaved with great kindness and propriety and liberality.[16]

Some controversy was to attend the young gentleman's claim to the title of chief of the MacKinnons, but as the family property which he wished to have was not the MacKinnons' Mishnish estate, the question does not concern us here.

Scott's reservations about Ranald Macdonald may be compared with Necker's, in that they both imply that the laird is more attentive than other absentee lairds, but at the same time identify absenteeism as a principal cause of emigration. James Macdonald, another favoured guest of Staffa's, and an official reporter on agriculture, commissioned to produce an account of farming in the Hebrides, visited between 1808 and 1810.[17]

James Macdonald was impartial in his praise of a group of landowners which included Maclean of Coll and the Duke of Argyll. To the other proprietors we shall return in a later chapter, but just now Ulva is under the microscope. To this author we are indebted for a more accurate statement about Staffa's residence on his island, which was for 'the greatest part of summer and autumn'. James Macdonald uses the word 'elegant' to describe Staffa's hospitality, and praises the quality and organisation of the kelp, at that time at the height of its profitability. He is full of admiration for Staffa's concern in the education of the tenants' children, no fewer than 126 being taught at school in 1809. Staffa is exemplary in this respect, as are the ladies of his family in their humanity and beneficence for the poor and the sick. But, the writer adds, the population is gradually increasing, and the tenantry live in very comfortable and easy circumstances.[18]

This distinction between 'population' and tenantry is one that recurs in Macdonald's book. By population, Macdonald means people, in large numbers, and by tenantry, the higher stratum of that population. In his general reflections on tenants and subtenants, he offers the information that subtenants or cottars rarely pay more than £3 yearly, and that even that low rent is rarely paid in cash, but is extracted in services by the higher from the lower strata. Almost all cottars support numerous families in a state bordering upon perfect idleness, and maintain grown children in this way rather than send them out into any kind of service. 'It is a common sight, on entering the cottage of one of these subtenants, to find five or six grown-up individuals, half-naked and savage looking, around a peat fire, watching a pot of potatoes (their sole food for nine months of the year) without any idea or wish of changing their manner of life; and on being demanded to work for hire, *asking the most extravagant wages,* or determined to remain as you found them.'

The cottars of Ulva were more than half of the population of the island, and it is now clear that Staffa, when speaking of the people in his care, was not including this class. The tenants' children were being taught in schools, and the tenants each had a boat, a garden, vegetables and fruit. It is clear too that the glowing pictures of life on Ulva were taken in the years 1790–1815, when kelp needed the maximum number of people, and it was expedient to keep the people. The charitable work of Mrs Macdonald, Staffa's mother, and of his sisters, was directed at these very poor people, but the laird's family were not responsible for keeping or removing those cottars.

In 1812, Ranald Macdonald of Staffa married Miss Elizabeth Seton Steuart, the only daughter and heiress of Sir Henry Seton Steuart of Allanton. The news was already going the rounds in November 1811, when Robert Campbell wrote to John Gregorson:

Staffa is to be married in a fortnight to Miss Stewart of Allanton by whom he gets £15,000 per annum and almost a certainty of the Touch estate, £4,000 per annum. He also gets the sheriffdom of Stirling, but of this say nothing at present.[19]

Staffa had certainly found a very rich bride, who was not to play any part in the history of Ulva as a personality. It is not known that she came to the island in the years between her marriage and her husband's financial collapse in 1817. Her father, Sir Henry Steuart, a noted authority on tree planting, came to the rescue of the Ulva estate after it had been offered for sale in 1816, when not a single enquiry was received from any potential buyer. With so much Mull property already about to go on the market, the price asked for Ulva, Gometra, the smaller islands offshore, and the section of the estate around Lagganulva was thought exorbitant. The years between 1816 and 1824 were very gloomy ones, and it was not until 1824 that a renewed effort was made to sell the estate in three parts, consisting of the isle of Ulva itself, the smaller islands, and the Mull land. Gometra was reserved for Staffa's sisters, Isabella and Jane Macdonald, and their mother Isabella, who had, after all, established themselves as benefactors over a period of twenty-five years, and wished to maintain their connection with the estate. In 1824, a printed booklet was issued, publishing the names of sitting tenants.[20] This document shows Ulva and Laggan with 600 inhabitants, the number of tenancies being sixty-nine. Only a very small proportion of the leases were shared, between brothers, or between fathers and sons. There were no joint small tenants in the style of the Lochbuy and Argyll estates. With average families of five, these figures suggest that there were just under 200 inhabitants without the security of a lease. These people, the cottars or 'scalags' were those afterwards referred to as the 'supernumary population'.

In spite of the serious fall in the price of kelp at the end of the wars with France, the population was still being referred to in 1824–25 as an asset, affording 'useful labour'. Kelp was still being manufactured, even if its profits had disappeared, and extension of the fisheries put forward as a possible development for the next owner of the island to undertake. The inhabitants were described as 'frugal and industrious', and it was to be hoped that interested would-be purchasers had not read James Macdonald's piece about the half-naked, savage-looking grown-up children standing watching a pot of potatoes boil.

But the only interested would-be purchaser was Colonel Charles Macquarie, a man who came from Ulva stock himself, and who knew exactly what to expect from the inhabitants.

As a distant relation of the old chief, Lachlan MacQuarrie of MacQuarrie, he had taken the old man under his roof in 1816, when the latter was 101 years old, and if a sort of apostolic succession had been operating, Charles was most fitted to be the anointed chief of Ulva. He watched from the sidelines as Staffa asked over £30,000 for the property, expecting that market forces would bring the price down to a more realistic level. He must have noted with dismay that Sir Henry Steuart's intervention would hold the asking price until the expected economic recovery made it look less outrageous. He offered himself as a guide to any buyer who came along, but none came. For reasons which will be divulged in Chapter 17, Charles finally became the sole offerer for Ulva, and entered into the little kingdom of his dreams in 1826. If the Macdonald reign had lasted less than a quarter of a century, this second kingdom of the MacQuarries was to be of less than ten years' duration, and would barely be remembered at all in the folk memory of the people.

As for Staffa, the married man, and sheriff of Stirling – like many another married man he began a new life, and even took a new name. His father-in-law saved him from the harsh realities of bankruptcy by making Staffa his heir, so that Sir Ranald Macdonald Seton Steuart of Touch and Allanton became a new star in the firmament. He retained his connections with the Mull presbytery, who had elected him Ruling Elder, asking him to represent their interests at the General Assembly in Edinburgh on many occasions. To the Mull ministers he remained 'Staffa' until his death in 1838. The island of Staffa, which had given him his distinctive title, was sold in 1816 to a series of trustees, some of whom used the territorial designation, but never with quite the same éclat as Ranald Macdonald.[21]

Rental of the estate of Ulva for the year 1824

		£	s.	d.	£	s.	d.
Ormaig	Widow Macfarlane	82	0	0			
	Archibald McArthur	14	2	6			
	Dugald Macdonald	8	1	0			
	Total of Ormaig				104	3	6
Cragaig	Donald McCallum	6	0	0			
	Charles McCallum	9	0	6			
	John McNeil and son	11	10	6			
	John Macquarie	13	10	6			
	Peter Macdonald and son	9	15	6			
	Hector Macdonald	11	10	6			
	John Morison	5	16	0			
	Total of Cragaig				67	3	6
Upper Kilvickewan	Lachlan Macdonald	21	10	0			
	Roderick Morison	8	8	0			
	Alexander McIntyre and son	22	7	6			
	Total Upper Kilvickewan				52	5	6
Lower Kilvickewan	Arch. and John Lamont	23	7	6			
	John and Dugald O'Henly	24	7	6			

		£	s.	d.	£	s.	d.
	Arch. Campbell	26	0	0			
	Total Lower Kilvickewan				73	15	0
Eolasary	Arch. Campbell and son	32	0	0			
	Lachlan McKinnon and son	14	19	0			
	John Macdonald	18	0	0			
	Total of Eolasary				66	0	0
Glaknagallan	John Macdonald	17	10	0			
	Lachlan Macquarie	14	19	0			
	John McDugald	9	13	0			
	Widow Macquarie	9	0	0			
	Niel Darroch	10	10	0			
	Total of Glaknagallan				61	12	0
Ballygartan	John Darroch	11	0	0			
	Niel Macdonald	14	15	0			
	Donald Macdonald	14	15	0			
	Robert Lamont	21	0	0			
	Total of Ballygartan				61	10	0
Berniss	Niel Macdonald	8	15	0			
	Donald McArthur	10	12	0			
	Malcolm McArthur	6	2	6			
	Donald Macdonald 11 50 " half of J. McKinnon's lot "	18	1	3			
	Total of Berniss				43	10	9
Culinish	John McKinnon	6	6	3			
	Malcolm Macdonald	11	0	0			
	Lachlan McKinnon	13	13	0			
	John Macdonald	14	19	0			
	John Ferguson	9	0	0			
	Archibald McKinnon	9	0	0			
	Total of Culinish				63	18	3
Aboss	Duncan McInnes	8	10	0			
	Archibald Darroch	11	19	0			
	Murdoch Black	12	14	0			
	Malc. and Donald Macquarie	11	19	0			
	Niel McNiel	8	0	0			
	Total of Aboss				53	2	0
Soriby	Niel and Arch. McArthur	15	2	6			
	Archibald McDugald	17	10	0			
	Donald and Robert Lamont	17	10	0			

		£	s.	d.	£	s.	d.
	Farquhar McArthur	14	5	0			
	Total of Soriby				64	7	6
Ferinanardry	Hector Macquarie and son	10	10	0			
	Donald Morison	6	0	0			
	Archibald Macdonald	7	10	0			
	John Currie	15	0	0			
	Donald Macdonald	5	0	0			
	John Macdonald	5	10	0			
	Andrew McFarlane	3	18	0			
	Guarie McQuarie	3	6	0			
	Total of Ferinanardry				56	14	0
Ardellum	Arch. Macdonald and Alex. McKinnon	9	6	6			
	Alexander Macdonald	9	6	6			
	William McLeod	9	0	0			
	John McPhee	10	0	0			
	Donald Campbell	9	0	0			
	Arch. Macdonald, wright	9	10	0			
	Donald McKinnon	5	10	0			
	Hugh Macdonald	4	0	0			
	John McGilvrae	14	10	0			
	Total of Ardellum				80	3	0
Salen Ruadh	Niel Macquarie	3	18	6			
Ulva Inn	Lachlan Macdonald	26	0	0			
Sound of Ulva	Norman Macdonald, smith	15	0	0			
	George Campbell, E.O.	8	8	0	53	6	6
Ardnacaillich and Cove farms	The Proprietor				120	0	0
Sound of U. Islands	The Proprietor				5	0	0
Laggan Ulva	2–3ds Arch. McPherson				86	0	0
Mansion House and Garden	For which has been offered of yearly rent				30	0	0
					1142	11	6
Kelp	100 tons p.a. @ £6 per ton				600	0	0
	Total of rents				1742	11	6*

* Rental of Ulva from GD174/1140/9. A similar list exists for Glenforsa estate from Whitsunday 1835 to Martinmas 1836, for the farms of Rohill (Raoill), Corachy and Pennygown. GD174/1146/11, in which MacPhails and MacQuarries are prominent.

Notes

1. Lochbuie Papers, GD 174/1.
2. Ibid. GD 174/18–19.
3. Mackenzie, Alexander, History of the Macdonalds and Lords of the Isles, Inverness, 1881 and Lochbuie Papers, NAS. GD 174/24–28.
4. A. Maclean Sinclair, *Maclean Bards*, pp. 39–41.
5. Literally, 'It comes upon me to arise' (and follow Charlie).
6. Carr, Sir John, *Caledonian Sketches*, 1809.
7. NAS. GD174/1148/19. List of non-payments of Ulva tenants (arrears) 1836.
8. The death of Oscar was a popular passage. The schoolmaster of Iona also knew it by heart.
9. Utz, Hans, *A Genevan's Journey to the Hebrides in 1807*. French edn, *Voyage en Ecosse*, vol. 3, p. 300.
10. Utz, op. cit., p. 65.
11. Sinclair, *Maclean Bards*, pp. 39–41. *Do Raonall Domhnallach Tighearna Stafa*.
12. Hector Macdonald WS, was one of Colin of Boisdale's sons from his first marriage, and added the name of Buchanan to his own when he married Miss Jean Buchanan in 1793.
13. Joanna Baillie had written a play, *The Family Legend*, about the lady of Lady's Rock, near Duart. Produced in 1810, it was much acclaimed.
14. Loch na Keill.
15. Grierson, H. J. C. (ed.), *Letters of Sir Walter Scott, 1808–1811*, p. 361.
16. William Alexander Mackinnon, 1789–1870, later MP for Lymington. The Mackinnons' Mull estate of Mishnish had been conveyed in 1757 to Macleod of Macleod, a tutor dative of the Mackinnon family, restored to Charles, sixteenth Mackinnon of Mackinnon, and sold again in 1774 to Campbell of Knock.
17. Macdonald, James, *General View of the Agriculture of the Hebrides … Drawn up under the Direction of the Board of Agriculture*, 1811.
18. Ibid. Appendix.
19. GRO. Uncatalogued MSS. Robert Campbell to John Gregorson, 19 November 1811.
20. NAS. GD174/1087/1. Particulars of the Estate of Ulva in Argyleshire.
21. John Forman WS, of Staffa (1775–1841) and his son, John Nairne Forman WS, of Staffa (1806–84).

15

Hail to the Chief:
young Murdoch of Lochbuy

At the age of thirteen, young Murdoch, the heir to Lochbuy, and his younger brother John, twelve, were fetched from Edinburgh by their aunt Elizabeth Campbell of Airds, because their father Murdoch was dying. Elizabeth had been at Lochbuy for some months tending her sister Jane whose health had been giving some anxiety for more than a year, presently complicated by a miscarriage at the beginning of 1804. But there had been a deterioration in Lochbuy's condition which suddenly made him the object of the doctor's attention instead of his wife. His complaint was 'the gravel', associated with an infection of the bladder. The household had been so preoccupied with Mrs Maclaine's illness that they had been unprepared for the laird's swift 'dissolution' as they called it. The doctor in attendance was yet another Allan Maclean, *doctair ruadh nam blath shuilean*, the 'red-haired doctor with the warm eyes', who, since leaving the army had lived at Ormsaig in Brolass. He had been at Lochbuy now for so many months that he was like a member of the family. A resident physician was a useful friend in a house where there were nine daughters between the ages of two and seventeen. The two boys had been at Mr Taylor's school in Musselburgh since November 1803, but the girls had a governess. In the previous year, the boys had had their tutor, Mr Andrew Halliday, who, being intensely interested in medical matters, had kept the parents in Edinburgh furnished with a journal of news about the health of the nine Lochbuy girls and all the people on the estate. Before we weep for the death of our friend Murdoch Maclaine senior of Lochbuy, whose varied life has bridged two centuries, it might be profitable to look at an epidemic of influenza which struck the island of Mull in 1803, so that the population was reduced by death as well as emigration, both in numbers which cannot be ascertained or guessed at.

Andrew Halliday, born in Lochmaben in 1781, was intended first for the ministry, but after completing his arts and divinity course at Edinburgh University he decided that he was more interested in medicine. Like most Scottish students he had to work his way through college, and was engaged by Murdoch Maclaine from 1801 over three summer vacations. By the summer of 1803, he was old enough and familiar enough with the household of Lochbuy to be left in charge of the family when Murdoch and Jane went to Edinburgh to seek medical advice and to be present at the auction of those lands which were being sold, under the terms of the entail, to pay outstanding estate debts.

On 8 June, the Rev. Mr Fraser had written to Murdoch and Jane from Gualachaoilish in his beautiful educated hand about the influenza which raged in 'the Country'.

> A fever, accompanied with a stitch has got among the people and proves mortal. It is so infectious that it is thought not safe to have any intercourse with the infected. Indeed I dread travelling the Country. The air now is getting denser and warmer, which will make it more dangerous.[1]

Andrew Halliday had the idea of writing Lochbuy news in the form of a journal for Murdoch and Jane. On 28 May, the first of many deaths was reported. 'Died this day of the Influenza at New Kinlochspelve, Archibald Lamont, tenant.' The weather, which had caused Mr Fraser to comment continued very fine. 'Many people sick at Kinlochspelve,' wrote Andrew on the 29th. 'We did not go to Church. Mary and Jarvis [the two youngest Lochbuy girls] continued to get better.' On 30 May, 'Died this day at New and Old Kinlochspelve, Duncan Currie's wife, and the Lady of Captain Rook [2] and the deceased Archibald Lamont's mother-in-law.' A day later, Andrew and the children saw 'one of Lord Selkirk's American transports cross the mouth of the loch under full sail.' This was said without any elaboration, remarked upon as casually as one might notice a beautiful bird flying from a crevice in the Carsaig cliffs on a summer's day. That it was a common sight in those first years of the nineteenth century is vouched for by a number of such throwaway remarks. Andrew Halliday spoke as if he had no difficulty in recognising an emigrant ship, and this was only one of many.[3] In December of the same year, Hector Maclean of Kingerloch wrote to Murdoch to say that he was unable to take emigrants.

> We set sail tomorrow for Nova Scotia. Our ship can't call in any harbours in Mull for emigrants, as she is cleared out of this Custom House direct for Pictou. If there are any of the people that wishes to go for America and that you should see them, you will have the goodness to inform them that my Brother-in-Law will have a Ship early in Spring going out. If they wish to go with him let them address to him, Major Fraser, care of James Skinner, Writer, Parliament Square, Edinburgh. If there is anything I can do for you in America, I beg you may command me to do anything in regard to your lands in that country. I beg you may let me know. I shall think no trouble too great if I can serve you.[4]

This was the first intimation that Murdoch had taken up land in the new world. What he did with it is not known.

A servant at Lochbuy, little Marion or Morag, had gone over the hill to look after her sick mother at Rossal. Aware that she might bring back the infection, Andrew made her change her clothes and bathe in the sea before she came into the house 'as it is a very infectious Fever her Mother labours under – indeed we were under some doubt whether Marrion should return or not. But I hope from our making her serve *Quarantine* there will be no danger.' That very evening the scribe wrote again.

> We are happy to hear the sale has taken place to your satisfaction and hope you will leave the Metropolis as soon as you can, for though we are all very well, yet as fevers are again raging in the Country, it makes us uneasy lest we should catch the infection. This day John Herd ventured out for the first time. John Currie and his wife are alive, and that is all. She is with her daughter and he is with his son. I have heard of no death since my last, but almost every person is sick. James's report is the labour is coming on very well. The crops are all looking tolerable. The peats are finished, and he is throng preparing the turnip ground. If the weather is good they will be sown this week, and he wishes you to return as soon as possible. No accounts of the meal vessel, and the people are like to eat us up for want of living.[5]

On 8 June, Andrew wrote,

> As Miss Catherine McLaine Senior of Gruline departed this life last night, I have thought proper to acquaint you of it, as it is a circumstance of which perhaps you would wish to be informed.[6] This being a letter out of order, I have not inserted the Journal, and as I wrote you only the day before yesterday, nothing material has taken place ... but the death of John Millar's wife[7] who was burried this day. John will not survive her long. We are still all in good health, thank God, and as busy as we can be. Altho' you mentioned nothing to me of the news, it is all over the Country. I hear that Captain Macquarie bought the lands at £10,000.
>
> MacTavish[8] paid us a visit today, but had no news to acquaint us with. This has been one of the finest days we have had this season, and if the good weather continues we intend to scringe the shores in a day or two;[9] The Herrings are making their appearance in Lochnagaul [Loch na Keall] they say, and upon our own shores we have the appearance of plenty of Salmon. The crops are looking very well since the good weather commenced. In short, every thing at present has a very beautiful aspect ...[10]

The journal for 4 June contained some information about the state of recruiting on the estate, and the degree of loyalty the tenants felt for Murdoch.

> This was His Majesty's Birthday, but I cannot say we have spent much Powder or Drink in rejoicing. It being a very fine day, MacTavish came and carried us over to Laggan, where we dined and drank tea.
>
> After finishing the Peats, the people went all off this day after dinner. When they were at Dinner I made John Roy speak to them to the following effect: 'Lochbuy was speaking something about Volunteers before he left the Country. Perhaps he may raise a Company or two when he comes home. Would you all be willing to enroll?' The answer was that 'they would all

sign that Minute if he chose.' There were present at the time upwards of fifty very handsome young men. Mrs Maclean Pennycross was this day safely delivered of a son.[11]

Murdoch, *our* Murdoch, the linchpin of this story,[12] the nineteenth of Lochbuy, died on 5 July 1804 at Moy, and was buried at Laggan. Shortly after the funeral, a dinner was held at the inn of Callachilly to christen the two parts of the Barony of Moy which had been sold to Murdoch's nephews, Major Lachlan and Captain Charles Macquarie. Lachlan had bought the lands of Callachilly, Salen, Gruline, Gederlie, Torlochan, Kilbeg and Bentalla, with the Bradils and Tomslea. These lands constituted an estate which he called Jarvisfield. Charles acquired Pennygown, Corrachy, Rohill, and the islands in the Sound of Mull called Glash Ellean, which he called, collectively, Glenforsa.[13] Murdoch had succeeded, before his death in transferring ownership of these significant pieces of Lochbuy land to relatives who were friendly to his family, and trustworthy. Both brothers had served him as factor, and both knew exactly what they were taking on. Although their careers had taken them away from Mull, and they were both to remain overseas for a number of years, they were able men who would delegate responsibility wisely. The change of ownership, however, was not achieved without some manoeuvering of tenants.

Lachlan was disturbed to find that under the terms of an existing lease, the tenant of Callachilly could not be moved to allow him to have that desirable house. But on both of the new estates, smaller tenants with shorter leases, and those cottars who had no leases at all, had been removed, or were in the process of moving. Eighty years later, in the course of a government enquiry, John McCallum, the Tobermory lawyer, was to lay at the feet of 'a Mr Macquarie' the blame for removing the best tenantry in Mull from Glenforsa.[14] Notable among the best tenantry were branches of the Macphails, an extended family of drovers and cattle dealers, who had lived in Glenforsa from time immemorial. Removal did not mean eviction. A landowner simply had the right to ask a tenant to take his roof with him to another place. The Macphails were accommodated at Corrinahenachy and Lussafoot, but loss of a traditional possession always helps to weaken the old bonds, and the Macphail descendants knew that the old order had passed away. Among the new generations born at Lussafoot instead of Rohill, was the poet Dugald Macphail.

The remaining estate was once more under trust until young Murdoch should come of age, and there were nearly eight years to go. Jane had been named by her husband as one of the trustees, along with Lieutenant-Colonel Lachlan Macquarie of Jarvisfield (promoted), Lieutenant-General John Campbell of Airds of the Argyle Militia, Jane's brother, Mr Donald Maclean merchant in Edinburgh, and Mr John Campbell WS. The lawyer presiding over them all was Donald Maclean WS, the up-and-coming 34-year-old solicitor son of the late Allan Maclean of Drimnin. At the first meeting of the guardians, one or two skeletons came out of the cupboard to be discussed. First, there was, still living, a natural son of John Maclaine of Lochbuy, Alexander Maclaine, a blind musician living in Edinburgh, who, it was revealed, had been supported since John Lochbuy's death by an annuity from our lately deceased and ever compassionate Murdoch. The guardians agreed to continue this during the lifetime of 'poor blind Sandy'.[15] Secondly, a woman called Isabel Maclaine appeared, with bona fide evidence of being Murdoch Maclaine's previously unsuspected illegitimate daughter. She was now Isabel Neilson, a widow with two children, but the guardians declined to help her, as Murdoch had told no one of her existence.[16]

Other business included an appeal from James Ferrier and James Maxwell, the Duke of Argyll's men of business, that the Lochbuy trustees should share the costs of a very important new road under consideration at the time of Lochbuy's death. Mr Ferrier was greatly worried that the death of Lochbuy, and the fact that the heir was a minor, would spoil the cherished scheme for a road which would open up the Ross of Mull. He wrote to Maxwell to press the point to the Lochbuy trustees.

> From the plan and estimate which have been made by Mr Donaldson, it appears that it will take £7000 to make the road and build the bridges betwixt the Ferry of Achnacraig & the Duke of Argyll's Fishing Village of Creich (where I find there is a remarkable good natural harbour) the distance being 35 miles. Under an Act of Parliament which passed last year, the land owners connected with the road have it in their power to receive from the public [funds] at this time £3,500 towards making that road, being one half of the whole expense, on their becoming bound to contribute the other half ...

The 'fishing village of Creich' was not present-day Fionnphort, which is a relatively modern development, but the stretch between the Bull Hole and Deargphort. The line of road, as it approached the coast opposite Iona, would swing towards Catchean, near what is now the Tormore quarry, then curve towards Fidden, and stop abruptly at the duke's tacksman's farm there. Fishing communities would be created at Catchean and Creich, which, joined with Kintra, would form a little conglomerate of industry, accessible by sea, and by land when the sea was boisterous. If the Lochbuy trustees and the few other heritors involved rejected this offer of a public subsidy, Mr Ferrier continued:

> There are others ready to grasp at it, and Ross will probably remain buried for some more centuries to come in the ruins of Icolmkill. If this offer shall be accepted, Mr Telfer, who is now here, will immediately advertise for contractors to begin the work early next Spring, and you and the heritors should encourage some of the natives to stand forward as undertakers.[17]

Mr Maxwell replied, reminding Mr Ferrier that some of the Lochbuy managers resided in Edinburgh, so that Ferrier might have a word in the ears of the two Mr Donald Macleans.

Thus it was that the trustees did not allow this opportunity to pass, and agreed to the proposal to share the costs of the new road, although their own surveyor was to comment two years later that the line of road only benefited the people of Rossal, Derrinaculen and Ardmeanach, and it would have been better to have made a branch to serve the people of Kinlochspelve.[18] As usual, the Duke of Argyll seemed to know exactly how to make his fellow heritors pay to his advantage.

But the Lochbuy guardians felt they were missing out on another important development of the nineteenth century. Everyone else, it seemed, was building a village. Tobermory had been growing since 1788, and as early as 1787 the duke had planned to make a fishing village at Bunessan, but had to wait until the farm's lease was up in 1799 before proceeding to divide it up for crofter fishermen. It was now halfway to being a village, having already had its inn and its mill, and its new church being under construction. The laird of Coll had begun on Dervaig on the Quinish lands in 1800. The guardians of young Murdoch felt that their young laird was being outstripped, and in 1806 invited the surveyor, Robert Reid to come and look at Lochbuy, to assess the problems and assets of the estate. Reid gave a damning report, which shocked Messrs Campbell and Maclean, and no doubt Mrs Maclaine also. Lochbuy, he said, was a rough and mountainous terrain with little arable soil. It had 122 tenants when it could support only fifty-one. (This meant heads of families, and was not a population figure.) Sheepfarming had been adopted, but was little understood. The present tenantry were wedded to their old prejudices. Some of them would remain obstinately attached to their present slovenly ways even to the end of a nineteen year lease. And as for villages, Robert Reid had considered possible sites, and found Scallastle to be the best, with its improveable mossy ground and its safe anchorage in Scallastle Bay; but the Scallastle lease had another twelve years to run. The second best site for a village was Fishnish, where there was a township. On the other side of the Lochbuy estate, Tiroran and Knockroy were good sites for villages, but these too had long leases, and could not be tampered with. The idea of a village, Reid said, had to be relinquished until Mr Maclaine of Scallastle's lease was out.

But what was the difference between this desirable thing called a village and the kind of township already existing all over Mull? Travellers were always commenting on the absence of villages with great surprise, and even with disdain. Had they not observed the townships clustered everywhere? In 1807 there were considerable communities of this kind on all the estates, and to give examples on the tourist's route from Achnacraig to Aros, we might list Ardchoirk, Kilpatrick, Scallastlebeg, Fishnish, Corrinahenachy and Aros itself. Two of these, Ardchoirk (pronounced rather like 'artichoke') and Fishnish, were exceptionally populous, each having over 100 souls in the early 1800s. Why were these not villages? The Gaelic word *baile*, or *baile-beag*, for village, is a prefix in many Mull place-names, and yet Mull was said again and again to have no villages. Clearly village meant something on the English or Lowland model, with all the essentials of village life – the shop, the mill, the church, the inn, the post office and the blacksmith's house. A township was what had been in Mull since people began to multiply – an inchoate, amorphous anachronistic mess of irregular boulders put together in the shape of houses, or worse, made of turf, with sods for thatch, middens at every door, hens and pigs wandering in and out at leisure, potato patches as near the dwelling as possible. Visitors referred occasionally to 'wretched huts' as seen on Iona and even on idyllic Ulva. Most of the time – like Sir John Carr, who admitted to short-sightedness – they did not see them at all, because grass and even small trees grew out of the roofs. But the characteristic which was conspicuously lacking in a township was community life, industry and mutual aid among skilled inhabitants.

Mr Robert Reid also pronounced on the mills he had seen in the parish of Torosay. The uncouth machines now in use were called Mullinders (no pun was intended); they had a horizontal water wheel, and the mill wheel moving upon the upper end of the axle – this kind of mill was slow, seldom grinding more than a boll per day, with waste of grain. Mr Reid was not, it has to be said, very impressed with the land or the people of Lochbuy.

Between Mr Taylor's school and the army, that is between 1806 and 1808, when he was commissioned second lieutenant in the 23rd regiment of Foot, there is a gap in young Murdoch's life, and in the progress of his estate, which has not yielded up its secrets, except for the hint in the minutes of his guardians that the people of Ardmeanach had left to go to America.[19] Also, a retrospective remark revealed that Mrs Maclaine used the resources of the estate rather too freely to pay for her nine daughters' upkeep. Then there was some evidence to suggest that young Murdoch spent time with the family of Donald Maclean WS in 21 Albany Street, Edinburgh while pursuing his 'educational plan'. The plan was not spelt out in the Minutes, but Lachlan Macquarie's opinion of his cousin, young Murdoch, was that he was 'not very bright – much fitter for a Mull farmer than a general'.[20]

In 1810, Young Murdoch was commissioned lieutenant in the 42nd, or Royal Highland regiment, and in 1812 he was serving in the Peninsular Wars in Spain and Portugal. No account of his experiences has survived. He seems to have longed to leave, and to take over the running of his estate, not because it was in less than capable hands, but possibly because he was indeed better suited to being a farmer than anything else. His mother and his nine sisters were all at Lochbuy House, and if he sold out of the 42nd and went home, they would be there still. The easiest way of tipping ten women out of his house was to return with a wife. She was not difficult to find, for his frequent visits to 21 Albany Street before his war service had introduced him to Christina Maclean, the eldest daughter of Donald Maclean, WS, chairman of the trustees of Lochbuy. Chirsty Maclean was pretty, and only seventeen years old when he decided to throw up his short career in the army. Her father, who had inherited some of the legal business of his master, Colquhoun Grant, had married Grant's daughter Lillias in 1793; by 1812, Donald Maclean and Lillias Grant had fifteen children.

Donald Maclean was the son of Allan Maclean of Drimnin by his second marriage to Mary or Mally Maclaine of Lochbuy. His father had also died in 1792, and the Drimnin estate had passed to Donald's half-brother Charles before being sold for debt in 1798. Donald was a very different kind of man from his Drimnin relations. Cautious and saving by nature, he worried excessively about the financial responsibilities thrust upon him in representing so many families of 'the Country' who were in the main penniless. A family of fifteen, soon to be sixteen, was a liability which did not allow him much leeway, and he warned young Murdoch that his daughter would have no dowry. The only portion she could offer the young laird was the common sense instilled into her by a father and mother who had to work very hard to make ends meet.

In March 1813, young Murdoch, still only twenty-one, obtained leave of absence and arrived in Edinburgh to marry Chirsty. His future father-in-law drew up an elaborate marriage contract, mostly concerned with the ramifications of the Lochbuy entail and their effects on the inheritance of the children of the marriage.[21] To introduce some element of romance during the endless and tedious discussions, Murdoch bought for his bride a fine silver-plated bridle engraved *Lochbuy*, a fine side saddle, a lady's whip, also engraved, and a new saddle for himself, with a special box to contain them. They were to be a good investment, for he at least was destined to spend the best part of the next thirty years in the saddle.

But such a youthful marriage, love match though it undoubtedly was, and traditional in the way it united two people with strong Mull connections, was not approved by Murdoch's cousin, Lachlan Macquarie, who had married first a young woman of fortune, then as a widower, married the sister of Jane Campbell of Airds. Lachlan, now governor of the colony of New South Wales, wrote to his brother Charles:

> I was also sincerely sorry to hear of Murdoch Lochbuy's foolish imprudent marriage, and I fear it will prove a most ruinous connection to him. His quitting the army too – at such a crisis and at his time of life, was disgraceful and highly improper.[22]

As for Murdoch Lochbuy's younger brother John, who was in New South Wales with Lachlan, well, the governor was quite sick of the Lochbuy family. They were all cursed. Lachlan had given up hope of John's reforming from his low vicious courses of drunkenness, low company and lying. He had talents and a good heart; he was brave and active; he had good sense which he made little use of, and his extravagance was unbounded. John had lived in Government House at Lachlan's expense as his ADC for nearly three years at an income of about £250, but was greatly in debt; the governor would be forced to pay about £300 just to get rid of him.

The gardener at Moy, or Lochbuy,[23] James Gillies, wrote to the young laird in Spain in December 1812, telling him how they all longed to have him home. His own wish was for some acorns, fresh larch seed, Spitzenburg apple trees, Jargonel and other pear trees. Young Murdoch's mother wanted weeping willow. In February 1814, when Murdoch was in Edinburgh, Gillies asked for grass seed, and trees for planting – larches, firs and a hundred each of oaks, beeches, spruce, alders, silver firs, and thorns. He added

> I wish you all manner of happiness of your young son, and hopes Mrs Maclaine and he are doing well. Your Mother was quite delighted at the news of being a grandmother. She gave all the servants a dance ... George has commenced his cod and ling fishing this day. He got about twenty-eight cod and ling.[24]

Most of the first wave of tree-planting in Mull seems to have been done in this phase of the Napoleonic wars, and Moy, Torloisk, Ulva and Quinish were to be transformed.

The new heir was yet another Murdoch, referred to as 'Murdie' in his babyhood. He was brought home in the spring of 1814 to the large mansion house at Lochbuy, built by the grandfather he had never known, and until recently filled with the voices of his nine aunts, and his grandmother. His mother, Chirsty, still under twenty years old herself, and a member of a very large family, was sorry to lose the company of her sisters-in-law, but to have nine of them would have been a little overwhelming. They had taken the house at Scallastle, vacated by Marie Maclaine, Gillean's widow, who had moved to Ledirkle.

Murdoch Maclaine, the twentieth of Lochbuy, found himself not quite his own master on the estate. His father-in-law, Donald Maclean, chairman of the trustees, still directed financial operations, and took it upon himself to guide his son-in-law in complicated matters such as repayments of debts which hung over from the reign of Murdoch the nineteenth. This was done in a genial, affectionate and knowledgeable manner, especially since Donald's clients included many other Mull heritors, and his legal friends in Edinburgh were lawyers like James Ferrier, commissioner of the Argyll estates, so that he was a practised exponent of suitable economic strategies. Donald was aware of the state of everyone else's finances, and knew the value of every Mull estate. In the course of their long family association he was to write 650 letters to Murdoch Maclaine, which were all preserved in the muniments room at Lochbuy. He enjoyed his role as manipulator, but as the father of sixteen children his need for fees meant that he was continually seeking more business in 'the Country'.

As Murdoch's personality was to have a bearing on the fate of Mull, his attitudes and social habits, as well as his economic problems have to be examined in some detail. Among his peers, he is notable for not having sought a rich wife. His neighbour and exact contemporary, Alexander Maclean of Pennycross, who was always regarded by Murdoch as a social equal, was extremely poor, and delayed marrying until he was middle aged. Hugh Maclean of Coll married two wealthy women in succession. Charles Macquarie, his cousin, married an heiress. Margaret Maclean Clephane of Torloisk was married shortly after Murdoch, to the son of an English marquis. Murdoch was the first Maclaine of Lochbuy to marry for love, and the first to have no illegitimate child. His sense of duty was strong, and his moral values inviolate. A social animal, his pleasures were hunting, shooting and drinking. He was a man of his time with his interest in 'improvement', and followed all the injunctions of James Macdonald, author of *A General View of the Agriculture of the Hebrides*. He valued hard-working tenants, but expected them to spring, ready made, from the soil of a land famed for its slothful inhabitants. He was prepared to make sacrifices for the sake of the welfare of his estate, but was irritated by the handicaps which held him back, such as the outrageous number of sisters he had been lumbered with, who cost the estate £50 a year in annuities, and the large number of relatives who still pursued ancient claims from the days of his predecessor, Archy Lochbuy, of whom he knew little, if anything.

Murdoch practised many economies, rationing his trips to Edinburgh, factoring his own estate, and, after five years of residence at Lochbuy, bringing his mother and the six sisters who were still unmarried back there to save the cost of another establishment. He had some harmless small extravagances, such as ordering goods by the new steamboat which began to operate between the Clyde and the islands after 1816. He was, as his father-in-law noted, apt to forget to plan, and left everything to the very last minute, so that special messengers had to speed to Edinburgh with payments or documents which a very efficient postal system was unable to deliver in time.

There was a touchiness about his character, which, combined with a certain pride in his birth, made him hold grudges – quite the opposite of his tolerant and forgiving father. For some reason which is still inexplicable, he resented his cousin Charles Macquarie, whose very first gesture of welcome to the bridegroom of 1813 had been to give Murdoch a gift of the debt the estate owed him, a sum of £350. Charles had run the estate for Murdoch's mother for the last few years of the heir's minority, had married about the same time as Murdoch, and was a fellow landowner, yet Murdoch would not turn to him for counsel. Charles was excluded pointedly from Lochbuy social events, to the great embarrassment of Donald Maclean and Murdoch's mother, Jane.

Murdoch could not help being a young man in tune with his times, and one of the developments in early nineteenth-century Highland life was the romantic gloss put on it by Walter Scott, which led to a reverence for tartan, clan life, family crests and coats of arms. The chieftain of the Maclaines of Lochbuy began to take up the old notion of a feud between Macleans and

Maclaines, and became a violent partisan of the view that the Lochbuy Maclaines, not the Duart Macleans, were the true chiefs of the clan. Murdoch would need only a few glasses of whisky to get on to his hobby horse. The confusion of his guests, many of whom were Macleans, had to be cloaked in a humorous indulgence, and the solution was that Murdoch was referred to always as 'the Chief', a jocular ploy which allowed the chief himself to bore everyone to his heart's content. He sent his father-in-law on a search for a true Maclaine tartan, which, in the end, had to be ordered in Edinburgh in batches of thirty yards. When it was discovered that the Lochbuys had never matriculated arms, Murdoch had to climb down, unable to afford the fee of £110 asked by the Lyon Court.

These foibles apart, Murdoch possessed a gift for friendship for those who had had no past history of which he might be jealous, and was generous and kind to underdogs. He was firm and affectionate with his eleven children, striving to educate them in an unpretentious way, which usually meant sending them to live with Chirsty's parents at 21 Albany Street, Edinburgh so that they could attend Edinburgh day schools. Chirsty was continually pregnant, for, like other members of the Mull gentry, she employed nurses for her babies, which freed her for the next pregnancy. Among the commoners, an interval of two years was normal as each child was breast-fed for over a year.

Little Murdie, the only child not to be born at Lochbuy, was crammed, according to his Edinburgh grandfather, with porridge and soup, became an indifferent pupil at school, and entertained ambitions to become MP for Argyll. His interests were in dogs, horses and shooting. The second son, Donald, born in 1816, was determined to succeed in commerce, for which he showed early flair. The later sons, John-Campbell, Allan, Alexander and Colquhoun, were simply to be younger sons, of whom little is known. Murdie and 'Dod' were the boys who were to make an impact, in very different ways, upon the estate and family of Lochbuy.

As Murdoch the twentieth settled into the everyday routine of a Mull landowner, constrained by the budget laid down by his father-in-law, and with an ever-increasing family of his own, he began to develop friendships and antipathies which were to change the social configuration of an island which was already in the throes of a greater change. In spite of his father's sale of the Glenforsa and Gruline lots on the estate to the Macquarie brothers, Murdoch was the principal resident heritor on the island. But the sixth Duke of Argyll had begun to sell sections of his estate, and Murdoch looked with covetous eyes on two parts of these old Duart lands. He would have cheerfully borrowed money to add Duart itself to the Lochbuy acres, for the Argyll possessions divided his farms in such a way that he could not ride from Moy to Garmony without crossing a foreign country, managed by descendants of the old Campbell tacksmen. Achnacroish, Achnacraig and Ardura were all in Campbell territory, and their appearance on the open market, at a time when his mentor, Donald Maclean, was lecturing him daily about economy, would be most galling. What was even more painful was that his father-in-law was acting as agent for several of the bidders, and was organising loans of money for men whose prospects were no better than Murdoch's own. One by one the Argyll lots went to families who had been mere tacksmen or tenants, and who now sold their very souls to be able to own the farms their fathers had farmed. These were not 'strangers'. Indeed, Donald Maclean was so much a man of 'the Country' that he favoured those whose pedigrees he had known from boyhood, like John Gregorson of Ardtornish (in Morvern), Hugh Maclean of Coll, John Stewart of Achadashenaig, Charles Macquarie, John Campbell of Knock, and Allan MacAskill, a relative of the Macleans of Coll. Even the duke's brother, Lord John Campbell, was said to be interested in the Torosay, Knock and Aros lots. From 1816 to 1825, a fever of speculation about the purchase of the Argyll lots led to still more land being offered for sale (in addition to the Ulva group, which had been on offer all along), as proprietors thought of switching their possessions. Rumours abounded about certain Argyll lots being taken off the market as successful sales eased the duke's debts. The Pennycross Macleans put their land on the market in 1818, in lots which included Carsaig and Kinloch, while, on the edge of the Ross of Mull territory (which was not to be disposed of), Torrans was due to be auctioned on the same day as Carsaig. Every seller was in need of money, and every would-be buyer was short of money. Cattle prices had plummeted, food was scarce, yet land not only held its price, but was fetching sums which Donald Maclean WS considered quite mad.[25]

When the excitement died down, Murdoch the twentieth of Lochbuy found himself and his estate surrounded by heritors already known to him. Some, like Sheriff John Gregorson of Ardtornish, had changed from being a much respected tacksman to being an owner. In spite of the fact that Mr Ferrier and Mr Maxwell had opposed the chopping up of units of land, Achadashenaig had been cut out of the Aros lot to oblige John Stewart, also a former tacksman, while Charles Macquarie had bought the strip from Killiechronan for his brother, the governor of New South Wales. Hugh Maclean of Coll had added the northern part of Aros and the swathe of land south of Dervaig to Quinish, but had failed in his bid for adjacent Penmore.

Mornish, including Penmore, Treshnish, Kilmaluaig, Frachadil, Sunipol and Inivea, was bought by Captain Allan MacAskill. He happened to be one of Staffa's creditors, who had been briefly tempted by Ulva, but as one of the club of Macleans, and represented by his dear friend Donald Maclean WS, he had resisted the blandishments of the enemy. Captain Allan had retired from his career as captain of an East Indiaman, and was living in Stockbridge, near Edinburgh, within walking distance of 21 Albany Street. He was the son of the minister of the Small Isles, Malcolm MacAskill, but was infinitely qualified for membership of Mull's best families through his mother, Mary Maclean of Coll, sister of 'Young Col', the guide of Johnson and Boswell. Allan's mother Mary was a respected poetess, who had written a lament for her brother when he was tragically drowned off Ulva in 1774. Her next brother Alexander, who had succeeded Young Col as heir, was Captain Allan MacAskill's uncle, and laird of Quinish in 1817, when Captain Allan bought Mornish from the sixth Duke of Argyll's trustees. Captain Allan, having made some money from his east Indian voyages, was keen to invest in a Mull property, but had no legitimate heirs. He was, it seems, a rough diamond compared to his Coll relations, but when he began to build a rather splendid house on the site of the existing tacksman's house at Calgary, in a new neo-Gothic style, he was not rejected by that family, who were not known to have any 'side' to them. The Macleans of Coll had instructed Donald Maclean WS to buy Penmore for them, since it was so near Quinish, but he had replied that they would not be successful, as a 'friend' of theirs, whose name he was not at liberty to disclose, was certain to acquire it. When the sale was accomplished, some sensible arrangement was made, without rancour, between the Coll family and the captain, as to grazing, just as, many years before, Hector of Torloisk had leased the land of Penmore from the Duke of Argyll. The 'castle' was completed in about 1819, and Captain Allan installed his sister, Miss Mary MacAskill, as housekeeper. In 1821, the Kilninian parish register records, retrospectively, the birth of a son, Donald MacAskill, in India, to Captain Allan and his mistress, Mary Wilson.[26] If Mary Wilson and young Donald ever lived at Calgary, they are not acknowledged as being there in any correspondence of the time. But Murdoch Maclaine of Lochbuy seems not to have approved of the household. In spite of his father-in-law's constant nagging, he felt himself unable to pay a social call on the MacAskills. As Donald Maclean had been the law agent in the purchase of Mornish, and greatly enjoyed the company of the captain, this pig-headed refusal to meet the new heritor troubled him greatly. 'I wish you would write Captain and Miss MacAskill ... asking them to their Christmas. I am certain they will not accept, but it will show your good wishes,' the despairing father-in-law wrote in 1819. Every year he renewed the entreaty, and still Murdoch would not make a gesture to the chatelain of Calgary. 'I entreat and beg you may go and see Captain Mac-Askill ... I truly regret you have not seen Captain MacAskill ...' Murdoch's stubborn refusal meant that he was excluded from Captain Allan and Hugh Coll's shooting parties to Rum, which might have been expected to tempt him, and when Donald Maclean was a guest at Calgary in 1824, Murdoch found himself too much engaged to accompany him. When Captain Allan died on 6 June 1828 at Calgary, one of the Lochbuy set was to remark, '*Sic transit gloria mundi.* Even elegant castles will not save us from the grasp of death.'[27] It would seem that it was the castle which rankled most in the hearts of the Maclaines.

The captain's will did not favour his natural son, Donald MacAskill, who had become a student at Edinburgh University, a singularly deep young man with long silky hair and literary interests, who would not, his father had fore-seen, make a practical landowner. Instead, the Mornish estate was bequeathed to Hugh MacAskill, the captain's nephew, who was twenty-nine years old, and a tacksman in Talisker in Skye.[28] Captain Allan had made a fatal decision, for *Eoghainn Mór*, or Big Hugh, was destined to be no friend to the Mornish people. An absentee landlord, who preferred living in Skye, and whose reputation as an evictor there was to be unsurpassed, Hugh showed no interest in Mull, and began to clear the population of the townships in the first years of the 1830s. He sold Ardow in 1837 to Kenneth Campbell and David Watson, brothers-in-law from Airth in Stirlingshire, and by the 1840s had removed thirty to forty families from the area around Calgary.[29] It is unfortunate that Captain Allan MacAskill's name, and not that of his nephew, has been associated with those evictions.[30] At this period, resident proprietors in Mull with strong family connections, did not evict with the same abandon as absentee landlords, or incomers.[31]

One of two new proprietors who found favour with the prickly Murdoch twentieth of Lochbuy was John Gregorson of Ardtornish, whose admission into a history of Mull people may be regarded with some puzzlement, because of the fact that he was a Morvern man. John Gregorson was appointed sheriff of the area which included Mull in about 1816, and was a powerful presence on the Mull stage. The Gregorson family, originally MacGregors, had been tacksmen to the Dukes of Argyll since the mid-eighteenth century. Some had held tacks in Mull, and some had been hereditary ferrymen at Achnacraig, where the dukes had a monopoly in transporting cattle to the mainland. But the principal family lived at Ardtornish, opposite Garmony, on the Sound of Mull. The patriarch of the family was James Gregorson of Correctled who had moved into the Argyll fold in about 1722, when he married a daughter of the Campbells of Airds. His son Angus Gregorson was tacksman of Ardtornish, who married another Campbell, and whose thirteen children were to be intimately associated with Mull through their marriages and their farming interests. The oldest of Angus's sons was John Gregorson, born in 1775. John was one of the declining number of nineteenth-century notables who had known Murdoch the nineteenth of Lochbuy, and whose memory could even serve him well enough to remember Gillean Maclaine of Scallastle, John Tacksman of Gruline, Dr Andrew Maclaine, and others of that generation, with all their unhappy associations.

In his youth, John had happily escaped the fate of marrying into the family of the Maclaines of Scallastle, when Julianna Maclaine's infatuation with him had incurred the wrath of her mother, Gillean's widow Marie. But Marie had been unable to prevent the marriage of Gillean's heir, Allan Scallastle, and John's sister, Marjory Gregorson. This regrettable alliance took place in 1797, when Marjory was just eighteen, and will be followed up in Chapter 19. In the meantime, John Gregorson's bachelor life was to be extended to the year 1820, when, having bought his father's farm of Ardtornish in the duke's sales, he married Young Murdoch's little sister Mary when he was forty-five, and she was twenty.

John Gregorson was now a much respected landowner and sheriff, known from the moment of his appointment as 'the Sheriff'. Donald Maclean WS saw the marriage as a most suitable and pleasing event, and Murdoch, whose pleasure in the marriages of his sisters was always tempered by the unpleasant duty of having to give them their portion, which was never available in cash, came to see that it was a good match. His approval of John Gregorson was endorsed by the very fact that his father-in-law never quite trusted the sheriff, because he was not given his legal affairs to manage. But Ardtornish and Lochbuy were now joined socially and politically, and Murdoch had a solid ally, whose opinions of small tenants coincided with his own. The new Mrs Gregorson was the least demanding of Murdoch's sisters, more inclined to give than to take, so that Murdoch and Chirsty were more and more inclined to take their barge, the *Delphine* to Ardtornish for Christmas, and for old and new New Years, for birthdays and anniversaries, and all the new kinds of celebrations which were being introduced into the Highland calendar in these hard times, to keep people's minds off the sober realities of life.

The second new proprietor to be welcomed wholeheartedly by Murdoch was Colonel Alexander Campbell of Possil, whose arrival on the scene will be explained in Chapter 17, but whose injection of all that was charming, cultivated, benevolent and good-humoured into the rather stale Mull scene must be briefly alluded to. 'Possil' arrived in 1826, with his beautiful wife, Harriet MacLachlan, and a family of one son and five daughters. Their house would be hard to find today, as it is now assumed to lie under the foundations of present-day Torosay. Like Mary Gregorson, Harriet Campbell was a compassionate and charming woman, and like Chirsty Maclaine, she had been married for about fourteen years. She brought new standards of gentility and *noblesse oblige* to the Mull community, supporting the established church in a way which had never been known before in that godless society. The Lochbuy Maclaines and the Scallastles had not even given lip service to the church, regarding the 'parsons' (as they were called with derogatory intent) as pests, and the church door as merely a place where sales of land or roups of belongings were advertised to *hoi polloi*.

Such allusion to the doings of the gentry may not seem to be very relevant to the lives of the common people, but this clique of friends was to have its influence on Mull affairs. The common denominator of the three families was that they were extremely sociable, conservative in politics and religion, and even if one of them had not matriculated his arms, staunch in their belief in good Highland blood.

Much of young Murdoch's life is to be observed by others in the following chapters, but the great sorrow of his life was not to be truly appreciated by anyone except his wife, his father-in-law, and, it is to be hoped, the author and readers of this book.

Little Murdie, whose birth in Edinburgh in 1814 was celebrated with a dance for all the tenants at Lochbuy, was, like many heirs apparent, watched over rather too anxiously by his parents. He also had fifteen aunts, ten uncles, two grandmothers, one grandfather, and a great-grandmother, the last being no other than Mally Maclaine of Lochbuy, who lived until 1831, in Edinburgh, as 'old Mrs Maclean of Drimnin'. When Murdie was twelve, his grandfather, Donald Maclean WS, was writing to Murdoch and Chirsty that the boy was 'playing up' when they returned to Mull without him, and that visits to his grandmother only made him worse. 'Murdoch is still very low in his class, still inattentive … he never knew what study was before', the grandfather wrote, from 21 Albany Street, in 1827, when Murdie was attending the High School. By 1829, he was reported as being 'very proud … I gave him a long lecture which I trust will do good. He has a great deal of good sense, and I trust it will prevent the flattery of the lower people about him doing him harm.' The Albany Street household had a cook from Mull, who filled him with stories about the prowess of his ancestors, which must have been, from what we know of the Lochbuy record, highly coloured. By 1830, an army career was being talked of, and Murdie obtained a commission in the 91st or Argyllshire Regiment of Foot in January 1834. Letters home from Limerick, St Helena, Cape Verde and Cork, showed him fluctuating in his ambitions throughout his twenties, but as the 1830s drew to a close, he was giving grave concern. Gambling debts began to be talked of. Men who had lent him money wrote to the father to ask for repayment. The son wanted to sell his commission. But more serious still was young Murdoch's conviction that he could, by consulting lawyers in Edinburgh, have the entail reduced so that his father's, and soon, he hoped, his own, obligations to pay estate debts would be lessened. Murdoch senior, so quick to take offence, was shaken by his son's indifference to his own position.

> Your letter of the 13th ult. I received in due course, but really I must say I was at a loss how to answer it, and I still feel my unfitness to give an opinion on a subject which to me is very distressing, as being one which anticipates my own dissolution, and which will, when that event takes place … leave you a perfect beggar. Reflect before it is too late. You have a commission which gives you pay perfectly to support yourself as a gentleman and an officer, but certainly not to dissipate at play, or guzzle at Champagne & Claret. I do not know the exact nature of the transaction you propose with the Insurance, but any advance made by them I fear will make your luxuries rather *pepperish*. You have now come to that time of life that you ought to be able to judge for yourself. Had you gone to India in the regiment into which you were promoted, you would now have all the comforts & enjoyments of the East without looking to me 'now' or occasioning your own ruin 'hereafter'. Your letter of the 2nd I also received, and have forwarded cash to Edinburgh to retire your draft for £22. There need not be a repetition, as I assure you I cannot afford ourselves the common necessaries, and of course will not make advances merely to assist

your extravagance ... I shall now be done of those subjects for the present, and, I hope, for ever.[32]

But young Murdoch, who sent letters when he had a scheme afoot, and remained silent when he had not, went on his merry way, until in 1841, the father wrote:

The wild scheme of opposition you hinted at formerly, of endeavouring to aid me in the prosecution of my action for getting rid of the entail – I shall expect you fulfil your part without any further delay ... I fear much that you are again falling into your former habits. As you again lose your character, no endeavour of yours will ever replace you in that Society which it ought to be your wish to be in. Do take some consideration for the feelings of us, your parents ... I understand your friends Messrs Patten & MacDougall are proceeding against you, and that you will more than probably receive this in jail.[33]

A month or so later, having had no reply, the father was in despair.

I fear no words of mine will recall you from your vicious and disgraceful habits. Murdoch, is it your determination by obdurate silence to drive me to the only resource left, of your being put in jail by your distressed Father?[34]

As week followed week, Murdoch senior wrote his last word on the subject, and received no response. Murdoch Junior's bills from jewellers and wine merchants were redirected to Lochbuy, adding to the parents' despair. Late in 1842, there was a form of forgiveness in an invitation to the prodigal son to return and repair his health in Mull. The cessation of the letters indicates either a total estrangement, or the return of Murdoch to be fed once more with wholesome soup and porridge. Comments from exiled sons and daughters of 'the Country' all predate 1842, but confirm the situation. 'I am very sorry for Lochbuy's fate in so worthless a son as his eldest seems to have turned out,' said Hector Scallastle, with detectable *Schadenfreude*.[35]

On an August night in 1844, Murdoch Maclaine, elder of Lochbuy, collapsed and died. 'Seized with the cramp, I suppose,' said one lamenting friend, 'in his stomach, from gout. He would be cut off in a few minutes, and before Dr Maclean could attend from Ceann-lochspelbh. Alas for his widow and poor numerous children depending on the bounty of the Heir!'[36]

Notes

1. NAS. GD174/1611. AF to MM, Gualachaoilish, 8 June 1803.
2. Captain Rook is unidentified.
3. Lord Selkirk, a proponent of emigration, corresponded at length with Charles Maclean, Gallanach, Coll, about Mull settlers. EUL. Laing MSS, La. II. and Laing Report, p. 735.

4. NAS. GD174/1615. Hector Maclean to MM, Fort William, 14 December 1803.

5. NAS. GD174/1600/6. Andrew Halliday to MM, Moy, 6 June 1803.

6. This was 'Miss Ketty', sister of the tacksman of Gruline. Her brother had died in 1792.

7. John Millar and John Herd were both occupational nicknames. The miller was John Maclaine.

8. Dugald MacTavish, tacksman of Laggan, 1750–1828. He was the son of a former minister of Torosay parish, Archibald MacTavish, 1711–78.

9. Scringe: to fish the bottom of a sea loch, inshore, using nets.

10. NAS. GD174/1600/7. Andrew Halliday to MM, Moy, 8 June 1803.

11. NAS. GD174/1600/6. Andrew Halliday's Lochbuy Journal. 4 June 1803. John Roy was speaking to the men in Gaelic. This recruitment was for the militia, or home guard, and did not involve leaving home. The Pennycross birth was probably that of Hector Maclean (d. 1834) later a banker in London.

12. MM was the linchpin because he preserved every letter and bill which makes this book possible, and taught his son to do the same.

13. NAS. Index to Argyll Sasines, 1781–1830.

14. Napier Commission, p. 2247. Evidence of John McCallum, 1884.

15. Blind Sandy was also supported by subscriptions raised by Mrs Clephane, always sympathetic to musicians.

16. NLS. MS. 20758. ii. Memorandum of Isbell Maclean, November 1804.

17. NAS. GD174/1858. James Ferrier to James Maxwell, Edinburgh, 31 July 1804. 'Mr Telfer' was Thomas Telford, the civil engineer who built many Highland roads as well as the Caledonian Canal in a remarkable government-aided plan to improve communications in the Highlands.

18. NLS. MS. 20758ii. Report on the estate of Lochbuy by Robert Reid, 1806.

19. NLS. MS. 20758ii. 'The tenants of Killiemore could be accommodated in the lands vacated by Ardmeanach people going to America.' Minutes of a meeting of the Tutors of Lochbuy, 24 April 1806.

20. NLS. MS. 3039. LM to CM, 1 December 1812.

21. NAS. GD1/1003. Marriage contract of Murdoch Maclaine and Christina Maclean, 1813.

22. NLS. MS 3039. LM to CM, [NSW] 28 May 1814.

23. The old name of Moy was still used for new Lochbuy House, which was built within 200 yards of both the tower house and John Lochbuy's dwelling house.

24. NAS. GD174/1035. James Gillies to MM2, December 1812 and February 1814.

25. Information on land sales, and names of buyers is from the correspondence of DMWS in GD174/1628 and from his letter book, NLS. MS 20758, as well as from Argyll Sasines. Sasines, however, confuse the issue by showing financial transactions between lenders and purchasers of land. There were also long delays in the registering of sasines.

26. Kilninian and Kilmore OPR, August 1821. 'Allan MacAskill Esq., Proprietor of Mornish and Mary Wilson, had their natural child Donald born at Calcutta, 10 January 1821.

27. DMWS's entreaties from NAS. GD174/1628 – letters to MM2. The remark about the captain's death from GRO. LMD's Journal, 8 June 1828.

28. Son of Donald MacAskill, MD, who had been drowned in 1817 on his way to Eigg. Hugh is supposed to have been connected with the founding of the Talisker Distillery, the best thing that can be said of him.

29. Poor Law Enquiry (Scotland), pt II, vol. XXI, 1844.

30. A quite reputable publication, HMSO's *Argyll 3*, p. 242, quotes unreliable 'local tradition' as a source.

31. For further information on the MacAskills see 'The MacAskills of Rudha An Dunain', Clan Macleod magazine, 1951.

32. NAS. GD174/1682/29. MM2 to MM3. Lieutenant 7th Royal Irish Fusiliers at Dublin. Lochbuy, 11 November 1838.

33. NAS. GD174/1682/41, 42. MM2 to MM3, 1841.

34. NAS. GD174/1682/43. MM2 to MM3, 1841.

35. GRO. D3330. Box 16. H. Maclaine to Mrs Craig, 10 June 1840.

36. GRO. LMD diary, Wednesday 21 August 1844.

16

A Writer to the Signet:
Donald Maclean WS

Donald Maclean of Drimnin,[1] son of Allan, son of Charles, son of John, son of Allan, son of Charles (which is how the bards would have sung his pedigree) was not simply the father-in-law of Murdoch Maclaine of Lochbuy. He was a Mull man in his own right, through owning land in Brolass from 1818 until his death in 1853. His estate was called Kinloch, and he too was known as Kinloch, now that the estate of Drimnin had passed out of his family. However, his long-term reputation was to gain nothing from being proprietor of Kinloch, for this area, perched on the shores of Loch Scridain, on the poor soil of Brolass, and contiguous to the very distinctive lands of the Ross of Mull, was to be, during the poverty-stricken times that lie ahead of us in this chronicle, a miserable place – a veritable Slough of Despond.

Donald Maclean was born in 1770, to Mally Maclaine, second wife of Allan Maclean of Drimnin. Donald was therefore not heir to anything. His father had a son called Charles who was to inherit Drimnin, as well as a particularly obnoxious second son called Allan, whose iniquities are in the first league of wickedness, even by 'the Country's' standards. These sins will be forgotten for the sake of brevity. The heir to Drimnin, Charles, was not an admirable man either, but although married to a daughter of Sir Allan Maclean, a girl who once read from the prayer book to Dr Johnson, he was without children, and did not do a great deal of harm beyond some minor evictions which will be referred to later.

Donald Maclean, Mally's son, had to make his own way in the world, and by his father's recommendation, he was indentured to Colquhoun Grant, the Jacobite lawyer, in Edinburgh, in 1789. Colquhoun Grant has been mentioned before as a successful legal agent for many Argyll families. He was a handsome man and a colourful character, and Donald Maclean was influenced by his jovial manners and by his daughter, Lillias. It was said that Donald found a girl with a goodly portion, but such stories tend to be exaggerated, and the couple's large family diffused any financial advantage. Donald and Lillias Grant married in 1793, shortly after Colquhoun Grant's death, and 'dear Lilly' bore sixteen children, the third being Chirsty, who married Murdoch the twentieth of Lochbuy.

After a few years of living in rented accommodation in Edinburgh's North Castle Street, Donald bought a whole house at 21 Albany Street, in the north-east of the New Town. Here he had his office, which was constantly visited by Mull and Morvern clients. Before the death of Murdoch the nineteenth of Lochbuy, Donald had begun to handle his business. During the minority of young Murdoch, as we have seen, Donald held the trust meetings. Young Murdoch met Donald's daughter in Albany Street, and the seeds were sown for the 'very foolish imprudent marriage', so called because Donald had no fortune to bestow on the bride. Donald and Lillias knew that by the kind of careful budgeting they themselves did, all would be well with the house of Lochbuy.

Albany Street was a second home to the Lochbuy family, and Donald was even referred to by Mull people as 'Mr Maclean Albany' in an adaptation of their own style of territorial designations. The Lochbuy girls, Jane, Margaret, Elizabeth, Catherine, Phoebe, Flora, Harriet, Mary and Jane Jarvis, all stayed there, went to 'finishing' classes in a variety of seminaries from this address, and learned their social graces from Edinburgh assemblies. Their sisters-in-law, Mary, Lillias, Ann, Margaret, Sibella and Jane, were not so indulged, being forced to teach each other. Donald's boys were all a disappointment to him, except for Allan and Alexander, who both died in 1818. The lawyer's letters to his son-in-law give a picture both of Mull life, and of the social world of Edinburgh, which he could not afford to live in. 'I am most scrimp for money' was his favourite expression.

Donald may have detected the deadly sin of pride in his daughter's husband, which he countered with lectures about compassion. The Highlands had always been a place where chiefs and people lived in harmony, and without ceremony. One very important and commendable trait in Murdoch was his insistence on speaking Gaelic, and although the writing of Gaelic was not considered a necessary attribute, Murdoch the twentieth was probably the only Lochbuy who wrote letters in his native tongue.[2] Donald's compassion for small tenants and cottars was demonstrated in his advice to Murdoch: 'You cannot blame your poor people for buying meat[3] in preference to paying you. If you could get them to cultivate their land in a proper manner, most of them could well supply themselves.'[4]

At the same time he was aware that the growing number of impecunious small tenants was detrimental to Murdoch's interests: 'the ruin of your estate'. Murdoch should go about the estate, encouraging his people, and approving when they made an effort. 'I am very sorry at what you say in regard to removing any of your people. Still, you must look to yourself. I thought they were all doing very well at Ardmeanach.'[5]

And in 1819, when hunger was everywhere, and few rents were paid: 'I would not sequestrate. It is a most distressing thing to a proprietor to see his tenants going to ruin. I entreat, stimulate them all to *improve.*'[6]

His vicarious pleasure in running the estate of Lochbuy led Donald to make a speculation which he was to regret. In 1818, in the midst of the Argyll estate sales, the Pennycross family, at the end of their tether, and unable to sustain the estate which straddled the present day route from Kinloch to

Carsaig, had placed their possessions under trustees, to be sold. Donald was at the meeting at which it was announced that no suitable buyer had emerged, and using his position, but conscious that he was in possession of what would now be called 'inside information', he offered £9,500 for the estate, put it in Murdoch's name, offered the Pennycross family a lease at £400 a year, and wrote immediately to Murdoch to explain the stratagem. There were to be four benefits from the strange transaction. The Macleans of Pennycross would stay on their land, Murdoch would appear to be a bigger landowner than he was, Donald would have the use of part of the estate, and would be able to take his large family to Mull in the summers when the courts rose, and strangers would be kept out of Mull. Donald had arranged his own funding. Murdoch would pay nothing.

Thus, by a hairbreadth, the Pennycrosses were enabled to remain in Mull, sheep farming on a large scale. Various complicated arrangements about the renting of grazing existed between Sandy Pennycross and Murdoch Maclaine, which no stranger could have continued. Sandy and Murdoch were almost like foster brothers in their closeness, which did not prevent Lochbuy from being exasperated with Pennycross. Sandy was as dilatory as most Mull lairds – in payments, in decision making, in replying to letters. His father, Archibald Pennycross, remained mysteriously in the background all his days; he had perhaps never recovered from the shock of having made the transition from tenant to heritor in 1796, when he bought his portion of Brolass from the bankrupt Charles Maclean of Drimnin and Kinlochaline. And here, a small deviation must be made, to explain why Charles Maclean of Drimnin, Donald Maclean's half-brother, should have had the estate of Brolass at all.

It may be remembered that when Sir Allan Maclean, 'the Knight', lost his case [7] against the Duke of Argyll in 1783, he was described as being like King Lear, with his two sons-in-law grasping at the money they hoped to fall heir to. Charles Maclean had married Maria Maclean in the expectation of such a windfall, but instead, his wife received only a third of Brolass, and Charles had to buy her sisters' portions. Charles and Maria settled at Kilfinichen, but soon found that they had over-extended themselves, so that both Brolass and Drimnin were sold in the late 1790s. The Macleans of Pennycross, already called 'Pennycross' although they were not proprietors, did what the Gregorsons of Ardtornish were to do twenty years later, but they too found the expenses of gentility too great for them. Related to the Macleans of Torloisk through a common ancestor who had lived in the seventeenth century, the Pennycrosses enjoyed the approval of Marianne Maclean Clephane, a commendation rarely bestowed and highly valued. It is now too late to discover the reason for the Torloisk patronage. Sandy Maclean of Pennycross and his brother Allan Thomas both had a university education, and were possibly able to discuss things of the mind with the Torloisk bluestockings. Sandy was the same age as Margaret Douglas Maclean Clephane. Perhaps an unassuming character combined with misfortune made Sandy attractive; perhaps his grandfather, Dr Alexander, had been Lachlan Torloisk's doctor. The Pennycross role in Mull society, at this stage of their history, must remain unfathomable.

Now Donald Maclean had thrown in his lot with the Pennycross family, who seemed to repay him for saving their possession by making the house of Carsaig available in the summer. But with a family of fourteen (like the green bottles, Donald's family was to reduce one by one for many years) who all had to be well enough to travel, Donald's preparations often came to nothing. In 1819, his son Colquhoun was giving trouble.

> For the last two days I did not expect Colquhoun to live ... inflammation and obstruction of the bowels ... He is *at best* the most thoughtless of God's Human Beings ... torment of my life ... and John, if possible, worse.

When Colquhoun recovered he was sent to Lochbuy to recuperate, and Murdoch and Chirsty were warned about what to expect.

> You must say to Colquhoun that I have had a letter from Lord Melville ... he must just support himself the best he can in the Merchant Service. He has been my curse since he could move, and I long foresaw what he was to come to. When he gets everything his own way it's all very well, but he has neither judgement nor resolution to act with common sense on any emergency, and I have myself seen him *as mad as any Bedlamite*. I never wish him to enter my door, or to meet him until he can do it with some credit.[8]

In 1821, Donald was complaining that Colquhoun was 'lost past redemption', but in the following year the son was off in his merchant ship. After much changing of his mind over coming to Mull, Donald was writing to Murdoch on 10 August:

> I this day received the sad news of my beloved Colquhoun's death at the very instant I had secured his promotion. He died of fatigue on the coast of Africa, beloved and respected by all who knew him. He was as gallant a sailor as ever lived, and could I have allowed him a moderate sum for his necessary expenses, he could have been everything the fondest father could have wished. Unfortunately my own situation forced me to be most illiberal to him, and that made both him and me unhappy. Mrs Maclean is sadly afflicted. He was always her darling.[9]

Margaret and Sibby, two of Donald's daughters, were staying in Mull, a visit that stretched over several months. With a large family at Lochbuy, one or other of Murdoch's sisters was always getting married, another having a baby, another causing a scandal through impropriety (Jane Jarvis was inclined to ride all over 'the Country' without her brother's consent). In 1823, Donald announced by letter to Mull, 'I dare say you will have heard that Dugald Laudle is to be married to Miss Stewart. If not, say nothing yet until you have it from others' authority. I think he could not have done a wiser thing. She is an excellent girl, and I think in every respect the proper wife for him.' [10]

'Dugald Laudle', Dugald MacLachlan, son of Eun MacLachlan of Laudale in Morvern, was one of an extended family who had long been associated with Morvern, and with lands belonging to the Dukes of Argyll at Achnacraig, in the south of Mull. Like the Stewarts of Achadashenaig, they were tacksmen, who became proprietors because of the sale of ducal land. This was the reason for Donald Maclean regarding Isabella, daughter of Robert Stewart, as a 'proper wife'. The Stewarts of Achadashenaig were not only of a similar social background, but had acquired a reputation for integrity, intelligence, common sense and sound judgement. Robert Stewart had died in 1813, and his son John was now one of the most sought-after 'birleymen', in Mull. Birleymen, or arbiters, saved a great deal of the expense of going to law. They could not afford to be anyone's crony, or drinking companion, so Stewart and James Maxwell were possibly the most sober men in 'the Country'. It is not known that the MacLachlans ever achieved such a respectable reputation, but they were solvent enough to buy a small slice of the two-penny land of Kilfinichen in 1801, a slice which included the farms of Killiemore, Ulvalt, Dererach, and Ardvergnish. At Killiemore, on Loch Scridain, the site of the house built by Charles in 1791, Dugald had been infeft in 1821, by Donald Maclean, and it was to this place that Dugald and Isabella moved on their marriage in 1823.[11] Their neighbouring property, Ardmeanach, belonged to Lochbuy, and was set aside as the provider of rents which would go to pay the annuities and portions of all the female Maclaines of Lochbuy, and, if it was sold, the capital sum was to be reserved for the same purpose. But Ardmeanach provided little in the way of rents, while stirring not a whit of interest in any would-be buyer. It was in an awkward place, hemmed in by Robert Macdonald's Burg and Gribun on one side, and by Kinloch on the other. Donald Maclean's most frequent cry was 'If only Colonel Macquarie would buy Ardmeanach.' But Charles Macquarie had more exciting estates in view, as will be seen in another chapter.

Our Writer to the Signet was appointed in 1822, Solicitor to the Court of Exchequer [12] which provided him with an extra income and not too much extra work. His 'Carsaig purchase' gave him nightmares, as he told Murdoch. 'I can with truth assure you that present appearances are very bad for Highland proprietors and I will ever repent that I became one. You might make an arrangement as to painting the house, but for heaven's sake try to get it free of rats.' But a visit to his daughter and son-in-law on their home ground was giving him more grounds for worry, and when he returned to Edinburgh, he sat down to give Murdoch 'some advice for your future conduct, which will add to your comfort and respectability ... given in the greatest love and affection ... don't know anyone possessed of more good qualities than you. I know not one on earth a better husband, parent or son ... no man of more good sense. Am I to suppose or hope that you are infallible?' And with this Donald launched into a list of corrective hints reminiscent of the Statutes of Iona. Murdoch was never to delay business; he must regulate his pecuniary business in a diary and not have messengers going here and there at the last moment. He was not to have messengers to Glasgow on every steamboat, and he was not to drink to excess. Water with a little whisky was enough for any active man. As for sitting up at night – had his father, Murdoch Lochbuy, lived, he was 'a perfect pattern to mankind in this respect. He took what was good for himself, and gave the same to his friends.'

The characteristic in Murdoch which most irritated Donald WS was the idea that he was the true chief of the clan Maclean and Maclaine.

> Kingerloch claimed it and he was laughed at by all. I have heard Coll claimed it, but I do not believe it. I think he has too much sense. You are the head of an old and respectable family, and so long as your own conduct is in every respect correct you will get every credit. I have thus my dearest Murdoch shortly mentioned to you the points which I consider most essential to your happiness, and if my beloved Allan and my dear other children were to rise from the grave,[13] I could not with more anxiety recommend anything to their consideration than I now do as I write to you … I hope you will receive it as it is meant and that it may do you good.

Murdoch must have taken this in good part – the warning on the outside of the letter said that it was 'most private', and only to be opened after due consideration. That no offence was taken is shown by the letters of 1824 in which Donald was planning a summer at Carsaig. He began to worry again about Murdoch's tendency to sequestrate for non-payment of rents. As a member of one of the old families (Murdoch had lost his father when a child, and had not learned about some of the old ways) Donald knew that a 'Mull Game', not unlike the one that Duncan Forbes of Culloden had once encountered, was always played between tenants and landlords.[14] The pattern was as follows: the rent was overdue, tenants would plead poverty, the landlord would press, the tenant would go as far as he dared, right to the edge of eviction, and if he were of a gambling disposition he might even wait for the sequestration notice before producing the rent, saying that the drover had come home at last. This was not an excuse. It had become a way of life. It was a way of life to be in arrears, and to wait for a reduction of rent, so that larger tenants as well as very small tenants and cottars never paid due rents, but only managed to dispose of arrears. Murdoch objected to the custom. If Marianne Maclean Clephane boasted that she gave rent reductions at Torloisk, he could not afford to do the same. The sequestration notice was a printed sheet, so familiar to all the tenants and cottars that they didn't need to be able to read in order to recognise it at a glance. The wording had not changed since 1775, and notified the tenant that he must *Fflitt and Remove himself, his Wife, Bairns, Family, Servants, Subtenants, Cottars, Dependers,*

Goods and Gear furth and from his occupation and possession of the said lands of . . .

The document, large and wordy, was known as a precept of Removing and Ejection.[15] The inclusion of servants, subtenants, cottars and dependers in the notice explains why it is often assumed that eviction was arbitrary and 'illegal'. In fact, it was a costly business, sanctioned by law, to take out an official precept of removal, but one notice issued to a tenant with several cottars, aged parents, cousins, siblings and children might secure the eviction of at least fifty souls. The more able bodied might go to America, or to the Low Country, but cottars with no resources could appeal only to other relatives, perhaps on other estates, for a piece of land where they could park themselves and their cow. In June 1824, when the Whitsunday deadline had passed, and Murdoch spoke of reluctant evictions, the father-in-law wrote:

> I would be sorry you would press your tenants too much, and for heavens sake avoid sequestrations as much as possible. It is a ruinous expense besides the reflection attending such proceedings. It is wonderful how your worthy excellent mother holds out so long. Death would be an happy relief to herself. I believe few are better prepared for it.[16]

The *non sequitur* was about Jane's last illness. The young Jane Campbell of Airds, Murdoch the nineteenth's 'lovely fair' had become 'old Mrs Maclaine', and was living in seclusion in Lochbuy House. She had succeeded in marrying off eight of her nine daughters, although, given the headstrong character of most of them, it is unlikely that she pushed any into marriage. Her worthless son John had died in 1818, and she exited from the Mull stage leaving young Murdoch happy in his marriage, apparently doing right, and little Murdie, aged ten, with no visible signs of future decadence. Donald Maclean WS was in Mull for the summer, and was one of the twelve gentlemen in the funeral procession from Moy to the *Caibeal Mheamhair*, Laggan. One hundred and seventy commoners also attended. At Highland burials only men go with the coffin to the grave.[17]

This summer, Donald was making what he called a round of visits, staying with Captain Allan MacAskill at Calgary 'Castle', the Macleans of Coll at Quinish, and Dugald MacLachlan at Killiemore. As solicitor to the Court of Exchequer he knew which people from 'the Country' had been fined for possessing contraband whisky. 'For heaven's sake take care of yourself in that respect,' he wrote Murdoch. Coll had paid him for the purchase of Aros, a most heart-warming and unusual state of affairs for a man like Donald, who was always close to 'complete ruin' at the hands of his clients. In reporting this to Murdoch, after his return to Edinburgh, Donald said:

> Coll Young and Old settled with me on the most liberal terms. In fact they left me to charge what I pleased for the purchase of Aros. Still it did not put one penny in my pocket for I was the whole time in their debt, but it

was a blessed way of paying it. Why not, my dear Murdoch, follow the example of your excellent Father. Had he a weekly bread box to Glasgow? Bake in the house what bread you require, and always have good oat and barley bread. You must be sensible that a radical change in your expenditure is necessary, for you cannot help seeing that otherwise absolute ruin is the consequence. I do fully agree with old McDougall that these steam boats will be the ruin of the Country. They take every shilling out of the Country, but nothing into it. I know that you do not like lectures ...[18]

Donald's ambivalent attitude to his estate of Kinloch had him preparing for his next year's trip one moment, and speaking of selling the next. He was aware of the disadvantage in being an absentee landlord, unable to supervise improvements. As most of the land was Sandy Pennycross's sheepwalk, Donald was not talking of agricultural improvements, but of repairs to piers, roads and dykes.

I am still most anxious that the roads at Pier should be made, for I have a purchase in view for it and I want all the old houses cleared below the road as you come from Pennycross. In short I wish it to have as decent an appearance as possible, and Sandy is so occupied in adorning Pennyghael that he can attend to nothing else. I think it will prove his ruin, furnishing, etc., without the means of doing so. I will be most anxious to hear from you on this subject ... For any sake, get free of rats.[19]

A week or two later, Donald's mysterious buyer was asking to see a specimen of the freestone used in the building of Carsaig, and Donald was longing to be there.

I hope to enjoy a little peace and quiet there and to see a few of those friends I most value [this was a hint about Captain Allan's good company] ... without show or expense ... I have written to Sandy in the most earnest manner to destroy the dogs so as to allow the hares to increase and not to shoot any grouse, as I hope his Father and I will be able to kill a few next season. Sandy has hurt the grey mare by leading stones to his new house. That house has absorbed every other idea or consideration, and I fear, in the end will prove his ruin.[20]

But the sale apparently came to nothing, and the pretence of Kinloch/Carsaig being part of Murdoch's estate was still maintained. Selling or not selling filled Donald with equal despair.

I much fear it will be impossible to make Carsaig so as to enable me to live there with any comfort, and unless it is so, I would much rather never go near it. I cannot to save me from death go into a heavy expense, for I have not the means to defray it ... Then altho distressed by it in the meantime, the money expended is not lost, and press Sandy to have the roads to both harbours made good.

Possil and the Sheriff leave this on Wednesday and go by the *Ben Nevis* next Thursday. Possil positively is to examine Duart. I pray Heaven he might be the purchaser on your account. Betwixt you you would soon have some good roads ... Fraser will be a great acquisition to Morvern and Possil to Mull. The more strangers that come to settle in a Country so far behind all others in improvements so much the better – I think you will see the effect of it in Mull and Morvern beyond all belief.[21]

Donald had changed his tune about strangers, swept off his feet by the talk of changes all around him. He prevented a friend from going to see Duart, lest Possil should not succeed. In April Donald was purchasing Ardow, between Penmore and Calgary, for Dr Lachlan Maclean, Gallanach. 'I never, bless Almighty God, had so much to do.'

The year 1825 was, for Donald Maclean WS, as happy as a year can ever be for a worrying kind of man, constantly on the edge of ruin. He was only sorry that his son-in-law was not sufficiently worried about his financial ruin to take steps to pay all his bills on time. Donald was in two minds about going to Carsaig in the summer; after his purchase of Ardow for Dr Lachlan, he was longing to go, but the business of the sale of Duart occupied him so greatly that by the end of April he was in doubt. 'The sale of Duart renders my stay in Edinburgh absolutely necessary. I am happy it is sold, and I am happy that Possil has got it, and I truly think it well worth the £40,000.[22] I admit the rent is not equal to such a price, but it can be improved to any extent. I trust he will enter keenly into the spirit of improvement, which will do himself and the Country much good.'[23]

As to Carsaig, Sandy Pennycross was still not fulfilling his part of the bargain as custodian of Donald's lands. 'I entreat, press Sandy regarding the roads and clearing the fields of the stances of old houses. I have been quite unhappy at the idea of going to Mull without seeing you all, but I am now quite relieved by not going at all.' In June he was hoping to go. 'The expense will exceed all bounds, and I expect no pleasure or comfort in it. A vessel is now engaged to carry coals and all the articles that can be got ready – tea, sugar, soap ... I send all the wine I require, and all the spirits except whisky. I trust to Robert Stewart getting a cask or two.[24] If I can get workmen, they will go by the next steam boat. I will look most foolish to send my family to a pig stye at an expense far beyond my means. I have bought a dining table ... and an immense quantity of chaff for beds – what will fill ten.'

In the end, he accompanied his family to the pig stye, and returned to Edinburgh in July to finish the business of the legal year. The house in Albany Street was empty except for his son John's dog, forgotten in the bustle of leaving. 'I found John's ugly dog Connon in the house, without meat or drink. I cannot think that any person could be so cruel as to leave him there. I gave him both, altho I detest him.' On 13 August, however,

Donald was in Carsaig with his family, enumerating the pleasures of bucolic life. 'I have as good mutton here as I would ever wish to eat. We have more fish than we can consume, and the finest possible – the variety great from your bountiful supply of salmon. If tomorrow is a good day, we must go to Kilfinichen church.' (The minister of Ross, Donald Campbell, had succeeded his father, Mr Dugald, in the charge, and preached in turn at Kilfinichen, Bunessan and Iona.) In October he had returned to Edinburgh, leaving his family at Carsaig, for Chirsty was about to give birth to her eighth child, and her mother was to be with her. With the safe arrival of the infant Mary Ann, he was to take the steam boat once more, and supervise the complicated operation of moving his wife, four sons and four daughters, two of their sons being blind, back to Albany Street.

It had been a summer of good weather and camaraderie. Mrs Maclean Clephane had been in residence at Torloisk, two of Gillean Maclaine's sons, Archibald and Hector, had come back to Scallastle after a long absence, to stay with their mother and sister-in-law, as if time had stood still. There had been trips to Staffa, walks to the Carsaig Arches, and parties at every house on the island which had a claim, by having a second storey, to be called a 'mansion house'. On Monday 31 October, with the new Lochbuy child christened by the Rev. Mr Alexander Fraser, a dinner was held, at which twenty-eight sat at table. These, Lochbuy and his lady apart, included ten from the family of Albany Street, Dr Allan Maclean, '*doctair ruadh nam blath shuilean*' and his wife Flora Lochbuy, Sandy Pennycross and his sister Miss Julian, the impetuous Miss Jane Jarvis Maclaine of Lochbuy, Mr Duncan and Mr Colin MacTavish of Laggan, the tutors for the two families, and two lady houseguests. The minister, Mr Fraser, whose wife had died eleven years before, said grace. Last, but far from least of the guests, was the man who has painted the scenes of those years for us (for how should we otherwise know who was at that Lochbuy dinner party?) – Lauchlan Maclaine, bachelor, fiddler, cottar, music collector, Gaelic scholar, army captain and diarist. He had walked from Garmony to Moy for the christening of the child, with his pointer Carlo, and his gun, and on Wednesday he attended Donald Maclean and his family to Grass Point, where they were to join the steam boat for Glasgow. From there he returned to Garmony, where he wrote his diary, telling us what the weather had been like, and that the Lochbuy dinner had been three courses, served on china, and very elegant.

The blindness of Donald's sons, John and Charles, was an affliction which had burst into the life of the family in 1819, when two of the children had recently died, and two others were acutely ill. Donald bore it with his usual blend of despair and indignation, with the knowledge also that the costs of doctors would bring him to total ruin. The boys, at school in England, had contracted a form of ophthalmia when they were fourteen and thirteen years old.

Two days ago I had the most afflicting news of my dearest Charles. He has got the ophthalmia to the greatest degree, and they have every apprehension of his forever losing his eyesight. May the Almighty God avert such an evil. I expect him home tomorrow or next day. The medical people there recommend it ... This is likely to stop Mrs Maclean's journey to Mull. She has long denied herself every enjoyment and promised herself much happiness for two months in the society of your family ... to the will of the Almighty God we must now submit.[25]

Alternately, John and Charles gave most anxiety. When their condition stabilised into certain blindness, they were sent to St Andrews to finish their education. Charles was the more optimistic of the two, John more resigned to his fate. Charles, hearing that a blind man had been accepted as a probationer in the Church of Scotland, read Divinity at Edinburgh, but having come through his course with distinction, was turned down by the church. Frustrated, and conscious of his own indomitable spirit, Charles at twenty-two was giving Donald much trouble, and at Carsaig, in 1828, Donald was unable to go to visit his friend Coll, at Quinish. 'Truly it is necessary for me to remain at home if it was nothing more than to look after Charles, who is the most impertinent and worst-tempered young man I ever knew. He is a tyrant with his brothers and sisters, and to myself insolent beyond belief. I make great allowances for his situation, otherwise he would not have remained an hour under my roof if he did not alter his conduct ... gets every person here he can collect, in my absence, and no one dare find fault with him ... if he does not check his behaviour, his ruin and disgrace must be the consequence.'

'Thrown on the wide world completely destitute ... totally incapable of doing anything for himself', was the father's opinion, but Charles insisted on travelling to London on his own, constantly seeking official support. The only person who believed in him was Jane Jarvis Maclaine of Lochbuy, four years his senior, and now one of only two unmarried Lochbuy girls. Charles's passion for Jane Jarvis was regarded by both families as entirely unsuitable, but she was well-known for her candour and demonstrativeness, and cared little for what the world thought. In this uncomfortable situation, Charles suddenly announced that he was going to America. The father was despondent: 'So absurd and mad a scheme ... He says he is to carry £500 with him. It can only be from Archy and Fitzroy.[26] I see nothing but ruin ... He from infancy could not be controlled ... perverse disposition ... if I could contrive it I would leave town the day before he sets out.'

Instead, against all his principles, Donald was forced to give a party for the departing son, 'to show his last mark of affection for Jarvis'. 'I believe he has given up every thought of her, and she acted with great propriety. I never in the course of my life grudged anything more.' Before leaving for America, Charles wrote to his brother-in-law Murdoch a moving and lucid account of his struggle with his father Donald and of his hopes for his life in the new world.[27] 'My mind will often be in Mull, where I have spent so many happy days.' In Canada he was to marry a girl who had lived at Carsaig, and their descendants were to be of Drimnin and Lochbuy stock.

Charles's brother John remained at Albany Street, a bachelor, living longest of all Donald's children. He little knew, however, as he saw Mr Fraser christen a scrap of a baby girl at Lochbuy in 1825, that Mary Ann would be his support at the end of his days.

When Charles left, his father was a widower, for the death of his 'dearest Lilly' had come on 30 December 1833. The serious decline in Murdoch's fortunes of the late 1820s, dating in fact from the dinner party in October 1825, had produced some differences of opinion in the two men, and caused Donald to give up most of his dealings with Lochbuy. His partner, Mr Giffen, now attended to Murdoch's business, and it was only when he appealed to Donald to use his influence with Murdoch over the paying of a bill that the father-in-law mentioned money. In this period he still went to Carsaig in the late summer, but sprints to Mull became a thing of the past. 'Chirsty expresses a wish that I would go to Lochbuy to the Christmas. I might as well think of going to Africa.' In 1831, while in Carsaig, Mr Giffen had had to write to Donald over a problem in Murdoch's payments. 'I declare to God,' Donald wrote in a note sent round to Lochbuy, 'that to have my *arm amputated* would not give me such pain as writing to you in unpleasant terms, but it is out of my power to avoid stating plain facts.' In 1831 his mother, old Mrs Maclean of Drimnin, died and he attended her funeral 'with much pain'.

But although Murdoch had spoken out once or twice against the 'forebodings' of his father-in-law, no real breach in the relationship occurred until the death of Colonel Macquarie, then in Ulva, showed up the most fundamental of all differences in their attitudes. This concerned the question of sequestration. For the very strange reason which will be addressed in Chapter 17, Charles Macquarie had named Murdoch Maclaine and Donald Maclean as trustees, so that the winding up of the estate of Ulva, and its subsequent sale was in their hands. The scale of arrears of rents in Ulva was so great that in legal terms the trustees had every right to apply for sequestration orders upon most of the tenantry before offering the island for sale. But the minister, the ground officer, Donald Maclean and the factor all disagreed with the idea of sequestration, and, as Donald said, thought that this was the majority view. Donald had imagined that they might go into the trustees' work 'with affection, hand in hand'. Instead, Murdoch had assumed an authority 'that nothing could justify'. Donald spent Christmas day writing from Albany Street, to remind Murdoch of what had happened.

> You have done everything in your power to thwart me and if you did not shake me the last time you was alone with me, you did everything *but* do so, and certainly used your hands to prevent me leaving my own room.

You deliberately showed the malevolence of your heart towards me and my family in all the rancour and revenge you could display, and I now beg in conclusion to say that any further intercourse betwixt us ... is utterly impossible.

In a memorandum, Donald reminded Murdoch of the trustees' walk through the island of Ulva, where the houses were marked for sequestration like houses in the days of the plague. 'The factor, the clergyman,[28] and ground officer all decided there was not to be any sequestration, and in my humble opinion there never was a wiser decision.'

Lochbuy's answer, copied on the memorandum, indicates that he was still of the opinion that sequestration would benefit the estate funds, and did not retract his view. For nearly three years there was correspondence of an intermittent and cool kind, with no family news. What Chirsty felt about this was apparently not considered. But in 1839, a touching request came from a Murdoch who had been seriously ill to his father-in-law.

There is a feeling which embitters my already much weakened constitution, and which you alone can alleviate. That is the terms on which you and I are. My ardent and earnest wish is for a Reconciliation, and if the Most High, whose Almighty power I acknowledge should remove me it would be an happy thought in yielding up my breath that you and I had parted in this world as I could have wished we had always lived.

If the great God should otherwise be pleased to grant me some time longer with my family, it will be a source of happiness to me to reflect that I have made this advance for a renewal of our friendship, and which if successful it shall always be my endeavour to cultivate for our mutual benefit and happiness.[29]

The letter was delivered by Alexander Crawford, the husband of Donald Maclean's daughter Sibella, who was one day to join the circle of 'new men' in Mull. Donald replied (as he prayed) in 'the same good honourable and pious feeling' in which Murdoch had written. 'No individual of your family could feel more than I did at your severe and protracted illness, and it is my everyday's prayer ... I myself going to my long home ... My dear Murdoch, may the Almighty bless you and your family, and I remain affectionately yours. ...'

The Albany Street house became quiet and dark, in the way of houses inhabited by old men, blind men, invalids and maiden ladies. After the Lochbuy children stopped going there for their education, young Murdie occasionally stayed with his grandfather, and did so even after his father's death. Young Murdie's plans to reduce the entail, to find mistakes in the sasine of his grandfather, Murdoch the nineteenth, to discover lands in Canada which had been granted at the end of the American war, and to pick over every legal document for gain, can hardly have delighted his surviving grandfather, especially when Murdie's agents did find an error in the sasine. No letters survive between Donald and Murdie from this time.

The younger man spent his time avoiding letters, which were most unpleasantly concerned with debts, and the poverty of his people in Mull. Very young Murdoch moved from place to place, staying out of reach of his factor, and of the constant appeals for charitable contributions to his own tenantry. His grandfather was well-disposed towards Mull cottars, allowing the miserable waifs expelled from Ulva, Ardmeanach and Gribun to settle on his lands at Kinloch when they had nowhere else to go. It was probably a misplaced, but well-intended kindness. He could neither afford to pour money into eleemosynary projects nor to sell his estate, which he fondly hoped would provide a small income to 'poor John', when left alone in the world.

Donald died in 1853, and John lived on at 21 Albany Street for another forty years. The Kinloch estate was sold in 1860 for £10,200 to Donald Maclaine of Lochbuy (who happened to be Donald WS's grandson, and whose story will be told in Chapter 27). There had been no increase in value from the time of the flurry of land sales after the end of the wars with France. The money from the sale, after deductions, was to go to Donald WS's children or their heirs. The contents of the house in Albany Street were sold at a roup in Edinburgh on 28 April 1892, when the prices realised were abjectly miserable. The circular table in the drawing room sold for 8s. 6d., and two old family portraits for 2s.

Notes

1. A Writer to the Signet was able to conduct business with a 'seal' on it, such as Royal or prestigious legal work. The Society of WSS controlled its membership by a strict system of apprenticeship or indentures, which Archy had entered upon, but Gillean had not been able to aspire to. Advocates (barristers) had a separate organisation, the Faculty of Advocates.
2. Estate business letters were always written in English, but letters survive in Gaelic between MM2 and LMD who shared a belief that Gaelic should be preserved.
3. 'Meat' in the sense of food in general rather than 'flesh'.
4. NAS. GD174/1628/116. DMWS to MM2, 12 July 1817.
5. NAS. GD174/1628/48. DMWS to MM2, 29 April 1815.
6. NAS. GD174/1628/164. DMWS to MM2, 4 February 1819.
7. Or, as Maclean historians like to pretend, 'won' his case.
8. NAS. GD174/1628/165. DMWS to MM2, 20 February 1819.
9. NAS. GD174/1628/296. DMWS to MM2, 10 August 1822.
10. NAS. GD174/1628/314. DMWS to MM2, 2 March 1823.
11. Abbreviated Register of Argyll Sasines, 1801 and 1821.
12. The Court of Exchequer was concerned with sheriffs' accounts, Customs and Excise and crown debts.
13. NAS. GD174/1628/332. DMWS to MM2, 7 September 1823. He had by that time lost five of his sixteen children.

14. See chapter 3, in which Forbes had come up against a 'collusion' to sabotage the raising of rents, but the term can also be applied to practices which delayed payment indefinitely.

15. Examples of precepts from the 1780s are in NAS. GD174/813.

16. NAS. GD174/1628/379. DMWS to MM2, 28 June 1824.

17. GRO. Journal of LMD. Tuesday 24 August 1824.

18. NAS. GD174/1628/388. DMWS to MM2, 4 October 1824.

19. NAS. GD174/1628/393. DMWS to MM2, 8 November 1824.

20. NAS. GD174/1628/395. DMWS to MM2, 15 November 1824. DMWS was not averse to dogs, and knew his gun dogs. He often supplied expensive pointers to MM2. Sandy's dogs must have been expendable.

21. NAS. GD174/1628/404. DMWS to MM2, 26 March 1825. Wm. Fraser bought Acharn in Morvern in 1825 from John Gregorson of Ardtornish, and sold it thirteen years later to the notorious Patrick Sellar. ACP bought 'Duart' in 1825, the house being called Achnacroish. That estate was the foundation of present-day Torosay, which had Duart Castle cut out of it to restore to the Macleans of Duart their ancestral home.

22. Another source gives the price as £35,000. GRO. LMD's diary, 17 April 1825.

23. NAS. GD174/1628/407. DMWS to MM2, 22 April 1825.

24. Possibly a slip of the pen, DMWS calling John Stewart by his father's name.

25. NAS. GD174/1628/172. DMWS to MM2, 10 July 1819.

26. Charles' brothers, who had offered their shares of a small legacy.

27. NAS. GD174/1688/3. Charles Maclean to MM2, Edinburgh, 2 May 1834, prior to sailing from Greenock for New York on the *Lady of the Lake*.

28. Rev. Neil Maclean, previously a tutor to CM's children, and now minister of the *quoad sacra* parish.

29. NAS. GD174/1628/641. MM2 to DMWS, 20 June 1839.

17

'The duke does not care a fig': the Macquarie brothers' bid

Lachlan Macquarie, governor of New South Wales, requires no introduction to Australians. He has given his name to harbours, islands, rivers and universities, and his life has been celebrated by many writers.[1] Lachlan will be left mainly in the safe and more accomplished hands of his biographers, but the impact of his purchase of lands in Mull upon the people of the island will be noticed. His younger brother, Charles, has attracted little attention from historians of the Mull scene, yet Charles was, in many ways, the more intelligent, interesting, thoughtful, compassionate, complex, and perhaps the sadder figure of the two. This chapter, like Tom Stoppard's view of Hamlet, concentrates on his Mull family, and in particular on Charles, just as Stoppard concentrated on the minor characters of Rosencrantz and Guildenstern, taking them out of their subordinate roles in Shakespeare's *Hamlet*, and placing them in the centre of the stage.[2]

In the days when the future Murdoch Maclaine the nineteenth of Lochbuy was a linen merchant, and Gillean Maclaine was learning the law by copying documents in an Edinburgh office, Murdoch's sister Margaret, known as Peggy, lived in Ulva with a man called Lachlan MacQuarrie. The spelling of the surname, which mattered little in the time we are talking of, was later fixed as 'Macquarie' by their sons, so that it resembled the name of the chiefs of MacQuarrie, yet remained distinctive, and peculiar to the two brothers who were to make it widely known.

No parish registers have survived from Mull before 1766, so that the marriage and first children of Peggy and Lachlan do not appear in church records. But although it is known that four children were born to the couple before 1766, they (or a couple with exactly the same names) approached the minister of Kilninian in 1768, asking to be married, or remarried. Nearly three years later, on 22 September 1771, a child called 'Kealloch' was baptised to Lachlan MacQuarrie in Soriby and Margaret McLean. The baptism was celebrated at Ormaig, then the home of the patriarch of the Ormaig branch of the family, Donald MacQuarrie, over ninety years old, whose wife Margaret was a daughter of Hector Lochbuy. This vague connection with the Ormaigs is all that can be surmised of the paternal line of Charles, and therefore of his older brother Lachlan. There is a chance that Lachlan Macquarie, who was to be famous as governor of New South Wales, was born before his parents' marriage. In eighteenth-century Scotland, and in the islands in particular, this was neither unusual nor a handicap. The subsequent marriage of the parents legitimised the children.

The name given to the child, 'Kealloch' was a form of Tearlach, the Gaelic for Charles, an unusual Christian name among MacQuarries, but current among Macleans. None of Lachlan and Peggy's children could speak English until they were removed from the island for the very purpose of widening their chances in life by giving them a Lowland education. It is certain that Peggy and her daughters spoke Gaelic only, and that when Peggy's sons spoke later of having someone 'read' their letters to their mother, they meant 'translate'. Letters were written in English, and the ability to write Gaelic prose was a nineteenth-century accomplishment, exemplified by the well-wrought compositions of ministers and scholars, and some Gaelic-speaking chieftains like young Murdoch Lochbuy.

If Murdoch Maclaine had not been a merchant in Edinburgh, able to give his nephews a liberal education there, it is unlikely that they would have left Mull. The family moved from Ulva to Oskamull, on the other side of the Ulva ferry, and some time after the father's death in 1775, Peggy took Charles with her, and stayed with her daughter Betty, who had married the carpenter Farquhar Maclaine in 1771. Peggy shared the rental of the farm at Oskamull with her son-in-law, and insisted on sharing the work. It was a family arrangement like hundreds of others in Mull, and like many others also, the Macquaries had a blood relationship with the 'gentry' which they might not be able to identify in every detail, but which gave them pride in their birth. Peggy was a granddaughter of Hector the twelfth of Lochbuy, a niece of Ormaig's lady, and a granddaughter of Lachlan MacQuarrie the fourteenth of Ulva. In an island where families were much larger than anyone could remember generations later, ties could be tenuous and economically unadvantageous, but they were known to everyone. Men and women lived long. Peggy could speak of the manner of her great-grandmother's death on the island of Little Colonsay as if it had happened yesterday.

Her sons went into the army. But first Lachlan was educated somewhere in or near Edinburgh. Murdoch Maclaine was not lavish with his avuncular aid, but he was kind, and if Charles' experience (which we know about) resembled Lachlan's (which is not known about), it was a sound, practical preparation for a better than average life. Lachlan had gone out into the world before Charles arrived at Writers Court in Edinburgh in 1779, a small lad who spoke Gaelic when he spoke at all. He was unable to communicate at first with his aunt, Anne Learmonth, but his cousin Donald, left in charge of Murdoch's business while Murdoch sailed to America and back on his military missions, had been given orders to find a school for the boy, and was mercifully a Gaelic speaker. Cousin Donald was 'scrimp' (as he confessed himself) in his habits, and suggested cutting costs by sending 'Je-Je' to Fife, but Anne asserted her rights as domestic supervisor, accused Donald of coming from a 'sett of beggars', and kept Charles with her. 'The boy is not big,' Donald reported to

Murdoch, of the eight year old. 'He now begins to speak English, and understands a great deal of what is said. As soon as she will let him out of her house I will do as you directed.'[3] Eventually, Charles was placed with the schoolmaster of Liberton, then a village outside Edinburgh, and was soon making good progress, but the family waited in vain for an intimation of his chosen vocation. At ten, he longed for his home in Mull, and for his brother-in-law Farquhar's trade of carpentry. Nearing eleven, he was learning book-keeping. 'He is boarded with a good schoolmaster,' Donald wrote in 1782. 'He is a very genteel, fine-like boy. He'll be a very large man if he is spaird.' And again, 'Charles is a very good schoollar, but no Business as yet.' Lachlan was also taking an interest in Charles' development. 'I am sorry I cannot say anything particular or decisive anent Charles Macquarie,' Donald replied to Murdoch, as the army, in which Lachlan, like Murdoch, was now serving, prepared to return to Britain, 'he is attending the Branches of Education ordered by his Brother.'

Lachlan, who had been in Jamaica with his regiment, arrived in Greenock on 29 February 1784, grateful to be alive after a perilous voyage of seventeen weeks and five days.[4] He was 'sorry to find the name of Maclean so much diminished by the death of so many of our friends,' but looked forward, in his affectionate way, to seeing his uncle in Edinburgh after the reduction of their regiments. 'I am sorry to hear that my Brother Charles is losing his time in Mull. I wrote my Mother and him yesterday by a man going to Mull from Lady Lochbuy's.'[5] At that very moment, Archy, in New York, was 'triffling and playing' in the Lowthers' house with Barbara, and Lachy's uncle Murdoch would have appeared to have no closer association with the house of Lochbuy than he had himself. Lachlan's respect and love for Murdoch derived from all the kindness that had been shown to him and to Charles.

When the news of Archy Lochbuy's murder reached Mull towards the end of the year, and Murdoch flew off to London, it was Lachlan Macquarie who was given charge of affairs at Moy, rather than the tacksman of Gruline or Gillean Maclaine. Murdoch, although he had been staying with Gillean at Scallastle, or perhaps because he was with Gillean, now had even more reason to distrust him. When the entail suddenly appeared out of the blue, Murdoch was even more cautious about taking Gillean into his confidence.[6] Lachlan, unlike Gillean, was a model of integrity, a man who treated everybody with courtesy. To Lachlan, Murdoch gave the task of sealing up the repositories at Lochbuy, in accordance with the custom of the time, so that independent arbiters could decide on questions arising from the executry.[7] Throughout the years 1785 and 1786, Lachlan Macquarie was to keep a close watch on business at Lochbuy, and to keep accounts for the incompetent John of Gruline, with Charles as his understudy. Lachlan was either away on Murdoch's business, or attending Murdoch's marriage to Jane Campbell at Airds when Gillean arrived with his boat and his henchmen to open the closet at Moy with his own key, and remove, as Miss Ketty was to recall, 'a sealed writing desk, two sealed trunks, and two swords'.[8] What Lachlan Macquarie and Gillean Maclaine felt about each other is undocumented,[9] but when Gillean and Marie asked Lachlan to Scallastle for the Christmas of 1786, the future governor refused politely, saying that he had a 'rather tedious complaint – nothing more than a scorbatic irruption on the back of both my hands' which confined him at home in Oskamull.[10]

When Lachlan re-entered the army a year later, Charles succeeded him part of the time as Murdoch's right-hand man in the running of the estate. It was an interim arrangement only, as Charles was now trying to find a niche for himself in India, but knew that Lachlan, who had gone there in 1788, was not influential enough to obtain a position for his younger brother. Charles also spent two winter sessions in Edinburgh in 1789–90 and 1790–91, attending classes in law which would qualify him to be a notary public. George Andrew, a lawyer in the office of Allan MacDougall, was keeping a kindly watch over him, and his admiring remarks to Murdoch Lochbuy were: 'A very agreeable obliging young man' and 'I see your nephew Mr Macquarie of whom I entertain a very good opinion, and have put some books into his hand to read, of which he seems disposed to make the best advantage, but I am apprehensive his progress cannot be such that he can be admitted Notary this session: and consequently that his attendance during a considerable part, if not the whole of the ensuing winter session will be requisite.'

Charles was beginning to feel discouraged by the consensus among friends that India was not a place for an unpromoted young man, and in 1793, Lord Breadalbane offered him a lieutenancy in the 99th Regiment, which was confirmed, but not implemented. In the meantime Charles busied himself in Mull, looking after the estate while his uncle Lochbuy served in the Argyllshire Fencibles. Charles' task was made more difficult by the death of John, tacksman of Gruline, from a fall in May 1792. In Mull, a dead man's affairs were frequently impossible to put right, but John Gruline's were worse than any other, and it took ten years to go through the books and papers.[11]

Charles' first army years were filled with negotiations to find himself a better place and with recruiting enough young men to improve his bargaining position. But men were scarce, and in 1794, in Glasgow, he had to employ agents to help him to achieve his final total of 375 recruits, most of whom were Highlanders. Lord Breadalbane's Regiment being drafted into the 42nd or Royal Highland, Charles was appointed captain in 1795, and sailed for Gibraltar first, then Minorca.[12] His letters to Mull between 1794 and 1801, when he returned to Spithead, are full of concern for the 'little ones' of the Lochbuy family, now numbering ten. Paternal feelings were perhaps aroused by the fact that four months after he left for London in 1794, a son had been born to him and a young woman called Janet Maclean, at Moy. The mother's name is recorded in the old parish register only.[13] Nothing else is known of her. She may have worked for the family at Moy when the child was conceived.

She may have married, and given up the child. Charles, in Minorca with his regiment in 1800, wrote to Murdoch and Jane, 'I am happy to find the boy Hector is at Lochbuy.' Hector, or the 'Hero Hector', as Lachlan was to call him, was only a year or two younger than the two Lochbuy boys, and was to spend some of his time with them.

Charles arrived at Spithead on Christmas Day 1801. He had received a severe wound in the head at the battle of Aboukir, but had been well enough to meet and talk with his brother Lachlan at Alexandria in Egypt,[14] when they discussed their plans to buy the lands Murdoch Maclaine was selling to pay the debts of the Lochbuy estate.[15]

Alexander Maclean of Coll, John Campbell of Airds, John Campbell of Knock and Colin Campbell of Achnacroish had all come forward willingly with the money that was needed for the purchase by both Macquarie brothers because their funds were locked up. These were not any old loans, but true debts of gratitude on the part of some of the lenders, such as Knock, whose son had died in India, and who had been in correspondence with Lachlan about the young man's effects. Lachlan, who had lost his 'angelic wife' Jane Jarvis in 1796, had inherited most of her £7,000 fortune, and Charles, whose army life had not been as expensive as Lachlan's Indian service, had saved prudently, after having had the astonishing good luck to win £900 with a shared lottery ticket in 1796. ('You will no doubt consider me a lucky dog', Charles had written Murdoch, and had straightway locked up the prize.)[16] Pennygown, Gruline and Ardmeanach were to go on the market as soon as the Scallastle family had been defeated in its attempt to stop the sales. It was such a very small Mull world overseas that Lachlan encountered Scallastle boys in India (he had indeed helped them to go there) and a batch of Mull soldiers in Alexandria. In 1802, reporting on the silly habits and extravagance of Gillean and Marie's younger sons, Lachlan said, 'I am sorry to find that they make so very bad use of their money as to remit it home to their foolish Mother, to enable her to fee designing lawyers to give you trouble and throw obstacles in the way of the sale of the Lochbuy lands … you may depend upon it that the foolish stories their ridiculous Mother circulates in Mull about the riches, etc. etc., of her sons are all without foundation. I am however very much concerned that she should be able to find funds anywhere to give you so much trouble and vexation.'[17]

As related in a previous chapter,[18] the sales went ahead, the only unscheduled part being that it was Murdoch Maclaine himself who bought, on behalf of all the daughters whose provision he now had to secure, Ardmeanach – separating it from the estate so that its rents might supply a personal income for the 'Lochbuy girls', who, with the advent of the baby Jane Jarvis, named for Lachlan's late 'angelic wife' were now nine. The rest of Murdoch's days we know about. It is only to be regretted that when the Macquarie brothers managed to be together in Mull in 1804 to celebrate their purchases, the man to whom they had both written for so many years, who had supplied them with the means to write so fluently and to judge their fellow men so clearly, had entered into his long rest at the *Caibeal Mheamhair.*

The brothers' estates, Jarvisfield and Glenforsa, were now left in the hands of managers while Lachlan served in London and India, and Charles in Ireland, Spain and Portugal.[19] Lachlan was appointed governor of New South Wales in 1809. From that period the two men corresponded as best they could in the days when a letter from New South Wales could take eight months to reach a European destination. Uppermost in their minds was the strong desire to increase their holdings in Mull, or to adjust them to their taste. Unlike most of the people who already owned estates, Charles and Lachlan had resources of money. Lachlan had his angelic wife's legacy and his own governor's income. Charles had increased his lucky win on the lottery with his army pay, and in 1812, married Marianne Willison, one of the daughters of George Willison, an Edinburgh portrait painter who had made a fortune in India.[20]

In the ten years between the death of Murdoch the nineteenth of Lochbuy and young Murdoch's assumption of control in about 1813, relations between the Macquarie brothers and the house of Lochbuy were as close and cordial as they could be at such a distance. Lachlan's attachment to Mull played a part in his choice of Jane Campbell's younger sister, Elizabeth Henrietta Campbell of Airds, as his second wife. There was no other person who could share with him the longing for home which played such a large part in his life in New South Wales from 1810 to 1822. Through Elizabeth, he could remain as intimate with Jane as distance would permit, and their new relationship of brother and sister, instead of nephew and aunt, was possibly gratifying to both.

Lachlan's gratitude to his late uncle, Murdoch, was without bounds, unlike his cousin Donald, merchant in Edinburgh, who did not carry indebtedness beyond the grave. Lachlan would send gifts of money for the education of the 'Lochbuy girls' and for little personal trifles for Jane. He did not tell the mother about her son John Lochbuy's 'vicious courses of drunkenness', for John had accompanied them to Australia. When the news of Charles' marriage finally reached the governor and Elizabeth, they sent two black swans to his 'pretty, good little wife to amuse her on Loch Ba, or on her own pretty river of Pennygown'. It is not known that the swans ever arrived.

It was late in the day when Lachlan heard at last of the sale of the Duke of Argyll's lands. 'I know that the duke does not care a fig for lands in Mull, and as far as depends on himself, I doubt he would prefer lands in England,' Lachlan pronounced, at first not affected by the fever of buying which was raging in 'the Country'. He was still dreaming of building a very populous, thriving and respectable village at Salen, with a water mill, distillery and post office. He had received Charles' miniature, which made him look a perfect *fright* – at least sixty, and ugly. He could not bear to look at this horrid picture.[21] But when he wrote in November, Lachlan was coveting the farms along the north shore of Loch na Keill, and counting up his money, reckoning himself worth £24,000, and before he had come to the end of the letter, he was so carried away that he was authorising Charles to buy all or any of the farms in the Loch na Keill lot.[22] If these farms were already sold, Charles should purchase Duart and its adjoining farms, by far the most beautiful and the most valuable. Lachlan, unlike any other buyers of Mull property, was thinking in terms of scenery, a very new idea for Mull in those times, or at least one that no one else had ever spoken of. 'But in this purchase,' added the governor, 'you will be *powerfully opposed* by old and young Coll, and all the monied Macleans in the world.' But the monied Macleans of the world must have been few, for there was no opposition when the time came for the duke to relinquish Duart.

Both brothers had a sentimental attachment to Ulva, and it was painful to Charles to see Ranald Macdonald of Staffa adhering to an asking price of £35,000 for the island. Because Staffa's father-in-law bought Ulva, as a device for keeping it in the family until the duke's sales should take rival properties off the market, the inflated price was upheld, and the female Macdonalds continued to inhabit the mansion house at Ardnacaillich, without the charismatic Staffa. The island was periodically advertised, but, as Donald WS reported, attracted no interest. Charles bided his time and looked after his own property and Lachlan's.

Since leaving the 42nd Regiment with the rank of lieutenant-colonel in 1811, and since his marriage to a rich young woman, Charles, living in Pennygown, had become an important heritor, representing both his brother Lachlan, and young Murdoch in the year before the new Lochbuy returned with his bride. Charles was highly respected by Donald Maclean WS, who kept singing his praises to his son-in-law. There was an age difference of exactly twenty years between the two newly-married men, and both had served in the Peninsula with the 42nd Regiment. If there had been any quarrel between them in the army, it was unmentioned. As early as January 1814, Murdoch referred Charles to 'aspersions in your letter to Mr Maclean'[23] so that it seems that some straightforward advice from Charles to Donald Maclean WS had caused offence. These remarks were about young Murdoch's lack of concern for his sisters, the nine Lochbuy girls. Of all the characters in the whole of this documented history of Mull people, Charles was the most incisive letter writer and the most logical thinker. For common sense and integrity he stood head and shoulders above every other *Muileach* in this array of personalities, although his diplomacy matched that of James Maxwell of Aros. Yet all that is known positively is that young Murdoch did not see eye to eye with Charles Macquarie, that he resented his advice and did not seek his company. They were bound to meet, if not at their own houses, then at Jane's after her removal from Lochbuy to Scallastle. Donald WS's allusions to the rift are always rather pained, in the manner of his reproaches to Murdoch for not visiting Captain MacAskill at Calgary. Charles wrote to young

Murdoch in the most affectionate manner, nudging him to remember to attend meetings, and humouring him over unpleasant matters such as the marriage of Murdoch's sister Eliza to Donald Campbell in 1819. When Murdoch resented people, he did so thoroughly, and was so ill at the idea of this alliance with a Campbell, son of 'the old fox' of Achnacraig, that he could not attend the ceremony. Charles and Donald WS remained good friends, pretending that they did not notice Murdoch's captious behaviour. But a further irritant was introduced when in 1821 the Writer to the Signet acted for Charles Macquarie in the surprising purchase of the Duke of Argyll's Duart lot.

Charles Macquarie's wife, Marianne, did not like her house at Pennygown, presumably for the reasons most wives do not like houses – that it was without the modern amenities of the day. Lachlan's house, Old Gruline, was more acceptable, so that in the years between 1815 and 1821, Charles and Marianne lived partly at Gruline, keeping it warm for Lachlan's return from Australia. Charles hankered after Ulva, and Lachlan sympathised, from New South Wales, with this longing to buy the ancestral lands of the MacQuarries. 'I am still not without hopes of your being laird of Ulva, for it never can sell for anything like what Staffa holds it up at,' the governor wrote in 1819, but the Macdonalds, in the shape of Staffa's father-in-law, Sir Henry Steuart of Allanton, still would not budge from their asking price. In the meantime, the trustees of George William, sixth Duke of Argyll, released the jewel in the crown, the lands of Duart, onto the market. As Lachlan and Elizabeth Macquarie were about to be quit of the irksome task of governing New South Wales, and were planning to return to Gruline, Charles made the decision to try for Duart, and instructed Donald Maclean WS to bid.

The lawyer duly acted, and was successful. Still pretending that there was no bad feeling between his son-in-law and the new master of Duart, Donald Maclean wrote elatedly to inform Murdoch of his cousin's success. 'You will be happy to hear that I have purchased Torosay [24] for Charles Macquarie. The price is great – £35,000.' Murdoch was not happy; he would have liked to add Duart to his own estate, but failing that, he would have liked to buy Ardura, if it had been offered as a separate lot. A keen deer hunter, young Murdoch regretted that his own hunting ground should be divided by the very pleasant strip of land around Ardura. His father-in-law, while keeping him to a stringent course of obliterating the debts of his estate, had invited and encouraged and helped Charles Macquarie into the duke's Torosay lands, which had been managed hitherto by a neutral agent, Mr James Maxwell. Now Murdoch was to endure the advice and criticism of Charles, and the humiliating knowledge that Charles had a very fine estate next door to his own. Duart Castle itself was, in 1821, a mere ruin, with the official presence of the military garrison reduced to a couple of men. But how sweet the sound of Duart with its associations with chiefdom, with the clan, with the bardic outpourings of old! The only house of any size and quality was Torgormaig, sometimes called Lower Achnacroish, a house which stood on the site of present-day Torosay Castle. In 1821, the castles of Duart and Aros were the only keeps on the duke's lands, and looked like being ruins for ever.

Murdoch did not rejoice at Charles' acquisition, or the prospect of having him as a neighbour. Charles' letters to Murdoch at this time are concerned with the Lochbuy girls, and the Lochbuy widow, Jane. Murdoch's impatience with the extravagance of the girls, and their unfortunate disposition to marry and to ask to have their portions paid out against his inclinations, was something which Charles could not easily accept, for he had known them all from infancy. They were his 'dear lambs' and he had known their mother, Jane, since she had come to Lochbuy as a bride in 1786. As marriages accelerated, and Charles advocated the proper payment of the allowances ordained by Murdoch the nineteenth, and as everyone praised the wise Colonel Macquarie, Murdoch's 'captious opposition' grew. 'Colonel Macquarie has acted in the most generous manner towards me. It is impossible to believe the extent of my obligations to him,' wrote Donald Maclean. 'Would to God you and he were as you ought to be.'[25]

Charles and Marianne moved to Torgormaig in 1821, with Lachlan pushing in the background for Charles' cattle to be removed in time for his return to Mull. Before his decision to buy Duart, Charles had asked his brother to swap Killiechronan for one of the Glenforsa properties, but Lachlan, who now had a six-year-old son, Lachlan Junior, was adamant that Killiechronan was destined for the boy. Young Lachlan would never forgive him for depriving him of Killiechronan.[26] Lachlan was so sorry that Cousin Donald had died in Edinburgh, but it had been most unkind and ungrateful of him not to leave some legacies to the poor Lochbuy girls. 'Indeed,' wrote Lachlan, 'from the affection he always professed for yourself, I did hope he would have left *you* a handsome legacy, but poor Donald had no real generosity or liberality, and was always a very covetous, narrow-minded man.' Cousin Donald Maclaine, seed merchant and merchant successor to the late Murdoch Maclaine, had had no children, and had died at 'a very advanced period of life'. His lack of generosity was greatly lamented in Maclean families in general, and the manner in which he had cheated the daughters of his benefactor was deplored.

Lachlan Macquarie, Elizabeth and young Lachlan arrived in Mull in September 1822, soon after the death of Lachlan's brother-in-law, 'honest Farquhar Maclaine'. Their house was not fit to live in.[27] Colonel Donald Campbell of Knock, who owned Mishnish, but was still known principally as 'Knock', invited the Macquaries to stay with his family until the weather improved and the house was more inviting. They were shocked by the state of Gruline, by the poverty of the people, and by the 'set of very idle fellows' who were in Charles' service. In less than a month, still staying with the Campbells, Lachlan decided to take Elizabeth and young Lachlan on a grand tour of Europe. As young Lachlan's schooling was not to be interrupted, he engaged a young man who was completing his arts and theology course at Edinburgh University, Robert Meiklejohn, to travel with them. Meiklejohn proved to be an excellent investment, even at the very generous salary of £100 a year.[28] He was to be a sharp-witted companion, a prudent factor and a spokesman for the Macquarie interest in Mull.

From Rome, Lachlan wrote to Charles, who was now settling, with Marianne and their three sons and two daughters, at 'Duart'.[29] Glenforsa still remained to be sold, and Charles was considering selling a desirable part of Duart while he waited. He was now hanging on for the right price for Glenforsa, just as Sir Henry Steuart was continuing to hold on to the ridiculous price he asked for Ulva. Lachlan, always a little more concerned with status and title than Charles (and less knowledgeable about the conventions and niceties of superiorities), asked if his brother could use the title of Duart. But this was the least of Charles' concerns. He spent more and more time at 14 Howard Place, Edinburgh, the home of his brother-in-law, Mr Scheniman, who was an accountant. His plan of financing Duart with the sale of Glenforsa was clearly unrealistic. His good friend, Donald Maclean WS had tried to interest Sir Fitzroy Maclean as early as 1816[30] in the advantages of buying back part of the clan heritage, and was trying again to plant the seed of the great project which was not to be realised until the twentieth century.[31] But the Duart Macleans were not rich, and Donald WS had to keep reporting failure to young Murdoch and to Charles. In 1820, Donald had had hopes that Lord John Campbell[32] would buy some of the Argyll lands from his brother the sixth duke. 'Lord John I understand is to be the purchaser of Torosay, Knock and Aros lots. I think you ought to pay every attention to him and Lady John,' Donald wrote Murdoch, just as he had to prod him to pay attention to Captain MacAskill and Colonel Macquarie. But not even a small section of Duart could be held out as bait to Lord John, who as the younger brother of a duke (and the most spendthrift of dukes), was no richer than Sir Fitzroy Maclean. Murdoch Lochbuy longed for Ardura with all his heart, but his father-in-law thought it would be 'madness' for Charles to sell this small slice. Donald WS enjoyed directing everyone else in the dance of the Mull estates, but he did not realise that it was precisely in the division into smaller parts that the future lay.

But one important piece of business which Donald did not have was the executry of Governor Lachlan Macquarie of New South Wales. For after the European tour, Lachlan had returned to Mull, perplexed by the end game of his own career, to find that their furniture was stormbound at Tobermory, and they must once more stay with the kind Campbells. In January 1824 they moved into their miserable quarters, and in April Lachlan travelled to London to wind up some business matters, never to return to Mull. In response to a letter posted in June in London, Elizabeth, Mr Meiklejohn and the ten-year-old Lachlan rushed to the capital to find the governor alive but only just.

When Charles was summoned from Mull, the whole island talked of the drama, and of whether or not Charles had found his brother 'in life'. Then there were conflicting reports of the coffin, and the route of the returning party, and whether Mrs Macquarie was accompanying the body. Every boat spotted in the Sound of Mull was assumed to be carrying the cortège. Lauchlan Maclaine in Garmony was keeping a diary at this time. On Friday 23 July he confirmed in his journal that 'the boat that passed down the Sound yesterday conveyed Mrs General Macquarie and her son, accompanied by Mr and Mrs MacDougall of Gallanach [33] as far as Salen ... I took a walk after dinner to Torgormaig to see Mrs Macquarie and her family and to learn if she had any late accounts from her husband. It appears that the last accounts were from near Aberdeen. The Corpse was so offensive that they were obliged to move it from the cabin to the deck. So much for the obstinacy and ignorance of his widow, who would not permit him to be put into a leaden coffin which would exclude the air, embalm him, or infuse the body in spirits, all of which would have preserved it.' [34]

The excitement caused by the death of the governor had deflected attention from the dying state of Jane Campbell, Murdoch the nineteenth's widow, at Lochbuy. On Sunday 1 August, Charles and Marianne attended Craignure Church in 'deep mourning', and the Rev. Mr Fraser gave a discourse in Gaelic and English. On the following Sunday, Mr Fraser lectured a congregation of three dozen people, and on the third Sunday, Jane Campbell was dead. On Tuesday 24 August the funeral procession of Mrs Maclaine of Lochbuy, Elizabeth Macquarie's sister, moved from Lochbuy House to the *Caibeal Mheamhair* at Laggan, attended, as the diarist recorded precisely, by 170 commoners and twelve gentlemen. As the gentlemen were traditionally invited to attend, and the commoners came unbidden to pay their respects, it is of interest to record (although the diarist made no comment) that Lochbuy, Lochnell, Coll, Sir John Campbell, Donald Maclean WS, Dr Donald Maclaine Callachilly, Captain Campbell of Ardnacross, Dr Allan Maclean Rossal and John Stewart Fasnacloich were the principal mourners, and that Charles, that loyal upholder of the deceased lady's interests, had not been invited. Nevertheless, the drinking and partying that dispelled the tension of the funeral was divided between Lochbuy and Torgormaig, with the diarist, that social chameleon, attending both, and on the 8 September, Donald WS and his wife Lilly went to call at Torgormaig while Lochbuy and Chirsty paid a visit to Elizabeth at Jarvisfield. In the month or two when her husband had been in London, Elizabeth had improved the house at Gruline, and since all socialising between Mull families in those days necessarily meant staying overnight, she was able to put up her nephew the laird and his lady.

In 1824, Sir Henry Steuart made a renewed effort to rid himself of Ulva, and a printed advertisement proclaimed its delights to a passive public. 'The estate consists of three main divisions – first the Island of Ulva extending to nearly 3,750 Scotch acres; secondly the lands of Laggan [35] or Lagganulva on the adjoining shore of Mull, extending to about 3,000; thirdly the numerous smaller islands which lie near the shores of both; in all about 8,500 English acres. The whole contains about 600 inhabitants, a circumstance which affords great facilities for manufacturing the kelp, extending the fisheries, or other useful labour.' [36] The mansion house of Ulva was surrounded with 200 acres of arable land, and, significant for later developments in Ulva, there was no Poor's Rate. Significant to anyone who was intimate with Ulva's past history was the remark that the island paid but a small feu duty to the Duke of Argyll. But who would remember Culinish now, and his advertisement in the newspaper warning any prospective buyer of inhibitions over the land? No one had ever written down the history of Mull, so how could anyone ever know?

The price of Ulva was calculated at twenty-seven years' purchase of the land rent, which was £29,460 19s. 6d. plus a fourteen years' purchase of the kelp, being £8,400, making the total purchase price £37,860 19s. 6d. [37] Charles offered to show prospective buyers round the island, but none came, even as birds of passage *en route* for Staffa. Within a year of his brother's death, the restless Charles, who still had not sold Glenforsa, had decided that only Duart was going to yield money, and to Duart he resorted for the price that was required to pay only a part of Ulva. Whether his relationship with young Murdoch, and Murdoch's implacable hostility and huffiness had anything to do with Charles' decision cannot be ascertained. But Murdoch's family circle, which included John Gregorson of Ardtornish, his brother-in-law, Dr Allan Maclean in Rossal, another brother-in-law, and Sir John Campbell of Airds, his cousin (although Charles was also his cousin) could not make overtures to Charles without offending Lochbuy. As we have seen, long discussions were necessary before Possil offered a price high enough for Charles to cover his costs in Duart. At last, in the spring of 1825, Charles and Colonel Alexander Campbell of Possil shook hands on the price, and Charles was free to buy back the ancestral home of the MacQuarries.

The Macquaries had long enjoyed the services of Neil Maclean as tutor to their children. Son of a Mull man, Charles Maclean, who had gone to Perthshire, and grandson of Iain Ban Mac Ailein in Acharn, Neil was doing what nearly every Highland minister was required to do when waiting for a call to a parish church – teach in the family of a heritor. He was born in 1796, and as his paternal uncle Allan Maclean *Ailean Sgoilear* was a schoolmaster in Iona, famous for his learning, Neil had lived with the uncle in Iona, and had received an exceptional education. He was just the kind of young man to appeal to Charles Macquarie, who did not care for the sports of the local gentlemen. Neither was Charles of a particularly religious bent. He could not bear poor Mr Fraser, the minister of Torosay, and was uncharacteristically mean when he reported Fraser to the presbytery for neglecting his duty in not preaching regularly at Salen. [38] But Fraser may have been a foolish old man, as he seemed to incur more than his fair share of animosity.

Neil Maclean was clever, and an able preacher, who took the service at

Craignure in Mr Fraser's absence, and who added to the interest of a visit to Torgormaig, for Lauchlan Maclaine the diarist at least. We shall see in Chapter 21 how Lauchlan mixed in the different worlds of gentlemen, commoners and intellectuals. And it was Lauchlan who would miss his evening stroll from Garmony to Torgormaig, gun and fiddle in hand, to talk to the colonel and the tutor, and to watch the progress of the colonel's children. 'Miss Elizabeth Macquarie shooting fast into the woman. She promises a fine person, with a comely expressive countenance', he noted, when she was eleven years old.[39]

The Macquaries flitted to Ulva at the end of May and beginning of June 1826, all the family, including Charles's son, the hero Hector, helping with the packing. A removal of this kind was carried out by boat, from Duart Bay to Loch Tuath. The diarist Lauchlan was invited to visit almost immediately after they had settled in, and noted that he had 'spent the day with Colonel Macquarie and his family most agreeably at Ardnacaillich[40] in Ulva where he is most comfortably situated – a good house, garden, offices, etc. Spent the whole day with them with the exception of a walk which Lieutenant Hector and I took to Laggan.' There was no mention of the 600 inhabitants. Neil Maclean had gone to Ulva too, having been appointed missionary there to relieve Dr MacArthur of part of the burden of the huge parish of Kilninian. Through Charles' recommendation, he was appointed in 1828 to be minister of the new parliamentary church, built to cater for the very large population of Ulva.

The family's enjoyment of Ulva was short-lived. Early in 1828, the 15-year-old Elizabeth became ill in Edinburgh, and Charles rushed to be with her, delayed at the Mull ferry by terrible storms. Although it had looked as if Charles and Marianne might have succeeded in limiting the number of their children (the last child, Marianne, having been born in 1820) Marianne had given birth to a son, Murdoch Maclaine Macquarie, on 29 February, and after her husband's departure she was reported to be seriously ill, attended by both Dr Donald Maclaine and Dr Daniel Maclean. In all the confusion, more anguish came with a letter from the Hero Hector[41] confirming the seriousness of his sister's state. How Death the Reaper managed to be so busy in Mull as well as in Edinburgh, weakening everybody before dealing his final blow, was startling to all. Alexander Campbell, 'the old fox' in Achnacraig, had had a stroke and lost his speech. Mrs Macquarie had had a relapse, Mrs Gregorson in Ardtornish had been desperately ill, and suddenly the young girl, Elizabeth, was dead. 'I this day attend the funeral of that charming girl Elizabeth Macquarie,' wrote Donald Maclean to Murdoch. 'The father is in the deepest distress, but more alarmed on her mother's account than any other thing.'[42]

Mr Fraser too was not spared. With an obstruction in his throat which did not allow him to swallow the smallest drop of water, he was able to converse 'with a degree of pleasantry', and remained in that state for seven weeks, dying at Gualachaolish on 3 July, four weeks after Captain Allan MacAskill of Calgary.[43] The roll call was still incomplete. Marianne Macquarie died on 3 September at the age of thirty-six, leaving a six-month-old baby boy. 'She is free from pain and happy,' wrote Lauchlan, 'but the Colonel I pity with his large and weak family.'

Elizabeth Henrietta Macquarie experienced that sense of elation and freedom which widows often discover after the first shock of a husband's death. After Lachlan's burial she had remained in Mull for only a month or two, and then, in accordance with the governor's wishes, she had gone south with young Lachlan and Mr Meiklejohn to a house in Putney, so that her son could go to school nearby. She was accompanied by her niece, the 31-year-old Miss Catherine Maclaine, fourth of the Lochbuy girls, and only slightly less giddy than the youngest, Miss Jane Jarvis. They were the only two still unmarried, and, following their mother's death, were as unruly as teenagers.

Catherine wrote to her brother Murdoch, who was not sure if he should be apprehensive about letting her loose, describing life in Putney with 'Aunt', a title which sounded primmer than Elizabeth actually was. She was meeting many old friends from Mull in Surrey. One was Andrew Halliday, the tutor who had come to Lochbuy when she was eight years old, and who had written an account of the influenza epidemic which had gripped half of the population of Mull. He was now Sir Andrew, a distinguished physician who attended the Duke of Clarence, and went to balls at Bushy Park.[44] Catherine was an incorrigible flirt, and 'longed for' visits from Dr Colin MacTavish of the Laggan family, Hector Pennycross, who worked in London, and other guests. She adored children, and bought presents for her nephews and nieces. Her letters are gossipy, and must have been alarming to her correct brother, who wrote to instruct that she must not return to Mull in the company of Mr Meiklejohn, as she suggested. Young ladies, of course, at this time, could not travel alone. Catherine was alternately ill and well, one moment asking Murdoch to come down to collect her because she was so ill: 'Aunt … will never be at the expense or trouble of going the length of her *toe* with me,' and the next moment being out of the house when the doctor arrived. 'Oh how I should delight to see you both *pop in*,' she told her brother in 1825 as Chirsty was beginning on her ninth pregnancy. 'I can't make out what has become of Colin MacTavish. I wish so much to see him.'

In March 1825, eight months after the death of the governor of New South Wales, Catherine and Elizabeth had had an expensive jaunt to London. 'She has taken a sudden desire for *gaity*,' Catherine wrote, 'and takes a drive into *London* three times a week, spends the day and returns home at night. Yesterday she entertained a party of twelve and was all day in the *highest glee* possible. If it would have the same effect I wish she had the same to entertain *every* day, but going into London every day quite ruins me … Lachlan seems to enjoy the most perfect health and good spirits. He is a great favourite at school.' [45] Mr Meiklejohn had returned to Mull before the 'jaunts' began. He had more serious things to think about, and now that young Lachlan was at school, he was attending heritors' meetings in Mull on behalf of the trustees, and turning up at presbytery. He also acted for Charles, who was frequently in Edinburgh arranging his troubling financial affairs. In spite of which, he was considerate of Murdoch's interest. 'I expressed my uneasiness to Colonel Macquarie,' Donald WS wrote, 'and he with the greatest expression of affection and kindness to you, said that whatever the consequence might be, he would raise the money.'

But Lauchlan Maclaine (who was exactly the same age as Charles, and a bachelor), sympathised. 'His asthmatic cough must always be troublesome to him in cold weather,' and 'no one is to be pitied more. He has no relation living to whom he can with pleasure commit the care of his children, the only respectable relative he has living (Lochbuy), being at variance with him. A father going to death under those circumstances, however well provided his family is, is much to be pitied.' Nobody fully appreciated the extent of Charles' financial difficulties, and as he grew more ill, his old wound was blamed. He was not a drinker, and must have been one of the very few men in Mull who did not overindulge.

His relations with his tenants and inhabitants were firm, but kind. He knew the Ulva people and their circumstances so well that he tended to give reductions to those who had no hope of finding their rent in cash. One such concession is in a letter to Donald Macquarrie 'Torquil' in Abass, of 18 February 1833.

> Donald,
>
> I am always well pleased when people wish to know how their account stands. You have your state[ment] on the other side [of the letter] reduced to a low rent. If you are to move, let me know immediately, as others will be glad to have your croft if I give it at £9, to which I have reduced it to help you, but I do not mean to give it to others at that rent.
>
> Yours, etc.
>
> C. Macquarie

Donald Torquil, about fifty years of age with six children, should have paid £10, and had arrears of over £15 in 1835. Such indulgence did not help Charles' own financial plight, but he remains one of the few proprietors to try standing in the shoes of the poor people. It was not surprising that when he died in March 1835, a fortnight after his sister-in-law, Elizabeth Henrietta had died at Gruline, 'a great concourse of common people were in attendance.' Again, our diarist, who dearly loved lists, enumerated Lochbuy, Young Lachlan Macquarie, Colonel Macdonald of Inch,[46] Charles' three sons, Charles, George and Lachlan, Dugald MacLachlan of Killiemore, Donald Campbell late Achnacraig,[47] Mr MacKinnon late Derriguaig,[48] the Revs Neil and Duncan Macleans,[49] the Rev. Dr MacArthur,[50] John Stewart of Achadashenaig, Mr

Lachlan Maclean Kilbrenan,[51] Mr Dugald Campbell Knock,[52] and Mr D. Stewart.[53] Because of the journey, Mr Donald Maclean WS had not been able to arrive until the following morning to convene a business meeting as Charles Macquarie's lawyer.

With the repositories sealed up in the usual manner, and the uneasy expectation that news of the financial situation might not be joyful, the main thing was to hear who had been appointed as trustees and guardians. These were to be Murdoch Maclaine of Lochbuy, Donald Maclean WS and Young Lachlan of Jarvisfield who had turned twenty-one the day after Charles' death. Charles' own sons were all minors. The factor of Ulva, Hector Campbell, was so drunk after the funeral that he had to be dismissed, and Mr Stewart, the tutor (like Mr Meiklejohn in similar circumstances) was requested to attend to all the inventory making and preparation of rentals and arrears which would be required. He was in fact to collect all the arrears. The heritable debt on the estate of Ulva, and on the as yet unsold Glenforsa, was estimated at £31,000.[54]

Charles Junior, who was not yet twenty-one, showed to his credit that he had no expectations. He wanted to be a ship's carpenter, and would learn the trade with his maternal uncle in Liverpool. His father had left a sealed and private letter for him, which remained private. George would go into the army, Lachlan would go to sea and Marianne was invited to go to Lochbuy to be with her cousins, Lillias and Jane being about the same age. The seven-year-old Murdoch was to be examined by doctors and pronounced upon. There was something not quite right about little Murdoch.

Charles Junior was concerned about the tenants and cottars of Ulva. He pleaded for an extension of time to allow them to pay arrears, and requested that they should not be sequestrated. Donald Maclean WS was of the same mind. Murdoch Lochbuy was convinced that the sequestration of bad payers would be an encouragement to potential buyers, who would not care to have 700 poor people on the estate. It was the difference of opinion between Donald Maclean and his son-in-law that led to the serious breach which has already been described in Chapter 16. Charles' motive in appointing Murdoch the twentieth of Lochbuy as an executor, guardian and trustee, when he must have known so well how impersonally 'the Chief' would treat his tenants and cottars, can only be attributed to some feeling of retributive justice, or strong faith in Murdoch's probity. Murdoch, usually so slow to deal with his own business, certainly regarded himself as the prime mover in Charles' affairs. In the summer of 1835 the two estates of Glenforsa and Ulva were exposed for sale. One man, Francis William Clark, a lawyer in Stirling, had already offered for Ulva on its own. He did not want Lagganulva, or any superfluous islands, and bid £28,500 for the island, reducing his offer to £27,000 on certain conditions. He did not want to be responsible for the church, or the roads on Mull. 'The gentleman from Stirling will not pay a fancy price,'

Murdoch observed to Young Lachlan, who was now in the Scots Greys. Murdoch had decided that Young Lachlan, having come into his inheritance, was an ideal buyer. Lachlan had not realised that his cousins were to inherit nothing in the way of land. He was surprised, and tempted by Glenforsa, which would make a good extension to Jarvisfield. At £12,500, Glenforsa would add a nice little piece of deer-hunting to Lachlan's property. And so it was that Glenforsa went to the heir of the governor in 1836.[55]

The young man had married, in January of that year, Isabella Campbell, one of seven daughters of Colin Campbell of Jura. His will and marriage contract made elaborate provision for the children they would never have. Instead, Lachlan transferred his affection to the bottle, and to his wife's sister, regarding whom there was a scandal which provided fodder for the prurient.[56] His increasing expenditure on drink and boisterous living was attended by an increase in debt, owed mainly to his friend, the Hon. William Henry Drummond, later Viscount Strathallan. After enlivening the Mull scene with unwonted scandal, Young Lachlan fell down a stone staircase at Craignish Castle, his father-in-law's home, in 1845, and died at the age of thirty-one. His body was taken to Gruline to join those of his parents in what is now the Macquarie Mausoleum.

The Macquarie proprietorship of Mull estates which in the old days had been owned by Lachlan MacQuarrie of that Ilk and his bibulous friend, John Maclaine of Lochbuy, as well as by the Macleans of Duart and the Duke of Argyll, had lasted thirty years, or one generation. The desire to possess land had been a driving force in two brothers, quite unalike in character. Inspired by the example of their uncle, Murdoch the nineteenth, who had applied commonsense principles to the management of an estate, and by his ability to rise from a state of overwhelming debt to a respected position among the heritors, they had begun their climb in the worst economic climate. Yet worse was still to come, and after their deaths, their children had not succeeded in carrying on their name in Mull. Charles, in particular, receives no recognition for the judicious manner in which he factored the Lochbuy estate, and for the extraordinary compassion he showed, at his own expense, to common people in an age when it was normal and right, and even wise to sequestrate and evict. In the public enquiries held in the late nineteenth century, those Mull men who gave evidence did not remember what the name of Macquarie stood for, unless it was the name of a man who had cut off the heads of ducks with his sword.[57] 'The evil that men do lives after them. The good is oft interred with their bones.'

Notes

1. His chief Australian biographers are M. H. Ellis and John Ritchie. The principal Scottish authority is R. W. Munro.

2. Stoppard, Tom, *Rosencrantz and Guildenstern are Dead.* 1967.

3. NAS. GD174/1329. Letters, DM to MM, 1779–1801.

4. NAS. GD174/1373. LM in Greenock to MM at Cecil Street Coffee House, Strand, 5 March 1784.

5. Old Lady Lochbuy, Archy's mother, was staying with her daughter Mrs Reid at Port Glasgow.

6. NAS. GD174/209/16. Jottings made by MM, 1799. 'the Tailzie which he airtfully obtained'.

7. NAS. GD174/1479/11. John Maclean Tacksman of Gruline (Nephew) to MM, 5 March 1800. Fifteen years later, John was asked by MM to question Miss Ketty on the events of 1784–85.

8. See Chapter 11 and ibid.

9. Although after GM's death, LM was much afraid that 'Poor Gillean' had not been as provident as a man bred up to the law ought to have been. NAS. GD174/1373/5. LM to MM, Bombay, 25 December 1789.

10. GRO. Uncatalogued MSS. LM to GM, Oskamull, 20 December 1786.

11. NAS. GD174/1410/166. John Stevenson, Oban to MM.

12. Munro, R. W., Gov. Lachlan Macquarie, etc., in *Scottish Genealogist*, 36, 1, 1989. CM's recruits were not all from Mull, but it is likely that 50 per cent were.

13. Torosay Old Parish Register, baptism 3 July 1794. 'Charles Macquarie and Janet McLean both in Moy, a child begotten in fornication – Hector.'

14. LM had been sent to Egypt from India with Sir David Baird after serving in the second siege of Seringapatam.

15. Munro, and NAS. GD174/1373/20.

16. NAS. GD174/1484/59. CM to MM, Edinburgh, 20 March 1796.

17. NAS. GD174/1373/30. LM to MM, Bombay, 6 December 1802.

18. Chapter 15, when Andrew Halliday had heard rumours of the Edinburgh sale.

19. NAS. GD174/1373/30. LM to MM, Bombay, 6 December 1802.

20. George Willison's money financed several loans in Argyll, e.g. to Allan Drimnin and his son Charles in 1785. NAS. Abbreviated Register of Sasines, Argyll.

21. NLS. MS 3833. LM to CM, 30 March 1816. Charles was forty-four.

22. NLS. MS 3833. LM to CM. 6 November 1816.

23. NAS. GD174/1627/2. Copy letter, MM2 to CM, Edinburgh, 20 January 1814.

24. 'Torosay' meaning the duke's lands in the parish of Torosay. Most of Torosay parish, except for the area including Duart Castle, Kilpatrick, Ardchoirk, Ardura and Achnacroish, belonged to the old Barony of Moy, and therefore to the Lochbuy estate.

25. NAS. GD174/1628/437. DMWS to MM2, 8 February 1827.

26. NLS. MS 3833. LM to CM, Sydney, 4 September 1820.

27. Ritchie, p. 198.

28. Robert Meiklejohn (1800–59), son of Professor Hugh Meiklejohn, was later minister at Alford.

29. The house is confusingly referred to as Duart, Torgormaig, Achnacroish and Torosay in Charles' time, and as Achnacroish in Colonel Campbell of Possil's day. After 1856, when David Bryce designed the present Torosay Castle for John Campbell, the estate was called Duart, and it was not until 1911 that the owner of today's Torosay returned the name of Duart to the restored castle on Duart Point.

30. Before Fitzroy had inherited the title through the death of his brother, Sir Hector, in 1818.

31. The Duart Macleans, with Fitzroy, were beginning to entertain the notion of restoring Duart as early as 1820. It took them ninety years to realise their ambition.

32. The future seventh Duke of Argyll.
33. Dugald MacDougall of Gallanach had married Margaret Maclaine, young Murdoch's sister, in 1815.
34. GRO. Maclaine Papers. Box 25. LMD's diary, 23 July 1824.
35. Laggan(ulva) – not to be confused with Laggan at Lochbuy.
36. See Chapter 14 for list of Ulva tenants.
37. NAS. GD174/1087/1/10. *Particulars of the Estate of Ulva*, 1824.
38. NAS. CH2/273. Mull Presbytery Minutes, 7 May 1817. Letter from CM read out.
39. GRO. Maclaine Papers. Box 25. LMD's diary, 15 August 1824.
40. Name of the area around Ulva House.
41. Hector Macquarie, Charles' natural son, who was now thirty-four years old.
42. NAS. GD174/1628/477. DMWS to MM2, Edinburgh, 5 April 1828.
43. See Chapter 15.
44. Who in 1830 became King William IV.
45. NAS. GD174/1634/12. Catherine Maclaine to MM2, Putney, 7 March 1825.
46. Colonel Robert Macdonald of Inchkenneth, younger brother of 'Staffa'.
47. Donald Campbell, husband of Lochbuy's sister, Elizabeth, so disliked by MM2, but accepted by CM.
48. Hector MacKinnon, an Argyll tenant in Derriguaig, had unsuccessfully appealed to MM2 for a reduction in rent in 1822, and had 'ended his tenancy'.
49. Rev. Neil, Charles' former tutor, now minister of Ulva, and Rev. Duncan, first minister of Salen Quoad Sacra parish.
50. Rev. Dr Donald MacArthur, minister of Kilninian.
51. Lachlan Maclean, Kilbrenan whose own death was 'anxiously wished for' by Alexander Shiells, see Chapter 12.
52. Dugald Knock, brother of Donald, who had given LM and Elizabeth hospitality on their return to Mull.
53. D. Stewart, tutor to the Macquarie sons, Charles, George, Lachlan and Murdoch.
54. NAS. GD174/35/1–5. Colonel Macquarie's trustees.
55. Correspondence, MM2 and LM Junior, NAS. GD174/1707. Abbreviated Register of Argyll Sasines, 1836.
56. Young Lachlan blamed a doctor resident in his house for a 'most diabolical report' that a hair comb belonging to Miss Mary Campbell, his sister-in-law, had been found in Lachlan's bed. NAS. GD174/1731. L. Macquarie to Colin Campbell of Jura, 14 January 1842.
57. MacCormick, John, *The Island of Mull*, p. 64. Charles Macquarie Junior disputed the will of Young Lachlan, claiming that his cousin was insane, and the story of the ducks' heads was given as proof of irresponsibility. Like every other challenge to a will in Mull history, this one failed, simply because judges were reluctant to question the will of the deceased. In this case, young Lachlan added several codicils as his debts to Drummond increased. For this reason, the bequest was perfectly valid, although LM had wanted his estates to pass to Charles' descendants if Lachlan did not survive.

Tha tighinn fodham eiridh. Words in Gaelic and English for the song James Boswell referred to as 'Hatyin foam'. (*Edinburgh University Library*)

18

Tha tighinn fodham eiridh:
it comes upon me to arise

James Boswell's favourite song, *Tha tighinn fodham eiridh*, which he called 'Hatyin foam'[1] refers to the desire to rise and go and follow Prince Charles Edward Stuart, but the boatmen who sang it with such passion for at least 100 years after the '45 may have been thinking of a different kind of going, and a very different destination. The excitement which Johnson and Boswell witnessed in Armadale with the 'dance called America' lay under the surface of life in many other island communities. When rents were too high, the weather too bad, or when hunger was forecast in disastrous harvests, emigration was a possible way out. America promised an alternative kind of hardship, for they had all heard stories of freezing winters without food, and of thick dark forests waiting to be cleared.

But over the years there were many different kinds of emigration, most of them obscured from our view by a total absence of documentation. The eighteenth-century emigrants were quite unlike the nineteenth-century ones, and even from decade to decade the pattern shifted. The first years of the nineteenth century were characterised by a new phenomenon, for just as the army's need for recruits brought the crimp sergeant into being, so the large numbers of wavering would-be emigrants created a niche for the emigration agent.

Before the agents and merchants came on the scene, emigration had been an adventure mainly for the middle classes. There is a belief that the 'late tacksmen' (referred to by Duncan Forbes of Culloden in his reorganisation of the Argyll estates in 1737 as 'harpies') emigrated to America. These were mostly Campbells, and it would be difficult to distinguish them from other Argyll Campbells who left at this time. Their association with Mull would not have lasted more than one generation. More identifiable, however, were the Macleans who went to Jamaica in the mid-eighteenth century. There was scarcely a family of Macleans in 'the Country' who were literate, and did not have a son or two in Jamaica. The Macleans of Brolass, Calgary, Drimnin, Duart, Garmony, Gruline, Inverscadale, Killunaig, Kingairloch, Lochbuy, Scallastle, Suie, Torloisk, and Torran all sported Jamaican connections. These young men had often gone first to Glasgow, Greenock or London, as Murdoch Maclaine had gone to Edinburgh, to follow a trade, had found themselves involved in West Indies business, and had begun by going out to establish links for their firms. Some stayed, some died young, but they all had a network of friends and relations of such dimensions that there was always a Maclean to turn to. Connections in Jamaica lasted long. Donald Maclean WS sent his difficult son Hector out in 1818, in the knowledge that some of the eighteenth-century emigrants would still be there to give him help.

> Hector goes off on Monday for Jamaica. I could make nothing better of him, and the sum for his outfit is very serious. If he is diligent and attentive he will get on. If not, he will not long live there, and his death would be preferable to his not doing well. I have written to Lachlan Maclean [2] and I have no fear of his not being placed in a comfortable situation if he makes good use of it. The misery I have suffered and suffer at this moment on his account is beyond all bounds. Sending an unfortunate thoughtless fellow at his age loose upon the wide world is a dreadful thought.[3]

The thoughtless fellow was one of those who did not last long in Jamaica, probably through not contacting his father's friend Lauchlan, for in November of the same year Donald was reporting his death.

> I have again to communicate sad tidings to you of my unfortunate family. My poor Hector I have forever lost. In going to Spanish Town, where a situation was provided for him, his mule threw him, and he died in consequence. The letter giving the account is dated so far back as the 5th August, yet I myself have no letter. Still, there can be no possible doubt as to the authenticity of the account. It is most strange that Lauchlan Maclean has not written.[4]

The West Indies attracted individuals who could afford the passage, and a few later landowners in Mull, like James Forsyth and Alexander Crawford, were the sons of men who had made money in Jamaica. It did not occur to this class of expatriate that they might not return to Scotland, since their exile usually provided the means to come back in style. But the next group of eighteenth-century emigrants were also the first wave of Highland soldiers to serve with the British army after the '45. The Seven Years' War of 1756–63 took a large number of Mull soldiers to north America, who afterwards settled in the colonies, and were recruited once more by Allan Maclean of Torloisk for the Royal Highland Emigrants in 1776. These men had brought families out, but did so on an individual basis, as was reported in a letter of 1773 to John Maclaine, tacksman of Gruline, by one Malcolm Maclean.

> Sir,
>
> I take this opportunity to let you know that I arrived at Boston in New England the 30th of October last in good health, Blessed be God for it, my wife and mother-in-law is in good health, and we all stay with John Livingstone, my father-in-law in a country place called New Boston about sixty miles from the Town of Boston. Sir, if it is possible that you could send me £10 sterling with the first opportunity of a sure hand, direct it to me

to the care of Mr James Anderson, merchant in Boston, for £10 would be of more service to me at this time than £20 at a twelve hence. I had the pleasure of seeing Captain John Campbell of Ardnacross, which told me he would write to you ... so that the money may be forwarded with safety and dispatch.

My brother Neil, I should be glad if he was sent to Hector McLean, tailor, to learn that trade, which I shall be at the expence of his prentice fee. I should have wrote to my father and mother[5] and all other friends, as Expect to be home in about two years, therefore my Cloaths that I left may remain till farther opportunity.[6]

The reduction of Scottish regiments in Nova Scotia after the American war, and the subsequent land grants in the area of Windsor, Nova Scotia, to men of the 84th Regiment do not seem to have led many Mull names to that quarter, although men in Murdoch Maclaine's company not belonging to Mull took up land.[7] In spite of Allan Maclean of Torloisk's claim that he had found 200 men of the name of Maclean in the Mohawk Valley alone, none of these appear to have been awarded land in Nova Scotia at the close of the war.[8] The only Maclean who settled in this region, having served in the 84th, was a correspondent of Murdoch's called Hector Maclean, who may have had Mull origins, but was born in Golden Square in London in 1751.[9]

The unhappy wreck of a ship off the American coast in November 1785, carrying families from Saorphein and Rossal, has been mentioned in Chapter 9, but these communications conveying news of random emigration must testify to only a tiny proportion of departures for the new world. Another indication of the extent of emigration, or of migration within Scotland, is in open-ended records in the baptism and marriage registers. In those registers the most fervent of adventurers and emigrants, the young, able-bodied unmarried men, are not represented at all, yet among couples who marry and have children, there is a constant disappearing which is too great to be put down to death or infertility, stillbirths or miscarriages, or the failings of missionaries and ministers in recording the data.[10] These disappearances are the more extraordinary because they happen to couples who began to follow the time-honoured pattern of marriage, which might be expected to bring them the average Mull family of 5.5 children, and then they simply cease to exist. When a married couple of the early nineteenth century stays in Mull, they can usually be picked up in the first census of 1841. But a study of marriages in the period 1807–27, for all three parishes of Mull, gives an astonishing 46 per cent return of disappearances taking effect between 1807 and 1841.[11] Not all of these couples went to north America; many are known to have gone to the Lowlands or other Highland areas, and there was a tendency to settle in Oban and other growing Argyllshire towns. But if we add to the number of missing persons an estimate of the young unmarried men who emigrated or served in the French wars, we might arrive at a total reduction of the population amounting to between 50 and 60 per cent. This depopulation was, however, being constantly remedied by the acquisition of new people, like the cottars from mainland areas such as Ardnamurchan and Morvern who were dispossessed in one fell swoop in 1828.

This picture of flux in the population may appear to resemble the activity of ants, but in fact there was nothing hectic about the movements in and out of the island in the first quarter of the nineteenth century. Torpor and indecision reigned. The tacksman of Tiroran, John Maclaine, was only one example of a head of family who had been thinking about emigrating for twenty years before he could bring himself to leave. In 1804, John Tiroran wrote to Murdoch Maclaine to object to a precept of removal which had been delivered to some of the poorest of the Ardmeanach cottars:

> I am very sorry that a Man of your Calling and Ranke, and of your throng family, could be moved against innocent people, and particularly against objects of Charity. The very people I now speak of, Hector MacNeil and Mary Obirn his wife, who is to be deprived of their poor portion of lands, is, in a manner, as great objects as are now in the three parishes. The said Hector MacNeil is for a long time on our poor list. He can neither walk, see or speak ... His wife is little better. God forbid that you wid distress such poor people. For Meen Malice which time and witness can prove, this case is so moving in itself that every Individuall ought to take the Allarm. Notwithstanding of all the Lands that was upon this Property or Estate, since your predecessor came from Ireland there was not a single instance of warning enny of the Obirns till now. The two innocent lads is now thinking of Emigration, like many other, and so ought every Individuall that can do it, or that intends well.[12]

As a man who had been keeping his eye on emigration for so long, John Tiroran knew that he might exploit the delicate situation that the lairds were in. They were now seen to be oppressors of the poor, and by his letter, John rubbed this in rather effectively by citing the case of poor Hector MacNeill. In 1803, legislation had been passed which, in a roundabout way, had put a stop to emigration. The Ship's Passenger Act purportedly improved conditions on ships bound for overseas destinations by making laws about provisions, health and accommodation, but in fact these new standards pushed up the price of the passage so much that the ordinary Highlander could not afford to take out a family. John Tiroran, who had sixteen children, must have found his prospects much diminished.

The trade in emigrants had become an industry in itself, attracting a new breed of emigration agent.[13] Ranald Macdonald of Staffa's brother, Hector Macdonald, a lawyer who had taken his wife's surname of Buchanan, was involved in curtailing the activities of the merchants, as well as trying to push through prosecution of tenants with leases, who were under legal obligations to remain with their landlords.[14]

We have seen in a previous chapter how skilled 'Staffa' was at putting
across a favourable view of the island of Ulva. He was also rather skilled at
publicising himself. In 1803 or thereabouts, he and his brother Hector were
'helping poor cottars to move to America' and negotiated with a certain
emigration agent, James Robertson of Prince Edward Island, for their accommodation. Mr Robertson had operated on the principle that the more he could
squeeze into a ship the better, and indeed, his success in recruiting emigrants
must have posed a threat to those landowners who wished to retain a large
labour force. The Boisdale Macdonalds, with their interest in kelp, were keen
to find a judicious balance in the emigration of the superfluous inhabitants
and the retaining of their kelp workers. Influential in the Highland Society,
which argued against emigration, the Boisdales, as represented by 'Staffa' and
Hector Macdonald Buchanan, engaged Robertson in a process which would
add weight to the arguments against emigration, and which helped the passage
of the Ship's Passenger Act. The Act, which appeared to be for the public
good, in that it did change conditions on board ship, with regulations limiting
numbers of passengers, ensuring clean water supplies, and providing food, by
indirectly raising the price of passage to North America, prevented families
who had saved enough money from emigrating, but Staffa was able to explain
to his own people from Ulva, and his neighbours in Mull, that the changes
were of great benefit to them, although he was also making sure that an
enormous outflow of kelp workers was stemmed. The poet John Maclean [15]
decided to put into shape a poem about Ranald Macdonald, Lord of Staffa,
'young Ranald, the man who takes such pains for the people' because the other
bards were beginning to forget what he had done for them when they sailed
away in the early years of the nineteenth century.

> Bha'n Robastanach eucorach
> Gan eigneachadh air bòrd;
> Chuir e gu mór an teanntachd iad,
> Gur gann a dh'fhan iad beò.
> B'i sin an naidheachd uabhasaich,
> Bha'n tuagh aige 'na dhòrn,
> 'S e maoidheadh air a' cheann thoirt diubh
> Mur tionndadh iad ga 'n deòin.
>
> B' e òrdagh teann don stiùramaich'
> An cùrsa 'chur mun cuairt;
> Is b' éiginn daibh a sgriobhadh dha
> Gun d' thill iad ri an-uair.
> Gu dalma bhrist e 'chùmhnantan,
> 'S an cuid ga spùinneadh bhuap' –
> Cha tric a chunnacas aintighearna
> Cho giomach, aingidh, fuar.

Nuair chuala Raonall Dòmhnallach
Mun t-seòl a rinn a' bhéist,
'S mu fhulangas nan Gaidheal
Gun do rinn a nàdar leum,
Gu dian 'na aghaidh thòisich e
Ri connsachadh gu geur,
'S cha sguir e dheth 's am fògrar e
Gu còrsa Bhot'ney Bay.

The poet would not let the events of the emigration years sink into oblivion (as they undoubtedly have sunk) and these three verses are the most dramatic of the story. Exactly translated, they run:

Robertson was criminal in forcing them on board; he put them greatly in distress, that they could scarcely stay alive. That was the terrible story. He had his axe in his fist, threatening to cut their heads off if they would not bend to his will. It was a strict order to the steersman to put the course around; and they had to write to him that they had returned on time. Obstinately he broke contracts, robbing them of their possessions. It is not often that such a grasping, vicious, cold tyrant has been seen. When Ranald Macdonald heard about the voyage the beast had made, and about the suffering of the Gaels, his nature made a leap, he began disputing vehemently and sharply with him, and he will not cease till he (Robertson) is exiled to the coast of Botany Bay.[16]

If other nobility, the poet adds, would be like Staffa in good breeding, their subjects would respect them, and would gladly sacrifice their cattle, if the gentry would be as they ought to be – merciful, compassionate and zealous.

Murdoch Maclaine, like others of the landowning class at this time, was apprehensive about emigration for three reasons. First it interfered with the setts of his land and continuity of rents; second it took kelp workers from his shores, and he was hoping to have some of the kelping rights that Gillean had arrogated restored in a submission with Scallastle; and third, since Bonaparte was daily expected to invade England, and men were urgently needed, recruitment would be more difficult than ever. He had written to his nephew Lachlan Macquarie, who had now returned to London after serving in India for fifteen years, and who regularly saw the men who were making military policy. Murdoch asked Lachlan about the rumour that the Canadian Fencibles were attracting Highlanders who wanted a free passage to Canada, and if it were true that Colonel Thomas Peters had been authorised by the government to offer passages at public expense. Lachlan was 'sorry to tell that Colonel Peters had been fully empowered'.[17]

Thus it seemed that the landlords were being beseiged on all sides. Their people were becoming rebellious, and even tacksmen like John Tiroran, who had once signed his letters to Murdoch Maclaine 'Yours affectionately', was now berating his laird in the most audacious manner. Complaints were being voiced which would have lain dormant in the days of John Lochbuy. In 1803, Tiroran addressed Murdoch on the subject of the general discontent among the Ardmeanach people.

> I am sorry to find it the generall Voice amongst all your people that they consider themselves far behind in many respects that you could better them in, such as Volunteering, Roads, Churches and Schools, etc. All their Neighbours have the satisfaction of these things and many other pleasures forby. I remember that I and all hereabouts offered our service some time ago, and I have your letter in answer to our Proposall, wherein you say, Pray will you be an officer without pay? The very Moment I came home I went to Scoble and got them all together, and delivered your orders to them – for which I have very bad thanks. It is rather hard that a person should have Reflection from both Master and the Tennants. However I prevailed so far that Lachlan MacQuarrie is to go to Morrow to settle for the herrings.[18]

John Tiroran was a difficult man, but he had had his troubles to contend with, not least in his past quarrels with Gillean Maclaine, who had tried to take all the kelp of Ardmeanach into his own hands in the 1780s. Donald Maclean WS was to remember him with respect. 'Poor John Maclaine was at war with every neighbour he had, and was constantly involved in lawsuits and quarrels, yet on that farm he has brought up as Ladies and Gentlemen a family I believe of at least sixteen children, and I hope he will carry £500 away with him.'[19] As John himself said, it was hard to be reflected upon by both the master and the tenants, and the tenants were quite the most troublesome in Mull. His endless struggle to maintain a school at Tiroran was frustrated on all sides.

> The 9th of August last, it was proclaimed in Church[20] that the Schoolhouse should be thacked [thatched]. As I saw the Houss going to Ruine in November, I went to Scoble and offered the Tennants any resonable pay if they would thack the Houss, but they wid not. The day of the Great Storm the Houss was Stript, and will be of little use soon. Wid you approve of compraising the Timber by two people upon Oath, rather than it should be intirely lost. I wrote you when the people were paying their Rents, but was given not the least hearing.[21]

John was not above telling tales. He informed Murdoch that the Ardmeanach miller, Rory McMillan, intended to give him the slip, wriggling out of his lease by selling his cattle privately and going to Greenock, where he would stay with friends until he was able to get a passage to America. This was exactly the kind of conduct that Hector Macdonald Buchanan was trying to prevent, but it took so long to prepare the legal documents, and to gather the details of the lease, that many a tenant was able to scamper off in this fashion.

One of the characteristics of Mull people which operated against their desire to take French leave was their sense of duty to aged parents. They would wish to leave 'the Country' in a family group, but to abandon an old couple to be *mar Oisean an deidh na Féinne*, like Ossian after the Fian, or alone in their old age, was something they could not bring themselves to do. The old people were ill adapted to either the voyage or the subsequent hardship of living in such severe winters as they heard of from Canada. Mull was renowned for the longevity of its people, and cases are known where a very large family, hardly able to feed itself, and desperate for land, would have to remain with a parent until death released them. In Torosay parish, an extended family of Lamonts delayed their emigration for as much as seventeen years because the patriarch, Malcolm Lamont, lived into his eighties, and could not be left behind.[22] Reluctance to emigrate, or procrastination, was not the result of a lack of will, but often betrays to us the shadowy figure of a lingering parent. Dr Norman Macleod, minister of St Columba's, in a poetic Gaelic essay about an emigrant ship,[23] quotes an old man whose daughter and grandchildren are leaving.

> On no journey will I go, until the great journey begins which awaits us all; and when that comes, who will bear my head to the burial? You are gone; you are gone; today I am left alone, blind and aged, without brother or son or support.

'Who will bear my head to the burial?' was the question which disturbed the old and young alike. It has been seen how the only savings a *Muileach* ever made was the sum he entrusted to the laird to pay for his burial. In spite of the undignified behaviour we have observed at funerals, and in contrast to the remarkable absence of marked gravestones from the eighteenth and early nineteenth centuries, all the treasure laid up on earth was destined to pay for the conspicuous consumption of whisky and the honour of having a long line of mourners. There was something in the attitude to the grave itself which was reminiscent of the tradition of spoken Gaelic poetry, which Dr Johnson had refused to believe in. Just as poetry was committed to memory and relayed from generation to generation, so the whereabouts of a grave was remembered down the years, and pointed out to descendants. The burial grounds which survive today – if we think about the size of the population in ages past – have the appearance of being relatively empty. Tiny markers of stone indicate the presence of a coffin, or even a less substantial covering – for wood was scarce. Elsewhere, where men fell, cairns mark the spot, and were added to by every passer-by who knew exactly who lay there. 'Who will remember where my grandparents' bones lie?' might just as well be the macabre question asked by intending emigrants from a society which knew the names of its begetters as though they were written in the book of Genesis.

Emigrant merchants were still operating in Mull until government took the initiative in the 1840s to provide assisted passages. The names of the merchants are as elusive as the names of ships or passengers have ever been, but one mentioned in 1829 was 'Mr McNiven', who may have been an Islay man.[24] By this time, the notoriety of such agents had died away, and they were not generally charged, as they had been at the turn of the century, with puffing up foreign lands and opportunities in an irresponsible way, or of threatening to cut off the heads of their passengers. By 1829 the people were recognised as being 'supernumary', even by themselves. There was no longer any conflict between lairds and people over the moral or practical issues. The agents were now helpful organisers, who often had to advise a family about difficult arrangements like transport to Glasgow or Liverpool, for fewer ships left from local ports. There was now no thought of preventing the people from leaving. 1836 was a year of famine which might be said to have been worse than the famous year of the potato blight, but for the fact that historians have concentrated on 1846 as the year of 'the Great Famine'.[25] In the spring, the people had no seed to plant. In May the solar eclipse prophesied hardship to come, the summer and autumn were exceptionally wet, and as early as October severe frost and snowstorms began to indicate that God was wreaking revenge on his people. 'Glenbyre House came down yesterday', Donald McPhee wrote to Murdoch Maclaine on 23 December. The back wall had fallen in, but the shepherds, living in the two ends, had escaped with 'a fright'.[26] With its mixed bag of afflictions, 1836 was, therefore, for those who took the risk of remaining in Mull until 1846, the practising ground for the year of the potato blight. All through the 1830s, the herring also deserted Hebridean waters[27] so that the *raison d'être* of Tobermory, its status as a fisheries station, was removed, and the village was hardly more than a refugee camp for people who had not been able to pay their rents, and who had been evicted as a result. Before the 1841 census, when the population of Mull was estimated at 11,026, it was recommended that 4,000 people should be removed to bring the island to a viable number.[28]

The agitation for an amendment of the Poor Law which began in the 1840s worried landowners and people alike, for the existing Poor Law, or recommendations for the relief of the poor, barely extended to conditions in the Highlands, where parishes had to conduct their own charitable relief. The presbytery, when it was not dealing with incest, bigamy, adultery and fornication, none of which were very widely practised in Mull, but which took up a disproportionate amount of time, yearly calculated how the collection for the poor at the church doors, augmented by fines for sexual misdemeanours, was to be distributed. Again, with the emphasis on the importance of burial, the dead scored over the living as recipients of charity, as coffins, costing 5s. each, were granted to those too poor to have laid up their mite against the day of their burial. A few epileptic and 'fatuous'[29] parishioners were given small sums of money to enable them to stay alive. With such need to provide for, the pennies in the church box could not possibly support people who were merely starving. To be a recipient of poor relief would have been to take money from the disabled and the dead, and would be regarded as shameful. Anyone who was not ashamed to beg nevertheless went to Coll or Tiree to do so, rather than be seen or talked of in Mull. Coll and Tiree beggars came to Mull, and were generally well received. Relations, of which everyone had scores, would always give some kind of food to the less fortunate of their blood line.

But the Poor Law Enquiry, like most public enquiries, was set in motion by a government which had already decided that an amendment to the present legislation was necessary, and the new arrangements would have to cover widely differing conditions, from towns like Glasgow, Paisley, and Greenock to rural Highland parishes. In June 1843, the commissioners visited Mull, after sending out a number of questions in the post to selected individuals. In the parish of Kilninian,[30] they listened to the views of Dr MacArthur, Captain Campbell in Quinish,[31] Mr Donald Campbell the minister of Ross, John Stewart of Achadashenaig; Dr Hector McColl, surgeon in Tobermory; Alexander Sinclair, farmer in Erray; Neil MacPhail, merchant in Tobermory, and Dougald McColl, teacher in Tobermory; Henry Nisbett, banker and procurator fiscal in Tobermory. This was a remarkable group of witnesses, demonstrating the presence of a new middle class of mostly Mull-born people. At least two of them might be described as 'radicals' in that they had, only weeks before, joined the ranks of the Free Church.[32] Asked to describe the condition of the poor, they were unanimous in their belief that a legal contribution instead of the voluntary contributions already in existence would do great harm to the social order. Every witness stressed that the tenants and farmers were remarkably good to the poor, and that if tenants and heritors were, by a new law, bound to support their poor neighbours, they would cease to give anything. All were agreed that the effect on the recipients of poor relief would be to make them dependent on the poor fund, so that they would stop trying to obtain work. As might be expected, Tobermory's incomers from Morvern and Ardnamurchan were in the greatest state of poverty. Each witness mentioned attitudes to emigration, and the numbers that had chosen to leave in the last few years. Twenty-seven families who had been removed from Calgary by Hugh MacAskill had gone to Australia and America. The largest 'supernumary' population was in the Ross of Mull, which still belonged to the Duke of Argyll.[33]

The Act for Amendment and Better Administration of the Laws relating to the Relief of the Poor was passed by parliament on 4 August 1845. Half of the poor assessment was to be imposed on owners of land, and the other half on tenants or occupants according to the annual value of the land. This *blunder*, as Mr Robert Somers [34] was to call it three years later, fulfilled every expectation of the reasonable men who had given their opinions to the commissioners, and was to be responsible for a strangely varied set of reactions from owners and tenants alike. Heritors and long-term tenants sent for copies

Captain Lauchlan Maclaine's assessment for the support of the poor under the new Act, based on his rent of £8 10s. in Oban in 1846. (*GRO. Maclaine Papers*)

of the Act and perused it with dread and loathing. Some, like Francis W. Clark, the new owner of Ulva, were swift in their vengeance. Some, like the new Lochbuy, Young Murdie, buried their heads in the sands or went into hiding. Others, like Hugh Maclean of Coll began to cut the umbilical cord, making plans to sell. Some, like the Northampton family, saw the need to reduce their own populations and begin again. Others, who were not even owners, but mere lessees, without the means to pay the assessment, asked their subtenants to go, and to take 'their' cottars with them. Christian charity was one thing, but the survival of one's own family came first. In spite of present-day preconceptions about wicked and greedy aristocrats sending the poor to the colonies in shiploads, it has to be said that many who acted as a result of the Poor Law, were modest, hard-working farmers who simply could not be squeezed for another penny.

Notes

1. See Chapter 8.
2. This was Lauchlan Maclaine, the diarist ('LMD') son of Gillean, who had gone out as a planter in 1789 and who spent nearly thirty years in Jamaica, returning to Mull once in 1812–16, before retiring to Garmony in 1824. DMWS always spelt his name 'Maclean'.
3. NAS. GD174/1628/136. DMWS to MM2, 4 April 1818.
4. NAS. GD174/1628/148. DMWS to MM2, 7 November 1818.
5. 'Mother' inserted as an afterthought.
6. NAS. GD174/1294. Malcolm Maclean to JMG, Boston, 20 December 1773. Malcolm had probably left cattle with John to be sold by drovers, and so had some credit. This kind of small transaction was what made John's papers, all tiny notes, so chaotic. see Chapter 11.
7. Duncanson, *Rawdon and Douglas: two Loyalist Townships* …
8. Duncanson, p. 393.
9. A most interesting writer, his letters to MM are in GD174/2154. His descendants listed by Duncanson.
10. Author's card files of Mull heads of families, extracted from OPRs and censuses.
11. Author's study, unpublished, *Marriages in Torosay, Ross and Kilninian, 1804–1824.*
12. NAS. GD174/1485/35. John Maclaine to MM, Tiroran 30 March 1804. The predecessor from Ireland refers to someone very far back in the annals of LB.
13. The most detailed treatment of this development is in Bumsted, *The People's Clearance.*
14. Bumsted, p. 132.
15. Yet another poet of the name, this John came from Tiree and lived 1787–1848.
16. Maclean Sinclair, *Maclean Bards. Do Raonall Dòmhnallach Tighearna Stafa.* Trans. Charles Coventry.
17. NAS. GD174/1373/39/1. LM to MM, London, 25 January 1804.
18. NAS. GD174/1485/34. John Tacksman of Tiroran to MM, Tiroran 11 November 1803.
19. NLS. MS 20758. Letterbook of Donald Maclean WS. Letter to D. McIntyre, 22 January 1817.
20. The church building was used for announcements of a secular kind, as well as for presbytery matters. Roups, roadworks and even warnings to quit were read out at the church door in what might seem today a rather unseemly way, but it was the best way of catching the people in one place.
21. NAS. GD174/1485/24. John Maclaine, Tacksman of Tiroran to MM, Tiroran, 25 January 1801.
22. Censuses, LMD's diary, letter from Allan Lamont from Canada West. See Chapter 28.
23. Translated into English, this forms Chapter 20 of *Reminiscences of a Highland Parish.*
24. GRO. LMD's diary, Saturday 7 February 1829. 'Mr McNiven the emigrant merchant called and dined with me.' Dugald MacArthur in an article 'Some emigrant ships from the West Highlands' *in Trans. Gaelic Soc. of Inverness*, 1987, mentions a 'notorious' Archibald McNiven of Islay, who was said to have transported 12,000 Highlanders to Cape Breton, Nova Scotia, PEI and Upper Canada between 1821 and 1832.
25. Devine, *The Great Highland Famine.*
26. NAS. GD174/1120/45. Donald McPhee to MM, 4 September 1836. Glenbyre was admittedly always falling down, and even today, when it is still used as a sheep station, the two ends are the only sturdy parts.

27. First Report of the Select Committee on Emigration: Minutes of evidence, 1841, p. 6.
28. Emigration report, p. 21.
29. Fatuous being the word employed for the mentally handicapped in the census of 1851.
30. Kilninian as it had once been, embracing the new *quoad sacra* parishes of Tobermory, Ulva and Salen.
31. Factor to Hugh Maclean of Coll, whose territory included Tenga and Aros.
32. For the effects of the Disruption, or breaking away of the Free Church from the established church in 1843, in Mull, see Chapter 22.
33. Poor Law Inquiry (Scotland) Reports from Commissioners, 7. HMSO 1844, vol. XXI. Synod of Argyll, Presbytery of Mull.
34. Somers, Robert, *Letters from the Highlands; or the Famine of 1847*. See Chapter 26.

19

Of hubris in the affairs of men

Hubris (in Greek tragedy) an excess of ambition, pride, etc., ultimately causing the transgressor's ruin.

Collins Dictionary of the English Language

Edmund Burt, in his *Letters from the North of Scotland*, first published in 1754, was fond of pointing out a particular weakness of the Highlander – an excessive and unjustifiable pride. His extremely funny and underrated book is full of images of dignified chiefs living in hovels and Highland ponies walking on precipices unshod, because their owners could not afford blacksmiths; or lairds with high-sounding names who claimed that they were short of money because of the vast sums they gave in marriage portions to their daughters.

James Macdonald, a later commentator, in his *General View of the Agriculture of the Hebrides* of 1811, spoke of the 'amazing powers of the common Hebridean in conversation, which, interlarded with reflections upon the character and conduct of their superiors, and upon the hardships of their own condition, fills up their leisure hours. They have an idea that they deserve a better fate than that which is fallen to their lot. Nothing can convince them that poor people in other countries want the benefit of leases, and are turned out of their lands ... or in short, suffer all the same distresses resulting from indolence, poverty or misfortune, precisely like themselves. They always suspect that they are peculiarly ill-treated, and live under an ungrateful government and oppressive landlords.' [1]

Girls, Burt said, were vain of being with child of a gentleman – so great is their esteem for gentility. The girls concerned were mostly servants, and were thus put into close contact with 'gentlemen', but Burt did not observe that to be in service was not deemed a good thing. Things may have changed between the eighteenth and the nineteenth centuries. In the nineteenth, people did not like to be described as servants, and older women boasted that they had never been in service. Work extracted in part payment of rent was extremely unpopular, and often disregarded by cottars, who never appeared voluntarily to fulfil their contract, but always had to be sent for. In 1798, a tenant in Kilbeg, Hugh Morison, although very poor, felt he was demeaning himself by allowing his son to work for Murdoch the nineteenth of Lochbuy, and wrote to the laird to stipulate conditions for this degrading work. The boy must not clean knives in the kitchen, or herd cattle, 'or any suchlike as would be a *disparagement* to him in future, in case by the help of friends I could direct him to something better.'²

Donald Maclean WS had trouble finding servants in the Carsaig area. 'I will not have Marion McInnes on any terms. She was *officious, proud*, and, with these, their ordinary concomitant, *ignorant*.'³ The enumerators of the 1841 census had difficulties in fitting people into the categories provided. The rules laid down indicated that the term 'agricultural labourer' had to be used for anyone of the servant class, but in Mull everyone was a farmer and nobody's servant, no matter how small his potato patch. Statutory labour on the roads was particularly resented. 'I would like to know,' Alexander Shiells wrote, in 1830, 'what is the reason Mrs Maclean's⁴ servant man does not work for the statute labour at the roads. Mrs Clephane's own work people are obliged by law to work at the roads, and do work at them, and no other workman is exempt, and cannot be ...'⁵ But the small rate of remuneration, even for a penniless head of family, was insufficient to compensate for his loss of status. '*Is fhearr tàmh na obair a nasgaidh*,' the Gaelic proverb said. It is better to rest than to work for nothing.

All these were perfectly understandable instances of self-respect in a community where leisure time was important to the dignity of man. It was difficult for a man of good family to come to terms with the fact that there was no suitable employment for him. Schoolmasters were quite strictly examined on their knowledge of English, Gaelic and even Latin, which made it difficult for the average man to apply. Advertisements for newer posts such as collectors of customs, inspectors of the poor (required after the Poor Law legislation) and road surveyors were responded to with enthusiasm, but in the end usually went to outsiders.⁶

Pride and dignity, however, did not seem to extend to the conditions of houses, and tourists commented endlessly on the smokiness of the interiors. As early as 1732, Sheriff Campbell of Stonefield reported that 'their houses are all wattled of the inside from top to bottom, and instead of stone, which is not scarce with them, they build with green turf or sods, which soon melts or smoulders away, and needs to be yearly repaired.'⁷ Burt found houses on the mainland to be like 'fuming dunghills' ... the chamber pot a hole in the ground beside the bedside.' Frédéric Mercey, traversing Mull in about 1840, was led in the dark to a lodging at Bunessan, and was so exhausted by his walk through the glen that he lay down gladly on a bed of heather placed between stones, on top of which his guide had thrown his own partly dried plaid as a covering. In the morning, the French traveller was wakened by a cock crowing in his ear, actually right inside his room. 'La pièce que nous occupions était une succursale du poulaillier.'⁸

> The room we were in was a hen roost. I rose in the midst of a great clucking, opened the wattle screen and found myself back in the room we had supped in. Our guides were already up, one of them lighting lumps of

damp peat which were piled up in the centre of the room on a sort of altar, a foot and a half high, called a fireplace. The smoke, which was not channeled or confined or chased outside by any breath of wind, spread freely through the room, which had beams varnished glossy and black, shining like a scene in an interior by Rembrandt. We went out to get some fresh morning air. Only then did I have a clear view of the pleasure house we had been sleeping in. Imagine a hut about twenty feet high, with walls going in all directions, built of rough pebbles, and over this two rows of rough squares of turf, tied with strong wooden pegs on the west side, and with string made out of heather, then alternating rows of stones, and the spaces filled in with mud. The ceiling was constructed of long poles with little bunches of thatch and heath, on top of which (as in all mountainous places) boulders were placed to stop the house from flying away in a gale. Half a dozen of these savages' huts, with even smaller sheds attached to them, form a Hebridean village. Since these houses have the same reddish grey colour as the heather, unless they are built on a summit you can hardly distinguish them from the ground. You have to touch them to know that they are there. We had breakfast with eggs, tea and redcurrant jam. Then we left Bunessan to go by pony to a small bay where a boat was waiting to take us to Iona. It belonged to a fisherman with whom our guides had been bargaining the previous evening.

Although many smoke-filled cottages had been described, with a roof with a central smoke hole, it should be remembered that this was Bunessan in 1840, not 1740. The Mull people had been for many years travellers in other lands, and had seen other habitations. The people in Ross went for seasonal work to the Lowlands every summer, and knew what the Lowland houses were like. Yet they appeared to strangers to have no pride about their houses, or simply regarded the smokey 'dunghill' as blessedly comfortable. 'Highlanders,' said Burt, 'love the smoke. It keeps them warm.'

Robert Louis Stevenson visited Mull before he wrote *Kidnapped*, and the experience he gives to David Balfour, of landing near Fidden, was probably very similar to his own. He arrived at a house which was roofed with turf and built of unmortared stone, in which lived an old gentleman. 'I call him so because of his manners,' says the hero, 'for his clothes were dropping off his back. He took me by the hand, led me into his hut, for it was no better, and presented me to his wife, as if she had been the Queen, and I a duke. The house, though it was thick with peat smoke, and as full of holes as a colander, seemed like a palace.'

The most significant advance in the cleanliness of houses came in 1832, and had nothing to do with increased pride in the appearance of a house, or of the order within. The plague of cholera was approaching 'the Country' so quickly, brought into Argyllshire by people returning from Glasgow, that a meeting of heritors and church representatives was convened in each of the

Mull parishes. Inspectors were appointed to call upon all householders and instruct them to scrub the interiors of their dwellings, to wash the walls with lime water, to wash the cabbers of their beds with the same, to keep the spaces under their beds empty and clean, to replace the bedding with fresh straw, and to wash, occasionally, their bedclothes.[9] The occupants had to remove their dunghills to a distance from their doors, to lay down clean gravel in front of their houses to prevent mud from accumulating. They had to remove daily the droppings of their poultry from the hen roosts, and 'of those houses where the cattle occupy one end, remove every particle of dung'. Where possible they were to remove the cattle to outhouses, and pigs were on no account to be permitted to remain in the dwelling houses. M. Mercey's stay in the house of what he called '*un bon habitant de Bunessan*' was happily undertaken under these new improved conditions.

The chief manifestation of pride in the people of Mull was in family connection, and in not being 'reflected upon', a state of being to be anxiously avoided.[10] Among the gentry, Murdoch Maclaine seemed to be free of pride when he was a linen merchant and an officer, but was accused of having become 'high and mighty' after succeeding to the estate. Mrs Clephane was always described as haughty or cold, but had learned these attitudes in England. Colonel Campbell of Possil was a perfect gentleman whose courtesy to one and all was exemplary, although he was cut off from dialogue with the humbler people by his ignorance of the Gaelic language. Colonel Greenhill-Gardyne, in a time we have not yet reached, was loved by the Gaels and had Gaelic panegyrics composed in his honour. Young Murdoch the twentieth was foolish in his insistence on being chief of the clan, but he always had Gaelic at his command. His foible was that he was prickly in his relations with anyone who got above himself, like the pushy Hector Maclean Bunessan when he rented Carsaig, or Francis William Clark when he wrote an over-familiar letter. And yet young Murdoch was a clubbable man, popular with those he approved of, and able to drink with the best of them.

It is often women who are responsible for false pride in birth, and for an exaggerated idea of their husbands' and sons' importance in the world, and nobody was more guilty of this than Gillean's widow, Marie. A young, motherless girl like Mally MacQuarrie, courted by her father's bachelor lawyer, and longing to leave home, is unlikely to be put off by her lover's illegitimacy. There were many dashing natural sons in the eighteenth century, and this one must have seemed to her particularly talented. She would have known little of the business he was conducting with her father and MacQuarrie of Ormaig, and Gillean must have informed her that he was helping them. Later commentators like Colin Macdonald of Boisdale noted that he had been earmarking payments from the Ulva reversion for the use of himself and his heirs. Few women in the eighteenth century (excepting Murdoch Maclaine's two very practical wives) would have known what their husbands were up to, and Marie MacQuarrie was very uneducated and very stubborn. It was Marie who, according to Murdoch, was the 'promoter and conductor of the present trouble.' [11]

Even the most intelligent woman, giving birth to twelve children in seventeen years, hardly has time to look into her husband's business. Marie respected, feared and loved Gillean, and was often separated from him when she had to go to Crosscauseway in Edinburgh for the sake of the older children's education. But after his death she became like a lioness with her cubs, asserting herself, complaining, whining about her loneliness and her children's poor weak orphan state. All of her sons and daughters were brought into service to write the letters she could not write, like so many secretaries of an illiterate queen. The best amanuensis, her stepson Lauchlan, was sent off to Jamaica to fend for himself so that he would take nothing out of the mouths of her 'dear little ones'. Marie always pleaded poverty, but managed to buy ensigncies and other commissions for her sons. Apart from a very possible secret source of funds provided by Gillean, she had the rents from subtenants of Scallastle, Garmony and Ledirkle, and the income from kelp, which was profitable in the years between her husband's death and 1815. As she paid a fixed rent of £45 per annum to Lochbuy, she must have been one of the few solvent widows in the Country in these years. Marie, and Allan under her tutelage, always used the expression 'our family' of the Scallastles. This meant herself, her ten living children, and, reluctantly, Lauchlan. It did not include her own father, Lachlan MacQuarrie of that Ilk, or even her mother Alice's brothers and sisters. It is significant that although Marie was a first cousin of Mrs Clephane of Torloisk, there is no evidence of any communication between them. As for Marie's Allan, a second cousin of Margaret, he seemed like a creature from a different planet from the clever young woman who was to marry Lord Compton.

When Gillean died, Murdoch Maclaine had had no sons, so that Gillean may have imagined the entail taking its course, and his son Allan becoming laird of Lochbuy, although Lachlan Maclean of Torloisk had taken the unusual step of making his daughter his heir. But the Lochbuy entail, drawn up purportedly in 1776, had specified male heirs, and Gillean had Allan. If the entail dated from December 1784 (which was surely impossible, since it bore Archy's unmistakeable signature), the Lochbuy estate had four Scallastle boys to safeguard the future of the Maclaines of Lochbuy.

Marie was fiercely protective of her boys' rights, and acted like a queen mother grooming her oldest son for kingship. Even after the birth of young Murdoch in 1791, she must have hoped for and expected his demise. When Allan came of age, he joined her in the management of what they considered their 'estate' of Scallastle. Allan quickly developed a reputation for unreliability, and even his feckless grandfather, Lachlan MacQuarrie, once chieftain of the clan, blamed his own daughter for Allan's unlovely characteristics. When Allan told his mother that he was about to marry Marjory Gregorson of Ardtornish,

Marie was 'riotous' because she did not consider Marjory quite good enough for a prince of the blood.

Allan, as has been related already, put a great deal of effort into not answering letters and accounts, and refusing to communicate when there was any legal matter to settle between himself and Murdoch Maclaine, to whom he spoke in a patronising manner, as if Murdoch were managing Allan's estate in a temporary kind of way. For this reason, Allan would not pay even his low rent of £45 to Murdoch, considering that it was more likely Murdoch owed him rent. The idea, incubated and encouraged by the mother, became a kind of paranoia. Marie sent letters to Murdoch, which, dictated as they were, carried a tone of deep hurt and offence, which one might be forgiven for thinking Murdoch had induced by a harsh and hectoring approach, were it not for the fact that Marie kept all of Murdoch's letters to herself and to Allan, and that they are kind, patient and long-suffering.[12]

One of Allan's first acts when he returned to Mull at the age of seventeen, by his position as heir to Gillean, was the issuing of a number of decreets of removal to his own tenants through the office of Robert Campbell, sheriff-depute of Argyll. The people who were sentenced in 1789 were Alexander MacDougall, Neil Fletcher, John Fletcher, Duncan Black, Alexander Black, Duncan Currie, Alexander Currie, Neil MacInnes and Donald MacLaine, 'all pretended subtenants and possessors of the lands of Ledirkle'; also Hector MacVurich,[13] Hector Maclaine Senior, Malcolm Currie, Hector MacLaine Junior, Donald MacPhail and Neil MacCarmaig, pretended tenants and possessors each of a house and garden acre and grazing upon the lands of Garmony; Donald MacDonald, Changekeeper,[14] Alexander MacLaine, Workman, John Currie, Workman, Donald MacLaine, Herd, Neil MacNeill, Herd, John MacInnes, John MacLaine, Donald MacLaine, Weavers, and John Mac-Dougall, Shoemaker, pretended tenants and possessors each of a house, garden acre, and grazing upon the lands of Scallastle, ordaining them by the act of 1756 to 'flitt and remove themselves, wives, bairns, families, servants, subtenants and cottars,' etc. by Whitsunday 1789.[15] No reason was given for the order, but it is most likely to have been for non-payment of rent. At the very least, 100 people were likely to have been dependent on these men, for once again cottars are of an unknown quantity. Desirable as it might be to try to trace the fate of those two dozen men, it can only be said that in the 1790s, most of the names are present in the register of baptisms for Torosay, but names are so repetitive that one cannot assume that a Duncan Currie in Kinlochspelve in 1794 [16] is the same man as the Duncan Currie evicted from Ledirkle five years earlier. Similarly, Hector MacVurich or Currie in Garmony was only one of many Hector Curries, a name that was to continue in Garmony for more than fifty years. Even more problematical for the historical sleuth is the fact that in 1800, Sheriff Robert Campbell of Asknish once more issued decreets of removal to tenants of the same farms.[17] In Garmony, Hector MacLaine Senior, Hector MacLaine Junior, Charles MacLaine, Duncan

Maclean Junior, John Maclean, Widow Mary Maclean, John Currie, Hugh MacLaine and Malcolm Currie were all 'pretended subtenants'. In Ledirkle, John Fletcher Senior and John Fletcher Junior [18] were also to be ejected in 1800, with no reason given in the precept, although presumably a reason had been given verbally before the sheriff's decreet. In this case too, John Fletchers are in evidence in Mull records after 1800, so that it is impossible for us to know whether these two, senior and junior, left the island. This problem of the duplication of names prevents all attempts to draw conclusions about the contribution of precepts of removal to depopulation and emigration.

However, an idea of the kind of reasons for delivering a decreet of removal is apparent in a letter sent by Allan Maclaine of Scallastle to the sheriff one week after the Ledirkle notices of April 1800 had been sent. Alexander MacDougall, the tenant who was being evicted, was the innkeeper at Scallastle.

> Dear Sir,
>
> I received yours covering a copy of Alexander MacDougall's defences which astonishes me very much. When he came to the house [19] he had it equally good with the former possessors. I certainly promised him a few years possession if he had been at the expense of paying the Masons, but in place of his paying them I was obliged to settle with them ... In the next place he was at no expence whatever about rebuilding the said house further than his being idle, and he and his son leading a few stones to the builders. He never pays his rents regularly, and I am very often obliged to take spirits from him in payment of his rents, so that I am resolved to turn him out of possession. In the next place, against my will & orders he has kept goats & mares on the possession. In short he is by no means a man that I would wish to have in the said house.
>
> I now declare that the above is true, and that it is not for any advanced Rent that I am turning him off, but for his misbehaviour in not paying his rents and keeping oversoums on the grass, so that you better take out a decreet against him without loss of time.[20]

Apart from the incredible fact that Allan was totally blind to his own very similar 'misbehaviour' in not paying his due rents to Murdoch Lochbuy, this is an informative missive about how a very bad landlord, though only a tenant himself, could eject a subtenant who clearly did not have a written lease for the 'few years' possession' he had been promised. The sheriff would have been able to send out a decreet on the basis of the oversouming. But if one cannot accuse Allan Maclaine of Scallastle of random eviction of tenants, he certainly has a poor record when it comes to his venomous obsession with obstructing the sales of Lochbuy land. From Edinburgh in 1796, Allan wrote to his brother Murdoch in Scallastle:

> Dear Brother,
>
> As your Mother and me requires money immediately to carry on our law

pleas with Lochbuy ... go to Mr Colin Campbell Achnacraig and get his letter of security for Alexander McKinnon Derrichuaig, and recover my money from him instantly. Go to him yourself with Mr Campbell's letter. Write me instantly now Murdoch. Do not neglect this, as we can do nothing untill such time as we receive the money. Get a Draft for it from some person and send it to me with the account you neglected sending me before ... Mr Moore the accountant will not proceed further untill we have money to give the Advocates.

You may judge my situation for the want of the needdy if this does not answer, see if our friend Mr Campbell will do something for me. I saw your friend Lochbuy off in his carriage on his way to Gerrensay,[21] I saw Colonel Cliphen of the 20th Regiment[22] yesterday, so my friend I hope you may stay in Mull other six months yet. We cannot find out what regiment your uncle has got John into as yet ...[23] As I know he is a better farmer than you, let him be attentive that they do not pulfer and the workmen does there work properly. Murdoch see and get the money for me, if not I do not think I will be home untill the month of March unless I get it. I am certain these rascaly Tennants might give you some [money] which you might enclose me by letter likewise along with the Draught. With compliments to all our friends and all the family wherein your Mother & the family here joins.

I am

Your affectionate Brother, Allan MacLaine.

This epistle was worthy of his mother, Marie, who had the grace to be ashamed of hers, and employed a writer for her correspondence. Allan, who rarely wrote letters except when there was some prospect of money, was unpractised in the art. But he and his mother spent, as the letter suggests, many months in Edinburgh preparing litigation against Murdoch, of whom they spoke to their lawyers as if he was an erring factor on their estate. This letter of Allan's and his disreputable methods of scraping money together, and indeed the whole ignominious conduct of his life, makes Marie's indignation at his marriage with a Gregorson of Ardtornish quite unintelligible. But she was unable to divert him from his purpose, as she had diverted three of her daughters into regrettable marriages. The influence of the Gregorson family appears to have reconciled Allan to Murdoch Maclaine of Lochbuy, and although the process was going ahead to remove the Scallastle family's opposition, the letters between the two protagonists are more polite, although Murdoch's applications for the payment of Allan's rents were met with excuses: 'no money owing to the cursed set of people I have got in the farms.' On 28 February 1800 Allan reported to Murdoch the birth of a 'fine stout boy', but added that since Marjory was brought to bed at her parents' house at Ardtornish 'I intend taking him home and getting a nurse for him, and on Monday first I intend to get him baptised, and here, if I was not afraid to hurt the feelings of his Mother by bringing him home so soon. I shall be advised by you,' said Allan with uncharacteristic submissiveness, 'how to behave at the present period. I can assure you they have endeavoured to scandalize [24] me so much that I am afraid of my temper getting the better of me.'

The baptism of Angus, entered in Torosay parish register on 3 March 1800, suggests that Allan had not waited for advice before bringing the newborn child across the Sound of Mull. Over a year later, Murdoch the nineteenth of Lochbuy, who, at the age of seventy-one was now a respected elder statesman, heard rumours of a confrontation among the younger men of the island in the course of a convivial evening at the Inn of Achnacraig. As a JP he was entitled to know about breaches of the peace. He wrote to John Gregorson for an explanation.[25] John complied.

> Dear Sir,
>
> Mr Eun Maclachlan [26] has put into my hands a letter expressive of your disapprobation of some circumstances which occurred here on Saturday evening. I shall give a simple statement of the facts in so far as I am concerned, and shall refer every comment to yourself. Allan Scallastle had a great part of the evening directed his discourse to Dr D. Maclaine,[27] sometimes in a soothing strain and sometimes in an opposite strain. At length Allan rose from his seat and placed himself right opposite to me, and aside the doctor. He then made some allusions indicative of his suspicion of the doctor's having an intimacy with his wife and decorating his brow with horns. The doctor, being perhaps warmed with liquor, made some smart replies, although I clearly perceived that Allan's conversation was as much levelled at me ... yet I took no notice of it from my determined resolution of passing over everything from him. After the company broke up, I met Allan in the passage ... talking disrespectfully of Dr Maclaine ... my temper being heated beyond its usual temperature, I was urged by a sudden impulse of passion to apply my hand to Allan's breast, and to tell him that he had better keep quiet, for every person despised him. With that he asked me if I meant to grapple ... This excited still more my rage, but I was just then carried away by some friend – Major Maclachlan or Pennycross, and immediately became calm. Allan all the evening blustered a great deal and threatened to beat and do me up in every sense ... I indeed remarked that the occasion we were at was a most unfit one to quarrel with each other.[28]

This kind of pub brawl is hardly the stuff of history, and common enough in any place. There is no need to prove that Allan Scallastle was anything but a worthless, spendthrift, dishonest knave who in his paranoiac delusions thought himself a laird, and who evicted tenants in the same spirit as he accused his neighbours of cuckolding him. Murdoch Lochbuy hardly needed to have the incident explained to him. It was the kind of behaviour expected of many factors and representatives of the landed classes. Yet in this case, the landed classes decided to take action, and in September 1801 a meeting was held to resolve the problem of the intolerable conduct of Allan Scallastle. Gentlemen of 'the Country' were to decide all differences between Allan and those he had fallen out with, in the traditional manner of the birleyman. Mr Angus Gregorson of Ardtornish was to accept this arbitration on condition that Allan wrote a letter to say he was wrong in having accused his wife of adultery.[29] But this Allan would not do, and the consequence was that not only did Lochbuy press his law plea, but Mr Gregorson, Marjory's father, and everyone else wronged by Allan set the full force of the law upon him. In the courts, Marjory was awarded a judicial separation with aliment, and Allan was ordered to pay back her portion. A few years later, Allan was officially pronounced insane, or 'cognosced as fatuous'.[30] John Gregorson, his trustworthy brother-in-law, was put in charge of Allan's 'estate', and appointed, along with Sir Archibald Maclaine, Allan's younger brother, guardian of the two promising sons, Gillean and Angus. Allan was hidden away in Gordon Castle, near Musselburgh, not far from Edinburgh. 'No man', pronounced his brother Archibald, on a visit to Edinburgh, 'in Britain who converses with him half an hour but must pronounce him mad.' [31]

'The best laid schemes o' mice an' men gang aft agley': Gillean's revenge on John Maclaine of Lochbuy for fathering him, on Archy for being the true and legitimate son, and on Murdoch for coming before him in the succession, however he had tried to thwart him, had failed. In the words of Lachlan MacQuarrie of Ulva, Allan's own grandfather: 'his mother was his ruin, and this jaunt will finish the work she began.' [32] Allan's financial debt to Marjory, his spouse, was restored to her from the rents of Scallastle, and many of the tenants mentioned above, who could not absolutely be identified, seemed to return to their former holdings.[33] Marie, very much chastened, retired to Ledirkle with two unmarried daughters, so that her daughter-in-law Marjory Gregorson might inhabit Scallastle. Marjory's sons Gillean and Angus, were now, with their Scallastle uncles who were all in the army, heirs of entail, but the terrible phrase was never uttered. Marjory brought up her sons to think of other things, to be interested in ideas for their own sake, to wish to succeed on their merit, and to be considerate of others. Surrounded by the protective care of a very large family of Gregorsons in Ardtornish, young Gillean and Angus crossed the Sound of Mull as often as the Maxwells and the Macleods went back and forward. In 1813, the two boys matriculated together at Glasgow University,[34] and wrote regular letters to their uncle and guardian, John, full of excitement about their studies in the Logic class, their activities in the Debating Society, and the literature of the day. 'I saw in a newspaper', Angus wrote, at the age of fourteen, 'a few extracts out of *The Lord of the Isles,* a poem lately published by Walter Scott. The scene lies chiefly at Ardtornish, which is represented as the residence of Kenneth, the

Lord of the Isles. A description is also given of the Battle of Bannockburn, after which Bruce visits Ardtornish. If this work be as good as his former poems, I dare say you will soon see crowds of Englishmen landing at the point to examine the ruins of that castle where the conquerors of their ancestors met after having driven them out of Scotland.' [35]

If Marjory Gregorson had suffered grievously at the hands of Allan Scallastle, her husband, she was now granted every recompense in her two clever and attentive sons. When they had finished their college courses, young Gillean went to a mercantile house in London which was quite Dickensian in its modes of business and treatment of its clerks, but this training allowed him to enter a firm in Java in the early 1820s. Here, this highly educated and hard-working young man applied himself to making money, and in eighteen years had become a successful businessman, trading coffee with an importer in Rotterdam. Angus, who excelled in debating and public speaking, read theology and entered the Church of Scotland, being licensed by the Presbytery of Mull in 1823, and admitted minister of Ardnamurchan in 1827, so that he returned to the scenes of his youth, continually sailing across the Sound of Mull to visit his mother in Scallastle [36] and his guardian John Gregorson at Ardtornish.

Marie MacQuarrie, or Maclaine, after the difficult years of her extended legal process with Murdoch Maclaine of Lochbuy, must hardly have known what to do when her adversary died. She had maintained an inexorable hostility to him, which he had not reciprocated, treating her kindly and courteously. In the year her cherished son Allan was at last cognosced insane, one of her twin boys, Murdoch, was killed at Maida. The other twin, Captain Archibald, in the 94th Regiment, paid a brief visit to his mother in Mull in 1805, and was recorded in the parish register as fathering 'a child in fornication', Colin Campbell Maclaine, upon a girl in Ledirkle.[37] Captain John, Marie's fourth son was in the 73rd Foot, and will reappear in Chapter 20. Her fifth and last son, 20-year-old Hector, was by 1806 a captain in the 64th Foot.

Of her five daughters, the three youngest were unmarried in 1806, and Marie remained with them at Ledirkle, having nothing to do with the management of the 'estate' of Scallastle, as she continued to call it, since it was to remain under Gregorson control until the lease ended. Although her father lived to the age of 103, dying at Pennygown in 1818, Marie had never allowed him to live in 'our family' (a phrase which excluded him), but had left him to the care of her half sister, Miss Ann MacQuarrie. About the time of her father's death, however, Marie left Mull at over seventy years of age, and lived with her daughters at 12 Warriston Crescent, Edinburgh, a little more than a mile from Donald Maclean WS's house in Albany Street. She had not been expected to come through the troubles of 1806, but Warriston Crescent seems to have agreed with her better than Mull, as she was always reported to be younger looking than anyone else, 'quite extraordinary' and in 'good spirits' like her father.

In the correspondence of her sons, thirty or forty years after the death of Murdoch Maclaine of Lochbuy, Murdoch was still referred to as a rogue, a villain and a usurper. 'The chicanery of the late Lochbuy' was a description used by Sir Archibald, and when the third Murdoch inherited, the Scallastle Maclaines still corresponded among themselves with bitterness and acrimony about what this new villain might be doing to 'their entail'. Until the advent of Donald Maclaine of Lochbuy in the middle of the nineteenth century, the Scallastle Maclaines were still consulted as heirs of entail when there was any talk of selling part of the estate.

In 1816, Hector Maclaine of Scallastle married Martha Osborne of Kyneton, or Kington, in Gloucestershire. Martha corresponded from Gloucestershire with the two unmarried Scallastle girls, Flora and Mary, in Edinburgh, who still wrote all their mother's letters, Marie being just as illiterate as she had always been. The tangled web of deceit, woven by Gillean Maclaine and thrown over 'our family' by Marie, still operated in 1837, when Martha wrote, most innocently from Kington to enquire about a little matter she had never quite understood about the Scallastle Maclaines.

1st February

My dear Mary,

Bad weather and illness confining me to the house is the reason you are so soon again bored with my tediousness. Moreover, I wish you to ask your Mother a few questions which Hector is unable to resolve for me. When the body is inactive, thoughts become doubly busy, so I have been teasing Hector to know how and in what way you are related to Lochbuy (if you really are related) and what relation your Father bore to the late Lochbuy, who, I understood when I heard the story, came almost unexpectedly into the estate. I want in fact to know what degree of kin rendered you heirs of entail? Was your Father one of the younger brothers of the Lochbuy house? Did he reside there in his youth, or if not, where was he born, and had he any brothers or sisters, and if so, did they leave any family, supposing them (the brothers and sisters) to be dead? I wish to know all this on William's [38] account, as I think it right everybody should know who their kith and kin are, especially if they can look back to them with any gratification, from their station or other qualities. The same questions I wish apply too to your Mother's relationship to Mrs Clephane. Was your grandmother a Maclean of Torloisk,[39] a sister of Mrs Clephane's Father? I will thank you to be very particular in answering these questions, for in a short lapse of time, so little is known relative to such matters. ... I must now tell you a little bit of romance connected with Mrs Clephane, that will revive your Mother's girlish recollections. A neighbour and friend of ours speaks of having met her at Perth Hunt Ball in the year 1787 with the greatest warmth. She was then Miss Maclean the heiress of Torloisk, and he says, 'Never can I forget her appearance. I had never seen so beautiful and lovely a creature. Her divine mind beamed through her lovely eyes ...' [40]

All the women in the world who have ever begun to be interested in tracing their Mull connections will sympathise with Martha Osborne Maclaine and her 'teasing' of her husband Hector to find out more about his ancestors. Hector was the least contentious of Gillean and Marie's sons, and was popular among all branches of Maclaines. It is certain that he did not deliberately hide from his wife the few facts he had at his command. When his father Gillean died he was only three years old; he had entered the army as an ensign at the age of eighteen, and was not involved, like his older brother Archibald, in the family's action against his brother Allan Scallastle. His military career kept him abroad, and his marriage to the beautiful, charming and intelligent heiress, Martha Osborne, had given him a new role as an English landowner. For Hector, that old story of Gillean and Murdoch was buried in the past, and was of no interest. If Mary Maclaine ever answered Martha's questions by appealing to her 90-year-old mother, her letter has not been discovered among the Thornbury correspondence.[41] Within eighteen years the three remaining Maclaine women in Warriston Crescent in Edinburgh were to die, taking the secrets of Scallastle to the grave. Marie died on 25 January 1846, at the age of ninety-eight, her daughters Mary and Margaret Anne in 1855.

But what did the family matter? Had Gillean's schemes, apart from holding up the progress of the real heirs to Lochbuy, actually influenced the course of Mull history? Had Allan Scallastle's selfish life had any more effect than to inconvenience a generation of tenants and cottars in one small corner of the island? And had Marie's profound ignorance, or her father's amiable slothfulness made the slightest dent in the lives of the population of Mull? It is arguable that they did not even supply the people with a long-lasting subject of gossip. Not a place, not a house, not a river and not a song is called after any one of them. The successful whitewashing of Gillean's life is not unusual, but it reminds us to pause before claiming a connection with a family with a sweet-sounding and apparently proud name.

Notes

1. Macdonald, *A General View* ... pp. 109–10.
2. NAS. GD174/1389/35. Hugh Morison to MM, Kilbeg, 13 May 1798.
3. NAS. GD174/1628/447. DMWS to MM2, 9 April 1827.
4. Mrs Maclean of Kilbrenan, or Flora MacQuarrie, sister of Marie and widow of John Lagganulva.
5. GRO. Uncatalogued MSS. Alexander Shiells to Miss Jean MacQuarrie, 12 March 1830.
6. NAS. GD174/1913. Letters of application for the post of road surveyor for the island of Mull.
7. NAS. Stonefield Papers. GD14/10/3. Report, 1732.

8. Mercey, F. *Scotia – souvenirs et récits de voyages.* Emeritus Professor Alan J. Steele of Edinburgh University directed me to this description of Mull.
9. GRO. Maclaine Papers, Box 25. Journals of LMD. Entry for Monday 26 March 1832.
10. The term is constantly used in correspondence between tenants and lairds.
11. NAS. GD174/209/16. Jottings.
12. The uncatalogued letters in GRO unwittingly testify to the strange fixations of the woman who preserved them.
13. Hector McVurich was Hector Currie, Currie being the anglicised form of the Gaelic surname.
14. Changekeeper: innkeeper. The Scallastle inn was a public house.
15. GRO. Uncatalogued MSS. Maclaine papers, Box 18. Robert Campbell of Asknish and Tenants … Inveraray, 4 April 1789.
16. Torosay OPR. Baptism of Dugald, lawful son of Duncan Currie and Mary Currie, Kinlochspelve, 13 April 1794.
17. GRO. Uncatalogued MSS. Robert Campbell and tenants, 4 April 1800.
18. 'Senior' and 'junior' were not used in the modern sense of father and son, but to distinguish an older and younger man of the same name in a list of tenants.
19. That is, the 'Change House' or inn.
20. It was not for any advanced rent. Bidding for lands was competitive, and Allan meant that MacDougall was not being turned off for not bidding high enough, but for 'oversouming' – which was keeping a larger number of grazing animals than the stipulated number that grass could support. Extent of ground was expressed not in acres but in souming.
21. MM was back in army service, his regiment based in Guernsey.
22. William Douglas Maclean Clephane, husband of Marianne Maclean of Torloisk.
23. John Maclaine, fourth son of Gillean and Marie was eighteen. As was the custom of the times, Gillean's sons relied on graft and the intervention of relations like Marie's uncle, Allan Maclean of Torloisk, to acquire commissions in the army.
24. 'Scandalize', meaning to attach scandals to Allan.
25. JG, the future sheriff of Mull, was then twenty-six years old, son of Angus G. of Ardtornish, and brother of Marjory, Allan's wife.
26. Eun MacLachlan of Laudle, Morvern, an uncle by marriage of JG.
27. Dr Donald Maclaine, medical man in Torosay parish, lived at Pennygown, a respectable married man with seven children.
28. The occasion was probably a funeral. NAS. GD174/1555/3. JG to MM, Achnacraig, 12 August 1801.
29. NAS. GD174/1427/42. LMQ to MM, Scallastle, 3 September [1801].
30. GRO. Uncatalogued MSS. State of debt due by Allan McLaine, tacksman of Scallastle, 1806–09.
31. GRO. Uncatalogued MSS. Archibald Maclaine to JG, St Bernard's Row, Edinburgh, 30 September 1806.
32. 'He is surely mad … forever ruined as to character …' NAS. GD174/1427/37. LMQ to MM, Colonsay, 17 February 1800.
33. GRO. State of debt, see above. This document includes a list of tenants at Scallastlebeg, Scallastlemore and Garmony.
34. In the early nineteenth century boys entered the Scottish universities at an average age of fourteen.
35. GRO. Maclaine Papers, Box 16. Angus Maclaine to JG, Glasgow, 21 January 1815.
36. Marjory Gregorson moved out of Scallastle to accommodate Jane Maclaine of Lochbuy and her nine girls in 1814. This suited everyone, as Marjory went to Glasgow when

her sons were students. She returned to Scallastle after Jane's return to Lochbuy, and stayed there until her death in 1836, staying intermittently at Ardtornish and at Ardnamurchan.

37. The mother was Mary Fletcher in Ledirkle. Torosay OPR. Baptism, 24 August 1806.
38. William Osborne Maclaine of Kington, Thornbury, Gloucestershire, Martha and Hector's only son.
39. Martha was now asking about Alice Maclean, Marie's mother, who was a Maclean of Torloisk.
40. GRO. Maclaine Papers, Box 16. Martha Osborne Maclaine to Mary Maclaine, 1 February [1837].
41. Time might reveal the reply, as the Maclaine Papers in the GRO are on deposit, and therefore uncatalogued.

20

The organ grinder comes:
Sandy Campbell's quest

A teanga líonmhur, bhríoghmhur, bhlasda, bhínn,
  'san chan'mhain thartrach, líobhtha, ghasta, ghrínn.[1]

Even in the early days of the eighteenth century there was a fear that Gaelic was being abandoned. 'It has been sold in the court for a new speech dating from only yesterday', the poet Maighstir Seathan said in 1705, but hoped that the attentions of the grammarian Edward Lhuyd would bring a renaissance, and that the withering away of Gaelic would be arrested. Maighstir Seathan did not know that a large man (whom many took to be a sage), wearing a ridiculous wig and riding a Mull sheltie, would pass the door of his own church, where he himself would be lying – a handful of grey ashes in his grave – and would later argue from profound ignorance that the Gaelic language had no literature, because nothing had been written down. And if nothing had been written down, Dr Johnson argued, no manuscripts could exist, and if no manuscripts existed, MacPherson could not have translated Ossian, and therefore, said Dr Johnson, Ossian and Fingal, and all their poetic company were fakes.

Dr Johnson was but an Englishman, and did not have the breadth of understanding of our later visitor to Mull, Necker de Saussure, whose more measured conclusion was that if James MacPherson had only used the word *adapted* instead of *translated*, all would have been well.[2] But MacPherson by his unwise choice of word, and Johnson by his unyielding prejudice, together did much harm to that sweet and melodious tongue which was in so much danger of being exterminated. There was no doubt that Ossianic stories had been transmitted orally from generation to generation, and that the stage on which the tales were enacted was Morvern and the surrounding country, but the bitterness of the debate which followed MacPherson's publication of *Fingal*, and the fact that the 'translator' went too far in giving the literature his own particular trademark, combined to give Gaelic a strange reception in the world. MacPherson's books were madly popular. New tourists poured into the Highlands to see the lands of Ossian and Fingal, quoting with reverence the lines of their favourites. Mull and Morvern families also enjoyed the cult of Ossian, and felt pleasure and pride in the tradition, which their ministers and

Gaelic scholars defended. The Gregorsons of Ardtornish called their boat the
Malvina. Maclaine dogs were given the names of Ossianic hounds – Bran,
Oscar and Connan. Scenery was suddenly appreciated as the backdrop to noble
deeds and sentiments. Yet many commentators still chose to despise both the
scenery and the language which fell upon their ears. MacCulloch, after his
virulent criticism of 'Mullish dreariness' and his pronouncement that 'it is a
detestable island, trackless and repulsive, rude without beauty, stormy, rainy
and dreary' went on:

> To all this we may add the impending abolition of the Gaelic language;
> that obstacle, which, as long as it remains unremoved, will render all other
> efforts vain, but which no fondness of exertion can now preserve from its
> natural and hastening death.[3]

But the Ossian controversy had had the good effect of bringing the Highland
Society of Scotland into the fray as the Scottish counterpart of the *Académie
Française*, investigating the authenticity of the Ossian works, instigating
correspondence with Gaelic scholars and collectors of manuscripts, and under-
lining the importance of preserving Gaelic culture. This body [4] was to be the
patron of Alexander Campbell, 'organ grinder' and song collector.

In the summer of 1815, a man no longer young and wearing Highland dress
arrived in Mull and made his way at once to Ledirkle, where the widow Marie
Maclaine, née MacQuarrie, was now living. His name was Alexander Campbell,
but he was not one of the breed of Campbells injected by the Dukes of Argyll
into Mull. He had been born in Perthshire, the son of a carpenter. The
father had saved diligently, and in the manner of the day, had placed his
savings in the hands of his laird, who had become a bankrupt, so that the
poor carpenter was forced to move with his sons to Edinburgh and begin life
again. But so great were his troubles that he died of a broken heart, and
young Alexander, called 'Sandy', was brought up by his older brother John.
The two boys were remarkably musical. John became precentor of the Canongate Kirk in Edinburgh, and he and Sandy taught music to some illustrious
Edinburgh folk, including the family of Sir Walter Scott.[5] John was also a
great friend of Robert Burns in the days when the poet was being lionised in
Edinburgh. Sandy could therefore boast (if he needed to) of being intimate
with the two finest and most popular Scottish poets of his day. Sandy was a
Jacobite of the sentimental kind who flourished (like Mr Colquhoun Grant,
and even Donald Maclean WS in his youth) long after the extinction of that
cause.

Sandy Campbell was an enthusiastic writer on music, and was one of the
few musical theorists able to explain the peculiarities of the 'Scottish scale'
which had so interested Necker de Saussure.[6] His attempts at poetry included
the now forgotten *Grampians Desolate*, exposing the depopulation of the
Highlands and the plight of those who had had to flee. Sandy was instrumental

in the founding of the Destitute Sick Society in Edinburgh. He married a widow [7] who was able to afford to put him through Edinburgh Medical School as a mature student. He took his doctorate in medicine, but returned to the less profitable practice of music teaching, and in 1812 applied for the patronage of the Highland Society of Scotland in a tour of the western Highlands which would enable him to salvage the fast disappearing songs of that area. He was perfectly qualified, being fluent in Gaelic, and able to note down any tune from a single hearing. 'He is a real good musician,' wrote Sir Walter Scott, 'accurate in taking down music from singing, and indefatigable in collecting it – an enthusiastic good hearted Highlander besides – so that I have done all I could to help him to a little cash.' [8] Sandy had also been an organist in an Edinburgh episcopal church, and as such inspired considerable mirth among those who knew him, probably more for going among the 'piscies' and being a comic than from any shortcomings in his playing. He received the nickname of 'the organ-grinder'. The caricature by John Kay, entitled 'A Medley of Musicians', shows Sandy as the most dignified of a group of cacophonous creatures, and this portrayal was to make him better remembered in Edinburgh than any of his own serious and worthwhile works.

Dr Campbell's journey in Mull can be told in his own words, from the report he made to his patrons of the Highland Society.[9] His mission was a sensitive one: because of the controversy surrounding Ossian, every source had to be identified and authenticated, then presented in the Gaelic original with an English translation. The very popularity of MacPherson's work had not been without its influence on Sandy Campbell himself, and he noted with pleasure when crossing Connel Ferry, that he was among scenes 'where Fingal lived'. From Lismore he crossed the Sound of Mull, and arrived at Grass Point.

Being now in the Isle of Mull I took the road to Ledirkle, the present residence of my much valued friend Mrs Maclaine senior of Scallastle.[10] I had received a letter from her, mentioning that her stepson Mr Lauchlan Maclaine had made a collection of Gaelic songs, which he had carried with him to the Isle of Wight, where he then was, on his way to join his regiment.[11] And, naturally, thinking that his sisters at home who sing and perform on the Pianoforte would gladly communicate the best of the pieces their brother had selected, I put their instrument soon after my arrival in proper tune. In the forenoon of the next day, namely 1st August, I prepared to note down the melodies and words of many beautiful songs, which I knew the young ladies of Scallastle were in possession of, but their usual gaiety was clouded with the gloom of solicitude occasioned by a letter to their mother from their brother Major John Maclaine, who had been wounded severely in the battle of Waterloo ... In the course of the day it was whispered among the servants that the brave youth was no more, and in the course of the next day, i.e. 2nd August, the Post brought a letter confirming the report. My intended operations were suspended … after mingling my tears with those shed for the departed hero, I silently withdrew by the break of day, i.e. 3rd August, and set out for the Isle of Ulva, on the way to which I overtook our learned secretary Staffa's brother [12] accompanied with Dr Hamel, the celebrated Russian traveller; and, traversing the isthmus from Aros to Loch na Keill, we embarked for Ulva, and landed safely in that island, time enough for dinner. It was here that I expected to commence my laborious task in earnest. And it was under Staffa's roof that I did so. For, knowing of my coming, he had with great precision prepared everything requisite for obtaining the object I was in pursuit of. Soon after my arrival here, the persons most reputed for local antiquarian knowledge, oral tradition, recitation, and singing were convened. And the fruits of my industry, in which I was assisted by Mr John Currie, school-master,[13] are 24 iorrams,[14] boat songs, etc. Before I left Ulva, I visited the islands of Staffa and Iona, or Icolumkill. In the principal cave of the former I heard the effect of the great Highland bagpipe, which excites so much wonder and admiration in the mind of those who can relish this sort of melody. The resounding tones of the piper … with the thundering noise of the Atlantick dashing into the farther end of the cavern, is awfully sublime. The performer, Staffa's piper, played with pathos the *Lament for the slain on the fatal field of Culloden*. He is a pupil of Lieutenant Donald MacCrimmon, the celebrated professor … I had spent many days in Ulva, and taking leave of my friends … I departed with regret. Passing over the sound, to Laggan Ulva, part of the property of Staffa in Mull, I ascended the heights and pursued my route by a shortcut over the hills to Ballochroy, where I arrived a little before dusk the evening of 16th August, the morning of which was spent in getting Staffa's attestation to each piece I had taken down from vocal recital … I had a letter of recommendation from Sir John MacGregor Murray to Mrs McKenzie, whose house was just opposite (in the village, Dervaig) to the Inn of Ballochroy, where I lodged. And by what I heard and *read* of this celebrated Gentlewoman, I was eager to pay my respects, and anxious to commune with her on the subject of my excursion to Mull. Accordingly, on the 17th August, about noon, I put my letter of introduction into the hands of Mrs McKenzie, who received me with that suavity and ease so natural to a person of breeding and understanding. I was now conversing with the identical Miss McLean, who, to use the words of her admirer, Dr Samuel Johnson, 'was born and had been bred at Glasgow, having removed with her father to Mull, added to other qualifications a great knowledge of the Erse language, which she had not learned in her childhood, but gained it by study …' I can bear witness that this sensible and accomplished lady, still, at the advanced age of *three score and ten*, nay, upwards [15] is in perfect possession of her various qualifications, her faculties being quite unimpaired; and her appearance such that, altho' she is not in all respects a *Ninon de Lenclos*,[16] yet there remains sufficient to give an idea that forty-two years ago, he must have been a sturdy moralist indeed, or love-proof, who could withstand the fascinating manners and graces of this agreeable woman.

I spent several days at Dervaig examining the MSS of Gaelic poetry and melodies which the father of this lady (Dr McLean) and she herself had collected.[17] And having marked several pieces for transcription, she is under promise to transmit them to me with all possible dispatch. I have in my possession what she gave me on the spot, viz. A sheet in the handwriting of the present Countess of Compton, late Miss McLean of Torloisk,[18] containing besides sixteen Highland melodies, three harp airs, the same as were played by Murdoch Macdonald, harper to the laird of Coll.[19] This minstrel was the last of our Hebridean harpers and died in 1739. Mrs McKenzie, who remembers him perfectly,[20] has promised to furnish me with a few biographical notices regarding him; and she has likewise engaged to give me some authentic particulars concerning John McLean, the bard of Mull, several of whose pieces are in her MS collection. 'The voice of Harps' may yet be heard in the Highlands and Western Islands. As a proof, it is well known that the accomplished ladies of Torloisk are admirably skilled in handling the harp. And I myself, while in Mull, was delighted with the tasteful execution on the improved harp of Mrs McLean at Cuinish.[21] This instrument, as an accompaniment to the voice, is well adapted to support, and give effect, in what is called *Musical Expression*, to say nothing of its being the best calculated to exhibit, in performance, the symmetry and grace of the female form to bewitching advantage. It might be considered rather a romantic, if not a wild idea, to suggest the possibility of restoring harp music and consequently the re-establishment of the ancient order of Harpers in Scotland and the Isles. And why not encourage *harpers* as well as *pipers?* Premiums, so as to excite generous emulation might do great things ...

Having made those arrangements with Mrs McKenzie, I, on the 21st August, set out early in the morning on an excursion to that district of Mull which belongs to the Duke of Argyll. I went first to Sunipol, a farm which is presently possessed by a namesake.[22] It was here, but in a different family of the same name,[23] that the author of *The Pleasures of Hope* was for some time preceptor.[24] And finding in the like capacity a young man (a namesake also) of considerable knowledge, I availed myself of his willingness to oblige, and readiness to communicate everything he knew regarding the objects of my research. It was here I accidentally fell in with an elderly man of the name of McLeod, who, while I was making a sketch, sat down by me and recited several ancient pieces, or rather fragments of poetry ascribed to Ossian. The scene I was delineating was that well known headland called the point of Calliach, on which, it is said, the author of *The Pleasures of Hope* was wont to study, and not infrequently, in the midst of storms and tempests of the great Atlantick – thus impressing his mind with the awfully sublime effects of the contending elements raging along the rugged shores of Mull.

During my short stay at Sunipol, I went to examine the Gaelic school, established for a short time by an association of well-meaning persons in Edinburgh. And altho' but remotely connected with my present pursuit, yet from a hint suggested by a particular friend, a member and director of the Highland Society, I judge it expedient to embrace this opportunity of observing on the spot what benefit there was likely to arise from itinerant teachers instructing the natives in their vernacular language, without the medium of another, of which they were entirely ignorant. I am decidedly of opinion that under proper regulations, and sanctioned by *proper* authority, the experiment is likely to succeed ... The young man who teaches this school, whose name is Munro, a native of Ross-shire,[25] has promised to write down such pieces of the fragments alluded to from the recitation of McLeod, the man mentioned above, and to transmit them to me.

22nd August. This day I crossed an arm of the sea to Treshnish, on a visit to Mr Campbell. While on my passage thither, the boatmen sang several iorrams and rowing songs, some of which were excellent and very well sung. I was to have returned to Sunipol in the evening, and appointed one of the boatmen (the best singer) to take down from his chanting two or three of the songs which had so much pleased me. But I could not get away from my namesakes at Treshnish [26] and I had great cause to be satisfied with my visit. For he himself is not only a neat performer on the violin, but a young man of the name of Maclean, a native of Breadalbane, touches that instrument sufficiently well for my purpose, and possesses several songs and dancing measures, five of which I noted down. But what is of much greater consequence, is the promise that Mr Campbell of Treshnish has made, of using his influence to procure for *Albyn's Anthology* the valuable MS collection of the Reverend Dugald Campbell, minister of Kilfinichen, in the Ross of Mull. ...

23rd August. On my way from Treshnish to Sunipol it was pointed out to me the spot where the remains of Murdoch Macdonald, the last of our Hebridean harpers were laid. Having spent the remainder of this day at Sunipol, and engaging the three young preceptors, Messrs McLean, Munro and Campbell as correspondents, I next morning, i.e. 24th August, returned to Ballochroy, the post town of this district of Mull, the greater portion of which is the property of the Laird of Coll, from whose daughter, Miss Breadalbane McLean,[27] I obtained permission to select and transcribe from her MS music book eight original Gaelic airs ... After bidding adieu to Mrs McKenzie, I set out for Mingary, whither I had been kindly invited by its present possessor, Mr McLean, whose wife is a namesake of mine, a sensible agreeable lady.[28]

At Mingary I fortunately found a person of whom I was in search, and was agreeably surprised to find him when I least expected. Islanders, it is well known, are the merriest of mortals, and the inhabitants of Mull of all classes are not a whit behind those who indulge almost to excess in dancing in the neighbouring islands. The minstrel of the present merry-making at Mingary was the very man I was in quest of, namely Angus Macdonald, cabinet maker in Clachy near Aros, Mull.[29] This singular character is a sort of Universalist, or Jack-of-all-trades, and among other qualifications, he draws a bold rough fiddle stick, and is no mean dab at a dancing measure of any sort. He and I, as if by a kind of congenial instinct, became instantly acquainted, the result of which was a faithful promise that his MS collection of Gaelic poems, the labour of his leisure hours since he was quite a lad, being now upwards of fifty, would be made available. As an earnest of his entering at once into my present views with perfect zeal, he writ down with his own hand the first stanza of *Sean Oran Gaoil* or ancient love song, the composition of a daughter of MhicCalein or Argyle.[30] The son of this Universalist is a true chip off the block. And scrapes lustily the fiddle too, and from him I noted down, when I had pricked the melody to the love song, a popular dancing-tune or reel called *Linn Mhullach*, the Sound of Mull. These two pieces are attested by Hector Maclean Esquire, under whose hospitable roof I reposed for the night. I sojourned here the greater part of 25th August, and after dinner set forward on my way to Tobermorie, a well-known haven on the Sound of Mull. I travelled without a guide, consequently to disadvantage. But Mr McLean and the tutor in his family, the Reverend Mr Ferguson,[31] having accompanied me a short distance to point out those marks by which I was to find my way over the hills to Tobermorie, we shook hands heartily and parted.

But I had not proceeded one third of the trackless, rough extent till I observed the night clouds gathering in the east, indicative that darkness was fast approaching. I soon found myself in the sad plight of a traveller benighted. Even the faint glimming was gradually fading, and I was now left in all but total darkness. I heard the brawl of a rapid brook, as if at no great distance, on coming to which I plunged in. And reaching the opposite bank – for there was no bridge – I found the wretched pathway, if it could be considered such, and endeavoured to grope my way the best manner I could. When I had passed over two mountain streams I thought I heard the distant murmur of waves, and it was no auricular deception. It was the roar of the Atlantick coursing through the Sound of Mull. Hearing soon after the tones of a human voice in the act of calling a cow to be milked, I naturally concluded that it was at no great distance to the wished-for haven. And now having met the female that was in quest of her cow, she directed me distinctly, and I soon found myself at the door of the inn, into which I gladly entered, and enjoyed that repose so sweet and refreshing to a weary way-worn traveller. Had I remained at Mingary, I should have found it impossible to travel next day. I had scarcely plunged under the bedclothes when I heard rain fall heavily, and the wind piping loud, indicating the near approach of a tremendous tempest – and it so happened. For, on looking out early, at the peep of day, the mountain torrent that falls into the harbour of Tobermorie was in full volume, and seemed to be charged, in accelerated velocity, with all the mountain streams of this rugged district of the island.

26th August. It cleared up, however, in the course of this day, and toward the evening it became quite fair. I went abroad to view the surrounding scenery, made a sketch of the harbour and opposite coast of what was once 'woody Morvern'. And lofty shores of that ample inlet of the Atlantick called Loch Sunart. On returning to my quarters at the inn, I learned with satisfaction that a vessel had just dropped anchor in the bay, bound immediately for the Long Island. Loch Boisdale in South Uist was the sea arm I wished to enter. But the packet was to sail directly to Lochmaddy, the place of her destination. I had but the alternative left of either going to the Long Island in this vessel, or of waiting a chance of a herring bush, or some worse sort of small craft to carry me to an uncertain haven, and many days might intervene before even this chance might favour my wishes. So I determined to go in the packet for North Uist, and accordingly on the 27th August I went early on board ...

When Sandy Campbell missed Lauchlan – Marie's stepson – at Ledirkle, Lauchlan had been gone for just eighty-nine days. He had gone first to Greenock, where the new steam boats were busy in the Firth of Clyde, then proceeded to Ayr to see his half-sister Margaret before going back to Glasgow to visit Allan Scallastle's natural daughter, Aemilia. It was a round of farewells, as he did not know if he would ever see any of his relatives again. On Monday 8 May 1815, he set off by the four o'clock coach to Edinburgh, where he arrived at eleven o'clock at night, staying at Mackay's Hotel. His baggage had been sent ahead of him from Mull, to the carriers' quarters in the Grassmarket, but had not arrived, and the Leith smacks were leaving for London at two o'clock. Suppressing his anxiety, Lauchlan walked down to Albany Street and called on Donald Maclean WS, who told him that Mrs Maclean Clephane was staying nearby in the Dumbreck Hotel. There, Lauchlan sent in his compliments without reflecting that 'Mr Maclaine from Mull' was hardly going to identify him to the lady. He was told that Mrs Clephane was 'rather busy', and he became indignant when no response came. He then sent a simple message in, requesting that if Mrs Clephane had any commands for Colonel Maclaine or any of her friends in the West Indies, Colonel Maclaine would be glad to carry them. He was on the wing when the boy came rushing back to ask him to step into their sitting room. Mrs Clephane was not, she said, to know who it was. There were so many Mr Macleans in Mull. The Maclean Clephane girls, Anna Jane and Wilmina were there (but not Margaret), and a gentleman who was a stranger to Lauchlan. This was, he presumed, Lord Compton, but the etiquette of the time did not allow an introduction unless the social superior should request one, and so Lauchlan remained unintroduced. He could not learn why Miss Margaret was missing, nor whether he should soon address her by another name. 'Not yet. By and by,' said Mrs Clephane, evasively.[32] 'I am perfectly of opinion that it is the fault of our own family that this lady is so very distant,' Lauchlan thought, as he took his farewells. 'On a near approach, I have not only found her polite, but kind, as much so indeed as I could possibly expect.' [33]

On his way to Leith to see if his bags had arrived, Lauchlan called in at Leith Walk to see Donald Maclaine, merchant and seedsman, nephew of Murdoch Maclaine the nineteenth of Lochbuy, where he took a glass of wine with the man who was later to be criticised for leaving no legacies to the Lochbuy girls, and with his niece Miss Flora, who was to receive all his money. The bags had arrived, and were dispatched. Lauchlan then executed his own personal errands in Edinburgh. He was to take to the West Indies new violin strings, a new flute, a Gaelic Bible, an English Bible, Dr Smith's edition of the Gaelic poems of Ossian and John Stuart's collection of Gaelic songs. These things were to fortify Lauchlan in the years ahead. It was unfortunate that two musicians with similar tastes, and a shared delight in Ossian, should have been travelling in different directions in the summer of 1815, and that it was Lauchlan in fact who had penned the letter from London to Marie Maclaine in Ledirkle, breaking the news of her son's death at Waterloo.

The poet who was mentioned with such reverence in Sandy Campbell's report, and in connection with Sunipol, was Tom Campbell, whose association with Mull was much exaggerated by nineteenth-century writers as a result of the popularity of his *Pleasures of Hope*, published in 1799 when he was only twenty-two years old, four years after his stay in Mull. His poem, 'Lord Ullin's Daughter' made the title of 'chief of Ulva's isle' famous, in its fictitious and unidentified setting. Tom Campbell was a great-grandson of Campbell of Kirnan,[34] who had addressed a complaint to the Duke of Argyll in 1740, but he did not possess his ancestor's interest in the practical issues of life in Argyll, and although his stay with his relations at Sunipol placed him in the centre of an area of Mull which is particularly destitute of description, the young poet's letters were rather frivolous and immature, and mentioned nothing of life on the island apart from his own ennui at having to be there at all. Unlike the Lochbuy tutor, Andrew Halliday, Tom did not mention his pupils, and showed no interest in any of the local people or their way of life. His achievement, for those of us who are interested in the island and the people, must remain unimpressive. His most memorable phrases, 'distance lends enchantment to the view' and 'like angel visits few and far between', also remain exasperatingly insubstantial.

The organ grinder had not ventured beyond the parishes of Torosay and Kilninian in his quest for music and song. But in the parish of Kilfinichen and Kilvicheoun, had he only known it, a very young woman, Mary McLucais, or MacDougall [35] who had been born in Brolass, at Torranuachdrach [36] was living at Siaba, the newly married wife of Neil Macdonald. As Mary Macdonald, her fame as a poetess and hymn writer was to outlast the renown of Tom Campbell. She made her name with one hymn, *Child in the Manger*, which was to be selected for publication in many hymnaries, and which is still sung today, to the tune *Bunessan*. But Mary's hymn was slightly longer, and her title more beautiful, *Leanabh an àigh*, 'child who was wondrous'. Her second stanza was to be omitted from the version sung around the world.

> Ged a bhitheas leanaban
> Aig righrean na talmhainn,
> 'N greadhnachas garbh
> Is anabarr mùirn,
> 'S geàrr gus am falbh iad
> 'S fàsaidh iad anfhann,
> An àilleachd 's an dealbh
> A' searg san ùir.[37]

Mary and her husband Neil Macdonald lived in a township which today seems almost unearthly in its beauty. Siaba lies well above the shore, on the south side of the Ross of Mull, looking out towards Colonsay and Jura. In the early nineteenth century, a track led over the higher land, which was not violently indented like the shores below, to Scour, Kilvicheoun, the old township of Saorphein, Ardchiavaig, Ardchy Ardalanish and Tirergain. In these seven farms there were 355 people in 1779[38] and when Mary MacDougall was twenty-six (in 1815, the year the organ grinder came to Mull) there were certainly more than 500 in the same group of farms. The couple had ten children in Siaba, and in 1841 Neil was a crofter of five acres at Ardalanish Point. Ardalanish itself was a fertile place, but the Point was barren. It is not known how many of their ten children survived. Coll, born in 1833, was a lobster fisher, probably the best employment for a boy who could take his catch to Oban. Between 1851 and 1861 the family was evicted from Ardalanish, and moved to Knockan, a hamlet in Ardtun, on the northern shore of the Ross.[39] Like many other families, they had grandchildren living with them. In the meantime, the Siaba people had left for Canada, and most of the inhabitants of the townships on the track from Siaba to Ardalanish had gone. Mary died at Knockan in 1872 at the age of eighty-three, known to all who remained as *Màiri Dhùghallach, bean Néill Dhòmhnullaich ann an Ard Tunna*. She was a different being from the men and women Sandy Campbell had visited in the north and east of Mull. As a member of a prominent Baptist family in the Ross of Mull, Mary was affected by a set of circumstances which will be discussed in Chapter 24.

Notes

1. John Maclean, *Rainn*, trans. Colm O Baoill. 'A widely-spoken, vigorous, sweet and melodious tongue, a strong, polished, beautiful and accurate language.'
2. See Chapter 14.
3. Macculloch, pp. 228, 232.
4. Operating today as the Royal Highland and Agricultural Society of Scotland.
5. Paterson and Maidment, vol. 2, p. 100. Mr John Campbell, precentor. A precentor led the singing in churches where there was no instrumental music. Sir Walter Scott describes his old music teacher in a MS letter in EUL. MS. Gen. 1732.
6. See Chapter 14. Campbell published his description in *A Dialogue on Scottish Music*, part of *An Introduction to the History of Poetry in Scotland*, 1798.
7. His second marriage was to the widow of Ranald Macdonnell of Keppoch.
8. EUL. MS. Gen. 1732. But Scott in the same letter called Sandy 'a crack-brained original'.
9. EUL. Laing Collection. *A Slight Sketch of a Journey*. A shorter version formed the introduction to his *Albyn's Anthology*, published 1816 and 1818. A projected third volume did not materialise.
10. Marie Maclaine, née MacQuarrie had moved to Ledirkle before 1811 as a result of the Scallastle settlement with the trustees of MM2. Her daughter-in-law, Marjory lived partly at Ledirkle, partly at Ardtornish, and in Glasgow when her sons attended college there. Sandy Campbell probably knew Marie from her Edinburgh days, when he may have taught music to her children.
11. LMD had joined the 7th West Indian Regiment at some time during the French wars, after being a civilian in Jamaica. His collection of Gaelic songs still survives in GRO, Maclaine Papers, Box 17. A microfilm copy in EUL and Inverness.
12. Ranald Macdonald of Staffa's brother, Colin, was on a visit to his mother, Isabella, at Ulva.
13. John Currie (1758–1828). His daughter, Bell Currie, was married to Alexander Shaw, a relative of CM who had the inn at Ulva in 1832. His wife, Mary McInnes came from Scallasdale, and John was originally from Torosay parish, like most Mull Curries.
14. Rowing songs.
15. Mrs Mackenzie would be about seventy-four in 1815.
16. Anne de Lenclos, seventeenth-century Frenchwoman, famous for her wit, charm, intellect and liaisons with distinguished men.
17. The collection was given by Mrs MacKenzie to the Tiree poet John Maclean, who took them to Canada. They form the nucleus of *The Maclean Bards*, ed. by A. Maclean Sinclair. Microfilms of the collection are in EUL and other Scottish university libraries.
18. Margaret Maclean Clephane had just married Lord Compton that summer.
19. In *Albyn's Anthology* as item 3.
20. It is unlikely that she remembered him if he died in 1739. He was probably Murchadh Clarsair, harper to Maclean of Coll.
21. Quinish. This was either Mrs Maclean senior (Catherine Cameron of Glendessary), wife of Alexander of Coll, or her daughter-in-law, Janet Dennistoun, who married Hugh, Younger of Coll, in 1814.
22. Duncan Campbell.
23. The family of Captain Archibald Campbell, d. 1790 and Janet Campbell.

24. The poet, Thomas Campbell was tutor here in summer 1795 to the Campbell children, Donald, John, Alexander, Margaret and Jean.

25. Alexander Munro. He began teaching for the Society for the Support of Gaelic Schools in June 1815, and wrote a report in 1816, which was published by the Society. In 1817 he was moved to Benmore. Teachers were 'ambulatory'.

26. Another Duncan Campbell, b. 1766, m. 1798, Grizel Campbell, daughter of John Campbell, Tacksman of Frachadil and Florence Campbell. He was the son of Archibald Campbell, Tacksman of Treshnish, and Catherine Campbell, and the writer of a letter in this very year, 1815, to Charles Selkrig in Edinburgh about his poverty, see Chapter 13.

27. Daughter of Alexander Maclean of Coll, she remained unmarried, later living at Retreat Cottage, Dervaig, and was noted for her charitable work.

28. Hector Maclean, 'Eachann Ruadh', b. c. 1760, formerly in Ensay, married Miss Helen Campbell in 1800. She was the daughter of Mr Donald Campbell, Chamberlain of Tiree. There were seven sons in succession of this marriage, then four daughters in succession (Kilninian OPR).

29. Possibly Callachilly, or Clachaig, although the latter is not very near to Aros.

30. Mac Cailein Mor, 'son of great Colin' – Gaelic name for the Duke of Argyll as chief of Clan Campbell.

31. Alexander Ferguson (1790–1833) was missionary at Salen, Ulva and Kilfinichen before becoming minister of Tobermory in 1828. He married Catherine Macdonald, Dererach in 1825 (Edinburgh Annual Register).

32. Mrs C. was justifiably evasive, as she had just received a letter from Walter Scott about his marriage negotiations with the Northampton family. There were points to be resolved before the deeds were signed. Grierson, *Letters of Sir WS*, vol. IV, 1815–17.

33. GRO. Maclaine Papers. Box 18; wrongly listed as journal of Gillean Maclaine, it is that of LMD, 1815–16.

34. See Chapter 4 for Kirnan's complaints.

35. The name of MacLucais, current in the Ross of Mull in the eighteenth century, became MacDougall in the nineteenth.

36. Two townships, Torranuachdrach and Torranbeg, south of Loch Scridain, were later called 'the Torrans' and are now called Torrans, so that the plurality has been lost to view.

37. 'Although there be children/born to earth's rulers,/awesome in majesty/and over-whelming in pomp/they will depart shortly,/grow weak [in body],/their form and their beauty/withering in earth.'

38. Cregeen, Eric R. (ed.), *Inhabitants of the Argyll Estate, 1779*. Census taken for the fifth Duke of Argyll.

39. Meek, Donald E., *Sunshine and Shadow*, and censuses of 1851 and 1861.

21

The fly on the wall:
Lauchlan Maclaine's diary

Lauchlan is first glimpsed on 9 June 1788, his seventeenth birthday, in Crosscauseway, Edinburgh, in the household of his stepmother, Marie. He and his half-brother, Allan, were attending classes in the college, and Lauchlan was writing to his father Gillean at Scallastle in Mull.

Dear Father,

I am happy to tell you that all your family here are in good health and going on with their education as fast as they can, only Mrs Maclaine herself has got a cold, but, I hope, will soon get the better of it. Allan entered with Masterton for Arithmetick and writing a few days ago, and attends four hours with him. The rest of his time he applies to the study of Latin with Mr Thornton, who is still here and is in hopes of getting a family in town. The three boys are keeping up with the classes pretty well, but I'm afraid will feel the loss of Mr Thornton's going away; I give copies to them and the two girls dayly, and I see a great alteration upon their hands since I began them, although I cannot by any means pretend to write well myself.[1] Alicia is done of the boarding school, but Julian [2] is not, on account of not being well for some time, but will be soon done. After which their Mother means to send them to the Miss Stewarts and Miss Nicholson's to get a sketch of Millinery and Mantua-making; I myself have gone through one set of Book-keeping, and am revising it dayly, but would be nothing the worse of a second set to make me thoroughly acquaint with it.

Professor Robertson [3] was drinking tea here once since you went away, and asked them all what they were doing, and among the rest asked me what classes I attended. I told him I attended two, one for writing and another for Geography, but he said I should know a little French and Mathematicks along with that.

Jean [4] goes off for Glasgow to her Aunty Betty [5] Monday come eight days, and your friend Mr Beaton has got a family in the New Town, one Mr Hunter's, a Writer to the Signet,[6] and has twenty-five pounds sterling bed, board, washing, etc. a year. I have had no answer from my uncle at London [7] but Archibald Maclean told me that if you had wrote him for those things you sent for, you should have them. Things are going on very well here unless the money be going too fast. I compute our expences since you went away to be about forty pounds sterling and odds, but you need not let anything on about that in your letters lest my stepmother should be displeased at me for writing you anything about it. I have nothing more particular to tell you, but that my Noverca[8] progresses, and that I stand in need of a new Coat. All the family have their compliments to you.

> I am
> Dear Father,
> Yours
> Lauchlan McLaine

Gillean Maclaine died at the end of this year, and apart from this letter, there is very little evidence about the relationship between the father and his natural son. Lauchlan's real mother, Janet MacPhail, married a widower in his forties, John Buchanan, when Lauchlan was about two years old. The Buchanans were, in Gaelic, McPhananichs, who lived in Ardchoirk, a large township on the Duke of Argyll's Torosay parish property, half a mile from the present-day village of Lochdonhead. About six stone ruins bear witness today to the existence of this populous community, which in 1779 had eighty-three people in it. The curious combination of surnames borne by the inhabitants, such as Colquhoun, MacGregor, Buchanan and MacFarlane, all hailing from the country north and east of Loch Lomond, and the fact that most of them were tenants rather than cottars, suggests that one of the Dukes of Argyll had awarded land holdings at the beginning of the eighteenth century to supporters, so that these families were planted, like the Campbells. Janet MacPhail and John Buchanan increased the numbers of Buchanans by at least three sons and a daughter.[9] Lauchlan was now in the curious position of having ten Maclaine half-brothers and sisters at Scallastle, and four Buchanan siblings at Ardchoirk. The first family claimed affiliation with the gentry, spoke Gaelic and English, wrote English (with the exception of Marie), sent its sons into the army, and aspired to the inheritance of the estate of Lochbuy. The second family was mainly Gaelic speaking, but were, unlike Lachlan Kilbrenan (so much despised by Marianne Maclean Clephane for being unable to speak English) aware of the need to spread their wings. Janet MacPhail's own relations included MacPhails who had gone to London to learn a trade. The Buchanans and MacPhails were active in a changing world.

Lauchlan had known from early childhood that he would not be as favoured as his Maclaine brethren. His stepmother accepted that he would be educated with her children, but as soon as he was ready, he must go out into the world and fend for himself. In 1789, he was placed with a planter in Jamaica, and sailed out. He was reported to be doing well there, but he was only a clerk. He returned to Mull some time after Allan's committal, stayed at Ledirkle, and was helped by Archibald, his half-brother, to enter the 7th West India Regiment in 1814. He was a colonel in 1815, but had to borrow money from the generous John Gregorson, his half-brother-in-law, to finance the next stage in his advancement. It is here that we catch up with Lauchlan, travelling back to the West Indies after missing an encounter with Sandy Campbell, the organ grinder.

He was only too aware of his impecunious state. He had had to finance his own army career. Marriage was, he considered (much as he longed for it), out of the question, partly because of his birth, and partly due to the tiny pension which was to come his way when he retired, in the early 1820s. He was not alone in being hard-up. The unusually long peace which followed Waterloo reduced thousands of officers to half-pay, and made the economy sluggish everywhere. But Lauchlan was induced, by love of country and Gaelic roots, as well as a sense of duty to his mother, Janet, to return to Mull. John Gregorson, now Sheriff of Mull and Morvern, persuaded his brother Peter to let Lauchlan have a humble abode in a two-roomed cottage at Garmony, and there, after drawing breath, in about 1824,[10] Lauchlan commenced the diary which was to record life in his little corner of the island for twelve years, in all its minute detail and painful sparseness.

Captain Lauchlan Maclaine was now fifty-three years old, and had in his day talked with princes and commoners. Now, his day (as befitted someone who had been concerned with planting in Jamaica), was devoted to preparing ground and sowing seeds at Garmony, but he at once found that the cottars and 'workmen' who lived around Scallastle, Garmony and Fishnish were unwilling to 'delve'. As Lauchlan progresses in the writing of his diary, describing the weather every day, and the reluctance of his people to work for him, the social structure of the community slowly reveals itself. Peter Gregorson was tenant of the lands, Lauchlan was subtenant in his cottage. The cottars were tolerated in their 'huts', provided they still offered services, something which the Duke of Argyll had abolished in 1737. Services largely consisted of help (usually transport) with peats and potatoes and sea ware. The Gregorson family, who had the tack of the land (which in turn was owned by the Lochbuy family) controlled their subtenants, who were allowed to avail themselves of the pool of labour provided by cottars and scalags. The system on the Lochbuy estate was less clear than on the Argyll estate, since the issue was very much clouded and obscured by the question of services, but vague services and toleration of the cottars who were living almost rent-free, were preferable to giving cottars a lease. Cottars were a liability when there was any thought of selling land, and as we have seen from the workload of Donald Maclean WS, land was being sold off all around, or new and better tenants were being sought. On the Scallastle land a township called Scallastlebeg had grown up. At first it had been small, but in 1825 it was spreading over good arable ground and pasture. John Gregorson wrote to young Murdoch about the problem:

> As I deemed it of great consequence to the farm of Scallastle that the cottars should be all removed from Scallastlebeg, where their houses were in the middle of pasture and arable grounds, to a more secluded part of the farm,

and where less injury would be done, I directed them to pull down their present houses and erect new houses.

I consider that a few cottars will be always necessary to the farm, therefore a new establishment of houses for them in a secluded corner may be considered a permanent improvement. The enclosed list they gave me of timber that may be requisite for them. I therefore hope you will give them an order to get the timber at sight of your wood officer, in the woods generally appropriated for the use of the Estate. Buck and blackwood, which is not much good for sale (indeed I find such unsaleable) is good enough for them ...[11]

Like Donald Maclean wishing to clear unsightly old houses from Carsaig the year before, John Gregorson was becoming conscious of the extent and miserable appearance of the cottages as well as their position on prime sites. Fifteen houses with sheds attached, peat stacks and dunghills in front, as well as plots walled in stone to keep animals out of corn and kale added up to a considerable built-up area. Between Lauchlan's cottage at Garmony and Corrinahenachy, there were four such townships, and from them Lauchlan drew his labour for the very small tasks he required to be done at Garmony. He also recruited from the townships the girls who cooked and cleaned for him, although they were often his own Buchanan relations. His cottage, which lay close to the road to Salen and Tobermory, had to house his mother, who had come to live with him, his maidservant and many passing guests who stayed overnight.

When Lauchlan was writing the second of his series of foolscap journals, Charles Macquarie and his family were living at the house called Torgormaig, or Lower Achnacroish, on the estate of Duart, which Charles had bought in 1821.[12] Lauchlan and Charles were exactly the same age, and perhaps because of the coolness between young Murdoch and Charles, enjoyed convivial evenings at Torgormaig, although Lauchlan was a frequent guest at Lochbuy also. When you are a gifted fiddler, you are likely to be much in demand in Highland households, especially where there are young ladies who love to dance. Lauchlan was fond of ladies, but as the ones who appealed to him most were educated gentlewomen, he had nothing to offer them in material terms. In his unique social situation, he had no equals of the opposite sex, although he observed sympathetically of Bell MacArthur [13] that she was 'a lassie come of a leg like myself'. 'It's a pity people could not wait to say grace before they fall to,' he observed of a very young girl who gave birth to an illegitimate daughter at Killean in the same year. He was reduced to worshipping girls from afar, without the prospect of a happy union, and the one he loved most, for her merry personality, her kindness, looks and charm, was Mary Maclaine of Lochbuy, second youngest daughter of Murdoch the nineteenth, who married John Gregorson of Ardtornish in 1820. She was twenty years old, and John forty-five, at the time of the marriage. John had recently bought Ardtornish, where his father had been tacksman for forty years. Mary Gregorson stepped into the role of mistress of Ardtornish with grace, making the old house into a centre for New Year and other festivities.[14] Her marriage was approved by her brother, young Murdoch, who grew closer to the Gregorsons as a result, and soon the Sound of Mull was buzzing with the coming and going of Maclaines and Gregorsons visiting for christenings and funerals and even for churchgoing. Lauchlan's birlinn [15] performed well, and was kept near Garmony Point, the nearest embarkation place for Ardtornish. He ferried Marjory Gregorson back and forward on her visits home to Scallastle, and since Marjory was his sister-in-law, his relationship with the Gregorsons was similar to Lochbuy's, although he owed a greater debt to John. In August 1815, when the wars with France abruptly ceased, and Lauchlan was being kept waiting while the war office decided what to do with all the alerted troops, he had written to John, 'Long ere this did I expect to be in the West Indies reaping a golden harvest which might enable me quickly to repay your kind loan, but Government will take its own time, and there is a fate in these matters.' [16] Both the Gregorsons and the Lochbuys constantly supplied Lauchlan with mutton and roasting beef, possibly to help him to be hospitable on his small income when they themselves dropped in at his cottage on their way up and down the road, to take their mutton with him, and to stay overnight. Among other overnight visitors at Garmony were the ministers of Torosay and Salen. But Mrs Gregorson exceeded even such small considerations in her kindness in sending food and drink. 'Wrote to my dear friend Mrs Gregorson for her kind and substantial present to me yesterday, various instances of whose good will towards me I have frequently experienced. She is the property of a good honest man. Let my friendship then keep within bounds, nor covet the goods of another. I hope I may admire without coveting.' [17]

His admiration of cultivated young women got him into trouble when he dared to admire Miss Anna Jane Maclean Clephane of Torloisk. He had had early warning of Marianne's fears on her daughters' account in July 1824.

Took a ride to Kilbrenan to see Mrs Maclean and extended it to Torloisk to see the family there. Received in a very formal manner by Mrs C., and ordered rather *coldly* to sit down. Lord Compton, his lady, his daughter, Lady Mary Anne Compton, and his two oldest sons and Wilmina I found there. Her Ladyship was too heavy to move off her seat.[18] Miss C.[19] was disposed to pay me some attention and her sister Miss Wilmina looked a great deal of good nature. His Lordship was as polite and attentive as perhaps a first interview would permit. Took a glass of water and a crust and departed. A daughter of Mr Maclean of Coll was there, Miss Breadalbane whom I would have examined but for my embarrassment from my reception. Returned to Oskamull for dinner.

A year later, when Lauchlan was visiting Ulva, Mrs Clephane had his trunk sent to Torloisk, a kind of peremptory invitation which he could hardly ignore. 'A strange, most clever woman,' he pondered, and was entertained on that occasion with music from the harp, which inspired him to write a little thank you note to Anna Jane, and slip it into the instrument. 'Miss Clephane tuned her harp to every lay / Maid of Torloisk who with such magic Art / Each emotion can so well inspire/Attuned must be that soul which can impart/ Such living powers unto the silent Lyre.' On St Valentine's Day, a festival much celebrated by the Argyll gentry, Lauchlan sent a Valentine song with music to Miss Anna Jane, and was attacked in a 'scurrilous note' by Mrs Clephane. 'Her friendship I never had', he concluded sadly. 'Improper pride.' He put a letter into the post at Ballifraoich, but met the postman [20] and asked for it back, since it was too severe. 'By it I would not only make her my enemy, but her daughters, and some of my own relations.' Lauchlan decided to restrict his attentions to females to a goose called Elizabeth which Marion Currie had brought him. 'A very fine goose which I will call Elizabeth after her oldest daughter.' Friday 17 March 1826: 'Made a house for the goose Elizabeth this day.' Monday 20 March 1826: 'Elizabeth Goose laid this day.' But even the goose fled to Salen.

The arrival in the parish of the family of Colonel Campbell of Possil in 1826 brought a new kind of heritor to the island. Alexander Campbell and his wife Harriet MacLachlan came from Argyll families who no longer spoke Gaelic. They were affluent and attractive people, and began at once to introduce agricultural methods which had long been taken for granted in other parts of Scotland. Colin McKillop became a gamekeeper for the Possils, a post that had not really existed before. Bounties for birds of prey were publicised. A captured or killed eagle commanded 5s., a hawk 6d., hoodie crows 2d. each, kingfishers 2d., and eaglets out of the nest 2s. 6d.[21] Colonel Campbell's compassion for poor families was considerable, and he paid for the funerals which neither the family nor the poor box could afford. His support for the church at Craignure was always generous, and included the gift of a church bell in 1829. His loft in Craignure Church was generally thronged with visitors and relations, who all gave equally generously to the poor box, on the scale of 6s. compared to the average 6d. of the other gentry families. Mrs Campbell, who kept a dispensary at home, sent nourishing food such as cornflour to sick people in the community who were in the habit of eating nothing but potatoes and milk. Her own daughters were encouraged to do charitable work, something which the Argyll gentry families had given little thought to in the past. The idea of old Lady Lochbuy, John Lochbuy's wife, who had owned one pot, and who was always scrabbling for money herself, giving to the poor, was quite unimaginable. Even her successor, Jane Campbell, with her nine daughters, was hardly in a position to throw largesse to the crowds. And young Murdoch's Chirsty was positively told by her careful father to spend nothing. The elegant Harriet in the role of Lady Bountiful was quite unnerving for the cottars of the Duart estate such as the people of Ardchoirk.

Lauchlan, whose heart was always susceptible to the charm of a lady, felt, being a bachelor, young and bashful and full of boyish admiration. He 'supped elegantly' with the Possils on their arrival in 'the Country', and was a frequent guest, with his violin, at parties, where there was dancing and singing. In 1832 he was anxious to see Miss Susan Campbell on her arrival from London. 'She is a fine figure, and has a great deal of the sweet expression of her Mother in her countenance.' Miss Susan and a large party of Campbell relations took an interest in the opening of a new Sunday School, but had to have the Gaelic proceedings translated by Lauchlan. In May 1834, Lauchlan, who was given to expressing himself in hopeful epistles, wrote what he called an imprudent letter of admiration to Miss Susan, gave it into the care of her brother Johnnie [22] who handed it to her mother, and found himself in hot water. That Harriet Campbell should take so seriously the attentions of a bachelor of sixty-three as to be 'implacable' was interesting, but the colonel, 'the true gentleman, the soldier, the man of the world' went up to Lauchlan at Craignure Church the following Sunday, and shook his hand as usual. The rest of the gentlemen in his loft followed suit, so that Lauchlan was not regarded as a threat to the good order of the family of Duart. His 'love ditty' (so similar to the indiscretion with the Torloisk family) took some time to be forgiven by the ladies. 'My Dulcinea would be distant', wrote Lauchlan in July. 'My flame looks rather pale', he was observing in 1836, 'and on taking her hand I am sensible my face flushed, and I believe kept so during my stay, which must have been near two hours.'

But Lauchlan's great enthusiasm, apart from his partiality for young ladies, was the practice of alternative medicine. He had learned some recipes in Jamaica, among them being an antidote for contagious fever made with wormwood, tansey, peppermint, camomile, and rhubarb root.[23] When typhus fever was killing Mull people in 1831, he prepared some of his 'bitters'.

> Malcolm Lamont, my old blind dancing-school fiddler and his wife some days ago fell victims to the typhus fever at Kilpatrick. A fine young man their son died of it yesterday. The infection will be greater and the disease more virulent from the number of deaths, and the evil must be spread as people must be employed as nurses and to bury the dead.

His panacea for everything from sore eyes, toothache, grazes and rheumatism was his 'oleum', which he made at home in Garmony from palm oil, possibly mixed with seaweed. There was no doctor for the very poor in Torosay parish. Dr Donald Maclaine, who had been accused of cuckolding Allan Maclaine in the inn at Achnacraig in 1801, was now about seventy years old, and refused most requests to attend to the sick. His removal in 1829 to Gualachaolish with his large family of adult children had put him beyond the reach even of those patients who were willing to pay his fee. Colonel Campbell and young Murdoch Lochbuy had tried to engage a doctor for the parish when the fear of cholera was at its height, but without success. Torosay was therefore doctorless when typhus was a reality and cholera a spectre moving ever closer. Lauchlan's interest in medicine, and his touching faith in his oleum made him a willing medical practitioner, but above all it made him an interesting commentator on the physical condition of the people at a time when poverty had restricted their diet to the basic fare of potatoes and milk. The community in which he worked as an unofficial doctor was principally the area north of his cottage at Garmony, including Ballameanach, Balifraoich, Ledirkle, Fishnish and Corrinahenachy. It was the same community which supplied the workmen who helped him with his peats, his thatching and his potato lifting, as well as other odd jobs like whitewashing and the filling of rat holes, delving and haymaking. The cat, given him as a present by the ever-kind Mrs Gregorson, had turned out to be, in his words, a 'carpet cat', which did not hunt rats and mice, but kept the rats at bay by its frequent mewing. 'The servant man is whitewashing my room,' he wrote in the diary in June 1827. 'My room now looks as gay as a young bride, fleecy white in wedding attire. A rat, the first I have seen here for some years, walked into my room as I was writing this, and went below my bed.'

He had trouble with his 'servants' – not surprisingly, as their payment seemed to be sometimes (for thatching) a fixed 6d. a day, and at other times (for peat cutting) a dram and some tobacco. His most difficult employee was Neil McNeil in Balifraoich,[24] whose wife had died in 1828, and who was unwilling to give services, and simply did not turn up when sent for. 'Neil McNeil did not come today. His daughter Ann, who came to beg for a plate of salt, says that he is sick. It may be so, for I believe he starves at home, and feeding heartily with me perhaps injures himself'. And in 1831, when Neil was sixty-seven years old:

> Archibald McNeil, son to Neil McNeil, Balifraoich, an active, fine young man, was cut suddenly off this day about 1 o'clock p.m. by a violent stitch or spasm. He has been complaining for some days of a violent pain in his chest, sometimes moving towards his shoulders, and sometimes his throat. I gave him some of the oleum to try and remove it, and he felt so much better he slept well that night, and yesterday *foolishly* went to assist his father to delve some ground. No doubt he overheated himself, which increased the stitch and quickly cut him off. Gave his brother half a crown to purchase boards for his coffin, for the family are all miserably poor.

Neil McNeil was always taking shortcuts, such as patching Lauchlan's roof with sods, which he did in November 1831, with the help of Hugh Macdonald, shepherd in Fishnish. 'My room, which was thatched by Hugh Macdonald looks near the fireplace as bad as ever. Sent for him to see it, and he has tried to mend it by putting sods on the roof.' This was a method which cost least effort, and Lauchlan did not approve. Clearly it was practised all over Mull, not least by Mercey's '*bon habitant de Bunessan*'. Lauchlan asked Neil McNeil heal chum an galar so chumail air falbh. 'Se dleasdanas gach fir-tighe, uime sin, aire churamach a thoirt dhoibh 'na theaglach fein.

TIGHEAN.

Chum tighean a chumail glan, tha e ro-fheumail gach torran salachair, agus gach dun-aolaich a chur fad air falbh, agus sin gun dail, o gach tigh-comhnuidh.

Tha e feumail, mar an ceudna, gach slochd agus tobar uisge mu 'n tigh a chumail glan; agus gach salachar a chur air falbh le sruthaibh uisge.

Feumar gach Seomar aiticht chumail glan le bhi gu tric ag sguabadh, agus a glanadh airneis; agus deadh fhaile chumail ann araon le teine math, agus le aile an Adhair a leigeil a stigh.

Feumar eudach leapa, araon olainn agus anairt a chumail glan, agus gach cuil mu 'n leabai a sguabadh; agus na sean bhrogan, agus na broineagan, agus gach salchar eile a tha gu tric air a thilgeil an sin, a chur a mach. Feumar gach ni a thogas droch-fhaile, no boladh breun air bith u chur a mach gun dail.

PEARSA.

Feumaidh gach neach a phearsa fein a chumail glan le bhi gu tric 'g a nigheadh, agus le bhi muthadh eudaich.

Feumar gach Srann ghouithe, agus aile na h-oidhche chumail a mach an am cadail.

Tha e iomchuidh eudach ollainn no flannel a chaitheadh am fagus do 'n chraicionn; gu h-araidh mu 'n mhionach; agus na casan agus na luirginean a chumail blath le ossain ollainn; agus an truscan a mhuthadh gun dail, an uair a tha e fliuch.

LON

A thaobh loin, tha aran, no buntata air a bhruich gu math, gle fhallann; ach feumar gach gne bhidh a sheachnadh a tha doilich a chnamh, no dhuisgeas seirbhe no gaoth air a ghoile.

Air doigh araidh feumar gach seorsa dibhe laidir agus Shearbh a Sheachnadh, agus gach ni a dhuisgeas faireachadh searbh no goirt sa Ghoile.

Mar chreutairean a tha 'n crochadh air cumhachd Dhe, se dleasdnas nan uile bha cridheal sunndach, agus gach eagal trailleil a chumail air falbh; oir tha eagal a lagachadh dhaoine air a leitheid sin a dhoigh, 's gu bheil e 'g am fagail buailteach do 'n phlaigh so.

'Se dleasdnas dhaoine feum a dheanamh do na riaghailtibh mar mheadhonaibh tearuinnteachd le earbsa umhal iriosal ann an comhnadh agus dion an Uilechumhachdaich; agus aonadh le cheile ann an urnaigh ri Dia gu 'n cumadh e air falbh o 'n duthaich, o 'n cairdibh, agus uapa fein a phlaigh uamhasach so,

Tha crioch ghlic aig Dia 's gach amhghar a tha e tarruing air daoinibh; agus, an uair a tha Dia a' bagradh, ma ni daoine dearmad air an slighean a leasachadh, air an droch chleachdan a chur air cul, air a pheacadh a tha gu furas ag iathadh umpa a threigsinn, feudaidh gu 'n cuir e peanas an gniomh orra airson cruas an cridhe, agus an dimeas air a rabhaidh leis a phlaigh sgriosach so a tharruing orra.

" Oir an uair a bhios breitheanais an Tighearna air an talamh, foghlumaidh luchd-aiteachaidh an t'saoghail fireantachd."

OKSELLER, OBAN.

Cholera poster in Gaelic, emphasising clean houses, personal hygiene and diet. In the *tighean* section it recommends that all dunghills and middens be removed to a distance from the dwelling house. (*GRO. Maclaine Papers*)

to return to do the traditional thatching, in a coxcomb, what was called, in Gaelic, a '*frighann*'.

Lauchlan's nephew, his mother Janet MacPhail's grandson, came to help sow the vegetables with which Lauchlan liked to vary his diet. They were carrots, turnips, leeks, broccoli, Normandy candy-heart, cress, mustard, celery, peas, beans and Indian corn, as well as red and white beetroot and swedes. As cottars and crofters did not care for vegetables, there was no danger of these being stolen when they were ready for eating, but his gooseberries were often plundered in the night just as they came to ripeness. When he at last bought himself a filly to carry him on his many journeys over Mull, and let her feed in his own 'black park': 'The farm servants, jealous that my Horse be feeding in the Black Park, though all their own cattle use it for *free quarters* there, had recourse to letting the Stallion loose at her, careless of consequences to me or her. As I am now in the enemy's camp, I require all my prudence, caution and patience ...'

His mother, Janet MacPhail, who also fell into disputes with the neighbours, and whose principal self-indulgence was the smoking of tobacco in a pipe, began to feel that her end was near in 1830, and arranged to bequeath her small and precious possessions among her legitimate children. These were a chest, a Paisley shawl, a plain gold ring, a silver brooch set with garnets and a spinning wheel. 'The greediness of Anne Buchanan', Lauchlan said of his half-sister,[25] 'makes her plague her Mother, even in the painful state she is in, to alter the disposal of the articles. She would fain have everything herself. She vexed me so much that I am determined to keep nothing that a Buchanan or a Currie can have any pretension to. The silver brooch which my Mother desired me to wear, I decline.' His mother died on 17 August, and he was faced with the predicament of avoiding a battle royal at the funeral.

> Donald Currie finished her coffin, a plain and neat one. I myself making a twenty pint cask of whisky toddy for the funeral, which takes place tomorrow. A fine warm fair day. The Northern Lights shining very splendid for these three nights back ... As usual in this Country, got a number of my neighbours (of the lower class, for I invited no gentlemen) from Ledirkle, Balifraoich and Garmony to collect to breakfast. But instead of making them bearers, dismounted the Body off one of the carts, and fixed the Coffin on the frames – the cask of toddy close by it – seated a woman on the same, and gave her charge of a jar of whisky. The Coffin covered with the Mortcloth ... accompanying this was a Horse and Creels full of bread, cheese and whisky in bottles to serve such as should *fall in* on the way to the burying place at Kilpatrick. A great concourse of her old friends and relations met us at the Grave. A fine warm dry day with N W wind.[26]

Lauchlan was a keen shot, and the long miles he walked were enlivened by his interest in game.

Monday 29 November 1824. Took my gun and dogs, and accompanied by my new servant Archibald Maclaine proceeded for Moy going across the hill to Rohill [27] by Ishribh [28] where I took a draw near Peggy Currie's, from whence I kept down through the glen. Found Lochbuy and family all well. ...

Shooting excursions after a funeral were favoured, because the men were conveniently gathered together. Lochbuy himself was a particularly good shot, but as the younger generation grew up, young Murdie, Dod [29] young Lachlan Macquarie and the three Macquarie sons of Colonel Charles joined the men. By this time Lauchlan's lameness was beginning to hold him back, and he lent his best pointer to Murdie Lochbuy to shoot over.

Monday 26 March 1832. On my way home was overtaken by Murdoch Maclaine Junior of Lochbuy, and Mr Johnnie Campbell, Possil. My old dog Norrie, who accompanies young Murdoch Lochbuy, scarcely recognises me! I never met with ingratitude in a dog before. But he seems to say, 'You have got old and lame, and cannot afford me sport. I have therefore transferred my affections to one who can.'

Two days after Janet MacPhail's funeral, Lauchlan had been out on an August deerhunt: 'called by young Murdie for the amusement of his cousin, the young heir of Jarvisfield, vulgarly called Gruline. Attended by Mr John Gregorson, Ardtornish, and Dr Neil Campbell, Frachadil. After hunting Fraochmore, a hind came out at Mr Gregorson's pass, which he shot, and which was immediately sent to Lochbuy.' [30]

Lauchlan disagreed with the policy of burning heather.

Monday 14 May 1827. Large fire at back of Corinahenach Hill, by which I have no doubt a good many moorfowl nests burnt. What a shame! But an example is shown by the Sheriff himself, whose hills were blazing last week. But O Lauchlan! What concern do you take in other people's matters? Mind your own affairs, and keep your mind at ease.

Lauchlan was able to prescribe his oleum for most ailments, but was defeated by the case of Marion MacKinnon's labour. Marion MacKinnon had married John MacEachern [31] in June 1830, both Fishnish people, and in June 1832, Lauchlan began to worry about her condition and the lack of a doctor.

John MacEachern's wife at Fishnish, Marion MacKinnon, Baldy's daughter,[32] in labour since Saturday last. I was only informed of her case this morning. Gave her some oil of peppermint, some Hailsham to smell at, and an injection of castor oil and warm water, which operated soon on her. I feel she is too long without a surgeon.

Friday 24 February. Sent a message to Mrs Colonel Campbell of Possil to use her influence with Dr Donald Maclaine to come and see her. She replies Dr Donald from age and sickness is unable to go. John MacKinnon, learning that Surgeon McColl,[33] a man midwife, was lately at Colonel

Campbell's,[34] Knock, I recommended him to proceed there.

Saturday 25 February 1832. Soon after breakfast crossed the hill to Fishnish to see the woman in labour, when happily I found Dr McColl the man midwife before me who was just arrived from Knock, where he had been attending Miss Campbell with Erisepelis. He pronounced the child dead, and delivered her with much labour on his part and excruciating suffering on hers, in the space of five hours. Got the doctor afterwards to come and dine with me, and afterwards accompanied him back to his patient carrying a dish of castor oil with fifteen drops of laudanum to be taken by her tomorrow night. Her husband John MacEachern paid him his fee reduced to the lowest degree – £1. Snow on the hills. A fine dry day. SSW wind.

Sunday 26 February 1832. As Mrs Campbell of Possil extends her charity to all such objects in her neighbourhood, informed her of the MacEacherns' helpless situation, and she is to send her necessaries – in the meantime gave me some arrowroot, epsom salts and some sugar for her.

Another of Lauchlan's services to posterity was the compiling of a private census of every person who lived in the triangle between Fishnish, Corrinahenachy and Balifraoich in 1829, with their ages. They amounted to 205 people, and of these, nearly every one was mentioned at some time in his diary, including children and infants. Many were not reported upon favourably, but the reluctance of men to work belonged to that strange phenomenon which is observed in many countries afflicted with hunger, a passive inertia which gathers momentum as hunger becomes a way of life. From about 1815, this lack of nourishment became prevalent, then turned into habitual hunger, then, in the 1830s, starvation. Lauchlan observed of his own brother, Hugh Buchanan, that he was thin, and underfed. His sister-in-law, Mary McKillop, asked Lauchlan for £1 to 'see her through hard times'.[35] 'The potato crop, I fear, will be short this year', Lauchlan observed, on 1 June 1835, 'as much of it has rotted in the ground.' On 3 August this was confirmed by the Scallastle potatoes being in a bad state from disease, Lauchlan's own potatoes not being free from it, but he could not complain, compared with some of his neighbours. Pigs were dying from feeding on rotten potatoes.

> *Monday 20 July 1835.* Saw Hector Maclaine's daughter who was lately delivered of a still-born child. She is not getting strong in a hurry, for a good reason. I fear that they are all starving, and can ill help her. The beast of a father (the father of the child), John McKillop, should assist her, but I blame that close-fisted father of his more than himself. They shall be made to pay in the end if justice is to be had.

Lauchlan's own income was restricted to his half-pay, but as a member of the half-gentry, his neighbours overestimated his resources, and constantly asked for loans. He tried to give these in the form of gifts of food, and by inviting his mother's relations to eat their Christmas dinner with him. The carpenter,

Presumed silhouette of Lauchlan Maclaine the diarist, *c.* 1831,
when he was about sixty. (*GRO. Maclaine Papers*)

Donald Currie, and his wife, Lauchlan's sister Anne Buchanan, were generally
unwilling, and only the younger members of the family would appear – Gillean,
Lachlan, Isabella and Hector. To them, Lauchlan presented Gaelic testaments,
in the hope of planting some seeds of learning, but their needs were more
material. 'Poor Donald Currie the Carpenter lost his boat in a storm, by an
extraordinary high surge, dashed into pieces against the rocks at Ledirkle.'
'Gave Donald Currie's wife for the use of her family fifty herrings, seeing
them eating their potatoes *per se.*' At the same time, Lauchlan was receiving
presents from his own social superiors (who may have felt more compassion
for the plight of a man raised as a gentleman than for the flighty cottars) –
raspberry jam and blackcurrant jelly from the Drimnin Macleans,[36] salmon
from Lochbuy, lamb from the Possils, and constant supplies of good things
from Mrs Gregorson at Ardtornish.

Advanced in his notions of hygiene, Lauchlan was made a member of the 'Health Board' which inspected the houses of the people in the cholera precautions. He mentioned having 'close stools' made by the carpenter for his own house. As a host to several lairds who stayed at his cottage overnight, he required such refinements. No mention was made of the sanitary problems of women, who menstruated less than modern women, being often either pregnant or nursing, and bearing children right up to the menopause; the age of a woman at the birth of her last child was usually forty-five or forty-six. He did, however, report the case of Miss Mary Maclean, daughter of Hugh Callachilly, who went through several surgical operations for cancer of the breasts in the 1820s. He also gave details of his own toothache, when he could not persuade Dr Donald Maclaine in Gualachaolish to pull the tooth, because, said Dr Donald, the weather was too frosty. Lauchlan had to pay the price of staying with the doctor's family for several days, reading, chatting and playing backgammon, until the weather turned wet, stormy and mild, and the tooth could be drawn. What the cottars did when they had toothache, without such social skills to interest the doctor, or the wherewithal to pay, must be imagined. It was a complaint Lauchlan himself did not attempt to treat.

Dr Donald Maclaine, previously of Callachilly, who was married to the daughter of the minister of Lismore,[37] a 'sensible woman', was one of those Mull fathers whose children never left home. In 1831, the year of Lauchlan's toothache, he had three daughters in their thirties, and four sons between fifteen and thirty-three, living at Gualachaolish, the former home of Alexander Fraser, the Torosay minister. This extraordinary predisposition to remain within the confines of the family, and not to marry, was a characteristic of so many Mull families that it was unfortunate that Lauchlan did not comment on it, although he loved to list all the sons and daughters he found at home whenever he visited. In 1841, after the doctor's death, six grown-up children were to be found at Kentallen, and in 1871 the remnant, Janet, Mary and Andrew, were living at Aros Bridge.

In December 1831, Lauchlan set off on the kind of round of visits which was typical of this time, taking his nephew, little Hugh Buchanan with him as his 'valet'. He spent one night at Salen manse, after a deluge of rain, with the Rev. Duncan Maclean, then moved on to Tighanlone Inn, and from there to Ulva Ferry. Over Christmas, Lauchlan stayed for ten days at Ulva with the widowed Colonel Charles Macquarie. Charles now gave sanctuary to the daughter of his old chieftain, Lachlan MacQuarrie of Ulva, the spirited Miss Ann MacQuarrie, who acted as an honorary aunt to the Macquarie children. Here, on Ulva, the Rev. Neil Maclean, formerly tutor to the children at Torgormaig, was minister of the quoad sacra parish of Ulva. He gave a 'good Gaelic discourse' which nobody from the big house attended except the current tutor, Mr Stewart.

Monday 19 December 1831. Walked about with the colonel viewing his improvements. One field which gave 1000 bolls of carrots and potatoes.[38]

Monday 26 December. Left Ulva for Lochbuy, making a call at Inch on Colonel Macdonald,[39] who was kind, pressing me to spend the day with him. Passed the night at Kilfinichen with Mr Dugald McLachlan and his family ... Ferryman to Gribun one shilling ... Walked to Dererach, where I engaged a boat to shove me to the head of the loch to save walking. With drams, the cost 1/6. The name of the person who kept the boat a McColl, a schoolfellow of mine, he says, at Salen, with Lachinn Mac Donich Bhain, the schoolmaster, who was a maternal relation of mine. Arrived around about nightfall.

Wednesday 28 December 1831. After breakfast took a walk to look at the new house building at Laggan – a substantial good farmhouse. Met Mr McAndrew, who told me that the primrose leaf and root is good for gravel.

Thursday 29 December 1831. Mr Duncan MacTavish [40] returned this evening from Ardtornish ... all well. Lochbuy, soon after the dinner was over, appeared with the joyful tidings of the birth of a fine boy.[41] A son and heir to the Ardtornish estate. He and I drank to the health of the boy with three times three cheers. Frost. Dry. NW wind.

Saturday 31 December 1831. A great shintie match, Hogmanay and the New Year brought in.[42] An argument between the Chief and me, not always conducted coolly!

Thursday 5 January 1832. This being Christmas Day Old Style ... a throng shintie playing at Ardtornish and Ledirkle.

Thursday 12 January 1832. New Year's Day Old Style at Ardtornish. The usual salutations of a good New Year with a bumper of Old man's Milk before breakfast. A shintie match in the evening previous to the various parties and balls.

Friday 13 January 1832. After breakfast walked down to the Castle [43] and called to Donald Currie to send over his boat for me, which arrived soon after, and in which I crossed to Mull ...

Monday 30 January 1832. Crossed over to Ardtornish from Balifraoich in the Packet, preceded by the Sheriff's yawl, which carried Mrs Maclaine and Mr Gillean Maclaine Ross [44] from Scallastle. Before 3 p.m., Lochbuy, Colonel Campbell of Possil, and the Reverend Mr Angus Maclaine [45] appeared. Found the Reverend Mr John Macleod [46] before us, who, in his Holy Vocation gave a name, Angus, to the young Gregarach, the heir and representative of John Gregorson Esquire of Ardtornish. Among other good things, the Sheriff made a bowl of whisky today in which a child might swim, which made us all loquacious, and gave wings to my feet in the dance, forgetting my rheumatism at the moment. Such are the magic powers of women, wine and music.

Lauchlan had said in 1828, after one of his early confrontations with the

Garmony people: 'Altho' I wish to have nothing to say to the servants here, still they annoy me, sensible that I see a number of things ... and altho' they quarrel like a parcel of tinkers among themselves, they are agreed *in this point, that if they could drive me out of this, the loaves as well as the fishes would be all their own.* God knows, altho' I vegetate here, I have not much enjoyment and never looked upon my present situation as an inheritance. I do not wish to desert an aged Mother with one foot in the grave, but when it is the will of the Almighty to call her hence, I shall resign my cottage without much regret.'[47] In 1836, he did receive a polite and kind letter written in Gaelic from Lochbuy indicating that Garmony was to be let to a Lowlander. He and 'the Chief' had a good understanding – hence the Gaelic letter, for that language would not have been used in business correspondence, and the mode of address, *Fhir mo Chridhe* – man of my heart – was friendly. Lauchlan replied in the same spirit and, with a year to find another humble abode, he could entertain without resentment Mr Young the stranger who was to take his place and improve Garmony beyond recognition. But of course, the cottars and workmen and 'scalags' must go too; this was the order of things. The cottars of Balifraoich were at least duly warned, but Mr Young, pleased to try them out, gave them a year's reprieve, which set him high in Lauchlan's estimation.

1836 was one of those years when many leases were to come to an end, and Murdoch Maclaine of Lochbuy, no longer so young, but forty-five years old, was casting about for good tenants. Scallastle was at last free, by Marjory Gregorson's removal, after almost a century of being in the vice-like grip of Gillean's family, to be let at an economic rent. Three years before this juncture, Lauchlan had suddenly realised that there was no one left in Mull who remembered Gillean. All his descendants were now in England or in Edinburgh, and Lauchlan too would sooner or later quit the island. He first asked Mr Clark, minister of Torosay, if he might see the parish register, but found that the baptism register for the years before 1793 had been lost; removed, it was thought, by the family of Mr Patrick MacArthur.[48] He began to reconstruct the birth dates of his half-siblings, and discovered that the page from *Buchan's Family Physician,* where Gillean had recorded his children's births, had been torn out. 'All my sisters in conclave devoted to the destruction, as a libeller, of this useful volume, so often consulted by their good father, as it developed their ages, who, in their wisdom, would be forever young.'

Their good father! Not even Lauchlan, as the oldest child, had an inkling of all that had gone before, in that remote century that few cared about. He was convinced that his father was good and noble, and he would put up a monument to his memory. Lauchlan interviewed the ancient men of Mull, riding down to see Donald MacPhail, the drover, at Pennygown, who was eighty-seven. Donald thought that Gillean and John Campbell of Knock and the 'Old Fox' Alexander Campbell and Allan Maclean of Torloisk had all been schoolfellows.

This was a warning to all to pay no attention to the warblings of venerable age. At last, Lauchlan had the cross made, and erected at Scallastle, where few were to see it, and even fewer care. On the back he had engraved, *Ego Lauchlanus erexi,*[49] *1833.*

The proceeds of the roup of stock, furniture and books held at Scallastle were to go to the heirs of Allan, Gillean and Angus Maclaine, apart from some Gregorson items that were the property of the sheriff. Lauchlan bought an ashet and a dining table, and like the sale of items at Killiemore thirty-eight years before, the rest circulated in the island of Mull. Some chest belonging to Gillean and Marie may yet survive. On 27 May 1836, Lauchlan walked up to Scallastle.

> Scallastle House is a silent empty house indeed today, for not a voice is to be heard or a face to be seen in it but the plasterers. Aultcreich, late Dugald MacLachlan's hotel is also very solitary. His house dog, the only object to be seen, which by accident was left behind, gave a degree of sadness to the scene. I was sorry to see a number of the Scallastle sheep feeding upon his corn, and a patch of land in sown grass, which ought to be preserved. A dry, very warm day, with SE wind in the forenoon which changed to the north in the evening.

In 1837, Lauchlan moved into a house, 'up a stair, in a close, through a big entry, East End, Shore Street, Oban.'[50]

Here everyone in Mull dropped in as they arrived in or departed from Oban. The town of Oban was still called a village, but the harbour bustled with steamboats and yachts, and Lauchlan continued to write the diary, which will still be referred to in the course of this story. All the young people dropped in for what they called – influenced by Indian parlance – a 'snack', and his even more humble abode thronged with Lochbuy sons and daughters arriving for the pleasures of the Oban Regatta. In 1839 he was described by a new figure on the scene, Angus Gregorson, Soroba, Lochbuy's nephew, and newly appointed factor, as 'poor Lauchlan ... experimenting on his own unfortunate limb, employing his own oleum to cure his pains, and dosing himself with quack stuffs.' He kept in touch with the scattered Scallastle Maclaines, particularly with the Rev. Angus of Ardnamurchan. The shifting of his scene to Oban was to frustrate no one but the very few twentieth-century people who have so far read his diaries, and appreciated his invaluable vignettes of Mull life in the time before the great exodus. As a collector of Gaelic songs, and recorder of life in the small West Highland town of Oban from 1837 until 1847, he is yet to be discovered.

Notes

1. LMD was learning a kind of shorthand. Mr Thornton was the tutor, who travelled from Scallastle with the older children.

2. Julian was a girl, born 7 August 1775. Alicia was the oldest daughter, born 16 May 1774.

3. Professor William Robertson (1721–93), historian and Principal of Edinburgh University.

4. Miss Jean MacQuarrie (c. 1755–1835) youngest of LMQ's daughters by Alice, and Marie's sister.

5. Betty Maclean, unmarried younger sister of Hector, Lachlan, Allan and Alice Maclean of Torloisk.

6. Mr Beaton was a tutor. John Hunter WS of Doonholm (1746–1823). His son Alexander Hunter WS was a friend of Flora Lochbuy, see Chapter 23, and married Maria Maclean of Coll.

7. LMD's mother's brother, a MacPhail from Mull.

8. Perhaps a reference to Marie's pregnancy, 'noverca' being Latin for stepmother? GRO. Box 17.

9. Cregeen, *Inhabitants ... 1779*, and LMD diaries referring to his Buchanan brothers and sisters.

10. It is not clear when LMD settled in Garmony, as journals 1 and 6 are missing from the GRO collection. Eight volumes survive.

11. NAS. GD174/1638/21. JG to MM2, 28 September 1825.

12. The house which was demolished when Torosay Castle was built on the site.

13. Natural daughter of Finlay MacArthur. Diary, 23 September 1836. Finlay later married Marjory MacKinnon and lived in Garmony.

14. Old Ardtornish House, built c. 1760, with about twenty-two rooms, was dismantled in 1896 and demolished in 1907. Gaskell, p. 168.

15. Originally a chief's barge, but in LMD's case a strong serviceable boat suitable for transporting goods.

16. GRO. Uncatalogued MSS. LMD to JG, Portsmouth, 19 August 1815.

17. LMD. Diary, 25 January 1826.

18. Never a sylph, Margaret Maclean Clephane grew enormously plump after her marriage, not helped by her repeated pregnancies.

19. Anna Jane, the middle sister, who took over the correspondence with Scott, and remained unmarried.

20. Malcolm MacKinnon, 'Calum Post', a well-known Mull personality, who knew everyone's secrets.

21. NAS. GD174/1114. Bounties paid for destroying birds of prey, 1831.

22. John Campbell of Possil, later to build the house now known as Torosay Castle.

23. GRO. D3330. Box 25. LMD. Diary, 19 November 1831.

24. Born about 1764. Neil McNeil's wife, Mary McCallum, died only a few days after his daughter Mary's death, and he was one of those who had no money to pay for a coffin, and for whom Colonel Campbell paid.

25. Anne Buchanan, born in 1777, married Donald Currie, carpenter at Ballameanach in 1807. Their children, Mary, Isabella, Lachlan, John, Hector and Gillean were only some of Janet MacPhail's grandchildren to remain in Scotland after the exodus of the 1850s.

26. LMD gives a report on the weather every day throughout the twenty years of his diary.

27. Now called Rhoail.

28. Ishriff. This was the normal walking route from Salen to Lochbuy.

29. Donald Maclaine, later of Lochbuy, born 1816.

30. MM2 had retained the shooting rights over this part of the lands.

31. Women were always known by their maiden names although married, but the wives of gentlemen were referred to as 'Mrs M'.

32. Archibald MacKinnon, seventy-four years old, in Fishnish. They still had four adult children at home in Fishnish at this time.

33. Dr Hector McColl (1799–1891), later a surgeon in Tobermory, was born at Ledmore, and should not be confused with Dr Duncan McColl who was born in Lismore in 1810 and later practised in Salen.

34. Colonel Archibald Campbell, son of John Campbell of Knock.

35. Mary McKillop was the wife of George Buchanan, and had seven children in 1731.

36. The new family at Drimnin were also called Maclean of Drimnin, but were not connected with the old.

37. Donald McNicol (1735–1802), who published a reply to Dr Johnson's assertion that no Gaelic MSS existed.

38. About 448 lbs to a boll meant that the crop was 448,000 lbs.

39. Staffa's brother, Robert Macdonald of Inchkenneth.

40. 'Big Duncan' MacTavish, Lochbuy's 'henchman', son of Dugald MacTavish.

41. After the birth of stillborn twin boys to the Gregorsons in 1827, the birth of Angus Gregorson was a blessed event.

42. In Mull, old and new Christmas and old and new New Year were (and still are) all celebrated, making four festivals.

43. The ruined Ardtornish Castle, on the seaward side of the old house at Ardtornish. From here, on a still day, one can call across the Sound of Mull.

44. Marjory Gregorson and her nephew Gillean, son of Gillean and Marie's daughter Julian, who had once nearly married John Gregorson of Ardtornish, Marie becoming 'riotous' at the idea.

45. Rev. Angus, minister of Ardnamurchan, second son of Marjory Gregorson and Allan Maclaine of Scallastle.

46. Rev. John Macleod, the 'High Priest of Morvern' (because of his great height), son of the Rev. Norman Macleod.

47. LMD. Diary Monday 4 August 1828.

48. Patrick MacArthur (1740–90), minister of Torosay, 1779–90, when he was drowned in the Sound of Mull. His family probably assumed that the parish register belonged to his private papers.

49. Lauchlan's cross was subsequently moved to Pennygown Church where it can be seen today at the foot of Gillean's memorial.

50. Address of Mr Lauchlan Maclaine on a note from Murdoch Maclaine, 'Chief' of Lochbuy, 1838.

22

The tent in the gravel pit

Modern observers of the ecclesiastical scene in Scotland in the eighteenth and nineteenth centuries cherish the idea that ministers of old derived some kind of vicarious pleasure from their constant investigations into sexual immorality. The presbytery of Mull, the church court mediating between the kirk session and the Synod of Argyll, and eventually the General Assembly of the Church of Scotland, from its erection in 1726, was based at Aros. It had responsibility for the parishes of Mull itself, then numbering three, and for the neighbouring charges of Ardnamurchan, Morvern, and Coll and Tiree. An eavesdropper at a meeting of the presbytery of Mull at Aros in March 1744 might have been surprised to hear the ministers of these parishes discussing a case of incest which had been committed, not by a parishioner, but by one of their own number, the missionary at Strontian, in Sunart. The Rev. Mr Francis Macdonald had indulged in scandalous and indecent behaviour with his sister, Miss Catherine, which was carefully written up in a report by Mr John Stewart, drover, of Achadashenaig. The miscreant, who had been a 'Papist Priest' in his time, was so attached to his sister that she had borne him two children, and he was accused of 'sensual and brutal delectation in her person and company'.[1]

Only ten years before, the minister of Ardnamurchan, Mr Daniel MacLauchlan, had been charged with singing indecent songs, profaning and drinking to excess. During an absence from his parish, he had been imprisoned in London as the suspected author of a pamphlet entitled 'An essay upon improving and adding to the strength of Great Britain and Ireland by fornication'. He was excommunicated in 1737.[2] The areas of Morvern and Ardnamurchan had always given trouble. The ministers of the presbytery of Mull were not sheltered from the darker sides of life.

But the Mull members of presbytery were good and able men, who were not easily corrupted. Occasionally a 'Popish Priest' slipped in among them, as in 1729, when a Mr John Campbell had had the assurance to preach and say mass at a very small distance from Mr John Maclean's preaching house in the parish of Kilninian and Kilmore, 'a most intolerable insult' according to Sheriff Campbell of Stonefield, 'spreading the venom of their pernicious principles', but Maighstir Seathan had defended his ground. 'I am very hopeful,' said the sheriff, 'that Mr McLean, whom I always found zealous for the Cause, will not neglect his duty.'[3]

The ministers had many miles to cover in their own parishes, and many more sea miles to traverse to meet each other at presbytery, so that the minister of the joint charge of Coll and Tiree had enough difficulty moving between his islands, without attempting to attend winter presbyteries at Aros. Missionaries were employed in outlying areas who were fully qualified for the ministry, and it was often one of those who stepped into the shoes of a late incumbent. Mr Alexander Fraser, one of Mr Roderick Macleod's Aberdeen graduates, began by being a missionary in Coll, and was then ordained assistant to Archibald McColl, minister of Tiree, in 1780. In 1788, both Mr McColl and his young assistant, Mr Fraser were in trouble with their older colleagues, when it was discovered that Mr Fraser was living in a state of marriage with a Miss Isabella Maclean in Coll.

'It was moved,' said the presbytery minutes, 'that in regard to the reports concerning the Minister of Coll's marriage being clandestine, and that Mr McColl, minister of Tyrie, the alledged Celebrator is now present, the Moderator should interrogate him concerning that affair. Which motion being agreed to, the said Mr Archibald McColl was interrogated from the Chair whether or not he was the Celebrator of Mr Alexander Fraser of Coll's marriage, to which he answered in the affirmative. Being then interrogated if there was any previous publication of banns, and whether there were any witnesses present at the marriage, he answered to both in the negative. He was then interrogated if the parties were known to cohabit together from the date of their marriage, to which he answered he believed they did not cohabit. He was further interrogated what time after the date of the marriage elapsed before it was publickly known or notour in the neighbourhood, to which he answered he believed it might be three years or there about.' [4]

Mr McColl had made no entry in the register, and had given no marriage lines to the bride and groom. The presbytery therefore summoned Mr Fraser and his lady to their next meeting at Kilchoan to receive 'privy censures', but not before both ministers had been made to feel just how close they had come to ending their careers by the practice of irregular marriage. To ensure the regularity of the alliance, the couple were reunited in the eyes of the Lord, and Mr Fraser's contrite heart and faithful performance of his ecclesiastical duties brought forgiveness in 1791, when, after the tragic drowning of Mr Patrick MacArthur in the Sound of Mull, he was presented to Torosay parish by the commissioners for John, fifth Duke of Argyll.

Such an example had had to be made, even of a good and faithful servant, in the interests of propriety, and even more careful investigation was made into the conduct of bigamists, adulterers and fornicators, not because of any prurient interest in the circumstances on the part of the ministers, but for the very practical reason that every effort must be made to prevent an attitude of promiscuity which would throw illegitimate children upon the charity of the parish and its meagre resources. Poor relief was entirely in the hands of the kirk sessions, and as we have seen, the poor box was miserably empty, and its contents already spoken for. Fathers were sought out assiduously, and made to admit paternity, then take responsibility for the child. One reason for the absence of gentry fathers from the interrogations of presbytery and session was the fact that men like Gillean Maclaine and his sons Allan and Archibald Maclaine of Scallastle quite happily claimed paternity, gave the mother a very small allowance and put a few mites in the poor box, so were not required to compear. Some said that there was a tradition of testing virility on another girl before marriage.[5]

Ministers in the lands belonging to the Dukes of Argyll, and in particular, the third, fourth and fifth dukes, were fortunate, for these ducal heritors made no complaint about paying stipends, and even if they did not supply a manse and a glebe, they made an allowance in compensation. The Dukes of Argyll were powerful patrons who directed the presbytery in its encourage-ment of candidates for the ministry, and as the presbytery came to be dominated by the duke's presentees, it naturally approved the duke's recom-mendations. Mr Fraser was favoured by the fifth duke because he was a nephew of Mr Paul Fraser, minister of Inveraray, and through the uncle's marriage, he was related to the Campbells of Airds. This was not, however, a connection which recommended him to Murdoch Maclaine, the nineteenth of Lochbuy.

In the century between 1750 and 1850, apart from the dukes, and the Macleans of Coll, the Mull heritors were a rather ungodly lot, barely acquainted with religion, either in its politics or in its doctrines. Murdoch the twentieth was one of the few who expressed any sentiment of piety in moments of distress. Colonel Campbell of Possil was deeply supportive of the established Church of Scotland, but any deviation from its moderate tenets was like a red rag to a bull, just as any mention of the Reform Bill, or calls for the abolition of patronage made him angry. Lachlan Maclean of Torloisk had been a good Christian. He had attended presbytery meetings, but his daughter Mrs Maclean Clephane entered into litigation with her minister over his perfectly natural desire for a manse, and the Macdonalds of Staffa and Inchkenneth liked to be elders in the refined manner of the Edinburgh moderates. 'Staffa' represented the parish of Kilninian and Kilmore long after his financial collapse, as a ruling elder. Captain Allan MacAskill of Mornish, although a son of the manse,[6] was, like many sea captains, not a pious man, and his nephew and successor, Hugh, said himself that he had been denied the ordinances of the church in Skye.[7]

The principal reason for the unpopularity of the clergy with the heritors was their irritating tenacity when it came to demanding their rights in the form of manse and glebe and stipend. Some of them were without a church, because they were unable to persuade heritors to repair existing ones, and churches fell a prey to raging gales and torrential rain. Many people believe that Scottish churches were destroyed by angry mobs and violent partisans of the Reformation, but the weather was a greater enemy to church buildings, as was sheer neglect of upkeep. The ministers of the eighteenth century, although cultivated men, did not consider rebuilding pre-Reformation churches, but constructed cheap preaching houses in make-do fashion, which in their turn fell down after twenty years. When John Stevenson of Oban was calculating the costs of a new church at Bunessan, he offered the presbytery a discount if he was allowed to use some of the stones from the thirteenth-century church of Kilvicheoun nearby, a church built in a uniquely beautiful, if complicated fashion, and the presbyters and heritors who were considering the estimates accepted this suggestion with alacrity.[8]

From the moment in 1762 when the Rev. Mr Neil Macleod drew the attention of his fellow ministers to the acts of the Scottish parliament which authorised churches, manses and glebes in every parish, the long suffering ministers decided to take the law into their own hands, and understanding that by an act of 1573 glebes could be taken from old church lands, they identified those lands in Mull and Iona, and began their 'perambulations' and 'visitations', taking with them a surveyor and a builder who estimated on the spot for the manse and measured out the glebe. Recognising their right so to do, the Duke of Argyll compromised when they chose a site on Iona, by proposing an 'excambion' or exchange of land when it did not suit him to make such church land available. In the Ross of Mull, he offered the land of Assapol in exchange for the Iona site, but the minister would have to wait for the expiry of the present lease on that farm. In the meantime, the minister, who rented the farm of Ardchrishnish, would receive an allowance in lieu of manse, glebe and grass. From this relative success, the ministers chanced their luck with a similar exercise at Killean, in the parish of Torosay, which, with another medieval church, was assumed to be church land which had fallen into the clutches of the Macleans, and then had become the property of the duke, only to pass to the Drimnin family. They reckoned without the aggressive anti-church sentiments of Allan Maclean of Drimnin, who went out to meet the party of ecclesiastics invading his land in a furious temper, challenging the 'honest and discreet men' who had come along as arbiters. 'The Devil a word will I allow them to confer,' he cried, in a passion. 'Nor have they any right to walk on my ground, nor will I allow them to fix any bounds.' And violently setting his hand to the breast of each of them, he shouted, 'I stop you, I stop you, and you ...'.[9]

The incumbent, Mr MacArthur of Torosay, received some help from the duke, who was a smaller heritor in Torosay. He was given the farm of Gualachaolish on the same terms as the minister of Ross had received Ardchrishnish, and the duke duly paid his own proportion of stipend and compensatory allowance in lieu of glebe and grass. Murdoch Maclaine was not so accommodating, however, for with poor Mr Fraser's induction in 1791 there began thirteen years of ignoble strife between the heritor and the 'parson', as he was disparagingly called. Lochbuy was employing his Fabian tactics, stalling every kind of payment including the stipend of the unfortunate minister and the desperately small salary of the schoolmaster, to which he was obliged to contribute. Only one letter survives from the schoolmaster.

Sir,

I understand you had no time yesterday to speak with me as fully as I inclined. Therefore I take the liberty of writing you. When a man goes to Law he ought to be well versed in his own case, for then he cannot be imposed upon. How far I am so, time will soon disclose. It is about 100 years since all the school salaries in Scotland were stipulated by Act of Parliament; and in all that time none of your Predecessors ever refused to pay their Quota of the stent.[10] Murdoch Og as he was called, did not refuse it.[11] No, he knew better, for he was well acquainted with the law, and you may be sure he would not pay the stent, did he not see he was obliged. The only colour of plea you have is 'that you and your tenants have no benefit from the school.' But that argues nothing, for the inhabitants of the Highlands are so much scattered from one another that it is merely impossible to have a school convenient to all. The contrary is generally the case, for there are many more Heritors in the shire who receive no benefit from the Parish School than those who do. Dunstaffnage & McDougall receive no benefit from the school of *Kilmore* in Lorn. Yet they pay the stent, and must pay it. So, as for your 'not ever countenancing me as a schoolmaster, or not subscribing for me,' – that argues nothing, because I was countenanced by the majority of Heritors to whom the minority must always yield. However, as you were not in the Country at the time of my admission, you were not therefore in capacity to give your concurrence. In fine, the Gentleman who advised you wrong makes you lose about 5 or 6 guineas, and he himself loses the double of it. My wife has been in great distress for a long time. I am sorry I cannot do for her as her situation requires; but she has her Cousins the McLean lairds to thank for that, who, out of pure friendship to her, a mighty mark of their esteem for her indeed, who, I say, oppress me by keeping back my salary. If they wanted to retain salaries, it was not with me they should have begun. They might have allowed me to pass. Mrs McLean Coll, and many others, are attentive. She flatters herself that if you knew her distress, as she is not able to move a foot, you would be as attentive as the rest. If you please to send her anything, the Boy, who is her own son, will bring it to her. I am, Sir, with much esteem, Your most humble servant, Alexander Campbell.[12]

This was only one of many schoolmasters and ministers who were forced to go to law to have paid to them their infinitesimally small remuneration, and the main offenders were those heritors who struggled against all the odds to keep their estates – the Macleans of Pennycross, the Lochbuys, and in their day, the Mackinnons of Mishnish. Mr Archibald Maclean,[13] the minister of the Ross of Mull, although remunerated by the Duke of Argyll, preached in Kilfinichen, in the territory of the Maclaines of Lochbuy, and in 1752 Lochbuy had paid not a penny of his share of the assessment. 'I was not able to go your length,' Mr Archibald wrote to one of the trustees, 'being both old and

sickly, to know from you what you propose to do in my affair. I am in great
need ... I have no pleasure to force payment by the dint of Law.' [14]

Poor Mr Fraser was to write over 500 letters to the two Murdochs in the
thirty-seven years of his ministry asking for credit on the security of the
stipend he had not received for two years. He too arranged to go to the Court
of Session, upon which Young Murdoch, Donald Maclean WS and Charles
Macquarie raged against him. 'The parson's only object is to plague his
heritors', Donald wrote. Charles and young Murdoch retaliated by making
complaints about poor Mr Fraser's preaching (always excellent according to
Lauchlan the diarist). Mr Fraser did not, of course, withhold his ministerial
attentions to the offending families. Between the courteous requests for
payment, the minister turned up at Lochbuy to baptise a total of seventeen
Maclaine infants and to marry seven Lochbuy girls. 'I am pleased Miss Mary
is to be joined to a man of so respectable a character,' he wrote sweetly to
young Murdoch about the future husband, John Gregorson, as he accepted
the summons to join the pair in matrimony. At Elizabeth Lochbuy's wedding
to Donald Campbell, Murdoch had so hated the bridegroom that he had been
laid up with a sick headache.[15]

After more than fifty years of the Mull presbytery's asking for a manse
and glebe for its Torosay minister, plans were at last afoot for the handsome
house at Craignure which was to reward so much turning of the other cheek.[16]
But Mr Fraser did not live to move in. Always a chatty man, he was seized
with an obstruction of the throat just as his manse was being prepared for
occupation, and when Lauchlan Maclaine from Garmony walked out to
Gualachaolish on a fine warm day in May 1828, he found the minister unable
to swallow even a liquid. 'His spirits were sound in entering into conversation
with me, which he carried on even with a degree of pleasantry.' In this state
the minister survived for seven weeks. At his funeral at Gualachaolish on 8
July, 'a great concourse of the lower orders attended, and there were a good
many gentlemen.' [17]

In spite of having no manses, no glebes and very often no stipends, with
enormous parishes to traverse in wild, boggy, mountainous areas in what was
possibly the worst climate in Europe, the ministers gave of their best, and
were respected by the people just as much as they were disdained by most
of the heritors. They contributed to the scholarly translations of the Bible
into Gaelic,[18] and as far as they were able, in the face of opposition from the
heritors, promoted schools in their parishes. Only the Dukes of Argyll seemed
to treat the ministers well, encourage them in their teachings, and present
them to their charges. The fifth duke, ably assisted by Mr Maxwell, was one
of the few who recognised the long-term benefits of educating the people to
make them better and more responsible tenants.

But the issue of the lack of churches, manses and glebes unfortunately took
up so much presbytery time and energy that by the 1820s, when a large

evangelical presence was making itself felt in the General Assembly of the Church of Scotland, the Argyll clergy were being attacked for not attending to the spiritual needs of their congregations. At the 1824 Assembly a speech was heard which claimed that these ministers were all 'Moderates' who were hostile to the pious young men who tried to go among them, preaching the true gospel.[19] The following year the Assembly published a leaflet entitled 'A statement as to the want of schools and catechists in the Highlands and Islands', and set up special 'Assembly schools' in competition with the SSPCK foundations and the parish schools. In 1826 a parliamentary report on emigration produced 'sensational evidence as to Highland conditions' which disturbed all right-thinking people in the Lowlands.[20] In the same year large-scale evictions from the neighbouring island of Rum were instigated by a mere tenant, Lachlan Maclean of Gallanach, who had purchased Arivelchyne, Ardrioch and Duchorin in Mull; people began to feel uneasy. Up till now the Mull clergy, obsessed by the ruinous condition of their buildings, had expressed no political views on social issues such as eviction, and at this point it is safe to say that no clearances had taken place in Mull in the manner of the Rum exercise. People had been warned, and sent away on most of the estates, for non-payment of rents, unpaid arrears, or non-fulfilment of leases, and in many cases dependent cottars had had to leave as a result of the eviction of members of the class immediately above them. Even the removal of the cottars of Glenforsa, supposedly cleared for the entry of Charles Macquarie into his new estate, can be categorised as the effects of the moving of tenants, who had to take their cottars with them. Now that many of the people who had chosen to go to Canada had gone, those remaining, who were not able to go, knowing little of their rights, but having had the conviction that they could not be 'flitted' as long as they paid their rents, looked for leaders who could tell them what to do.

The clearance of Rum had indeed been a bad omen. Within a few years, the farm of Frachadil on the estate of Mornish, once a stronghold of Campbell tacksmen, was, as a result of the intensified threats of litigation from the clergy, being prepared for the accommodation of the minister of Kilninian, Dr MacArthur. It was unfortunate that the long sought for and rightful accommodation of the minister should be associated with clearances, but the cottars of Inivea and other townships within the bounds of Frachadil were, to use the ugly word now coming into being, 'supernumary'. The heritor in question, Hugh MacAskill, '*Eachann Mòr*', was an outsider who lived in Skye. In issuing precepts of removal, he was not concerned about the fate of these cottars. In the event it seems that most of the six families served with precepts were accommodated within the parish, and that Dr MacArthur (whose epitaph gives him a good name) may have helped them. The names peculiar to the township of Inivea, Gillies, McIlphadraig[21] and MacArthur, did not immediately disappear from the parish.

Before this 'evacuation' of Inivea, which in some traditions was said to be the result of a plague of mice,[22] more than 1,000 emigrants had left for Cape Breton.[23] In 1831 the Reform Bill went through its capers of being introduced, withdrawn, amended and rejected. In 1835, alarm was expressed at a presbytery meeting about dissent in the parish of Kilfinichen and Kilvicheoun, mainly in the Ross of Mull area. Anabaptist notions had infiltrated the people, and the minister, Mr Campbell, could not cope with the problem. A visitation was arranged, and the ministers, now increased in number by the addition of parliamentary churches at Tobermory, Salen, Ulva and Kinlochspelve, agreed to preach in rotation at Bunessan for the duration of the dissent, which they spoke of as if it were an infection, like cholera. At about the same time, there were deep divisions of opinion in the selection of a new minister for Salen. The laird of Coll, Hugh Maclean, was found to be attempting to introduce a candidate of his own, with 'enthusiastic' principles, and the other heritors complained that they had not been consulted. The question of Patronage[24] was raising its head even in Mull.

In Torosay parish, a new minister, Mr Duncan Clark, presented by the sixth Duke of Argyll and therefore not of a radical persuasion, began his ministry as a bachelor, living in the fine manse at Craignure which had been built to accommodate a family of ten. For the first six years of his incumbency he was preoccupied with acquiring the necessary wife, observed by his friend Lauchlan, a watchful elder of the church. 'I learned that Mr Clark was off again by steam for the North, which seems to have powerful attractions at present, his needle always pointing towards the pole.' In no time the minister had returned. 'Rode up this forenoon to the Torosay Manse to congratulate the young pair on their marriage. Mr C. seems very happy and the wife I have no doubt, no less so. She is comely, handsome and affable. Some of her wedding cake decorated with light blue ribbons … I will place under my pillow tonight.'[25]

The new heritor of Duart, Colonel Alexander Campbell of Possil, and his wife Harriet, were well pleased with the character of the minister at Craignure. The friendship between the Possils, the Maclaines at Lochbuy and the Gregorsons at Ardtornish was cemented by the views they held in common. The generosity of the Campbells did not cease when the dreaded new Poor Law was passed. The Colonel had a policy of employing local labour in his schemes for improvement and Harriet's provision for the poor now included a weekly allowance for the very needy in her area, and a further sum for the education of their children.[26] Their factor, Mr Middleton, had told the Poor Law Enquiry that the cottars on the Possils' estate had barely bedding or bedclothes, and that many lay on the ground on heath or straw. Nevertheless, he said, their poor people were infinitely better off than those on neighbouring estates, and a legal assessment would be a very great evil. But now the legal assessment had been enforced, and Mr Middleton was about to be proved right.

The issues of emigration, patronage and a new, but very quiet kind of religio-political awareness were beginning to join forces when in 1837, a shipload of emigrants were given an emotive farewell sermon in Gaelic by the Rev. Finlay MacPherson of the *quoad sacra* parish of Tobermory.[27] In the following year a 'fine large ship' left Tobermory for Australia with 400 emigrants, as John Campbell Maclaine, one of young Murdoch's sons, reported to his brother Murdie. John Campbell himself would follow it in 1841, for the gentry families too began to see in Australia the land of the future.

Very few rumblings were heard by the Establishment in Mull prior to the Disruption of 1843 (unless 'Anabaptist error' be classed as rumbling), but news of disquiet spread from the mainland. Lauchlan the diarist, who had gone to live in Oban in 1837, noted when his minister had gone off to take over the charge of the Gaelic chapel in Edinburgh, that 'the Secession church would be full', in his absence. In 1841, he was unhappy that two ministers had been invited to preach in his church *against church patronage*.[28] In Mull, a few ministers and schoolmasters were beginning to show an inclination to embrace the new apostasy. When the crunch came, and 450 ministers walked out of the General Assembly of the Church of Scotland in May 1843, excitement at the formation of a new Free Church of Scotland was great, although the man with the greatest influence on 'the Country', Norman Macleod, son of the manse of Fiunary in Morvern, had remained in the Established Church. The Mull presbytery sadly noted the names of its own seceders – Donald McVean, minister of Iona, John McQueen and Donald McInnes, teachers in Kilfinichen, Mr Dugald McColl, parliamentary teacher in Tobermory, the two John MacCormicks in the Ross, and many more schoolteachers.

It was ironic that apart from Iona and the tip of the Ross of Mull, the greatest concentration of Free Church sympathisers should be at Lochdonhead, on the estate of Colonel Campbell of Possil. Seeking sites for free churches, Mr Graham Speirs had written to Colonel Campbell, and had been refused. Several landowners had been alarmed by the aggressive language of some Free Church oratory, and the use of verbs like 'vanquish' and 'destroy' in relation to the Church of Scotland. Colonel Campbell, a staunch supporter of the Establishment, was, like his friend Hugh Maclean of Coll, unwilling to favour a bunch of bandits. But Mr Auldjo, proprietor of Pennyghael, had, although an Englishman, and a member of the Church of England, given a site for a Free Church near Loch Scridain, and was promising a manse and a schoolhouse as well.[29] The blacksmith at Lochdonhead, John McKane, who was an incomer to Mull, lent the Torosay people a lean-to shed to worship in, when they were forced to hold their services out of doors, and was threatened with eviction; as he was gone from Lochdonhead in 1851, it is assumed that the threat was carried out. The Free Church congregation acquired a tent, but as Colonel Campbell had forbidden any kind of worship on his lands, they had to go to a site between the marks of high and low tide.

This was the infamous 'gravel pit', which became a symbol for the hardship and lack of sympathy suffered by the Torosay dissenters.

'The tent in the gravel pit' made a good newspaper story, as it would today, and a sketch of the poor suffering congregation of Highlanders during the administration of the Holy Sacrament, huddled inside and outside the tent near the head of Lochdon,[30] with the wind blowing and the rain falling from angry clouds, was published in November 1845. The scene is taken from life, and the Free Church minister, Mr Finlay MacPherson, is truly represented. According to Mr MacPherson's testimony, between forty and fifty adherents took communion that day in the tent in the gravel pit.[31]

Donald Fletcher, road contractor in Torosay, later allowed the congregation to worship in his house; the fact that he had a lease, and was not a tenant at will, protected him from eviction.[32] Colonel Campbell of Possil was genuinely distressed by the obstinacy of the Free Church people, believing that he was doing all he could to prevent schism from becoming final in Mull. At the end of August 1846, the Lochbuy factor wrote to Murdie Lochbuy in Edinburgh, 'You will regret to hear that poor Possil has had a fit of apoplexy. He is still alive, but that is all. I am afraid there is no hope.'[33] He was about fifty-seven years old, and lingered in his hopeless state for several months. When he died, Achnacroish went to his son John, who began shortly afterwards to make plans for what was to become Torosay Castle.

When the chairman of the Select Committee investigating the question of sites for churches in Scotland in April 1847 asked his witness, the Rev. Finlay MacPherson, 'What class of people are the Torosay people? Are there any wealthy people among them?' he was exercising that kind of judicial naïvete which was a feature of all government enquiries, still in use by judges today, and which appears to waste a great deal of time. The answer was: 'There are not; they are generally small farmers and cottars, and perhaps tradesmen and fishermen.' 'Then', said the chairman, 'generally speaking they are a humble class?' 'Yes.' The witness had no opportunity of enlarging upon this simplistic conclusion. But in fact, humble as they undoubtedly were, the leaders of the Free Church movement in Mull were the intellectuals of the community, mostly undervalued schoolmasters who doubled as postmasters, like Allan Lamont at Lochdonhead, who had to give up his school when he 'came out', and Donald Fletcher, the road contractor in the same place, who was later to be sheriff officer at Tobermory, and who was related to the highly talented Fletchers once in Penalbanach. There was also, at the Free Church breeding ground at Lochdon, Dugald MacPhail, joiner and miller there, later to become the much-loved poet in exile, writer and public speaker. In Brolass, an important supporter of the new church was Archibald Mackinnon, the respected tacksman of Torrans, whose farmhouse was home to Free Church probationers and students of divinity, and whose wife was Flora Shaw, daughter of the Kinloch Shaws.[34] In the Ross of Mull, the MacCormicks, free churchmen to a man, supported Mr McVean, the minister of Iona and Ross, who was the first man to declare himself 'out' in 1843. In Kilninian, land for a new Free Church was granted at Ardow soon after the Disruption, but Tobermory was quickest off the mark under its leader Peter Maclean, while Salen had a church by 1846, at Achadashenaig.[35] The huge increase in emigration between 1843 and 1853, however, was to reduce the numbers of Free Church members and Baptists, and was to empty the parliamentary churches as well.

Notes

1. NAS. CH2/273. Mull Presbytery Minutes, LVIII. 7 March 1744.
2. Scott, Hew (ed.), *Fasti Ecclesiae Scoticanae*, vol. 4, Synods of Argyll, Perth and Stirling.
3. NAS. GD14/10 f. 273. Stonefield Papers. Letterbook, 26 March 1729.
4. NAS. CH273/2. Mull Presbytery Minutes, 26 March 1788.
5. Hall, James, *Travels in Scotland*, p. 549. 'It is thought little or no disgrace for a servant maid ... to have a natural child; and some young men prefer these when about to marry, before others, as by this they know that they probably will have children.'
6. He was son of Rev. Malcolm MacAskill (1723–87), Minister of the Small Isles.
7. Third Report from the Select Committee on sites for churches (Scotland) PP 1847, p. 67.
8. NAS. CH2/273/2. Mull Presbytery Minutes, 1785.
9. NAS. CH2/273/2. Mull Presbytery Minutes, 1781.
10. Stent: parochial assessment.
11. Recalling 'Young Murdoch' – in this case Murdoch the thirteenth of Lochbuy, who died *c.* 1727, is a rhetorical device. The style of the letter, like a great deal of English prose written by Gaelic speakers (cf. the anonymous letter to Alexander Shiells in Chapter 12), owes much to the rhetoric of St Paul in his Epistle to the Romans, in which the law referred to was religious, not secular.
12. Alexander Campbell was the schoolmaster in Laggan, appointed by the SSPCK through the presbytery. NAS. GD174/1449.1790.
13. Rev. Archibald Maclean (1683–1755) grandfather of John Maclean of William and Mary College, USA, and of the Macleans of Ardfenaig, father-in-law of Mr Neil Macleod.
14. NAS. GD174/1239. Rev. Archd. Maclean to JMLB or trustees, Ardchrishnish, 20 April 1752.
15. MM2 was not wrong in his judgement of Campbell, who was reckless with money and frequently drunk.
16. Still standing, and a Bed and Breakfast at the time of writing.
17. GRO. D3330. Box 25. LMD diary, 8 July 1828.
18. Mr Archibald MacArthur of Kilninian was a notable translator in the period 1783–1801.
19. *Account of the present state of religion throughout the Highlands and Islands of Scotland*, by a lay member of the Established Church, 1827.
20. Adam, Margaret I. 'Eighteenth-century Highland landlords and the poverty problem' in *SHR* 19, 75, 1922. And PP IV, 1826–27.
21. Later McIlphadraigs were to change their name to Paterson.
22. Oral evidence of a local farmer in conversation with the author.

23. Hunter, p. 113.

24. The issue which was to lead to Disruption ten years later.

25. GRO. Box 25. LMD. Diary, June 1836. Mrs Clark, née Mary McCallum died six months later.

26. Poor Law Enquiry (Scotland). Reports from Commissioners. Evidence of James Middleton, Factor for Colonel Campbell.

27. *Quoad sacra*: a parish constituted for ecclesiastical purposes, and without civil significance. In Mull the original parishes were divided to provide churches for large concentrations of population remote from the parish, or *quoad omnia* church.

28. Against the Established Church's policy of allowing landowners to appoint ministers.

29. First Report from the Select Committee on sites for churches (Scotland), PP 1847.

30. The site of the gravel pit was on the shore just below the place where a free church was eventually built.

31. First Report ... etc. PP 1847, p. 80.

32. Annals of the Disruption.

33. NAS. GD174/1186/56. Angus Gregorson, Oban to MM3, 1 September 1846.

34. Archibald's father, Murdoch Mackinnon, had lived to the age of about 100 at Torrans, one of a family who had been in that place since the seventeenth century.

35. Achadashenaig is now called Glen Aros. The church was leased for thirty years, and was one mile from Salen. After the expiry of the lease, a new church was built at Salen in 1883. Ewing, *Annals of the Free Church of Scotland*, vol. 2.

23

Doctair ruadh nam blath shuilean:
the tale of the red-haired doctor

In 1722, a dashing young Maclean officer, Captain Allan Maclean, of the family of Brolass, died at Stirling, leaving 'one or two' natural children.[1] One of these is known to have been a girl, four years old, called Christina. In her late thirties she married a Dr John Maclean,[2] *Iain Dhòmhnaill Mhic Theàrlaich*, and three children grew to adulthood. Allan, the older son, was born about 1759 or 1760, Donald was a lieutenant in the Cameron Highlanders, and Miss Marion, the only daughter, remained devoted to her brothers, and did not marry.

From many chance comments in letters we know that Allan, who followed his father's profession, and became an army surgeon, was an exceptionally attractive man. Miss Catherine Maclaine 'met a Mrs General Maclean on Monday. Tell the doctor she particularly asks for him, indeed went the length of saying she was *quite in love with him*, and so it will not be safe for his wife to let him loose again alone to London, stealing all the widows' hearts.'[3] Two Gaelic poems about him suggest that he was irresistible to the opposite sex; the poems must be read rather warily however. Just as in Homer, the epithets 'white-armed Hera' or 'Danae of the fair ankles' are used as standard descriptions of goddesses, so in Gaelic poetry there are traditional expressions such as 'warm eyes' and 'calves like a salmon' which should not be taken too literally. Nevertheless, it is tempting to think that the red-haired doctor deserved what was said of him by the Ross of Mull poet Donald Maclean,[4] in his song, *Oran don Dotair Ailein Mac-Gilleain*, when he was going on a voyage to the Isle of Skye:

> Something is missing in this place
> We feel it is long since he left us;
> He is the red-haired doctor of the warm eyes;
> He has the appearance and dignity of a duke.
>
> Every week is like a year
> Since you left us for Talisker
> Cold and storm came upon us
> It seems a long time.
>
> Well the scarlet coat becomes you
> New from the tailor's hands;
> You are like a rose in the middle of the garden,
> Growing in the dark of winter.

Your fine white calves
Are like a salmon in clear water;
Yours is a graceful foot in a watertight shoe,
Which you used to lace up with silk.[5]

After his career as an army surgeon, Doctor Allan had decided to settle at his parents' home at Beach, near Ormsaig in Brolass, following the death of his brother Donald in 1799. His mother was then eighty-one, his father seventy-five, and his sister was their only child at home. An honourable Mull man could not desert such worthy people in their old age. They were a family who carried a certain weight in the parish of Kilfinichen and Kilvicheoun, the father having been a doctor in the area made famous by the Beaton family who had lived at Pennycross as physicians to the Macleans of Duart.

Here a small speculative digression is required to explain the preponderance of physicians in this corner of Mull, between Beach and Pennycross. The Beatons had not practised for very long after the exile of the Duart Macleans, but the grant of the lands of Pennycross to a succession of physicians, if they should be suitably qualified, remained with the family until the 1760s,[6] when they were bought by Dr Alexander Maclean. It should also be added that the lands remained with the Beatons only after certain vicissitudes and feuds between tenants, factors and possessors. After the death of Malcolm Beaton of Pennycross about 1718, his sister Ann Beaton was threatened with the loss of her tack of Dererach, which she held jointly with her husband, by that arch mischief-maker John Maclean of Killean (who had so provoked John of Lochbuy into imprisoning him in the Castle of Moy), because she would not surrender to John Killean her late brother's papers.[7] Whatever dwelling house was at Pennycross[8] in the middle of the eighteenth century, it was let, in the absence of Edmund Beaton in London and Jamaica, and stripped of wood by John Killean.[9] The possessors of the land do not sound as if they might be the kind of men who would take care of the old Physick Garden of the Beatons at Pennycross, yet it is possible that the Killunaig or Gruline Macleans did in fact keep the botanical plants going, and that the presence of the garden was one of the main attractions for Dr Alexander Maclean when he bought the tiny property from Neil Beaton of Pennycross and his wife, Martha Hall.

When Dr Johnson and James Boswell rode across the 'Mull Alps' in 1773 from Ardchrishnish to Lochbuy, they visited Dr Alexander at Pennycross, and were given dinner there.[10] The doctor was, said Boswell, 'one of the stoutest and most hearty men I have seen, more of the farmer than of the doctor.' The dinner was pronounced very good. But there was no mention of the Beatons' herb garden. Perhaps both visitors were unlikely to be interested in herbal medicine; or a physick garden, being a well-known feature of both Edinburgh and London, was not worth mentioning. Or the doctor may have talked proudly of it, and was simply not recorded. The fact remains that the hale and hearty Dr Alexander and the red-haired doctor's father Dr John lived, at about the same time, within an easy ride of the Beaton herb garden.

Dr Alexander Maclean of Pennycross was to add to his small estate in 1781 with Pennyghael, and again in 1796 his family extended his lands to include the strip between Kinloch and Kilpatrick.[11] Meanwhile, his fellow physician, Dr John Maclean, in Beach, had no property of his own. He lived as tacksman of the farm, surrounded by three dozen tenants and cottars and workmen and children. He had two manservants and one maid.[12]

Christina Maclean, Dr John's wife, was a poet, and also wrote about her son's disposition to depart from Brolass, as he had to in order to earn a living. Her song, complete with a chorus, was entitled *Criomagan de Dhuanaig*, 'Fragments of a little song', and some of the fragments are these:

> You left me yesterday to go abroad,
> My earnest wish is for your safe return.
> You left me yesterday to go abroad.
>
> It is no surprise that she is sorrowful,
> The sister whom you left on her own.
> Lovely would her young shoulders be
> If you would be staying near her.
>
> Your fingers most elegant playing music,
> The most handsome foot on the floor,
> And I am certain you'll not be refused
> When you set your mind on a sweetheart.[13]

The praise imagery might be traditional, and the sentiments part of a poetic mode, but there is some historical truth in the situation described, since the young doctor was known to play the fiddle, and left with his regiment for Quebec in the same ship as Murdoch Maclaine of Lochbuy in 1779. His friendship with Murdoch was lasting, and in 1804, having left the army, he was staying in Lochbuy House tending both Murdoch and Jane in their illnesses. One of the nine Lochbuy girls at home at this time, and being taught by a governess, was Flora, aged seven, and although there were older sisters in their teens, Jane, Margaret and Elizabeth, and ten-year-old Catherine, it was Flora who was one day to be the sweetheart of the not-so-young doctor. In 1808, the doctor's parents, Dr John and Chirsty Maclean of Beach, died within a few days of each other, and full of years.[14] In 1813, before young Murdoch himself was married to Chirsty Maclean, the 16-year-old Flora Maclaine of Lochbuy and the 54-year-old doctor with calves like a salmon were married by Mr Alexander Fraser.[15]

Lachlan Macquarie in New South Wales wrote indignantly over a year later to his brother Charles, 'Elizabeth and myself were shocked and grieved to hear that Flory Lochbuy had made so mean and preposterous a marriage with a low vulgar man who might almost be her grandfather.' [16] It was a strangely contemptuous remark from the son of a carpenter about a man whose parents had led a gentle life, and who was so admired by his own kin. No other reactions to the alliance seem to have survived, other than practical arrangements between Donald Maclean WS and young Murdoch to make the farm of Rossal, on the route between Beach and Lochbuy, available to the couple. Their first child, John Allan, was baptised in Torosay in June 1814, and between that date and August 1826, Flory gave birth to another five sons and three daughters at Rossal. Miss Marion, the red-haired doctor's sister, who had been so sorrowful on his departure to the wars, moved in to the household, and was apparently a difficult sister-in-law.[17]

The doctor, although living at Rossal, was retained by the family of Lochbuy in all medical matters, and considering that there were ten women and a succession of infants there, he was kept busy. He and Flory were included in most of the social events, like the christening and dinner of 1825 with the family of Donald Maclean WS at Lochbuy. They were also at Ardtornish and Airds, and it was clear that Dr Allan was valued by his wife's family, if not by the governor of New South Wales. But 'dear Rossal' was their much-loved home, and the Maclean children who grew up there were to dream of it when they were gone, and long to go back. Their sons, John Allan, Murdoch, Donald, John, and Neil [18] were taught by a tutor, Mr McNaughton at Rossal, whom the family shared with the Ardfenaig Macleans, descendants of John Maclean of Killean. Theirs was otherwise a frugal existence, and their sensible policy of living within their means was upset when in 1826, the red-haired doctor became ill, and was in such pain that he had to seek medical advice in Edinburgh.

It was 'the Stones', and Donald Maclean WS reported on the progress of the painful operations the doctor underwent to remove them. 'The doctor had four large stones extracted on Saturday.' 'The poor doctor is extremely ill.' 'The doctor is again greatly better, but to undergo more operations when he can bear it. From my heart I wish Liston had been applied to.' [19] Flora stayed with her husband in Edinburgh throughout the ups and downs of his treatment. In July, Donald was writing, 'The doctor and Mrs Maclean dine here today, and he considers himself in perfect health.' In October, Lauchlan the diarist noted, 'Heard this day the account of Doctor Allan Maclean of Rossal, his death.' [20] Dr Allan had written, in his own hand, an unusual last will and testament.

As we have no 'continued city here', it is incumbent on all, and especially the aged, as I am, to make spiritual and temporal preparations for that 'journey from whose bourne no traveller returns', I therefore wish this to be considered as my last will, and hope it will be considered by my heirs as valid ... I commend my Soul to that Omnipotent King who gave it. I trust my Wife and Children to the same father of Mercies who said, 'Leave your fatherless children to me, and I will preserve them ... and let your Widows trust in me ...'

I nominate and appoint Flora MacLean my Spouse as sole executrix of all my personal and heritable subjects ... If circumstances should induce my said Spouse after my demise to enter into the Bonds of Wedlock with another, then, and in that case, I appoint Mr John Maclean Bunessan, Captain H. H. Maclean, h.p. 93rd Regt. and their brother, Charles Maclean, A.S. 53rd Regt.,[21] to be joint trustees and guardians to my orphans, with Murdoch Maclaine, Esquire of Lochbuy. Having seen inconveniences arising from the nomination of too many guardians, and having little to bequeath, I do not name any others.[22] I trust that I have many wellwishers and that the family of Archibald MacLean Esq., of Pennycross [23] will believe me when I say that my charges against him for professional attendance never amounted to one half of what I might have legally demanded, and I trust they will not forget my orphans. I request that no expences that can be avoided shall be incurred at my funeral wherever it is. I would wish some of my Boys to follow mechanical professions if they do not evince much reluctance to it. I cannot advise my Spouse, if she survives me, to keep by this farm at its present rent, which no doubt was offered and promised by myself.[24] I need not recommend to my Beloved Spouse to pay all my lawful debts, particularly servants' wages, as expeditiously as she can.

In witness of this, being my last will and testament, I subscribe this, my holograph disposition & instrument written on this and the preceeding page at Rosehall this nineteenth day of July one thousand eight hundred and twenty two years [signed] Allan MacLean.'

No will could have been less practical, or less concerned with actual sums of money or articles of value, but it can be seen that this one was infused with a spirit which the doctor's wife Flora could recognise and live by. Her loneliness and misery are expressed in her letters to her brother Murdoch, who had not, fourteen years after her marriage, paid her her marriage portion. He had in fact paid very little of any of the marriage portions of his sisters, and the interest which they were entitled to apply was mounting to a considerable sum, so that his usual response to letters from any of his sisters was not to respond at all. As a result, a large pile of desperate pleas accumulated, asking for 'states' or statements of account with all of the eight girls, which, most of the time, he neglected to answer. Even Catherine, the unmarried, and Jarvis, who married relatively late, had the idea that he should pay their debts.[25]

Flora began her widowhood at the age of thirty-one at Rossal, where a roup was to be held for the sale of her husband's stock, farm implements and most of their furniture. It was only the roup which delayed her leaving the farm, as the doctor had advised. Meanwhile every small tragedy assumed great proportions. Her well-written letters give a poignant picture of life at Rossal through the winter and spring.

> *20 February 1828*. My beautiful foal drowned ... God help me, nothing but losses and hardships in this world. The poor grey mare came herself to the door to give warning of her distress.

> *May 5 1828*. John Ban [26] has just come in ... poor Mrs Maclean, Ardfenaig has given McNaughton £6 as her share [27] ... Peter MacArthur has crawled this length tonight. Such a figure may I never see. I cannot tell how I pity his poor wife when she sees him. [28]

> What a melancholy accident happened at Bunessan on Friday. Poor James Morison drowned when coming home with a load of wrack from the shore of Ardfenaig. He has left a large weak family, and his poor wife, *our cousin*, one of the Uiskens at the down-laying and very destitute.[29] Mr Peter MacArthur has never yet arrived. He got a tumble down the stairs at Bunessan, which cut his mouth so dreadfully that his companions thought it best to cut off his life ... He is now there in that state. Poor Pennycross is also still unable to move from Assapol. I am none the worse of my ducking ...[30]

Flora left Mull with her children in June 1828 to live in Ayr, where the Ayr Academy was a school with an excellent reputation. She was hardly settled in Newton Ayr when she had a visit which she related to her brother Murdoch. 'I cannot help telling you a circumstance that has happened. The principal doctor in this town, who has been here for the last two years, on hearing my name, called to know if it was possible this could be the family of his late and much valued acquaintance who was here in the Breadalbane Fencibles, and who gave his son a *drum*. He actually wept when talking of him, and made so much of Lachlan and Christina's eyes, which he said will be soon cured without any strong medicine, merely ointment to rub at night, for they all look so healthy it would be a pity to disturb them with medicine. *This doctrine* agreed with *me*. It was what I was *used to hear*. This gentleman's name is Dr Whiteside, a respectable looking old man. He said he would often look in upon us. Adieu almost in distraction, your ever affectionate sister, Flora Maclean.' [31]

Flora had no exaggerated view of her own importance, or false pride which would prevent her children from working for a living. Her duty as she saw it was to provide them with a home in a humble narrow little house on two floors in Newton Green, where the parlour was converted into a schoolroom, and the emphasis was placed on giving them an education and then sending them into the world. 'To be in debt is my horror,' she told Murdoch, but he had still not given her an account of her money from the roup at Rossal on 14 May 1828, possibly since he himself was the principal buyer, spending £116 compared with the average farmer's £9 or £10.[32] Flora wished for solitude and wept in secret. 'Often and often in my solitude have I been reading over my beloved husband's dying letter to myself, in which he says he is deprived of rest or sleep thinking of all the hardships I have to come through.' The children were frequently dangerously ill, as all children were in those days before vaccination. 'The doctor very kind and attentive.' When she was unable to pay her bills, Elizabeth Macquarie sent her an unexpected sum of money. 'No debts, due to Aunt Macquarie's kind assistance.' And still fond of 'dear Rossal' she asked what the new tenant, Mr Macdonald was giving in rent.[33]

'Your silence is past all comprehension,' she wrote to Murdoch in July 1829, having asked him for her 'state' again. 'As we were all stepping into bed Friday night, who walked in but *unfortunate* Miss Marion, bag and baggage, her account of her treatment and suffering beyond conception.[34] God forgive me … I am inclined to attach blame to her own proceedings, as to her friends particularly, *from what I know of old* … her woeful tale … in spite of me I could not but laugh. If I had Mrs Maclaine [35] we should enjoy ourselves.' In 1830 Miss Marion was still paying her 'call', which she insisted it was. Murdoch was sailing to Buenos Aires as a midshipman. Young John was to go on a trial voyage. Donald would try the mercantile line at home. John Allan was apprenticed to a surgeon.

> *17 February 1831.* The parting from darling John, who has sailed … our good friend Dr Whiteside took pity on us, and at his own expence was so kind as to take him to Greenock and see him safe on board. He was then in high spirits again. My dear Donald has just got rigged out for Jamaica.

In 1831 her good friend Dr Whiteside proposed marriage. Flora wrote to Murdoch and received an unpleasant and disapproving letter in reply. But her uncle Airds [36] had been delighted and had invited Flora and her future husband to 'dear Airds' on their marriage jaunt. Murdoch was sulking in his tent, much as he had done when his sister Elizabeth had married Donald Campbell. Nothing could move him. This must be a low fellow, an old man, quite taking advantage of her – 'disparity of years' – Mr John Gregorson was consulted about the 'reprehensible' union, and agreed, he who had himself married a wife twenty-five years his junior. But when Flora and 'Dr William' arrived at Ardtornish on their wedding jaunt, before risking the wrath of the laird of Lochbuy, the bridegroom was discovered to be only three years older than Flora. Ardtornish adored him: Flora was very fortunate – his father [37] so beloved in Ayr – his sister married to the distinguished Dr McLagan of Edinburgh – Sir John Campbell at Airds thought so highly of him. In no time they were all standing around the pianoforte: the doctor had such a good voice; an excellent singer of the old Scots songs. By the time the married pair arrived at Lochbuy, the laird had been well prepared for a change of tune. He must also have been enraptured with this new member of the family, for in reply to a letter Murdoch wrote to him, Mr Donald Maclean WS replied:

I did not notice Mrs Doctor's marriage sooner, as from your letter, I took the same view you did of it, but I am happy to find that you are all much mistaken as to Dr Whiteside's age – and that his character is the best possible. Hunter [38] informs me he is much of her own age, that he is an excellent character, an uncommon fine young man. All *his* relations countenanced this marriage.[39]

On her way home from her jaunt, Flora called on Donald Maclean WS in Albany Street. Even with the happy outcome of their stay at Lochbuy, she had still been unable to persuade her brother to give her a statement of what he owed her. Perhaps Mr Maclean Albany could help. She was still struggling to be independent, as far as her own children were concerned, of Dr William's help. At the age of eighteen John Allan wrote to his uncle to ask if he could count on his mother having a payment, which he needed to go to university. Even Hector Bunessan,[40] exiled through bankruptcy to Campbeltown, but one of Dr Allan's chosen guardians for his children, wrote to Murdoch in defence of John Allan's claim. There is no record of Murdoch Maclaine's eventual response, but Dr William's firm character and winning ways had their effect, for in 1834 a discharge was issued by 'Flora Maclaine, relict of Allan Maclean, surgeon at Ormsaig, and spouse of Dr William Whiteside in Ayr', to her brother Murdoch of all financial claims.[41] Flora Lochbuy was probably the only member of her family who had a sincere and earnest wish to live within her means, and a conscience about being in debt. Talented and level-headed, compassionate, hard-working and attractive, she probably deserved the only laurels posterity might award to her clan. Flora and Dr William were to have two daughters born in Ayr. She and her husband had thirty years of married life together, and Flora died in 1869, not by any means the last of the nine daughters of Murdoch and Jane to leave what Flora had once called 'a life overburdened with grief'.

Notes

1. Maclean Sinclair, 467.
2. John Maclean, Member of the Faculty of Physicians and Surgeons of Glasgow, 1753.
3. NAS. GD174/1634/7. Catherine Maclaine of LB to MM2, Putney, 10 December 1824.
4. The poet lived at Leob, near Kilpatrick in Ross.
5. A. Maclean Sinclair (ed.), *Maclean Bards*, vol. 2. pp. 23–4. Trans. by Anja Gunderloch.
6. NAS. CH2/273/1. Mull Presbytery Minutes. The Rev. Neil Macleod addressed 'Mr Beaton' of Pennycross, a heritor, about his application for a manse and glebe, 26 November 1762. This was probably Neil Beaton of Pennycross. See Bannerman, John, *The Beatons.*
7. NAS. GD14/10/1. Letterbook of James Campbell of Stonefield, *c.* 1728.
8. Then near Pennycross. Confusingly, because of the Maclean family's residence at Carsaig for a time, Carsaig was called Pennycross.

9. NAS. GD174/133/2. Summons, Beaton against Lachlan McLain and John McLean of Killean. Also Bannerman, p. 34.

10. Fleeman, who edited Johnson's account, thought that the doctor lived at Rossal, and John Bailey, another editor, thought he lived at Kilfinichen.

11. Index to Argyll Sasines and letter, NAS. GD174/1387/82. AM to MM, London 12 May 1796. The 'strip' cost £7,500.

12. Cregeen, *Inhabitants*, p. 103. Beach sits above the road from Kinloch to Bunessan, on the left.

13. Maclean Sinclair (ed.), *Maclean Bards*, vol. 2, pp. 173–4.

14. Their joint gravestone in Kilpatrick Burial Ground commemorates 'John McLean, surgeon, died 5 March 1808, aged 84. Christina McLean his spouse, died 2 March 1808, aged 90.'

15. Torosay OPR 22 April 1813.

16. NLS. MS 3833. LM to CM, NSW 28 May 1814.

17. NAS. GD174/1634/57, 62. Flora Maclean to MM2.1829.

18. A daughter Jane, baptised in 1818, may have died young. Two other daughters, Alexandrina Christina and Christian were too young to be educated at Rossal, and Lachlan Macquarie Maclean, the youngest child, was born in 1826.

19. NAS. GD174/1628. DMWS to MM2, 1826. Robert Liston (1794–1847) then in Edinburgh, and renowned for his 'dexterity with the surgeon's knife'.

20. GRO. D3330. Box 25. LMD. Diary, 14 October 1827.

21. Three sons of Lachlan Maclean of Bunessan, changekeeper of the Inn there (now the Argyll Arms), they were grandsons, through their mother of Hector Maclean of Torrans, brother of Dr Alexander Maclean of Pennycross.

22. John Gregorson was added on 16 August 1827.

23. Dr Alexander of Pennycross had died in 1786, and was succeeded by his son Archibald, who was not a doctor.

24. Rossal was part of the Lochbuy estate, which operated a system of giving a farm to the highest bidder. There was no relaxation of rent for members of the family.

25. All the sisters' letters to MM2 are in GD174/1634.

26. John Bàn Maclean, Bunessan, who was a merchant in Glasgow, but returned to Bunessan to run his father, Lachlan Bàn's inn.

27. 'Poor' because she too was a widow. This was Susanna Macleod, daughter of the Rev. Neil Macleod of the parish of Ross, whose husband, Dugald Maclean, grandson of John Killean, had been drowned in 1818. She could little afford to pay for the tutor shared with Flora. Her son, Hector Neil died in this year, another reason for being pitied by Flora.

28. Peter MacArthur had married Flora Maclean, Kengharair, in 1824. They lived at Ardura, whence he had presumably 'crawled', drunk.

29. James Morison, merchant in Bunessan. His wife was Janet or Jessie Maclean (*c.* 1789–1869), daughter of Duncan Maclean, Uisken and Mary Maclaine, Gruline. Janet was about to give birth to her daughter, Jemima Morison.

30. NAS. GD174/1634/37. Flora Maclean to MM2, Rossal [May 1828].

31. NAS. GD174/1634/39. Flora Maclean to MM2, Newton Ayr, 4 June 1828.

32. But many of the buyers, in fairness to MM2, did not pay their roup bills, with 'John Bunessan' sending a new excuse for non-payment every few months, and eventually being threatened with the law.

33. NAS. GD174/1634/1–52. Flora Maclean, Rossal and Ayr to MM2, 1828–29.

34. Miss Marion, the red-haired doctor's sister, probably now about sixty-six. It is not known where she had been living.

35. Murdoch's wife, Chirsty.
36. Her mother, Jane Campbell's brother, Sir John Campbell.
37. Dr Philip Whiteside, who lived with the couple in Ayr and was to be shocked by the bad manners of Flora's sister, Jarvis.
38. Alexander Hunter WS (1790–1858) of Doonholm. He had married a daughter of Alexander Maclean of Coll, and had taken some law business away from DMWS, but he helped Flora when she was in Ayr, and tried to induce MM2 to pay her her dues.
39. NAS. GD174/1628/582. DMWS to MM2, Edinburgh, 23 June 1831.
40. After a most bitter exchange of letters, Hector H. Maclean and MM2 went to law, and Hector had to leave 'the Country'.
41. NAS. GD174/515. Discharge, 21 March 1834.

24

'No Jews, negroes, gipsies, foreigners, or people born in England'

Item. Shiaba this toune is set upon tennents in full mealls.
The soume thereof foure score Kows, foure scoire sheep,
twenty horse, twenty-foure bolls sowing.

Item. Scurre. The soume thereof is fourty-eight Kows,
fourty-eight sheep, sixtein horse, twenty-foure bolls and ane
boll beere sowing.

Item. Killviceown ane pennie thereof set upon donald mcallan
for 130 marks and ye other pennie upon tennents viz: Duncan
McIan ane farthen thereof and ye fourth pairt of ane farthen
full duties Allan McAllan vc laughland and Ivour duy
mcCartna, three clitags full meals. John baine and his good
son halfe a pennie full meals.

This extract from a rental of the Earl of Argyll of 1662 [1] gives an idea of
land use in the Ross of Mull in the seventeenth century. It tells of three
contiguous places, Siaba, Scour and Kilvicheoun, the first being set in 'mealls'
or parts for which rents were accepted in kind, from a group of joint tenants,
the second having simply a 'soume' or souming, an allocation of animals which
the land was deemed to be able to support, and the third being set to particular
men in penny and farthing parts, with Allan and Ivor receiving three clitags.
A clitag was a tiny area with grass for only one cow, a kind of precursor of
the croft. [2]

  The rental of 1662 is of interest because of the names of inhabitants of the
Ross of Mull, the most indigenous, unchanged people of the island. Townships
mentioned in the rental, such as Siaba, Saorphein, Ardchiavaig, Tirergain,
Ardalanish and Upper Ardtun, were hardly on the beaten track. Indeed there
was no beaten track to anywhere. Pilgrims may have walked from Grass Point,
Killean or Croggan in the days of the medieval monastery of Iona, but when
the buildings fell into ruin there were few civilised visitors to Iona and the
Ross of Mull. The seventeenth century was more likely to have seen sorners,

beggars, plunderers and invaders, and so the people stayed on relatively high sites, usually at a safe distance from the sea. The preference for an inland habitat had also been long ago determined by the position of fertile grazing for black cattle, the chief resource of small farmers.[3] The names of some of these small farmers in the earl's rental were, to give some real examples, James Beton (a surname), in Assapol, Finlay McIan Vc Velane in Assapol, Neill Mc Donald Vc Innes in Ardchiavaig, Ferqhard McIan Vane in Ardachy, and Charles McIan Vc Donald Vc Charles in Ardalanish. These names were patronymics mixed with descriptive words such as 'vane' for ban or fair. The presence of James Beton, or Beaton, in the list, demonstrates the shifting ground of the list-maker, who was living in an age of transition from Gaelic styles to the English or Lowland form of inherited surname.

The earl's list[4] shows also that long before the Maclean chiefs were personally ousted from Mull, rents were being collected from inhabitants of the Ross of Mull, but unlike the Argyll tenants or possessors of those parts of the Duart estates situated in Mornish, Aros and Torosay, the Ross of Mull and Iona did not generally pay rent in money. Donald McAllan in Kilvicheoun was an exception. This concession alone marked them out as different. The people had no access to money, so could not pay in cash. Their geographical remoteness, their untranslated names, their concealed townships and the very small number of tacksmen they had to supervise them all combined to leave them almost a century behind the rest of Mull.

The minister who wrote the first statistical account of Ross was interested, as a scientist might be, in the composition of his parish and its remarkable static character. In the census of 1779, made by the fifth Duke of Argyll of his own estates, names in the Ross are identifiable as belonging to the same families who were in the 1662 rental, even if the arbitrary adoption of surnames is sometimes bewildering. But elsewhere in Mull, there has been an influx of new names almost everywhere except for the Torloisk and Ulva estates. The sale of Ulva to the Macdonalds of Boisdale in the late eighteenth century brought in scores of Macdonalds (or made it expedient for native Ulvaichs to change their names), who multiplied until they almost outstripped the native MacQuarries. In south-east Mull, people called Fletcher, Currie, Buchanan,[5] Carmichael, Colquhoun, MacPhail and MacGregor were brought in by the Argyll family for reasons which are now forgotten, and became naturalised. In the Ross of Mull, however, there was little new blood. Hardly any strangers appeared in that parish other than the sporadic bands of pilgrims who were beginning to venture again over the hill from Achnacraig via Lochbuy to Rossal and who followed the line of the present road to Iona.

The Ross of Mull, Brolass, Ardmeanach and Burg still look entirely different from the rest of the island. Going from east and north to the south west has always been rather like travelling from the east of Ireland to Galway. Until about 1865, emergence from Glen More must have revealed straggling groups of cottages near the shore of Loch Scridain, all emitting smoke from damp peat. In 1861, 207 people lived at the head of Loch Scridain, on the estate called Kinloch, which had just been sold by the trustees of Donald Maclean WS. The cluster of farms between Torrans and Kilpatrick burying ground had 170 inhabitants. But the most populous area of all, Ardtun, to the north of the road as one passed Kilpatrick, had 346 men, women and children. The absence of resident heritors meant that houses were uniform in style and size.[6]

The minister of the parish of Kilfinichen and Kilvicheoun, Mr Dugald Campbell, counted the population of his parish in 1791 and listed the names of 3,002 persons.[7] Among those, there were, as he put it, 'no Jews, negroes, gipsies, foreigners, or persons born in England, Ireland or the colonies'. If he had added that there were none born on any other island, or on the mainland of Scotland, it would not have been surprising. 'No people are more attached to their native country,' said Mr Campbell, 'and it is only necessity that obliges them to leave it.'

With few resident heritors, and a few people who were called tacksmen simply because they could write and keep lists, but who did not have a lifestyle very different from the commoners, the parish was undifferentiated in character. Mr Dugald Campbell felt that his flock was sober and industrious. They went to the Lowlands for seasonal work, and therefore detachedly observed Lowland ways. They had served in the army, and knew what America was like. But the most important factor in their survival was that they were left out of the sixth duke's extensive sales of his estates between 1816 and 1826. The Ross of Mull people remained virtually undisturbed through George William's reign (until 1839). It is hard to say whether this was a good or a bad thing. 'My grandfather's successor,' said the eighth duke (who disliked George William so much that he never referred to him in any other way but this, rather as if he had been a changeling, and not related to himself), 'lived for thirty-three years [8] during the whole of which time the powers of ownership may be said to have been suspended. He was a perfect type of the kind of landowner who was adored in Ireland – one who never meddled or interfered with the stupidities of Custom. Celtic usages were allowed their course. Subdivision went on at a redoubled rate, and population kept up even more than pace.'[9]

It could be said that Duke George William not only undid all the good that his father had done, but, by his *laissez-faire* attitude compounded the harm that natural increase of population had done to the estate. In the tiny hamlet of Kintra, which had been set up as a fishing station by Duke John in the early 1790s, but where the fishermen were without the means to buy boats and tackle, sixteen families lived in 1844, with only three cows between them.[10] In those parts of the parish with other heritors (Ardmeanach, Gribun, Inchkenneth, Pennyghael, Kilpatrick, Killiemore, Kinloch, Burg and Carsaig) the population was being reduced, so that the inhabitants of the duke's lands were even more noticeable in their destitution. In 1844, only three heritors out of eight resided in the parish.[11] The duke held most of the land.

When George William died in 1839,[12] he was succeeded by his brother, Lord John Campbell (who had once considered buying some of the Mull lands), described by Madame de Staël as 'possessing those charming manners which we in France have lost,'[13] and who had never seen eye to eye with his brother. But the seventh duke was elderly, and ill, and by the time of the disastrous potato blight of 1846, he was finding it difficult to travel over his estates. Many of his duties were taken over by his son, George Douglas Campbell, twenty-three years old, active, practical and strong-minded. It was in the year before the potato blight that a chamberlain was appointed to look after the ducal estate of the Ross of Mull. He was an Islay man, forty-five years old, tall, and with facial features which were definitely of a Campbell cut. His name was John Campbell of Ardmore, and he was to be known for the next twenty-five years as 'Factor Mór', the big factor. Ardfenaig, a house which had been inhabited for more than fifty years by the family of the Macleans of Killean, as tacksmen, had been enlarged and improved to accommodate him and his wife, Flora. Their farm servants and in-servants came, in the main, from Islay. For the first few years, Factor Mór's ploughman was a Torosay man, Alexander Maclean, but he emigrated in 1852, with his wife Cirsty, and four children, to Australia, and was replaced by an Islay man, Donald McPhee.[14]

Near Ardfenaig, at Tirghoil, lived the Baptist minister Mr Duncan Fergusson, ministering to a large congregation which had sprung up in the townships on the south side of Ross – in Ardachy, Ardchiavaig, Uisken, Ardalanish, Tirergain and Knocknafenaig. Mr Fergusson was moved to Lee, north east of Scour, in the 1850s. His congregation consisted of cottars, many of them paying no rent, but nevertheless in a state of great poverty and hardship. One of these Baptist families had been moved from Siaba to Ardalanish Point – Mary MacDougall and her husband Neil Macdonald – when the entire population of that township was asked to leave in 1847. Factor Mór's first ten years as chamberlain were like a game of chess, in which he was constantly moving the pawns. Large farms, which were tenanted by his Islay friends, seemed to become larger, and the cottars, who out-numbered the crofters, were crowded into smaller areas. Cottars could be moved many times, for they had no leases and no rights.

The potato blight, which was not at first recognised as an affliction affecting the whole of the Highlands, was not identified until the autumn of 1846. Hunger was normal in the summer, and had been for almost a century, because the new crop of potatoes was not dug until about 31 July. When it was realised that there would be a crisis of great proportions, such as Ireland had already suffered, national sympathy was mobilised, and a relief fund organised. Sir John McNeill, of the Colonsay McNeills, who had an impressive record as a diplomatist through his career in India, Persia, and as a brilliant writer of reports such as his *Progress and Present Positions of Russia in the East,* was appointed chairman in 1845 of the Board of Supervision which guided the implementing of the new Poor Law in Scotland. As chairman, he led the special enquiry which was conducted in 1851 into the particular destitution of the Highlands and Islands. But before this enquiry found its way to Mull, a naval surgeon on half-pay, with even more relevant qualifications for his post, was appointed in 1847 to manage the distribution of relief to the destitute areas. This was David Boyter, who had, since 1836 worked for the Colonial Department in the emigration service, selecting emigrants for New South Wales. He had chosen families, including Highland ones, who were going to contribute most to their country of adoption. Now he was about to survey the lives of those who had not offered themselves, or had been left behind. He was to select the most helpless and the most desperate, and give them aid.[15] David Boyter moved ahead of the relief itself, pinpointing need and shifting distribution workers from one centre to another if he suddenly came across cases of extreme hunger. While the purpose of the fund from public subscription was to buy meal and flour [16] for the hungry, the administrators of the Board of Supervision re-interpreted this purpose as to provide food for the helpless (the very old, the very young, and the disabled sick) while the able-bodied were to be provided with work,[17] so that the population did not come to rely on charity, as everyone in the Poor Law Enquiry had expected them to do. The crofters and cottars were unsure about the distinction between these two kinds of assistance, and when they were told that they would have reduced meal allowances if they were able-bodied, but refused to work on any of the schemes to provide employ-ment, and when they saw also that the landowners were hastening to join the schemes which would drain their lands and build roads, piers and breakwaters, they were understandably suspicious. Such was the confusion over the 'trickery' of the landowners and the Board of Supervision combined, that some of the poorer people refused to labour on the roads. David Boyter wrote on 9 April 1848:

> A strong party of Irish labourers were landed here [Tobermory] on Tuesday by the *Tartar* under an engagement with the contractor of the great line of road from Salen to Ulva, although his contract especially mentioned the employment of the people of the district, but finding great difficulty, he followed that plan which was not well accepted in an area where so many people are destitute ... we have on our list a hundred people who have been driven from other places on the island for want of food and shelter, and as they express their wish for work, I see nothing for it but giving them work on the roads. The population of Tobermory in addition to all the *outcasts* of the other districts on the island have assumed a character that requires caution and management to prevent the worst circumstances and con-sequences. So far no steps have been taken to repress any violence. I may

mention that at the sheriff court here last week, up to 600 summonses of removal were issued.[18]

Yet violence did not erupt. In 1847 he had gone to the parish of Kilfinichen and Kilvicheoun:

So on to Bunessan on the vessel *Porcupine* to land stores under the charge of Mr MacQuarrie.[19] The following morning we arrived at Kilfinichen, where distress prevails to a considerable extent. A number of people collected about Mr Maclean's[20] house, and asked for supplies to appease hunger. I despatched a messenger to Mr MacQuarrie at Bunessan to share with the people here the supplies he had received. I also found Mr MacLaughlan's[21] district equally destitute, so I despatched a messenger to Tobermory to Captain Rose[22] to forward supplies immediately ... On Saturday His Grace the Duke of Argyll[23] arrived in Bunessan and requested to see me. He expressed himself highly gratified with the extraordinary kindness displayed by the Board to his poor Tenants and Cottars, and we agreed to the absolute necessity of removing a considerable number of his people to some other locality, or abroad, and measures to that effect would be attempted next spring ...[24]

'Next spring' was 1848, and in May of that year, Dr Boyter walked with Mr Campbell, the minister of the established church, to inspect the making of a road which was to join Bunessan and Uisken. The port at Uisken was to be a fishing station and the road would enable fishermen to bring catches from Bunessan without risking the treacherous sea passage round the tip of the Ross and the Torran rocks. He reported:

I counted only thirty-five at work instead of fifty or sixty, mostly old men and boys. Many of the older men seemed discontented and admitted their unwillingness to work. The young boys on the contrary, whose work was to wheel barrows of gravel, seemed delighted to harrass the older by the constant succession of empty barrows waiting to be filled. This competition was new to me and goes far to show that much can be made of the rising generation. I have also observed the evident improvement in young girls whose cleanliness and neat dresses and manners would almost indicate a change in the race of the land. The road to Port Uisken will require every effort to be completed by the end of the season. On Wednesday 24th I met all the fishers, being aware that Mr Maclean,[25] a merchant in Bunessan, would be an agreeable agent for them, I would appoint him our inspector of fishings on a remuneration of 12s. a week, instead of commission on the produce of fishing. I am happy to say that although our meeting was at first rather unruly and boisterous, everyone gave way to the advice and promises I made to them, which was to continue their employment as at present on the usual allowance of meal, one half pound more to the father of a family daily, and 2s. 6d. a week to buy cheese or anything they desired, and on being left to themselves the use of the boats and tackle with one half of the profits of their labour, the other half to be used in any way the board may deem proper. All disputes of any kind to be referred to Messrs. MacQuarrie and Maclean without appeal. I have given them clearly to understand that anyone who withdraws from his engagement would not again, or his family, be recipients on the Fund list.[26]

Dr Boyter died in 1850, before the Board of Supervision under Sir John McNeill conducted its enquiry into the effects of the new Poor Law and of the poor relief following the potato blight. He did not describe his encounters with John Campbell, 'Factor Mór', but between 1846 and 1851, the chamberlain had been busy moving his pawns around the board, and moving them backwards. Probably because of his belief that his own farming activities were more profitable, not to mention exemplary, to the neighbourhood, his activities seemed to be aimed at taking over grazing lands for the consolidation of the larger farms of Ardfenaig, Fidden and Ardalanish, and making crofts in the marginal areas such as Kintra, Creich and Ardtun. One of his crofters, Donald MacLachlan, a blacksmith, who had been born at Ardachy in 1804,[27] worked at Bunessan from his marriage in 1825 to Annabella Macdonald, Knockna-fenaig. They moved to Creich in 1830, to Aridhglas in 1835, and to another croft at Creich in 1850. Donald gave evidence at the McNeill enquiry which indicated that the last of these moves had not been his own choice, although he was much better off than most of his neighbours, but, as he had no lease, he was reluctant to improve the croft at Creich, lest he should be removed and his croft given to a higher bidder.[28] He ploughed four acres of arable ground, sowed three bolls of oats, four bushels of barley and some turnip. He had grazing for two cows and one horse, and used his horse and cart to earn money transporting seaweed, shell sand and other commodities for neighbouring crofters.[29]

His was an enterprising family, whose alliance with the intelligent tribe of MacCormicks in the Ross of Mull underlined their abilities.[30] His extended family of Macdonalds, Grahams, MacCormicks, Blacks and MacLachlans were the very backbone of their community. Those who were still around in 1850 were not, as has been often supposed, the dregs of Ross families. Donald MacLachlan told the enquiry that he did not believe that one in three of the small crofters and cottars, his neighbours, would remain if they could find the means of emigrating.[31]

Donald's treatment at the hands of the chamberlain rankled so much with his friends and relations that it was brought up again during the course of evidence to the Highlands and Islands (Crofters') Commission in 1883. 'Do you remember,' Alexander MacFarlane was asked during the enquiry at Bunessan, 'Donald MacLachlan and Donald MacGillivray who were crofters in the township about thirty years ago?, Are they still living?' Alexander replied that MacLachlan was still alive. 'Why did he leave the estate?' 'The

place was taken from him.' 'Is the country poorer now than it was then?' ...
'In a certain sense, matters are worse now ... rents are more than double.'
The questioning was designed to confirm instances of land being taken away
from families settled in that area for generations, and Donald MacLachlan the
smith was only one of scores in the Ross of Mull who had suffered. He had
not emigrated, but had 'retired' to Ballygown, in Kilninian parish, where he
was to die in 1889. At this enquiry many crofters who had been afraid to
speak during the lifetime of the factor came forward to enumerate injustices
such as the raising of rent at a time of hardship, the giving of crofts to
non-crofters [32] and the taking away of hill pasture. The remit of the commission
was to establish that crofters had been removed from their crofts, and side
issues were not investigated in depth, although a sympathetic interest was
shown by the commissioners in stories of unfair treatment. It seemed that
many of the delegates had come more to talk about grievances dating from
the factor's arrival in 1845 than their present poverty and land hunger.[33]

Duncan Campbell,[34] who had lived in Knocknafenaig in the 1840s, made
improvements in his house there in 1843. 'I went on with the improvements
until 1846, and in that year Mr Campbell the factor came. In 1854 a tenant
came in, and six of the crofters were dispossessed of their crofts for the sake
of this one man ... I was left without a place ... my forefathers were there,
and my father was put out for the sake of this man ... Mr McNiven.[35] The
duke did not know anything of this. The late factor I think reported to the
duke that the people were in arrears. It is not the duke's fault.' All the people
who spoke about Factor Mór, even many years after his death, believed that
the duke did not know of his chamberlain's activities, and would not have
condoned them. Professor Donald Mackinnon, one of the commissioners, who
came of Mull crofting stock himself,[36] made a little Campbell joke of the kind
that was well understood in Mull. 'How did it come about,' he asked, 'when
you were not in arrears, *and you a Campbell*, and the factor was a Campbell
and the proprietor is the head of the Campbells ...' ('the *Chief*' interrupted
the witness with relish) ... 'How did it happen that you were dispossessed in
favour of a McNiven?'

The Commissioners who visited Bunessan in 1883 were unable to land on
Iona because of storms, and an extra hearing was arranged in Glasgow.
Malcolm Ferguson, who lived in Iona and was the nephew of Duncan
Fergusson, the Baptist pastor lately at Lee,[37] went to Glasgow to give evidence,
and did not enhance the reputation of the late Factor Mór. In 1847, he said,
in the middle of the people's greatest distress, the big factor had increased
most of the rents of Ross and Iona by 50 per cent. But this was no secret,
for John Campbell had been interrogated by Sir John McNeill in 1851, and
had put his cards on the table. 'The cottars on the duke's property pay no
rent. The classes amongst whom destitution exists, or is to be apprehended,
are the cottars and small crofters. I am of opinion that the rents on the duke's
property are lower than anywhere in Mull. The rents in Iona were raised at

Whitsunday 1847, but they are lower than on other parts of the property. The reason for raising the rents was that from the superior quality of the soil the lands were under-rented, and the people became indolent and careless, as they could pay their rents without making any great exertion, and I think that it had the effect of stimulating them to greater exertions.' Even the factor's successor, James Wyllie, was unable to explain why this policy should have been adopted in a year of hunger, and kept protesting, when questioned by Lord Napier, that he knew nothing of anything that had happened before his time. If Factor Mór had had his favourites, James Wyllie chose to be bland, impartial and completely unaware of all that had gone on before his time.

John Campbell, the factor, was unparalleled as a focus for resentment in 300 years of Mull history. Even Francis W. Clark and James Forsyth, two proprietors yet to be encountered, did not inspire such dislike. He was perceived to have taken land from crofters to expand his own farm and the farms of his favourites from Islay. Even the island of Islay has hardly recovered from its association with Factor Mór in the minds of Ross of Mull people.

The report of Sir John McNeill's investigation of 1851 chronicled the population increase and its decrease by emigration and death. In the ten years since the 1841 census, the parish had actually lost 1,114 inhabitants. In 1846–47, a large number of the middle rank – crofters – had emigrated to America at their own expense. In 1849 a still greater number of cottars and small crofters emigrated. In 1847, the trustees of the Lochbuy estate had sold Ardmeanach (which was in the parish of Kilfinichen) to Mr Alexander MacArthur, and the crofters had left in a body in 1850.[38] Yet there was little apparent improvement in the conditions of life of those remaining. It appeared that even more emigration was needed to give those who survived the next cull a chance to live with a minimum degree of comfort.

Who were the people left after the first wave of emigration? In 1851, the most common names in Brolass and the Ross were MacGilvray, Maclean, Macdonald, Campbell, MacKinnon, MacArthur, MacEachern,[39] Beaton, MacCormick and McInnes, followed by less frequent names such as MacCallum, Rose, Graham, Lamont, Black, Shaw and Cameron. These names were found in greatest density in the townships, where there were clusters of cottars who paid no rent. In the parish of Kilfinichen and Kilvicheoun there were 160 crofters and 250 cottars. 'I am intimately acquainted,' said Charles MacQuarrie, 'with the condition of the people generally in the parish; it is at present very miserable, especially that of the cottars who have no land. It is a mystery to me how they contrive to exist. In the Bunessan district of the parish, including Iona, there are 206 families of cottars consisting of 1,101 individuals. This number is taken subsequent to the last emigration, and it is therefore the actual present number. I am not aware that these cottars pay any rent.'[40]

Creich and Catchean, in the vicinity of present-day Fionnphort[41] were poor, and full of crofters whose land had been reduced as their rents had been raised, as well as cottars who had no land except for a potato patch. But they were not the poorest in the parish: that distinction was reserved for that proverbially poor area of Brolass, and the land called Ardmeanach, which John, Tacksman of Tiroran had once referred to as 'this remote unhappy districk', 'this unhappy place' and 'this side of the hill'. Poverty was endemic among the Obirns [42] and the McNeills. With the exodus of the majority of the Ardmeanach people, the remnant had joined the poor in Kinloch, at the head of Loch Scridain.

The Crofters' Inquiry in 1883 produced a remarkable witness from the rural slums of Kinloch. He was a 40-year-old crofter called Alexander Mac-Pherson [43] who possessed no apparent qualifications for writing a statement of extraordinary cogency, but whose testimony would have made a strong man weep. In it, the commissioners were introduced to proprietors who were not in the first rank of villains, or of gentlemen, and who in fact were hardly heard of. No great landowner was at the head of this estate. Instead, Kinloch's history was that it had belonged to the Macleans of Pennycross, and had been bought in the strange manner recounted in Chapter 16 by Donald Maclean WS; it had then been sold by Donald's trustees to Donald Maclaine of Lochbuy, who had died very shortly afterwards, and his son had sold it to a pair of strangers and brothers called Mitchell. The elder brother, Andrew Mitchell, had made changes similar to those of Factor Mór in the Ross. He had raised the rents, taken away the hill pasture, deprived fifteen families of their crofts, and squeezed the remainder into the part of Kinlochscridain which was regularly flooded by the tide. 'Nearly the whole of the crofters' population and nearly all the cottars are like so many half-water half-land plants studded over the poorest parts of the slopeland ... never properly drained for seed; in short the Kinloch crofters are placed on the only spots in the district of this sort of land.' The two farms which gained from this redisposal of land were Rossal (once possessed by the red-haired doctor) and Kinloch Inn, which was not really a farm at all. 'All the meal and all the other necessaries have to be provided out of the wages earned elsewhere, and that they are alive at all on the dismal spots which they occupy is an abundant refutation of the wanton charge of laziness. The only employment the proprietor ever gives is an occasional spell at sheep shearing and the like, and the people give their work for no other wages than one meal of food a day.' 'I suppose,' said one of the commissioners sympathetically, 'when this proprietor bought the estate he found crofters rather in the way of what he wanted it for?'

What Mr Mitchell wanted was to graze sheep, and for the next fifty years the crofters and cottars of Mull were to see the question as a simple one – proprietors 'preferred' sheep to people. Angus MacKechnie, a Gaelic poet writing in the 1920s,[44] expressed the sentiment with remarkable absence of anger:

Tha gach raon fo chaoraich bhàna;
Fàs gun àiteach tha na glinn;
'S an còir-bhreith rinn Breatann àicheadh
Do na h-àrmainn chaidh g'a dion.[45]

Among the homogeneous inhabitants of the Ross of Mull, a handful of families, all Macleans, were notable for being what Allan Maclean of Torloisk had once called, in exasperation, the 'half gentry'.[46] They were literate, spoke English,[47] and the only careers they felt able to consider were medical or military. In the early nineteenth century we have seen the family of the red-haired doctor in Brolass; in the Ross there were three Maclean families who were half gentry – the Macleans in Ardfenaig, the Macleans of Scour, and the Macleans of Uisken.[48] All had tenuous connections with one or other of the Maclean lairds, and all three families were impoverished enough, at some time or another, to appeal to Lochbuy or Torloisk for meal or money. They lived in small thatched houses in these three locations, and married the sons and daughters of cadet branches of the heritor families or of the ministers, who had similar origins.

The Uiskens, who were, according to Flora Lochbuy, 'our cousins', married Fletchers, Macdonalds, MacPhersons and Morisons in the first two decades of the nineteenth century. James Morison, a merchant in Bunessan, husband of Janet Maclean, was drowned in 1828,[49] and Catherine Maclean, married to Hugh Fletcher with nine children, left Tirghoil for Canada in the 1850s with hundreds of others in the wake of Factor Mór's changes. Lieutenant Duncan Maclean, their brother, had two natural children by Margaret Macdonald. But the oldest brother, Lieutenant-Colonel Alexander Maclean, had no wife and no children, and accumulated, apparently by saving and investing his army pay, the large sum of £20,000. When he died in 1859, his will was found to be a document upon which he had expended much time and thought. In his retirement his chief recreation appeared to have been amending the disposition of his own fortune.[50] Such a document requires no elucidation in this story, but in the event, the principal sum bequeathed was to provide funds for the education of boys of the name of Maclean in conditions so circumscribed that yet once more, enmity within Mull families was to provide work for the lawyers' willing hands. Once again, a dead man's relations were to enter into litigation because the fortune had not come to them.[51]

The process, which came to the Court of Session in June 1861, was an action for Reduction brought by the Mull relatives of Colonel Maclean of Uisken, who, having come to dislike his family extremely, had gone to considerable lengths to exclude them, if not positively to provoke them. The pursuers were Janet Morison, Bunessan, her sister Catherine Fletcher in Canada, Marion Macdonald, John Ralph Maclean in Uisken, Lilias Maclean in Uisken, Margaret Alicia Maclean in Uisken, Mrs Margaret MacCallum in Canada, and John Maclean in Canada. Needless to say, they had no means of knowing the fate of such actions in Mull's unlucky past, and even Janet

Morison's son,[52] who was a lawyer in Edinburgh, seemed incautious in advising, when the only legal challenge to a will rested upon the deceased being shown to be 'facile', as in the case of Maclaine *v.* Maclaine so long ago, or upon some form of fraud. The pursuers lost, and much research would be required to discover whether the money was taken up by deserving boys of the name of Maclean.[53] The case, which provided a diversion from the iniquities of Factor Mór, is recalled here mainly to show that it was not only the cottar and crofter classes who had gone to Canada, but descendants of the diluted ranks of Mull's half gentry. The rather parasitical reputation which they had acquired in Mull would be shed for ever in the new world, where they were to be valuable acquisitions.

In 1872, a bachelor by the name of Uisdean Ros, or Eugene Rose,[54] living in the one-roomed cottage at Achnahaird in Ardtun, to which he had been ignominiously consigned by Factor Mór many years before, heard of the death of the big factor, and composed a poem – some might have called it a lament – which began:

> Tha sgeul anns an dùthaich, 's tha sinn sunndach ga
> h-éisdeachd,
> Gu bheil am Bàillidh 'na shineadh, 's gun trìd air ach léine,
> 'S e gun chomas na bruidhneadh, gun sgriobhadh, gun
> leughadh;
> 'S gu bheil cùl-taice nan Ileach 'na shineadh 's chan éirich.[55]

As recently as the mid-twentieth century, the remaining population of Ross told stories about the big factor, but often against themselves. They would speak of him as if he was living among them still, but tales of the extra-long coffin he had required would reassure them that no retribution could result from a few humorous anecdotes, and a kind of retrospective, belated *esprit d'escalier* began to manifest itself. 'There was this man called Donald Beaton, who went to the factor and asked for a cow's grass, and Factor Mór said "Why should I give you that when you give nothing in return?" and Donie Beaton thought and thought, and then like a flash it came into his mind ...' and here a different rejoinder was given for every suppliant.[56] Such an intimation of his own immortality and such merriment would have surprised the factor, who had tried to inculcate habits of hard work, sobriety and prudence in the people, for the approval of the duke, the satisfaction of Victorian critics and the betterment of all.

Notes

1. ICP. Argyll Rentals. Microfilm copy in EUL.
2. The word probably came from the Gaelic or ON word for a ridge, and was used in

rentals from the seventeenth to the nineteenth centuries as the minimum size of holding usually granted to widows.

3. Discussion of settlement patterns in the Ross of Mull with Mr Attie MacKechnie, Fionnphort, 1998.

4. The list also has farms in Torosay, Aros and Mornish, but with very few personal names.

5. I am grateful to Mary Buchanan and Edna Stark of the Glasgow and West of Scotland Family History Society for pointing out that the Mull Buchanans came from Appin, and were unconnected with the southern Buchanans. In the anglicising of Gaelic surnames, an existing name was rather arbitrarily adopted as a translation.

6. Figures from 1861 Census.

7. Unfortunately this list does not seem to have survived. If it had been part of the duke's census, it would not have covered the whole parish.

8. Meaning that he was the sixth duke for thirty-three years.

9. *Scotland As It Was and As It Is*, by the Duke of Argyll. [George Douglas Campbell, eighth duke, b. 1823, d. 1900], p. 432.

10. Poor Law Enquiry (Scotland) part 2, vol. XXI, 1844. Minutes of Evidence.

11. Maclean of Pennycross, Dugald MacLachlan of Killiemore and Colonel Robert Macdonald of Inchkenneth.

12. A very gentle death, at the dinner table at Inveraray Castle.

13. Germaine de Stael to Meister, Coppet, 1803, in R. McNair Wilson's *Germaine de Stael.*

14. Censuses, 1851, 1861. Author's file on lives of Mull people. NAS. Highlands and Islands Emigration Society.

15. Information on Dr Boyter (1788–1850) from St Andrews University Archives.

16. In July 1847 the barque *Polly* arrived in the Clyde with flour and peasemeal from Toronto, beef and oatmeal from Montreal, sent by Highland emigrants in sympathy with their people at home. Boyter Report.

17. Devine, T. *The Great Highland Famine.*

18. Boyter Report, 1848.

19. Charles MacQuarrie (1806–61) son of Lachlan MacQuarrie (1779–1821) and Mary Shaw. He was a leader of the Baptist church group in the Ross, a merchant in Bunessan and a member of the parochial board and inspector for Ross and Iona. Not known to be related to LM or CM.

20. Possibly Alexander Maclean of Pennycross's house, Pennycross Farm.

21. Ewan MacLachlan, aged twenty-two, son of Dugald M. of Killiemore, was inspector for the Kilfinichen and Pennycross districts.

22. The inspector for Wester Ross, who was at Tobermory to replenish stocks for his own area.

23. The eighth duke had succeeded on the death of his father in 1847.

24. Boyter Report, 1848.

25. Donald Maclean, postmaster in Bunessan. His wife Margaret Dewar was daughter of the minister of Kilmartin.

26. Boyter Report, May 1848.

27. His family was in Ardachy in the ducal census of 1779, when an ancestor, Robert MacLachlan, born *c.* 1745, was smith.

28. McNeill Report, Appendix (A) 1 February 1851.

29. Donald's son-in-law, Robert Graham, was a wheelwright, and lived with his in-laws.

30. His daughter Annabella (1838–1932) married Neil MacCormick (1836–1925), son of

John MacCormick and Margaret Black. They were third cousins. CR Marriage, 1859. His son John MacLachlan (b. 1830) married Mary MacCormick in 1855.

31. McNeill Report, Appendix (A).

32. The Free Church minister got croft land, as did the quarry workers at Tormore. Napier or Crofters' Enquiry, Minutes of Evidence.

33. Report, and Evidence taken by HM Commissioners of Inquiry into the condition of the crofters and cottars in the Highlands and Islands of Scotland, vol. III, 1884. [Napier Commission].

34. Duncan Campbell (b. *c.* 1814) son of John Campbell and Mary McGilvra.

35. Angus McNiven, born *c.* 1810 in Islay. Tenant of Ardalanish.

36. Donald MacKinnon(1839–1914), first professor of Celtic at Edinburgh University, was the son of Duncan MacKinnon, son of Angus MacKinnon. He was related to MacCormicks and MacKinnons who had left Mull in 1831 for Canada.

37. Malcolm Ferguson (1835–1920) son of Alexander F. and Isabella Black, grandson of Malcolm Ferguson and Mary McIntyre.

38. McNeill Report, p. xvi.

39. The name MacEachern was changed to MacKechnie after 1850, apparently partly owing to the recommendations of Dr Alexander MacKechnie, general practitioner at Bunessan, who found the latter version more acceptable. Information from Mr Attie MacKechnie, Fionnphort, 1998.

40. McNeill Report, Appendix (A), p. 3. Evidence of Mr Charles MacQuarrie, Bunessan.

41. The name Fionnphort, pronounced Fin-a-fort, was unknown before the late nineteenth century.

42. The provenance of this name is unknown.

43. Alexander MacPherson, son of Hugh MacPherson, Penmore, and Catherine McKenzie.

44. Angus MacKechnie (1870–1944), descendant of MacEacherns in Penalbanach in Mishnish, and of the Glenforsa MacPhails.

45. Every pasture is under white sheep / Desolate without dwellings are the glens / And Britain renounced the birthright / Of the heroes who went to protect her.

46. NAS. GD174/46. AM to MM, London, 3 December 1789. 'What you write about Hugh married to my niece does not surprise me. He and all your Mull half gentry have conceived an idea that you and I must serve them right or wrong, and must sacrifice our own interest to please them.' His niece Marion, daughter of the strong man of Reudle, Donald Maclean, had married Hugh Maclean of Ardchrishnish, later in Rossal, and known as 'Hugh Rossal'.

47. According to Burt, 'a gentleman's bairns are to be distinguished by their speaking English.' Burt, p. 238.

48. Lachlan Ban Maclean of the inn at Bunessan does not seem to have had a close kinship with any of the lairds.

49. See Chapter 23, in which Flora Maclaine of Lochbuy was concerned about Janet, left with seven children, and pregnant.

50. GRO. D3330. Box 16. Deed of Settlement by Lieutenant-Colonel Alexander Maclean and two relative codicils, 1856, 1858, 1859.

51. The most recent instance of litigation had been Colonel Charles Macquarie's children challenging the will of Lachlan Macquarie Junior.

52. Archibald Maclean Morison or Morrison, b. 1819. Like many Mull people of this period, he acquired his middle name, usually the mother's maiden surname, in later life.

53. In a codicil the cavilling colonel had excluded boys who spelt their names 'Maclaine' from his bounty. The fund was later administered by Glasgow councillors. It

apparently does still provide help for Maclean students. Information from Nicholas Maclean-Bristol, 2000.

54. Eugene Rose, baptised 1804, son of Lachlan Rose and Mary MacFadyen. Many of the Ross of Mull Roses seem to have come from one David Rose, a farmer in Killiechronan, Kilninian parish.

55. Meek, Donald E. (ed.), *Tuath is Tighearna, Tenants and Landlords.* The translation is: 'There is news in the land that we rejoice to hear – that the Factor is laid out without a stitch on him but a shroud/without the ability to speak, and unable to read or write;/the champion of the Islay folk is laid low, and will never rise again.'

56. Personal memories from the author's childhood.

25

'I cried for madder music
and for stronger wine'

It was not only young Murdie Lochbuy who drank too much, 'guzzling at champagne and claret'. The little aqua vitae observed by Dean Munro, taken by every *Muileach* as a corrective to the weather, was becoming strangely more necessary to everyone. 'I am convinced drinking is the bane of all society,' Donald Maclean WS had written to his son-in-law in 1821, but his conviction did not stop him from loading gallons of whisky on board a steamer for his own summer holiday in Mull. In 1829 he had not brought enough, and sent a note round to Lochbuy from Carsaig, 'My whisky is nearly finished. If you can spare six or seven gallons, take it with you the first time you come.' [1]

Since one of the criticisms levelled at the hungry islanders when they were receiving meal from the Destitution Fund was that they could afford to eat if they stopped drinking, Sir John McNeill thought he should include a note in his report stating the actual amount of alcohol consumed by Mull people in one year, 1847–48.

It is a remarkable fact that the consumption of whisky appears to have increased since 1845. In that year, according to the returns made to the Excise Office, the quantity sold or sent out by spirit retailers in the district was 8701 gallons of undiluted spirit; and in the year ending 10 October 1850, the quantity of duty paid for consumption, by retailers, was 10,212 gallons. From a report made to the General Assembly of the Church of Scotland in 1849 by the Rev. Mr Ross of Tobermory, it appears that the stock taken by the revenue officers in the hands of the spirit dealers in Mull for the year ending 10 October 1848 was – whisky 8464 gallons; rum 720 gallons; brandy 108 gallons; total 9292 gallons of undiluted spirits. It is the practice of all retailers of whisky to add one fourth of water before giving it to customers. Thus diluted, it is sold at one shilling the half mutchkin (half pint) when drunk upon the premises, or at two shillings and sixpence the quart bottle. To 8464 gallons of whisky, add one fourth, or 2116, and we have 10,580 gallons to be retailed, which, at one shilling the half pint, gives about 20 shillings the gallon, or £10,580; but estimating the stock of whisky at 13 shillings, rum at 13 shillings, and brandy at 24 shillings per gallon, the value of the stock taken would be £6,099 ... we thus have an expenditure of £6,099 on ardent spirits in a year of distress. But as all the more wealthy classes purchase the spirits they consume in larger quantities at wholesale prices, the sum above stated represents the expenditure on this account of the labouring classes and crofters. The value of bolls of meal distributed by the destitution committee in Mull during the year 1848, estimated at 15 shillings a boll, would be £3,202. It may therefore be assumed as an established fact that there was expended by the inhabitants of Mull in 1848, on ardent spirits, a sum equal to double the amount of extraneous aid necessary to relieve destitution in that year.[2]

It might be argued very powerfully that if one lived in a damp, cold house, sometimes without glass windows, sometimes without fitted doors, with only peat to burn, and if one had no waterproof clothing or footwear, and the recorded rainfall was 90in a year, the winds boisterous, and there were no hot drinks such as cocoa, or soup mixes, coffee and tea, one would be glad of ardent spirits as a corrective to the weather. There was no temperance movement in Mull until the 1840s, and when Donald Maclean WS warned his son-in-law about immoderate drinking, 'moderate' drinking was probably about half a pint of whisky a day. 'Whisky, though a strong spirit, is to them like water,' Burt said of the Highlanders. And who could blame the poor people if the government should choose their own native drink for a punitive tax, outlawing private stills. Customs officials were of that new professional group of men, like inspectors of the poor and road overseers, who were always being given crofts taken from the crofters. The Rev. John Macleod of Morvern, who did not say no to a drink himself, gave a very special discourse in Gaelic in Craignure church on 15 March 1829, on drunkenness, but by that he meant unruly and violent behaviour of the kind found at funerals.[3] Several visitors noted that the people emerged from church and went straight into the nearest inn to drink. Lauchlan Maclaine often went with the minister himself into Mrs MacDougall's at Craignure. It would have been very foolish to allow all one's friends to depart immediately after sermon, where they had all been gathered together. 'Mr Donald Campbell,[4] Achnacraig treated the Parson, the Elders, etc., to a dram in the name of his two eldest sons, Sandy and Murdoch, who for the first time came to church,' Lauchlan Maclaine wrote in his diary on Sunday 21 September 1827. Everyone lingered at the church door, which was the place where all secular announcements were made after the service, and even threats of eviction and sequestration would be read out there, as well as new estate regulations. Tenants might be reminded in 1829 that there was a rule on the estate of Lochbuy, NO GOATS, NO COTTARS.[5]

In the 1820s, both gentles and commoners were poorer than they had ever been, and a little more was required in the way of a corrective. In midwinter, things were particularly gloomy, and the tradition, since the Sassenach introduction of an alien Christmas and New Year, was to celebrate both twice – the 'real' Christmas and New Year being honoured with deeper potations than the official ones. In the lowlands, Christmas had almost been forbidden because of its Popish associations, but there were no such reservations in Mull

– at least among the gentles. Marriages were celebrated at 'new' New Year among the commoners, because there was not very much to do on the land. If you took off the amount of drink required for weddings, and the unavoidable flowing cups of funerals, the number of gallons quoted by the Rev. Mr David Ross seemed paltry.

The innkeepers of Mull were mixed in their respectability and their conviviality. In 1806, an anonymous traveller arriving at Ulva found no one in the inn, and called several times in vain. 'We sallied out and were met in the door by a figure by all the world like a wax baby moved mechanically. She was a tall thin woman, apparently upon the borders of eternity.'[6] This woman's husband, however, was found to be 'a very different personage from his wife, a good looking, clever, obliging fellow' who acted as boatman and wisely engaged a piper to accompany the visitors to Staffa and Iona, a ploy which always distracted attention from the dangers of the voyage. The innkeeping couple were Macdonalds, like so many of their fellow Ulvaichs of this period, who were given small areas of land by Ranald Macdonald or his father Colin Macdonald of Boisdale.[7]

Mrs MacDougall in Craignure [8] seemed to be the most sociable and efficient of the innkeepers, although Craignure was not, in the early nineteenth century, a port of departure for the ferry. Weddings were held at the inn, and gaiety was encouraged. 'Charles McDugald [9] produced a fiddle,' Lauchlan reported on 21 January 1829, 'and they must needs all hear me play. I told them that on condition they should dance I would, and recommended to Elder John McKillop,[10] aged eighty-two to dance the first reel, which he did with alacrity, and all the other grey beards followed his example. I myself danced at last to my own music.' Mrs MacDougall was a sister of the second wife of Lachlan MacQuarrie of Ulva, Ann MacQuarrie (who had had her kiln house at Ardnacaillich burnt by an arsonist), but must have been very much younger, which was not impossible in an age when women spent twenty-five years in childbearing. Charles MacDougall became involved through this relationship in one of the most protracted disputes to involve Mull families. Since this chapter is about drink and hilarity in Mull in the period leading up to what has been called the great famine, it might be of interest to tell a digressive story concerning the greatest drinker of all, Lachlan MacQuarrie of that Ilk, and his daughter Miss Ann MacQuarrie, one of the merriest of Mull ladies.

In 1817, Lachlan MacQuarrie, former laird of Ulva, chief of the clan MacQuarrie, was 102 years old. He lived at Pennygown farm, which had been made available to him by his kinsman, Colonel Charles Macquarie, on his Glenforsa estate. Charles and his wife Marianne had taken pity on the old man, who had been moved on from Little Colonsay, then Gribun. They did not take him into the bosom of their family, as has been occasionally supposed; they were meanwhile living in the house of Lachlan Macquarie of New South Wales at Gruline. But the chief, who was now blind, was cared for by his daughter, Miss Ann MacQuarrie, the sole remaining child of his second marriage. He sadly missed the kindness of Murdoch the nineteenth of Lochbuy, who had supplied him with money from time to time. But after Murdoch's death in 1804, there had been few to respond to his polite scrounging. There was some little matter of a sum owed to the heirs of his last wife's sister, which sum would just see him through till the end of his life if paid to his daughter Ann. The trustees of young Murdoch had been unapproachable, and Ann's approaches to the new young laird himself had found no favour. Now, in 1817, the ancient chief dictated a letter to his daughter which Lochbuy received in August of that year.

> Hearing that Mr Maclean, your father-in-law is arrived, which was the time you fixed upon for settling with my daughter Ann, I now beg leave to remind you of your promise, and fondly trust you will not only put matters in a train of settlement at your earliest convenience, but actually pay her the sum of £30 at the present period, it being her intention to leave Mull in the course of the autumn ... All that she wishes is to have a certain sum at her command as she may have occasion for it ... Should her presence be necessary at Moy, she shall do herself the pleasure of waiting on you there ... Give my respects to my dear friend your respected Mother and the young ladies her daughters, my sincere congratulations to my friend Mr Donald Maclean on his arrival in the Highlands. To your spouse, and to the dear young ones your children, present the blessings of an old man ...[11]

Young Murdoch replied that neither he nor his trustees had any knowledge of this debt, but if there were incidentals which Miss Ann claimed, he would be glad to see her. He was not going to law for any reason. But in November Miss Ann herself wrote: her father was very weak; perhaps Murdoch would remit some money on the return of the drovers. She daily expected her father's death. MacQuarrie died on 14 January 1818, and it was not until 1830 that Miss Ann took up her pen again. Some time after the death of her father, Charles Macquarie had again come to her rescue [12] and brought her into his household on Ulva to be a kind of aunt to his children. From Ulva House she asked young Murdoch's lawyers for interest on the principal of the sum owed. The claim was based on a bill to her mother's sister Mrs Christian Maclaine, who was owed £128 by Murdoch the nineteenth. This was typical of many claims in Mull, which went back four decades or more, and attracted interest, and it was only one of many claims Murdoch was facing at that moment, including those of his own sister Flora, and the MacGilvrays of Pennyghael (nearly all women). In 1834 the sum was £199, and Miss Ann had engaged Edinburgh lawyers in the time-honoured manner. Some shadow of justification must have been there, for young Murdoch was suggesting in 1835 a meeting at Aros, but for whatever reason, Miss Ann preferred the clout of the lawyers, and probably suspected that Lochbuy's compensation would be small. About this time, Charles Macquarie died, Miss Ann gave her services to the poor orphaned children in Ulva, Murdoch was tied up with the affairs of the estate, and the sum grew and grew, while the lawyers wrote and wrote.

Litigation was so much a way of life among Mull families that there was no deep depression visible in any of the participants. Lauchlan had seen Miss Ann frequently at Ulva, and reported on her teasing, playful ways. She was a bundle of fun, a 'caution', and full of kindness. Like Miss Catherine of Lochbuy, she moved around her family, staying with her half-sister Marie in Warriston Crescent in Edinburgh, with the Schenimans, Colonel Macquarie's in-laws, and other dwindling relations. When Lauchlan went to live in Oban, she visited him in Shore Street, and gave him a problem in choosing a dinner companion who might make a suitable third at table. She died suddenly at the end of December 1842.

Miss Ann had no heirs closer than Charles MacDougall of the inn at Craignure, so that the expected sum of money now had another destination, which was male. It appears to have been an attitude of the time, and not just a funny little prejudice of Murdoch's, that mere females did not require money. His sisters' payments were ignored until (as in Flora's case) a strong and influential husband appeared on the scene. Miss Ann was to be stalled indefinitely. But when he was informed that Charles MacDougall was now the heir to the disputed bill, Murdoch wrote in an amiable and co-operative manner, 'it would appear that Mr Charles MacDougall and his brothers and sisters are Miss Ann's next of kin, and in that case I shall be very glad to have it in my power to be useful to Mr MacDougall and his family in establishing their claim ...'.[13]

At the beginning of young Murdoch's reign, in 1814, his father-in-law Donald Maclean WS, had set the scene by writing – of female babies – 'We want no daughters. We have abundance of females in our families already – but you must say nothing of this to the ladies.' [14]

Pennant, writing in 1772, had said, 'The isles I fear annually experience a temporary famine: perhaps from improvidence, perhaps from eagerness to increase their stock of cattle.' Of the people of Rum, he had said, 'They are a well-made and well-looking race, but carry famine in their aspect.' He might have been speaking of Mull in the 1830s. In that decade hunger was greater than usual, resistance to disease was low, children did not go to school, and Lauchlan Maclaine's neighbours, his 'blackguards' were 'up to their old tricks'. They sneaked their cattle into the fields of the unsuspecting Lowlanders who were now being offered leases. The women borrowed money from Lauchlan, and the Garmony farm servants or scalags worked at his peats for a dram and a reel. When the Lowland tenant Mr Young came to Garmony, Lauchlan observed, 'People of Garmony and Balifraoich cutting peats for Mr Young refuse to drink the whisky toddy he made for them. They want it *pure*.' [15]

1832 was the happiest year for all of the people. The summer was a good one, possibly one of the best ever recorded, with 'fine dry day' following 'fine warm day' in Lauchlan's diary from the beginning of April to September. Although the spectre of cholera was in the background, it seemed that the measures that were being taken by the parochial boards of health were having their effect. 'Dugald McInnes [16] has commenced in good earnest to scrub clean and whitewash his house with lime. I wish a few more would follow his example.' As Dugald was one of the most intractable and insolent of the cottars at Garmony, this was a remarkable victory for the Torosay board of health. For a people who might go for an entire lifetime without experiencing a truly warm summer of more than a few days' duration, these golden days of 1832 had to be seized and enjoyed. On Saturday 12 May Lauchlan set out for Achnacroish for four days of merrymaking with the Campbells of Possil, 'at the desire of the younger part of the family making my boy carry my violin … gave the young folks a dance and joined with them in a reel.' [17] On the 17 May sailing conditions were so perfect that 'the Sheriff set to and rigged out the *Malvina* with new sails and sent her in the evening off for Balnacarry with Mrs Gregorson, Angus and Gillean Ross … *a fine dry warm day with north wind.*' On the 18th, the *Malvina* had returned to Mull. 'Mr P. Gregorson, Mr Macleod and I took a sail in the *Malvina*, there being a fine breeze in Duart Bay, to see Colonel Campbell's fine lifeboat, which, being at anchor, we had nearly run down by getting foul of her cable. The Colonel looking on we went ashore [18] and apologised for the accident, which happily terminated without injury to the boat. Beat back to Ardtornish in fine style with a strong north west wind. *A fine dry day.*'

After the sheep shearing on 11 June, the parties resumed, bringing music, dancing and singing, with all the other good things of life.

> *Thursday 21 June.* Accompanied Mr Thomas Campbell to fish on the lake at Glennan where he caught a fine dish of trout. On our return home found all the gentlemen at a roup of cattle etc. at Glennan made by Archibald McKillop, former tenant at Leidag but now removed to this place. Everything sold well. At night resumed the song and dance with merry glee in which I took my part …

Among the poor, weddings and funerals provided the principal occasions for drinking. The marriage of John Buchanan in Ardchoirk and Mary McKillop, daughter of Charles McKillop (brother of the elder, John McKillop, who had danced a reel with alacrity) was celebrated at Mrs MacDougall's inn at Craignure on 1 February 1833, and was very well conducted, according to Lauchlan, who attended, and found a 'party of very fine young men and girls, old men and women.' A snowstorm had blown up in the evening, during which nine of Lauchlan's geese had flown away. It was not until the next day that the bridal couple heard that Mary McGhiel,[19] a cousin of the bride from Ardchoirk, after dancing and being joyful, had perished in the snow as she walked back home alone. Inadequate clothing, poor footwear and liquor had probably played their part, but a meagre diet would not have helped.[20]

In 1836, the gentles of Torosay parish and of Morvern were more sociable than ever. In September the once-derided Dr Whiteside brought his revered brother-in-law Dr McLagan to visit Lochbuy, and this was an excuse for a grand party. 'Music song and dance,' Lauchlan reported delightedly from Moy. 'Dr Whiteside sings well.' It was one of Lauchlan's last parties in the incessant round going from Ardtornish to Barnacarry to Lochbuy and to Achnacroish. He was to leave for Oban, but not to run out of material. In August 1838 everyone arrived for the Regatta.

> More yachts arrived in the harbour, and the *Maid of Ilay* brought Walter F. Campbell Esquire of Ilay, Member for Argyll County. Among other yachts, that of the Rev. Mr Maclean of Tiree came into harbour today. Lochbuy and his lady and two oldest daughters, his son John and Major L. Maclaine, late Royals crossed over in the morning. The town of Oban is 'bumper full'. Many, I learn, cannot get beds! And I further hear that in some of the houses they are charging a Guinea for the night!! I have given my spare room to Mr Chamberlain at the recommendation of Mr John Maclaine Lochbuy ...
>
> *Thursday 30 August.* The ticket for the Ball seven and sixpence. Some beauty and a deal of fashion at the Ball. Some of the gentlemen appeared in the Highland garb – Ilay, MacDougall, Glengarry, Captain MacKenzie, Raasay, etc.
>
> *Friday 31 August.* 'Attended the public dinner, ticket ten and sixpence ... a number of ladies.
>
> *Saturday 1 September.* Sheriff Gregorson here and rather unwell from a renewal of the *tic doloreux*.

But the 'merited chastening of the Almighty', as the presbytery of Mull described it, came, for the commoners, in the year 1836. In March 1837, Dr Norman Macleod, speaking at the Mansion House in London about distress in the Highlands moved his audience with his account of suffering:

> There are many entire parishes in these island districts without meal, and having no more potatoes (their sole subsistence) than sufficient to keep the people in existence for a few weeks, while a fearful proportion of them are without peat (or turf) for fuel, or an article of food to maintain life, except the miserable substance obtained from shellfish and seaweed collected at low water; huddled together for want of blankets or bedclothes, under a covering of dried ferns or rushes, and as a population without seed, either of corn or potatoes, for the ensuing season ... Every source has failed them; the kelp manufacture; the employment arising from harvest work in the south has failed them; the herring fishing has failed them; and above all the crops have miserably failed! In many places disease has attacked their flocks 'the fields yield no meat ... the tongue of the sucking child cleaveth to the roof of its mouth for thirst, the young children ask bread, but no man breaketh it with them.' [21]

Dr Macleod asked for 'an immediate exertion to arrest the progress of famine which has already commenced, and will ere long reign through almost every part of that interesting country.' The fire had gone from the eye of the poor Highlander. 'But,' said this friend of the Gael, 'He said, "I was hungry and ye gave me meat; naked and ye clothed me; forasmuch as ye have done it to one of the least of these, ye have done it to me."' What the minister called his imperfect English (he claimed that Gaelic was the only language he spoke correctly), together with his powerful Christian rhetoric, brought to the attention of the outside world a famine more significant than the potato failure to come.

In the same year, a report was drawn up by Mr Robert Graham and ordered to be printed by the House of Commons, expressing the view that destitution was due, not to any special oppression by the owners, by way of rents, tenures, the introduction of sheep or enlargement of farms. Instead, the evil consisted in the want of occupation for the great mass of the population in any way which would pay for the maintenance of life.[22]

In 1838, as a result of minimal nutrition and lack of resistance to disease, there was a great mortality from smallpox at Tobermory. Lauchlan, who, like everyone in Mull, knew 'John Bunessan'[23] the son of Lachlan Ban Bunessan, very well, wrote in his Oban diary, 'Mr John Maclean Bunessan's sister, Mrs MacCallum I hear has died of the smallpox, leaving a large and young family behind, and a no less pitiable object in her brother, her house being his quarters for some time back. It is my fervent hope that my dear friend Mrs Sheriff Gregorson of Ardtornish will take her family away from it to Ardtornish before any infection takes place among them.'[24]

Notes

1. NAS. GD174/1628/532. DMWS to MM2, n.d.
2. McNeill Report, pp. xv–xvi., 1851.
3. GRO. Box 25. LMD. Diary, 15 March 1829.
4. Donald Campbell, son of 'the old fox' Alexander Campbell, and husband of Eliza Maclaine of Lochbuy. A particular *bête noire* of MM2, he would, when drinking, 'give his name for £1000 to any man', according to DMWS.
5. The regulation was written in after 1829, when Archibald and Donald Macdonald in Rossal and their father Neil signed a seven-year lease at £85 per year agreeing to this condition. This was yet another reason for the squeezing of cottars into marginal land.
6. UAHC. MS1023. Travel Journal, f. 27.
7. Lachlan Macdonald was innkeeper in 1824, but as he was married in 1808 to Flora MacPherson, he is unlikely to be the innkeeper described here in 1806, unless the wax doll was really on the borders of eternity.
8. In the inn which still stands today, and has not been altered.
9. Mrs MacDougall's son, then only seventeen.
10. John McKillop was a tenant in Ardchoirk in 1779, when he was said to be thirty-four.

His wife was Sarah McColl. His brother Charles was also a character in Torosay parish. They were intermarried with Buchanans and MacGregors, all from Ardchoirk.

11. NAS. GD174/496/2. LMQ to MM2, 15 August 1817.
12. Probably at the time of the last illness of his wife, in 1828.
13. NAS. GD174/496/32. MM2 to David Campbell WS, 1843.
14. NAS. GD174/1628/19. DMWS to MM2, 2 July 1814.
15. GRO. Box 25. LMD. Diary, Tuesday 7 June 1836.
16. Dugald McInnes, born *c.* 1890, married to Isabel McKay. Five sons and one daughter in Torosay OPR, who were, according to LMD, a rough tribe. Dugald was the man who was sent for to kill pigs, lambs, etc. When he confined a horse for twelve hours without food or water, LMD said 'I called him a slaightire, which in English is a rascal, a villain.'
17. GRO. Box 25. LMD. Diary. Saturday 12 May 1832.
18. On the shore below the present Torosay Castle.
19. Mary McGhiel, called by her maiden name, as every woman was, was the widow of Neil Rankin, the 'late infamous miller' at Glennan. They had married in 1821, Mary being called McGhiel alias MacGregor in the OPR entry. The McGhiels had changed their name during the proscription of the name MacGregor.
20. GRO. Box 25. LMD. Diary. 1 and 2 February 1833.
21. Macleod, John N. *Memorials of the Rev. Norman Macleod Senior, DD.,* pp. 127–32.
22. Letter from Mr Robert Graham to Mr Fox Maule on Highland destitution, 6 May 1837, quoted in Margaret I Adam, 'Eighteenth-century Highland landlords and the poverty problem' in *SHR*, XIX, 75, April 1922.
23. John Maclean, a bachelor, once a merchant in Glasgow, had returned to Mull after Lachlan Ban's death to run the inn at Bunessan. His sister Catherine was married to John MacCallum, joiner in Tobermory. One of their sons was the Tobermory lawyer John MacCallum.
24. John Gregorson, as Sheriff of Mull district, held courts in Tobermory, and the family stayed there from time to time.

26

The potatoes fail; Mr Somers investigates; Mr Clark has a remedy

Two of the daughters of Murdoch the nineteenth of Lochbuy and Jane Campbell married Gregorsons of Ardtornish, the first being Phoebe and the second Mary Maclaine. Mary Maclaine has featured in this narrative as Mrs Gregorson of Ardtornish. Phoebe, who had married Donald Gregorson, and was widowed in 1829, lived at Soroba [1] during the 1830s, a handsome house which was visited by many members of the extended family. Her son Angus, a banker and lawyer in Oban, was appointed by his uncle, young Murdoch of Lochbuy, to be a factor of the Lochbuy estate in 1837.

Angus Gregorson Oban and Murdoch the twentieth of Lochbuy worked well together, and Lochbuy must have wished that his own son and heir had had some of the gravitas and common sense of this young man, who was about the same age as Murdie. Instead, Murdie was in Dublin, drinking, cheating, and even spending some time in jail.[2] After Murdoch the twentieth died in 1844, the heir surprised observers by conducting himself at the funeral with great propriety which gave promise for the future.[3] Angus Gregorson continued as factor, but the new Lochbuy was as restless as that far-off predecessor, Archy, had been in the 1770s. Like Archy he had various schemes afoot to raise money, quite apart from his constant recourse to lawyers in his efforts to discover ways of getting round the entail. Angus Gregorson was left to deal with the day-to-day running of the estate while Murdie stayed in the United Services Club in Edinburgh. Constant references were made to his state of health, but his ailment was not named, and it might be surmised that it was drink related. He was involved in a variety of legal cases, most of which he seems to have lost. He confided in no one, except when a wild scheme popped into his head, and then alarm and despondency were spread through his family. His next brother, Donald, or 'Dod' was in Java, where he had joined the firm of Gillean Maclaine in the 1830s. The next brother, John Campbell Maclaine, had gone to Australia, and the next, Allan, was not known for his persevering qualities. Murdie's mother, Chirsty, stayed at Lochbuy after her husband's death with five daughters and two younger sons, Alexander and Colquhoun. Being a woman, and the widow of a man who did not give women responsibility (unlike his father, Murdoch the nineteenth), she had very little influence on the running of the estate, and relied on Angus Gregorson's advice and Murdie's ultimate authority.[4]

After behaving quite well for a few months, Murdie had gone to Edinburgh, leaving the servants at Lochbuy with no indication whether they were to be kept on or dismissed. They were 'quite discouraged', Angus reported at the beginning of 1845. A year later, Murdoch (whose name must now be allowed to mature, even at the risk of confusion with his father and grandfather) was still in Edinburgh when, on 31 March 1846, Angus wrote, 'I have tonight John McLaine's [5] account of his potatoes. It is lamentable. He is to blame that he did not examine and turn them before.' Thus, at first, poor John was blamed for what turned out to be a catastrophe on a national scale. But Murdoch was contemplating 'vast changes' of another kind on his lands, from his retreat in Campbell's Hotel in Princes Street. He asked Angus to collect his rents because he needed cash, but Angus was extremely reluctant. 'The Dumbarton Market is on. The principal tenants are there. It is useless to try to collect before their return, and to make such an *ineffectual* attempt would give tenants the victory over you.' It was hurtful to Angus that Murdoch should even consider such an invidious plan – 'no idea of the *damage* it did' – and in August 1846 when the full scale of the potato blight had made itself known, 'I really do not know what to say at your continued stay South when your own immediate concerns as well as the interest of your estate and people so much require your presence in the country. The failure of the potato crop is universal, and such a calamity requires deep consideration and prompt attention. It is a matter that cannot be deferred.' To this was attached a note from Hugh Gillespie to say that the crop was ready, but the shearers would not cut. 'They say they won't be paid.' [6]

All the heritors had agreed to support the poor of the parish of Torosay except the principal one, whose liability was £18. 'Really I do not know what you can be about – you are allowing yourself to be out of all repute in this country.' Angus's embarrassment was compounded when Sir Edward Pine Coffin [7] gave him 'a pretty rowing' for not having the meal from the Destitution Fund sent out. But Murdoch had moved on to contribute to the unseemly quarrels which had arisen over the schemes for work on the roads, objecting to the proposal to provide Ulva with a road from Salen. Angus was unable to conceal his anger. 'You have certainly made a mess of your Road Dispute. What on earth has sent you into the Court of Session about them? You surely had enough to bother you without *this crowning folly*. It will be no joke.' [8]

Angus's uncle, Sheriff John Gregorson, who had been in financial difficulties since his purchase of Liddesdale, had, after a great deal of waiting in the hope that things would improve, finally put Ardtornish on the market in 1838, and in 1844 had succumbed reluctantly to overtures from the notorious Patrick Sellar.[9] 'I have been told,' said Angus, 'that Sellar had a great hankering after Scallastle.' [10] Since Sellar had made it a condition of his purchase of Ardtornish that the surviving crofters be cleared before he moved in, it seems that Scallastle, with its many crofters, cottars and scalags, had narrowly escaped a purge.[11]

Alexander Mark, supervisor of the scheme for working on the roads, and a member of the parochial board, found Murdoch's silence disturbing. He wrote to Angus:

Dear Sir,

I wrote Mr McLaine of Lochbuy for the last half year's aliment to the paupers on his estate, that is for the half year preceding 4th August last.

I sent him a copy of the amount, as also a full copy of the Minutes of Meeting of the Parochial Board of this parish, held on 4th August. I have however received no answer, and do not know what to do, as immediate payment was ordered by the Board at that meeting, which he must see from the Minutes sent him.

I have received instructions from the Board of Supervision to give them a full report of all proceedings connected with the poor of this parish as soon as possible. But before I give in that report I wish you could advise me about that Money. I shall wait your reply, and if you cannot advise me yourself, perhaps you had better write Mr McLaine. I will not give in the report till I hear from you.[12]

This appeal came at the time of greatest distress, and on the very day that Colonel Campbell of Possil had a fit of apoplexy, and was 'alive and no more', so that the two principal proprietors of Torosay parish were, for different reasons, absent from the gatherings of the distressed poor, who even travelled to petition Angus outside his office door in Oban. The potato blight did not simply annihilate the crop of one season, but lasted for several years, so that the Destitution Fund became an institution, and its organisers skilled at the art of preventing the recipients of aid from becoming, in Factor Mór's phrase, 'indolent and careless'. Dr Hector McColl, an inspector at Tobermory, was still writing to Murdoch Maclaine in 1849, asking if he intended to state how much he was willing to refund for the relief of his destitute poor. Unlike the Duke of Argyll, Murdoch was not organising or requesting help with emigration. In fact he was planning a trip of his own to St Vincent. 'You are fortunate,' wrote Angus, 'in having arranged to sail out to St Vincent, for a trip there will, I hope, re-establish your health. I trust however, you will not leave without seeing that the arrangement for an allowance for your Mother is effected. If you do you leave the Family in a most deplorable state, without money and without credit, and I cannot conceive how they are to exist through the winter.'[13] Murdoch was deeply concerned in the Ulva Feud and ready to take on Francis W. Clark (that steely heritor who is shortly to be introduced). 'For any sake reconsider before you commit yourself to this step,' wrote Angus in what resembled anguish. 'What will be the use of your showing your Teeth unless you can make them felt? Besides, there is no hope of getting the new Members at once to take a side against Clark, especially Forsyth,[14] who must always hear both sides of a question and act from Conviction ... do not spoil your character by acting rashly.'[15]

Four weeks later, Murdoch was in Torquay, and still keeping up the road squabble, with which his grandfather, Donald Maclean WS (who was still a heritor in Kinloch) would have nothing to do. Donald, eighty and still living in Albany Street, had withdrawn from business. In July, Murdoch must have been very weak, for Angus had stopped scolding. 'I hope you gain strength', he said. Murdoch died on the 7 August 1850, at the age of thirty-six, his estate in trusteeship and also under sequestration, with about 300 souls on the estate designated 'needy' or 'very needy'. The next brother, Donald, was in Java, but it seemed there was nothing left to fall heir to. Instead, Donald Maclaine paid off £7830 13s. 10d., his brother Murdoch's personal debts.[16]

In the autumn of 1847, a young journalist, Robert Somers,[17] who had, at the age of twenty-two, published a trenchant pamphlet on the Poor Law Amendment Act, visited the Highlands to 'help forward the cause of the suffering Highlanders', and published his findings in a series of 'letters', some of which appeared in the *North British Daily Mail*.[18] Delays in finding ferries and boatmen had left very little time for his visit to Mull, so that on his arrival in Tobermory he resolved to begin at once by interviewing the poor in their own homes. For at least twenty years now Tobermory had been a place of refuge for cottars who had lost their homes on various estates in Mull, but the influx of homeless people had accelerated over the last few years. If it should be imagined that investigative journalism was invented in the twentieth century and carried to extremes in the twenty-first, Mr Somers' method must speak for a much earlier origin. His eye, like a camera, swept round the rooms of the poor, pausing in one case to note that a hungry tailor possessed two clocks, and in another that a miserable den was so full of smoke that a candle would not burn in it. In a 'back house' (an enduring feature of Tobermory life)[19] he observed an infant asleep on the floor. Mr Somers found it a matter of wonder that the people, debarred from making a livelihood from the soil, should have derived so little benefit from the treasures of the sea. The brief and irregular manner in which the men turned to the sea had given them the reputation for a kind of flighty laziness. Mr Somers calculated that before the potatoes failed, a man and his wife needed to work at them for only two months to feed themselves and a family of six for a year. The fickle herring had a season of three months, during which the people '*lolled* about the shore in anxious yet idle expectancy'. When it was established that the herring had arrived, the men went out to fish, and in a few days had enough to augment their families' diet for a year. Mr Somers' contention was an interesting one: it was that far from being a good thing for the Highlander, the ease with which he had been able to secure his food in the past was permanently damaging to his character, making him idle, and content with the most miserable fare. It was very remarkable that those two dietary resources should have failed at the same time, for the herring had gradually disappeared over the ten years preceding the ultimate potato blight. 'It seems,' added Mr Somers, 'as if Providence had determined to destroy the baneful system on which the population of the Highlands has so long grown poor and wretched.'

His observations did not end there. He did not think that there was any guarantee that the poor Highlanders would use fishing gear if they had it. They required masters – masters to secure their remuneration, to direct their operations, and to keep them steadily and constantly at work. 'But, as I have often remarked, the indolence of the monied classes in the Highlands is a worse obstacle to improvement than the indolence of the poor. The same evil taint infects society from its top to its base, being the more fatal and inexcusable the higher it is found in the social scale.' [20]

When Mr Robert Somers was observing, analysing and condemning the social structure of the Highlands, an incomer called Francis William Clark had already been in possession of the island of Ulva for eleven years. At the time of Mr Somers' visit, Mr Clark was forty-six years old, a married man with a son of twenty. He had been born in Elgin, studied law at Edinburgh, served as a lawyer in Stirling, and married a woman from Stirling. 'Mr Clark is a writer in Stirling who got a considerable fortune by his wife,' Murdoch the twentieth wrote to Lachlan Macquarie Junior, a fellow trustee of Colonel Charles Macquarie's estates.[21] The trustees (or at least Murdoch, who regarded himself as principal trustee) had received Mr Clark's overtures with a certain degree of coolness, for he was full of legalistic quibbles, and he did not want the numerous smaller islands which surrounded Ulva, or the lands of Laggan Ulva on the adjoining shore of Mull. He did not want to have responsibility for the upkeep of the parliamentary church on Ulva, and wished to save money by agreeing certain matters with Murdoch personally instead of going through the Edinburgh courts. Mr Clark's tone in a letter to Murdoch (in which he addressed him as 'Mr Maclean') possibly irritated the Chief still further. They were certainly not to be chums in the manner Mr Clark was hinting at when he said, 'Were we to meet, I have not the smallest doubt that in ten minutes we would at once settle the matter to our mutual satisfaction.' [22]

When the former owner of Ulva, Colonel Charles Macquarie died in 1835, it will be remembered that Donald Maclean WS and his son-in-law had almost come to blows over the question of the sequestration of the Ulva tenants and crofters who were in arrears, with Donald urging leniency, and Murdoch taking a hard line. This difference of opinion had caused a falling-out which lasted several years. The list of arrears of rent in 1835 was extensive, and Charles had been indulgent. It is almost certain that the Ulvaichs were gambling on the possibility of being excused their rents, or on a reduction of rent. Like so many Mull tenants, they had come to depend on a remission of rents in all bad years.[23] Every chance to delay the payment of rent was seized by the people, and the death of a proprietor always gave hope of evasion. Young Mr Charles Macquarie, full of the compassion of youth, begged that the people be given more time to pay, for he had seen, as he went rent collecting with his tutor, Mr Stewart, the pitiful state of many of the households. An interregnum on Ulva saw Mr Charles, Mr Stewart the tutor (who had been charged by the trustees with settling with the tenants) and Mr Clark's parents all together in Ulva House. 'Accompanied Mr Charles and Lachlan Macquarie [24] to Ulva House,' wrote Lauchlan the diarist, 'to see Mr Stewart, and was introduced to Mr Clark the father of the purchaser of Ulva, who I found a pleasant and intelligent man. He must needs treat us to a bottle of wine before dinner, after drinking which we returned to Kilbrenan carrying a good many oysters, a present from Mr Clark to Mrs Craig.' [25]

In May 1836, Mr Stewart, the tutor, reported, 'Mr Clark had them [the people of Ulva] all collected yesterday, and I am much mistaken if he thinks more of his bargain after the interview. All who did not give more or less are to be sequestrated immediately, and in that case the sooner you get clear the better.' [26] Mr Clark therefore began his reign with some sequestrations, *pour encourager les autres*, making it clear from the start that he would be a firm master.

Towards the end of the 1830s, a *New Statistical Account* was in preparation. Contributions were generally made by the parish minister, but Dr MacArthur was either indisposed or too busy to write the account of the parish of Kilninian, and Francis William Clark took on the task. The parish included Ulva for this purpose, and Mr Clark paid scant attention to Kilninian before passing to the subject he knew best, which was his own island.

It would appear that a custom prevailed in this country, even so recently as forty years ago, of the inhabitants setting off to the hills with their flocks at the beginning of summer, and bivouacking in the vicinity of the best upland pastures, and where all the families of the district took up their residence till it became necessary to descend to the low grounds in the month of August, when the hill pasture became bare, and when their crops required attendance. Frequently has the writer of this listened with delight to the tales of pastoral life led by the people on these occasions, – when free from care they tended their flocks among the pastures of the upland common. The men occasionally visited the low grounds to attend their simple husbandry then in use, or to procure some of the delicious fish which abound along the coast; some engaged in the chase, or followed the game; and richly did they deem themselves rewarded for their toil. When returning to the family circle, the produce of the flocks and dairy were put before them, and the feast enlivened by the pure essence of mountain dew, joined to the heart-stirring strains of the bagpipe. Nor in this pastoral encampment were the women idle; much of their time was occupied in the labours of the dairy, in preparing an abundant stock of butter and cheese for winter. When 'baughting-time' was over, the females used the distaff and spindle, and, congregating on the sunniest bank, enlivened the task of providing the tartan clothing for the family by the simple yet innocent strains of their mountain songs.[27]

Mr Clark was waxing lyrical about his island quite as Ranald Macdonald of Staffa had done, and mentioned also his own success with wheat and potatoes. Three of his potatoes this year had weighed 2 lbs each. But between the writing of his account and its publication, the new Poor Law changed things. Kelp prices were dealt the final blow, the potato failure came, and 'finding that the crofters could not pay their rents, and that my private resources were diminishing from year to year, I had no alternative but either to surrender my property to the people, or resume the natural possession of the land. I therefore very reluctantly resolved to promote the removal of the crofters, and proceeded to warn off a certain number yearly for the last four years until now. The population which was originally about 500, is reduced to 150. This diminution has been accomplished in five years. Five of the families removed got crofts on other properties. Two of the cottars are in Tobermory – all the others went to America, Australia, or to the south of Scotland.'[28]

He had said himself that the population of the island of Ulva had been, in 1837, 604 people,[29] and others were to say that very large numbers had come into Tobermory, not just 'two of the cottars'.[30] To Sir John McNeill he also gave his opinion that 'the relief afforded by the destitution fund has had the most pernicious effect upon the character of the people; that it has altogether demoralised them. I am aware,' he went on, 'that many were induced by the desire to share in the distribution, to make false statements as to their condition and circumstances; and that altogether the tendency of the eleemosynary aid was to deteriorate their moral character generally. It has taught them habits of *chicane* which formerly they would have scorned.'[31]

It was not until 1883 that a witness from Ulva dared to refer to Mr Clark's removals. Speaking of seventy-three families evicted from Ulva, Lachlan McQuarie, a 73-year-old shoemaker in Salen remembered:

Some of these evicted families were first removed from sufficient farms to smaller ones, then they were reduced to a house and grass for a cow or two, then to nothing at all, and when they would not clear off altogether, some of them had the roofs taken off their huts. When one of them asked Mr Clark for a house, the answer given was 'No, I am not the father of your family.' In another case there was a very sick woman with her daughter in one of the houses which Mr Clark wished to pull down. Notwithstanding the critical condition of the woman, he had the roof taken down all to a small bit right over the sick woman's bed. On other occasions he went and pleaded with the inmates to go, he giving biscuits to the children as inducements. One of the inducements offered in another case was that the parties appealed to would get good treatment in the Tobermory Poor House, as he (Mr Clark) was a member of the parochial board. By one means or another he got the people away, now one lot, and then another lot of them, according as he was able to stock the land. Some poor people got permission to build huts on a point which no one else thought worth having.[32] By way of making the place look nicer they planted some trees; but as that went to give them a more permanent feeling and appearance, he actually pulled up the plants and ultimately sent the people away too. ... After the failure of the potato the present proprietor (Mr Clark) cleared off the crofters from about the half of the island first, and put sheep in their place; and as his stock was increasing he gradually cleared off the rest till he had all the island cleared, with the exception of one small place. ... I also remember a poor woman being at the well one day when she, terrified at seeing Mr Clark coming, ran away and left her kettle at the well, which Mr Clark took hold of, and smashed to pieces. Another poor woman left her body clothes to bleach by the same roadside, and on Mr Clark coming, he saw them and tore them in pieces.[33]

Mr Clark (who had taken the trouble to learn Gaelic so that he could make himself understood to all his islanders) seemed to spend a great deal of time walking on his roads and encountering cottars, and it might be wondered if his kettle-smashing and tearing up of clothes were legal. But he was not a stranger in the Sheriff Court in Tobermory, where, soon after Sheriff John Gregorson sold Ardtornish to Patrick Sellar and left 'the Country', Mr Clark was up before the new sheriff on a charge of deforcement, resisting and obstructing an officer of the law in the execution of his duty. He had deforced Neil MacPhail, a sheriff officer who was taking possession of a boat lying on the shore at Ulva, part of the poinded effects of Alexander Maclean.[34] 'The said Francis Clark Senior did by threats and otherwise, deter and prevent the said Neil MacPhail from carrying the said warrant into execution. Mr Clark pleaded guilty to the charge, and was fined two guineas, to be imprisoned at Tobermory until the fine was paid.' [35] It is to be hoped that Mr Clark happened to have two guineas in his pocket.

During the hearings of the Crofters' Inquiry in 1883, Francis William Clark was still alive and well in Ulva, aged eighty-two. His son Francis William had married Catherine, daughter of Dugald MacLachlan of Killiemore, at a point when his father's clearances had been completed. She was a grand-daughter of the Stewarts of Achadashenaig, but her father Dugald was in constant financial embarrassment, being 'blackballed' by the Oban bank, and trying to support a very large family. Francis William Clark Junior was Sheriff of Lanark at the time of the Napier Report, and there are faint echoes of a myth in Mull suggesting unseemly quarrels between father and son. Francis Junior, who spoke in public in a most romantic vein about the Highlands, was never to inherit the isle of Ulva, for he predeceased his father by ten months, and although there was yet another Francis William Clark to come – in Francis and Catherine's son, about twenty-eight on the death of his grand-father – the later generations of the family could offer nothing in the way of notoriety to match the first owner of Ulva. From the point of view of tracing Mull families, a more interesting study might be made of the family of the sister of the first Francis William Clark of Ulva, Miss Clementina Clark, who married Neil Maclean, minister of Ulva, nephew of *'Ailean Sgoilear'* of Iona, and tutor to the children of Charles Macquarie when they were in Torgormaig (Duart). It was his company, and his discourses in Craignure church, in the absence of Mr Fraser, which had stimulated Captain Lauchlan Maclaine, diarist of Garmony.

Mr Clark's remedy for the state of affairs in which, as he saw it, he was expected to be the all-providing father to his people, was brutal. It was inconsiderate because the village of Tobermory was burdened with refugees, and the poor there became poorer as a result. It was also remarkably conspicuous. The *Muileach* fear of being 'reflected upon' was absent from his make-up. He seems to have had no conscience about his actions, for he spoke about them quite openly. His brother-in-law, the minister of Ulva, who had been a restraining influence on Murdoch the twentieth of Lochbuy when he had advocated sequestration, left the island in 1844 for a charge in Halkirk. Francis William Clark was a most unusual landowner because he knew exactly how many persons lived on his estate before the amendment of the Poor Law; other estate records have lists of tenants, and some small parts of estates have detailed lists of 'souls'. Although there had been censuses before 1841, they had given the total number of people in parishes, not on estates. In the days of the fifth Duke of Argyll, accurate lists had been made of the people on his lands: tacksmen, tenants, cottars, workmen and women. But during the sixth duke's time, no command came from on high to enumerate the people. Other estate papers have not survived, or have not emerged. Mr Clark knew very well just how many paupers he had in 1845, and how many potential paupers, who would have to be supported by the heritor and the parish. Mr John MacCallum, a lawyer in Tobermory, blamed the Poor Law. 'We ought to have a general poor law instead of having so many parochial systems here and there; because if it is a national defect it ought to be nationally administered, and at far less expense and trouble; and for this reason – that if such a law had existed, Mr Clark of Ulva and other proprietors would have had no inducement to send their people to the next proprietor ... It was fear of paupers that made Mr Clark send his crofters away. I have heard it said that if the people had not been sent away by him, they would have sent him away. I believe they would pay their rents by the lobsters on the shores.' [36]

Mr Clark's remedy was all the more conspicuous because he owned an island. 'He was slipping them away just as fast as he could get them across the ferry,' said John Campbell of Dervaig in evidence in 1894.[37] But at about the same time other heritors were applying every Procrustean rule in their own leases to lose unwanted tenants and cottars, and 'unwanted' simply meant those whose 'subject' was insufficient for the regular payment of rent. Francis William Clark was different in that he operated on a large scale, within a short time, and had no atavistic sense of his 'clann' or children to stay his hand.

Notes

1. Soroba, then a country house, is now in the town of Oban, and is a hotel at the time of writing.
2. NAS. GD174/1719/5.
3. GRO. Box 25. LMD. Diary. Tuesday 27 August 1844.
4. Angus Gregorson's references to her and her letter to MM3, 18 April 1850. NAS. GD174/1861/206.
5. John Maclaine, tenant in Ledirkle, b. *c.* 1790, married 1827, Ann Cameron.
6. NAS. GD174/1186/55. Angus Gregorson to MM3, 25 August 1846.
7. Sir Edward Pine Coffin, director of the relief operations for the destitute.
8. NAS. GD174/1186/70 and 88. Angus Gregorson to MM3, January and May 1847.
9. Patrick Sellar (1780–1851), factor of the Sutherland estates, and blamed for clearances there.
10. NAS. GD174/1186/111. Angus Gregorson to MM3, 3 January 1848.
11. Gaskell, p. 41. Napier Commission evidence, 1884.
12. NAS. GD174/1186/56. Alexander Mark to Angus Gregorson, 31 August 1846.
13. NAS. GD174/1186/200. Angus Gregorson to MM3, 2 December 1849.
14. James Forsyth of Dunacht, who had just bought Sorne.
15. NAS. GD174/1185/202. Angus Gregorson to MM3, 9 February 1850.
16. NAS. GD174/290/131. List of debts of Murdoch Maclaine Esq. of Lochbuy, paid by his brother.
17. Robert Somers (1822–91) b. Newton Stewart of an English father and Scottish mother, later an acknowledged expert on questions of banking, education, law, trade and commerce.
18. Somers, Robert, *Letters from the Highlands, or the Famine of 1847*, London, 1848.
19. 'Back houses' were often sheds constructed in the back gardens of houses where the principal tenant retreated in order to make some money from the letting of rooms. While in Tobermory several rooms might be let to poor families with many children, the custom had a different aspect in Iona, where the main house was let to holiday makers. Visitors to Knocknacross, in Iona, who took over the whole house in the summer, had to contend with their landlady's presence in 'Katie's Back'.
20. All from *Letters from the Highlands.* The final chapter, XXXII, condemns sheep-walks, deer forests, waste of animal manure, the frittering away of money by proprietors, absentee landlords, waste of labour on peat cutting, unfenced land, idleness, entails and unemployment.
21. NAS. GD174/1707/2. MM2 to Lachlan Macquarie Junior, 3 August 1835. Mrs Clark was Agnes Wright, daughter of James Wright, Writer in Stirling and Mary Powell.
22. NAS. GD174/1148/1. Francis W. Clark to MM2, 17 October 1836.
23. Burt had noted in the 1730s that it was customary for Highland lairds to give remission of rent, and this remained a habit of the old indigenous families. Mrs Clephane had given her tenants remissions in the bad years of the 1820s.
24. Lachlan Macquarie Junior, son of LM of NSW, first cousin of Mr Charles Macquarie. They were both twenty-one.
25. Margaret Craig, Marie and Gillean's youngest daughter, was staying with her aunt Flora at Kilbrenan.

26. NAS. GD174/1148/30. D. Stewart to MM2, Ulva House, 24 May 1836. MM2 was to conclude negotiations and balance accounts so that he would not be charged with the cost of sequestrations.

27. *New Statistical Account*, vol. vii. Kilninian and Kilmore, drawn up by Francis William Clark, Esq. of Ulva, 1845, but prepared some years earlier.

28. McNeill Report. Minutes of Evidence. Mr F. W. Clark examined, 13 February 1851. Appendix (A) pp. 10–11.

29. *New Statistical Account*, as above.

30. The Rev. David Ross on being examined on 15 February 1851 said that in 1850, seventy-eight ejected from Ulva at Whitsunday had settled in Tobermory 'where they still remain'. McNeill Report. Minutes of Evidence, Appendix (A) p. 12.

31. McNeill Report. Minutes of Evidence. Mr F. W. Clark, 13 February 1851. Appendix (A) p. 11.

32. One of the very few pieces of documentary evidence for the story of 'Starvation Point'.

33. Report, HM Commissioners of Inquiry into the Condition of the Crofters and Cottars (Napier Report) Minutes of Evidence, pp. 2253–5.

34. There were very few Macleans on Ulva, and no Alexanders in the 1841 census or 1835 rentals. This man was probably concealing his boat from the sheriff officer by leaving it on Ulva.

35. NAS. SC59/8/1. Criminal trials. 14 September 1847.

36. Report, HM Commissioners of Inquiry into the Condition of the Crofters and Cottars (Napier Report), vol. 3, p. 2249.

37. Royal Commission Highlands and Islands, 1892. Minutes of Evidence vol. 2, p. 897.

27

'I dreamt I dwelt in marble halls':
the new men

I dreamed that I dwelt in marble halls
With vassals and serfs at my side.[1]

The census for 1851 was to be taken on 30 March, and the enumerators prepared to fill in their schedules with accuracy. It was fortunate that census day was so early, because Whitsunday old style[2] was the date on which many small tenants, crofters and cottars were due to be removed from their holdings, and some estates would be altered beyond recognition in a month or two. The Rev. David Ross remarked on the schedule for Tobermory:

> Having examined this schedule I find it correct. I cannot but express my regret that it does not show the number who can read and write, and the religious denomination to which each adheres, as valuable information on these points could be more easily and accurately obtained by this method than by any other.

Even more valuable would have been the question, if it could have been put to the population: 'Are you expecting to leave this country in the next few months?' Whitsunday 1851 would see a great removal of cottars, including the remnant of Mr Clark's people and the bulk of Mr Forsyth's. For a new bogey man had come to join the ranks of Clark and Factor John Campbell.

In 1833, a Mr James Forsyth of Kingston, Jamaica, inherited the lands of Dunacht in the parish of Kilbride and Kilmore, in mainland Argyll, from his uncle Alexander Forsyth, an Edinburgh Writer. During the Poor Law Enquiry, when he had owned this small estate for ten years, he commented that there was a population in Oban composed of crofters and cottars driven from their possessions in the neighbouring islands, who were not yet eligible for parish relief in Kilmore, but who increased the destitution of the place. Their numbers increased yearly, and the rooms in which they lived were divided and subdivided in order to find lodging for them. Mr Forsyth could not give the precise reason for their distress, but thought it was partly a result of the insecurity of their holdings. If they had leases they might do better. But on the other hand they were not very good at bringing wasteland into cultivation. They were not good spadesmen. There was a want of steady persevering industry among the Highlanders, which was common to all uninstructed people whose employment had been desultory.[3] Mr Forsyth was an incomer in his parish, and not very well known, as he had married an English wife with a foreign name, and spent part of his time in the area of Bristol.[4] Mr Forsyth was unknown to Lauchlan the diarist when he heard his name mentioned in Oban, but he would, before long, be known to many people in Mull. Nevertheless, his obscure origins were, in the eyes of the ordinary Mull people who preferred landlords from 'the Country' to strangers, a reason for despising him, in that inimitable manner which they indulged in private. He was described long after his death by a tenant as 'an individual calling himself James Forsyth, Esquire of Dunach, a total stranger to us'.[5] The acquisition of a territorial title carried no weight with the local people unless, as in the case of the Macleans of Coll, the pedigree could be recited, and recited in Gaelic to boot.

In 1849–50, the lands of Sorne, part of the old Mishnish territory in the far north of Mull, were sold to Mr Forsyth by the trustees of Mr John Stewart, whose relation, Lieutenant-Colonel Donald Campbell of Knock had been proprietor for some time.[6] Mr Forsyth, eager to enter into his possession and to become one of the twenty-one heritors of the island of Mull, arrived at Whitsunday 1850, and began immediately on his 'improvements'.[7] The Stewarts' tenants and crofters had been in arrears, just as the Ulva tenants had been after the death of Colonel Charles Macquarie when Mr Clark arrived in 1835. Perhaps the small tenants should have taken fright from the very similarity of the situation, for both men were quick in action, and anxious to test the industry of the people. Forsyth recovered some arrears in rent from the year 1849–50, and expended £496 on wages in 1850–51. He also erected some agricultural buildings at a cost of £800. Between May 1850 and the spring of 1851, when he gave evidence to Sir John McNeill, Mr Forsyth had summed up the 260 inhabitants of his new estate.

> I have made an unsuccessful attempt to improve the condition of the crofters, and have found it necessary to resume the natural possession of the whole property ... I have at the same time offered to such of the crofters as may be disposed to undertake the task, and whom I consider capable of carrying it out, lots of waste land to improve, and employment for wages until their lots have returned their produce, and been brought into a proper state. Some are disposed to accept it. I have at the same time allowed those who surrendered their lands last year to remain in their houses, maintaining themselves by the employment which I afforded; and I should have no objection to permit such as those who are to surrender their lands at Whitsunday, as may not have taken crofts elsewhere, or otherwise provided for themselves, to continue for a time to occupy their houses.

As early as February 1851, Mr Forsyth had decided that no amount of exertion on the part of a proprietor would induce the present race of small tenants to

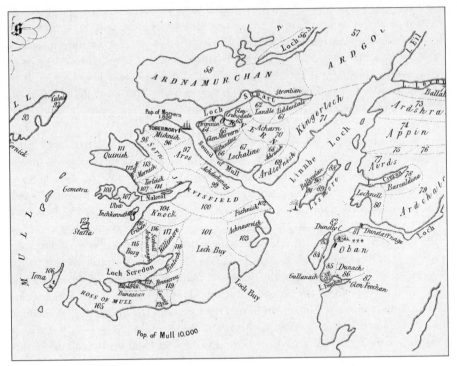

Map of the Destitute Areas of Hebrides, showing estates in Mull, Morvern, etc., *c.* 1850.
The numbers refer to a key distributed round the outside margin of the original map,
with proprietors' names. (*NAS. Highland Destitution Papers*)

engage heartily in improvements, and concluded that a 'moderate amount of emigration, judiciously conducted, would be beneficial to the people themselves'.[8]

Mr Forsyth's view of his crofters seemed to be contradicted by the evidence of John Macdonald,[9] a father of two sons and five daughters, whose account of his own industry was convincing. He had no arrears, and had accepted labouring work from the proprietor, but had nevertheless been given notice to quit. He told Sir John McNeill that Mr Forsyth had begun by taking away the hill pasture. John Macdonald's main worry was that he 'was at a loss which way to turn'. Mr Forsyth had declined to take his animal stock at an independent valuation, and his fate looked as if it might be the usual one of going to Tobermory and waiting to know whether he would have enough to pay his family's fares to America, during which time the little he did have might be used up in rent. John Macdonald's information to the board was concise, factual and courteous, but he was not in the 1861 census. It was not until 1884 that a more graphic description of Mr Forsyth's methods was given to another set of commissioners.

The people had been well off with the previous owner, John Stewart; so John McKinnon, an 83-year-old carpenter in Tobermory, told the commissioners.

Lachlan Kennedy, a carrier in Dervaig, following the evidence, plunged into the cause of the troubles right away. 'Our grievances,' he said, 'may be said to have commenced when the late Mr Forsyth [10] bought the Quinish estate in 1857,' and went on to list Mr Forsyth's iniquities. But here, a brief digression must suffice to deplore the passing of a family which was loved in Mull by people as diverse as the Maclean Clephanes, Young Murdoch of Lochbuy, old Lachlan MacQuarrie of Ulva and the people of Dervaig – the family of Maclean of Coll.

The Macleans of Coll, proprietors in both Mull and Coll, and very often resident in Aberdeen, Doncaster, Edinburgh and London, had nevertheless been active enough in Coll and Mull to endear themselves to their tenants and their clan. Cultivated and urbane, they had enjoyed the attentions of bards and musicians. Alexander the father and Hugh the son had carried on that traditional partnership of Elder and Younger so well understood by their followers. In about 1800, Alexander had designed the village of Dervaig, building the houses in pairs, and giving verbal promises of eternal life to the agreements. In 1814, Hugh the son had married the first of two rich and beautiful young wives, who bore him four daughters and died. A few years later, he married Jane Robertson, noted by Lauchlan the diarist for her beauty. In 1821, Donald Maclean WS had bought the Aros lot of the sixth Duke of Argyll's lands for 'Young Coll,' [11] although he had been quite convinced that Lord John [12] was going to buy Duart, Knock and Aros. The Quinish estate was also extended by the purchase of the strip of land south of Penmollach and Dervaig which included Druimnacroish and Tenga. The addition of Baliscate to the Coll empire in 1827 on its release by the British Fisheries Society, gave the family an interrupted circle of land, and when Alexander of Coll died in 1835, there was no hint that the Colls were bowing out. Hugh had sons from his second marriage, and, like Colonel Campbell of Possil, appeared to be one of the few Mull landowners weathering the economic storm.

But Hugh Maclean of Coll benefited from the fond memory people had of his father and his grandfather, and his uncle 'Young Col'. When Alexander died at Quinish, the patriarchal spirit died with him, and Hugh showed signs of wishing to become a new kind of landlord. The transition may not have been noticed at once by his people. Since the deaths of 'young' Murdoch of Lochbuy in 1844, and Lauchlan the diarist in 1847, no letters and diaries from the other Mull families chronicle the changing character and eventual demise of the Colls. But the evidence given to commissions of enquiry by the people of the Coll estate enshrines the family in a golden age in which laird and people understood and respected each other. 'To whom did Quinish belong before Mr Forsyth bought it?' asked Mr Fraser-Mackintosh of Lachlan Kennedy, the Dervaig carrier, in 1884. 'To the laird of Coll.' 'You were quite happy under the laird of Coll?' asked the commissioner. 'Every person was,' replied Lachlan.

Mr Forsyth added the Maclean of Coll lands of Quinish to his estate of Sorne in 1857. Like John Gregorson of Ardtornish, whose trustees had sold Ardtornish to the notorious Patrick Sellar, Hugh Maclean of Coll must have known that he was betraying his people by handing them over to a well-known and rather self-righteous reformer, one who adorned his intrusive new house at 'Glengorm' with the Prayer Book's injunction, *Except the Lord build the House* ... It would be interesting to know whether Hugh Coll slept well at nights in the four years of life remaining to him, having delivered his 'children' to a man whose characteristics were already familiar to the cottars and crofters of Sorne. But Hugh Maclean's reputation was not as unsullied as Lachlan Kennedy supposed: he had had considerable practice in sleeping through evictions when he authorised Lachlan Gallanach to give the people of Rum notice to quit in 1825.[13]

The first act of James Forsyth on his Quinish estate had been to raise the rents, the next was to remove the common pasture on the hills of Monabeg and Torr, which changed the identity of the twenty-seven Dervaig heads of families from crofters to possessors of houses and gardens only. There was now nowhere to graze cows and horses, and Forsyth offered to buy the dispossessed animals. His agent and factor, an outsider,[14] had manners as endearing as Factor Mór's in the Ross of Mull. When one of the Dervaig crofters, Duncan Livingstone,[15] craved summer grazing for one cow, he was advised by the factor to cut the cow's throat, and when the crofters were unable to dispose of their horses in the market, the factor proposed drowning them.[16]

'It was a bad day for Dervaig when the laird of Coll sold it?' asked the sympathetic Mr Fraser-Mackintosh, who was doing the questioning about thirty years after the events described. 'Yes, all the world knows that,' replied Lachlan Kennedy, who had been an 11-year-old schoolboy at the time.

Hugh of Coll, before leaving his hereditary estates, had indulged that curious whim which seized so many landowners on the point of extinction – the desire to build a grand house in a modern style on his property. Whether the cost of building in itself precipitated insolvency, or whether it was considered that an estate would not sell easily unless it had a fine modern mansion to attract buyers, the phenomenon was exemplified in Mull by Coll's building Druimfin, and by Colonel Campbell of Possil's son, John, undertaking the ambitious scheme of turning a sufficiently attractive dwelling house at Achnacroish, very similar to Lachlan Torloisk's pretty early mansion, into Torosay Castle. Hugh Maclean of Coll, at the time of his second marriage, engaged the architect William Burn to design a Tudor house, simple in its lines, but heavy and bleak compared to his father's house at Quinish, and quite discordant with the Mull landscape. It did not look like a house where a bird might wish to build a nest, but there is no knowing whether Hugh's bride was pleased with its fashionable appearance. The lands and new house of Druimfin, or Aros,[17] were sold to Alexander Crawford in 1845, he being yet another Scot whose father had been 'sometime of Kingston, Jamaica'. Crawford was also the husband of Sibella Maclean, daughter of Donald Maclean WS of 21 Albany Street, Edinburgh. But Alexander Crawford died in 1856, at the early age of forty-five, and Aros passed to Farquhar Campbell, a 36-year-old captain in the Black Watch, and member of an Argyllshire family of note.

It was ironic that the next owner of Aros, Bryce Allan, and his son Alexander Allan, the next again,[18] should have made money from the emigrant trade across the Atlantic from 1820 onwards. The activities of Alexander Allan, an exponent of teetotalism, are outside the scope of this book. His predecessor in Aros, Alexander Crawford, like his father-in-law, Donald Maclean WS, was remembered for his liberal attitudes in such matters as the non-payment of rents in times of trouble. He owned a large part of Tobermory, and it was to this area that evicted cottars were resorting in the years following the Poor Law Amendment Act. It is not known that Donald WS dispensed to this son-in-law the same amount of control and advice as 'young' Murdoch received, but the later son-in-law was delicate, and gave more anxiety. 'I feel very uneasy about poor Alexander Crawford,' Donald reported in the mid-1830s, after an illness during which he had despaired of the young man. 'Such a long confinement, with no animal food.'

The united estate of Jarvisfield and Glenforsa had been joined when young Lachlan Macquarie, son of the governor of New South Wales, had bought Glenforsa from the trustees of his uncle, Charles Macquarie. Lachlan had willed this combined estate to his friend, trustee and creditor, Lord Strathallan, and his will had been upheld in the courts against the challenge of Charles Macquarie's son. The Strathallan family had sold their interest to a son-in-law, Mr Greenhill, later Colonel Greenhill-Gardyne, who was also to build a somewhat grander house beside the old farmhouse of Gruline, where John of Gruline had once lived, and where the governor of New South Wales had been so disappointed in his property and his Mull servants. The focal point of the estate was now the village of Salen, which in 1861 had a population of about 200 people, of whom about two-fifths were children of fifteen or under. The governor had once referred to it jocularly as Port Macquarie, but like Tobermory and Dervaig it fell far short of his vision of village industry.

In the farms on this estate and on Glenaros, formerly Achadashenaig, a large number of the tenants were strangers of lowland origin, mostly shepherds, and the native people occupied cottages and were described as agricultural labourers, herds and ploughmen. Colonel Greenhill-Gardyne, however, did not arouse any animosity in his tenantry, as had James Forsyth. Being an amiable and likeable fellow, he spoke some Gaelic, and was rewarded with tributes in the Gaelic language from those who regarded themselves as descendants of the bardic tradition. His agricultural measures, which included the first creation of a deer forest in Mull (well known to require the minimum number of estate workers), were not met with resentment, nor did there seem to be, between himself and his tenants, any of the monumental misunderstandings which plagued relationships between the people and men like James Forsyth. Conflict between master and men would appear to be particularly intense in cases where the landowner or factor took the view that the *Muileach* were lazy, and needed to be taught a lesson. Strong religious conviction and crusading zeal were features of the characters of James Forsyth and John Campbell of Ardfenaig, but their manner of speaking and methods of punishment were unappreciated by their people, who, had they been treated like gentlemen, might have responded in time.

James Forsyth's son, James Noel Muller Forsyth of Quinish, who succeeded in 1862, was, like Francis William Clark the Younger, a very different man from his father, who wished to distance himself from the reputation of the master of Glengorm. Many of the monsters of Highland estates in the earlier years of the nineteenth century – Sellar, Clark and Forsyth being examples from 'the Country' – begat quiet academic descendants, who would have done anything rather than express rigid disciplinarian views on the life style of Highlanders. Mrs Forsyth, widow of 'the individual calling himself James Forsyth Esquire of Dunach', spent much of the remainder of her life in Mull engaged in charitable works, like a medieval lady on a stained glass window doing penance.

In the middle of the century, those who were left of the indigenous population settled down with a new view of themselves. They now expected no protection from the new men, and nothing from the old lairds. New issues, such as the constant struggle between educational theories of the efficacy or otherwise of teaching English in schools through the medium of Gaelic, created schisms. The minister of Kinlochspelve, Angus Macintyre, insisted on Gaelic being used in school, but the parish schoolmaster could do nothing but deplore the children's want of English. 'Progress is very slow, as children have so little command over the English language,' the teacher wrote in the log book in 1866.[19] The vast majority of children born since the potato blight of 1846 spoke Gaelic only, and the schoolmasters were only echoing the view expressed by Mrs Maclean Clephane in 1804, when she accused John Lagganulva of neglecting his son's prospects by not insisting that he learn to read and spell in English.[20] The timidity and shyness of Gaelic-speaking children was hard to overcome. Accounts which have come down in the oral tradition of schoolchildren being beaten for speaking Gaelic in the playground were the unfortunate consequence of a genuine belief that Gaelic was a handicap which would prevent young people from making progress on the mainland or overseas – the only places where any profitable future could now be envisaged.

In Java, an island of the Dutch East Indies, some enterprising young men from Mull had settled in the 1820s and 1830s. Among these were Gillean Maclaine,[21] Donald or 'Dod' Maclaine of Lochbuy,[22] and John Argyll Maxwell.[23] Others went out to try their fortunes with the increasingly successful coffee-exporting firm of Maclaine Watson, founded by Gillean Maclaine, and it seemed that Java had taken over from Jamaica as the place where Macleans and Maclaines could succeed in business, and send money home to relations. Here the clever and industrious Gillean met his Dutch wife, Catherine Cornelia van Beusechem.[24] When Donald Maclaine of Lochbuy joined Gillean in 1836, at the age of twenty, he wrote to his older brother Murdie:

> I fancy I have not much chance of seeing you out in this part of the world. I should like very much that John[25] came out to New Holland, as I am sure that in a very short time he would make a fortune. You will have heard that Maclaine[26] is going home with all his family. He intends leaving this in February if all things go well ... I am as happy as the day is long here, in town[27] all day making money, and in the country all the evening making love, so what could you wish for more than that? ... When Maclaine goes home ... no one shall miss him as much as I will. His kindness to me is more than a father's could have been, and I shall never forget it to him or his family. When he takes his sisters-in-law to Lochbuy, I hope you will pay them all attention. They are as fine a family as I ever saw. I tell you, but of course in hopes that you will not tell, I am in love with the youngest, and intend following her home or getting her out here again as soon as I can. You will of course give her most of your attention for my sake ...[28]

But when this finest of families, consisting of Gillean, his wife, mother-in-law, two small children and two sisters-in-law embarked for England on the *Regina* in March 1840, nothing was heard of them for many months, and it was not until the beginning of 1841 that hope was lost, and it was assumed that they had all perished. Gillean had been everyone's correspondent, writing newsy letters to his grandmother Marie in Edinburgh, to his uncles in Gloucestershire and Morvern, and to his brother Angus in Ardnamurchan. His mother, Marjory Gregorson, had mercifully died in 1836. In Oban, the diarist Lauchlan Maclaine read the news of the tragedy in the *Caledonian Mercury* of 2 January 1841. The Rev. Angus Maclaine, Gillean's younger brother, had gone out to Adelaide, Australia, in 1839, requesting leave of absence from the presbytery of Mull on grounds of health. A clutch of Mull families had settled in South Australia, and Gillean had bought a small estate there, which had been named 'Ardtornish'. Donald Maclaine of Lochbuy was reported to be returning to Britain from Java for the sake of his health, but no one of course knew of his love for Gillean's lost sister-in-law, and that he would suffer from more heartache than the rest of them. He was unable to settle at Lochbuy, but wandered restlessly from island to island, apparently under medical directions to do very little. He visited Lauchlan the diarist in Oban, and sat in his 'parlour', listless and distracted. On one return to Mull, on 22 June 1842, the steamboat, the *Toward Castle*, was filled with people going to the roup of the Rev. Angus's goods and chattels in Ardnamurchan.

Angus was giving up the ministry, and would return to Batavia and Adelaide to attend to Gillean's financial affairs. Gillean had left such a fortune that Angus no longer needed to be a clergyman: in the most painful of circumstances he was the sole heir.

Gillean had been, according to Lauchlan the diarist, the only one of his relations who was truly generous. Sir Archibald Maclaine [29] was always talking of helping his old nurse in Torosay or his other dependants who could not be named, or even Lauchlan himself, but it always slipped his mind. Gillean on the other hand had heard from Angus about destitution in the Highlands and had at once made a fund available for the poor in Torosay parish. Lauchlan had been put in charge of the distribution of money, and his list of recipients survives.[30] Forty-two people, mostly poor widows, were to be chosen every year to receive five shillings each. Lauchlan too received a generous 'slush fund' from Gillean, which made his last years in Oban, 'up a stair, in a close, through a big entry, east end of Shore Street' more comfortable than they might have been.[31]

Donald Maclaine of Lochbuy was restless, and after a year of island-to-mainland hopping, was off for Java once more. His father had not been well. Furthermore, this was the time of his unhappy correspondence with Murdie which has already been related in Chapter 15. Murdie had been in deep disgrace, and even in jail, and the father was despondent. Donald had possibly heard about the meddling with the entail, the plan for getting money from the insurance policy, and every other mad scheme designed to break his parents' hearts. Donald did not wish to remain. Back in Java, he married a young Dutch woman, Emilie Guillaumine Vincent, the daughter of an Amsterdam businessman. He had probably not yet heard of his father's death in 1844. On 1 September 1845, their first son was born in Java, and named Murdoch Gillean after his grandfather and the brilliant young entrepreneur who had founded the firm in Java and lost his life so tragically at sea.

As Angus Gregorson, the Lochbuy factor, had predicted, Murdie Lochbuy left his mother and sisters unprovided for. For several years after his death in 1850, they lived in a state of uncertainty and penury at Lochbuy. Not one of the five girls had married. Two of Chirsty's sons had died by 1853.[32] Another three sons went via Java to Australia, but did not have Donald's perseverance in business.[33] The Rev. Angus had put very clearly his views on the qualities that were necessary for survival in the Australian bush.

> I fear the colony is little understood at home. Nothing will do here but the strictest economy in expenditure, and close attention to business. Young men have much drudgery, and to those who are fond of ease, much hard work to encounter, which can only be surmounted by perseverance and a steady determination to let nothing interfere with the one object of obtaining independence. This independence and a comfortable home may certainly be much more surely attained by young men who act so than at home, while

the making of fortunes which will enable them to live at home, and leave their property here under the superintendence of others seems to me out of the question. None should come to be Colonists who don't intend to make the Colony their home. Those who had most capital have done worst through neglect of business and extravagance. If John does not resolve *to go through with it*, the sooner he leaves the better. Though he has not shown any *flinching* yet, there is a possibility that he get tired of a bush life, like hundreds of others.[34]

It was not easy to go to Australia on preferential terms. Colin Campbell of Kintraw, who had married the oldest daughter of Murdoch Maclaine and Jane Campbell, negotiated with HM Colonisation Commissioners for South Australia, and with the South Australian Company in 1838.

I mentioned to you in August last our intention of going to South Australia if we could accomplish it, and Jane would tell you when last at Lochbuy that we were making the necessary arrangements in the best way we could. Here we cannot live, through suffering severe privations, and occasioning trouble to our friends. No doubt we must suffer hardships at the commencement where we are going, but by care and frugality we expect to get forward, and the children who are a burden to us here, will be of the greatest benefit to themselves and us in that Colony.[35] I have been in correspondence since Jane's return from Mull with her Majesty's Colonization Commissioners for South Australia, and with the South Australia Company. The latter offer apparently very favourable conditions to those renting farms from them (for they sell none), upon a lease of 21 years with a break at the end of every seven; but then they are very particular as to the improvements to be carried on, and to the buildings to be erected, and although the tenant at the end of every break in the lease has it in his power to purchase his farm at £5, £6 or £7, yet I consider it more hazardous than treating with the Government Commissioners, who will sell eighty acres of good lands for £80 without any reservation of woods ... after comparing the conditions of both parties ... The Commissioners will also allow me to take shipping at Greenock; the Company wish to ship the emigrants in their own ships in the Port of London, paying their own expense till taken on board.[36]

These middle-class emigrants to Australia were very different from the Mull emigrants who had been flooding to Canada, and who would never recross the Atlantic. Many of them returned home after a taste of hardship. The family of Charles Macquarie, son of Charles Macquarie of Ulva, tried Australia in 1838, but returned to Scotland in 1845, in spite of having 'a fine farm up the Paterson River'.[37] They went first to Moidart (from the remote fastness of which Charles challenged the Will of his cousin, Lachlan Junior of Jarvisfield), and then rented Baliscate, near Tobermory. But the luxury of a change of mind was denied to families like the Penders in Tobermory, or the well-educated but penniless Macleans of Ardfenaig.

The Lochbuy estate was sequestrated in 1845, having been in the hands of trustees since 1831.[38] From Java, Donald conducted a correspondence with the Edinburgh lawyers. He had tried to find out from his brother Murdie what was happening at home, but Murdie had written rarely, and Donald heard only vague accounts of Lochbuy having to be sold. 'When our *dear Lochbuy* is on the market,' Donald wrote to Murdie, 'I see that you will require about £30,000 to pay all ... It is quite out of my power to assist you with funds.'[39] After Murdie's death, Donald's attempts to keep in touch with the situation at home were reminiscent of Lachlan Macquarie trying to act incisively from New South Wales forty years before, when the sixth duke was selling land. Donald Maclean WS, Donald's grandfather, for whom he had been named, had long ago given up all legal work for the Lochbuy family, and died in 1853 at the age of eighty-three. In Java, Donald Maclaine was annoyed at not having been told that his grandfather's estate of Kinloch, at the head of Loch Scridain, was for sale. He bought it in 1860, after a brief flirtation with the idea of buying Inchkenneth and Gribun when they were exposed for sale in 1858. Between 1853 and 1858 every title deed concerning the old Lochbuy estate had been scrutinised for inhibitions. Donald was at last advised that he might now, like any member of the public, offer the upset price of £31,000 for Lochbuy, and become the new owner, free of entails or mortgages. Having a clean bill of health over the property, Donald could now attend to his title, and enter himself heir to his father Murdoch, to become the twenty-first of Lochbuy.[40] Dear Lochbuy had been rescued from the administrations of strangers, and Kinloch too. Yet those two properties, with the exception of the pauperised village of Tobermory, where every evicted person sought refuge, were the most distressed areas in the whole of Mull. It is difficult to know whether Donald acted out of personal sentiment, or whether he had any plans for the amelioration of the conditions of his people. Not one reference to his tenantry emerges from his letters, and when he finally returned from Java to take over his purchases, he was to live for only three or four years more. Donald Lochbuy, coffee exporter in Java and saviour of the estate, died in Edinburgh only twelve days short of his forty-seventh birthday, grey-haired, grey-bearded and weary looking. People blamed the climate of Batavia for his premature death.[41] A monument at Loch Uisg inadequately outlines his identity and his achievement. He was little known in Mull, his principal legacy being the name he gave to the house he built for his mother and sisters – Java Lodge. It was not a beautiful house, and the Java ladies were not happy in it. Until the end of the nineteenth century they tried without success to let it in order to provide themselves with an income as they became more and more impoverished.[42] Like Aros House, Java Lodge was demolished in the 1960s, but a group of modern houses north of Craignure, built around the site, preserves the memory of a fortune made in Asia by one enterprising member of the family of Lochbuy.

Now the estate did go without let or hindrance to his two sons, Murdoch Gillean and Anthony Vincent. On Saturday 1 September 1866, the coming-of-age of Murdoch Gillean was celebrated with a dinner for the tenants, and bonfires. It was a day of unclouded sunshine, quite different from the torrential rain which had marked the Marquis of Lorne's majority on 6 August. It ended with a ball in the marble halls of Java Lodge. Lochbuy House was let to a shooting tenant.[43]

In 1866, the formidable Miss Catherine Maclaine of Lochbuy attended the coming-of-age celebrations for her great-nephew, Murdoch Gillean. Born in 1793, she had reversed the temporary trend of the births of boys into the Lochbuy family. Charles Macquarie, who was fond of babies, had announced her birth to Murdoch, her father, as of a 'fair daughter'. In fact her resemblance to her father was uncanny. She had the same long, narrow nose, humorous brown eyes and fair colouring. 'Your little woman', Jane had called her when writing to her husband about the infant. Miss Catherine had been the only daughter of Jane and Murdoch to remain unmarried, in spite of her flirtatious disposition and fondness for men. Occasionally in trouble with her brother, 'young' Murdoch, over her outlay on dress, and her resentment of the fact that she had to pay him £35 a year for bed and board at Lochbuy, she travelled widely, as unmarried ladies did in those days, staying with aunts like Elizabeth Henrietta Macquarie, and with all her sisters. Her expenditure on kid gloves was remarkable, but they may have been given as presents to all her female relatives. She was a link between the eighteenth century and the nineteenth, frequently meeting another Lochbuy daughter called Mally Maclaine, who had belonged to the age of fostering and makalive cattle.[44] She was a link between the old Mull and the new, between that pulsing, pullulating world of overpopulated townships, kelp workers, singing boatmen, resident pipers and turf houses reeking with smoke, and the new etiolated Mull which had to reach out beyond the seas in order to speak to its own people. She, with her sister Jane Jarvis, had ridden side-saddle through the pages of Lauchlan Maclaine's diary. She expended much effort in concealing her true age; in the 1841 census she was thirty-nine when she was actually forty-seven. From time to time a lawyer to the family of Lochbuy would notice an annuity of £55 going out, and would write in a memo, 'Who is Miss Catherine Maclaine?' She avoided being consigned to Java Lodge with the younger Lochbuy women after her nephew Dod's death, and when the mansion house was let, she stayed on in a cottage at Lochbuy. There were no diarists to chronicle her last years, and it is not known what she thought of the later Lochbuy or 'Lochbuie' girls, with their novelettish names, Kathleen, Mabel and Edith.[45] When Miss Catherine died in 1894 at 'Lochbuie', in an alien world, there were no relations in the parish, and her particulars were given by her servant, Janet Currie. In the *Caibeal Mheamhair* at Laggan, burial place of the Maclaines of Lochbuy, her plaque bristles with mistakes of the kind which Lauchlan the diarist had so assiduously avoided in the case of his father Gillean.

In the first generations of new men, there were strangers like Francis W. Clark and James Forsyth, who came in without connections, but whose children married into families of 'the Country'.[46] Then there was a second type of new landlord, like Alexander Crawford, John Auldjo of Pennyghael (who was a son-in-law of William MacGillivray), Lord Compton, a grandson of Marianne Torloisk, the Misses Macdonald of Gometra, sisters of Ranald Macdonald of Staffa, and the MacArthurs in Ardmeanach, who had some ties of blood with the old Mull people. In the early 1840s, the estate and headland of Burg, formerly belonging to the Argyll or Duart estate, was sold to Duncan MacIntyre, a Mull man of long pedigree, whose father Nicol MacIntyre had been tenant in Ardalanish since 1775, and whose ancestors had, he said, lived there for hundreds of years. In the power politics of Factor Mór, the MacIntyres lost their farm of Ardalanish to Islay favourites called MacNiven, but moved as tenants to Knockvoligan, and showed their independence of petty princes by the purchase of Burg. Burg provided grazing for cattle, but had no dwelling house of distinction. The MacIntyres, fervent Baptists, did not aspire to competition with the new men. Duncan MacIntyre was a unique heritor who composed Gaelic hymns and sacred verse. His son, another Nicol MacIntyre, supervised the family's farming interests from Knockvologan. Duncan and his wife, Mary Maclean, died in 1863, apparently free of the taint of evicting Burg tenants, although their neighbour, Mr MacArthur in Ardmeanach, was responsible for a clean sweep in his lands.

In Killiechronan, part of the united estate of Jarvisfield and Glenforsa, forty-three families were removed in about 1854, a very large number of 'souls'.[47] The Strathallan family, who had been guardians to young Lachlan Macquarie, the governor's son, had practised eviction during his minority, and again after his death, when his lands had reverted to them. This property, on the northern shores of Loch na Keill, had been notable for the number of old townships lying on its flanks, and one of those had actually been observed by an anonymous traveller in 1808. 'Passed a village of Highland huts, upon the north side of Loch Nakeal, in a beautiful situation. Here we first had a view of that charming little island of Inch Kenneth, the most delightful spot in the Hebrides. All the country around it is covered with black barren heath, but Inch Kenneth has the most luxuriant verdure imaginable.'[48]

In Penmore, once part of the Argyll estate, transferred to Hugh Maclean of Coll in the years of his empire building, and later acquired by Dr MacNab, half the people, or fifteen families, were evicted between 1856 and 1860.[49] The MacNabs, father and son, seemed to belong to the first category of unconnected heritors, the father an Ardrishaig farmer, and the son a doctor who practised in Bury St Edmunds.[50] Among heritors, it would seem that eviction was practised with the greatest aplomb by 'new men': Clark, Forsyth, Strathallan and MacNab, and Hugh MacAskill of Talisker. But in spite of the people's refusal to believe that their beloved Macleans of Coll could have betrayed them,[51] Hugh Maclean had had his share, while the Northamptons at Torloisk, the Macdonald sisters in Gometra, and the MacArthurs had not been shy in 'losing' their people. The seventh Duke of Argyll had been too ill to act incisively, but his son had sheltered behind the broad back of Factor Mór, while his tenants and cottars insisted that the good duke did not know what his factor was doing. If Factor Mór had a very pronounced view of how the people should be taught to work, he was also carrying out the policies of the duke. The Maclaines of Lochbuy were not blamed for evicting their cottars simply for the purpose of clearance, but continued to raise actions for non-payment of rent, and as their lands showed greater signs of poverty and distress than any other estate, their restraint appears to have come from the muddle of Murdie's reign and the absence of Donald during his, rather than from compassion.

Notes

1. Alfred Bunn, librettist. *The Bohemian Girl* (1843), Act 2.
2. Like Christmas and New Year, the lease dates were still old style, Whitsunday being 25 May.
3. Poor Law Inquiry, part 2, vol. XXI. 1844, p. 167.
4. James Forsyth, 1801–62 married 26 June 1834, Maria Magdalen Muller, of Farrs, Dorset, who died in 1890. They had one son and four daughters, one of whom was to marry a MacDougall of Dunollie.
5. Napier Enquiry, p. 2277. Evidence of John Campbell, 1884.
6. Abbrev. Reg. of Argyll Sasines. Donald Campbell had inherited Sorne, Lephein, Ardmore, Baliachtrach, Penalbanach, Erray, etc., from his father, John Campbell, in 1817, who had bought them from the MacKinnons.
7. McNeill Report, p. xviii.
8. McNeill Report, Minutes of Evidence, Appendix (A), p. 22.
9. John Macdonald and his neighbour Donald McInnes lived at Baliacrach, one of the townships of the estate called Sorne.
10. Forsyth died in 1862.
11. 'I have today purchased the Aros lot for young Coll at £15,000 and consider it a very great bargain.' DMWS to MM2, 14 April 1821. NAS. GD174/1628/233.
12. Lord John (Douglas) Campbell, the sixth Duke's brother and future seventh Duke of Argyll.
13. Love, J. A., 'Rhum's Human History'. In Clutton-Brock, T. H. and Ball, M. E. (eds), *Rhum, the Natural History of an Island.*
14. The factor was William Blair, b. 1800 in Port of Menteith. He was unmarried (1861 Census).
15. Duncan Livingstone, forty-six in 1861 census, but probably born in 1812, was a feuar in one of the original houses in Dervaig.
16. Crofters Report, Minutes of Evidence, p. 2251. Evidence of Lachlan Kennedy, Dervaig, 1884.

17. The Barony was called Aros, and this name was adopted for the estate in the 1850s.

18. Alexander Allan (1780–1854), originally a ship's carpenter, became part owner of a brig which traded from Greenock to Montreal. His son, Bryce Allan bought Aros in 1873, and died the following year, when his son Alexander Allan (1844–1927) became the owner of Aros.

19. ABDA. Log books of Kinlochspelve Parish School.

20. See Chapter 12.

21. Son of Allan of Scallastle and Marjory Gregorson, and grandson of Gillean and Marie.

22. Second son of 'young' Murdoch and Chirsty, and grandson of Donald Maclean WS.

23. Son of James Maxwell, chamberlain of the Argyll estates, and his wife Janet McNeill.

24. Munro, R. W., 'The MacQuarries of Ulva' in *The Scottish Genealogist*, 15, 2, 1968.

25. John Campbell Maclaine of Lochbuy (1818–85), third son of Murdoch and Chirsty.

26. Gillean Maclaine, born 1798, and so eighteen years Donald's senior.

27. Batavia, later Djakarta.

28. NAS. GD174/2343. DMLB to MM3, Batavia, 6 October 1839. MM3 was in Cork with his regiment.

29. Sir Archibald Maclaine (1777–1861). One of the twins of Gillean and Marie. He had no surviving legitimate children. His old nurse, Marion Maclean, died in abject poverty in 1829.

30. GRO. Uncatalogued MSS. List of people served on 20 July 1839 from the charitable bounty of Gillean Maclaine Esq., of Java.

31. MM2's jocular form of address. LMD blessed Gillean many times when the grocer, Mr Cumstie, sent his bill.

32. Colquhoun, the 6th son, died in August 1853 at the age of twenty-four.

33. John Campbell Maclaine (1818–85); Allan Maclaine (1822–75); Alexander Maclaine (1827–85).

34. Rev. Angus Maclaine, Ardtornish, Adelaide, S.A., 23 January 1843, to MM2 about his son John.

35. Colin Campbell and Jane Maclaine had several children born at Kintraw, followed by John Maclaine Campbell born in Mull in 1826 and Donald, Torosay 1829. Their eldest daughter Jane married the blind Charles, son of Donald Maclean WS, and lived in Canada.

36. NAS. GD174/2340/1. Colin Campbell to MM2, Oban, 27 April 1839.

37. NAS. GD174/2341. Lachlan Macquarie, Brisbane Grove, Paterson River, to MM2, 1 May 1839.

38. GRO. D3330. Gillean Maclaine to Hector Maclaine, 15 August 1831. 'Nearly three quarters of the Highlands are for sale. Ardtornish under trustees and I fear so is Lochbuy. Possil is the only man that stands his ground.'

39. NAS. GD174/2346/7. DMLB to MM3, Batavia, 26 September 1848.

40. The Lochbuy chieftains have been re-numbered, but the numbers of A. Maclean Sinclair are being adhered to here.

41. Batavia was built like a typical Dutch town, with canals, and was mosquito ridden.

42. The Java Letters. Collection in the possession of the author.

43. *Oban Times*, Saturday 8 September 1866. The house was let almost permanently from then until 1919, when Sir Stephen Herbert Gatty and Lady Gatty, tenants, raised an action against Kenneth Douglas Lorne Maclaine of Lochbuie for non-payment of interest on a loan or bond dated 1910. The case revolved around the meaning of the word punctual, a word which had not existed in the vocabulary of the eighteenth- and early nineteenth-century Maclaines. True to the style of JMLB, this Maclaine

challenged the stern judgement of the courts, and lost Lochbuy, which had been his security, to the Gattys.

44. Mally Maclaine was the mother of Donald Maclean WS, and therefore grandmother to Miss Catherine's sister-in-law, Chirsty. She lived in Edinburgh until her death in 1831, aged ninety-two.
45. Kathleen, Mabel and Edith were the daughters of Murdoch Gillean. Mabel married a Maclean of Pennycross.
46. FWC Junior married Catherine MacLachlan. Caroline Harriet Forsyth married a Macdougall of Dunollie.
47. This clearance probably accounted for some 200 people in Achronich, Acharn, Killiemore, Oskamull and Kellan.
48. UAHC. MS 1023. Anonymous travel journal.
49. Royal Commission (Highlands and Islands) 1892. Minutes of Evidence. Evidence of John Campbell.
50. Addison, Matriculations in Glasgow University.
51. The evidence of John Campbell is full of instances of Hugh Coll's evictions, at Mingary, Achnadrish, Teanga, and Ledmore.

28

An t-sobhrach Mhuileach:
the Mull primrose

Mo shòbhrach gheal-bhuidh', thlàth
D' an dùthchas a' choill' fhàsail;
Bha do bhreih is d' fhàs
Am bràighe Chreag-an-Iubhair.
A lilidh ...[1]

Tobermory had been, for nearly 200 years of this chronicle, part of an estate, like all other places in Mull, so that it belonged to heritors, just like all the small townships. In fact what is now Tobermory straddled two estates, Mishnish and Aros. In the eighteenth century these had belonged to the Mackinnons of Mackinnon, and to the Dukes of Argyll. In the last quarter of that century, Charles Mackinnon sold Mishnish to the Campbells of Knock, and in 1788, the fifth duke, one of the promoters of the scheme to make a fisheries station at Tobermory, sold a sufficient portion of his property to the British Society for Extending the Fisheries and Improving the Sea Coasts of this Kingdom. Mr Stevenson of Oban and Mr Maxwell, the duke's chamberlain, together organised work on the new village, but the criticism of the plan by another Mr Stevenson – Robert, engineer to the Commissioners of the Northern Lights – might be the ultimate judgement on Tobermory's failure to become a centre for fishing and trade. In 1814, Robert Stevenson told Walter Scott that he thought the village should have been built on the island of Calve, with a causeway linking it to Mull.[2] Thus the people who had been granted feus in the new upper village might have been nearer the fishing than they were in their houses on the hill.

Tobermory was rarely visited by strangers; Johnson and Boswell, Lord Mountstuart and William Daniell were exceptional in passing through. The latter thought the road from Achnacraig to Tobermory *excellent* in 1813, and commented on the neatness of the Tobermorians, the many pretty women, and the purity of the English spoken there. His drawing of the bay depicts an exceptionally neat woman, a tidy inn, and some well-built houses. But for many decades travellers, who were even then in a hurry, preferred to cross from Aros Bay to Loch na Keill on their way to Staffa and Iona. The trouble with this wonderful site, so often compared to a Roman amphitheatre, was that it had no hinterland where anything happened; there was no great navigable river opening into the sea; there were no industries producing exportable goods. The occupation which had sustained the people for hundreds of years – the breeding and selling of cattle – was, by the mid-nineteenth century, lost to them, since on every estate common pasture had been removed. Lowland shepherds had replaced small Mull farmers in houses improved or even rebuilt for their accommodation. The original feuars in the upper town of Tobermory had, like the crofters of Dervaig village, lost grazing, and could hardly keep a cow. Some took to letting rooms to dispossessed people, since this was one commodity always in demand. But few wanted to make a living from fishing. 'It is strange,' Mr Somers had said, 'that when people are debarred from making a living from the land, that they don't take up fishing, except as a secondary activity, and to provide food for themselves.' He was not alone in thinking it strange.

All Tobermorians were tenants or feuars until about 1820, when among all the property deals there suddenly appeared, in the Register of Sasines, some signs of market activity of a new kind. A number of sites with dwelling houses appeared in the lower village. Until that time, property had been about investment in land, and not about buildings. Houses were of secondary importance, and many good estates did not have a single house of any quality until the new men began to build in style. 'A neat white-washed house surrounded with several well-enclosed and well-cultivated fields' [3] represented the standard aspired to by tenants and owners in the early nineteenth century, and even the critical attentions of a constant stream of visitors had done little to improve the appearance of farmhouses. William Daniell had deplored the collapse of Sir Allan Maclean's house on Inch Kenneth, which was now roofless. In Tobermory, the feuars' houses were plain and neat, but it was only after Daniell's visit that the lower village was developed, and individual lots began to belong to people other than heritors.

The earliest property deal to be concluded by a member of the unlanded classes in Tobermory seems to have been the sasine granted in 1820 to Margaret MacLachlan, wife of Dugald MacLachlan, tailor, in security of an annuity promised to her in her marriage contract. [4] The house was described as having a court, a 'back house', and offices and gardens on the Low Street or Breast of Tobermory. In 1823, another Dugald MacLachlan acquired a piece of land in Portmore, Tobermory on the east side of the burn, with a dwelling house thereon. Dugald MacLachlan the tailor extended his property on the Breast. In October 1823, John MacCallum, carpenter in Tobermory, and son-in-law to Lachlan Ban Maclean Bunessan, acquired from the British Society a piece of ground in the Low Street, or Breast of Tobermory, with a dwelling house. The middle classes in Mull, who had taken so long to constitute themselves, were at last coming into being. Duncan Black, shoemaker, Alexander Graham, tide waiter, John Sinclair, merchant, [5] Hector MacDougall, spirit dealer, Duncan MacColl, shoemaker, and the wife of Robert Cuthbertson, fishery officer, [6] all rushed to join the charmed circle.

A hive of industry was forming itself throughout the 1820s, created by a new generation of Mull and Morvern people. In spite of the economic climate elsewhere on the island, the facilities created by the Portmore and Breast tradesmen were used, and attracted people to Tobermory from Torosay parish who might otherwise have gone only as far as Salen. Lauchlan the diarist would order a tartan waistcoat from Tobermory, and when he went to see his half-brother George Buchanan, he would stay, or dine, at one of the new boarding houses. But the growth of prosperity was halted after the first rural evictions that came with the Poor Law Amendment, and the character of the village began to change. The large-scale removals of Francis William Clark brought hundreds of cottars to huddle in back houses, and land changes in Morvern and Ardnamurchan brought more refugees. Sheriff John Gregorson had had to 'lose' many small tenants to meet with the requirements of the purchaser of Ardtornish – Patrick Sellar. This influx of the dispossessed changed the social balance of the population beyond remedy, and Tobermory became a focus of attention as a pauperised Highland village. Families who would have been ashamed to beg in the countryside sent their children begging now, for the refugees required a residence qualification before being admitted to the Poor Roll. Ostensibly, many families were waiting for a passage to Canada or Australia, but selection processes were long, and waiting became a way of life.

One of the best-known families of Mull were the MacPhails, said to have been in Glen Forsa for 'upwards of 800 years'.[7] Donald MacPhail[8] was one of the most successful of Mull drovers in the eighteenth century, whose sons and nephews were, for the most part, hard-working cattle breeders.[9] His grandson, Dugald MacPhail[10] was apprenticed to a cousin, Neil Fletcher, a joiner in Penalbanach, near Tobermory, and returned to Torosay parish to be miller and joiner there, in the years preceding the potato blight. It is unfortunate that Lauchlan Maclaine the diarist had gone to live in Oban, for some comments on the life and work of Mull's favourite poet would have been invaluable. Dugald himself was unduly reticent about his own life, deeming himself unworthy of attention. One of his few autobiographical statements came in a letter to Professor Blackie in 1876.

I was born in the year 1818 at Torosay, Island of Mull. My father at that time held the farm of Derrychullen. My first schoolmaster was a young man of a weak intellect, but well up in the three Rs. Like many others of his time he had committed to memory a large treasure of Ossian's poems, some of which he used to sing to wild plaintive airs, handed down no doubt from sire to son for many generations. The pure idiom of the pieces as sung by him and others whom I know, had, I believe, inspired me with an ardent love of Gaelic poetry and song. With my own poetic genius, however, I never felt satisfied, nor did the occupations and struggles of my chequered life prove favourable to the cultivation of the mind. I have written a good deal, such as it was, but never considered myself as possessed of true poetic genius, and had always a strong aversion to appear in print as a mere verse maker.

My early education was altogether of a low order. I had no difficulty in acquiring, while under twelve years of age, all that the parish schoolmaster could teach me, and beyond that I may say I have been self-taught. In early life I was bred to the joiner trade, but by persevering study of drawing, mathematics, etc., I qualified myself for the appointment of Clerk and Draughtsman with an architect in Newcastle on Tyne, where under a fit of Highland homesickness I wrote the *Eilean Muileach*, and while there in 1859 I gained the silver medal of the Edinburgh Celtic Society for an original Gaelic essay on the Highland Clearances ... I have contributed somewhat largely to *The Gael* ... under the signature of *'Muileach'*. *'Callum a Ghlinne'*, an original tale, is to some extent an autobiography of myself.[11]

But Dugald MacPhail's writings were immensely popular with the Highland diaspora in Glasgow where he now lived and worked. To the present day, his *Eilean Muileach* has been sung at concerts in Mull and elsewhere, wherever people from 'the Country' have gathered. He was a spokesman for the native Mull people, and one who had lived through the greatest troubles. His reflections on the events of the first half of the nineteenth century are surprisingly different from the conclusions which come from contemporary historians. His prize-winning essay on depopulation admitted the need for reducing the numbers of people, acknowledged the striving after profit of the landlords, but pointed out that the heritors had been debt-ridden from the start. Like Mr Somers, he blamed the Poor Law for what had happened. How Dugald MacPhail differed from other commentators was in his passionate nostalgia for the cultivated lands of his youth. The introduction of sheep farming on a large scale, and the eviction of the people who had, in their joint possessions cultivated corn and other crops, had changed the landscape from a colourful canvas of fields of waving cereals to a nettle-covered wilderness.[12] It is well known that sheep, when introduced on a scale which upsets the ecological balance, will ruin land, but no one has reminded us quite so poignantly of the colour and sweetness of the earth before they took it over.

Dugald and his wife, Janet Merry, daughter of one of the early Lowland farmers in Mull, lived in Edinburgh for some time after a sojourn of fifteen years in Newcastle and Dorset; a friend in Mull sent them a clump of primroses to plant in their garden. Dugald placed them beside a noble root of lilies, and, filled with emotion, wrote an exile song which would touch the hearts of his Gaelic audiences for a long time, but which has now passed out of the memories of all, in much the same way as the entire history of the island has been relegated to oblivion.

All over these bare fields
Where thistles will not grow
Heavy handfuls of them [the Mull primroses]
Will be found on every mound and hill.[13]

From Canada West (as it was then called) in 1853, the former schoolmaster at Lochdon, former postmaster at Achnacraig, and former session-clerk of Craignure church, Allan Lamont,[14] wrote to his son-in-law, Angus MacPhail, who had bid a high rent to Factor Mór for the farm of Culbhuirg in Iona. Allan and his family had sailed from Greenock in the previous year with a large number of neighbours and relations from the estate of the Campbells of Possil. At the Disruption of 1843, he had joined the Free Church, and had therefore been obliged to give up the parish school. He had been one of those who had worshipped in the Gravel Pit. His son, Donald Lamont, was assistant to Angus Gregorson, factor to the estate of Lochbuy, in Oban, and having a good job, and the prospect of a legal career, Donald had stayed in Scotland. A second son, Neil, had remained too, and Sally Lamont, who had married Angus MacPhail, had three small daughters in Iona. It was customary for men of 'the Country' to address each other in letters, and not to take very much notice of wives and daughters, just as Donald Maclean WS had always written to his son-in-law, and never direct to his dearest Chirsty. Married women were not to be distracted from other duties.

> Township of Grey
> Canada West.
> 9 August 1853.

My dear Son,
    Your letter of the 28 March I duly received, which gave us all great satisfaction to understand that you and family and all other enquiring friends enjoyed good health at the time of writing. I must admit that I should have written you before now, but I was waiting until I would be able to give you some account of the Climate and Crop of this new world. We had the most delightful summer that ever I remember seeing since I was born. I suppose the heat is sometimes beyond anything that I felt in the old Country. Still, there is a fresh breeze coming daily about noon which continues till the evening, or sunset, with a heavy dew at night. This is an instance of God's merciful kindness to his people in all parts of the Globe.
    Autumn is the most pleasant quarter of the year in Canada. It is neither cold nor too warm for any Scotchman. As for the other half year, there will be some sharp nights and mornings, but far easier to work in the wood with your trousers and shirt than with a suit of clothes in the Highlands of Scotland. There is another instance of God's merciful dealing with sinners in this country. If so much rain would fall in Canada in winter and spring as is falling in Scotland, it would inundate the whole of the country, owing to the place being so level, but this is not the case. There is no rain here

in winter at all. Instead of rain we have frost that shuts up our large Lakes, Rivers and Creeks, so that it is impossible for them to do any more harm to the province than in summer.

The Grain over here is above the average Crop, and secured in the Stackyards about the end of July and the beginning of August. But this is an old Settlement, where they sow autumn or Fall Wheat as they call it in this country. In new Settlements people are not able to sow this kind for the first year. They sow another kind they call spring wheat. This kind is sown between the 15th and 25th of May in new land. They allow one and a quarter barrels to the Acre, which will give 25 to 40 return according to the soil and season. I have 3 acres of spring wheat which I have sown between the 20th and 25th of May, and now is 5 to 6 feet in height, and will be ready for the Sickle in the course of a fortnight. This will give you some idea of the Climate and Soil of Canada West.

Whenever a person gets his wood burnt, and the ground cleared, he has nothing more to do farther than throwing the seed into the Ground, then harrow and fence it, and he may depend upon good Crops. I have 2 acres of potatoes, some India corn, Oats, Turnips, Cabbage, Savoy & Greens, Onions and Carrots, which are all thriving well. I am now preparing for the Fall Wheat, which must be sown between the 15th and 20th of September, so that the braird may be strong enough before the frost and snow come on. I intend to sow 6 Acres of this Fall Wheat in the uncleared ground which we are to commence burning the beginning of next week. ... On one of the Lots I have, there is a Meadow on which I have cut about 6 tons of Hay which has grown to the height of 5 feet in six weeks' time. There is no labour on Hay here except the cutting and stacking. It will dry in one day.

On this Meadow there is, I may say, an Orchard planted by the Counsel and Will of the Creator of all things, and not by the hands of men. All Vegetables and Fruits thrive here to perfection, and your Mother made a good deal of Jelly and Jam on the produce of this Garden. She made about 100 pounds of Sugar on the Sap of the Maple Tree ...

I see you want my opinion about such a man as you are, with a young family, coming to this country. In reply my opinion is that every person who is under a burden not easily carried should throw it off as soon as possible and emigrate to this quarter. I regret very much that I have spent the most of my days under so many Masters, – viz. Landlords, Writers, Chamberlains, Factors, etc. etc., and would require to be as humble to every one of those individuals as a mouse under the Cat's paw, and after being so, still not please any of them. Let me know if you had any account from Australia,[15] and what has become of Malcolm MacPhail,[16] and Dugald MacPhail.[17] Are they in Torosay or not?

As I gave you a long time for spinning and making your Web, I hope when it comes that it will be a long one. I must now conclude with my best Respects and Kind Love to you and family, to Duncan,[18] to your father and mother,[19] to my friends Mr and Miss Lamont,[20] and all enquiring friends. I am your most affectionate father. Allan Lamont.[21]

This letter was not the lamentation of an unhappy exile, but a declaration of delight in good weather, fine crops and the gifts of God. Allan Lamont's descendants are on the same land today.

Postscript

The Macleans of Duart, who have featured so prominently at the beginning of this account, went into exile in the late seventeenth century. Sir Hector made a brief appearance in Edinburgh in 1745, and was arrested. Sir Allan Maclean, 'the Knight', succeeded Sir Hector in 1750, and has been an important figure in this Mull story. Sir Allan's attempt to regain the Duart lands was unsuccessful. If he had had male heirs, and if those heirs had been able to restore the fortunes of his family, the history of Mull might have taken another course. Instead, he was succeeded by a very remote cousin, Sir Hector Maclean, who died unmarried and was succeeded by his half-brother, Fitzroy Jeffreys Grafton in 1818.

Sir Fitzroy Jeffreys Grafton Maclean and Donald Maclean WS were about the same age, married at about the same time, and had some bond which may simply have been a shared sense of humour. 'Poor Grafton', as his brother-in-law Brigadier Allan Maclean called him, went into the army, and Donald WS, as we know, into the law. In 1816, before poor Grafton had inherited the title, Donald WS had collared him on the question of purchasing Duart,[22] 'the seat of your ancestors'. A few months later Donald told Charles Macquarie, 'I do not believe Fitzroy will purchase an inch.'[23] Charles himself was to become the owner of Duart, if only for five years, and his brother Lachlan of New South Wales reported in 1824, 'Your friend Sir Fitzroy Maclean appears now very keen to purchase the Duart lot of your estate, and is actually going down to look in about a fortnight. I hope you have not yet closed with Lord John.' Three weeks later he pronounced Sir Fitzroy to be 'a great *Jaw*', who was always talking about the Duart lot,[24] but who did nothing about it. Everyone else seemed to think it a capital idea that the chief of the Macleans should buy Duart, and even Lauchlan the diarist wrote to urge his half-brother to use his influence. In 1827, when Duart belonged to Colonel Campbell of Possil, Sir Fitzroy went to Mull with his friend Donald Maclean. There is no record of his impressions of 'the Country', or of regrets about his missed opportunity. But it is certain that he could not afford the price of the estate. There is no record either of a meeting with young Murdoch of Lochbuy, who had begun to conceive of himself as Chief of the Clan Gillean.

However, it was about this time that the dream of regaining Duart was born, and handed down to the next generation. It was Sir Fitzroy's grandson, also a Sir Fitzroy, who finally took the step which he claimed his own father had longed to do.[25] The idea of buying only a tiny portion of the estate and restoring the castle itself had apparently not occurred to any of the chiefs as a solution agreeable to themselves and bringing a welcome little sum to the owner of 'Duart House', the most beautiful of the new wave of marble halls. As we have observed above, the importance of property lay in agricultural land, not in houses, until well into the nineteenth century. It was not until 1910 that an agreement was reached with the owners of Duart House, now Walter Murray Guthrie and his wife, that the Macleans of Duart should buy the totally ruinous castle and a fringe of ground surrounding it. The restoration of ruined castles was not at this time a popular pastime, but in this case it was a brilliant idea, a stunning experiment in public relations. The architect, Dr John J. Burnett, began work in 1911, and the ceremony marking the return of the castle to the descendants of the Macleans took place on 24 August 1912 in the presence of some hundreds of Macleans. Mrs Olive Guthrie's letter to Sir Fitzroy Maclean was read out.

> My dear Sir Fitzroy,
>   As the day draws near for you to formally hoist your banner on the Castle of Duart, so long the property of your ancestors, I feel strongly that I ought to change the name of my house and estate to what I believe it was formerly called, ie *Torosay*.[26] I wish to leave the name of Duart to you alone, who have certainly the senior right to it. I shall be glad if you will announce this desire on my part to your clansmen ...[27]

The Macleans of Duart moved back into their castle after an absence of more than 200 years, during which time nobody had known them very well. The family had lived, on and off, like so many other Macleans, in the West Indies. Having no possessions in Mull, they must have known very little of the social conditions prevailing there. They had been unaffected by all those severe tests of virtue which had beset their cousins, such as famine, emigration, overpopulation and the scrutiny of historians, travel writers and journalists. They had returned after the storm, and could never be called rapacious landlords or foolish gamblers or evictors. There had been no long-term calculation in all this, but Sir Fitzroy could have chosen no better time.

The Macleans of Duart moved into what was, incontestably, the finest dwelling place in Mull, with grace and dignity. They had lost their estate in days of terror and strife, and at the hands of a formidable enemy. The history of Mull had stopped at about 1745, and no one had a very clear idea of what had happened thereafter. Two centuries of discord in Mull families, of legal disputes over money and land, of sordid and underhand attempts to strip kith and kin of their assets, did not constitute 'real' history. The Macleans of Duart very wisely set up a museum in the castle which referred to bygone days and battles long ago. And elsewhere in the castle, where Archy Lochbuy,

Sir Allan, Gillean Maclaine of Scallastle and Lachlan MacQuarrie of Ulva had once drunk whisky grog with Governor Lane, and come to blows, photographs of plump Maclean babies and charming boys and girls were exactly what the public wished to see. 'Hail to the Chief ...'

Notes

1. From Dugald MacPhail's song, *An t-sobhrach Mhuileach.* 'My pleasant white-yellow primrose whose heritage is the untrodden wood / You were born and grew on the slopes of Craignure / O lily ...', trans. Charles Coventry.
2. See Chapter 13, and *The Voyage of the* Pharos, p. 100.
3. Description of Ardtornish in 1814.
4. NAS. Abbrev. Reg. of Sasines (3207), 10 October 1820.
5. John Sinclair was the most successful of the new property owners, running the distillery in Tobermory.
6. Isabella Maclean of Kengharair. She was to make her dwelling house into a successful boarding house.
7. Memorial in Pennygown churchyard.
8. Donald MacPhail (1746–1836). He married Sarah Fletcher (1755–1800).
9. His sons John (1794–1872) and Duncan (1796–1876) were tenants of Scallastle, Garmony and Tiroran.
10. Dugald MacPhail (1818–87) son of Donald MacPhail (1779–1832) and Catherine Campbell (1786–1864).
11. NLS. MS2632. Dugald MacPhail to John Stuart Blackie, Professor of Greek at EU and publicist for Gaelic causes and the Edinburgh Chair of Celtic. 24 May 1876.
12. EUL. Cameron Room. CR Box 5.65. *Oraid le Dughall MacPhail* (On depopulation).
13. *An t-sobhrach Mhuileach.* It was sung to the tune *Birlinn bhan a' Chubair.* Trans. Charles Coventry.
14. Allan Lamont (1793–1865) son of Malcolm Lamont in Killean, married Mary MacDougall (b. 1798). Their children were Donald b. 1817, Neil b. 1819, Marion or Sarah b. 1823 (all of whom stayed in Scotland) and Malcolm, Dugald, Catherine, Allan, Hugh, Archibald, Euphemia, and Mary who went to Canada.
15. Angus's sister, Marion, his two brothers, Hugh and Colin, and John Macdonald, Precentor, had emigrated in 1852.
16. Probably Malcolm MacPhail (1793–1879) in Ardura and later in Oskamull.
17. The poet, who had been a neighbour of the Lamonts in Lochdonhead. He married Janet Merry on 23 August 1853, and left Mull.
18. Duncan MacPhail (1812–90), elder brother of Angus and father of the Iona 'character' Angus MacPhail (1865–1931).
19. Duncan MacPhail Senior (1779–1863) and Flora MacKinnon (1791–1866) from Garmony and Fishnish.
20. Angus Lamont (1771–1856), son of Donald L. and Effy Black, Ulva, now tenant in Iona, and his daughter Mary (1810–93).
21. MS letter in the possession of the author.
22. NAS. GD174/1628/78. DMWS to MM2, 28 March 1816.
23. NLS. MS 20758. Letterbook of DMWS. Letter to CM, 11 November 1816.
24. NLS. MS 3833. LM to CM, 27 May 1824 and 21 June 1824.
25. Maclean, JP, *Renaissance of the Clan Maclean*, p. 24.

26. The estate, under the dukes, and in Mr Maxwell's time, was referred to as the Torosay part of the Argyll estate.
27. *Renaissance*, p. 83.

Bibliography

I. Manuscript Sources

Aberdeen University, Historic Collections
Anon.   Travel journal, MS1023, ff20–29.

Argyll and Bute District Archives, Lochgilphead
Kinlochspelvie Parish School. Log book. 1865–1869.

Clan Donald Visitor Centre, Skye
Macdonald of Inchkenneth Papers MS 17.1–32

Edinburgh University Library

Argyll, 6th duke of	Contract of marriage, La. Add. MSS. 5/15
	Misc. correspondence with the 6th duke's agents. MS. Gen. 886*
Argyll Rentals	[Microfilm from ICP] Mic. M. 674 and 676.
Campbell, Alexander	A slight sketch of a journey made through parts of the Highlands and Hebrides undertaken to collect materials for Albyn's Anthology, by the editor, in Autumn 1815. Laing Collection.
Campbell, Duncan	Memorial, DC, Tacksman of Treshnish to Charles Selkrig [c. 1817] Gen. 886* /9/24.
	Letters concerning the raising of Fraser's Highlanders, 1775. La. II 506
Maclean, Allan	Letter to William Lumsden, 1777. Laing MSS. La. II 509.955
McLean, Dr Hector	Collection of Gaelic poetry. [Microfilm of MSS in Nova Scotia]
McNicol, Donald	Letter to the Rev. John Walker, 22 March 1775. Laing Collection.
Scott, Sir Walter	Description of Alexander Campbell, n.d., MS. Gen. 1732
Symbolae Scoticae	[a series of scrapbooks of Scottish illustrations] Dh 6.69
Selkirk, 5th Earl of	Letters to and from Alexander Macdonald of Dalilea, 1811–1815. Laing MSS. La. II. 202
Wodrow, Robert	Queries & things to be done in ye Western Highlands, Laing MSS. La. III. 355

General Register Office for Scotland, Edinburgh
Censuses for 1841, 1851, 1861, 1871, 1881, 1891 for Mull parishes
Old Parish Registers (OPRs) for Mull parishes
Statutory Registers of births, marriages and deaths for Mull parishes

Gloucestershire Record Office, Gloucester
Maclaine of Scallastle Papers, D3330
Journals of Lauchlan Maclaine in Garmony and Oban, 1815–16, 1824–1836, 1838–1847. Box 25
Commonplace book of Lachlan Maclaine, c1790–1810. Box 17
Correspondence, estate and legal papers relating to Scallastle, Lochbuy and Ulva estates, 1699–1859. Box 18
Correspondence, legal papers and accounts of Allan and Gillean Maclaine, and Lachlan MacQuarrie of Ulva, 1739–1803. Box 17
Estate accounts of cattle, whisky, etc., of Gillean Maclaine of Garmony and Scallastle, 1755–1788. Box 17

Executry of Lt. Col. Alexander Maclean of Millport [Uisken] Box 16
Lachlan Maclean [of Kilbrenan]'s Trust Papers. Box 26
Personal correspondence of John Gregorson of Ardtornish, Morvern, 1802–1822. Box 25
Personal correspondence of Mrs Maclaine [Marjory Gregorson] at Scallastle and Ardtornish,
    1805–1833. Box 26
Personal, family and estate correspondence of the Maclaine family, Lachlan McLean, Kilbrenan, etc.
    1796–1852. Box 20

Isle of Mull Museum, Tobermory
Argyll transcripts [from ICP]
Aros estate papers (4) Alexander Allan
Papers of Donald Maclean WS

National Archives of Scotland (formerly Scottish Record Office), Edinburgh
Highland Destitution Papers HD2/17
Lochbuie Papers GD174 & GD1
Minutes of the Presbytery of Mull CH2/273
Stonefield Papers GD14
Tobermory Sheriff Court SC59

National Library of Scotland, Edinburgh
Argyll Papers	MS 3138
Blackie Papers	Letter of Dugald Macphail, 1876. MS 2632, f. 74
Calendar of MSS belonging to Colonel G. C. P. Campbell of Stonefield MS 3737	
Clephane, Margaret Douglas Maclean	
Clephane, Marianne Douglas Maclean	Letters to Sir Walter Scott, MS 3874–3913
Clephane, Anna Jane Douglas Maclean	
Culloden Papers	MS 2961–74
Jacobite Papers II	Sketch of Sir Hector Maclean. MS 1694–6
Maclean, Donald, WS	Letterbook, MS 20758. ii.
Macquarie, Lachlan	Letters to Charles Macquarie. MS 3833
Saltoun Papers	The Argyll estates in Mull, Morvern and Tiree 1717–1750. MS 17677–8.
Scott, Walter	Lines on Mr Macdonald of Staaffa [sic] MS 876
Sibbald Papers	Description of Mull, c. 1680. Adv. MS 33.3.20.
Stuart, John, Lord Mountstuart	Journal of the Tour round the Western Islands of Scotland, 1788. MS 9587
Wood, John	Journal of a Jaunt to the Island of Mull in the Month of October 1801. MS 3038

Private Collections
Gregorson Papers and albums	Collection of David Sillar, Esq.
Java Lodge Papers	Author's Collection.
Lamont, Allan	MS letter from Township of Grey, Canada West, 1853 (Author's Collection).
Maclean Clephane of Torloisk Papers	Collection of Capt. AAC Farquharson.

II. Broadsides

Verdict of an assize, Hector Maclean *et. al.* v. John McLaine of Lochbuy, 1758.
Protest of the General Assembly of the Church of Scotland.

III. Government Publications and Parliamentary Papers

Education Inquiry, Scotland, Accounts and Papers, session ... 1837, vol. XLVII ... [London] 1837.

Evidence taken by Her Majesty's Commissioners of Inquiry into the condition of the crofters and cottars in the Highlands and Islands of Scotland, vols III & IV, Edinburgh 1884 [Napier].

First report from the Select Committee on Emigration, Scotland, together with the Minutes of Evidence, London, 1841.

First Report from the Select Committee on Sites for Churches (Scotland) ... [London] 1847.

Report of Her Majesty's Commissioners of Inquiry into the Condition of the Crofters and Cottars in the Highlands and Islands of Scotland, Edinburgh, 1884 [Crofters' Report or Napier Report].

Report to the Board of Supervision by Sir John McNeill, GCB, on the Western Highlands and Islands [McNeill Report], Edinburgh, 1851.

Reports from Commissioners, Poor Law Inquiry (Scotland) Part II, Edinburgh, 1844.

Royal Commission on the Ancient and Historical Monuments of Scotland [RCAHMS]: *Argyll, an Inventory of the Monuments, vol. 2 Lorn ...*, Edinburgh, 1975.

Royal Commission on the Ancient and Historical Monuments of Scotland [RCAHMS]: *Argyll, an Inventory of the Monuments, vol. 3 Mull, Tiree, Coll & Northern Argyll ...*, Edinburgh, 1980.

Royal Commission, Highlands and Islands, reports from Commissioners, Inspectors and others, vol. 26, part 1, Edinburgh, 1895.

Second Report from the Select Committee on Sites for Churches (Scotland) ... [London] 1847.

Third Report from the Select Committee on Sites for Churches (Scotland) ... [London] 1847.

IV. Session Papers (Printed)

The petition of Lachlan McLean of Torloisk, February 24, 1775.

Answers for Allan McLean of Drimnin to the petition of John Duke of Argyle, September 27, 1777.

V. Pamphlets

Dewar, Daniel, *A letter to Sir James M. Riddell, Bart. of Ardnamurchan and Sunart, being a brief memorial on the state of the Highlands ...*, Edinburgh, 1819.

Free Church of Scotland, *Correspondence relative to the refusal of sites for churches, manses, etc.*, Edinburgh, 1846.

——, *Extracts from letters to the Rev. Dr McLeod, Glasgow, regarding the famine and destitution in the Highlands and Islands of Scotland*, Glasgow, 1847.

Mackenzie, Alexander, *The Highland Clearances: or a Strange Return by the Highland Chiefs for the Fidelity of the Clans*, Inverness, 1881.

Mackenzie, Henry, *Report of the Committee of the Highland Society of Scotland appointed to inquire into the nature and authenticity of the poems of Ossian ...*, Edinburgh, 1805.

Macphail, Dugald, *Oraid (Essay – on depopulation)*, n.p., n.d., EUL Cam. R. Box 5.65.

[Report of] the Society for the support of Gaelic Schools ... Edinburgh, 1817.

Sixteenth Annual Report of the Society for the Support of Gaelic Schools ... Edinburgh, 1827.

VI. Published Texts

Adam, Margaret I., 'The causes of the Highland emigrations of 1783–1803, in *The Scottish Historical Review*, 17, no. 66, 1920.

——, 'Eighteenth century Highland landlords and the poverty problem', in *The Scottish Historical Review*, 19, no. 75, 1922.

——, 'The Highland emigration of 1770', in *The Scottish Historical Review*, 16, 1919.

Alden, John R., *A history of the American Revolution*, New York, 1969.

Allen, Robert S. (ed.), *The Loyal Americans: the Military Role of the Loyalist Provincial Corps and their Settlement in British North America, 1775–1784*, n.p., n.d. [Exhibition brochure].

Anon., *An Account of the Depredations committed on the Clan Campbell ...*, n.p., 1816.

Argyll, 8th Duke of [George Douglas Campbell], *Autobiography and memoirs ...*, 2 vols, London, 1906.

——, 'On the economic condition of the Highlands of Scotland', in *The Nineteenth Century*, 72, 1883.

——, *Scotland As It Was and As It Is*, Edinburgh, 1887.

Bannerman, John, *The Beatons: a medical kindred in the Classical Gaelic tradition*, Edinburgh, 1986.

Beattie, William (ed.), *Life and letters of Thomas Campbell*, 3 vols, London, 1849.

Black, Ronald, *Mac Mhaighstir Alasdair, the Ardnamurchan Years*, [Coll], 1986.

Blackie, John Stuart, 'The Highland Crofters', in *The Nineteenth Century*, 74, *1883*.

——, *The Scottish Highlander and the Land Laws, an historico-economical enquiry*, London, 1885.

Boswell, James, *Boswell's Journal of a Tour to the Hebrides with Samuel Johnson, LL.D., now first published from the original manuscript ... with preface and notes by Frederick A. Pottle and Charles H. Bennett*, London, 1936.

Brander, Michael, *The Scottish Highlanders and their Regiments*, [Scotland], 1996.

Bray, Elizabeth, *The Discovery of the Hebrides, Voyages to the Western Isles 1745–1883*, Edinburgh, 1996.

Brown, Iain Gordon and Cheape, Hugh (eds), *Witness to Rebellion, John Maclean's Journal of the 'Forty-five and the Penicuik drawings*, [NLS] East Linton, 1996.

Brown, Keith M., *Kingdom or Province? Scotland and the Regal Union, 1603–1715*, Basingstoke, 1992.

Brown, Olive and Whittaker, Jean, *A Walk Round Tobermory*, Tobermory, 1988.

Bumsted, J. M., *The People's Clearance, Highland Emigration to British North America, 1770–1815*, Edinburgh, 1982.

Burt, Edmund, *Burt's Letters from the North of Scotland ... (Withers & Simmons)*, Edinburgh, 1998.

Cameron, Alan, *Bank of Scotland, 1695–1995, a Very Singular Institution*, Edinburgh, 1995.

Cameron, Sir Ewen, *Memoirs of Sir Ewen Cameron of Locheill ...* [Abbotsford Club], Edinburgh, 1842.

Cameron, Ewen A., *Land for the People? The British Government and the Scottish Highlands,c. 1880–1925*, East Linton, 1996.

—— 'Politics, ideology and the Highland land issue, 1886 to the 1920s' in *The Scottish Historical Review*, 72, no. 193, 1993.

Cameron, John (ed.), *The Justiciary Records of Argyll and the Isles, 1664–1705*, vol. 1 [The Stair Society], Edinburgh, 1949.

Campbell, Sir Duncan, *The Clan Campbell Abstracts of Entries relating to Campbells in the Sheriff Court Books of Argyll at Inveraray ...*, Edinburgh, 1913.

Campbell, J. L. and Thomson, Derick, *Edward Lhuyd in the Scottish Highlands 1699–1700*, Oxford, 1963.

Campbell, John Lorne, *Highland Songs of the Forty-five*, Edinburgh, 1933.

Campbell, J[ohn] L[orne], *Canna, the Story of a Hebridean Island*, Edinburgh, 1994.

Campbell, Marion, *Argyll, the Enduring Heartland*, Bath, 1977.

Campbell, R. H., 'Too much on the Highlands? A plea for change', in *Scottish Economic and Social History*, 14 (1994).

Campbell, Robert, *The Life of the Most Illustrious Prince John, Duke of Argyll and Greenwich*, London, 1745.

Carr, Sir John, *Caledonian Sketches, or a Tour through Scotland in 1807 ...* London, 1809.

Chantreau, Pierre Nicolas, *Voyage dans les Trois Royaumes d'Angleterre d'Ecosse et d'Irlande fait en 1788 et 1789*, Paris, 1792.

Charnley, Bob, *Iona and Staffa via Oban, Nostalgic Album Views*, Doune, 1994.

Checkland, S. G., *Scottish Banking, a History, 1695–1973*, Glasgow, 1975.

Clutton-Brock, T. H. and Ball, M. E. (eds), *Rhum, the Natural History of an Island*, Edinburgh, 1987.

Cohen, Lysbeth, *Elizabeth Macquarie, her Life and Times*, Sydney, 1979.

Cooke, Anthony *et al.*, *Modern Scottish History*, 1707.

Cooper, Derek, *Road to the Isles, Travellers in the Hebrides 1770–1914*, Glasgow, 1990.

Cowan, Edward J., *Montrose for Covenant and King*, Edinburgh 1995.

Cowan, Ian B., *The Scottish Reformation ...* London, 1982.

Craig, David, *On the Crofters' Trail, in Search of the Clearance Highlanders*, London, 1990.

Cregeen, Eric R. (ed.), *Argyll Estate Instructions, Mull, Morvern, Tiree, 1771–1805*, Scottish History Society, Edinburgh, 1964.

Cregeen, Eric R., 'The changing role of the house of Argyll in the Scottish Highlands', in *Scotland in the Age of Improvement*, Edinburgh,1996.

Cregeen, Eric R. (ed.), *Inhabitants of the Argyll Estate, 1779* [Scottish Record Society], Edinburgh, 1963.

Cregeen, E. R., 'The tacksmen and their successors, a study of tenurial reorganisation in Mull, Morvern and Tiree in the early eighteenth century' *in Scottish Studies*, 13, 1969.

Cummings, A. J. G., 'Industry and investment in the eighteenth century Highlands: the York Buildings Company of London', in *Industry, Business and Society in Scotland since 1700 ...*, Edinburgh, 1994.

Currie, Jo, *Mull Family Names for Ancestor Hunters*, Tobermory, 1998.

——, 'Mull People' *in The Scottish Genealogist*, 44, 1, 1997.

Daniell, William, *A Voyage Round Great Britain Undertaken in the Summer of the Year 1813 ... with a Series of Views ...* vol. 3, London, 1820.

Devine, T. M., *Clanship to Crofters' War, the Social Transformation of the Scottish Highlands*, Manchester, 1994.

——, *The Great Highland Famine, Hunger, Emigration and the Scottish Highlands in the Nineteenth Century*, Edinburgh, 1988.

——, 'Landlordism and Highland emigration', in *Scottish Emigration and Scottish Society ...*, Edinburgh, 1992.

—— (ed.), *Scottish Elites: Proceedings of the Scottish Historical Studies Seminar, University of Strathclyde 1991–1992*, Edinburgh, 1994.

De Watteville, Alastair, *The Isle of Iona*, Romsey, 1999.

——, *The Isle of Mull*, Romsey, 1994.

——, *The Island of Staffa*, Romsey, 1993.

Dodgshon, Robert A., *From Chiefs to Landlords. Social and Economic Change in the Western Highlands and Islands c. 1493–1820*. Edinburgh, 1998.

——, 'West Highland and Hebridean Landscapes: have they a history without runrig?', in *Journal of Historical Geography*, 19, 4, 1993.

——, 'West Highland and Hebridean Settlement prior to Crofting and the Clearances: a study in stability or change?', in *Proceedings of the Society of Antiquaries of Scotland*, 123 (1993).

Donaldson, Gordon, *The Scots Overseas*, London, 1966.

Dressler, Camille, *Eigg, the Story of an Island*, Edinburgh, 1998.

Duncanson, John V., *Rawdon and Douglas: Two Loyalist Townships in Nova Scotia*, Belleville, 1989.

Eckstein, Eve, *Historic Visitors to Mull, Iona and Staffa*, London, 1992.

Edgar, Gregory T., *Liberty or Death! The Northern Campaigns in the American Revolutionary War*, Bowie [Md], 1994.

Ellis, M. H., *Lachlan Macquarie, his Life, Adventures and Times*, Sydney, 1958.

Ewing, William (ed.), *Annals of the Free Church of Scotland*, vol. II, Edinburgh, 1914.

Fairfax-Lucy, Norah, *Hebridean Childhood, an Autobiography*, Glasgow, 1981.

Faithfull, Joan, *The Ross of Mull Granite Quarries*, Iona, 1995.

Faujas de Saint Fond, B., *A Journey through England and Scotland to the Hebrides in 1784*, 2 vols, Glasgow, 1907.

Ferguson, William, 'Samuel Johnson's Views on Scottish Gaelic Culture', in *Scottish Historical Review*, 77, 2, 183, 1998.

Fergusson, Sir James, *Argyll in the Forty-five*, London, 1951.

Firth, C. H. (ed.), *Scotland and the Protectorate, Letters Relating to the Military Government of Scotland from January 1654 to June 1659* [Scottish History Society], Edinburgh, 1899.

Fleeman, J. D., *Samuel Johnson: A Journey to the Western Isles of Scotland with introduction and notes*, Oxford, 1985.

Frazer, John, Δευτεροσκοπια, *or a Brief Discourse Concerning the Second Sight ...*, Edinburgh, 1707.

Fryer, Mary Beacock, *Allan Maclean Jacobite General: the Life of an 18th Century Career Soldier*, Toronto, 1987.

Garnett, Thomas, *Tour through the Highlands and Western Islands*, n.p., 1811.

Gaskell, Philip, *Morvern Transformed: a Highland Parish in the Nineteenth Century*, Cambridge, 1968.

Gibbon, J. Murray, *Scots in Canada*, London, 1911.

Gibson, John Sibbald, *Edinburgh in the '45, Bonnie Prince Charlie at Holyroodhouse*, Edinburgh, 1995.

——, *Lochiel of the '45, the Jacobite Chief and the Prince*, Edinburgh 1994.

Goodare, Julian, 'The Statutes of Iona in context', in *Scottish Historical Review*, 77,1, 203, 1998.

Graham, Henry Grey, *The Social Life of Scotland in the Eighteenth Century*, 2 vols, London, 1900.

Graham-Campbell, David, 'The younger generation in Argyll at the beginning of the eighteenth century', *in Scottish Studies*, 18, 1974.

Grant, Francis J., *The Commissariot Record of the Isles:Register of Testaments, 1661–1800* [Scottish Record Society], Edinburgh, 1902.

Grant, I. F., *Highland Folk Ways*, Edinburgh, 1995.

——, *The Macleods, the History of a Clan, 1200–1956*, London, 1959.

Grant, I. F. and Cheape, Hugh, *Periods in Highland History*, London, 1997.

Grant, Mrs K. W., 'Peasant life in Argyllshire in the end of the eighteenth century', in *Scottish Historical Review*, 16, 1919.

Grant, Neil, *The Campbells of Argyll*, London, 1975.

Gray, Malcolm, *The Highland Economy, 1750–1850*, Edinburgh, 1957.

—— (ed.), *The Statistical Account of Scotland, 1791–1799*, edited by Sir John Sinclair, vol. viii, Argyll, (Mainland), Wakefield, 1983.

Grierson, H. J. C. (ed.), *The Letters of Sir Walter Scott, 1808–1811*, London, 1932.

Haldane, A. R. B., *The Drove Roads of Scotland*, Colonsay, 1995.

——, *New Ways Through the Glens*, London, 1962.

Hamilton, Henry, *The Economic History of Scotland in the 18th Century*, Oxford, 1963.

Hannan, Thomas, *The Beautiful Isle of Mull with Iona and the Isle of Saints*, Edinburgh, 1926.

Haswell-Smith, Hamish, *The Scottish Islands, a Comprehensive Guide to Every Scottish Island*, Edinburgh, 1996.

Haythornthwaite, Philip J., *Who Was Who in the Napoleonic Wars*, London, 1998.

Henderson, Diana M., *Highland Soldier: a Social Study of the Highland Regiments, 1820–1920*, Edinburgh, 1989.

Hibbert, Christopher, *Redcoats and Rebels: the American Revolution Through British Eyes*, New York, 1991.

Hill, Ralph Nading, *Lake Champlain: Key to Liberty*, Woodstock, 1995.

Home, James A. (ed.), *Lady Louisa Stuart: Selections from her Manuscripts*, Edinburgh, 1899.

Hunter, James, *A Dance called America: the Scottish Highlands, the United States and Canada*, Edinburgh, 1994.

—— (ed.), *For the People's Cause: from the writings of John Murdoch, Highland and Irish land reformer*, Edinburgh, 1986.

——, *The Making of the Crofting Community*, Edinburgh, 1987.

Imrie, John (ed.), *The Justiciary Records of Argyll and the Isles, 1644–1742, vol. II, 1705–1742* [The Stair Society], Edinburgh, 1969.

Johnson, James, *The Recess, or Autumnal Relaxation in the Highlands and Lowlands*, London, 1834.

Johnson, Samuel, *A Journey to the Western Islands of Scotland, with an introduction and notes by J. D. Fleeman*, Oxford, 1985.

Johnston, Christopher N., *John Blaw of Castlehill, Jacobite and Criminal*, Edinburgh, 1916.

Ketchum, Richard M., *Saratoga: Turning Point of America's Revolutionary War*, New York, 1997.

Le May, Jackie, *Ardmeanach: a Hidden Corner of Mull*, Iona, 1995.

Leyden, John, *Journal of a Tour in the Highlands and Western Islands of Scotland in 1800*, Edinburgh, 1903.

Lindsay, Ian G. and Cosh, Mary, *Inveraray and the Dukes of Argyll*, Edinburgh, 1973.

McAnna, James, *The Ulva Families of Shotts*, Shotts, 1991.

Macarthur, Dugald, 'The *Breadalbane* 1844–1853 and her work for the Highland Destitution Committee', in *Transactions of the Gaelic Society of Inverness*, 55, 1986–1988.

Macarthur, Dugald, 'Some emigrant ships from the West Highlands', in *Transactions of the Gaelic Society of Inverness*, 55, 1986–88.

Macarthur, E. Mairi, *Columba's Island: Iona from Past to Present*, Edinburgh, 1995.

Macarthur, E. Mairi, *Iona* [with Colin Baxter], Grantown-on-Spey, 1997.

——, *Iona, the Living Memory of a Crofting Community, 1750–1914*, Edinburgh, 1990.

MacCormick, John, *An t-eilean Muileach: the Island of Mull, its History, Scenes and Legends*, Glasgow, [1923].

McCrorie, Ian, *Steamers of the Highlands and Islands*, Greenock, 1987.

Macculloch, John, *The Highlands and Western Islands of Scotland*, 4 vols, London, 1824.

Macdonald, Duncan, 'Eminent Highland doctors. Dr Hector McColl, Tobermory' in *The Caledonian Medical Journal* [The Journal of the Caledonian Medical Society],new series, vol. vi. July 1904–October 1906.

Macdonald, James, *A General View of the Agriculture of the Hebrides or Western Isles of Scotland*, Edinburgh, 1811.

MacDonald, Murdo, 'The droving trade in the records of the commissioners of supply of Argyllshire' in *Transactions of the Gaelic Society of Inverness*, 58, 1993–1994.

MacDougall, Robert, *The Emigrant's Guide to North America*, Toronto, 1998.

Macinnes, Allan I., *Clanship, Commerce and the House of Stuart, 1603–1788*, East Linton, 1996.

Macinnes, Allan, 'From clanship to commercial landlordism: landownership in Argyll from the seventeenth to the nineteenth century', in *History and Computing*, 2, no. 3, 1990.

Macinnes, John, *The Evangelical Movement in the Highlands of Scotland 1688 to 1800*, Aberdeen, 1951.

McKay, Margaret M. (ed.), *The Rev. Dr John Walker's Report on the Hebrides of 1764 and 1771*, Edinburgh, 1980.

MacKenzie, Alexander, *The History of the Highland Clearances ...* Edinburgh, 1997 [reprint].

Mackichan, David, *All you Need to Know about the Pilgrims' Way to Iona*, Craignure, 1987.

Mackinnon, Sir Alex. Downie, *Genealogical Account of the Family of Mackinnon ...*, London, 1883.

Mackinnon, Donald D., *Memoirs of Clan Fingon*, Tunbridge Wells, n.d.

Maclean, Charles, *The Isle of Mull: Placenames, Meanings and Stories*, Dumfries, 1997.

McLean, J. P., *An Examination into the Evidences of the Chiefship of the Clann-Ghilleain*, Glasgow, 1895.
——, *An Historical Account of the Settlements of Scotch Highlanders in America*, Cleveland, 1900.
——, *History of the Island of Mull, embracing Description, Climate, Geology, Flora, Fauna, Antiquities, Folklore, Superstitions, Traditions, with an account of its inhabitants* ... 2 vols, Greenville, Ohio, 1923.
——, Renaissance of the Clan Maclean ... Columbus, 1913.
Maclean, James M. N., *Reward is Secondary: the Life of a Political Adventurer and an Enquiry into the Mystery of Junius*, London, 1963.
Maclean, Loraine, *The Raising of the 79th Highlanders*, Coll, 1980.
Maclean-Bristol, Nicholas, *Hebridean Decade, Mull, Coll and Tiree, 1761–1771*, Coll, 1982.
—— (ed.), *Inhabitants of the Inner Isles, Morvern and Ardnamurchan, 1716* [Scottish Record Society], Edinburgh, 1998.
——, *Murder under Trust: the Crimes and Death of Sir Lachlan Mor Maclean of Duart, 1558–1598*, East Linton, 1998.
——, *Warriors and Priests: the History of the Clan Maclean, 1300–1570*, East Linton, 1995.
Macleod, John N., *Memorials of the Rev. Norman Macleod Senior, DD*, Edinburgh, 1898.
Macleod, Malcolm C. (ed.), *Modern Gaelic Bards*, Stirling, 1908.
Macleod, Norman, *Reminiscences of a Highland Parish*, London, n.d.
Macnab, John, *The Immunity from Consumption in the Hebrides*, Edinburgh, 1869.
Macnab, Peter, *Highways and Byways in Mull and Iona*, Barr, 1992.
Macnab, P. A., *Mull and Iona*, Newton Abbot, 1995.
McNeill, Roger, *On the Public Health of the Insular and Inland Rural Districts of Scotland*, Edinburgh, 1890.
Macphail, I. M. M., *The Crofters' War*, Stornoway, 1989.
Macphail, J. R. N. (ed.), 'Papers relating to the Macleans of Duart', *in Highland Papers*, vol. 1 [Scottish History Society], Edinburgh, 1914.
Macpherson, James, *The poems of Ossian, translated by JM*, in 2 volumes, London, 1796.
Mactavish, Duncan C. (ed.), *Minutes of the Synod of Argyll, 1652–1661*, Edinburgh, 1944.
Magnusson, Magnus, *Rum: Nature's Island*, Edinburgh, 1997.
Meek, Donald E., 'Evangelical missionaries in the early nineteenth century Highlands', in *Scottish Studies*, 28, 1987.
——, *Island Harvest: A History of Tiree Baptist Church, 1838–1988*, Tiree, 1988.
——, *Sunshine and Shadow: The Story of the Baptists of Mull*, Edinburgh, 1991.
——, *Tuath is tighearna, Tenants and Landlords, an Anthology of Gaelic Poetry of Social and Political Protest from the Clearances to the Land Agitation (1800–1890)* [Scottish Gaelic Texts Society], Edinburgh, 1995.
Menary, George, *The Life and Letters of Duncan Forbes of Culloden, Lord President of the Court of Session, 1685–1747*, London, 1936.
Mestern, Pat Mattaini, *Fergus, a Scottish Town by Birthright*, Toronto, 1995.
Michie, R. C., *Money, Mania and Markets, Investment, Company Formation and the Stock Exchange in 19th Century Scotland*, Edinburgh 1981.
Monro, Sir Donald, *Description of the Western Isles of Scotland called Hybrides, with the Genealogies of the Chief Clans of the Isles*, Glasgow, 1884.
Munn, Charles W., *The Scottish Provincial Banking Companies, 1747–1864*, Edinburgh, 1981.
Munro, Jean, *The Founding of Tobermory* [Coll], 1976.
Munro, Jean & R. W. (eds), *Acts of the Lords of the Isles, 1336–1493* [Scottish History Society], Edinburgh, 1986.
Munro, R. W. and Macquarrie, Alan, *Clan MacQuarrie, a History*, Auburn, Mass., 1996.
Munro, R. W., 'Governor Lachlan Macquarie and his family circle', *in The Scottish Genealogist*, 36, 1, 1989.
[——] , *Lachlan Macquarrie XVI of Ulva, with notes on some clansmen in India*, Karachi, 1944.
——, 'The MacQuarries of Ulva' *in The Scottish Genealogist*, 15, 2, 1968.
—— (ed.), *Monro's Western Isles of Scotland*, Edinburgh, 1961.
Murray, Mrs, *The Steamboat Companion and Stranger's Guide to the Western Islands and Highlands of Scotland*, Glasgow, 1820.
Newte, Thomas, *Prospects and Observations on a Tour in England and Scotland*, London, 1791.
Nicholls, Sir George, *A history of the Scottish Poor Law, in Connexion with the Condition of the People*, London, 1856.
O Baoill, Colm, *Eachann Bacach and other Maclean poets* [Scottish Gaelic Texts Society], Edinburgh, 1979.
Ogg, Diana, *Coll, island of the Hebrides*, London, 1988.
Orr, Willie, *Discovering Argyll, Mull and Iona*, Edinburgh, 1990.

Pennant, Thomas, *A Tour in Scotland and Voyage to the Hebrides, 1772*, Edinburgh, 1998 [reprint].

Phillipson, N. T., and Mitchison, Rosalind (eds), *Scotland in the Age of Improvement: Essays in Scottish History in the Eighteenth Century*, Edinburgh, 1996.

Pottle, Frederick A. *see* Boswell

Reid, Stuart and Chappell, Mike, *18th Century Highlanders* [Men-at-Arms series, 261], Oxford, 1993.

Ritchie, Alec & Euphemia, *Iona Past and Present*, Edinburgh, 1934.

Ritchie, John, *Lachlan Macquarie: a Biography*, Melbourne, 1986.

Sacheverell, William *An Account of the Isle of Man ... with a Voyage to I-Columb-kill ...* [The Manx Society], Douglas, 1859.

Scott, Hew, *Fasti Ecclesiae Scoticanae: The Succession of Ministers in the Church of Scotland from the Reformation, vol. 4, Synods of Argyll, and of Perth and Stirling*, Edinburgh, 1923.

Scott, Walter, *The Lord of the Isles*, Edinburgh, 1815.

———, *Tales of a Grandfather: A History of Scotland, 1033 to 1788*, London, 1893.

———, *The Voyage of the Pharos, Walter Scott's Cruise around Scotland in 1814*, Hamilton, 1998.

'A Seneachie', *An Historical and Genealogical Account of the Clan Maclean*, London, 1838.

Seymour, William, *The Price of Folly: British Blunders in the War of American Independence*, London, 1995.

Simpson, John M., 'Who steered the gravy train, 1707–1766?', in *Scotland in the Age of Improvement*, Edinburgh, 1996.

Sinclair, A. Maclean, *The Clan Gillean*, Charlottetown, 1899.

Sinclair, A. Maclean, *Na Baird Leathanach: The Maclean Bards*, 2 vols, Charlottetown, 1898.

Skene, William F., *The Highlanders of Scotland, their Origin, History and Antiquities ...* 2 vols, London, 1836.

Smith, Paul H., *Loyalists and Redcoats: A Study in British Revolutionary Policy*, Chapel Hill, 1964.

Smout, T. C. *et al.*, 'Scottish emigration in the seventeenth and eighteenth centuries', in *Europeans on the Move: Studies in European Migration, 1500–1800*, Oxford, 1994.

Somers, Robert, *Letters from the Highlands; or the Famine of 1847*, London, 1848.

Steer, K. and Bannerman, J., *Late Medieval Monumental Sculpture in the West Highlands* [RCAHMS], Edinburgh, 1977.

Stevenson, David, *Highland Warrior: Alasdair MacColla and the Civil Wars*, Edinburgh, 1994.

Stewart, David, of Garth, *Sketches of the Character, Institutions and Customs of the Highlanders of Scotland*, Inverness, 1885.

Storrie, Margaret, *Islay: Biography of an Island*, Islay, 1997.

Tayler, Henrietta, 'John, Duke of Argyll and Greenwich' *in The Scottish Historical Review*, 26, 1, 1947.

Thomson, Derick S. (ed.), *The Companion to Gaelic Scotland*, Glasgow, 1994.

Thornber, Iain, *Rats: an old Morvern Song*, reprinted from *Transactions of the Gaelic Society of Inverness*, LV, 1989.

Utz, Hans, 'A Genevan's journey to the Hebrides in 1807: an anti-Johnsonian venture' *in Studies in Scottish Literature*, 27, 1993.

Walker, D. M., *The Scottish Legal System: An Introduction to the Study of Scots Law*, Edinburgh, 1992.

Walker, John, *An Economical History of the Hebrides and Highlands of Scotland*, 2 vols, London, 1812.

Whyte, Henry ['Fionn'], *The Rankins, Pipers to the Macleans of Duart, and later to the Macleans of Coll*, Glasgow, 1907.

Wiener, Christine, *Mull: a Traveller's Guide*, London, 1991.

Wimsatt, William K. and Pottle, Frederick A. (eds), *Boswell for the Defence, 1769–1774*, Melbourne, 1960.

Wright, David F. (ed.), *The Bible in Scottish Life and Literature*, Edinburgh, 1988.

——— *et al.* (eds), *Dictionary of Scottish Church History and Theology*, Edinburgh, 1993.

Youngson, A. J., *Beyond the Highland Line: Three Journals of Travel in Eighteenth Century Scotland: Burt, Pennant, Thornton*. London, 1974.

Landownership maps

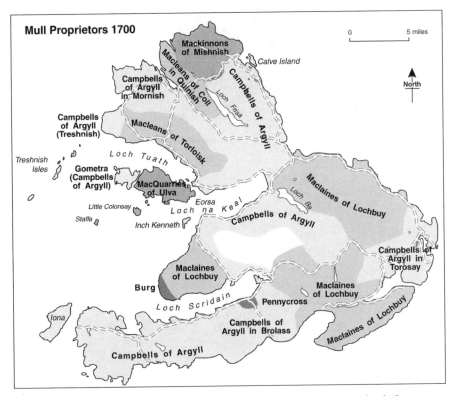

Mull Proprietors 1700

0   5 miles

Mackinnons
of Mishnish

Calve Island

Macleans of Coll in Quinish

Campbells
of Argyll
in Mornish

Loch Frisa

Campbells of Argyll

North

Campbells
of Argyll
(Treshnish)

Macleans of Torloisk

Treshnish
Isles

Loch Tuath

Gometra
(Campbells
of Argyll)

MacQuarrie
of Ulva

Eorsa

Macleans of Lochbuy

Loch Ba

Little Colonsay

Loch na Keal

Staffa

Inch Kenneth

Campbells of Argyll

Campbells of
Argyll in
Torosay

Maclaines
of Lochbuy

Maclaines
of Lochbuy

Burg

Loch Scridain

Pennycross

Maclaines of Lochbuy

Iona

Campbells of
Argyll in Brolass

Campbells of Argyll

The Earl of Argyll had now been in formal possession of the old Duart lands for some years, after a struggle which lasted for most of the seventeenth century. The Campbells of Argyll are therefore the principal landowners in terms of acreage. Church lands in Iona and Ross, granted to the Macleans of Duart, were appropriated with the rest of the Maclean property, but the Torloisk Macleans were able to keep Torloisk, and the lands of Brolass, leased to the Macleans of Brolass, were under a wadset arrangement. The number of proprietors was only six, if the special dispensation to the Beatons in Pennycross be included.

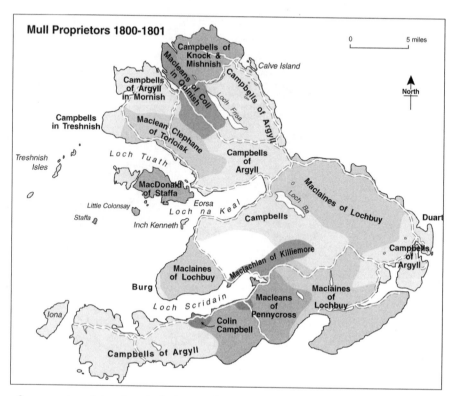

Mull Proprietors 1800-1801

0   5 miles

North

Campbells of Knock & Mishnish

Macleans of Coll in Quinish

Campbells of Argyll in Mornish

Campbells of Argyll

Calve Island

Loch Frisa

Campbells in Treshnish

Maclean Clephane of Torloisk

Campbells of Argyll

Treshnish Isles

Loch Tuath

MacDonald of Staffa

Little Colonsay

Eorsa

Loch na Keal

Maclaines of Lochbuy

Loch Ba

Staffa

Inch Kenneth

Campbells

Duart

Campbells of Argyll

Maclachlan of Killiemore

Maclaines of Lochbuy

Burg

Loch Scridain

Macleans of Pennycross

Maclaines of Lochbuy

Iona

Colin Campbell

Campbells of Argyll

Over a century later, the principal ownership changes are in Ulva, now possessed by the Macdonalds of Boisdale, and in Mishnish, purchased from the Mackinnons by the Campbells of Knock, formerly tacksmen to the Dukes of Argyll. But the MacLachlans of Laudale are about to acquire Killiemore (Kilfinichen) on the north side of Loch Scridain, and the Macquarie brothers are negotiating with Murdoch Maclaine of Lochbuy to buy swathes of his estate under the terms of the entail. The fifth Duke of Argyll released Torrans in 1801 to Archibald Maclean of Pennycross, who had also bought, in the bankruptcy sales of Charles Maclean of Drimmin and Kinlochaline (successor to Sir Allan Maclean in the titles) at the end of the eighteenth century, a large section of Brolass, extended even farther by a private arrangement with McGilvra of Pennyghael. 'Pennycross' was thus an important new heritor. In the Tobermory area, the Fisheries Society acquired land from both the duke and the Campbells of Mishnish.

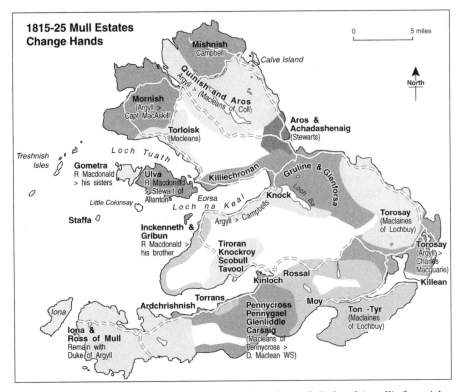

1815-25 Mull Estates Change Hands

0   5 miles

North

Mishnish
Campbell

Calve Island

Quinish and Aros
Argyll > (Macleans of Coll)

Mornish
(Argyll >
Capt MacAskill)

Aros &
Achadashenaig
(Stewarts)

Torloisk
(Macleans)

Treshnish
Isles

Loch Tuath

Gometra
R Macdonald
> his sisters

Ulva
R Macdonald
> Stewart of
Allanton

Killiechronan

Gruline & Glenforsa

Loch Ba

Little Colonsay

Eorsa

Loch na Keal

Knock

Staffa

Argyll > Campbells

Torosay
(Maclaines
of Lochbuy)

Inckenneth &
Gribun
R Macdonald >
his brother

Tiroran
Knockroy
Scobull
Tavool

Torosay
(Argyll >
Charles
Macquarie)

Rossal

Killean

Kinloch

Torrans

Moy

Iona

Ardchrishnish

Pennycross
Pennygael
Glenliddle
Carsaig
(Macleans of
Pennycross >
D. Maclean WS)

Ton -Tyr
(Maclaines
of Lochbuy)

Iona &
Ross of Mull
Remain with
Duke of Argyll

Convulsions in land ownership had been caused by the sixth Duke of Argyll's financial troubles. Land was released by his trustees after the passing of a special Act of Parliament. His commissioner, James Ferrier, advocated the sale of lots to sitting tenants, trying to retain the configuration of the Argyll farms. The Macleans of Coll bought upper Aros, and extended their Quinish property down to Tenga. The Stewarts of Achadashenaig bought lower Aros, including their own house, known today as Glenaros. Captain Allan MacAskill bought Calgary with Treshnish and Sunipol. The Macquarie brothers extended their estates with the purchase of the north shore of Loch na Keill (Lachlan) and the Torosay lands of the Campbells around Duart (Charles). Ranald Macdonald of Staffa, whose ownership of Ulva had officially passed to his father-in-law, Henry Steuart of Allanton, and of Gometra to his sisters, had not relinquished his interest in Ulva, for which Charles Macquarie was to pay too high a price in 1826. In Brolass, the Pennycross Macleans, having overextended themselves in the early 1800s, entered into a complicated arrangement with Donald Maclean WS, who bought Kinloch and Carsaig ostensibly for his son-in-law, and allowed the Pennycrosses to continue the management of the estate while legally retaining Pennyghael. A new MacGillivray, William, appeared in 1819, to augment Torrans with part of Pennyghael. Inchkenneth, the jewel in the crown of Brolass, had become the property of Robert Macdonald, Staffa's brother. As Charles Macquarie considered offers for the prestigious Duart lands to finance his dream of buying Ulva, a prospective buyer appeared in the shape of Colonel Campbell of Possil, whose successors were to alter the balance of land ownership in Mull.

Genealogical tables

1	Maclaines of Lochbuy	419
2	Later Maclaines of Lochbuy and Macleans of Drimnin	420
3	Macleans of Duart and Brolass	421
4	Macleans of Torloisk and Pennycross	422–3
5	Maclaines of Scallastle	424
6	Gregorsons of Ardtornish	425
7	Campbells of Argyll	426
8	Family of Lauchlan Maclaine	427
9	Macleans of Drimnin and Kinloch	428
10	Clarks of Ulva	429
11	MacQuarries of Ulva and Ormaig	430–1
12	Macquarie brothers	432
13	Maxwells and Macleods	433
14	Macdonalds of Boisdale, Staffa and Inchkenneth	434

TABLE 1.

MACLAINES of LOCHBUY (1).

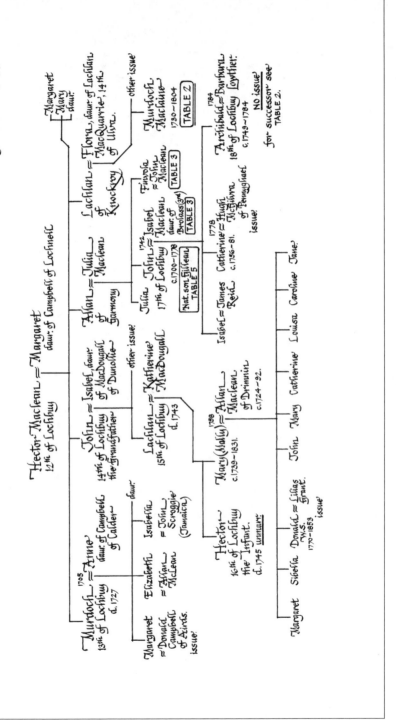

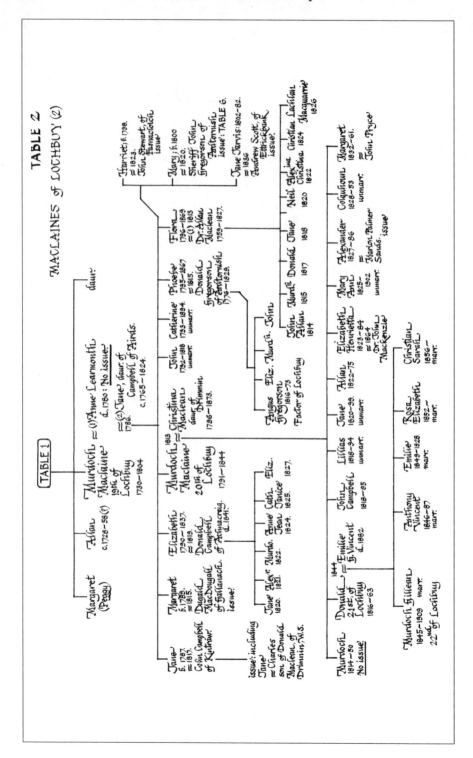

TABLE 2

MACLAINES OF LOCHBUY (2)

TABLE 3.

MACLEANS
of DUART & BROLASS

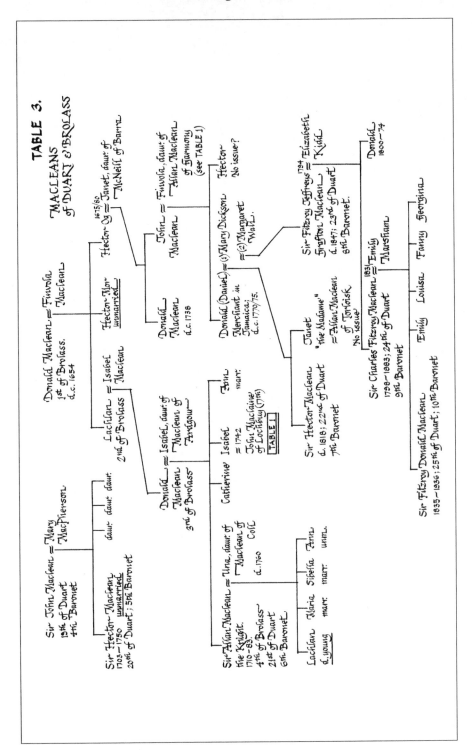

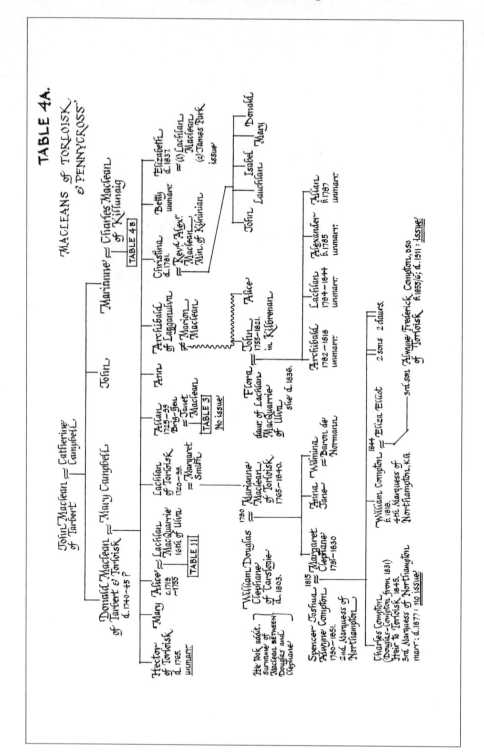

TABLE 4A.

'MACLEANS of TOROLISK & PENNYCROSS'

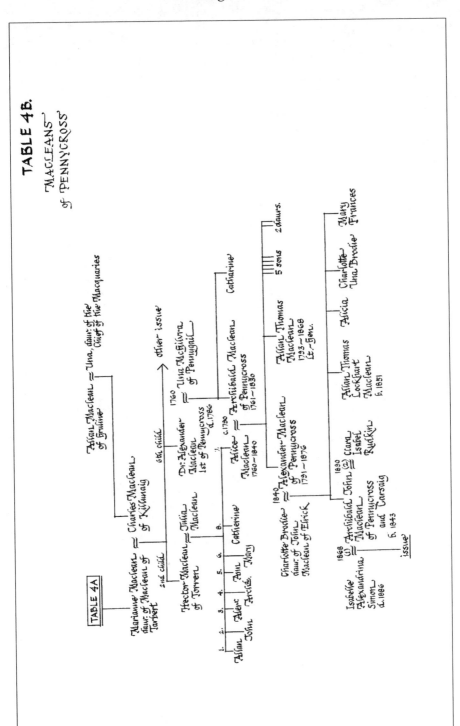

TABLE 4B.

"MACLEANS"
of "PENNYCROSS"

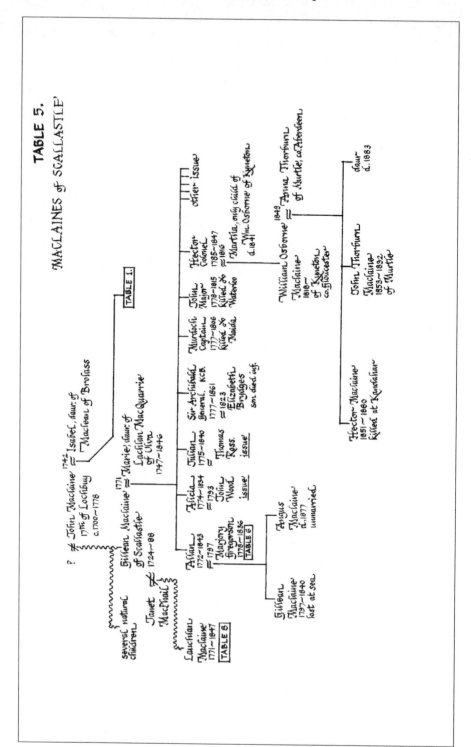

TABLE 5.

MACLAINES of SCALLASTLE

? ⚔ John Maclaine 1742 = Isabel, daur. of
17th of Lochbuy   Maclean of Brolass
c.1700~1778

Gillean Maclaine = Marie, daur. of
of Scallastle 1771 Lachlan MacQuarrie
1724~88   of Ulva
                    1747~1846

several natural
children

Janet ⚔
MacPhail

TABLE 1.

Lauchlan
Maclaine
1711~1847
TABLE 6

Allan   Alicia   Julian   Sir Archibald   Murdoch   John   Hector   other issue
1772~1843   1774~1854   1775~1840   General, KCB   Captain   Major   Colonel
= 1797   = 1793   = Thomas   1777~1861   1777~1806   1778~1815   1785~1847
Marjory   John   Ross.   = 1823   killed at   killed at   = 1816
Ferguson   Wood   issue   Elizabeth   Maida   Waterloo   Martha, only child of
1778~1836   issue   Brydges   Wm. Osborne of Kyneton
TABLE 6   son died inf.   d.1841

Gillean   Angus   William Osborne 1849 = Anna Thorburn
Maclaine   Maclaine   Maclaine   of Murtle, co. Aberdeen
1797~1840   d.1877   1810~
lost at sea   unmarried   of Kyneton
                                                                                     co. Gloucester

                                               Hector Maclaine   John Thorburn   daur.
                                               1851~1880   Maclaine   d.1883
                                               killed at Kandahar   1853~1892
                                                                                     of Murtle

TABLE 6

GREGORSONS of ARDTORNISH'

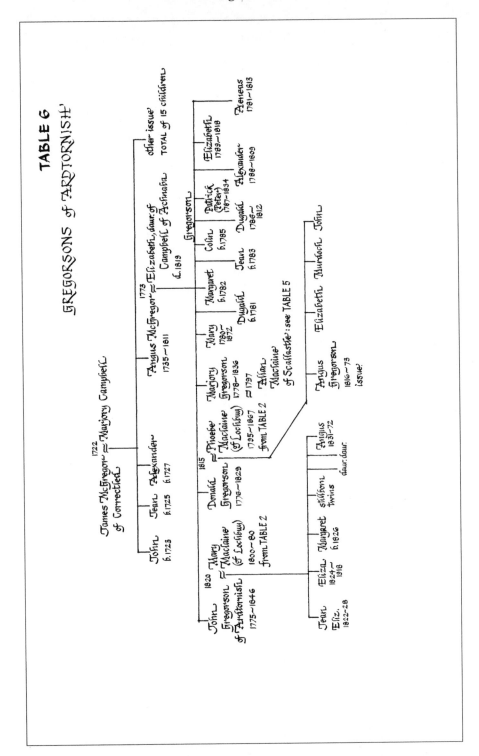

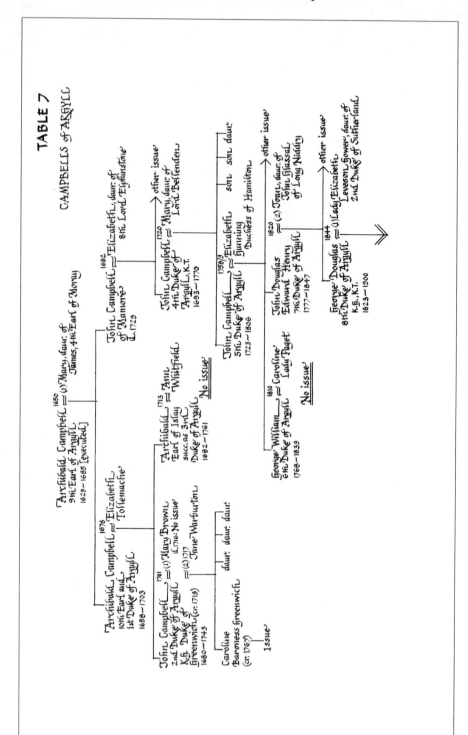

TABLE 7

CAMPBELLS OF ARGYLL

TABLE 8.

LATERAL RELATIONS of LAUGHLAN MACLAINE

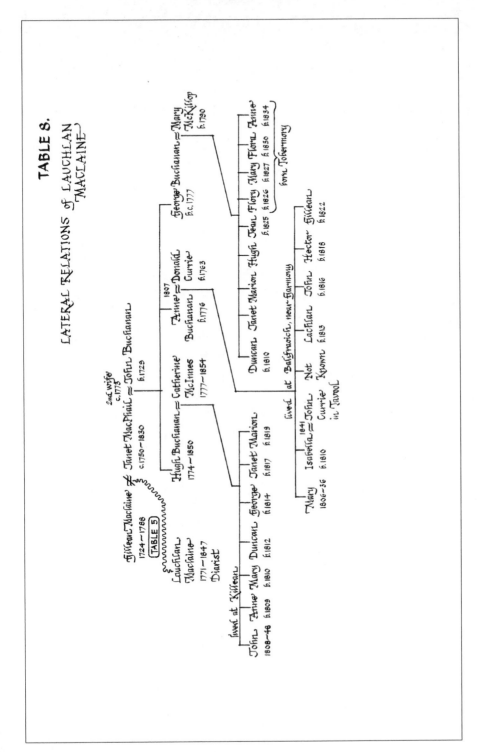

TABLE 9

MACLEANS of DRIMNIN and KINLOCH

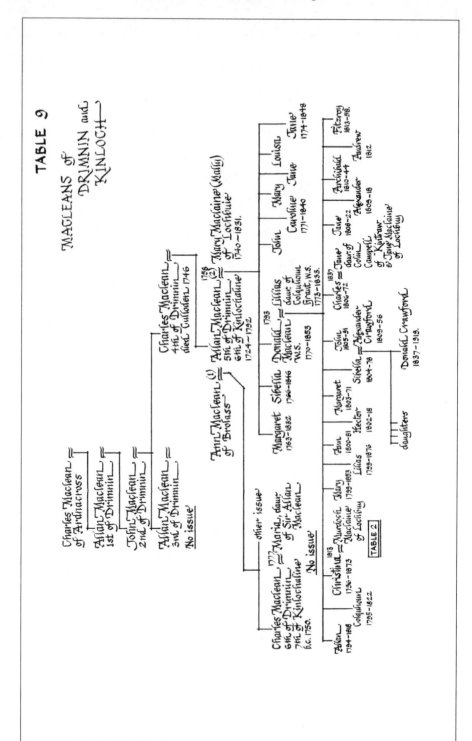

TABLE 10

CLARKS of ULVA

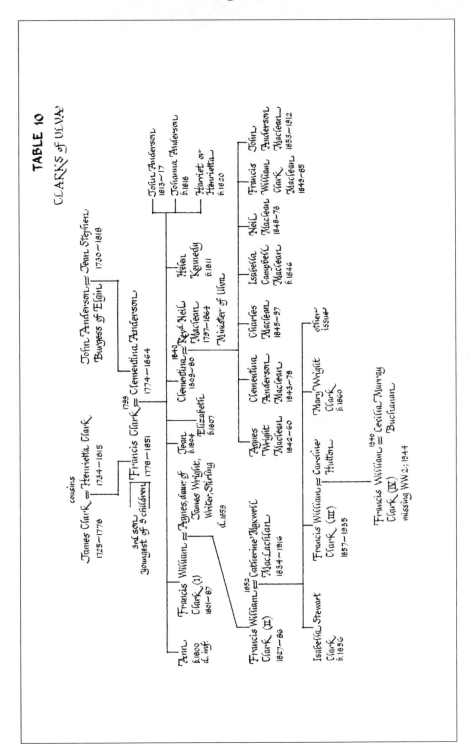

James Clark = Henrietta Clark
1725–1778   1734–1815

cousins

John Anderson = Jean Stephen
Burgess of Elgin   1730–1818

3rd son
youngest of 9 children

Francis Clark = Clementina Anderson
1778–1851   1774–1864
(married 1799)

John Anderson
1813–17

Johanna Anderson
b.1816

Harriet or Henrietta
b.1820

Ann
b.1800
d. inf.

Francis William = Agnes, daur. of James Wright, Whitor, Stirling
Clark (I)   d.1859
1801–87

Jean
b.1804

Elizabeth
b.1807

Clementina = Revd Neil Maclean
1809–80   1797–1864
(married 1840)   Minister of Ulva

Helen Kenneth
b.1811

Francis William = Catherine Maxwell MacLachlan
Clark (II)   1834–1916
1827–86
(married 1852)

Agnes Wright Maclean
1842–60

Clementina Anderson Maclean
1843–78

Charles Maclean
1845–97

Isabella Campbell Maclean
b.1846

Neil Maclean
1848–78

Francis William Clark Maclean
1849–85

John Anderson Maclean
1853–1912

Francis William = Caroline Hutton
Clark (III)
1857–1935

Mary Wright Clark
b.1860

other issue

Isabella Stewart Clark
b.1856

Francis William = Cecilia Murray Buchanan
Clark (IV)
(married 1940)
missing WW 2; 1944

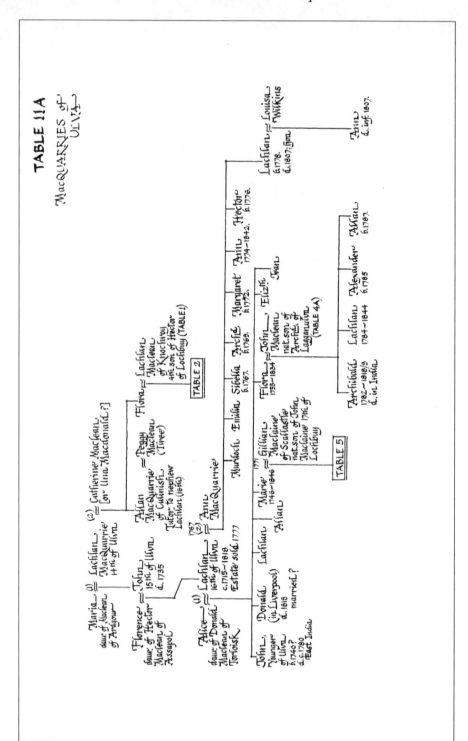

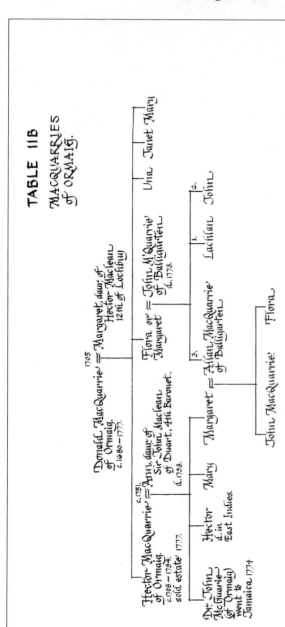

TABLE 11B

MACQUARRIES
of ORMAIG.

Donald MacQuarrie' 1705 = Margaret, daur of
of Ormaig.   Hector Maclean
c.1680–1777.   12th of Lochbuy

Hector MacQuarrie = Ann, daur of   Flora or = John M'Quarrie'   Una   Janet   Mary
of Ormaig.   c.1751. Sir John Maclean   Margaret of Ballygartan
c.1708–1794.   of Duart, 4th Baronet.   d.1773.
sold estate 1777. d.1753.

Dr. John   Hector   Mary   Margaret = Allan MacQuarrie'   1.   2.
McQuarrie   d. in   of Ballygartan   Lachlan   John
of Ormaig)   East Indies.
went to   John MacQuarrie'   Flora
Jamaica 1774

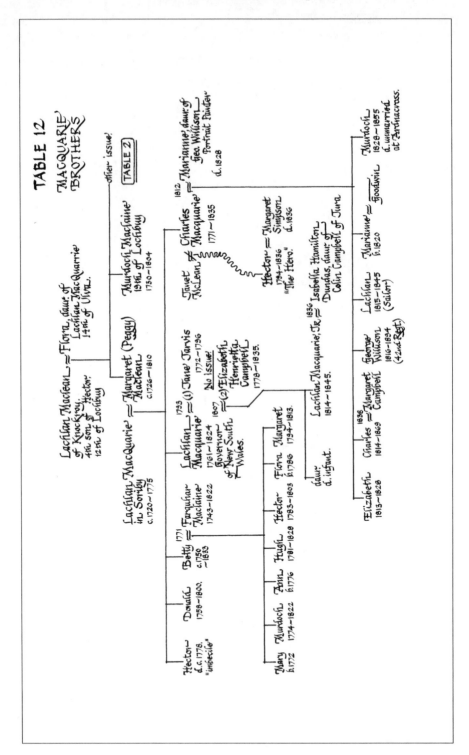

TABLE 13
MAXWELLS and MACLEODS

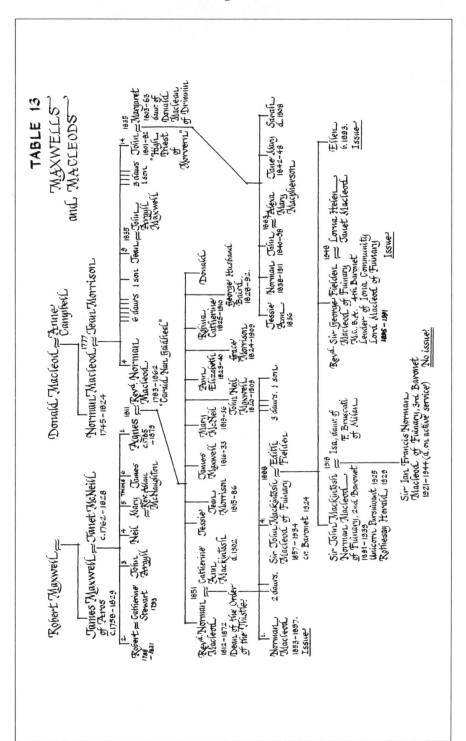

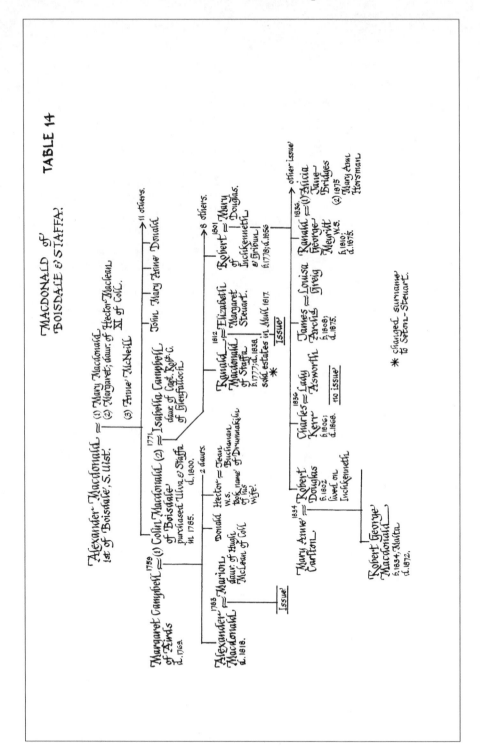

TABLE 14

MACDONALD of
BOISDALE & STAFFA.

Index of Placenames

selected references excluding personal and territorial titles

D/A = Duart/Argyll estates   LB=Lochbuy

PG=Pennyghael   PX=Pennycross

Aboss (Ulva) List of tenants in, 208

Achadashenaig later re-named Glen Aros; on 18th C. route from Aros to Ulva, 113; one of principal farms of D/A, 189; a hospitable house, 193; bought from Argyll trustees by Stewarts, 197; 222; Free Church for Salen area set up at A., 1846, 334; 335: n.35; as 'Glen Aros' estate employs lowland shepherds, 386

Achnacraig (Torosay) Ferry port; JB and SJ leave Mull from A., 112; a principal farm on D/A in 1770s, 189; also known as Grass Point, 192; Gregorsons ferrymen at A., 224; convivial evening at Inn of A., 286

Achnacraig (Kilmore) Near Dervaig; Charles Maclean, Jacobite, in A., 44

Achnacroish (Torosay) Part of D/A lands, bought by CM, who lives there; bought by ACP, 1825; one of principal farms of D/A in 1770s, 189; Possils arrive at A., 225; Torgormaig [Achnacroish] the only house of quality on Duart estate, 252–3; CM and Marianne move into A., 253; Torgormaig the destination of LMD's evening strolls, 257; LMD plays fiddle at, 308; ACP and family move in, 310; frequent parties at A., 311; ACP has fit of apoplexy at A., 333; LMD has four days of merrymaking at A., 366; John Campbell plans building of new house at A., 385; owners of A. (Duart House) agree to sell D. Castle, 404; house to be re-named Torosay, 404

Achnahaird (Ross of Mull) Argyll estate; hamlet in Ardtun, home of Uisdean Ros, 357

Aird, Ard (Kilfinichen) Part of Killiemore, set to same tenant, 138

Airds (mainland – Appin) MM & JC married at A., 154; J. Stevenson doing masonry at A., 154; MM's first child reared at A., 157

Ardachy (Ross of Mull) Argyll estate; land going to waste in 1748, 139; linked to other townships by track, 302; name of tenant in A. in 1662, 347

Ardalanish (Ross of Mull) Argyll estate; land going to waste in 1748, 139; linked to chain of Ross townships, 302; Neil Macdonald and Mary MacDougall crofters at A. Point, evicted, 302; name of tenant in A. in 1662, 347; MacIntyres tenants in, 393

Ardchiavaig (Ross of Mull) Argyll estate; going to waste in 1748, 139; linked by track to other Ross townships, 302; name of tenant in A. in 1662, 347

Ardchoirk (Torosay) D/A, near Lochdon – example of populous 18th C. township, 134; 216; home of Buchanans, 306; A. inhabited by people not native to Mull, 306

Ardchrishnish (Brolass) Loch Scridain, sett to minister of Ross, 138; JB & SJ visit A., 110; Charles Maclean of Drimnin infeft there in 1786, 148

Ardellum (Ulva) List of tenants in, 209

Ardfenaig (Ross of Mull) Argyll estate, sett to John Maclean of Killean in 1750 and inhabited by that family for nearly 100 years; improved for new chamberlain in 1845, 349

Ardmeanach LB; kelp industry causes increase in population, 98; to be sold to pay LB debts, 161; people of A. leave for America, 217; 228: n.19; A. set aside to provide for LB girls, 234; people expelled from A. settle at Kinloch, 243; precepts of removal issued to cottars of A., 1804, 268; discontent of people of A. voiced by tacksman, 271; A. sold to Mr MacArthur, 354; 393; people of A. poorest in parish, 355

Ardnacaillich (Ulva) Situation of Ulva House; GM spends time there on legal business, 80; GM marries Marie MacQuarrie at A., 81; arsonist attacks house & kiln of, 93; JB and SJ visit, 106; new, larger house built before 1800, 199; in list of tenants of Ulva, 209; RM's mother and sisters remain at A. when Ulva is for sale, 251; CM moves into A., 257; CM's death at A., 259–60; Miss Ann MacQuarrie goes to live at A., 364

Ardnacross One of principal farms on D/A, 189; small tenants of A. removed to Ardtun, 189

Ardnamurchan (mainland) Angus Maclaine becomes minister of, 288; earlier minister of A. excommunicated, 324; roup of possessions of the Rev. Angus Maclaine in A., 388–9; people evicted from A. swell population of Tobermory, 399

Ardow (Kilninian) Usually referred to in group, Arivelchyne, Ardrioch and Duchorin; part of D/A lands; Dr Lachlan Maclean takes possession, but A. is sold to Kenneth Campbell and his brother-in-law, David Watson in 1837; land granted at A. for Free

Church, 334; DMWS purchasing A. for Dr Lachlan Maclean, 1825, 238

Ardtornish (Morvern) Pact subscribed at Castle of A., 3–4; bought by Gregorsons from Argyll trustees, 197; 222; Gregorsons of A. described, 224; young Gillean and Angus Maclaine products of Ardtornish, 287; A. a centre for parties, 309; Gregorson heir born at A., 319; shintie played at, 319; Flora LB and Dr Whiteside visit A., 342

Ardtun (Ross of Mull) Small tenants from Ardnacross removed to A., 189; population of 346 in A. in 1861, 348

Ardura Part of D/A lands in Torosay; sett to Archibald MacTavish in 1750; MM2 wishes to add it to LB, 252; 254

Ardvergnish (Brolass) Administered by Argyll estate in wadset; MacLachlans buy farm of A., with purchase of Killiemore, 234

Arin D/A, becoming waste in 1748, 139; 11 families removed from, c.1814, 194; 198: n.13

Arivelchyne Part of D/A lands in 18th C., when A. was known as 'Arvoulchein'; grouped with Duchorin & Ardrioch; sold to Kenneth Campbell and David Watson in 1837, 224; Lachlan Maclean of Gallanach acquires A., 1826, 330

Arle D/A; part of lot bought by Macleans of Coll in duke's sales.

Aros (old) D/A land; chiefs summoned to meeting at A., 5; earl of Argyll gets charter of, 7; castle uninhabited in 1680, 8; Latin school set up in, 86; soil of A. in bad condition, 1748, 139; one of principal farms of D/A, 189; lived in by duke's chamberlain, 189; main landing-place in late 18th C.,189–90; Maxwell settled at A., 190; township at A. has 57 people in 1779, 190; A. [now Aros Mains] a hospitable house, 193; 6th duke visits, 194; small window in wall at A., 196; Hugh Maclean of Coll buys northern part of A. from Argyll trustees, 222; 384; Coll's promptness in paying for purchase of, 236–7; children of Dr Donald Maclaine living at A. Bridge, 318; Mull presbytery meets at A., 324

Aros (House) D/A, formerly Druimfin, near Tobermory, name changed mid-19th C., causing confusion with old Aros; Hugh Maclean builds new house, 385; sold to Alexander Crawford, 385–6; to Farquhar Campbell, 386; Allan family in Aros House, 386

Assapol (Ross of Mull) Argyll estate; sett to small tenants in 1750; Maxwell ascertains boundaries near A., 191; A. is offered as site of minister's house, 327; Archibald Maclean of PX ill at A., 341; names of tenants in A. in 1662, 347

Aultcreich LB, near Craignure; an Inn in the time of LMD; deserted in 1836, 321

Baliacrach Mishnish estate; on JB & SJ's route to Ulva, 106; as example of Mull

township, 134; tenants of B. give account of Mr Forsyth, 383; 394: n.9

Baliscate One of principal farms on D/A in 1770s, 189; considered as chamberlain's residence, 189; arable land of B. required for settlers in Tobermory,189; house at B. rented by Charles Macquarie Jr., 390

Ballameanach (Torosay) Near Fishnish; site of marketplace referred to by LMD

Ballifraoich (Torosay) LB, at Garmony, part of GM's tack of Scallastle, Garmony & Ledirkle; home of LMD's workmen; post office at, 310; misfortunes of McNeils in B., 312; LMD compiles list of 30 inhabitants of, 1829, 316; cottars of B. to be removed, 320; reprieved by Mr Young, 320

Ballinaheine Part of lands of Brolass along with Balnahaird and Balmeanach, which went with Inchkenneth; sold to Macdonalds along with Inchkenneth in 1803.

Ballochroy Coll estate; Inn at Dervaig pre-dates village; Sandy Campbell stays at Inn of B., 296; 298

Ballygartan (Ulva) List of tenants in, 208

Ballygown Torloisk estate, 181; family of schoolmaster at, 187: n.44

Balmeanach (Kilfinichen) Gribun; sett with Tenga, 138; Charles Maclean infeft in B., 1786, 148

Balnahaird Sett to small tenants, 1748, 138; Charles Maclean infeft 1786, 148

Beach (Brolass) Farm near Ormsaig in Brolass; in tack to parents of Dr Allan Maclean, 337

Bentalla Part of LB until 1804; in tack to Dr Andrew Maclaine for cattle rearing, 163; bought by LM as part of estate to be called Jarvisfield, 214

Berniss, Bernice (Ulva) List of tenants in, 208

Bradil LB; JMG tacksman of, 67; sold to LM under terms of entail, 1804, 214

Bradiluachtrach Part of LB until 1804, when sold to LM, 214

Brolass Part of Duart estate which Campbells of Argyll mortgaged to Macleans of Brolass, so that terms of its control by dukes of A. were unlike those of other Duart lands; more than six Maclean tacksmen remained in B. Charter of B., 1637, acquired by earl of Argyll, 7; leased by AMB, 46; 'worst spot in Mull', 46; no house of quality in, 138; B. on different footing (wadset) from other Duart/Argyll lands, 141; AMB's attempt to regain Duart lands successful only in B., 142; south side of B. sold by Charles Maclean of Drimnin and Kinlochaline, to Pennycross, 148; people of B. a 'parcel of rascals', 148; Charles Maclean's possession of Brolass, 232

Bunessan (Ross of Mull) Argyll estate; joint farm in 18th C.; a good farm going to waste in 1748, 139; JB and SJ rowed into bay of, Inn at B. kept by Lachlan Ban Maclean, 109; new village planned at B., 191; new village to be divided for crofting, 216; house at B.

described by F. Mercey, c.1840, 279–80;
John Stevenson estimating for new church at
B., 327; rota of preachers arranged for B.
because of Baptist infiltration, 331; James
Morison, merchant in B. drowned at B.,
1828, 341; road from B. to Uisken begun by
statute labour, 351; Crofters Enquiry at B.,
1883, 352–3; numbers of cottars and crofters
in district of B., 354; Inn managed by John
Bunessan, 369, n: 369

Burg (headland) Barony of Duart, then
Argyll estate, bought by Macdonalds of
Boisdale, 1807; sold to Duncan MacIntyre,
393

Burgh, Burg Torloisk estate, 181

Caibeal Mheamhair Chapel of remembrance
of LB family, at Laggan; MM buried at, 214;
JC's funeral procession to, 236; 255; Miss
Catherine's plaque at CM wrongly dated, 393

Cairnburgh (Treshnish Isles) Stronghold of
Maclean resistance to Campbells, 16;
description of, 21: n.24

Calgary Part of Argyll estate in 18th C., 89;
sett to Alexander Maclean in 1750; sold as
part of Mornish lot by Argyll trustees to
Capt. Allan MacAskill, 1817, 222; Capt.
Allan builds neo-Gothic house at, 223;
Calgary 'Castle' resented by Maclaines, 223;
inherited by Hugh MacAskill, 224; DMWS
visits, 236; Capt. Allan dies at C., 258; 27
families removed from C., 274

Callachilly LB until 1804; dinner held at Inn
of, to celebrate LM's purchase of Jarvisfield,
which included C., 214

Calliach D/A in 18th C., 89; eight families
removed, c.1814, 194; 198: n.13

Calve (Island) D/A, at Tobermory – island
a better place for building village, 190; 397

Camus (Kilfinichen) LB, bought by
MacLachlans of Killiemore early 19th C.

Carsaig PG property (MacGilvras) until
1781, but under terms of wadset similar to
AMB's conditions; transferred to Dr
Alexander Maclean of PX; stone from C.
used for new house at LB, 154; C. for sale
by PX family, 222; DMWS goes to C. in
summer vacation, 235; C. (house) impossible
to make comfortable, 237

Carvolg Pendicle sett with Beach in 1748,
138

Catchean (Ross of Mull) Argyll estate, part
of planned development of fishing in Ross,
215; poverty of C. in 1840s, 354; rents
raised and land reduced, 355

Cillchroisd, Gilchrist D/A, parish of
Kilninian and Kilmore, 89; becoming waste
in 1748, 139

Clachandow (Torosay) D/A, alternative
name for Lochdonhead; postmaster at C.
distributes *Gaelic Messenger*, 196;
schoolmaster leaves post, being adherent of
Free Church, 333

Colonsay (Little) D/A until 1801, when RM
buys island, 200

Corkamull D/A, close to Lagganulva, and
subject to boundary disputes in 18th C.

Corrynachenchy Township of LB; C. as
example of Mull township, 134; northern
limit of LMD's neighbourhood; heather
burning on hill at C., 315; LMD compiles
list of 50 inhabitants of, 1829, 316

Cragaig (Ulva) List of tenants in, 207

Craignure (Torosay) D/A and LB; boundary
of two estates runs through present-day C;
name C. not found in rentals, C. only comes
into prominence with church and Inn;
village at 'Scallastle' recommended by
surveyor, cannot be developed by LB
trustees due to GM's long lease, 216;
sermon on solar eclipse preached in church
at C., 185; English language service at C.,
197; CM and Marianne attend church in
deep mourning after LM's death, 255; Rev.
Neil Maclean preaches at C., 257; Possils
generous supporters of church at, 310; fine
manse built at C., 331; Mrs MacDougall's
Inn at C., 362–3; wedding at Inn at C., 366

Crannich D/A property in south Aros lot.

Creich (Ross of Mull) Argyll estate; new
village planned at C., 191; road from
Achnacraig to C. planned, 215; a 'remarkable
good natural harbour', 215; poverty of C. in
1840s, 354; rents raised and land reduced,
355

Croggan LB estate at entrance to Loch Spelve

Cuin (Quinish) Coll estate, home of
descendants of Charles Maclean, Jacobite, 44

Culbhuirg (Iona) Argyll estate; prosperous
farm rented by MacPhails from 1848, 401

Culinish (Ulva) Allan MacQuarrie ousted
from lands of, 1754, 90–1; list of tenants in,
208

Dererach (Brolass) Argyll estate (wadset
land); sett to small tenants in 1748; 138;
MacLachlans buy D. with purchase of
Killiemore, 234; LMD walks to D. from
Killiemore, 319; Ann Beaton in D.
threatened by John Killean, 337

Derrychulen, Derrinacullen Farm on D/A;
birthplace of Dugald MacPhail, 399; only
people from D. benefit from road, 216;
becomes property in turn of CM and ACP;
Donald MacPhail, father of poet, has farm of
D., 399

Derryguaig, Derrychuaig D/A, in Torosay
parish, but recorded in Kilfinichen, later in
QS parish of Salen; sett to MacKinnons from
1750; Hector Mackinnon the last tacksman
takes Tiroran (LB) in 1816–17, but ends his
tenancy in 1820s, 263: n.48

Dervaig Coll estate; Alexander Maclean in
1799 builds new village at, 99; Sandy
Campbell visits Mrs MacKenzie at D.,
296–7; people of D. happy under Macleans
of Coll, 384; crofters of D. have hill pasture
taken by Mr Forsyth, 385

Drimnin (Morvern) House of D. burned,
1746, 42; position of D., 147

Druimfin D/A, bought from Argyll trustees by Maclean of Coll, 197; Hugh Maclean of Coll builds new house at, 385

Druimgigha Torloisk estate, 181

Druimnacroish Coll estate of Quinish; Q. extended from D. to Tenga, 384

Duart Stronghold of Macleans of Duart, besieged by earl of Argyll in 1690s; castle has spacious hall in 1680, 8; garrisoned by Cromwellian forces, 14; earl of Argyll unable to approach D. by sea, 19; disarming held at D., 1716, 26; Governor Lane entertains AMLB, AMB and LMQ at D. with whisky grog, 68; 405; duke of Argyll rejects plan to keep soldiers at, 164; Duart as part of Argyll estate comes on market, 221; estate of D. to be examined by ACP, 238; purchase of D. by ACP from CM, 238; DMWS acts for CM in surprise purchase of D., 252; MM2 envious of CM's purchase of D., 252; ACP and CM agree to price for D., 256; cottars on estate of D. better off than most, 331; DMWS presses Sir Fitzroy Maclean to buy D., 403; Macleans dream of buying D., 403–4; Macleans of Duart move into restored castle of D., 404; museum of Maclean history set up at D., 404–5

Duchorin Part of D/A lands, usually referred to in charters and conveyances as 'Arivelchyne, Ardrioch and Duchorin'

Ensay Part of Torloisk estate in 1820s, 181

Eolasary (Ulva) List of tenants in, 208

Erraid Island off tip of Ross of Mull, part of church lands of Iona

Erray (Mishnish) Mishnish estate; house built by Mackinnons c.1725, 29; a 'strange confused house', 105; retained by Heir of Provision to Mishnish estates, 46; rusty parrot lives at E., 82; JB and SJ visit, 105

Fanmore Part of Torloisk estate, 181

Ferinanardry (Ulva) List of tenants in, 209

Fidden (Ross of Mull) One of the principal farms in Ross, occupied by Campbell tacksmen in 18th C.

Fionnphort (Ross of Mull) Argyll estate; village of recent development, now port of departure for Iona

Fishnish (Torosay) Second-best site for a new village on LB estate, 216; cottars at F. unwilling to work for LMD., 307; case of difficult childbirth at F., 315–16; LMD compiles list of 87 inhabitants of, 1829, 316

Fiunary (Morvern) D/A in Morvern; Macleod family in F., 196

Frachadil (Kilninian) One of principal farms on D/A in 1770s, 189; sold by duke's trustees to Allan MacAskill in 1817 as part of Mornish estate; prepared as manse and glebe for Kilninian, 330

Garmony (Torosay) Lands given to Allan Maclaine of LB by his father Hector, 1705, 27; GM gets tack of, 1751, 61; GM probably

raised at G., 61; JMLB casts envious eyes on G., 64; GM and Mally settle at G., 81; two commoners drowned at G., 1768, 101; precepts of removal issued to tenants of, 1789, 283; problem of identifying Curries in G., 283; further precepts issued in 1800, 283–4; LMD settles at G., 307; [There is no evidence of a 'superior' house at G. before building began in 1836. LMD's cottage may have been the one lived in by GM in 18th C.] cottars at G. unwilling to work for LMD, 307; lairds & ministers stay overnight with LMD at G., 309; description of fruit and vegetables grown at G., 314; people of G. quarrel like tinkers, 320; LMD has to quit G., 320; farm servants at G. perform services without payment and drink only neat whisky, 365

Gedderlie, Gederlie LB estate till 1804; becomes part of Jarvisfield when bought by LM, 1804, 214

Gilchrist (*see* **Cillchroisd**)

Glacknagallan (Ulva) List of tenants in, 208

Gleannan, Glennan D/A land in Torosay, once site of a mill and shop; LMD fishes loch at G, roup of cattle at, 366; Neil Rankin, miller at, 369: n.19

Glenbyre LB at end of hill route, Kinloch to LB, 110; house at G. falls down in storm, 273

Glencannel D/A land in centre of Mull, in tack to Stewarts of Achadashenaig from 1750.

Glenforsa LB; name assigned to estate purchased by CM under conditions of LB entail, 1804, 214; best tenantry in Mull said to have been removed from G., 214; G. to be sold to pay for CM's purchase of Duart, 254; debt on G. disclosed on CM's death, 260; MM2 influences Lachlan Macquarie Jr. to buy G., 261; G. added to Jarvisfield and bequeathed to Lord Strathallan, 386; Col Greenhill-Gardyne becomes owner of united estate, 386

Glen Forsa Name of the glen, not estate, part of LB, leased to Dr Andrew Maclaine for cattle breeding, 163; most of its inhabitants drovers; traditional inhabitants MacPhails, drovers, 399

Glengorm Modern name for combined farms conveyed to James Forsyth from parts of Mishnish and Quinish; Forsyth adorns G. with quotation from Prayer Book, 385; his son does not keep name or estate of Glengorm, 387

Glenlidle (Brolass) Bought by Archibald Maclean of PX, 1803, and later within DMWS's purchase of Kinloch.

Glen More Change in character of scenery and people when emerging from, 348

Gometra D/A in 1750 when Ardskipnish was set to small tenants; George William sells G. as soon as he inherits it [1806]; G. and Ulva seldom had same owner; crew of *Pharos* shelter at G., 179; bought by RM, 1807, 200; G. reserved for sisters of RM, 206; some evictions from G., 394

Gortenbuy With Glencannel, part of D/A lands, in tack to Stewarts of Achadashenaig.

Grass Point (Torosay) At Achnacraig, D/A property with main landing point for travellers in 18th C., 192

Gribun Descriptive name for precipitous coastline between L. na Keall and Loch Scridain, not used in sasines; LMQ moves to, 95; land in G. bought by Boisdale Macdonalds, 1803, 200

Gruline Part of LB estate until 1804; JMG becomes tacksman of, 67; farmhouse to be improved, 154; bought by LM, 1804, and becomes part of Jarvisfield, 214; CM and Marianne go to live at G., 252; LM and Elizabeth shocked by G., 253; Macquaries move into G., 1824, 254; Elizabeth improves house at G. after LM's death, 255; Elizabeth dies at G., 259; young Lachlan buried at G., 261

Gualachaoilish Former church land; sett as farm to Rev. Archibald MacTavish in 1750; reserved from sale of Killean to form manse and glebe for Torosay minister, 192; Mr Fraser dies at G., 258; 329; becomes farm again when manse is built at Craignure; Dr Donald Maclaine moves to G. with family, 1829, 311; LMD has tooth extracted at G., 318; Rev. Mr MacArthur gets farm at G., 327

Haunn D/A, part of Treshnish or Kilmaluaig farm, bought by Capt. Allan MacAskill.

Icolmkill (*see* Iona)

Inch Kenneth (Kilfinichen) Referred to as 'Inch'; its fertility extolled in 1680, 8; visit by JB and SJ, 107; possessed by Macleans of Brolass, 138; let to Lady Brolass, 1748, 138; I. goes to Charles Maclean of Drimnin & Kinlochaline, 148; bought by Macdonalds of Boisdale, 1803; LMD calls on Col. Macdonald at, 319; ferry from I. to Gribun costs LMD one shilling, 319; DMLB thinks of buying I. in 1858, 391; the most delightful spot in the Hebrides, 393

Inivea (Kilninian) D/A, Mornish, sett to small tenants in 1750; example of an extended township, 134; becoming waste land, 139; four families removed, c.1814, 194; 198: n.13; sold to Capt. Allan MacAskill in 1817 by Argyll trustees, 222; cottars of I. cleared, 330

Iona Charter of I. granted to Macleans of Duart, 4; East End sett to John Maclean 1750; West End sett to small tenants, 1750; JB and SJ arrive at, 109; 6th duke visits, 194; Rev. Neil Maclean educated by his uncle in I., 256

Jarvisfield Name given to estate bought from LB by LM, 1803, comprising Callachilly, Salen, Gruline, Gederlie, Torlochan, Kilbeg, Bentalla, 214; named for LM's late wife, Jane Jarvis; 'J' used meaning

Gruline House as in case of MM2's visit, 255; J. joined with Glenforsa estate, 386; bequeathed to Lord Strathallan in payment of debts, 386; passes to Col. Greenhill-Gardyne, 386

Java Lodge (Torosay) Formerly LB, part of Scallastle tack, near Craignure; built by DMLB for his mother and sisters, 391; demolished, 391; party at J. for coming-of-age of Murdoch Gillean Maclaine, 392

Kellan Argyll estate, north side of Loch na Keall, important for its mill

Kengharair Torloisk estate, let to Maclaine family (Callachilly); later factor's house, 181

Kilbeg LB until 1804, when sold to LM under terms of entail, 214; Hugh Morison, tenant in K., 278

Kilbrenan Torloisk estate, 181; open bidding for, after funeral of Flora Maclean, 184; LMD rides to K. to visit Macleans, 309

Kilfinichen Statistical account of the parish of, 1790s, 116–7; Maria Maclean inhabits house at, 148; roup at, 149; teachers in K. join Free Church, 332; population in 1791, 348; food distributed in K., 351

Killean Church lands associated with pilgrim route to Iona – its acquisition by Campbells, 73:n.11; Maxwell and Ferrier persuade MM to support manse and glebe at K., 192; farm of K. 'kept out of the hands of the Roman Catholics', 192; Mull ministers go to K. to measure land for manse and glebe, 327

Killiechronan One of principal farms of D/A on Loch na Keill; 189; CM buys K. for LM, 222; CM asks LM to swap K. for Glenforsa property, 253; LM wishes his son to have K., 253; 43 families removed from, c.1854, 393; numerous old townships near K., 393

Killiemore (Kilfinichen) Charles Maclean of Drimnin and Kinlochaline infeft there, 1786, 148; MacLachlans buy land at K., 234; Dugald MacLachlan moves into house at, 234; LMD stays with MacLachlans at, 319

Killumar, Killuman Brolass part of Argyll estate, at Gribun; sett to small tenants, 1748, 138; to Charles Maclean 1786, 148

Killunaig (Brolass) Argyll estate; sett to Donald Maclean in 1748, 138

Kilmaluaig (or Treshnish) D/A; sold with Mornish by Argyll trustees to Capt. MacAskill, 222

Kilmore Old parish, joined with Kilninian, on JB and SJ's route to Ulva, 106

Kilmory Part of Torloisk estate, 181

Kilninian Statistical account of the parish of K. (and Kilmore), 1790s, 115–6; services still exacted in parish, 116; part of Torloisk estate, 181; minister of Kilninian refused farm at K., 181; 186: n.39

Kilpatrick (Brolass) The boundary between Brolass and Ross was the Lealt burn; K. the 'worst spot in Brolass', 46; sett to A. Macdonald, Tiree, 138; Charles Maclean of Drimnin infeft in, 148

Kilpatrick (Torosay) D/A, one of duke's farms in Torosay in 1770s, 189; becomes part of CM's estate, then of ACP's; typhus fever at K., 311

Kilvicheoun (Ross of Mull) Statistical account of the parish of (with Kilfinichen), 116–7; linked to other Ross townships by a track, 302; tenants of farm of K. in 1662, 346; population in 1791, 348

Kilvickewan (Ulva) List of tenants in, 207

Kingharair (see Kengharair)

Kinloch(scridain) Possessed by John Maclean ('Killean') 1748, 138; exposed for sale by Macleans of Pennycross, 222; DMWS known as 'Kinloch', 230; K. sold, 1860, to DMLB, 243; 355; 391; over 200 people in K. in 1861 (after exodus), 348; history of K's troubles, 355; the Mitchell brothers in K., 355

Kinlochspelve LB; 'Flu epidemic at, 212; problem of identifying Duncan Currie in K., 283; Gaelic insisted upon in school at, 387; children have no English, 387

Kintra (Ross of Mull) Argyll estate; new fishing village planned at K., 191; road from Achnacraig to Catchean planned to help fishing, 215; poverty of fisherman in K., 348

Knock D/A; one of principal farms in 1770s, 189; retained by Argyll family; Col. Campbell's at K. a hospitable house, 193; LM and wife stay at K. when Gruline is unfit, 253; Lord John Campbell expected to buy K., 254

Knockan (Ross of Mull) Argyll estate; Mary MacDougall, poet, dies at K., 302

Knocknafenaig As example of township, 134; tenants give evidence about treatment by factor, 352–3

Knockroy LB lands given to Lachlan Maclaine (father of MM) by his father, Hector, 1705, 27; possible childhood home of MM, 75; considered a good site for a village by surveyor, 216

Knockvologan (Ross of Mull) Argyll estate; MacIntyres become tenants of, 393

Lag D/A, Mornish, 89; sold by Argyll trustees to Capt. MacAskill, 1817, 222

Laggan LB estate; LMD sees 'a substantial good farmhouse' being built at, 319

Lagganulva Squabbles over lands of, between Macdonalds and Macleans of Torloisk, 177; part of Torloisk, 181; FWC does not want to buy L., 260

Langamull D/A, Mornish estate, rented mainly to Torloisk family, 181; MMT's factor offered house at, 181

Ledirkle Near Fishnish, added to GM's tack, 1751, 61; precepts of removal issued to tenants of L., 1789, 283; sheriff issues further precepts in L, 1800, 283–4; Marie, GM's widow, retires to L., 287; Mary Fletcher in L. gives birth to Sir Archibald Maclaine's natural son, 288; 292: n.37; Sandy Campbell visits L., 294–296; LMD stays at

L., 306; LMD compiles list of 38 inhabitants of, 1829, 316; carpenter's boat at L. destroyed in storm, 317; shintie played at L. at Christmas Old Style, 319

Ledmore D/A on Loch Frisa; with Ledbeg, sett to small tenants in 1748; birthplace of Dr Hector McColl, 323: n.33

Lee (Ross of Mull) Argyll estate; Baptist pastor moved to L., 349; 353

Leob Argyll estate, near Kilpatrick, on borders of Ross and Brolass; home of the poet Donald Maclean, 336

Lettermore D/A, conveyed to Macleans of Coll, 1820s

Little Colonsay D/A until 1801; LMQ takes lease of, living in his 'hermitage', 95; RM buys island, 200

Loch Ba Boundary loch between Gruline [LB, later sold to LM] and Argyll land at Knock; LM sends black swans to CM for Loch B., 250

Lochbuy Name of estate, of village, and of house; later houses continue to be called 'Moy', from name of castle; LB the best harbour in Mull in 1680, 8; advice to tenants in, 1764, 87; MM oversees management of, 151; plan of management for, 153; new mansion house built by John Stevenson, 154; AM and his wife Janet visit LB, 160; tenants asked to volunteer for fencibles, 213–4; sheep farming not understood in LB, 216; dinner party at LB, 239; Dr Whiteside at LB, 342; 367; MM3 ignores plight of people in LB, 371–2; Miss Catherine pays rent at LB and retains a cottage at, 392; LB lost to Maclaines when Sir Stephen and Lady Gatty raise action in 1919 for non-payment of interest on a loan, for which LB was security, 395–6: n.43

Lochdonhead D/A; after Possil's purchase of estate, L. has large number of Free Church adherents, 332; blacksmith at L. lends shed for worship of dissenters, 332; tent in the gravel pit erected at L., 333; Mull poet, Dugald MacPhail living at L., 333; Allan Lamont schoolmaster at L., 401

Loch Frisa On D/A land, later conveyed to Macleans of Coll

Loch na Keill Farms on coast of coveted by LM, 250–51

Loch Scridain JB and SJ visit Ardchrishnish on Loch S., 109; Kinloch's position on, 230

Loch Spelve Sea loch with LB and Argyll properties on its shores

Lussafoot (Torosay) Macphails removed from Glenforsa to L., 214

Mingary (Kilmore) Quinish; Sandy Campbell visits Hector Maclean at M., 298–9

Mishnish Territory of Mackinnons in Mull; John Dubh Mackinnon attainted 1715, imprisoned 1746, for participation in Jacobite uprisings; another John Mackinnon ['Mishnish'] made Heir of Provision for duration of forfeiture; estate sold privately by him in 1751; Mishnish regained for Charles M., heir of line, who sells it in 1774 to John Campbell of Knock, 210: n.16; 397

Mornish (Kilninian) Families cleared from, c.1814, 194; 198: n.13; bought from Argyll trustees by Capt. Allan MacAskill, 197; Capt. Allan makes Hugh MacAskill his heir, 224; Hugh removes people from townships of M., 224

Moy LB; Moy House built by JMLB, 1752, 49; doubt about the Grandfather living at Castle of M., 55; Hector Killean forces doors of, 60; JB and SJ visit M., view dungeon, 110–12; AMLB refuses to repair castle of M., 120; GM removes papers from M., 154–5; 247–8; AMLB grants lease of house to MM, 167; gardener's plans for planting at M., 219

Ormaig (Ulva) GM advises MacQuarries of O. to sell land, 78; Ormaig to be sold, 79; CM baptised at, 245; lists of tenants in, 207

Ormsaig (Brolass) Once lived in by Macleans of Brolass, 138; Charles Maclean of Drimnin infeft in, 148

Oskamull D/A; LM's family move to, 246; reported as waste ground, 1748, 139; LM's mother Peggy living at O., 162; LM confined at O. with scurvy, 248

Penalbanach On Mishnish estate, sold by Charles MacKinnon to Campbells of Knock 1774; Fletchers in P. a talented family, 333; Dugald MacPhail serves apprenticeship in P., 399

Penmollach Name often interchangeable with Quinish, estate of Macleans of Coll

Penmore (Kilninian & K.) Part of D/A lands, 89; P. a township in late 18th C., 134; land leased by Torloisk Macleans, 145; to be used for flax, 145; sold after adjustment with Capt. Allan MacAskill, to Hugh Maclean of Coll, 222; Dr MacNab acquires P., 15 families evicted from, 393

Pennycross Originally Duart lands, granted to Beatons as physicians; due to Maclean/McGilvra marriages, and to money-lending on bond secured by land, between families, ownership of PG and PX is confusing, 150: n.30; JB and SJ visit Dr Maclean at P., 110; 337; PX put on market, 1818, 222; DMWS's involvement with PX, 231–2; DMWS wishes old houses to be cleared on road from P., 237; P. as home of Beaton physicians, 337; a tiny property, sold by Neil Beaton to Dr Alexander Maclean, 337; hungry people gather outside farm of P, 351

Pennyghael Possessed by MacGilvras/MacGilvrays of PG until 1781, but still lived in by that family; private arrangements between MacGilvrays of PG and Macleans of PX [in 1801] obscure ownership of, 150: n.30; Lady LB tries living at PG, 159; Sandy PX 'adorning' PG., 237;

new proprietor of PG, Mr Auldjo, supports Free Church, 332; PG added to PX, 338

Pennygown Old name for parish of Torosay when (now ruinous) chapel of P. was in use, 115; lands of given by Hector LB to his son John, 1705, 27; LB family lives there when Moy Castle becomes derelict, 48; home of Isabel MacDougall, 55; Dr Andrew Maclaine lives at P., 163; CM buys property, to be named Glenforsa, 1804, 214; CM lives at P., 251; Marianne his wife dislikes P., 252; LMQ dies at P., 1818, 288; LMD visits Donald Drover at Pennygown, 320

Portmore (Tobermory) Originally a farm on Mishnish estate, later part of Tobermory.

Quinish Estate of Macleans of Coll in Kilmore parish, Mull, 29; reserved for 'Young Col', 188; Sandy Campbell hears the harp played at Q., 297; Mr Forsyth buys Q., 384

Reraig R an example of a township, 134

Reudle (Kilninian parish) Part of Torloisk estate, 181

Rhoail, Rohill In Glen Forsa; part of LB estate, bought in 1804 by CM to become part of his Glenforsa estate, 214; LMD walks from R. to Ishriff, 315

Ross of Mull South western peninsula of Mull, formerly church lands of Iona Abbey; charter granted to Macleans of Duart, 4; medicinal springs in, 8; increase in population due to kelp industry, 98; farms in R. go to waste after reforms of Forbes of Culloden, 139; road planned to R., 215; people of R. go south annually for work, 280; religious dissent in, 331; teachers from R. join Free Church, 332; R. behind the rest of Mull, 347; people of R. left undisturbed in 6th duke's time, 348; Baptists increase in south of R., 349; duke agrees people must be removed, 351; consolidation of large farms in, 352; duke connives at his factor's policies, which were in fact his own, 394

Rossal LB estate; JB and SJ go to LB via Rossal, 110; R. made available for Flora Maclaine and her husband AMD, 339; called 'dear Rossal' by family of AMD, 339; tutor employed at R, 339; roup at R. in 1828, 340; R. enlarged at expense of Kinloch, 355; conditions of Macdonalds' lease in R., 368: n.5

Salen Originally LB, no village until 1800s; also name of a quoad sacra parish established 1828, taken from Torosay and Kilninian parishes; 18th C. church placed near S. because it was 'centrical' to farms, not due to population; part of LB until 1803, acquired by LM, 214; Maxwell interested in church at S., 191; LM's ambitions for Salen village, 250; LMD stays at manse of, 318; S. has Free Church at Achadashenaig in 1846, 334; road from Salen to Ulva to be made by

Irish labour, 350; focal point of
Glenforsa-Jarvisfield estate, 386; population
of 200 in 1861, 386; LM calls S. 'Port
Macquarie', 386

Salen Ruadh (Ulva)   Tenant of, in 1824, 209

Saorphein (Ross of Mull)   People from S.
lost in shipwreck on way to America, 134; S.
a 'good farm likely to be waste' in 1748,
139; once linked to other Ross townships,
302

Scallastle   Part of LB; house at S. [original,
on same site, burned down in 19th C.]
home of GM's family, who are called 'the
Scallastles'; Bay of S. used by government
ships, 1745–6, 41; farm of S. added by
stealth to GM's tack after death of
Alexander Campbell, 61; GM and Mally
move to S., 1772, 81; MM stays at S. in
summer 1784, 85; S. a 'cake-house' for
tourists, 113; surveyor recommends as best
site in Torosay for a village, 216; JC and
nine daughters move to S., 219; S.
considered an estate by Marie and Allan,
282; precepts of removal issued to tenants of
S., 1789, 283; eviction of innkeeper at S.,
284; Marjory Gregorson goes to live at S.,
287; cottars at S. unwilling to work for
LMD., 307; potatoes at S. diseased, 316;
monument to GM erected at S., 321; roup of
stock, furniture and books at S., 321; Patrick
Sellar hankers after S., 371

Scallastlebeg   LB; township of cottars
providing services for tacksman of Scallastle;
JG directs cottars of S. to pull down their
houses, 307–8

Scallastlemore   LB; township of cottars
providing kelp workers for GM; *see* above.

Scobul (Ardmeanach)   Township of LB
estate, 134; people of S. resent MM's orders,
271; tenants of S. refuse to thatch
school-house, 271

Scour (Ross of Mull)   Argyll estate,
remaining in possession of dukes of Argyll;
linked to other townships by a track, 302;
souming of S. in 1662, 346

Siaba, Shiaba (Ross of Mull)   Shipwreck off
S., 1792, 100; S. as example of township,
134; home of Mary MacDougall, 302; beauty
of S., 302; description of S. in 1662, with
souming, 346; whole population has to leave,
1847, 349

Soriby (Ulva)   List of tenants in 1824,
208–9; place of origin of LM and CM, 245

Sorne   Part of the lands of Mishnish,
Mackinnon/Campbell of Knock/Caldwell/
Stewart/Forsyth; probably on JB's and SJ's
route to Ulva, 106; example of Mull
township, 134; Mr Forsyth comes to S.,
382–3

Sound of Mull   Rev. Patrick MacArthur
drowned in, 325; boat passes down Sound
with body of
LM, 255

Sound of Ulva   Tenant's name in 1824, 209

Staffa   JB and SJ pass by S., 109; Wm.

Thornton stays in hut on S., 173; S. sold in
1816, 207

Suidhe, Suie (Ross of Mull)   Argyll estate;
tack of S. held by Allan Maclaine, father of
JMG, 67

Sunipol   Part of D/A, 89; one of principal
farms in 1770s, 189; sold, with Frachadil,
Inivea, Lag, Calgary, etc., to Capt. Allan
MacAskill in 1817, 222; Sandy Campbell
goes to S., 297; Tom Campbell tutor at S.,
297–8; 301; Gaelic school at S., 298

Tayinlone   Site of Inn serving travellers
from Salen to Ulva; LMD stops at Inn en
route for Ulva, 318

Tenga, Tangie   D/A; site of cattle fair;
populous township; sold by Argyll trustees
to Maclean of Coll, in 1817, 197; Quinish
estate extended to include T., 384

Tenga (Gribun)   Small tongue of land near
(and sett with) Balmeanach, 138; passes to
Charles Maclean of Drimnin,1786, 148

Tiraghoil, Tirghoil (Ross)   Argyll estate;
home of Fergusson family, Baptists, 349

Tirergain (Ross of Mull)   Argyll estate; in
chain of Ross townships once linked by a
track, 302

Tiroran   Farm on LB; good site for new
village, 216; schoolhouse at T. going to ruin,
271

Tobermory   Part D/A; part Mishnish
(Mackinnons); not in existence until 1789;
plan for its commercial development not
followed up, 31; harbour used by
government forces 1746, 45; JB and SJ's
impressions of, 104; marked out for building,
113; population of 300 in 1790s, 115;
Maxwell involved in planning of village,
189; drift of dispossessed begins c.1812–16,
194; description of T. in 1807, 202; fishing
neglected in, 202; T. a refugee camp, 273;
Free Church established at T., 334; violence
anticipated in T., 350–51; smallpox at T.,
368; Robert Somers investigates conditions
in T., 373–4; FWC appears in Sheriff Court
at T., 377; T. burdened with refugees, 378;
back-houses in T., 373; 379:n.19; site of T.
criticised, 397; seldom visited by strangers in
18th and early 19th C., 397; inhabitants
neat, women pretty, good English spoken in,
397; drawbacks of position of, 397–8; feuars
of T. lose grazing, 398; inhabitants reluctant
to fish, 398; new ownership of property in
T., 398; influx of dispossessed changes
character of T., 399

Tomslea   Glen Forsa; part of LB until 1804,
when sold to LM under terms of entail, 214

Torgormaig   Name used for Lower
Achnacroish, later rebuilt as Duart House,
afterwards Torosay Castle; *see* Achnacroish;
also 262: n.29

Torlochan   Part of LB until 1804, then part
of Jarvisfield; LMQ wishes to use wood from
T. for his boat, 100; LM buys T. as part of
Jarvisfield, 214

Torloisk Estate in north west Mull granted by Macleans of Duart to a kinsman, and protected from Argyll claim by separate charter and role of family of T. as tutors of Duart; humble cottage before new house was built, 145; 173; treeless site, 145; 173; spinning school set up at T. [by Miss Mary Maclean], 145; estate of T. supervised by Archibald Maclean, 170; LMT builds house, 1782, 170–72; T. on dry platform, 173; hospitality at T., 173–4; MMT imports soil for T., 181; MMT worried about legal ownership of, 181; 60 families on T. estate in 1820s, 182; inhabitants of T. go to Kilbrenan funeral, 182–3; names of tenants in T., 185: n.9; LMD coldly received at T., 309; listens to harp at, 310; evictions carried out at T, 394

Tormore (Ross of Mull) Granite quarry; workers receive croft land, provoking resentment in crofters, 359: n.32

Torosay (parish) Statistical account of parish of, 1790s, 115; LMD finds parish register is missing, 320; nature of people of T., 333; outsider surnames in T., 347

Torosay Castle House on site known as Torgormaig or Achnacroish; John Campbell of Possil makes plans for a grander house, 333

Torranbeg (Brolass) Under wadset arrangement with Argyll estate, so that Maclean tacksmen, not Campbells, control Brolass; sett to Hector Maclean, 1748, 138

Torrans (Brolass) *See* above; plural form (in English) of the two townships, Torranbeg and Torranuachtrach, and referred to as 'the Torrans'; Charles Maclean of Drimnin and Kinlochaline infeft in, 1786, 148; sold to Archibald Maclean of PX, 1801, due to be auctioned in 1818, 222; collective name, 304: n.36; tacksman of T. supports Free Church, 333; population of T. in 1861, 348

Torranuachtrach (Brolass) *See* above; populous township, sett to Hector Maclean [Hector Torran] 1748, 138; birthplace of Mary MacDougall, author of *Child in the Manger*, 301–2

Tostary Part of Torloisk estate, 181

Treshnish Part of D/A [Kilmaluaig], 89; becoming waste ground, 1748, 139; one of principal farms in 1770s, 189; tacksman's complaints, 195; sold to Capt. MacAskill by Argyll trustees, 222; Sandy Campbell visits T., 298

Uisken (Ross of Mull) Port planned in 19th C., road from Bunessan begun by statute labour, 1848, 351

Ulva Property of MacQuarries, 29; U. and Gometra have different owners, 7; U. sold to Dugald Campbell, Charles Campbell, and Colin Macdonald, 89; transferred to Ranald Macdonald, 89; U.'s greatest asset kelp, causing population increase, 97–8; nothing worthy of observation in U., 107; sale of U. deliberately postponed by LMQ, 175; Ulva House one of four hospitable houses in Mull, 193; complications of sale of U., 199; poor tenants go to America, c.1802–4, 200; island becomes showpiece, 200–5; difference between cottars and tenants in U., 201–2; 205; Walter Scott visits U., 203–4; estate transferred to ownership of Sir Henry Steuart, 206; on market at high price, 206; population of, 1824, 206; names of tenants of, 1824, 207–9; CM offers for U., 207; value of kelp in U. in 1824, 209; sequestration of tenants of U. a cause of dispute between DMWS and MM2, 241–2; no buyers for U. when advertised, 251; renewed effort to sell U., 1824, 255; description of extent of lands, 255–6; CM buys U., 1825–6, 256; CM's flitting to U., 257; Neil Maclean appointed minister of, 1828, 257; CM compassionate towards people of U., 259; estate of U., found burdened with debt at CM's death, 260; people of U. to pay arrears of rent, 260; MM2's role as executor of estate of U., 260; RM helps poor people to emigrate to America, 269; Sandy Campbell visits U., 296; LMD stays ten days with CM at, 318–19; reasons for large number of Macdonalds in U., 347; FWC as proprietor of U., 374–9

Ulvalt (Brolass) Farm in tack of Sir Allan Maclean, but controlled by Argyll estate, sett to small tenants in 1748, 138; later tenanted by Macdonalds and Mackinnons; Charles Maclean of Drimnin and Kinlochaline infeft in, 148; MacLachlans buy Kilfinichen land including U., 234

Index of Personal Names

b. = born or baptised.

c. = approximate date of birth or death calculated
from age on another given date.

d. = died

fl. = floruit – flourished at this date, or between this span of dates
(where life dates are not known).

n.k. = unidentified. Kings & Queens in caps.

For abbreviations of names of principal characters *see* Abbreviations page.

Abercorn, Lady (1763–1827), friend of Sir Walter Scott, 203

Agnew, Rev. John (fl. 1786), guardian of Barbara Maclaine in London, 131, 135n.

Allan, Alexander (1780–1854), ship owner, in emigrant trade to Canada, 395n.

Allan, Alexander (1844–1927), proprietor of Aros estate and part of Tobermory, 386, 395n.

Allan, Bryce (d. 1874), steamship owner, proprietor of Aros, 386, 395n.

Amherst, Jeffrey (1717–1797), governor general of British North America, 60

Anderson, James (fl. 1773), merchant in Boston, 267

Andrew, George (fl. 1790), lawyer in Edinburgh, 248

ANNE (1665–1714), 32

Arnold, Benedict (1741–1801), American patriot in attack on Quebec, later joining British, 83

Auldjo, John (fl. 1830s & 1840s), of Pennyghael, son-in-law of William MacGillivray, 197, 332, 393

Baillie, Joanna (1762–1851), poetess, dramatist of *The Family Legend*, 203

Banks, Sir Joseph (1743–1820), explorer, visitor to Staffa in 1772, 109, 112

Beaton, Ann (fl. 1720–1730), sister of Malcolm Beaton of Pennycross, 337

Beaton, Edmond (d. 1758–9), of Pennycross, 337

Beaton, Rev. John (c. 1645–1708) minister of Kilninian, 22

Beaton, Malcolm (d. 1718), of Pennycross, 337

Beaton, Neil (d. c. 1768), of Pennycross, 337, 343n.

Beton, James (fl. 1662), tenant in Assapol, 347

Beusechem, Catherine Cornelia van (d. 1840), wife of Gillean Maclaine, grandson of GM, 388

Black, Alexander (fl. 1770–1789), subtenant in Ledirkle, 283

Black, Duncan (fl. 1770–1789), subtenant in Ledirkle, 283

Black, Duncan (fl. 1800–1830s), shoemaker in Glasgow and Tobermory, 398

Black, Effy (b. 1740s), married Donald Lamont, Ulva, mother of Angus L., Iona, 405n.

Black, Margaret (c. 1797–1882), wife of John MacCormick in Iona, 358–9n.

Blackie, John Stuart (1809–1895), professor of Greek at EU, 399

Blair, Moggie (fl. 1745), landlady in the Canongate, Edinburgh, 44–5

Blair, William (b. 1800), factor to James Forsyth, 385, 394n.

Blaw, John (c. 1692–1767), Jacobite, 45

Bonaparte, Napoleon (1769–1821), emperor of the French, 270

Boswell, Alexander (1706–1782), of Auchinleck, father of JB, 28

Boswell, James (1740–1795), JB, biographer of Dr Johnson, 24, 49, 66, 71, 82, 91, 93, 96, 99, 104–12, 126, 134, 137, 138, 141, 148, 174, 199, 200, 222, 265, 337, 397

Boyter, Dr David (1788–1850), in charge of famine relief in Mull, 350–2

Breadalbane, Lord (1762–1834) [John Campbell] 248

Browne, Mary, (d. 1717), first wife of 2nd D. of A., 23, 32

Buchanan, Anne (b. 1777), half-sister of LMD, wife of Donald Currie, joiner, 314, 322n., 317

Buchanan, George (1777–1870), half-brother of LMD, in Tobermory, later in Colonsay, 399

Buchanan, Hector Macdonald, WS (d. 1828), brother of RM, 203, 268–71

Buchanan, Hugh (c. 1774–1850), half-brother of LMD, 316

Buchanan, Hugh (b. c. 1819), son of George Buchanan, nephew of LMD, 318

Buchanan, John (b. 1729), husband of Janet MacPhail, LMD's mother , 306

Buchanan, John (1808–1848), from Ardchoirk, husband of Mary McKillop, 366

Burgoyne, John (1722–1792), British general in American revolutionary war, 70, 71, 119

Burn, William (1789–1870), architect of Aros House, formerly Druimfin, 385

Burnett, Dr John J. (1857–1938), architect for restoration of Duart Castle, 404

Burns, Robert (1759–1796), poet, 294

Burt, Captain Edmund (d. 1765), writer, road contractor, 31, 55, 75, 172, 183, 278–80, 362

Caille, Monsieur (fl. 1784), French official at Dunkirk, 126

Cameron, Catherine (d. 1835), of Glendessary, wife of Alexander Maclean 15th of Coll, 297, 328

Cameron, Sir Ewen (1629–1719), of Lochiel, 15–16, 26

ARGYLL, DUKES & EARLS OF:

Campbell, Archibald (1576–1638), 7th earl, 7

Campbell, Archibald (1607–1661), 8th earl and marquis (Gillespie Gruamach), 4, 7, 13–17

Campbell, Archibald (1629–1685), 9th earl, 15–18, 346

Campbell, Archibald (d. 1703), 10th earl and 1st duke, 17, 19, 23

Campbell, Archibald (1682–1761), 3rd duke, formerly Earl of Ilay, 23, 37, 40, 91, 145, 194

Campbell, George Douglas (1823–1900), 8th duke, 348, 349, 351, 358n., 372

Campbell, George William (1768–1839), 6th duke, 144, 164, 180, 188, 193–4, 196, 197, 203, 204, 221, 250, 252, 297, 348, 349, 358n. 391

Campbell, John (1678–1743), 2nd duke, 17, 23–5, 28–9, 32–7, 39–40, 193, 301

Campbell, John (d. 1770), of Mamore, 4th duke, 37, 40, 42, 44, 86

Campbell, John ('Jack') (1723–1806), 5th duke, 16, 40, 98, 112, 132, 140, 141–2, 164–6, 175, 188–90, 193, 194, 196, 325, 327, 329, 347, 348, 378, 397

Campbell, John Douglas (1777–1847), 'Lord John' later 7th duke, 188, 222, 254, 349, 384, 394 & n.

Campbell, John Douglas Sutherland (1845–1914), 9th duke, governor-general of Canada, as marquis of Lorne, 392

Campbell, Alexander (fl. 1690s–1740s), of Kirnan, 39, 101, 301

Campbell, Alexander (d. 1756), tenant of Scallastle, 61

Campbell, Alexander (1764–1824), 'Sandy', 'the Organ Grinder'; compiler of *Albyn*, 293–302, 303n., 307

Campbell, Alexander (d. 1828), 'the Old Fox' in Achnacraig, 252, 257, 320

Campbell, Alexander (fl. 1790), schoolmaster in Laggan, on LB estate, 328, 334n.

Campbell, Col. Alexander (1778–1847), ACP, 'Possil', of Possil and Achnacroish, 197, 225, 238, 256, 281, 310–12, 319, 326, 331, 332, 333, 366, 372, 384, 403

Campbell, Alexander (b. 1821) 'Sandy', son of Donald C., 362

Campbell, Archibald (1696–1777), AC, of Stonefield, chamberlain of Argyll estate, justice-depute of Argyll, 6, 28, 32–6, 41, 42, 153, 279, 324

Campbell, Archibald (fl. 1740), tacksman of Killiechronan, half-brother to Stonefield , 44

Campbell, Col. Archibald (d. 1840), son of John C. of Knock, 315–16, 323n.

Campbell, Archibald (c. 1750–1790), army captain, tenant of Sunipol in 1780s, 303n.

Campbell, Capt. (fl. 1820s), Ardnacross, 255

Campbell, Caroline (1717–1794), dau. of 2nd D. of A., later countess of Dalkeith, 36

Campbell, Charles (fl. 1760s–80s), of Barbreck, 89, 93, 199

Campbell, Colin (1747–1806), tacksman of Achnacroish, 249

Campbell, Colin (1772–1848), of Jura and Craignish, father-in-law of LM Jr., 261

Campbell, Colin (fl. 1796), in Achnacraig, 285

Campbell, Colin (b. c. 1780), of Kintraw , husband of Jane Maclaine of LB, 390, 395n.

Campbell, Donald (d. 1775), of Airds, chamberlain of Mull, 138, 153, 189

Campbell, Donald (fl. 1747), tacksman of Knock, 44

Campbell, Col. Donald (b. c. 1764), of Mishnish, son of John C. of Knock, 181, 193, 253, 382

Campbell, Capt. Donald (c. 1783–1870), factor of Quinish, 274

Campbell, Donald (1785–1841), husband of Eliza Maclaine of LB, 252, 259, 329, 342, 362, 368n.

Campbell, Rev. Donald (1786–1855), minister of Ross, 239, 274, 331, 351

Campbell, Donald (b. 1829), son of Colin C. and Jane Maclaine of LB, 395n.

Campbell, Dugald (fl. 1770s), of Achnaba, purchaser of Ulva, 89, 199

Campbell, Rev. Dugald (1746–1824), minister of Ross, 115, 116–17, 191, 239, 298, 348

Campbell, Dugald (fl. 1760s–1835), in Knock, 260

Campbell, Duncan (1707–c. 1790), chamberlain of Mull and Morvern, 113, 172, 189

Campbell, Duncan (fl. 1747), innkeeper at Aros, 43

Campbell, Duncan, (b. 1766 d. after 1816), tacksman of Treshnish, in Sunipol in 1815, 194–5, 298, 304n.

Campbell, Duncan (b. c. 1814), in Knocknafenaig, 353, 359n.

Campbell, Elizabeth Henrietta (1788–1835), of Airds, wife of LM, 154, 211, 218, 250–5, 258–9, 338, 342, 392

Campbell, Farquhar (1820–1881), son of Farquhar C., proprietor of the Aros estate from 1856, 386

Campbell, Flora (b. c. 1806), wife of John Campbell of Ardmore in Islay ('Factor Mor'), 349

Campbell, Grizel (b. 1772 fl. 1816), dau. of John C. tacksman of Frachadil, wife of Duncan Campbell, Treshnish, 304n.

Campbell, Hector (fl. 1750s), in Rossal, 58

Campbell, Hector (fl. 1835), factor to CM in Ulva, 260

Campbell, Isabella (d. 1837), second wife of Colin C. of Boisdale, mother of RM, 89, 199, 205, 206

Campbell, Isabella Hamilton Dundas, (fl. 1830s), dau. of Colin C., Jura, wife of Lachlan Macquarie Jr., 184, 261

Campbell, James (d. 1731), of Stonefield, justice-depute of Argyll, 24, 26, 28, 40

Campbell, Jane Phoebe (d. 1800), of Stonefield, 'Lady Airds', mother of JC, 153, 157

Campbell, Jane (c. 1761–1824), of Airds, JC, wife of MM, 153, 154, 156, 160, 161, 162, 211–12, 216, 218, 220, 236, 247, 249, 250, 251, 253; death of 255, 310, 338, 343, 370, 392

Campbell, Jane (b. 1820), dau. of Eliza Maclaine of LB and Donald C., Mrs Charles Maclean, 241

Campbell, Jean (b. c. 1789), dau. of Capt. Archibald C. in Sunipol, 304n.

Campbell, John (fl. 1729), Catholic priest visiting Kilninian, 324

Campbell, Captain John (fl. 1770s), of Ardnacross, in America in 1773, 267

Campbell, John (c. 1750–1795), precentor in Edinburgh, friend of Burns, brother of Sandy C., 294

Campbell, John (c. 1727–1808), of Knock and Mishnish, 46, 116, 190, 222, 249, 320, 394n.

Campbell, Sir John (d. 1788), of Airds, father of JC, 153

Campbell, Sir John (1767–1834), of Airds, brother of JC, 214, 249, 255, 256, 342, 345n.

Campbell, John WS (fl. 1790), 'that villan',[perhaps JC of Smiddygreen] 161, 166–7, 216

Campbell, John (1816–1885), younger of Possil, 'Johnnie', or 'the Dragoon', 311, 322n., 315, 333, 385

Campbell, John (1800–1872), of Ardmore in Islay, 'Factor Mor', 349–57, 385, 387, 393, 394

Campbell, John Maclaine (b. 1826), son of Colin C. and Jane Maclaine of LB, 395n.

Campbell, John (1831–fl. 1894), son of Duncan C. crofter in Dervaig, witness in 1883, 1894 enquiries, 378, 394n.

Campbell, Kenneth (c. 1795–1875), proprietor of Ardow, 224

Campbell, Marion (c. 1700–1764), mother of JMG, 67

Campbell, Mary (d. 1762), mother of LMT, AM, etc., of Torloisk, 76

Campbell, Mary (fl. 1830s), dau. of Colin C. of Jura, sister-in-law of Lachlan Macquarie Jr., 261

Campbell, Murdoch (1822–1834), son of Donald C., 362

Campbell, Neil (b. c. 1750), son of Alexander C. in Scallastle, later sheriff of Dumbarton, 65

Campbell, Dr Neil (b. 1786, fl. 1830), sixth son of John C., tacksman of Frachadil, 315

Campbell, Robert (fl. 1700–1745), biographer of John, 2nd duke of Argyll, 17

Campbell, Robert (fl. 1750s–1800s), sheriff-depute of Argyll, 205, 283

Campbell, Susan (b. 1813), dau. of ACP, LMD's flame, 311

Campbell, Susanna (fl. 1730–1760s), widow of Alexander C. in Scallastle, 62, 65

Campbell, Susanna (fl. 1760s), of Airds, 76

Campbell, Thomas (1777–1844), poet, tutor in Mull in 1795, 297, 301, 302, 304n.

Campbell, Thomas (fl. 1800–1830s), brother of ACP, 366

Campbell, Walter F. (1798–1855), of Islay, MP for Argyll, 367

Carr, Sir John (1772–1832), writer, traveller in Mull in 1807, 98, 192, 200–2

Chamberlain, Mr (fl. 1836), friend of LB family, guest of LMD in Oban, 367

Chantreau, Pierre Nicolas (fl. 1770–1800), 'Citoyen Chantreau', 113–14

Choffard, Pottineau (fl. 1784), French consul in Jamaica, 126

CHARLES II (1630–1685), 14, 15, 16, 17, 18

Clark, Clementina (1810–1880), sister of FWC, wife of Rev. Neil Maclean, 378

Clark, Rev. Duncan (1790–1878), minister of Torosay, 320, 331

Clark, Francis (1778–1851), father of FWC, 375

Clark, Francis W. (1801–1887), FWC, proprietor of Ulva, 149, 185, 260, 275, 281, 354, 372, 374–9, 381, 387, 393, 394, 399

Clark, Francis William Jr. (1827–1886), son of FWC, 377, 387, 396n.

Clark, Francis William 3rd (1858–1935), of Ulva, grandson of FWC, 377

Cleland, Mr, alias of Sir Hector Maclean of Duart during 1745 uprising.

Clephane, Anna Jane Maclean (b. c. 1794), dau. of MMT, 180, 182, 185, 300, 309, 322n., 310

Clephane, Margaret Douglas Maclean (c. 1791–1830), of Torloisk, later Lady Compton, Marchioness of Northampton, 178–80, 181, 182, 220, 232, 282, 297, 300–1, 304n., 309, 322n.

Clephane, Mrs, *see* Maclean, Marianne

Clephane, Gen. William Douglas Maclean (c. 1760–1803), of Carslogie, husband of MMT, 176, 285

Clephane, Wilmina Maclean (b. 1803), dau. of MMT, 180, 300, 309

Clinton, Sir Henry (1738–1795), commander-in-chief of forces in North America, 84

Cobbett (fl. 1653), Cromwellian officer, 14

Coffin, Sir Edward Pine (1784–1862), commissary general, director of famine relief operation, 371, 379n.

Compton, Charles Douglas Maclean (b. 1816), of Kirkness and Torloisk, 180, 393

Compton, Lady Mary Anne, dau. of Lord Compton and Margaret, dau. of MMT, 309

Compton, Spencer Joshua Alwyne (1790–1851), later marquis of Northampton, 178–80, 282, 300, 303n., 309

Compton, William (b. 1818), son of Lord
Compton and Margaret, dau. of MMT, 180

Cornwallis, Gen. Charles (1738–1805), earl of
C., commander (under Clinton) in North
America, 84

Crawford, Alexander (1809–1856), of Aros,
son-in-law of DMWS, 242, 266, 385–6, 393

Cromwell, Oliver (1599–1658), Protector, 14,
18

Cromwell, Richard (1626–1712), son of Oliver
C., 15

Cumberland, William Augustus, duke of
(1721–1765), son of GEORGE II,
commander at Culloden, 41–2

Cumstie, William (c. 1805–1859), shopkeeper in
Oban, 395

Currie, Alexander (fl. 1770–1789), subtenant in
Ledirkle, 283

Currie, Donald (b. 1763), joiner in Balifraoich,
husband of Anne Buchanan, LMD's sister,
314, 316–7, 319

Currie, Duncan (fl. 1765–1800s), subtenant in
Ledirkle, 283

Currie, Duncan (fl. 1770–1803), tenant in New
Kinlochspelve, 212, 283

Currie, Gillean (1822–1916), son of Donald C.
and Anne Buchanan, 317

Currie, Hector, or McVurich (fl. 1770–1789),
tenant in Garmony, 283

Currie, Hector (1818–1906), son of Donald C.,
joiner in Balifraoich, 317

Currie, Isabella (b. 1810), [wife of John
Currie, Tavool] dau. of Donald C. and Anne
Buchanan, 317

Currie, Janet *see* Livingstone, Janet

Currie, John (1758–1828), schoolmaster in
Ulva, 296, 303n.

Currie, John (fl. but probably dying in 1803),
213

Currie, John (fl. 1770–1789), workman and
tenant in Scallastle, 283

Currie, John (fl. 1775–1800), subtenant in
Garmony, 283–4

Currie, John (fl. 1824), in Ballameanach, 183

Currie, Lachlan (b. 1813), son of Donald Currie
and Anne Buchanan, 317

Currie, Marion (c. 1755–1855), donor of LMD's
very fine goose Elizabeth, 310

Currie, Mary (fl. 1824), sister of John C. in
Ballameanach, 184

Currie, Malcolm (fl. 1770–1789), tenant in
Garmony, 283

Currie, Malcolm (fl. 1775–1800), subtenant in
Garmony [perhaps same as above] 283–4

Currie, Peggy (b. c. 1775), in Ishriff, wife of
Malcolm Black, 315

Cuthbertson, Robert (fl. 1790–1832), fishery
officer in Tobermory from 1814, 398

Daniell, William (1769–1837), landscape
painter, 200, 397, 398

Defoe, Daniel (1660–1731), as anonymous
author of *Use and abuse* ..., 155

Dickson, Mary (fl. 1720–1760), wife of Daniel
Maclean of the Duart family, 143

Dorcas (fl. 1784), a 'negro wench' bought by
AMLB, 132

Douglas, Heron & Co., bankers, proprietors of
the Ayr Bank [crashed 1772], 81

Drummond, William Henry (1811–1886), later
Lord Strathallan, 261, 386, 394

Duff, Capt. Robert (fl. 1746), captain of HMS
Terror, 40, 41

Emerson, Captain (fl. 1645), governor of the
garrison at Duart, 14

Faujas de Saint Fond, B. (1741–1819),
geologist, author, 113, 132, 172–4, 176, 189,
200, 202

Ferguson, Adam (1723–1816), professor of
philosophy at EU, 63

Ferguson, Rev. Alexander (1790–1833), tutor
in house of Hector Maclean, later minister of
Tobermory, 299

Ferguson, Malcolm (1835–1920), son of
Alexander F., crofter in Iona, 353, 359n.

Fergusson, Duncan, (1800–1882), Baptist
preacher in Ross, 349, 353

Ferrier, James WS (1744–1829), agent for D.
of A., [father of Susan F., novelist] 189,
192, 194, 219, 222

Fletcher, Catherine, *see* Maclean, Catherine

Fletcher, Donald (1808–1884), road contractor,
sheriff officer, postmaster at Lochdonhead,
333

Fletcher, John (fl. 1740s–1760s), foster-father of
Mally Maclaine, 55

Fletcher, John (fl. 1770–1789), subtenant in
Ledirkle, 283–4

Fletcher, John, Junior (fl. 1800), in Ledirkle, 284

Fletcher, Mary (fl. 1806), in Ledirkle, mother of
nat. dau. by Sir Archibald Maclaine, 292n.

Fletcher, Neil (fl. 1770–1789), subtenant in
Ledirkle, 283

Fletcher, Neil (c. 1800–1879), joiner in
Penalbanach, later in Salen, 399

Fletcher, Sarah (1755–1800), wife of Donald
MacPhail, 405n.

Forbes, Duncan (1644–1704) of Culloden,
father of DF, 19, 22, 26

Forbes, Duncan (1685–1747), of Culloden, DF,
friend of Duke John, 22, 32–7, 42, 43, 45,
62, 138, 235, 265

Forbes, John (b. c. 1711), of Culloden, son of
Duncan F. (1685–1747), 33–5

Forsyth, Alexander (fl. 1770–1832), writer in
Edinburgh, uncle of James Forsyth, 381

Forsyth, Caroline Harriet (1847–1930), dau. of
James Forsyth, 396n.

Forsyth, James (1801–1862), of Dunacht, later
of Glengorm, 266, 354, 372, 379n., 381–7,
394n., 393–4

Forsyth, James Noel Muller (1844–1923), of
Glengorm, later called 'of Quinish', son of
James Forsyth, 387

Fraser, Rev. Alexander (1758–1828), minister
of Torosay, 191, 192, 212, 239, 241, 255–7;
death of, 257; 318, 325, 326, 327, 329, 338,
378

Fraser, Rev. Farquhar (1606–1678), chaplain to

Sir Lachlan Maclean and minister of Tiree, 12, 23

Fraser, Rev. John (1647–1702), minister of Tiree, son of Rev. Farquhar F., 12, 23

Fraser, Rev. Paul (1731–1827), minister of Inveraray, uncle of Rev. Alexander F., 326

Fraser, Gen. Simon (1726–1782), raises Fraser's Highlanders in 1755, [later part of 84th or RHE] 114, 140

Fraser, William (b. c. 1800), London solicitor, son of Alexander F., buyer of Acharn (Morvern), 238

Fraser-Mackintosh, Charles (1828–1901), MP for Inverness, commissioner in Napier Enquiry, 384, 385

Gardyne, Charles Greenhill, *see* Greenhill-Gardyne

Garnett, Dr Thomas (1766–1802), [MD Edin., 1788] traveller in Mull, 172, 174

Gatty, Sir Stephen Herbert (1849–1922), tenant of LB, 395n.

GEORGE I (1660–1727), 24

GEORGE III (1738–1820), 72, 123, 213

Germain, Lord George (1716–1785), previously Sackville, Lord Commissioner of Trade and Plantations, 94

Giffen, Mr (fl. 1830s –1840s), partner of DMWS, 241

Gillespie, Hugh (fl. 1846 n.k.), tells MM3 shearers won't cut crop, 371

Gillies, James (b. c. 1770. fl. in 1819), gardener at Moy and Torloisk, 213, 219

Glich, Lieut. (fl. 1777), German officer on British side at Bennington, 70

Graham, Alexander (fl. 1820s), tidewaiter in Tobermory, 398

Graham, Henry Grey (c. 1843–1906), historian, 22

Graham, James (1612–1650), 5th earl and 1st marquis of Montrose, 11–15

Graham, John (1648–1689), 'Bonnie Dundee', 18

Graham, Robert (1816–1896), wheelwright, nat. son of John G., schoolmaster in Bunessan, 358n.

Graham, Robert (fl. 1820s–1830s) author of a letter on Highland Destitution, 368

Grant, Colquhoun WS (1721–1792), father of Lillias G., 42, 56, 58, 128, 142, 147, 164, 165, 218, 230, 294

Grant, Lillias (1773–1833), dau. of Colquhoun G., wife of DMWS, 147, 218, 230–1, 233, 239; death 241, 255

Greenhill-Gardyne, Lieut. -Col. Charles (1831–1923), laird of Finavon and Glenforsa, 281, 386–7

Gregorson, Angus (1735–1811), father of JG, 224, 287

Gregorson, Angus (1816–1873), factor on LB estate, 321, 370–3, 389

Gregorson, Angus (1831–1872), son of JG, 319, 323n.

Gregorson, Donald (1776–1829), brother of JG, 370

Gregorson, James (1699–1759), of Correctled, patriarch of Gregorsons of Ardtornish, 224

Gregorson, John, (1775–1846), JG, Sheriff of Mull and Morvern, 184, 198, 205, 222, 224–5, 256, 286–8, 306, 307–9, 315, 319, 321, 329, 342, 366, 367, 371, 377, 385, 399

Gregorson, Marjory (1778–1836), wife of Allan Maclaine of Scallastle, 224, 282–3, 285, 287–8, 309, 319, 320, 323n., 388

Gregorson, Peter (1787–1834), brother of JG, 307, 366

Gunning, Elizabeth (1734–1790), duchess of Argyll, wife of 5th duke, 188, 194

Guthrie, Olive Louisa Blanche, *see* Leslie, Olive Louisa Blanche

Guthrie, Walter Murray (c. 1869–1911), of Torosay Castle, or Duart House, 404

Hall, Martha (fl. 1740s–1760s), wife of Neil Beaton of Pennycross, 337

Halliday, Andrew (1781–1839), tutor at LB, later physician to William IV, 211–14, 258, 301

Hamel, Dr (fl. 1815), 'celebrated Russian traveller', 296

Hamilton, Alexander, senior (1739–1802), professor of midwifery at EU, 84

Hardie, John (fl. 1715), captain of Duart Castle, 27, 47

Hay, John, 4th marquis of Tweeddale (d. 1762), interviews Sir Hector Maclean, 44–5

Hill, Colonel John (fl. 1690), governor of Inverlochy, 18–19

Howe, Admiral Richard (1726–1799), English admiral of the fleet in American war, 70

Howe, Gen. William, (1729–1814), 5th viscount, commander in Staten Island in 1776, 70

Hume, David (1711–1776), philosopher, 37, 44

Hunter, Alexander WS (1790–1858), of Doonholm, [married Maria Maclean of Coll] 322n., 343, 345n.

Hunter, John WS (1746–1823), of Doonholm, 305, 322n.

JAMES V of Scotland (1512–1542), 4

JAMES VI of Scotland, I of England (1566–1625), 4, 5, 6

JAMES II & VII [of Scotland] (1633–1701), 17, 18, 22

Jarvis, Jane (d. 1796), first wife of LM, 249, 250

Jervis, John, Lord St Vincent (1735–1823), 163

Johnson, Samuel (1709–1784), SJ, lexicographer, 24, 48, 71, 81, 82, 91, 93, 96, 99, 104–12, 114, 115, 137, 138, 140, 141, 142, 154, 173, 174, 199, 200, 202, 222, 230, 265, 272, 293, 296, 337, 397

Kay, John (1742–1826), caricaturist, 99, 295

Kennedy, Lachlan (1849–1920), carrier, son of Charles Kennedy, crofter in Dervaig, 384, 385

Knox, Andrew (1559–1633), Bishop of the Isles, 5

Lamont, Allan (1793–1865), schoolmaster, session clerk, Torosay, later in Ontario, 196, 333, 401–3, 405n.

Lamont, Allan (b. 1833), son of Allan L., went to Ontario, 405n.

Lamont, Angus (1771–1856), son of Donald L. and Effy Black Ulva, later in Iona, 403, 405n.

Lamont, Archibald (d. 1800s), tenant in New Kinlochspelve, 212

Lamont, Archibald (b. 1838) [twin of Euphemia], son of Allan L., went to Ontario, 405n.

Lamont, Catherine (b. 1831), dau. of Allan L., went to Ontario, 405n.

Lamont, Donald (b. c.1740), merchant in Ulva, father of Angus L., guide in Iona, 405n.

Lamont, Donald (1817–1890), son of Allan L., assistant to Angus Gregorson Oban, 401

Lamont, Dugald (b. 1827), son of Allan L., went to Ontario, 405n.

Lamont, Euphemia (b. 1838) [twin of Archibald], son of Allan L., went to Ontario, 405n.

Lamont, Hugh (b. 1836), son of Allan L., went to Ontario, 405n.

Lamont, Malcolm (fl. 17–18), LMD's old blind dancing teacher, 311

Lamont, Malcolm (1760-c.1848), in Killean, Torosay Parish, 272, 405n.

Lamont, Malcolm (b. 1827), son of Allan L., went to Ontario, 405n.

Lamont, Mary (1810–1893), dau. of Angus L. in Iona, 403, 405n.

Lamont, Mary (b. 1842), dau. of Allan L., went to Ontario, 405n.

Lamont, Neil (1819–1887), second son of Allan L., [later in Renfrew] 401, 405n.

Lamont, Sarah (Marion or Sally) (b. 1823–fl. 1870), dau. of Allan L., wife of Angus MacPhail, Iona, 401, 405n.

Lane, John (fl. 1740–1770), governor of Duart Castle garrison, 68, 127, 405

Lauderdale, earl of (1616–1682) [John Maitland], Secretary of State for Scotland, 16

Learmonth, Anne (d. 1780), first wife of MM, 75–80, 84, 128, 246–7

Learmonth, Charles (fl. 1720s), father of Anne L., 75–6

Lemaitre, Charlotte (fl. 1770s–1780s), mother of AMLB's nat. son, Washington Maclaine, 131–2

Leslie, General David (d. 1682), covenanting general and opposer of Cromwell, 7, 12, 13

Leslie, Olive Louisa Blanche (1872–1945), proprietor of Torosay Castle or Duart House, 404

Lewis, Matthew 'Monk' (1775–1818), friend of 6th duke of Argyll, 194

Lillburne, John (1614–1657), political agitator, 14

Lhuyd, Edward (1660–1709), Celtic scholar, 28, 293

Liston, Robert (1794–1847), surgeon in Edinburgh, 339

Livingstone, Duncan (b. 1812), feuar in Dervaig, 385

Livingstone, Janet (c.1822–1901), servant to

Miss Catherine Maclaine of LB and wife of Hector Currie, 393

Livingstone, John (fl. 1770s), Mull emigrant in New Boston, 266

Lowther, Barbara (b. c.1768), wife of AMLB, 85, 117, 124–31, 147, 151, 159, 247

Lowther, Thomas (fl. 1760s–1780s), brother of Barbara L., 124, 130

Lowther, William (fl. 1740s–1800s), father of Barbara L., 126, 129–30, 132

McAdam, John, Lord Craigengillan (fl. 1720–1770 ?), John LB resembles him, 110

Mac Ailean, Iain (fl. 17th C.), bard, 19, 141

McAllan, Allan (fl. 1662), tenant in Kilvicheoun, 346

McAllan, Donald (fl. 1662), tenant in Kilvicheoun, 346–7

MacArthur, Alexander (c. fl. 1800- 1850s), proprietor of Ardmeanach, 354, 393

MacArthur, Rev. Archibald (1734–1810), minister of Kilninian, 115, 116, 191, 334n.

MacArthur, Archibald (c.1775–1834), piper to RM ('Staffa'), 296

MacArthur, Bell (fl. 1805–1835), dau. of Finlay M. in Garmony, 308, 322n.

MacArthur, Rev. Dr Donald (1772–1864), minister of Kilninian, 181, 184, 257, 259, 274, 330, 375

MacArthur, John (b. c.1827), proprietor of Ardmeanach, writer in Inveraray, 393

MacArthur, Rev. Patrick (c.1740–1790), minister of Torosay, 101, 115, 320, 323n., 325, 327

MacArthur, Peter (b. c.1800 ?), in Ardura, husband of Flora McLean, 341, 344n.

MacAskill, Captain Allan (1765–1828), of Calgary, Mornish, 197, 222–4, 236, 237, 251, 254, 258, 326, 334n.

MacAskill, Donald (n.k.), nat. son of Capt. Allan M., 'a young man of colour, a surgeon', 223

MacAskill, Hugh (1799–1863), 'Eoghainn Mor' of Talisker and Mornish, 224, 274, 326, 330, 394

MacAskill, Rev. Malcolm (1723–1787), minister of the Small Isles, 222, 334n.

MacAskill, Mary (1775–1866), sister and housekeeper of Capt. Allan M., 223

MacCallum, John (c.1793–1836), joiner in Tobermory, 369n., 398

MacCallum, John (1822–1909), writer in Tobermory, [pupil of DMWS in 1840s] 214, 369n., 378

McCallum, Margaret (fl. 1780–1815), wife of John Maclean, schoolmaster Ballygown, 187n.

MacCallum, Mary (d. 1837), wife of the Rev. Duncan Clark, 331, 335n.

McCarmaig, Neil [or McCormick] (fl. 1770–1789), tenant in Garmony, 283

McCartna, Ivour duy (fl. 1662), tenant in Kilvicheoun, 346

McColl, Rev. Archibald (1746–1814), minister of Tiree, 325

McColl, Dougald (fl. 1840s), parliamentary teacher in Tobermory, 274, 332

McColl, Duncan (fl. 1770s–1840s), in Dererach, schoolfellow of LMD, [father-in-law of Joseph McIntyre] 319

McColl, Duncan (fl. 1780s–1830s ?), shoemaker in Tobermory

McColl, Dr Duncan (c. 1810–1882), from Lismore, medical practitioner in Salen, 323n.

McColl, Dr Hector (1799–1891), surgeon in Tobermory, 274, 315–16, 323n., 372

MacColla, [or Macdonald] Alasdair (d. 1647), son of Coll Ciotach, ally of Montrose, 11, 12, 14

MacCormick, John (c. 1785–1879), SSPCK schoolmaster in Creich, [married to Mary Macdonald] 332

MacCormick, John (1795–1861), shoemaker, session clerk in Iona, later teacher in Catchean, 332, 358–9n.

MacCormick, Neil (1836–1925), quarry manager in Ross, husband of Annabella MacLachlan, 358–9n.

MacCrimmon, Donald (d. 1825) [Donald Ruadh MacCrimmon], 296

MacCulloch, John (1773–1835), author of A description of the Western Isles, 294

Macdonald, Alasdair Mac Mhaighstir Alasdair (c. 1695–c. 1770), poet, 45

Macdonald, Alexander (d. 1818), of Boisdale, son of Colin M., 89, 199

Macdonald, Angus (fl. 1815), cabinet-maker near Aros, 299

Macdonald, Annabella (1805–1893), dau. of John M., Knocknafenaig, wife of Donald MacLachlan, smith in Creich, 352

Macdonald, Archibald (fl. 1748), in Tiree, tenant in Kilpatrick, Brolass, 138

Macdonald, Catherine (b. c. 1725 ?), sister of Rev. Francis M., 324

Macdonald, Colin (d. 1800), of Boisdale, 89, 92, 93, 98, 116, 175, 177, 199, 281, 363

Macdonald, Colin (fl. c. 1780–1815), brother of RM, 296, 303n.

Macdonald, Coll (b. 1833), lobster fisher, son of Mary MacDougall or Macdonald, hymn writer, 302

Macdonald, Donald (1770–1789), changekeeper, tenant in Scallastle in 1789, 283

Macdonald, Flora (1722–1790), Jacobite heroine, 41, 89

Macdonald, Rev. Francis (fl. 1740s), missionary at Strontian, Ardgour, 324

Macdonald, Hector, WS (c. 1780–1828), of Boisdale family, later Buchanan, 203, 268–71

Macdonald, Hugh (fl. 1830s), shepherd in Fishnish, 312–13

Macdonald, Isabella (fl. 1770s–1850s), sister of RM, later proprietor of Gometra, 206, 393

Macdonald, James (fl. 18th–19th C.), author, 200, 204–5, 206, 220, 278

Macdonald, Jane (1770s–1860s), sister of RM, later proprietor of Gometra, 206, 393

Macdonald, John (b. c. 1808), tenant in Rossal, 342

Macdonald, John (fl. 1800–1850), tenant in Baliacrach in 1850s, 383, 394n.

Macdonald, John (1823–1887), precentor in Iona, son of Donald M., went to Australia, 405n.

Macdonald, Margaret (fl. 1820s), mother of John and Gillean Maclean, Uisken, 356

Macdonald, Murdoch (d. 1739), harper to laird of Coll, 297, 298

Macdonald, Neill Vc Innes (fl. 1662), tenant in Ardchiavaig, 347

Macdonald, Neil (c. 1790–1878), in Siaba, Ardalanish Point and Ardtun, 302, 349

Macdonald, (fl. 1773), 'Provost' in Iona, 109

Macdonald, Ranald, (1777–1838), RM, 'Staffa', 89, 98, 175, 177–9, 185, 192, 193, 199–209, 222, 251, 252, 268–70, 296, 326, 363, 376

Macdonald, Robert (c. 1779–1856), of Inchkenneth, son of Colin M. of Boisdale, 95, 234, 259, 319, 323n., 358n.

MacDougall, Alexander (fl. 1770–1789), subtenant in Ledirkle, 283

MacDougall, Alexander (fl. 1800), from Kerrera, innkeeper at Scallastle [married Kate MacQuarrie, 1776], 284

MacDougall, Allan WS (d. 1807), of Gallanach, 70, 71, 80, 99, 119, 128–9, 153, 157, 163–5, 248

MacDougall, Catherine Mrs MacDougall, innkeeper at Craignure, see MacQuarrie, Catherine 'Kate'

MacDougall, Charles (1795–1871), son of Mrs Kate MacDougall at Craignure Inn, 363, 365, 368n.

MacDougall, Donald (fl. 1773), servant boy to AMB, 110

MacDougall, Dugald (fl. 1780–1824) of Gallanach, husband of Margaret Maclaine, MM2's sister, 255

MacDougall, Hector (b. c. 1800), spirit dealer in Tobermory, 398

MacDougall, Isabel (1685–1759), wife of John 14th of LB, 'the Grandmother', 55–6

MacDougall, John (fl. 1770–1789), shoemaker, tenant in Scallastle, 283

MacDougall, Katharine (fl. 1720s–1750s), wife of Lachlan of LB, the prodigal, 48, 55, 60

MacDougall, Mary or McLucais (1789–1872), (Mrs Neil Macdonald), hymn writer, 301–2, 349

MacDougall, Mary (b. 1798), wife of Allan Lamont, schoolmaster in Lochdonhead, 402, 405n.

McDuffy, Donald, alias Fie, see McPhee, Donald in Ardfenaig

MacEachern, Donald (b. 1717), in Assapol, 191

MacEachern, John (d. 1840s), in Fishnish, husband of Marion Mackinnon, 315–16

MacFadyen, Lachlan (fl. 1842), tenant on LB estate, 184

MacFarlane, Alexander (c. 1815–1887), crofter in Creich, witness in Napier Enquiry, 352

MacFarlane, Hugh (b. 1713), in Ardchrishnish, 191

McGhiel, Mary (1799–1833), dau. of Malcolm

M., Ardchoirk, widow of Neil Rankin, miller in Glennan, 366, 369n.

MacGillivray, Donald (*c.* 1790- d. 1863), crofter in Creich, ferryman, widower of Bell MacArthur, 352

MacGillivray, William (fl. early 1800s), of Montreal and Pennyghael, 393

MacGilvra, Alexander (1684–1778), of Pennyghael, 43

MacGilvra, Duncan (fl. 1690s–1748), brother of Alexander M. of Pennyghael, 138

MacGilvra, Hugh (fl. 1740–1780s), of Pennyghael, 111, 120, 154, 159

McGilvra, Rev. Martin (*c.* 1620-before 1687), of Pennyghael, 12

McGuarie, Dr John (fl. 1750s–1770s), of Ormaig, [went to Jamaica 1774] 132

McIan, Charles Vc Donald Vc Charles (fl. 1662), tenant in Ardalanish, 347

McIan, Duncan (fl. 1662), tenant in Kilvicheoun, 346

McIan, Ferquhard Vane (fl. 1662), tenant in Ardachy, 347

McIan, Finlay Vc Velane (fl. 1662), tenant in Assapol, 347

McInnes, Donald (*c.* 1780–1860s), charity schoolmaster, Gribun, later in Free Church, 332

McInnes, Dugald (b. *c.* 1890), cottar in Garmony, of 'a rough tribe', 366, 369n.

McInnes, John (fl. 1770–1789), weaver, tenant in Scallastle, 283

McInnes, Marion (*c.* 1793- fl. 1841), servant at Carsaig and LB, 279

McInnes, Mary (fl. 1770–1806), wife of John Currie, schoolmaster in Ulva, 303n.

McInnes, Neil (fl. 1770–1789), subtenant in Ledirkle, 283

Macintyre, Rev. Angus (1815–1887), minister of Kinlochspelve, 387

MacIntyre, Duncan Ban, (1724–1814), poet, 116, visits Mull *c.* 1787, 118n.

MacIntyre, Duncan (1777–1863), son of Nicol MacIntyre, proprietor of Burg, Baptist hymn writer, 393

MacIntyre, Nicol (b. 1721), tenant in Ardalanish, 393

MacIntyre, Nicol (*c.* 1803–1878), son of Duncan MacIntyre, grandson of Nicol M., 393

McKane, John (1818–1882), blacksmith at Lochdonhead in 1840s, 332

MacKechnie, Angus (1870–1944), poet, ship's captain, postmaster in Bunessan, 355–6, 359n.

MacKenzie, Duncan (b. 1743), husband of Miss Maclean, 106

MacKenzie, Mrs (*c.* 1740–1826), *see* Maclean, Christina, or Mary, 105, 106, 296–8

McKillop, Archibald (fl. 1830s), in Glennan, his roup, before emigrating to America, 366

McKillop, Charles (1773–1850s), tenant in Ledirkle [married Catherine McGregor], 366

McKillop, Colin (*c.* 1800–fl. 1845), gamekeeper to ACP, later innkeeper, [married Anne Campbell] 310

McKillop, John (b. *c.* 1745), Elder in Torosay parish, 363, 366, 368n.

McKillop, John (b. 1811), father of stillborn child of dau. of Hector Maclaine in Fishnish, 316

McKillop, Mary (1789–1864), wife of George Buchanan, 316, 366

McKillop, Mary (b. *c.* 1806), dau. of Charles M., wife of John Buchanan, 366

Mackinnon, Alexander (1731–fl. 1796), tacksman of Derrichuaig [Derriguaig], 285

Mackinnon, Archibald (b. 1757), 'Baldy', in Fishnish, 315, 323n.

Mackinnon, Archibald (*c.* 1784–1858), tacksman of Torrans, 333, 335n.

Mackinnon, Charles (b. 1753), of Mackinnon, son of John Dubh M., 46, 190, 397

Mackinnon, Charles (fl. 1750s), in Kilfinichen, 58

Mackinnon, Prof. Donald (1839–1914), commissioner in Napier Enquiry, 353, 359n.

Mackinnon, Flora (1791–1866), Fishnish, later Corrynachenchy and Iona, wife of Duncan MacPhail, 405n.

Mackinnon, Hector (d. 1837), tacksman of Derriguaig, [married to Catherine Maclean] 259

Mackinnon, John, (d. 1737), of Mackinnon, builder of Erray, 29, 105

Mackinnon, John (d. 1759), of Mishnish, Heir of Provision, 43, summoned by presbytery, 46

Mackinnon, John (b. 1804), brother of Marion Mackinnon, 315

Mackinnon, John (1801–1890), carpenter from Tobermory in 1884 report, 383–4

Mackinnon, Malcolm (1787–1873), 'Calum Post', son of John M., Tobermory feuar, 322n.

Mackinnon, Marion (b. 1799–fl. 1851), Fishnish, Baldy's daughter, wife of John MacEachern, 315–16

Mackinnon, Murdoch (*c.* 1744–1842), father of Archibald M., tacksman of Torrans, 335n.

Mackinnon, Neil (fl. 1750), in Rossall, 134

Mackinnon, William Alexander (1789–1870), claimant to title of Mackinnon of that Ilk, 204

MacLachlan, Annabella (1838–1932), dau. of Donald MacLachlan, 358–9n.

Maclachlan, Catherine (1834–1916), dau. of Dugald M. of Killiemore, wife of FWC Jr., 377, 396n.

MacLachlan, Donald (1804–1889), blacksmith in Creich, 352–3, 358n.

Maclachlan, Dugald (b. 1723–fl. 1784), of Laudle [Laudale], tacksman of Achnacraig, 163

Maclachlan, Dugald (*c.* 1790 –1852), of Killiemore, 233–4, 236, 259, 319, 358n., 377

Maclachlan, Dugald (fl. 1790–1836), innkeeper in Aultcreich, 321

Maclachlan, Dugald (*c.* 1785–1868), tailor in Tobermory, 398

Maclachlan, Eun (1757–1820), of Laudle [Laudale], 163, 286, 351, 358n.,

Maclachlan, Ewan (1825–1888), son of Dugald
M. of Killiemore, 351, 358n.

Maclachlan, Harriet (*c.* 1792–1880), wife of
ACP, 225, 310–11, 315–16, 331

Maclachlan, Janet (fl. 1770–1797), wife of Dr
Andrew Maclaine, 163

Maclachlan, Margaret (*c.* 1800–1850s), wife of
Dugald Maclachlan, tailor; early proprietor
in Tobermory, 398

Maclauchlan, Mr Daniel (*c.* 1710–*c.* 1745), excommunicated minister of Ardnamurchan, 324

McLagan, Dr David (1785–1865) [married
Jane Whiteside, 1811], 342, 367

Maclaine, Alexander (fl. 1740–1780s), 'Sanders'
in Callachilly, 71, 82

Maclaine, Alexander (fl. *c.* 1730–1804), nat. son
of JMLB, blind musician, 215

Maclaine, Alexander (fl. 1770–1789), workman,
tenant in Scallastle, 283

Maclaine, Alexander (1827–1886), son of MM2,
221, 370, 389, 395n.

Maclaine, Alicia (1774–1834), dau. of GM, 305,
322n.

Maclaine, Allan (b. *c.* 1685 ?), of Garmony, 48,
61

Maclaine, Allan (*c.* 1728–1758 ?), elder brother
of MM, 75

Maclaine, Allan (d. 1747), Tacksman of Suie, 67

Maclaine, Allan (1772–1843), of Scallastle, son
of GM, 81, 98, 120, 121, 128, 151, 158, 159,
161–2, 166–7, 216, 224, 282–8, 290, 305–6,
311, 321, 326

Maclaine, Allan (1822–1875), son of MM2, 221,
370, 389, 395n.

Maclaine, Amelia (b. 1796), nat. dau. of Allan
M. of Scallastle, [Mrs Allan Gillies] 300

Maclaine, Dr Andrew (1748–1795), surgeon
and drover, 71, 163–4, 224

Maclaine, Andrew (1814–1891), son of Dr
Donald Maclaine, 318

Maclaine, Rev. Angus (1800–1877), son of
Allan Maclaine of Scallastle, 285–6, 287–8,
319, 321, 323n., 366, 388–9

Maclaine, Anthony Vincent (1846–1887),
second son of DMLB, 392

Maclaine, Archibald (1749–1784), 18th of LB,
'Archy Lochbuy', 49, 62–72, 76, 78, 83–5,
marriage of, 85, 86, 104, 117, 119–32, 143,
145–7, 151, 156, 158–9, 166–7, 204, 220,
247, 282, 287, 370, 404–5

Maclaine, Sir Archibald (1777–1861), twin son
of GM, 152, 239, 287–90, 306, 326, 389,
395n.

Maclaine, Archibald (fl. 1824), LMD's servant,
315

Maclaine, Catherine (d. 1803), sister of JMG,
'Miss Ketty', 67, 154, 213, 247

Maclaine, Catherine (*c.* 1756–1828), dau. of
JMLB, [Mrs Hugh McGilvra] 66, 111, 120,
156, 159

Maclaine, Catherine (1793–1894), dau. of MM,
'Miss Catherine', 231, 258, 336, 338, 340,
365, 392–3

Maclaine, Charles (fl. 1770–1800), subtenant in
Garmony, 283–4

Maclaine, Charles, (b. 1792), in Fishnish,
attacks Mary Currie after a funeral, 184

Maclaine, Colin Campbell (b. 1806), nat. son of
Sir Archibald Maclaine and Mary Fletcher
in Ledirkle, 288

Maclaine, Colquhoun (1828–1853), son of
MM2, 221, 370, 395n.

Maclaine, Donald (d. 1820) DM, seedsman in
Edinburgh, nephew of MM, 76, 77, 84, 85,
119, 130, 142, 146, 151, 161, 162, 214, 216,
246, 250, 253, 301

Maclaine, Donald (fl. 1770–1789), weaver in
Ledirkle, 283

Maclaine, Donald (fl. 1770–1789), weaver,
tenant in Scallastle, 283

Maclaine, Donald (fl. 1770–1789), subtenant in
Ledirkle, 283

Maclaine, Dr Donald (1756–1834), Callachilly,
later Gualachaoilish, 32, 163, 255, 257, 286,
311, 315, 318

Maclaine, Donald (1816–1863), 'Dod', DMLB,
21st of LB, 221, 243, 289, 315, 355, 370,
373, 387–92, 394, 395n.

Maclaine, Edith (b. 1870s ?), dau. of Murdoch
Gillean M. of LB, 392, 396n.

Maclaine, Elizabeth or Eliza (1790–1837), dau.
of MM, 231, 252, 329, 338, 342

Maclaine, Farquhar (1743–1822), 'Honest
Farquhar', carpenter at Oskamull, 154, 162,
247, 253,

Maclaine, Flora (1783–1838), dau. of GM, 156,
289

Maclaine, Flora (1796–1869), dau. of MM,
'Flory Lochbuy', Mrs Allan Maclean, later
Mrs Whiteside, 231, 239, 338–43 , 356, 364

Maclaine, Flora Anne (fl. 1790s–1820s), 'Miss
Flora', niece of DM, merchant in Edinburgh,
301

Maclaine, Gillean (1724–1788), nat. son of
JMLB, 48, 50, 60–69, 75–80, marriage 81,
85–7, 92, 94, 96–8, 100, 101, 111, 113,
119–23, 128, 130, 141, 143, 146, 151, 153,
154, 155, 157–9, 161, 162, 163, 166–8, 192,
224, 245, 247–8, 249, 270, 271, 281, 282,
283, 287, 289–90, 305–6, 306, 320–1, 326,
393

Maclaine, Gillean (1798–1840), son of Allan M.
of Scallastle, 287–8, 321, 370, 387–9, 395n.

Maclaine, Harriet [Henrietta] (1798–1889),
dau. of MM, [Mrs John Stewart of
Fasnacloich] 231

Maclaine, Hector (b. *c.* 1640), 12th of LB, 27,
47, 246

Maclaine, Hector, (d. 1745), 'the infant', 48, 49,
55, 75

Maclaine, Hector, [also spelt Maclean] (b.
1765), in shipwreck off American coast, 135

Maclaine, Hector, Senior (fl. 1770–1789), tenant
in Garmony, 283–4

Maclaine, Hector, Jr. (fl. 1770–1789), tenant in
Garmony, 283–4

Maclaine, Hector (1785–1847), Scallastle, son of
GM, later in Thornbury, Glos., 156, 227,
239, 288, 289–90

Maclaine, Hector (b. 1773), in Fishnish, 316

Maclaine, Hugh (b. 1735), in Kilvicheoun, father of Hector, who survived shipwreck in 1786. 134–5

Maclaine, Hugh (b. *c.* 1750 ?), brother of Dr Andrew, vintner in Tobermory in 1795, later in Kengharair, 163

Maclaine, Hugh (fl. 1800), subtenant in Garmony, 283–4

Maclaine, Isabel (Bell) (b. *c.* 1745 ?), dau. of JMLB, 60, 66, 156

Maclaine, Ishbel, (b. *c.* 1750s ? fl. 1804), nat. dau. of MM, [married James Neilson, coppersmith, 1788] 215

Maclaine, Jane (b. 1787), dau. of MM, wife of Colin Campbell of Kintraw, 157, 231, 338, 390, 395n.

Maclaine, Jane Jarvis (1802–1882), dau. of MM, later Mrs Andrew Scott of Ettrickbank, 212, 231, 233, 239, 240, 249, 258, 340, 392

Maclaine, Jane (1820–1899), dau. of MM2, [unm. – died at Java Lodge] 260

Maclaine, Janet (b. 1797), dau. of Dr Donald Maclaine, 318

Maclaine, John (d. 1747), 14th of LB, 'the grandfather', 47–8, 55, 60, 75

Maclaine, John (*c.* 1700–1778), JMLB, 17th of LB, 'John Lochbuy', 48–9, 55–71, 75, 78, 80, 92, 96, 98, 100, 108, 117, 119, 126, 132, 140, 149, 151, 157, 159, 261, 287, 310, 328, 337

Maclaine, John, (d. 1792) JMG, 'John Gruline', 67, 71, 72, 82, 86, 87, 119–20, 124, 134, 144, 146, 152, 154, 156, 159, 163, 224, 247; death of, 248; 266, 386

Maclaine, John (fl. 1770s–1800), nephew of JMG, [perhaps same as John Maclean Jamaica] 152

Maclaine, John (b. 1757 d. after 1816), tacksman of Tiroran, 98, 195, 268, 270–1, 355

Maclaine, John (fl. 1770–1789), weaver, tenant in Scallastle, 283

Maclaine, John (fl. 1775–1803), miller at LB in 1803, when his wife dies, 213

Maclaine, John (1778–1815) son of GM, 152, 285, 288; died from wounds at Waterloo 295–6, 301

Maclaine, John (*c.* 1790), tenant in Ledirkle, encounters potato blight, 371

Maclaine, John (1792–1818), second son of MM and JC, 161, 211, 218, 236, 250

Maclaine, John Campbell (1818–1885), son of MM2 , 221, 332, 367, 370, 388, 389, 390, 395n.

Maclaine, Julian (1775–1840), dau. of GM, 224, 305, 322n.

Maclaine, Kathleen Emilie (b. after 1869), dau. of Murdoch Gillean M. of LB, 392, 396n.

Maclaine, Kenneth Douglas Lorne (1880–1935), of LB, 395n.

Maclaine, Lachlan (b. *c.* 1678 ?), of Knockroy, 75, 128

Maclaine, Lachlan (*c.* 1717–1743), 15th of LB, 'the prodigal', 47–9, 55, 60, 75, 111, 137, 151

Maclaine, Lachlan (fl. 1760–1780, 'Lachinn Mac Donich Bhain', schoolmaster at Leiter and Salen, 319

Maclaine, Major Lachlan (fl. 1838), of the Royals, [later in Craignure] 367

Maclaine, Lauchlan (1771–1847), LMD, diarist, nat. son of Gillean M. and Janet MacPhail, 81, 158, 159, 239, 255, 257, 259, 266, 282, 295, 300–1, 305–21, 322, 329, 332, 339, 362, 365–8, 378, 382, 384, 388–9, 392, 393, 399

Maclaine, Lillias (1818–1894), 'Lily' dau. of MM2, [unm.] 260

Maclaine, Mabel Julia (b. after 1869), dau. of Murdoch Gillean M. of LB, 392, 396n.

Maclaine, Margaret (b. *c.* 1685), wife of Donald MacQuarrie of Ormaig, 245, 246

Maclaine, Margaret (*c.* 1726–1810), 'Peggy' sister of MM, mother of LM, 75, 76, 95, 162, 245–6

Maclaine, Margaret Ann (1788–1855), (Mrs Wm. Craig), dau. of GM, 156, 290, 300, 375, 379n.

Maclaine, Margaret (b. 1789), dau. of MM, [Mrs Dugald MacDougall of Gallanach] 231, 255, 338

Maclaine, Mary (1740–1831), 'Mally' dau. of Lachlan M. of LB, 55–8, 110–11, 137, 140, 147, 218, 226, 230, 241, 392, 396n.

Maclaine, Mary (1787–1855), dau. of GM, 289–90

Maclaine, Mary (b. 1799), dau. of Dr Donald M., 318

Maclaine, Mary (1800–1880), dau. of MM, wife of JG, 212, 224–5, 231, 257, 308–9, 312, 317, 329, 366, 368, 369n., 370

Maclaine, Mary Ann (1825–1902), dau. of MM2 [unm.], christening of, 239, 241

Maclaine, Murdoch (fl. 1643), of LB, 7, 8

Maclaine, Murdoch (d. 1727), 'Murdoch Og', younger of LB, later 13th of LB, 27, 47, 328, 334n.

Maclaine, Murdoch (d. 1747), 14th of LB, 27

Maclaine, Capt. Murdoch (1730–1804), MM, linen merchant, later 19th of LB, 50, 63, 66, 67, 68, 69, 70, 75–87, 92, 100, 119–24, 127–31, 142, 144, 145, 146, 147, 148, 151–68, 174, 192, 198, 203, 211, 224, 237, 242, 245–50, 261, 265, 267, 268, 270, 271, 278, 281, 282, 283, 285–90, 326, 327–8, 338, 343, 364, 370, 392

Maclaine, Murdoch (1777–1806), twin son of GM, 152, 284–5, 288

Maclaine, Murdoch (1791–1844), 20th of LB, MM2, ' the Chief', 'Young Murdoch', 161, 211–27, 230–42, 250–6, 273, 281, 282, 307–12, 315, 319, 320, 329, 332, 338, 339–43, 364, 367, 370, 374, 378, 384, 391, 392, 403

Maclaine, Murdoch (1814–1850), MM3, 'Little Murdie', 21st of LB, 168, 221, 225–7, 236, 242–3, 275, 289, 315, 332, 361, 370–3, 388, 389, 391, 394

Maclaine, Murdoch Gillean (1845–1909), of LB, 389, 392

Maclaine, Peggy (b. *c.* 1740), nat. dau. of JMLB, 60, 66

Maclaine, Phoebe (1795–1867), dau. of MM, [Mrs Donald Gregorson] 231, 370

Maclaine, Tibby (fl. 1750s), dau. of JMLB, 60

Maclaine, Washington (b. c. 1777), nat. son of AMLB in N. America, 131–2

Maclaine, William Osborne (1818–1906), 289

Maclean, Alexander (1753–1835), 15th of Coll, brother of 'young Col', 71, 99, 101, 114–15, 116, 121, 137, 161, 192, 216, 223, 240, 249, 251, 384

Maclean, Rev. Alexander (1721–1765), minister of Kilninian, son of Rev. John Maclean, 45–6

Maclean, Dr Alexander (1725–1786), of Pennycross, 110, 117, 148, 337–8, 344n.

Maclean, Alexander (fl. 1785), correspondent of MM in Kensington, 131

Maclean, Alexander (fl. 1740–1780s), in Callachilly, 'Sanders' [also spelt Maclaine] 71, 82

Maclean, Lieut. -Col. Alexander (c. 1777–1859), leaves £20,000 to educate boys named Maclean, 356–7, 359n.

Maclean, Alexander (1791–1876), of Pennycross, 'Sandy Pennycross', 181, 220, 232, 237, 238, 239, 351, 358n.

Maclean, Alexander (b. 1802), son of the schoolmaster in Ballygown, 183

Maclean, Alexander (fl. 1847), owner of boat left in Ulva, 377, 380n.

Maclean, Alexander (1809–1818), son of DMWS, 231

Maclean, Alexander (b. c. 1815), ploughman at Ardfenaig, 349

Maclean, Alexandrina Christina (b. 1822), dau. of AMD and Flora LB, 344n.

Maclean, Alice, of Torloisk (c. 1719– c. 1752–5), first wife of LMQ, 90, 145, 282

Maclean, Alice (1760–1840), of Torranbeg, wife of Archibald M. of Pennycross, 214

Maclean, Sir Allan (b. c. 1640 ? d. 1674), of Duart, 12, 14–16

Maclean, Allan (fl. 1747), of Totranald (Coll), 43

Maclean, Capt. Allan (d. 1722), father of Christina Maclean, 336

Maclean, Allan (1710–1783), 4th of Brolass, later Sir Allan, AMB, 'The Knight', 43, 46, inherits title 49, 50, 68, 76, 86, 107–12, 124, 132, 137–44, 148, 149, 230, 232, 398, 403, 404–5

Maclean, Allan (d. 1759), of Kilmory, 55, 58, 60, 64, 110

Maclean, Allan (1724–1792), 5th of Drimnin, 16, 41, 42, elopes with Mally Maclaine 56, 137, 140–2, 147–9, 161, 218, 230, 327

Maclean, Col. later Brig. Gen. Allan (1725–1797), of Torloisk, AM, 46, 70, 71, 75, 82, 84, 86, 91, 94, 120–3, 129, 130, 137, 139, 143, 144–7, 151, 152–3, 156–7, 159–62, 170–1, 174–5, 266, 267, 320, 356, 403

Maclean, Allan (fl. 1750s–1780s), second son of Allan Maclean of Drimnin and Ann of Brolass, 56

Maclean, Dr Allan (c. 1759–1827), AMD, the 'red-haired doctor', 132, 176, 211, 239, 255, 256, 336–40, 343, 355

Maclean, Allan (c. 1760–1853), 'Ailean Sgoilear', schoolmaster in Iona, 256, 378

Maclean, Allan (1794–1818), son of DMWS, 231, 235

Maclean, Allan Thomas (1793–1868), brother of Sandy Pennycross, 232

Maclean, Allice (b. 1750s ?), nat. dau. of John Maclean of Lagganulva, 171

Maclean, Ann (b. c. 1825), dau. of John Treshnish, 36

Maclean, Ann (d. c. 1755 ?), of Brolass, first wife of Allan Maclean of Drimnin, 56, 137, 140, 147, 148

Maclean, Ann (1800–1881), dau. of DMWS [unm.] 231

Maclean, Anna (b. c. 1757), dau. of AMB, 50, 142

Maclean, Anne (d. 1793), dau. of Sir John Maclean of Duart, wife of Hector MacQ. of Ormaig, 92

Maclean, Rev. Archibald (1683–1755), minister of Ross, 138, 328–9, 334n.

Maclean, Archibald (c. 1727–1782), in Lagganulva, brother of LMT, 80, 170–1, 175

Maclean, Archibald (d. 1772), surgeon in Jamaica, 132

Maclean, Archibald (d. 1768), in Torosay Parish, drowned, 101

Maclean, Archibald (1761–1830), of Pennycross, 175, 232, 286, 340, 341, 344n.

Maclean, Archibald (1810–1844), son of DMWS, 240

Maclean, Betty (d. c. 1792), sister of LMT, [unm.] 305, 322n.

Maclean, Breadalbane (b. 1793), dau. of Alexander M. of Coll, 298, 304n., 309

Maclean, Catherine (b. c. 1715 ?), of Coll, wife of Dr Hector Maclean, 105

Maclean, Catherine (d. 1770), of Brolass, sister of AMB, wife of Lachlan Maclean of Coll, 137

Maclean, Catherine (b. c. 1785), in Tirghoil, wife of Hugh Fletcher, later in Canada, 356

Maclean, Catherine (d. 1838 ?) dau. of Lachlan Ban M., wife of John MacCallum, 368, 369n.

Maclean, Charles (fl. 17th C.), of Ardnacross, great great-grandfather of Allan Drimnin, 147

Maclean, Charles (d. 1746), of Drimnin, 41, 42

Maclean, Charles (b. c. 1750 ?), of Drimnin and Kinlochaline, 42, 56, 117, 140, 142, 148–9, 161, 175, 218, 230–4

Maclean, Charles Roy (fl. 1780s), servant to JMG, 154

Maclean, Charles (b. 1770s), army surgeon, son of Lachlan Ban M., Bunessan, 132, 340, 344n.

Maclean, Charles (fl. 1745), in Achnacraig, near Dervaig, shakes hands with Bonnie Prince Charlie, 44

Maclean, Charles (fl. 1770–1832), father of Rev. Neil M., 256

Maclean, Charles (1806–1872), blind son of DMWS, 239–41, 395n.

Maclean, Charles Alexander (b. 1874), of

Pennycross, husband of Mabel Maclaine of LB, 396n.

Maclean, Christian (b. 1824), dau. of AMD and Flora LB, 341, 344n.

Maclean, Christina *see* Mary (*c.* 1740–1826), 'Miss Maclean', a. k. a. Christina, 105, 106, 296–8

Maclean, Christina (1718–1808), poetess, wife of Dr John Maclean, mother of AMD, 336–8, 344n.

Maclean, Christina (1796 –1873), 'Chirsty', dau. of DMWS, wife of MM2, 42, 217–21, 225, 226, 239, 241, 242, 255, 310, 338, 342, 367, 370, 389, 401

Maclean, Colquhoun (1795–1822), son of DMWS, 233

Maclean, Daniel (b. *c.* 1710 ? d. after 1770), merchant in Glasgow and Jamaica, 139–40, 143, 144, 146

Maclean, Daniel (fl. 1765), lawyer in Glasgow, 65, 167

Maclean, Dr Daniel (fl. 1828), doctor in Tobermory, 257

Maclean, Donald (17th C.), of Brolass, 8, 11

Maclean, Donald (1671–1725), of Brolass, 137–8, 149n.

Maclean, Donald (fl. 1747), tacksman of Calgary, 44

Maclean, Donald (*c.* 1780–1748), of Torloisk, 29, 44, 90, 144, 145

Maclean, Donald (fl. 1725–1779), in Pennygown, 82, 88n.

Maclean, Donald (fl. 1750), 'strong man of Reudle', brother-in-law of AM, 359n.

Maclean, Donald (1753–1774), of Coll, 'Young Col', 56, 69, 99, 101, 104, 106, 107, 110, 137, 188, 222–3, 384

Maclean, Donald (fl. 1740s), tacksman of Killunaig, 43, 138

Maclean, Donald (fl. 1780 ?), poet in Leob, Kilpatrick [Ross] 336, 343n.

Maclean, Donald (*c.* 1761–1799), Cameron Highlanders, brother of AMD, 336, 337

Maclean, Donald WS (1770–1853), DMWS, 58, 147, 197, 214, 216–20, 223–4, 226, 230–43, 251–5, 257, 260, 266, 271, 279, 288, 294, 300, 307, 308, 329, 339, 342–3, 348, 355, 361, 362, 364–5, 373–4, 384, 386, 391, 401, 403

Maclean, Dr Donald (b. 1815), son of Rev. Neil M., minister of Tiree; doctor in Kinlochspelve, 227

Maclean, Donald (1793–1897), postmaster, merchant in Bunessan [b. Knapdale], 351, 352, 358n.

Maclean, Donald (b. 1817), son of AMD and Flora LB, 339, 342

Maclean, Capt. Dugald (d. 1818), of Ardfenaig, 344n.

Maclean, Duncan (fl. 1740s–1760s), servant to JMLB, 76

Maclean, Duncan Junior (fl. 1770–1800), subtenant in Garmony, 283–4

Maclean, Rev. Duncan (1795–1871), minister of Salen, Gaelic scholar, friend of LMD, 259, 318

Maclean, Lieut. Duncan (fl. 1800–1820s) , of the Uisken family, 356

Maclean, Sir Fitzroy Jeffreys Grafton (*c.* 1770–1847), of Duart, 'poor Grafton', 144, 161, 254, 403

Maclean, Sir Fitzroy Donald (1835–1936), of Duart, 404

Maclean, Fitzroy Jeffreys Grafton, WS (1813–1858), son of DMWS, 240

Maclean, Flora (b. *c.* 1803 ?), of Kengharair , wife of Peter MacArthur, 341, 344n.

Maclean, Florence (b. 1720s), dau. of John M. of Treshnish, 36

Maclean, Florence [Flora] (fl. 17th C.), dau. of Hector Og, great-grandmother of MM and Peggy, 95

Maclean, Florence (fl. 1690–1720), of Assapol, mother of LMQ, 89

Maclean, Brig. Gen. Francis (*c.* 1718–1781), 94

Maclean, Hector (fl. 15th C.), of Duart, 4, 89

Maclean, Sir Hector (d. 1651), of Duart, 8, 13

Maclean, Hector (1688–1754), 11th of Coll, 'a judicious pretty gentleman', father of Una, wife of AMB, 49

Maclean, Rev. Hector (1696–1775), minister of Coll, son of Ewen of Treshnish, 43

Maclean, Sir Hector (1703–1750), of Duart, son of Sir John M., 26, 28, 44–5, 49, 109, 143, 403

Maclean, Hector (fl. 1658), of Torloisk, 7, 15

Maclean, Hector (*c.* 1718–1765), of Torloisk, lawyer in Edinburgh, 62, 65, 67, 76, 80, 90, 91, 139, 144–6, 166, 167, 170–1, 175, 223

Maclean, Hector (fl. 1747), Younger of Totranald (Coll), 43

Maclean, Hector (1689–1754), 13th of Coll, 43, 49

Maclean, Dr Hector (1704–1784), of Gruline, father of Miss Maclean, 105, 297

Maclean, Hector (fl. 1720–1760), of Torran, son of Charles M. of Killunaig, father-in-law of Lachlan Ban M., 43, 138, 344n.

Maclean, Hector (b. 1751), Adjutant in 84th Regt., settled in Nova Scotia, 151, 267

Maclean, Hector (fl. 1803), of Kingairloch, 212

Maclean, Hector (b. 1714, d. *c.* 1799), of Killean, later Ardfenaig, imprisoned by JMLB, 58, 60, 64, 110, 138

Maclean, Sir Hector (d. 1818), of Duart, 143–4, 151, 403

Maclean, Hector (fl. 1770s), tailor on LB estate in 1773, 267

Maclean, Hector (b. *c.* 1760), 'Eachann Ruadh', in Mingary, 298–9, 304n.

Maclean, Hector H. (1778–1840),'Hector Bunessan', son of Lachlan Ban M., 281, 340, 343, 344n.,

Maclean, Hector (1803–1834), brother of Sandy Pennycross, 214, 258

Maclean, Hector (1802–1818), son of DMWS, 266

Maclean, Hector Neil (1810–1828), son of Capt. Dugald Maclean of Ardfenaig and Susanna Macleod, 344n.

Maclean, Hugh (d. 1786), 14th of Coll, 89, 99, 104

Maclean, Hugh (1735–1785 ?), father of Hector Maclaine, survivor of shipwreck, 135

Maclean, Hugh (fl. mid-18th C.), possessor of Gribun lands in 1748, 138

Maclean, Hugh (b. 1720s ?), son of John Treshnish, 36

Maclean, Hugh (fl. 1747), of Grishipol (Coll), 43

Maclean, Hugh (fl. 1750s–1784), of Kingairloch, 79, 81, 82, 174

Maclean, Hugh (fl. 1720s–1765), lawyer in Glasgow, 171

Maclean, Hugh (fl. 1780s–1790s), 'Hugh Rossal', Ardchrishnish, archetype of Mull's 'half gentry', 356, 359n.

Maclean, Hugh (fl. 1750), son of Allan Maclean of Kilmory, 60

Maclean, Hugh (1782–1861), Younger of Coll, 220, 222, 223, 251, 255, 275, 331, 332, 384–5, 393, 394

Maclean, Iain (fl. 16th C.), 'Iain Ruadh', hereditary constable of Cairnburgh, 35

Maclean, Isabel (c. 1680–1753), wife of Rev. John Maclean (Maighstir Seathan), 50

Maclean, Isabel (fl. 1680–1760), of Ardgour, Lady Brolass senior, mother of AMB, 138

Maclean, Isabel (c. 1800–1799), of Brolass, wife of JMLB, 'Lady Lochbuy', 49, 58–60, 62, 69, 80, 110–12, 120, 131, 137, 156, 159, 247, 310

Maclean, Isabella (d. 1814), wife of Rev. Alexander Fraser; death of 239, 325

Maclean, Isabella (c. 1795–fl. 1834), of Kengharair, [Mrs Cuthbertson] lodgings keeper in Tobermory, 405n.

Maclean, Jane (1808–1822), dau. of DMWS, 231

Maclean, Janet (b. c. 1755), 'the Madame', wife of AM, 122, 143, 144, 160, 171

Maclean, Janet (fl. 1780s–90s), mother of the 'Hero Hector', son of CM, 248–9

Maclean, Janet (Jessie) (c. 1789–1869), dau. of Duncan Maclean, Uisken, wife of James Morrison, 341, 344n., 356–7

Maclean, Sir John (1670–1716), of Duart, 14, 16, 18–19, 22, 24, 26, 105

Maclean, John (fl. 1660s), of Ardgour, 15

Maclean, Rev. John (1680–1756), Maighstir Seathan, poet, minister of Kilninian, 22, 27–8, 34, 43, 45, 50, 293, 324

Maclean, John (fl. 1680–1720), poet in Inivea, 27, 105

Maclean, Dr John (1724–1808), in Brolass, father of AMD, 132, 336–8, 344n.

Maclean, John (b. 1729- c. 1785 ?), 'Iain Ban Mac Ailein', grandfather of Rev. Neil Maclean, 256

Maclean, John (fl. 1695–1760 ?), in Treshnish, later in Iona, 35–6, 42–3

Maclean, John (fl. 1747), brother to Lachlan Maclean of Gruline, 44

Maclean, John (fl. 1748), possessor of lands at Kinlochscridain in 1748, 138

Maclean, John (1755–1821), nat. son of

Archibald M. of Lagganulva, 171, 175, 176, 177, 183, 387

Maclean, John (fl. 18thC.), of William and Mary College, Virginia, 334n.

Maclean, John (d. 1810), of Langamull, 176

Maclean, John (fl. 18th C.), tacksman of Killean, father of Hector M., 43, 58, 71, 138, 337, 339, 344n.

Maclean, John (fl. 1750–1800s), of Inverscadale, 'Castle Dowart', 142, 152 and 'John Jamaica', 182

Maclean, John (fl. 1770–1800), subtenant in Garmony, 283–4

Maclean, John (1775–fl. 1838), merchant in Glasgow, son of Lachlan Ban M., 'John Bunessan', 340, 341, 344n., 368, 369n.

Maclean, John (fl. 1790s–1830s), schoolmaster in Ballygown, 183

Maclean, John (1787–1848), poet, later in Canada, 203, 269–70, 303n.

Maclean, John (1805–1891), son of DMWS, 238, his blindness 239–41, 243

Maclean, John (b. 1808), son of the schoolmaster in Ballygown, 183

Maclean, John Allan (b. 1814), son of AMD and Flora LB, 339, 342, 343

Maclean, John (b. c. 1819), son of AMD and Flora LB, 339, 342

Maclean, John (fl. 1820s–1860s), nephew of Lieut. -Col. Alexander Maclean, later in Canada, 356

Maclean, John Ralph (1827–1903), son of Lieut. Archibald Maclean of Uisken, 356

Maclean, Julia (d. 1760), of Torloisk, grandmother of GM, 61

Maclean, Julian (d. 1874), dau. of Archibald Maclean of Pennycross, 239

Maclean, Lachlan (fl. 15th–16th C.), nat. son of Hector M. of Duart, 89

Maclean, Sir Lachlan (fl. 17th C.), of Duart, 7, 11, 12, 23

Maclean, Lachlan (1650–1687), 2nd of Brolass, 18

Maclean, Lachlan (d. 1746), nat. son of Charles of Drimnin, 147

Maclean, Lachlan (fl. 1745), servant to Sir Hector Maclean, 44

Maclean, Lachlan (fl. 1700–1730), of the Coll family, 31

Maclean, Lachlan (1670–1751), of Gruline, 44

Maclean, Lachlan (fl. 1740s–1760s) schoolmaster, 58

Maclean, Lachlan (1720–1799), of Torloisk, LMT, 71, 78–9, 82, 113, 116, 132, 144–6, 161, 170–5, 188, 192, 233, 326, 385

Maclean, Lachlan (fl. 1758), son of Allan M. of Kilmory, 60

Maclean, Lachlan Ban (1751–1819), 'Lachlan Bunessan', innkeeper, 109, 368, 398

Maclean, Lachlan (1784–1844), son of John M. in Lagganulva, later in Kilbrenan, 176, 182, 183, 260, 306, 387

Maclean, Dr Lachlan (1789–1881), of Gallanach, leased Rum 1825–1839, later in Tobermory, 238, 330, 385

Maclean, Lachlan (fl. 1815–1840), SSPCK schoolmaster, catechist in Mornish, 298

Maclean, Lachlan Macquarie (b. 1826), son of AMD and Flora LB, 341, 344n.

Maclean, Lauchlan (d. *c.* 1754), infant son of AMB, 50, 139

Maclean, Lilias (b. 1823), 'Lilly', dau. of Lieut. Archibald M. and Sarah MacPherson, Uisken, 356

Maclean, Lillias (1799–1876), twin dau. (with Mary) of DMWS, [unm.] 231

Maclean, Malcolm (fl. 1770s), Mull emigrant in New Boston, 266–7

Maclean, Margaret (1737–1789), dau. of Rev. Archibald M., wife of Rev. Neil Macleod, 110

Maclean, Margaret (b. 1730s), dau. of John Treshnish 36

Maclean, Margaret (1803–1871), dau. of DMWS, [unm.] 231, 233

Maclean, Margaret Alicia (fl. 1820s–1850s), in Uisken, 356

Maclean, Margaret (fl. 1820s–1860s), [Mrs Neil MacCallum] of Uisken family, later in Canada, 356

Maclean, Maria (b. *c.* 1752), dau. of AMB, 50, 107, 140, 148, 149, 230, 232

Maclean, Marianne (1765–*c.* 1841), of Torloisk, MMT, later Mrs Clephane, 172–85, 199, 203, 232, 235, 239, 279, 281, 282, 289–90, 300–1, 306, 309–10, 326, 387, 393

Maclean, Marion (fl. 1740–1800 ?), mistress of Archibald Maclean of Lagganulva, 176

Maclean, Marion (*c.* 1750–1829), Mor Nigh'n Eughinn, [Mrs Malcolm Currie] Sir A. Maclaine's nurse, 395n.

Maclean, Marion (*c.* 1757–after 1830), sister of AMD, 'Miss Marion', 336, 337, 339, 342

Maclean, Marion (b. *c.* 1789), 'Little Marion' , servant at LB, 212–3

Maclean, Mary (b. *c.* 1718 ?), sister of AM, 130, 156, 157, 159, 160–1, 164

Maclean, Mary (fl. 1710–1740), wife of John Treshnish, 36

Maclean, Mary (fl. 1740–1781), sister of Alexander M. of Coll, mother of Capt. Allan MacAskill, 222–3

Maclean, Mary (b. 1730s), dau. of John Treshnish, 36

Maclean, Mary (b. *c.* 1752 ?), of Torrans, wife of Lachlan Ban M., 109

Maclean, Mary (*c.* 1740–1826), dau. of Dr Hector M., 'Miss Maclean', a. k. a. Christina, [Mrs Duncan MacKenzie] 105, 106, 296–8

Maclean, Mary (fl. 1750–1800), widow, subtenant in Garmony, 283–4

Maclean, Mary (1799–1853), twin dau. (with Lillias) of DMWS, [unm.] 231

Maclean, Mary (fl. 1790s–1820s) dau. of Hugh M. in Callachilly, 318

Maclean, Mary (*c.* 1777–1863), wife of Duncan MacIntyre, 393

Maclean, Murdoch (b. 1815), son of AMD and Flora LB, 339, 342

Maclean, Neil (b. 1730s), son of John M. of Treshnish, 36

Maclean, Lieut. Neil (fl. 1760s–1800), in Royal Highland Emigrants, 122

Maclean, Neil (fl. 1770s), brother of Malcolm M., intended as tailor's apprentice, 267

Maclean, Rev. Neil (1784–1859), minister of Tiree, 367

Maclean, Rev. Neil (1796–1864), tutor to CM's children, later minister of Ulva, 256–7, 259, 318, 378

Maclean, Neil (b. 1820), son of AMD and Flora LB, 339

Maclean, Rev. Peter (fl. 1843–1855), minister of FC in Tobermory from 1843, 334

Maclean, Sibella (b. *c.* 1756), dau. of AMB, 50, 107

Maclean, Sibella (1804–1878), 'Sibby', dau. of DMWS, later Mrs Alexander Crawford, 231, 233, 242, 386

Maclean, Susanna (fl. 1750s), housekeeper to John Mackinnon of Mishnish, [Heir of Provision] 46

Maclean, Una (b. *c.* 1733), dau. of John Treshnish, 36

Maclean, Una (*c.* 1728–1760), dau. of Hector 11th of Coll, marries AMB, 46, 49, death of 50, 137, 139

Macleane, Lauchlin (b. *c.* 1728), MD., supposed author of the Junius letters, 146

Macleod, Janet (b. *c.* 1730), of Talisker, wife of Hugh Maclean 14th of Coll, 99

Macleod, [perhaps John ?] an 'elderly man' in 1815, reciter of Ossian, 297, 298

Macleod, Rev. John (1801–1882), 'High Priest of Morvern', 319, 323n., 362, 366

Macleod, John Neil Maxwell (1820–1909), son of Norman M. and Agnes Maxwell, 193–4

Macleod, Julia (fl. 1740–1775), of Dunvegan, wife of Sir Allan Maclean 18th of Duart, 14

Macleod, Rev. Neil (1729–1780), minister of the Ross, 86, 109–10, 132, 138, 327, 343n.

Macleod, Norman (fl. 1750s), of Macleod, 46

Macleod, Rev. Norman (1745–1824), minister of Morvern, 196, 323n.

Macleod, Rev. Norman (1783–1862), 'Caraid nan Gaidheal', 196–7, 272, 332, 367–8

Macleod, Rev. Norman (1812–1872), son of Norman M. and Agnes Maxwell, author of *Highland Parish*, 198n.

Macleod, Roderick (fl. mid 18th C.), of Talisker, brother-in-law of Alexander Maclean of Coll, 99, 325

Macleod, Susanna (1768–1847), wife of Capt. Dugald Maclean of Ardfenaig, 341, 344n.

McLucais, Mary (1789–1872), *see* MacDougall, Mary (1789–1872)

MacMillan, John (fl. 1730–1750s), 'reputed rogue', 58

Macmillan, Ronald Dunbar (fl. 1730s–1750s), lawyer to Duke of Argyll, in jaunt to Mull, 33

McMillan, Rory (fl. 1800), miller in Ardmeanach, 271

MacNab, Archibald (*c.* 1805–1882), farmer in Ardrishaig, 393

MacNab, Robert (b. 1841) MD 1861, FRCS.

1866, GP in Glasgow, Bury, Brighton, Bath, 'of Penmore', 393–4

McNaughton, Mr (fl. 1820s), tutor to children of AMD, 339, 341

McNeill, Ann (b. 1795), dau. of Neil McNeill, in Balifraoich, 312

McNeill, Archibald (d. 1831), son of Neil McNeill, Balifraoich, 312

McNeill, Hector (fl. 1750–1804), in Ardmeanach, married to Mary Obirn, 268

McNeill, Hector (d. 1824), in Torosay, 183

McNeill, Janet (c. 1762–1828) (Jessie), wife of James Maxwell, 190, 196

McNeill, John (fl. 1780), writer in Inveraray, manager of estate of Ulva, 89

McNeill, Sir John (1795–1883), chairman, Board of Supervision [Poor Law], 349–50, 352–4, 361–2, 376, 382–3

McNeill, Neil (fl. 1770–1789), herd, tenant in Scallastle, 283

McNeill, Neil (b. c. 1763) [may be same as above] in Balifraoich, 312–3, 322n.

McNicol, Rev. Donald (1735–1802), minister of Lismore, opponent of SJ's views on Gaelic, 112, 163, 318, 323n.

MacNicol, Mary (1774–fl. 1830s), dau. of Rev. D. McNicol, wife of Dr Donald Maclaine, 163, 318

McNiven, Angus (c. 1805–1893), from Islay, tenant in Ardachy, 353, 359n., 393

McNiven, Archibald (fl. 1800–1832), emigration agent from Islay, 273, 276n.

McOsenag, Neil (d. 1768), in Torosay Parish, drowned, 101

MacPhail, Angus (1816–1862), farmer in Cuilbhuirg, Iona, husband of Sally Lamont, 401

MacPhail, Colin (b. 1828), brother of Angus M., went to Australia 1852, 405n.

MacPhail, Donald (1746–1836), drover in Pennygown, 320, 399, 405n.

MacPhail, Donald (fl. 1770–1789), tenant in Garmony, 283

MacPhail, Donald (1779–1832), father of Dugald M., the bard, 399

MacPhail, Dugald (1818–1887), joiner, miller, architect, poet, author of *An t-eilean Muileach*, 214, 333, 399–401, 402, 405n.

MacPhail, Duncan (1779–1863), in Corrynachenachy, later in Iona, 403, 405n.

MacPhail, Duncan (1796–1876), tenant in Garmony, [unm.] 405n.

MacPhail, Duncan (1812–1890), brother of Angus M., in Iona, 403, 405n.

MacPhail, Hugh (b. c. 1822), brother of Angus M., went to Australia 1852, 405n.

MacPhail, Janet (c. 1750–1830), mother of LMD, 80–1, 306, 307, 314, 315

MacPhail, John (1794–1872), tenant in Scallastle, later in Tiroran, 405n.

MacPhail, Malcolm (1793–1879), in Ardura and Oskamull, 402, 405n.

MacPhail, Marion (b. 1830), dau. of Duncan M., sister of Angus M., 405n.

MacPhail, Neil (c. 1794–1863), spirit merchant in Tobermory, later innkeeper in Ledaig, 274

MacPhail, Neil (fl. 1847), sheriff officer [may be same as above], 377

McPhee, Lieut. Donald (fl. 1836), tenant in Glenbyre and Laggan, from 1831, 273

McPhee, Donald (b. c. 1820), from Islay, ploughman at Ardfenaig, sometime at Scour, 349

MacPherson, Alexander (b. 1843–fl. 1883), crofter in Kinloch, 355, 359n.

MacPherson, Rev. Finlay (1796–1852), minister of Tobermory 1834–8, brother-in-law of Neil MacPhail, 332–3

MacPherson, James (1736–1796), translator of Ossian, 108, 112, 202, 293

MacPherson, John (n.k.), 124

Macquarie, Betty (c. 1750–1833), sister of LM and CM, wife of Farquhar Maclaine, 246

Macquarie, Charles (1771–1835), CM, proprietor of Glenforsa, Duart and Ulva, brother of LM., 76, 96, 162–4, 206, 218, 220, 222, 234, 241, 245–57, 259–61, 308, 315, 318, 329, 363–4, 374, 378, 382, 386, 392, 403

Macquarie, Charles Jr. (1814–1869), son of CM, 259, 260, 374, 386, 390–1

Macquarie, Elizabeth (1813–1828), dau. of CM, 257

Macquarie, George Willison (1816–1894), son of CM, 259, 260

Macquarie, Hector (1794–1836), nat. son of CM, 'the Hero', 248–9, 257

Macquarie, Lachlan (1761–1824), LM, governor of NSW, 76, 83, 96, 115, 132, 152, 153–4, 162, 218–19, 245–55, 338–9, 363, 386, 391, 393, 403

Macquarie, Lachlan (c. 1810–after 1883), shoemaker in Salen, once in Ulva, witness in Napier Enquiry, 1883, 376

Macquarie, Lachlan, Jr. (1814–1845), son of LM, of Jarvisfield, 184, 253–4, 258–9, 260, 261, 315, 374–5, 379n., 386, 393

Macquarie, Lachlan (1818–1845), son of CM, 259, 260

Macquarie, Marianne (b. 1820 fl. 1844), dau. of CM, later Mrs Goodwin, 257, 260

Macquarie, Murdoch Maclaine (1828–1855), son of CM, 257, 258, 260

MacQuarrie, Allan (fl. 1700–1750s), of Culinish, uncle to LMQ, 43, 89–93, 97, 145, 256

MacQuarrie, Allan (b. c. 1746), son of LMQ, 91

MacQuarrie, Ann (d. 1778), second wife of LMQ, 91, 92, 93, 96, 106, 110, 363

MacQuarrie, Ann (1774–1842), 'Miss Ann MacQ.,' dau. of LMQ by his second wife, 92, 96, 288, 318, 363–5

MacQuarrie, Archibald (b. c. 1769), son of LMQ by his second wife, 92

MacQuarrie, Catherine (b. c. 1760–d. c. 1830), 'Kate', Mrs Alexander MacDougall, Craignure Inn, sister of Ann MacQ., second wife of LMQ, 362, 363, 366

MacQuarrie, Charles, senior (1806 –1861), Baptist pastor, merchant, hymn writer, inspector of meal distribution, 100, 351, 352, 354, 358n.

MacQuarrie, Donald (*c.* 1680–1777), of Ormaig, 92, 245

MacQuarrie, Donald (d. 1818), son of LMQ, later in Liverpool, 91, 96

MacQuarrie, Donald Torquil (fl. 1833), in Ulva, 259

MacQuarrie, Elizabeth (b. *c.* 1752), dau. of LMQ, 91

MacQuarrie, Emilia (Emmy) (b. *c.* 1765), dau. of LMQ by his second wife, 91, 92

MacQuarrie, Flora (*c.* 1750–1836), dau. of LMQ, wife of John Maclean in Kilbrenan, 91, 176, 182–3, 279, 379n.

MacQuarrie, Hector (d. 1794), of Ormaig, 'our unluckie Cousin Ormaig', 29, 43, 79, 92, 199, 281

MacQuarrie, Hector (1776–1801or 2), son of LMQ by his second wife, 92, 96

MacQuarrie, Jean (1755–1835), dau. of LMQ, 91, 183, 184, 305, 322n.

MacQuarrie, John (d. 1735), 15th of Ulva, 29, 89

MacQuarrie, John (d. 1773), of Balligartan, 43

MacQuarrie, John (fl. 1740–1780), Younger of Ulva, son of LMQ, 76, 91

MacQuarrie, Lachlan (fl. 17th C.), 14th of Ulva, 246

MacQuarrie, Lachlan (1715–1818), 16th of Ulva, LMQ, 43, 49, 67–9, 78–9, 89–102, 104, 106–7, 110, 119, 132, 145, 155, 159, 176, 177, 199, 206, 261, 282, 287, 288, 318, 363–4, 404–5

MacQuarrie, Lachlan (fl. 17th–18th C.), of Ormaig, 43

MacQuarrie, Lachlan (d. 1775), father of LM and CM, 245–6

MacQuarrie, Lachlan (b. *c.* 1750 ?), son of LMQ, 91

MacQuarrie, Lachlan (fl. 1803), in Ardmeanach, 271

MacQuarrie, Lachlan (1778–1807), son of LMQ by his second wife, 92

MacQuarrie, Margaret (1772–1773), dau. of LMQ by his second wife, 92

MacQuarrie, Marie (Mally) (1747–1846), wife of GM, 67, 69, 77–81, 86, 91, 93, 96, 101, 155, 156, 158, 159, 162, 166, 173, 176, 219, 224, 249, 281–2, 285–90, 294–5, 301, 305–6, 321, 365, 388

MacQuarrie, Murdoch (b. *c.* 1763), son of LMQ by his second wife, 91, 92, 96

MacQuarrie, Peggy (fl. 1760s–1770s), passenger on LMQ's ship to Halifax, gives birth 94

MacQuarrie, Sibella (b. 1767), dau. of LMQ by his second wife, 91, 92

McQueen, John (fl. 1843), teacher in Kilfinichen, 332

MacTavish, Rev. Archibald (1711–1778), minister of Torosay, 44

MacTavish, Dr Colin (*c.* 1795–1856), son of Dugald M., Laggan, later in Islay, 239, 258

MacTavish, Dugald (1750–1828), tacksman in Laggan, 213, 228n.

MacTavish, Duncan (b. *c.* 1785 ?), 'Big Duncan', MM2's henchman, son of Dugald M. in Laggan, 239, 319

McVean, Rev. Donald (1808–1880), C of S minister of Iona, later FC, 332, 334

MacVurich, Hector *see* Currie, Hector

Mar, 11th earl of (1675–1732), [John Erskine] 'Bobbing John', Jacobite leader in 1715, 24

Mark, Alexander (b. *c.* 1803), road surveyor, inspector of poor, 372

Marriott, Sir James (fl. 1785), judge in trial of Daniel Munro, 131

Martin, Martin (*c.* 1660–1719), scholar, writer, doctor, 22, 23, 107–8

MARY Queen of Scots (1542–1587), 4

MARY II (1662–1694), 17–18, 26

Maxwell, Agnes (1785–1879), dau. of James M., wife of Rev. Norman Macleod, 196

Maxwell, James (*c.* 1757–1829), duke's chamberlain in Mull, 181, 188–98, 222, 234, 251, 252, 329, 397

Maxwell, John Argyll (1790–1855), son of James M., married Jean Macleod, 196, in Java, 387, 395n.

Maxwell, Robert (*c.* 1788–1821), son of James M., marries Catherine Stewart of Achadashenaig, 196

Meiklejohn, Rev. Robert (1800–1859), tutor to LM Jr., later minister of Alford, 254, 258–9

Melville, Lord (1771–1851), [Robert Saunders Dundas] First Lord of the Admiralty in 1819, 233

Mercey, Frederic (fl. 1820–1840), traveller in Mull in 1840, 279, 281, 312

Merry, Janet (*c.* 1830 –1915), dau. of John Merry, wife of Dugald Macphail, 400

Middleton, James (1791–1861), factor to ACP, later in Gualachaolish, 331, 335n.

Milton, Lord (1692–1766), [Andrew Fletcher] factotum of 2nd duke of Argyll in Scottish affairs, 37

Mitchell, Andrew (1708–1771), student friend of David Hume, under-secretary for Scotland in 1745, 44

Mitchell, Andrew (1842- after 1883), [BA Oxford, studied law at EU] proprietor of Kinloch, 355

Montgomery, Brig. -Gen. Richard (d. 1775), with Arnold in attack on Quebec, 1775, 83

Montrose, James Graham, 1st marquis of (1612–1650), 11–14

Morison, Hugh (fl. 1750–1798), tenant in Kilbeg, 278

Morrison, Archibald Maclean (b. 1819), lawyer, son of James M., 357, 359n.

Morrison, Janet *see* Maclean, Janet

Morrison, James (1764–1828), merchant in Bunessan, husband of Janet Maclean, 341, 356

Morrison, Jemima (1828–1909), dau. of James Morrison, 344n.

Mountstuart, John, viscount, later 4th earl of Bute, (1744–1814), visitor to Mull in 1788, 113, 172, 397

Muller, Maria Magdalen (*c.* 1808–1890), wife of James Forsyth, 387, 394n.

Munro, Alexander (fl. 1815), teacher in Gaelic school, 298, 304n.

Munro, Daniel (*c.* 1760–1799), inadvertent killer of AMLB, 127–31, 151, 152

Murray, Alexander (1687–1743), of Stanhope, proprietor of Ardnamurchan, mineral speculator, 31

Murray, John (fl. 1740–1770s), lawyer in Edinburgh, 58, 66–7, 78

Murray, Sarah (1744–1811), travel writer, 174, 199

Napier, Lord (1819–1898), chairman of the 1883 enquiry (Crofters' Commission), 354

Necker de Saussure, Louis-Albert (1786–1861), geologist, 200, 202–4, 293, 294

Neilson, Ishbel *see* Maclaine, Ishbel

Neilson, James – alias of Sir Hector Maclean, 44–5; *see* also Maclaine, Ishbel

Nisbett, Henry (*c.* 1810–1867), banker in Tobermory, 274

Northampton, 1st marquis of (d. 1828), father of Lord Compton, 179

Northampton, marchioness of (fl. 1815), mother of Lord C., 'full of a hundred littlenesses', 180

Obirn, Mary (fl. 1750–1804), wife of Hector McNeill in Ardmeanach, 268

Orme, Alexander (*c.* 1740–1789), lawyer in Edinburgh, 62, 63, 66, 67

Osborne, Martha (*c.* 1798–1841), wife of Hector Maclaine of Scallastle, 289–90

Ossian (3rd C.), legendary bard, 112, 113, 173, 293–5, 301, 399

Paget, Lady Caroline (d. 1835), wife of 6th duke of Argyll, 194

Park, Archy (b. *c.* 1765), older brother of the explorer Mungo P., customs man in Tobermory, 180–1

Park, Miss (fl. 1785), courted by MM, 85

Pemberton, Mr (fl. 1813), friend of Lord Compton, 178–9

Pennant, Thomas (1726–1798), traveller, naturalist, visitor to Mull in 1772, 101, 109, 365

Peters, Col. Thomas (fl. 1704), recruiting officer, 270

Pococke, Richard (1704–1765), visitor to Iona in 1760, 109

Rankin, Neil (died 1827–32), 'late infamous miller' in Glennan, 369n.

Reid, Robert (fl. 1780–1806), surveyor, 216–17

Riddell, Sir James (d. 1797), of Ardnamurchan and Sunart, 117

Robertson, James (fl. *c.* 1800), emigration agent, 203, 269–70

Robertson, Jane (fl. 1810–1830), second wife of Hugh Maclean of Coll, 384, 385

Robertson, William (1721–1793), principal of EU, historian, 158, 305, 322n.

Rook, Captain (fl. 1803 ?), whose wife died at Kinlochspelve in 1803, 212

Rose, Captain (fl. 1848), inspector of meal distribution for Wester Ross, 351, 358n.

Rose, Eugene (1804–1884), son of Lachlan Rose, Bunessan, poet, 357, 360n.

Ross, Gillean Maclaine (b. *c.* 1800), son of Julian Maclaine and Thomas Ross, 319, 323n., 366

Ross, Rev. David (1805–1891), minister of Tobermory 1844–1855, 361, 363, 380n., 381

Rousseau, Jean-Jacques (1712–1778), French writer and philosopher, 71, 116

Sacheverell, William (fl. 17th C.), author, traveller in Mull in 1697, 109

Scheniman, Ferdinand (1773–1843), accountant in Edinburgh, brother-in-law of CM, 254

Scott, Walter (1771–1832), advocate, writer, poet, 112, 114, 177–80, 190, 192, 196, 197, 200, 203, 204, 220, 287, 294–5, 397

Seaforth, 4th earl of (d. 1701), [Kenneth Mackenzie] Jacobite, foster-father of Sir John Maclean of Duart, 16

Selkirk, Lord (1771–1820) [Thomas Douglas], 5th earl of Selkirk, 212

Selkrig, Charles (fl. 1815), accountant in Edinburgh, trustee of 6th duke of Argyll, 195

Sellar, Patrick (1780–1851), advocate of clearance, in Ardtornish, hankers after Scallastle, 371, 377, 379n., 385, 399

Seneachie (fl. 1800–1840), historian of the clan Maclean, 45

Shaw, Flora (1802–1869), wife of Archibald Mackinnon of Torrans, 333

Sheridan, Tom (fl. 1790–1810), friend of 6th duke of Argyll, 196

Shiells, Alexander (fl. 1780s–1830s), factor to MMT, 181–4, 279

Shiells, Andrew (fl. 1820s), son of above, 182

Sinclair, A. Maclean (fl. 1850–1900), 49, 395n.

Sinclair, Alexander (*c.* 1793–fl. 1867), farmer in Erray, later in Knock, Morvern, 274

Sinclair, Daniel (fl. 1750–86), captain of the *Hero*, 127

Sinclair, Sir John (1754–1835), originator of the *Statistical Account*, 115

Sinclair, John (1770–1863), merchant, distiller in Tobermory, proprietor of Lochaline, Morvern, 398, 405n.

Small, John (1726–1796), commander, 2nd batt. 84th Reg., (Royal Highland), 70, 83, 121, 144, 156, 157

Smith, Adam (1723–1790), economist, 82, 97, 98

Smith, Margaret (b. *c.* 1745, lived after 1800), wife of LMT, 76, 145, 172, 174

Somers, Robert (1822–1891), writer , 274, 370, 373–4, 379n., 398, 400

Speirs, Graham (1797–1847), advocate, convenor of committee on Free Church sites, 332

Stael, Anne-Louise-Germaine Necker de (1766–1817), Swiss writer, 349

Steuart, Elizabeth Margaret Seton (fl. 1790s–1830s), wife of RM, 205–6

Steuart, Sir Henry (1759–1836), of Allanton,

father-in-law of RM, planter, 205, 206, 207, 252, 254, 255

Stevenson, John (d. 1812), contractor in Oban, 154–5, 157, 164, 327, 397

Stevenson, Robert (1772–1850), commissioner of lighthouses, 190, 397

Stevenson, Robert Louis (1850–1894), writer, 280

Stewart, Catherine (b. 1793), dau. of Robert S. of Achadashenaig [Mrs Robert Maxwell], 196

Stewart, Donald (fl. 1835), tutor to children of CM, collector of Ulva rents, 260, 318, 375

Stewart, Isabella (c. 1795–1869), dau. of Robert S. of Achadashenaig [Mrs Dugald MacLachlan], 233–4

Stewart, John (c. 1720–1770), of Achadashenaig, drover, 76, 324

Stewart, John (fl. 1780s), in Hampstead, 124

Stewart, John (c. 1790–fl. 1843), of Achadashenaig, 193, 222, 234, 259, 274, 382

Stewart, John (d. 1844), of Fasnacloich, husband of Harriet Maclaine of LB, 255

Stewart, Robert (1747–1813), of Achadashenaig, and Sorne, son of John S. and sheriff substitute, 160, 195, 234

Stoppard, Tom (b. 1937), playwright, 245

Strachan, Lord (fl. 1743), 37

Strathallan, Lord, *see* Drummond, William Henry, 261, 386, 394

Stuart, Prince Charles Edward (1720–1788), the Young Pretender, 40, 41, 44, 45, 75, 265

Stuart, James Francis (1688–1766), 'James VIII', the Old Pretender, 25–6

Thomson, David (fl. 1818–1835), in Torloisk, 182

Thornton, William (1759–1828), traveller in Mull, later in America [designed Capitol], 172, 173

Thornton, Mr (fl. 1788), tutor to GM's children, 305

Townshend, Charles, 2nd viscount, (1674–1738), 24

Tweeddale, marquess of, *see* Hay, John

Vincent, Emilie Guillaumine, (1826–1882), wife of DMLB, 389

Voltaire, Francois –Marie Arouet (1694–1778), French philosopher, 71

Wade, General George (1673–1748), demilitariser of the Highlands, road maker, 31

Walker, Rev. John (1731–1803), geologist and surveyor of Hebrides, 86–7, 97, 109, 112, 115

Walker, Mr (n.k.), tutor to LMQ's children, 93

Wall, Margaret (b. c. 1745), second wife of Daniel Maclean, mother of Sir F. J. G. Maclean, 144

Walpole, Sir Robert(1676–1745), statesman, 28, 37

Warburton, Jane (c. 1692–1767), second wife of 2nd duke of Argyll, 32, 37

Watson, David (c. 1796–1876), proprietor of Ardow, 224

Watts, William (1752–1851), illustrator and line engraver, 174

Wells, Robert (fl. 1785), Mr Lowther's agent in London, 129, 130

Whiteside, Dr Philip (fl. 1770s–1830s), surgeon in Ayr, father of Dr William W., 342, 345n.

Whiteside, Dr William (1793–1862), of Ayr, second husband of Flora LB, 341–3, 367

Wilberforce, William (1759–1833), philanthropist, 178

WILLIAM (1650–1702), of Orange, joint sovereign with MARY II, 17–19, 22, 26

WILLIAM IV (1765–1837), 258

Willison, George (1741–1797), portrait painter, father of Marianne W., CM's wife, 148, 250

Willison, Marianne (c. 1792–1828), dau. of George W., wife of CM, 250–55, 257; death of, 258, 363

Wilson, Mary (n.k.), mistress of Capt. Allan MacAskill, 223

Wolfe, General James (1727–1759), 60

Wright, Agnes (c. 1785–1859), dau. of James Wright, writer in Stirling, wife of FWC, 374, 379n.

Wyllie, James (fl. 1850–1884), duke's factor in Ross of Mull, 354

Young, Hugh (fl. c. 1810–1840s), tenant of Garmony, [later in Ardnadrochit] 320, 365